Behind the Bamboo Curtain

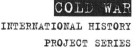

INTERNATIONAL HISTORY
PROJECT SERIES

James G. Hershberg
series editor

Brothers in Arms
The Rise and Fall of the Sino-Soviet Alliance,
1945–1963
Edited by Odd Arne Westad

Economic Cold War
America's Embargo against
China and the Sino-Soviet
Alliance, 1949–1963
Shu Guang Zhang

Confronting Vietnam
Soviet Policy toward the
Indochina Conflict, 1954–1963
Ilya V. Gaiduk

Kim Il Sung in the Krushchev Era
Soviet-DPRK Relations and the Roots
of North Korean Despotism, 1953–1964
Balázs Szalontai

Failed Illusions
Moscow, Washington, Budapest
and the 1956 Hungarian Revolt
Charles Gati

Behind the Bamboo Curtain

China, Vietnam, and the
World beyond Asia

Edited by Priscilla Roberts

Woodrow Wilson Center Press
Washington, D.C.

Stanford University Press
Stanford, California

EDITORIAL OFFICES
Woodrow Wilson Center Press
Woodrow Wilson International Center for Scholars
One Woodrow Wilson Plaza
1300 Pennsylvania Avenue, N.W.
Washington, DC 20004-3027
Telephone: 202-691-4010
www.wilsoncenter.org

ORDER FROM

Stanford University Press
Chicago Distribution Center
11030 South Langley Avenue
Chicago, IL 60628
Telephone: 1-800-621-2736

2 4 6 8 9 7 5 3 1

Library of Congress Cataloging-in-Publication Data

Behind the bamboo curtain : China, Vietnam, and the world beyond Asia / edited by
   Priscilla Roberts.
      p. cm. — (Cold War International History Project series)
   Includes index.
   ISBN-13: 978-0-8047-5502-3 (cloth : alk. paper)
   ISBN-10: 0-8047-5502-7 (cloth : alk. paper)
   1. China—Foreign relations—Vietnam (Democratic Republic) 2. Vietnam (Democratic
Republic)—Foreign relations—China. 3. Vietnam War, 1961–1975—Diplomatic history.
4. China—Foreign relations—1949–1976. 5. Vietnam—Foreign relations—20th century.
I. Roberts, Priscilla Mary. II. Series.
DS740.5.V5B44 2006
959.704'32—dc22
                                                                              2006015450

The Cold War International History Project

The Cold War International History Project was established by the Woodrow Wilson International Center for Scholars in 1991. The project supports the full and prompt release of historical materials by governments on all sides of the Cold War and seeks to disseminate new information and perspectives on Cold War history emerging from previously inaccessible sources on the "the other side"—the former Communist bloc—through publications, fellowships, and scholarly meetings and conferences. The project publishes the *Cold War International History Project Bulletin* and a working paper series and maintains a Web site (http://cwihp.si.edu).

In collaboration with the National Security Archive, a nongovernmental research institute and document repository located at George Washington University, the project has created a Russian and East-Bloc Archival Documents Database at Gelman Library, from Russian and other former Communist archives donated by the project, the National Security Archive, and various scholars. The database may be explored through a computer-searchable English-language inventory. For further information, contact the National Security Archive, Gelman Library, George Washington University, Washington, DC 20037.

At the Woodrow Wilson Center, the project is part of the Division of International Security Studies, headed by Robert S. Litwak. The director of the project is Christian F. Ostermann. The project is overseen by an advisory committee that is chaired by William Taubman, Amherst College, and includes Michael Beschloss; James H. Billington, librarian of Congress; Warren I. Cohen, University of Maryland at Baltimore; John Lewis Gaddis, Yale University; James G. Hershberg, George Washington University; Samuel F. Wells Jr., associate director of the Woodrow Wilson Center; and Sharon Wolchik, George Washington University.

The Cold War International History Project was created with the help of the John D. and Catherine T. MacArthur Foundation.

Contents

Part II The Widening War

Part III Documents

Preface

James G. Hershberg

When I first visited Hanoi, in the fall of 1995—with a delegation of historians accompanying former U.S. secretary of defense Robert S. McNamara, as surreal a voyage as anyone who lived through the Vietnam War could imagine—within a few hours of reaching the city, I walked over to the History Museum a few noisy blocks east of Hoan Kiem Lake. Though my Vietnamese language abilities were essentially nonexistent, it didn't take a linguist to grasp the meaning of the display cases dominating the vast hall on the second floor. One after another, with dates extending back more than a millennium, they held maps of present-day Vietnam and China, with blue arrows reaching down from the northern neighbor only to confront red arrows racing up to rebuff them. Each, it was obvious, described an epic Vietnamese struggle against a Chinese attempt at domination—centuries before the more familiar battles against the French or the Americans. Though I couldn't decipher the explanatory panels, several names leapt out at me, already familiar from the streets outside; every Vietnamese city, I soon learned, featured main thoroughfares named after heroes of anti-Chinese revolts or resistance.

For one immersed in the Cold War but a bit hazy about its precursors, this vivid lesson in the persistence and pervasiveness of conflict in Sino-Vietnamese relations reinforced two central truths: that the histories of these two countries were inextricably intertwined; and that the expressions of eternal ideological solidarity uniting Beijing and Hanoi loudly proclaimed during the Vietnam War masked a far more complex reality—something that experts knew or at least surmised at the time, but that was not really made evident until these two former allies fought a nasty little border war just a few short years after the communist conquest of Saigon in the spring of 1975. Among those few who noticed the incongruous newspaper head-lines—after the nightmare ended, most Americans did their best to forget Vietnam ever existed—there was considerable head scratching. Wait a minute: Hadn't we fought the war in the first place to stop Chinese expansionism? Weren't those communist regimes, headed by those grizzled revolutionaries Mao Zedong and Ho Chi Minh, fully in cahoots in their quest to topple imperialist dominoes? What were these "comrades in arms" suddenly doing at each other's throats? "There's something happenin' here," Buffalo Springfield had sung of the fighting in Vietnam a decade earlier. "What it is ain't exactly clear. . . ."

*   *   *

Finally, it is becoming clearer: Going behind the Bamboo Curtain, this volume penetrates and illuminates a relationship that for roughly a decade, beginning in the early 1960s, was as important to U.S. officials, and also as exasperatingly unfathomable, as any in the communist world. As the Vietnam War ascended to dominate America's foreign policy agenda and poison its domestic politics, those responsible for dealing with the turmoil in Southeast Asia found the mystery-enshrouded Beijing-Hanoi link both vital and vexing.

At every stage of the conflict, Washington's approach depended crucially on comprehending, or even influencing, the ties between the People's Republic of China (PRC) and the Democratic Republic of (North) Vietnam (DRV). The roots of the U.S. commitment extended back, in fact, to the communist victory in the Chinese Civil War of 1949–50, which helped push Washington, after much vacillation, to back the French wholeheartedly against the Viet Minh and view the fight for Indochina in a Cold War context, linking it to the danger of further communist expansion in Asia rather than a mere nationalist anticolonial uprising.[1] Then, in the Kennedy years, as crises flared up over communist insurgencies in both Laos and South

Vietnam, Washington blamed a belligerent Beijing for egging on Hanoi, encouraging and supporting the armed struggles. When Lyndon B. Johnson sent hundreds of thousands of U.S. troops to South Vietnam and began bombing the North, he feared military escalation might trigger a large-scale direct Chinese intervention, reprising the Korean disaster a decade before. Then, as the Johnson administration for long, bloody years sought fruitlessly to open negotiations with North Vietnam, it blamed Beijing (and a purported "pro-Chinese" faction in Hanoi) for being stubbornly determined to fight on until total victory against the "criminal imperialist aggressor." Finally, after U.S.-DRV talks started and quickly deadlocked in Paris, the Nixon-Kissinger strategy relied on "triangular diplomacy"—Washington's simultaneous cultivation of improved relations with both communist powers, the Soviets and the Chinese—to manipulate Beijing, through a blend of enticement and coercion, into pressuring Hanoi into making concessions that would permit a "peace with honor" and an American exit from the war.[2]

Yet, at the time and for decades afterward, the truth of what transpired between these communist leaderships remained hidden beneath multiple layers of ideological dogma, cultural unfamiliarity, and pervasive secrecy. Only now, as the Vietnam War and the Cold War itself recede into history, can scholars scrutinize and inspect the kind of evidence about which contemporaneous analysts could only fantasize. Melodramatic as it may sound, one may without exaggeration state that CIA spies would have literally killed—or at least paid substantial bribes—for the types of intimate information and revealing insights into the Sino-Vietnamese alliance this book contains.

Once the schism between Moscow and Beijing broke out, Western analysts could at least collect firsthand accounts from one side of the story, as numerous Soviet bloc officials maintained contacts with Westerners and increasingly shed their inhibitions about confiding feelings of exasperation, consternation, and mystification concerning the Kremlin's ex-ally. But Sino-Vietnamese ties were far different: U.S. intelligence analysts, both military and civilian, required to advise policymakers and engaged in their own frequently contentious debates over whether to accentuate cooperation or friction between Beijing and Hanoi, often had relatively little hard information to go on, and were at times reduced to the equivalent of reading the "tea leaves" of blustery public pronouncements issued by party mouthpieces like *Renmin Ribao* and *Nhan Dan,* or drawing broad inferences from cryptic military deployments or hearsay gossip.[3] This was by design, not accident: As a matter of culture and party discipline, both communist regimes kept a tight grip on information, permitted few outsiders to gain more than token access to their realms, and effectively concealed tensions between them behind militant protestations of ideological solidarity.

The process of uncovering this hidden history received a boost from the deterioration in Sino-Vietnamese relations following the communist victory in 1975. As their alliance degenerated into bitter recriminations, the two sides hurled historical accusations of betrayal and ingratitude, in the process disclosing previously secret episodes and details of such issues as Dien Bien Phu, the Geneva Conference, and the significance of aid to Hanoi during the war against the Americans. Those accounts, however, were highly selective and warped by clashing political aims.

Far more beneficial to history, however, has been the process of Chinese modernization, spearheaded by Deng Xiaoping, accompanied by the ending of the Cold War. Since the late 1980s, despite the persistence in power of a nominally communist regime, a flood of historical materials has emerged from the PRC on the post-1949 era, ranging from memoirs, hagiographies, and oral histories to *neibu* (restricted) compilations of party documents to, most excitingly, the gradual opening of archives in various provinces and, finally, in Beijing itself. Such sources have enabled, for the first time, such scholars as Zhai Qiang, Chen Jian, and Yang Kuisong to reassess China's involvement in three decades of Cold War conflicts in "Indochina" or, more neutrally, Southeast Asia, going beyond Sinological accounts based largely on public sources or intelligence estimates by outsiders.[4] Unfortunately, the declassification process in Vietnam itself has moved at a far slower pace, although, as this volume shows, the release of substantial fresh Chinese historical evidence—in addition to American, Russian, and other sources—is stimulating Vietnamese scholars to respond to a reinvigorated historical debate, and, one may hope, placing fresh pressure on Hanoi to reveal more of its own side of the story.[5]

The present volume builds on this foundation, gathering an international cross-section of scholars and primary sources—Chinese, Vietnamese, Western (both American and European), Russian—that, collectively, bring new information to the surface and advance original interpretations, addressing some old mysteries while also raising and examining previously unasked questions. Originally presented at a January 2000 conference at Hong Kong University in a bracing series of discussions that were collegial but at times grew heated—especially when Chinese and Vietnamese scholars disputed aspects of the breakdown in Sino-Vietnamese relations—the chapters, since extensively revised, present an up-to-date, kaleidoscopic panorama of perspectives in a fluid, fast-changing field. Naturally, they cannot claim to offer a comprehensive or definitive account—many sources remain off-limits, and there are simply too many broad issues to cover—but readers should find the contributions exciting in several areas of overlapping interest: Not only do the Vietnam War and Sino-Vietnamese relations receive attention, but the chapters also enhance our understanding of several complex dynamics that are now at the cutting edge of scholarly investigation, such as the interactions between the conflicts in Southeast Asia, the decolonization process as a whole, and the evolution of the Sino-Soviet split and Sino-American relations during the Cold War.[6]

Finally, as with the best of the new international Cold War history, *Behind the Bamboo Curtain* rewards readers in additional ways. It is replete with "fly on the wall" moments when one feels privy to the inner sanctum of history, when figures like Mao and Ho, Zhou and Giap, Kissinger and Khrushchev, spring from the page and come to life. It also pieces together from disparate archives and sources, in different languages, countries, and continents, Rashomon-like tales of international intrigue that even those directly involved, seeing only their own side, could not have discerned. Few, if any, countries were able to escape the reverberations of the Asian crisis. Ultimately, and most important, this volume represents a new point of departure, which should inspire further investigations, most immediately in China and Vietnam, but also in the United States, Russia, European states on both sides of the shredded Iron Curtain, and the rest of the world.

Notes

1. For an excellent new study on how the United States came to throw its full support behind the French, see Mark Atwood Lawrence, *Assuming the Burden: Europe and the American Commitment to War in Vietnam* (Berkeley: University of California Press, 2005).

2. Although China naturally surfaces sporadically in accounts of the American involvement in the Vietnam War, no focused study of U.S. policy toward China in the context of the war using declassified documents yet exists. The emergence of fresh communist and international evidence, highlighted by the present volume, suggests such a project might shed considerable light on U.S. policy toward both the war and the process of Sino-American normalization. For a start, a researcher might consult volumes of the *Foreign Relations of the United States* series on both Vietnam and China, which are now available (online at http://www.state.gov/www/about_state/history/frusonline.html) for the Kennedy and Johnson years and are being released for the Nixon administration.

3. For two important fresh sources on U.S. intelligence estimates on Vietnam and

China during the war, see *Vietnam 1961–1968 as Interpreted in INR's Production,* by W. Dean Howells, Dorothy Avery, and Fred Greene, declassified November 2002, accessible on the National Security Archive Web site (http://www.nsarchive.org); and the collection of declassified Central Intelligence Agency (CIA) analyses of the Vietnam War, accessible at the CIA's Freedom of Information Act Web site (http://www.foia.cia.gov/nic_vietnam_collection.asp).

4. For examples of this growing literature in English, see Zhai Qiang, "Beijing and the Vietnam Conflict, 1964–1965: New Chinese Evidence," *Cold War International History Project* [hereafter CWIHP] *Bulletin,* nos. 6–7 (Winter 1995–96): 233–50; Zhai Qiang, "Opposing Negotiations: China and Vietnam Peace Talks," *Pacific Historical Review* 68, no. 1 (February 1999): 21–49; Zhai Qiang, *Beijing and the Vietnam Peace Talks, 1965–1968,* CWIHP Working Paper 18 (Washington, D.C.: Woodrow Wilson International Center for Scholars, 1997); and Zhai Qiang, *China and the Vietnam Wars, 1950–1975* (Chapel Hill: University of North Carolina Press, 2000); Chen Jian, "China's Involvement in the Vietnam War, 1964–1969," *China Quarterly,* no. 142 (July 1995): 365–66; Chen Jian, *Mao's China and the Cold War* (Chapel Hill: University of North Carolina Press, 2001), chap. 8; Yang Kuisong, *Changes in Mao Zedong's Attitude toward the Indochina War, 1949–1973,* CWIHP Working Paper 34 (Washington, D.C.: Woodrow Wilson International Center for Scholars, 2002); and Odd Arne Westad, Chen Jian, Stein Tonnesson, Nguyen Vu Tung, and James G. Hershberg, eds., *77 Conversations between Chinese and Foreign Leaders on the Wars in Indochina, 1964–1977,* CWIHP Working Paper 22 (Washington, D.C.: Woodrow Wilson International Center for Scholars, 1998).

5. On the fitful release of Vietnamese archival sources, see, e.g., Mark Bradley and Robert Brigham, *Vietnamese Archives and Scholarship on the Cold War,* CWIHP Working Paper 7 (Washington, D.C.: Woodrow Wilson International Center for Scholars, 1993); Fredrik Logevall, "Bringing in the 'Other Side': New Scholarship on the Vietnam Wars," *Journal of Cold War Studies* 3, no. 3 (Fall 2001): 77–93; and Pierre Asselin, "New Evidence from Vietnam," *Passport* (Society for Historians of American Foreign Relations Newsletter), December 2004, 2–5.

6. For important new scholarly investigations of the interaction between the Sino-Soviet schism and the Vietnam War, see the dissertations (from Yale University and the London School of Economics and Political Science, respectively) and forthcoming books of Lorenz Luthi and Sergey Radchenko, both of whom extensively and creatively use Chinese, Russian, European (both East and West), U.S., and other sources in their narratives.

Acknowledgments

The conference from which this book arose was generously funded by the Louis Cha Fund for East-West Studies of the University of Hong Kong and the John D. and Catherine T. MacArthur Foundation. The staff of the Department of History of the University of Hong Kong and the Cold War International History Project worked long and hard to make the event happen.

Preparation of the conference papers was greatly facilitated by assistance from Christian Ostermann and Nancy Meyers of the Cold War International History Project. The Institute of European, Russian, and Eurasian Studies of George Washington University provided a stimulating, hospitable, and congenial home for the editor while revisions were in progress, during a sabbatical made possible by a Fulbright–Hong Kong Research Grants Council Fellowship. Special thanks are due to James Goldgeier, Vedrana Hadzialic, and Jennifer Sieck of the Institute for their never-failing assistance. Robert Brigham most kindly helped to track down one elusive contribution. James G. Hershberg, Joseph Brinley of the Wilson Center Press, and an unnamed third reader of the manuscript made particularly insightful suggestions for revisions and reorganization of the volume.

List of Abbreviations

CCP   Chinese Communist Party
CPSU   Communist Party of the Soviet Union
DRV   Democratic Republic of Vietnam (North Vietnam)
NIE   National Intelligence Estimate (United States)
NLF   National Liberation Front (Communists in South Vietnam)
PAVN   People's Army of Vietnam (North Vietnam)
PLA   People's Liberation Army (China)
PRC   People's Republic of China
VWP   Vietnamese Workers' Party (name of Vietnamese Communist
        Party, 1951–76)

Behind the Bamboo Curtain

Introduction: The Vietnam War in Its International Setting

Priscilla Roberts

For more than twenty years, from at least 1953 to 1973, Indochina served as the cockpit of Asia, a fulcrum where the interests of several great powers —notably China, the Soviet Union, and the United States—collided, competed, and conflicted, as did the regional interests of China, Vietnam, Laos, Cambodia, and other Southeast Asian nations. During the 1960s and 1970s, the Vietnam War became the subject of emotionally and politically super-charged debate in the United States, a millstone dragging down the successive presidential administrations of Lyndon B. Johnson and Richard Nixon, something reflected in the continuous torrent of books on the subject that began in the 1960s and still shows no sign of abating.[1]

Even today, for at least some Americans, Vietnam remains an open wound, its memory perennially bitter, as became apparent in the controversy provoked in the mid-1990s by former secretary of defense Robert S. McNamara's long-deferred memoirs, *In Retrospect,* when many of his former critics dissented bitterly from his stance that, although mistaken, he had acted in good faith first in greatly escalating his country's involvement

1

in the war, and then in failing to make public his growing private misgivings. McNamara's close involvement in the production of a 2003 documentary film, *The Fog of War,* covering his role in the making of major
Johnson and Kennedy administration foreign policy decisions, not just
Vietnam but also the Cuban missile crisis and others, predictably stirred up
yet more controversy.[2]

Though perhaps to a lesser extent, within Asia, the Indochina wars, like
their predecessors, have generated lasting tensions and, in particular, sensitive and disputed memories, as is readily apparent in the current press. For
many years the governments of China, South Korea, and the Southeast Asian
nations have attacked Japanese school textbooks for allegedly underplaying
the history of Japanese militarism and aggression against its neighbors during the 1930s and World War II, disputes highlighted in the spring of 2005
by major anti-Japanese riots in several Chinese cities.[3] In 2002, President
Jiang Zemin of China, while visiting Vietnam, "urged Hanoi to alter some
school history textbooks to make them less antagonistic towards China" and
"to make more clear . . . China's assistance to Vietnam during the Vietnam
War that ended in 1975." He also "voiced hope former Chinese dynasties'
repeated invasions of Vietnam, which followed thousands of years of Chinese domination, would not be linked to the current Chinese administration's
foreign policy."[4] Meanwhile China—apparently fearing that "unflattering
evidence" might emerge as to its role in bringing the Khmer Rouge to power
in Cambodia in the mid-1970s and its subsequent acquiescence in Pol Pot's
atrocities—in 2002 pressured President Hun Sen to scuttle the projected UN
tribunal, which had been supposed to put surviving Cambodian Communist
leaders on trial for their role in that regime's genocide.[5]

Yet, notwithstanding such continuing attempts to dictate what views of
the Vietnam War are currently acceptable, as international tensions faded
and new documentary materials, from Western, Asian, former Soviet, and
East European archives became more readily available in the 1990s, a new
era opened in the study of the Indochina wars and, indeed, in the broader
history of the Cold War in Asia and elsewhere. Initially, the great bulk of
the outpouring of scholarship and writing on the Vietnam War was American in origin, making it one of the very few wars, as three distinguished
historians with some irony pointed out, whose history was written primarily by the losers.[6] Given the persistent and traumatic impact of the Vietnam War upon the United States, this was to some extent understandable.
Over time, however, this emphasis has changed, and the past decade in particular has seen a slew of books and articles seeking to appreciate the wars
in Indochina in their international context.

The pioneering effort on this subject was undoubtedly R. B. Smith's ambitious multivolume work, *An International History of the Vietnam War,* some of whose numerous stimulating insights can now be proved, disproved, clarified, or supplemented by newly available archival materials.[7] Fredrik Logevall's acclaimed study, *Choosing War,* surveyed the United States' 1963–65 decisions on the dramatic escalation of military commitments in Vietnam in the context of America's relations with its allies in Western Europe, Canada, Australia, and New Zealand, finding that while none except Australia thought those decisions wise, with the exception of President Charles de Gaulle of France, allied leaders failed to make strong representations on the subject to American officials.[8]

Caroline Page, a former British diplomat, has studied the nature and effectiveness of official U.S. propaganda on Vietnam in the United Kingdom, France, and Germany, and its broader impact on American relations with these countries.[9] The Australian historian Peter Edwards has published two comprehensive volumes on his nation's involvement in the wars in Indochina, and two studies of Canadian involvement in Vietnam have also appeared.[10] Broadening the focus to U.S. allies in the Asian sphere, Robert Blackburn suggested that the response of the Thai, South Korean, and Philippine governments in contributing troops to the American war effort in Vietnam, as called for by President Johnson's "more flags" campaign, effectively meant that their soldiers were serving as "mercenaries."[11] Thomas Havens has also scrutinized the impact of the Vietnam War on Japan, the most significant U.S. ally in Asia.[12] From somewhat differing perspectives, Thomas A. Schwartz and John Dumbrell have assessed how the Vietnam War affected Johnson's ability to deal with both his country's European allies and the Soviet Union.[13]

Four collections of essays published in the past decade attempt to give some sense of the breadth of scholarship in some way related to the Indochina wars currently in progress. The first, edited by the British historian Peter Lowe, brought together perspectives from American, Australian, British, Chinese, Russian, and Vietnamese scholars on the war.[14] Two years later, a volume edited by two American historians, Lloyd C. Gardner and Ted Gittinger, expanded the focus to include not just the major protagonists, Vietnam, the United States, China, and the Soviet Union, plus Australia, but also the war's impact on a range of American allies—including the NATO alliance, South Korea, and Japan; its long-term effects on Southeast Asia; and how it affected U.S. flexibility in handling the Middle East.[15]

In 2003, Gardner joined with two German historians to produce an even more ambitious collection of essays, some of which drew analogies between aspects of the Vietnam War and comparable historical episodes and events. Others not only focused on a range of international relationships during the war—including the assorted alliance concerns of the NATO powers, Thailand, Australia, and North Vietnam, and the war's impact on the international monetary system—but also considered the influence the war and protests against it exerted within Italian, West German, and East German politics and the American women's movement.[16] Gardner and Gittinger followed this collection with a further compilation of essays by an international array of leading scholars from the United States, the United Kingdom, Russia, Japan, China, Germany, Canada, and France, who discussed the various ways in which all those states, plus North Vietnam, South Vietnam, India, and Czechoslovakia, played some part in the lengthy attempts of the 1960s and early 1970s to end the war through negotiations of some kind.[17]

Much though by no means all of the new scholarship of the past decade, which clearly generated a great overall upsurge in investigating the international ramifications of the wars in Indochina, has been due to or at least greatly facilitated by the novel availability of archival materials from the communist or former communist bloc. The United States–based Cold War International History Project, founded in 1991, with its initial mission to encourage the opening of archival sources and the development of scholarship in the communist and former communist world, has published extensive selections from such sources and from the new scholarship to which they have given rise.[18] Particularly notable, in relation to the current volume's broad themes, is the translation of *77 Conversations between Chinese and Foreign Leaders on the Wars in Indochina, 1964–1977,* a compilation of transcripts or excerpts from official conversations obtained somewhat surreptitiously from unidentified archives and other sources in China and, in a few cases, Vietnam.[19] A selection of these documents is included in this volume.

Although their provenance apparently varies, some of these documents may initially have been gathered or excerpted to serve as source material for China's *White Paper* of 1979, an official counterblast published in response to Vietnam's own *White Paper* justifying its own position on the war that had just erupted with China. In no country as yet is the complete archival record open, despite the extensive declassification of files in the United States, United Kingdom, and other Western countries. Indeed, after a period of rapidly expanding access in the early 1990s, some former Soviet archives were subsequently closed or sharply restricted, and many of their most significant sources were never generally open.[20] Still, former Soviet and, increasingly, East and Central European archives are providing new insight into the whole span of the Cold War foreign policies of Asian communist powers, offering information simply unavailable in the archives of Western countries, whose dealings with those states were the reverse of intimate. The Russian academic Ilya V. Gaiduk and the Norwegian scholar Mari Olsen have both used Soviet sources to elucidate Soviet involvement in Indochina over part or whole of the period from the Geneva accords to the reunification of Vietnam in 1975.[21]

As a rule, within Asia, the archival position is more restrictive. Many of the most significant mainland Chinese archives are closed, while in others often ill-defined rules of archival access, since the late 1990s all too frequently subject to draconian retrospective interpretation by the Chinese Public Security Bureau and courts, in many cases retard and discourage serious scholarly research. Yet China has also seen an upsurge of scholarly interest and productivity, with the publication of many significant official—sometimes restricted—documentary compilations, the compilation of oral histories, the production of memoirs, and the publication of serious and scholarly historical works on many topics.[22] As in present-day Russia, a new generation of younger Chinese scholars, often with doctorates earned in the United States, some of whom remain based in that country while others have returned home, are increasingly melding Chinese with Western, former Soviet, and other sources, while benefiting from the insights provided by their personal experience of spending their formative years in a still communist society to draw attention to the saliency in the Cold War of such issues as ideology and culture, which Western historians have often tended to discount and deemphasize.[23] Chinese scholars, whether based on the mainland or overseas, often show great ingenuity and creativity in exploiting the wealth of materials available in provincial, municipal, and specific bureau archives to illuminate the making and implementation of their country's foreign policy, and in correlating these with materials from other sources from different countries.[24] Sadly, at present it is still not always possible for them to provide complete citations of their sources.

Perhaps in partial response to China's flood of official, often *neibu* (classified), and semiofficial publications, the Vietnamese are publishing substantial volumes of official histories, documents, memoirs, and oral histories. In recent years, Western presses have also begun to publish translations of full-length Vietnamese works utilizing normally closed official sources.[25] Though Vietnamese sources remain considerably less accessible, especially to foreign scholars, than even comparable Chinese archives, valuable and enlightening material is slowly becoming available, a process that ongoing scholarly interchanges undoubtedly facilitate. And in both the West and Asia, some scholars have begun to publish studies based upon Vietnamese materials. Particularly notable are Robert K. Brigham's study of the Vietnamese National Liberation Front; Mark Bradley's volume on pre-1950 Vietnam; Ang Cheng Guan's works presenting the "Vietnam War from the other side," giving the perspective of North Vietnam; Stein Tønnesson's volume on the origins of the Vietnamese revolution of 1945; Christopher E. Goscha's and Thomas E. Engelbert's extensive studies of relations among the Vietnamese, Laotian, Cambodian, Thai, and other Southeast Asian communist parties; William J. Duiker's works on the years of war and revolution in Vietnam, and his biography of Ho Chi Minh; and Jeffrey Kimball's study of the Nixon administration's Vietnam policies.[26]

In international meetings from 1988 onward, Vietnamese and Americans also began to explore their often dramatically divergent perspectives on the Indochina wars. One early fruit of such encounters was a collection of essays, jointly edited by the American scholar Jayne S. Werner and the Vietnamese historian Luu Doan Huynh, the latter of whom participated in many of the events he described.[27] In 1995 the Watson Institute for International Relations of Brown University in the United States and Vietnam's Institute for International Relations in Hanoi began an oral history project that brought former officials and scholars from both sides together in several conferences and generated much provocative discussion, while McNamara's participation assured them copious press coverage.[28]

During the past decade, the Cold War International History Project, whose first director, James G. Hershberg, was much involved in the aforementioned Vietnamese conferences, has itself organized and cosponsored, with a variety of partners, several conferences with an Asian theme—on Sino-American relations, the Cold War in Asia, Sino-Soviet relations, and the insights that East European archives can provide into the Cold War in Asia. This book is based upon one such conference, "New Evidence on China, Southeast Asia, and the Vietnam War," which was held at the University of Hong Kong in January 2000.[29] This conference was itself the third of several held starting in 1990 at that institution centering on themes of international diplomacy that included numerous mainland Chinese scholarly participants, as well as Russian, American, European, Australian, Israeli, and Vietnamese scholars, most of whose papers utilized a broad international range of source materials. One of its most notable accomplishments was the opportunity it provided for sometimes heated interchanges between Chinese scholars and two Vietnamese counterparts, the redoubtable Luu Doan Huynh, and Doan Van Thang, both from the Institute for International Relations.

The most extensive study of Chinese involvement in the wars in Indochina, that of Zhai Qiang, gives an excellent survey of the quarter century from 1950 to 1975, but it can by no means serve as the last word on the subject; rather, it marks a beginning. No one historian, however diligent and talented, can hope to give definitive answers on every aspect of Chinese involvement in Vietnam, especially when new evidence is constantly becoming available in archives around the world, including in China itself. Various chapters of the present volume enlarge and elucidate upon themes raised by Zhai, such as the role of Mao Zedong, Chinese aid to Vietnam, Chinese efforts to limit the conflict, and the impact of the Vietnam War itself upon Sino-Soviet relations. In chapter 11 of this volume, Zhai himself provides a lengthy analysis of Chinese dealings with Cambodia, and other contributors have broadened the geographical focus to include the Soviet Union's views of both Vietnam and China in the mid-1950s, the role that long-standing U.S. hostility to China played in the decisions of 1964–65 to escalate the war, and French attitudes toward China and Vietnam.

Even so, this volume in no way pretends to give a complete picture of Chinese policy, or even Sino-Vietnamese relations, during the Indochina wars. Its contributors range from senior scholars and officials with decades of experience to young academics just finishing their doctorates, and even those from the same country are by no means committed to a single viewpoint. The chapters of this volume raise as many questions as they answer. It is to be hoped that, rather than being considered in any way conclusive, they will stimulate and indicate directions for further research, not least by many of the able contributors themselves.

Part I: From Colonial Rule to Escalation

For more than a quarter century after the foundation of new China, the mighty figure of Chairman Mao dominated Chinese politics, domestic and foreign, though it seems likely that from the late 1960s, as China reeled under the twin impact of the Cultural Revolution and ever more intense Sino-Soviet antagonism, Premier Zhou Enlai increasingly prevailed in the making of foreign policy.[30] It is fitting, therefore, that chapter 1 of this book—by Yang Kuisong, who has also written perceptively on Sino-Soviet and Sino-

American relations—surveys the entire span of Mao's policy toward Indochina.[31] Relying heavily on newly available published collections of Chinese documents, and also utilizing unpublished materials, Yang gives a nuanced account of the gradual evolution of Mao's thinking on Indochina,
which like recent studies by Chen Jian and Qiang Zhai emphasizes the close
early ties between the Chinese and Vietnamese communist movements, and
the reciprocal military assistance and even refuge which, before attaining
power, the two afforded each other (as, indeed, did the Chinese and Korean
movements).[32]

In chapter 1, Yang depicts Mao as both principled and pragmatic. Given
the genuinely international nature of Asian communism, Mao's very conscious sense that he sought to become the leader of nationalist, anticolonialist forces around the world, and Stalin's acquiescence in 1949–50 in
China's assumption of a vanguard role in such revolutionary movements in
Asia, retaining for the Soviet Union the captaincy of international proletarian revolution in developed countries, Chinese eagerness to assist Vietnam
is even more explicable. As early as November 1949, indeed, Stalin sought
to restrain Mao's eagerness to send Chinese troops to assist Ho's forces in
Vietnam.[33] Yang likewise demonstrates that Mao's support for Vietnam
changed over time. In 1954, he endorsed the policy advocated by Zhou and
the Soviets, of pressuring Ho and the Viet Minh to accept, at least temporarily, the division of Vietnam at the 17th parallel, a policy decision dictated in part by Chinese reluctance to encourage greater American involvement in Asia, and also by China's need, after many years of fighting in the
anti-Japanese War, the Civil War, and the Korean War, to concentrate upon
domestic development. Despite Mao's rather rambunctious determination
to enter the Korean War in 1950, it seems that the unexpected U.S. military
intervention in that conflict, and the protracted experience of fighting a
lengthy, stalemated war, may have had a certain sobering impact upon
him.[34] Yang also suggests that, in the mid-1950s, Chinese policymaking remained more democratic than it later became, leading Mao to yield to his
more pragmatic colleagues, something he later claimed to regret as a betrayal of Vietnam's revolution.

After 1958, however, as he found Soviet efforts to attain peaceful coexistence with capitalism increasingly irksome, Mao viewed North Vietnam's resumption of revolutionary struggle against the South as a validation of his own belief in revolution. In the early 1960s, he rejected attempts
by Zhou, Deng Xiaoping, and Wang Jiaxiang, the director of the Chinese
Communist Party's International Liaison Department, to restrain the con-

flict in South Vietnam to a low intensity, a position they favored partly because they believed China needed to concentrate on internal economic recovery from the damage wreaked by the Great Leap Forward and the withdrawal of Soviet aid, and also because they sought to minimize the possibility of large-scale U.S. intervention.[35]

Such policies reflected a broader switch in Mao's thinking, from the promotion of revolution and communism around Asia and elsewhere in the developing world through peaceful, democratic methods, to the assumption by China of the role of the "center of world revolution," with the establishment of training camps in China itself for young, foreign revolutionaries from Asia, Africa, and Latin America, to whom China then provided military and economic assistance. At least verbally, Mao went so far as to contemplate Chinese military intervention in Indochina in response to any potential American commitment of troops. Rather ironically, in 1963 and 1964 China even attacked Ho for being insufficiently revolutionary, particularly in his adoption of Soviet rather than Chinese models of land reform, and for attempting to remain neutral in the Sino-Soviet split, when China would have preferred strong Vietnamese endorsement of its own position. Even more infuriating was North Vietnam's acceptance from late 1964 onward of Soviet assistance in its struggle with the United States, aid that surpassed, in technological sophistication and eventually in quantity, anything China could match, and which brought Soviet influence to China's own southern borders.

Even so, Chinese aid to Vietnam, already relatively substantial between 1956 and 1963, grew dramatically in the years 1964 to 1968, and China even helped to transport some Soviet aid to Vietnam itself. Yet from 1965 onward, Mao repeatedly attacked Soviet efforts to facilitate negotiations between North Vietnam and its enemies, and when, after the Tet Offensive of the spring of 1968, peace talks were begun, China likewise considered this policy mistaken and a betrayal of the revolutionary cause. Such disputes effectively drove Vietnam away from China, forcing it into closer ties with the Soviets. From 1969 onward, however, Mao—disappointed by the substantial failure of his policies of world revolution, and alarmed by the 1968 Soviet invasion of Czechoslovakia, fierce Sino-Soviet border clashes, and Soviet threats of a nuclear attack upon China—showed himself "sober and capable of paying attention to the realities of power politics." He therefore endorsed Zhou's efforts to obtain protection against the Soviet Union by reopening relations with the United States, even though for two decades Chinese propaganda had depicted the latter as the chief and foremost of China's international enemies.

By the early 1950s, the complicated situation in Indochina had already made the area a nexus of international diplomacy, a region where all the world's major powers were, however reluctantly, to some degree involved. As the world's senior communist power and as a cochair, with the United Kingdom, of the 1954 Geneva Conference, the Soviet Union acquired a certain investment in Vietnam, a stake that, especially after Soviet president Joseph Stalin's death in 1953, it may well have found less than welcome. In a paper that previewed his larger study of pre-1964 Soviet policy toward Vietnam, Ilya V. Gaiduk confirmed the accepted view that, like their Chinese counterparts, Soviet representatives at Geneva pressured the Viet Minh to accept the temporary partitioning of their country.[36] In chapter 2 of this volume, Mari Olsen—a Norwegian scholar and the author of the only other study to date employing former Soviet archival materials to concentrate on Soviet–Vietnamese relations in this period—reminds us that the Soviets therefore had a vested interest in the implementation of the Geneva Accords, and scrutinizes Soviet policy in 1955, as it gradually became apparent that, with American backing, South Vietnam was likely to block the nationwide elections that settlement had envisaged for 1956.

By the spring of 1955, it seems, the Soviet Union believed North Vietnamese influence remained overly weak in the South, and that the North's efforts to block the replacement of French by American power there were insufficiently vigorous and energetic. The Soviets therefore recommended the establishment of a quasi-autonomous Southern national unification movement, with no overt connection to the North. They also urged Northern officials to moderate their criticism of the Southern government. Though the Soviets signed an economic assistance agreement for North Vietnam in 1955, until at least 1957, perhaps fearing that a stronger North might launch an outright attack on the South, they refused to provide military assistance or establish a military mission in Hanoi, and like China they failed to protest against the South's U.S.-backed abrogation of the Geneva accords. To the North's disgust, in 1957 the Soviet Union even suggested that both Vietnams might become members of the United Nations. Soviet officials may well have feared that, at a time when Nikita Khrushchev was moving toward peaceful coexistence with capitalist states, the outbreak of war in Vietnam would have forced them to choose between supporting the North, when broader foreign policy imperatives and the emergence of serious dissent in several East European satellites mandated caution, or abandoning a communist client. In 1955, the Soviets also refused to establish a joint Sino-Soviet economic mission in Vietnam, arguing that China already had well-established economic aid policies and initiatives there, possibly demonstrating continuing Soviet recognition of the internecine division of labor within international communist efforts Mao and Stalin had reached in 1950, and at this time they generally deferred to China on Vietnam.

Olsen argues that many of the inconsistencies in Soviet actions on Vietnam in the late 1950s derived from the dual audiences to which many Soviet international policies were directed: other big powers and world public opinion, on the one hand, and the international socialist camp, on the other. She suggests that, though prepared to allow China to bear most of the burden of assisting Vietnam in the later 1950s, as the Sino-Soviet split developed, the Soviets may nonetheless have expected Vietnam to follow the Soviet line in ideology. The need to compete with China may also have been one reason why, ten years after the Geneva Agreement was reached, the Soviet Union would ultimately decide to provide extensive aid to the North Vietnamese struggle.

In 1964 and 1965, as military hostilities within Vietnam intensified, three great powers, the United States, China, and the Soviet Union, each had to decide whether and to what degree they should escalate their military commitment to their ideological client states in Vietnam. For all three countries, considerations of international credibility played a major part in the decision for enhanced involvement; though for China, national security considerations intensified the need to prevent the United States from establishing a strong military presence near its southern border. Though China and the Soviet Union both provided limited aid to North Vietnam, during two decades the commitment of each communist great power to that country remained relatively modest and restrained, at least by comparison with the levels of support that, from 1964 onward, the United States accorded the Southern Vietnamese government. It seems, indeed, that President John F. Kennedy's steady enhancement of American involvement in Vietnam from early 1961 onward greatly disappointed Soviet officials, who did not consider Indochina an area of great strategic significance and had hoped to work out an acceptable modus vivendi there.[37] Debate still rages, exemplified, perhaps, in the work *Argument without End,* as to how it was that the United States, for which in the 1950s Vietnam was only one of numerous second-level overseas commitments, became so deeply, inextricably, and detrimentally involved in a highly divisive and destructive conflict that ultimately brought defeat, humiliation, and disillusion.

In chapter 3 of this volume, Noam Kochavi, a youthful Israeli historian who pursued postgraduate studies at the University of Toronto, addresses the still controversial questions of whether President Kennedy was, as his admirers, including former defense secretary McNamara and the filmmaker Oliver Stone allege, an innovative leader who intended, at least in his second term, to recognize China and withdraw from Vietnam or, as critics such as the historian Gordon Chang suggest, an unreconstructed Cold Warrior whose most original concept on China was his proposal that, with Soviet acquiescence, the United States might launch a first strike against Chinese nuclear facilities before they became operational.[38]

Much of the heat in this now decades-long but still continuing debate springs from the near-hagiographic treatment accorded Kennedy by many of his associates, especially after his assassination, the sense of lost opportunities to which this charismatic leader's tragic and premature death gave rise, and the counterdisillusionment that revelations of both his personal and political flaws subsequently provoked.[39] Kochavi provides an admirably balanced assessment of Kennedy's China policy, based upon in-depth archival research and wide reading in all the available literature. He suggests that, although within Kennedy's administration one can find evidence to support either view, overall the New Frontier exhibited a "deep fragmentation on China policy," a characteristic he blames on the compartmentalization of the American policymaking apparatus under Kennedy.

Kochavi argues that in mid-1962 and again in Kennedy's final months, revisionist thinking within the administration featured a "calm appraisal of China's capabilities and intentions" based upon the predicate that, vis-à-vis the United States, China was weak. Kennedy himself, Kochavi argues, vacillated between an image of China as intransigent and a regional, if not global threat, especially over nuclear policy and Vietnam, that must therefore be opposed, and a desire, particularly in late 1963, to reach some kind of modus vivendi with China, especially if this might reduce the American commitment in Vietnam. Overall, according to Kochavi, Kennedy's view of China and Mao leaned toward the inflexible and rigid, while he "tended to pay insufficient attention to constraints and pressures faced by the Chinese leadership, including those generated by Washington's own actions, evincing little understanding, for example, of Mao's fear of nuclear blackmail by the two superpowers." He leaves open the question "whether Kennedy was in the autumn of 1963 won over to the alternative image of China," but also argues that, in any case, Kennedy's record on China was no worse than that of most other American leaders; that in the early 1960s, as Chang suggests, Mao's renewed espousal of radical policies probably limited the scope for any rapprochement; and that Eisenhower, who ignored the genuine opening for Sino-American reconciliation that developed in China in 1955–56, probably bore more responsibility than Kennedy for missed opportunities in American relations with China.

Undoubtedly, however, Kennedy's fear that China was ultimately responsible for the increasingly embattled situation in South Vietnam was one major reason why, from 1961 to 1963, he dispatched increasing though still limited numbers of American military advisers to that country, setting the stage for his successor, Lyndon B. Johnson's, exponentially greater escalation of that military commitment. Ironically, only a few years later, under Richard Nixon, the massively expanded American involvement and the quest for escape from it would eventually propel the U.S. government toward reversing its lengthy refusal to entertain diplomatic relations with Communist China.

In 1964, however, Johnson was unwilling to entertain any such departures. Shortly after Kennedy's death, in January 1964, France recognized the People's Republic of China, the first of America's NATO partners to do so since the United Kingdom in 1950. In chapter 4 of this volume, Fredrik Logevall, the author of an award-winning work on the broader American failure in the mid-1960s to seek a peaceful solution in Vietnam, draws on British, French, and U.S. archives to explore the ramifications of France's decision for American relations with Vietnam. Lyndon Johnson, the new U.S. president, was already determined to reject any outcome in Vietnam that might remove the southern portion of the country from the U.S. sphere of influence. American officials, who feared the French move would increase pressure upon them to reach a neutralist settlement in South Vietnam, where the government of Diem had recently fallen in a bloody coup, made strenuous efforts to dissuade France from recognizing China; this was particularly the case because President Charles de Gaulle and other French representatives suggested that Paris's recognition of Beijing might help to facilitate such a settlement.

By this time, indeed, the readiness of some prominent South Vietnamese leaders to consider such an outcome to the growing conflict seriously alarmed U.S. leaders, who had acquiesced in the coup against Diem in part to preclude just such a resolution of the hostilities in Vietnam. When France ignored American concerns, senior American officials hastily affirmed that their commitment to South Vietnam remained unshaken, while endorsing a successful coup mounted on January 30, 1964, by the hawkish General Nguyen Khanh—who claimed, at least to the Americans, that the incumbents were neutralist and sympathetic to French suggestions for a negotiated peace—against the recently established South Vietnamese government headed by Duong Van Minh. These moves were intended to counter suggestions by de Gaulle that, with Chinese backing, a neutralized Vietnamese settlement was attainable, proposals that the American allies the United Kingdom, Japan, Canada, and most others welcomed.

Logevall argues that historians have underestimated the significance of the Khanh coup, which replaced a South Vietnamese leader eager "to keep the United States at arm's length and to shift the struggle from the military to the political plane to some degree" with an ineffective leader, during whose twelve-month hold on power "the Vietcong consolidated its hold on key areas of the South and war weariness and alienation from the GVN [Government of Viet Nam] became rampant at all levels of South Vietnamese society."[40] The failure of de Gaulle's neutralization proposals was also symptomatic of the profound U.S. disinclination at this time to consider any kind of negotiated settlement in Vietnam, an outlook which, Logevall contends, given the prevailing Chinese and Soviet reluctance to endorse a greatly expanded conflict in Vietnam, killed what may well have been a potentially fruitful opening to resolve the ever-escalating confrontation.

In 1964 and 1965, Chinese and Soviet officials alike had to determine how to respond to steadily increasing, though still limited, U.S. military involvement in Vietnam. In chapter 5 of this volume, Li Xiangqian, a researcher at the Party History Research Center of the Chinese Communist Party Central Committee in Beijing, suggests that in early to middle 1964, China still did not anticipate massive U.S. intervention in Vietnam, a viewpoint that, as Odd Arne Westad, one of its editors, points out, the volume *77 Conversations* seems to confirm.[41] (To arrive at this finding, Li draws largely on newly published Chinese documentary collections, memoirs, and biographical and historical works.) Indeed, the historian Ang Cheng Guan argues that one major objective of both North Vietnamese and Chinese policies before 1964 was to avoid taking actions that might provoke the commitment of a major U.S. military presence in Vietnam, which both felt would be strategically undesirable and hazardous to their own interests. Even when Hanoi increased its military activities in South Vietnam after the fall 1963 assassination of President Diem, the objective was still to win a quick victory before the United States could intervene.[42] Chen Jian and Yang Kuisong both argue forcibly that, more often than not, Mao used foreign policy primarily as a means to generate enthusiasm and popular and elite support for his often disruptive domestic policies of social mobilization for continuous revolution, a theme likewise sounded by Thomas Christensen in his study of Chinese and American policies on the Korean War and the Taiwan Strait crises.[43]

Li follows these researchers in arguing that Mao's mid-1964 decision to mobilize the country to aid Vietnam in a potential struggle with the United States bore more relation to his desire to sabotage the emphasis upon domestic economic recovery and rehabilitation after the Great Leap Forward given in the Third Five-Year Plan, issued in 1963, and substitute a new focus upon preparations for war, as opposed to light industry producing consumer goods, and the establishment of a Third Line of defense, removing Chinese industrial and defense plants to remote areas of the country far removed from potential American or Soviet attack. Starting in the spring of 1964—well before the Tonkin Gulf incident of August 1964 and the subsequent American escalation, and despite his belief that the risk of greatly expanded U.S. intervention in Vietnam remained small—Mao urged this viewpoint, primarily, it seems, with the objective of regaining control over the making of Chinese domestic and foreign policies and reinvigorating the policies of continuous revolution that were his personal contribution to international communist theory.[44]

Li also dismisses the belief that Mao feared war with the Soviet Union, suggesting that in practice he thought Khrushchev, the Soviet general secretary, was weak and that his country was a satiated power that, despite assorted bellicose pronouncements from Mao condemning the nineteenth-century "unequal treaties" prescribing the Sino-Soviet border, would not risk war with China. Li even suggests that Mao's readiness at this time to precipitate further domestic chaos was evidence that he did not contemplate Chinese intervention in a major war, mobilization for which would normally involve maintaining domestic stability while enhancing economic production.

Part II: The Widening War

In classic Chinese opera style, Mao's bellicose rhetoric often far surpassed his actual performance, and this was apparently the case in Vietnam. Whether or not Chinese leaders anticipated a major U.S. escalation in early 1964, once that event occurred, they rather swiftly mounted a major effort to limit the scope of both their own and the U.S. commitment there.[45] Interestingly, as early as April 1962, a British diplomat in Beijing reported Foreign Minister Chen Yi as informing him that the Chinese would not intervene in Vietnam unless they considered a serious threat existed to the continued viability of the North Vietnamese regime.[46]

For many years, allegations have circulated that in the mid-1960s China and the United States reached an implicit understanding that China would restrict its assistance to North Vietnam to economic and military aid and matériel and its troops to support roles, provided that the Americans refrained from invading North Vietnamese or Chinese territory, attacking the North Vietnamese system of irrigation dikes, or using nuclear weapons.[47] In chapter 6 of this volume—drawing on a wide array of British, U.S., Pakistani, Chinese, and Vietnamese archival and printed sources—James G. Hershberg and Chen Jian confirm that in essence this was indeed the case, and that, using British diplomats as intermediaries, in 1965 Beijing successfully conveyed such a message to top U.S. officials. Their wide-ranging study reveals that, in the mid-1960s, both Chinese and American officials had very much in mind the experience of the earlier Korean War, when the leaders of the People's Republic of China (PRC) indirectly warned their American counterparts that, should U.S.-led forces cross the 38th parallel separating North and South Korea, China would intervene militarily and, when this warning was ignored, did so. Though carefully and artfully leaving the precise triggers for Chinese military intervention somewhat ambiguous, Zhou specifically invoked this past experience to caution American leaders that if they were to again disregard China's sensibilities over Vietnam, they would risk a confrontation with the Chinese involving force.

Hershberg and Chen further suggest that, by the mid-1960s, China and the United States could draw on the experience of more than a decade of indulgence in bellicose rhetoric over Taiwan combined with a sedulous avoidance by both sides of direct military conflict, practices they transferred to the Vietnam theater. Hershberg and Chen go so far as to suggest that the tacit Sino-American mutual interest and collaboration in avoiding full-scale hostilities against each other in Vietnam helped to pave the way for the subsequent reopening of Sino-American relations a few years later.

Chinese involvement in the Vietnam conflict was nonetheless extensive and expensive. In this volume, chapter 7 by Shu Guang Zhang and chapter 8 by Li Danhui focus primarily upon the rather substantial economic and military assistance the communist great powers provided to Vietnam during the 1960s and early 1970s, giving nuanced accounts of the aid provided by China and the Sino-Soviet contentions, difficulties, and rivalries generated by the Soviet Union's own concurrent dispatch of assistance to Hanoi. Before discussing their chapters, however, it is important to describe a paper whose omission from this volume was unfortunately compelled by constraints of space. In that paper, Qu Aiguo, a senior researcher in the Department of Military History of the Academy of Military Science in Beijing, again presented the conventional view, that China consistently provided Vietnam with generous and effective support. He gave a detailed—though, because many of his sources remained classified, rather sparsely documented—account of the scale and scope of the assistance, both in economic and military supplies and auxiliary support troops, which China furnished Vietnam from 1962 onward, and he cited numerous North Vietnamese expressions of appreciation and gratitude for this aid and the part it played in their ultimate triumph.

According to Qu, the withdrawal of virtually all Chinese support troops in 1969–70 and the drastic cutback in Chinese aid were not the result of Chinese displeasure over Vietnam's opening of peace talks with the United States, but occurred at Vietnam's request, because these forces had by then completed their assigned tasks. He drew particular attention to China's actions in 1972 in providing mine-sweeping facilities to counter the U.S. mining of North Vietnamese harbors, and in laying oil pipelines to transmit gas and diesel fuel to Vietnam. Qu also argued that Chinese signals to the United States that, should American ground troops invade North Vietnamese territory, China would enter the war outright inhibited the United States from expanding the war, a determining factor in the ultimate North Vietnamese victory. Missing from his meticulous description of Chinese aid, however, was any acknowledgment of the manner in which, despite initially agreeing to do so, China failed to provide North Vietnam with Chinese pilots and airplanes to resist American bombing attacks, or any suggestion that China drastically reduced its aid to Vietnam in 1969, to signal Chinese disagreement with North Vietnam's decision to open negotiations with the United States, and possibly, too, Chinese resentment of growing Vietnamese reliance upon more technologically sophisticated Soviet assistance and the consequent geopolitical tilt toward the Soviet Union.[48]

However, in chapters 7 and 8, both Zhang and Li adopt a rather more skeptical approach. Zhang, one of the foremost American-trained mainland historians now based in the United States, uses both Chinese and American archival and printed sources to provide an overview of Chinese economic aid to Vietnam from 1956 onward, and its role in both Sino-Soviet and Sino-American relations. Zhang points out that, whereas Chinese aid to Vietnam between 1956 and 1963 was undoubtedly substantial—considerably surpassing Soviet aid, both Gaiduk and Ang suggest[49]—at this time it was by no means China's highest priority, and on several occasions in the early 1960s China refused Vietnamese requests for what it considered overambitious technical assistance. In 1963 the ramifications of the Sino-Soviet split and its potentially detrimental impact upon China's international position led Zhou, despite the damage caused by the Great Leap Forward and the competing demands of economic recovery, to institute a major Chinese foreign aid program as a means of regaining international influence. At this time, however, Zhou still anticipated that Africa, not Southeast Asia, would be the major recipient of Chinese economic aid, a priority that changed only after the Tonkin Gulf incident and the major escalation of American involvement that followed, and which seems to confirm that until then the Chinese had not seriously anticipated a massive U.S. military commitment in Vietnam. (It is, nonetheless, worth remembering that in subsequent years, Zhou would consider that 1962 marked the beginning of China's allocation of significant quantities of military aid to the actual armed struggle in Vietnam, a verdict that recent work by the historian Niu Jun endorses.[50])

With China still feeling the impact of both the Great Leap Forward and the withdrawal of Soviet aid, Zhang explains, in the spring of 1965 Zhou feared that, despite Mao's bellicose rhetoric, China needed substantial time for preparation before it could consider the possibility of direct military participation in any conflict in Vietnam. Instead, from the second half of 1964, Chinese leaders instituted a major economic aid and military assistance program for the North and for the Southern National Liberation Front, under the close personal supervision of both Mao and Zhou, a highly centralized enterprise that continued undisturbed throughout the height of the otherwise highly disruptive Cultural Revolution. China also dispatched support troops, with particular responsibility for mounting antiaircraft defense against American air strikes and for maintaining Vietnam's communications system, including vital links with China. The Chinese tried, though unsuccessfully, to persuade Vietnam to reject Soviet aid—arguing that, unlike their own assistance, Soviet help always came with undesirable political strings and ulterior motives attached.

According to Zhang, American officials, who in 1964 initially held China responsible for the growing intensity of Northern-backed guerrilla activities in South Vietnam, but later came to believe that the interests of Hanoi and Beijing were by no means identical, quickly noted China's limitation of its support to economic aid, and predicted both that this would inflict major strains on China's battered economy, and that it would generate substantial competitive tensions with the Soviet Union.[51] A desire to maintain a high level of Sino-Soviet discord was one major factor inhibiting any U.S.

expansion of the war to North Vietnam or to Southern China, which American officials feared might bring not only Chinese forces but also, in demonstration of fraternal solidarity, the Soviet Union into the conflict. From 1965 to 1968, American officials even rather vaguely considered trying to relax tensions with and to make diplomatic overtures to China itself, though at that time nothing came of such faint suggestions; by 1968, Soviet officials found them sufficiently alarming that they endeavored to suggest that, should the United States move toward China, "any hope of progress in U.S.-Soviet relations would be completely impossible." At best Chinese aid policy toward Vietnam could only be considered a mixed success, because, while undoubtedly helping Hanoi to survive a protracted war of attrition with the United States, it imposed heavy economic burdens upon a vulnerable China without winning the donor long-term leverage over or gratitude from the recipient.

When the United States escalated its intervention in Vietnam in 1964, after Khrushchev's fall from power, the Soviet Union—which had previously held aloof from the growing confrontation between Vietnam and the United States—responded by providing extensive military and economic aid to North Vietnam, assistance that helped to move that country into the Soviet orbit, and that China deeply resented but could neither match nor persuade its beleaguered Vietnamese ally to reject.[52] In chapter 8 of this volume, Li Danhui—one of China's leading scholars of the Cold War and the author of several major articles on aspects of Chinese foreign policy in the 1960s and 1970s—surveys the sometimes bitter Sino-Soviet disputes to which this aid gave rise between 1965 and 1972. Besides drawing on published Chinese documentary collections and memoirs, Li makes imaginative use of such sources as the archives of the Chinese Ministry of Railway Administration and various Chinese provincial archives, materials that mainland scholars are increasingly beginning to utilize for insights into a wide range of issues.

As Li shows, despite the tense relations between China and the Soviet Union, perhaps one-eighth of Soviet aid was conveyed to Vietnam through Chinese ports and along Chinese railroads, an illustration of the degree to which its commitment to international communist solidarity and support for an embattled ideological ally constrained Chinese freedom of action on this issue. So, too, did China's desire to cultivate the support of Vietnam in the ongoing Sino-Soviet split. One reason for the Chinese withdrawal of aid to Vietnam in 1969–70 was its displeasure over Vietnam's increasing reliance upon Soviet aid, in addition to its disagreement with the North Vietnamese decision to open peace talks with the United States. Chinese officials reacted with great suspicion to Soviet demands for access to Chinese airspace, even on occasion for dedicated air corridors or rights at Chinese air bases near the Vietnamese frontier, to deliver badly needed warplanes and other supplies to Vietnam, while Soviet propaganda made great play with Chinese refusals to accord such facilities. In 1965, China urged North Vietnam to reject an offer of Warsaw Pact "volunteers" to assist in the struggle, a course Vietnamese officials probably intended to follow in any case, because the Soviets did not expect their largely propaganda offer to be accepted, but which further exacerbated Sino-Vietnamese relations. Soviet nonobservance of prearranged port and railroad delivery schedules played havoc with Chinese rail timetables and freight arrangements and enormously irritated those Chinese officials involved. Even so, such logistical irregularities often occur, and Li rightly observes that, "had it not been for the existing friction between China and the Soviet Union, neither the rail nor the ocean transfer of Soviet aid materials would have caused any problems." Oddly enough, Li does not mention Soviet allegations that the Chinese skimmed the best of the Vietnam-destined military supplies for themselves.[53] Zhai has stated that on this issue the evidence is still inconclusive, but that due to the prevailing chaos in the Cultural Revolution, in 1966 and 1967 episodes undoubtedly did occur in which trains bearing goods destined for Vietnam were attacked and looted by Red Guards and other "feuding factions." It seems clear, however, that Zhou tried to restrain such activities and to obtain the return of seized weapons and other goods.[54]

As mentioned above, in 1969 and 1970, China cut back drastically on aid to Vietnam, an indication of its displeasure over the opening of peace negotiations. Vietnamese sources allege that, in October 1968, China unavailingly threatened to cut all ties with the Vietnamese Workers' Party unless Hanoi broke with the Soviet Union and ended the peace negotiations.[55] In August 1969, Zhou prevaricated on Chinese aid to Vietnam, refusing to make any commitments unless the Vietnamese pledged themselves to fight on to the end rather than accept a negotiated settlement, though a generous assistance agreement was eventually signed the following month. The historian Chris Connolly also suggests that, facing potential military conflict with the Soviet Union, Chinese leaders sought to reserve scarce resources for their own potential use.[56] According to Li, between 1970 and 1972, as peace negotiations began to show signs of success, China greatly increased its aid to North Vietnam and the southern National People's Liberation Front, apparently anticipating an embargo on such supplies after a peace settlement, and wishing to place the North and its supporters in an advantageous position to take over the entire country once a "decent interval" had elapsed after American withdrawal.

During this period, China also actively encouraged Vietnam to obtain more supplies from the Soviet Union, and—although disputes still arose, and China attempted to exclude Soviet officials from any role in the transshipment of such goods—was considerably more accommodating in storing Soviet supplies and facilitating their transportation through China to Vietnam. Such increases in aid may have been intended to induce North Vietnam to compromise at the negotiating table, which would in turn further China's ongoing efforts toward rapprochement with the United States. In addition, given the heavy fighting that characterized the final year before the Paris Peace Accords were signed in January 1973, they were probably designed to bolster North Vietnam's military efforts and leave the North Vietnamese in a good position for an eventual takeover of the South. Connolly further elaborates Li's suggestion that the death in 1970 of Ho Chi Minh, who had longstanding close ties to Chinese officials that his colleagues did not share, impelled Chinese leaders to treat North Vietnam generously as part of their effort to win North Vietnam's loyalties in any Sino-Soviet clash. Although no other historian to date has given so detailed a picture of Chinese aid to Vietnam in the final stages of the war, Li essentially validates Zhai's argument that in 1971 and 1972 "Beijing disagreed with Hanoi not over strategies but over tactics."[57] Her study also suggests that, whatever President Richard Nixon and Henry Kissinger, his national security adviser, may have hoped at the time or subsequently claimed to believe, in 1971 and 1972 the prospects for long-term Chinese acquiescence in the indefinite continuation of an independent South Vietnam or the Saigon government were virtually nonexistent. Indeed, as late as 1973 Chinese and Vietnamese leaders were in accord on the need to prepare for a protracted struggle to win control of the South.[58]

By the late 1960s, China's own sense of vulnerability, especially with regard to the Soviet Union, was a leading factor impelling Mao and Zhou to move toward a rapprochement with their long-term foe, the United States. In chapter 9 of this volume, Niu Jun—a leading scholar of Sino-American relations and a senior researcher at both Peking University and the Institute of American Studies of the Chinese Academy of Social Sciences—draws primarily on newly available Chinese published archival and documentary collections to provide a wide-ranging study of the background to the dramatic changes in China's policies at this time, to which the effects of the Vietnam War itself contributed significantly.[59]

Niu focuses first upon the threat which escalating U.S. involvement in Vietnam posed to Chinese national security, which led China both to extend aid to Vietnam and, as noted above, to warn the United States that the consequences of untrammeled expansion of its military campaign against North Vietnam might well include Chinese intervention. Niu notes that, during the Vietnam War, despite China's gaining a nuclear weapons capacity in 1964, "losing the military support its alliance with the Soviet Union had previously provided severely vitiated China's capacity to counter U.S. attacks, especially its ability to coordinate air and naval power"; this, in turn, led China to take strong emergency countermeasures against U.S. incursions, raising commensurately the possibility of direct combat between Chinese and American military personnel.

Meanwhile, Sino-Soviet border clashes, a feature of their relationship since 1960, intensified, and in 1964 talks between the two sides failed to reach any agreement, leading to further increases in the numbers of such confrontations over the next five years, culminating in the Zhenbao Island incident of early 1969. In the India-Pakistan War of 1965, China supported Pakistan while the Soviet Union backed India, and in January 1966 the Soviet Union signed a friendship and alliance treaty with another Chinese neighbor, the People's Republic of Mongolia. The forcible Soviet restoration of communist rule in Czechoslovakia in the autumn of 1968 was the final event that persuaded China that its northern neighbor, the Soviet Union, represented a greater threat than its southern and eastern opponent, the United States.

With Mao's backing, in late 1967 Zhou and his allies regained control of the Chinese Foreign Ministry, which had for two years been taken over by Cultural Revolution radicals, whose activities had discredited China abroad and alienated even its friends. Moreover, from 1965 onward, the common Chinese and Soviet sponsorship of North Vietnam's struggle exacerbated rather than alleviated tensions between the two. China initially vehemently rejected as ideologically unsound and unprincipled Soviet suggestions that the two should cooperate in helping to foster a negotiated peace in Vietnam, which would enable the United States to extricate itself from this entanglement. This stance, and the perennial disputes over the transit of Soviet aid through China to Vietnam, seriously alienated China from its Southeast Asian client, as did its opposition to the opening of peace negotiations in 1968. The souring of China's relations with both Vietnam and the Soviet Union in turn facilitated its decision, in 1968 and 1969, to consider reopening and improving its until then dormant, mostly hostile relationship with the United States.

In chapter 10 of this volume, Shen Zhihua, Li Danhui's husband and longtime academic collaborator, draws like her on a wide range of Chinese published and unpublished sources, combined with memoirs and other materials from China, Vietnam, the Soviet Union, and the United States, to focus specifically on the way in which, once China had decided to move toward the United States, Chinese leaders had to juggle their desire for improved Sino-American relations with their long-standing commitments both to Vietnam, a fellow communist ally, and also to their internationalist rhetoric supporting "liberation movements by peoples all over the world." He also focuses on China's need for security on its southern border after American withdrawal, something that an overly close Soviet-Vietnamese relationship would jeopardize.

In 1971 and 1972, Zhou seems to have made every effort to keep North Vietnam informed of the progress of his talks with the United States, and to reassure North Vietnam that China would not abandon its cause, in part through a major enhancement of the aid program that, a scant year or two earlier, China had drastically curtailed. In meetings with U.S. national security adviser Kissinger, Zhou held steadfastly aloof from issues relating to Vietnam, professing respect for that country's independence but only making rhetorical protests when, retaliating for Vietnam's spring 1972 offensive, in May of that year the United States launched heavy air strikes against the North and mined Haiphong and other northern harbors. China quickly dispatched massive amounts of economic aid to the North, agreed to assist with numerous industrial projects, and, most significantly, also dispatched mine-sweeping ships and troops to help clear northern seaways. In the second half of 1972 China, eager to facilitate the withdrawal of American troops from Vietnam, urged North Vietnamese officials to compromise on such matters as leaving the Nguyen van Thieu government at least temporarily in place in Saigon, but also exerted pressure on the United States to make concessions when necessary.

Once the war ended, however, Sino-Vietnamese relations quickly deteriorated, and later in 1973 China rejected North Vietnam's request for a huge aid package as beyond China's resources.[60] From 1971 the Soviets, hoping to entice Indochina into the Soviet camp on a permanent basis, had deliberately outmatched the aid China provided to Vietnam, a strategy Soviet officials continued and even escalated after the war was over, despite their suspicion toward many of Vietnam's leaders and their own distaste for Vietnam's desire to resolve all outstanding issues through military conflict.

Growing Soviet involvement in Vietnam in turn created new problems for China. In chapter 11 of this volume, Qiang Zhai now supplements his existing book-length study of China and the Vietnam war by focusing specif-

ically on Chinese policies toward Cambodia, based on extensive use of Chinese—and those few available Cambodian—published sources of every
kind, supplemented by some Western primary sources and numerous secondary works. Zhai demonstrates that Chinese fears of the burgeoning
Soviet influence in Indochina and, more broadly, China's desire to inhibit
the spread of Vietnamese domination in the rest of Indochina largely accounted for China's often somewhat contradictory, even paradoxical, policies toward Cambodian communism. At the 1954 Geneva Conference,
China urged Khmer insurgents to compromise and work with the Royal
Cambodian government headed by Prince Sihanouk, a strategy that remained effective until Sihanouk's overthrow in 1970 in an American-
backed right-wing coup headed by General Lon Nol. In the 1960s, Sihanouk
interpreted Cambodia's ostensible Cold War neutrality as permitting—for
a price—the transport of supplies from China to Vietnam, along the famed
Ho Chi Minh Trail, and allowed communist Vietnamese guerrillas to take
refuge in sanctuaries in Cambodian territory.

As Qiang explains, the Khmer Rouge Cambodian communist party developed largely in isolation from China, and as insurgency and civil war
against the Lon Nol regime intensified in the early 1970s, China urged the
formation of a coalition government including representatives of all Cambodian factions and headed by Sihanouk, who found a comfortable refuge
in Beijing after his overthrow. This stance derived not only from China's
long-standing comfortable relations with Sihanouk but also from Chinese
fears that the Khmer Rouge were too close to either or both the North Vietnamese communists and the Soviet Union. (Ironically, the fact that during
the 1960s North Vietnam benefited substantially from the accommodating
Sihanouk's policies likewise impelled North Vietnamese leaders to urge the
Cambodian Khmer Rouge, including Pol Pot, to form a united front with
Sihanouk rather than waging armed struggle to take over the country, and
to support Sihanouk after his overthrow.[61])

Visits to Beijing by such top Khmer Rouge leaders as Khieu Samphan in
early 1974 and the efforts of Pol Pot, the Khmer Rouge head, to eliminate
pro-Vietnamese members from his party, convinced Chinese officials that
most Cambodian communist leaders were largely independent of both Vietnamese and Soviet influence, whereupon they dropped their earlier insistence upon a negotiated coalition settlement and gave full support to Khmer
Rouge efforts to take over the entire country. In so doing, China may well
have sought to check any growth of pro-Hanoi forces in Cambodia. Chinese
assistance played a significant role in the final Khmer Rouge victory in

1975. Although Sihanouk was briefly restored to power as a figurehead chief of state, eight months later, the Khmer Rouge placed him under house arrest, and three years later, after the death of many of close family members in Pol Pot's purges, he fled the country. Until the late 1980s, the Cambodian Khmer Rouge remained close Chinese allies, while Vietnam's 1978 invasion of Cambodia triggered the brief Sino-Vietnamese war of 1979.

In chapter 12 of this volume, Stephen Morris, the author of *Why Vietnam Invaded Cambodia,* uses reports from Soviet diplomats based in Vietnam between 1970 and 1975 to shed further light upon the Soviet-Chinese-Vietnamese triangle at that date.[62] Morris challenges the accepted view that, as it had done for most of the 1960s, in the 1970s and 1980s, Vietnam attempted to balance between China and the Soviet Union, arguing that in fact its policies demonstrated a decided pro-Soviet tilt, which, in turn, provoked difficulties in Sino-Vietnamese relations.[63] Notwithstanding Chinese leaders' sedulous efforts to reassure North Vietnam, it seems that by mid-1971 distrust of China's progress toward Sino-American rapprochement persuaded Vietnam (which as Zhai demonstrates had in 1960 sought to bring about a Sino-Soviet reconciliation) to lean toward the Soviets in the two communist giants' ongoing feud.[64]

Yet as late as 1972, Morris shows, North Vietnam—though greatly irritated by Nixon's visit to China—was still trying to balance between its two patrons, and as Gaiduk points out, Soviet efforts toward détente with the United States regardless of their impact on Vietnam were an equally galling cause of concern to Vietnamese leaders, prodding them into concessions at the negotiating table.[65] The generous 1973 aid agreement the Soviets made with Vietnam—just as China, as described by Shen Zhihua, cut back requested Vietnamese assistance—may have been the factor that finally tipped the scales toward the Soviets. Certainly, in the autumn of 1975, Chinese officials informed Vietnamese leaders, including Le Duan, the secretary general of the Vietnamese Workers' Party, of their great displeasure over Vietnam's pro-Soviet inclination, further evidence of which came in 1978 when Vietnam joined the Council for Mutual Economic Assistance and signed a Treaty of Friendship and Cooperation with the Soviet Union.

Morris considers Vietnam's pro-Soviet affiliation the major cause of the 1979 Sino-Vietnamese war, though conflicts over Cambodia and Chinese resentment of Vietnamese discrimination against ethnic Chinese residents also played their part. In November 1977, the Vietnamese again privately urged Chinese leaders to heal the Sino-Soviet split and reach reconciliation with the Soviet Union. Morris argues that Hanoi desired to maintain a working relationship with China, but that other Vietnamese foreign policy goals were incompatible with this. Giving valuable insight into the still murky subject of internal Vietnamese divisions, Morris suggests that within Vietnam's communist leadership there existed pro-Soviet and pro-Chinese factions, though other issues often cut across these lines of demarcation.

As Mari Olsen and Gaiduk have done for earlier periods, Morris demonstrates that in the early to middle 1970s relations between Vietnam and its Soviet patrons remained extremely difficult.[66] Indeed, the Soviet ambassador to the United States, Anatoly Dobrynin, plaintively complained that the Soviets learned more of Hanoi's negotiating position from the Americans at their May 1972 summit meeting with Nixon than they did from the Vietnamese themselves.[67] In 1970, North Vietnam bluntly refused to coordinate its foreign policy with that of the Soviet Union, and insisted on maintaining independent relations with other members of the Soviet bloc in Eastern Europe and elsewhere and approaching them separately for aid, tactics the Soviets found confusing and irritating. Soviet diplomats in Vietnam were habitually subjected to numerous restrictions and close surveillance, and "the Soviet embassy complained that the Vietnamese army command tried to limit the Soviet specialists' activity in every possible way to technical assistance only," excluding them from all significant combat and policy decisions as well as intelligence data and captured American weapons. Draconian, quasi-Stalinist restrictions on Soviet personnel in Vietnam endured throughout the 1970s. Vietnam failed to inform the Soviet Union in advance of its major spring 1972 military offensive, and Soviet officials often felt that when dealing with them their Vietnamese counterparts were less than frank.

In chapter 13 of this volume, Luu Doan Huynh, a mid-level North Vietnamese official who participated in many of the events on which he was commenting, writes in a private capacity but nonetheless provides a Vietnamese perspective on both Chinese and Soviet behavior toward Vietnam. Huynh—already known for his forceful presentation of North Vietnamese viewpoints and perspectives to Americans in the Brown University series of conferences and other international scholarly gatherings—is equally trenchant in advancing criticisms of the positions of Vietnam's communist allies throughout the conflict. The sharply unflattering gloss he gives upon several essays by mainland scholars is a refreshing antidote to the rather complacent stance these take toward China's assistance to North Vietnam during the Indochina wars, shocking some but also serving to illuminate the starkly divergent Vietnamese perspective upon China's policies toward Vietnam.[68] He pays particular attention to Yang Kuisong's analysis of Mao's shifting policies toward the Vietnam wars in chapter 1, decrying the priority Mao consistently accorded to Chinese national interests as he perceived these. He also takes considerable exception to two papers, by Qu Xing and Wan Tailei and by Tao Wenzhao, whose omission from this volume was unfortunately dictated by considerations of space. In the past, the conventional mainland scholarly view of China's diplomacy throughout the Indochinese conflict was essentially celebratory, though also somewhat defensive, a perspective that to some degree informed both these papers.

In their paper, Qu Xing, a vice president of the Foreign Affairs College in Beijing, and Wan Tailei, one of his postgraduate students, focus upon two episodes: China's pressure upon North Vietnamese representatives at the 1954 Geneva Conference to accept a settlement that partitioned the country, while leaving Laos and Cambodia to make separate peace agreements whereby noncommunist governments retained control of those states; and China's deprecation of North Vietnam's 1968 decision to open peace talks with the United States, which ironically preceded its own decision to resume relations with the United States, something many Vietnamese leaders regarded as a betrayal of their own cause. In the first case, Qu and Wan argue that, by forestalling formal U.S. military intervention and obtaining a coherent, economically viable territory for North Vietnam, China effectively won it the preconditions for its success in subsequently unifying the entire country, something that protracted battle did not attain in Korea.

In the second instance, Qu and Wan stress China's continuing public rhetorical support for Vietnam during the second Indochina war of the 1960s, its extensive provision of military and economic aid and assistance, and its stated readiness, conveyed to the United States, to intervene militarily should the United States proceed too forcefully against North Vietnam. They suggest that virtually no progress occurred in the peace talks until 1970, and even imply that Zhou's sense that movement was finally developing in the stalemated negotiations was one reason for China's own decision to establish contact with the United States. They also point to the numerous occasions on which Zhou used his dealings with American officials to demand a complete U.S. withdrawal from Vietnam, a development that facilitated the ultimate North Vietnamese victory in 1975. They portray Zhou's efforts to keep Vietnamese officials closely informed of his talks with the Americans, and his advice in 1972 that the Vietnamese be more flexible and make more concessions in their dealings with the United States, as advantageous to Vietnam, because the Americans actively sought an opportunity to withdraw.[69]

Qu and Wan, drawing heavily on published Chinese accounts and official compilations of source materials, bolstered by some oral history interviews, essentially present the case for the Chinese defense against the charges brought in the Vietnamese *White Paper* of 1979. They do not consider the possibility, raised not only by that document and Huynh but also in Zhai Qiang's recent study of Chinese involvement in Vietnam, that once the United States had decided to intervene in Vietnam, in the mid-1960s China did not seek a swift Vietnamese victory but in practice preferred to keep the United States embroiled in a protracted, wearing, expensive, and domestically divisive conflict, one that weakened a major enemy at relatively little cost to China.[70] They pay equally little heed to the suggestion, by the editors of the *77 Conversations,* that China preferred continued fighting to the negotiation of a peace settlement that would leave North Vietnam effectively a Soviet client.[71]

Unlike Zhai, Qu and Wan omit to bring up the fact that in November 1971 Chinese officials turned down a request by visiting Premier Pham Van Dong to cancel the visit by President Nixon to China scheduled for February 1972.[72] They do not bring up Vietnamese rebuffs of Chinese offers to discuss the Indochinese situation on their behalf during Nixon's visit, or Zhou's assurances to Nixon that China did not contemplate military intervention in Vietnam, which emboldened the United States in its ongoing negotiations.[73] Nor, unlike Zhai, do they mention China's efforts, between 1973 and 1975, to persuade North Vietnam to defer its takeover of the South, which were accompanied by major reductions in Chinese aid to Vietnam.[74] Absent from their discussion, moreover, is any sense that, whether or not China's decisions on these occasions were ultimately beneficial to North Vietnam's efforts to unify the country, in both 1954 and 1968–72 China essentially gave priority to considerations of political expediency and its own interests—among others, the desire to exclude U.S. military forces from areas on its own borders and, in the late 1960s and early 1970s, to obtain American protection against the Soviet Union and keep the latter from the region—and that any advantageous impact upon Vietnam was primarily incidental to these.

A more sophisticated justification of Chinese policy toward Vietnam is the essay mentioned above by Tao Wenzhao, the deputy director of the Institute of American Studies of the Chinese Academy of Social Sciences and one of China's most senior diplomatic historians. By skillfully deploying both Chinese and U.S. published documentary sources and memoirs, he focuses exclusively on Chinese dealings with Vietnam between 1950 and 1954, giving a more detailed account than did Qu and Wan of both Chinese assistance to the Viet Minh in the conflict and of Chinese diplomacy at the

Geneva Conference. Tao also demonstrates the near veneration with which many senior Chinese academics still regard the much-loved and respected Premier Zhou, perhaps Communist China's one remaining secular saint. Tao emphasizes the reluctance of U.S. officials, especially Secretary of State John Foster Dulles, to reach any agreement on Indochina, and their eagerness to sabotage the Geneva Conference, a strategy that Zhou's able diplomacy successfully checkmated. Like Qu and Wan, Tao draws attention to the desirability of excluding American military forces from Indochina, to Zhou's skill in attaining this objective over in the face of U.S. obstruction, and to Ho Chi Minh's later endorsement of Zhou's priorities.

For Tao, as for Qu and Wan, Zhou's diplomacy at Geneva helped to lay the foundation of subsequent Vietnamese successes, winning the North a much-needed breathing space in which to establish itself economically and politically before proceeding toward unification. Though not denying that China—like the Soviet Union—exerted pressure on North Vietnamese negotiators, Tao argues that in the long term these tactics best served Vietnam's interests. Tao also hails Zhou's success in making himself a major, perhaps *the* major, diplomatic figure at the Geneva Conference, an event that marked new China's emergence as a force to reckon with on the international stage.[75]

In chapter 13 of the present volume, however, Huynh, still unconvinced by such arguments, summarizes his position in a thoughtful commentary. He clearly feels that on more than one occasion, most notably at the Geneva Conference but also when advising North Vietnam on peace negotiations during the 1960s, both great communist powers often consulted their own interests first and those of North Vietnam second. His commentary is ample confirmation of the extent to which, in the words of Stein Tønnesson, "the 1954 Geneva settlement was a time-bomb within the Asian communist fraternity."[76] At the level of detail, Huynh points out certain instances where the documentary record is still far from complete. He also warns that, when using archival evidence, to obtain the full picture one must compare materials gathered from different sources, not simply rely upon documents collected from one party in isolation, a caveat that leads one to wish that his own country's government would pay greater heed to his advice.

Huynh's commentary is striking evidence of the degree to which, however generous Chinese aid to Vietnam may have been, and however well-intentioned Chinese actions were on at least some occasions, perceived shortcomings in China's attitudes and policies toward Vietnam generated enormous resentment, which eventually climaxed in the 1979 war. Indeed,

recognizing the long-term Sino-Vietnamese acrimony and resentments that
the Geneva settlement ultimately generated, Chen Jian suggests that "the origins of the confrontation" that led to the Sino-Vietnamese War of 1979 "can
be traced back to their relationship at the Geneva conference of 1954."[77]

Even when they disagree sharply with Huynh's perspective, most of
those Chinese scholars exposed to it clearly find it an enlightening, if often
decidedly unpalatable, corrective to the overly complacent view of Sino-Vietnamese relations their own essays sometimes convey. Huynh provokes
debate as to whether the flaws that he perceives in Sino-Vietnamese alliance
relations—and, more broadly, the predominantly unsatisfactory relations
among large and small communist allies that during the Cold War were virtually inherent in all asymmetrical state-to-state dealings among communist powers, such as those between China and the Soviet Union—were inevitable in any alliance patron–client relationship or were derived from
broader systemic flaws intrinsic to the very nature of communism.

Documentary Evidence

The scholarly chapters in this volume depend heavily on new archival evidence from former communist archives, especially the Soviet Union, China,
and Vietnam. A few examples of documents from the latter two states are
included here in chapters 14 and 15, a mere sampling of the types of materials that are now becoming available.

Chapter 14 consists of a document that appears to be based on genuine
oral reflections on Sino-Vietnamese relations by Le Duan in 1979; it has
been translated by Christopher E. Goscha and is preceded by a commentary
by Stein Tønnesson. This document provides new and intimate insights into
Vietnamese perceptions of Chinese policies toward Vietnam over more than
thirty years. Tønnesson and Goscha rightly warn that Duan's perspective
was undoubtedly affected by China's war against Vietnam. Even so, his
memories of Sino-Vietnamese dealings provide perhaps the most revealing
glimpse to date of top Vietnamese officials' attitudes dealings toward their
often conflicted relationship with China. Interestingly, Duan, who visited
China frequently during the Vietnam War, managing some of the diplomatic
aspects of the relationship, makes it clear that he often deliberately kept
their Soviet rivals in ignorance of Vietnamese policies and strategies. His
relationship with Mao was obviously difficult, and he repeatedly chastises
the chairman for lack of resolution, even cowardice, in dealing with the
United States, suggesting that Mao fundamentally feared American power.

Morris suggests that Vietnamese leaders generally liked and admired Zhou, which was certainly true of Duan, perhaps because Zhou seems on occasion to have flattered him, a tactic the flexible premier likewise often used with Mao. Interestingly, Duan suggests that Zhou regretted the Sino-Soviet split, a division within the communist camp that—even if largely on the grounds that it disadvantaged Vietnam internationally—he himself deplored, and sought to mend, which perhaps confirms Westad's view that in the early 1960s the split might still have been repaired, and it was "Mao's resurgence in Chinese politics in mid-1962 and the ensuing confrontation over foreign affairs that in the end laid the Sino-Soviet alliance to rest."[78] On several occasions, indeed, in the mid-1960s and early 1970s, Soviet officials seem to have hoped for a more cooperative Sino-Soviet relationship on Vietnam, suggesting that even then scope for reconciliation existed, though on each occasion Mao blocked such overtures.[79]

According to Morris, Vietnamese leaders followed closely the intricacies of Chinese politics, and when Deng Xiaoping regained power in 1978 they hoped Sino-Vietnamese relations would improve. Duan clearly respected and perhaps regarded as a kindred spirit the bluntly outspoken Deng, to the extent that he believed that in 1979 Deng went to war against Vietnam largely because internal political pressures compelled him to do so. This may repeat a pattern apparent in Deng's behavior earlier in the 1970s, when political vulnerability seems to have caused him to take a harsher line with the United States on Taiwan than Chinese officials had previously done.[80]

Whatever Duan's feelings in 1954, by 1979 he clearly deeply resented the partitioning of Vietnam under the Geneva Accords, and he felt that in the later 1950s and 1960s China had pressured Vietnam to restrain the insurgency to a level of low intensity, so as not to provoke U.S. intervention. This may reveal the degree to which the Great Leap Forward crippled China's ability to project its power overseas. The depths of Vietnamese suspicions of China are well revealed in Duan's suggestion that, seeking a peace settlement in Vietnam, China endorsed the tough tactics of massive airstrikes against North Vietnam and mining Vietnamese harbors the United States adopted in 1972; and his allegations that, in a quest for lebensraum for China's surplus population, Mao sought to annex all of Southeast Asia to China.

Such sources as this offer intriguing evidence, and can only whet the appetite of historians for additional and far more extensive documentation from North Vietnam than is currently available.

Although documentation from China is also relatively scarce, in recent years the picture has improved somewhat, not least with the 2004 opening of the Chinese Foreign Ministry Archives in Beijing to research. The selected Chinese and Vietnamese documents included here in chapter 15, however, are of more ambiguous provenance—transcripts of all or part of conversations of top Chinese, Vietnamese, and Cambodian communist leaders on the Indochinese wars obtained by historians who are currently unable to specify their precise sources. The transcripts have a fly-on-the-wall immediacy not always apparent in the edited versions of such conversations published in various Chinese documentary collections.[81]

Interestingly and ironically, the documents included here allow us to judge the validity of Duan's exaggerated claims that he was extremely outspoken in meetings with Mao. It is also possible to trace just how strong was initial Chinese support for North Vietnamese resumption of armed struggle in 1963 and 1964; the perennial Chinese suspicion of Soviet intentions and involvement in Vietnam, a subject on which Chinese leaders issued repeated warnings to Vietnamese officials; the circuitous but determined efforts of Premier Zhou to signal U.S. officials to limit both American and Chinese military involvement in Vietnam and avoid a full-scale confrontation between the two countries; the early Chinese dissent from the Vietnamese decision in 1968 to open negotiations with the United States, and that policy's subsequent reversal; the detrimental impact on Sino-Vietnamese relations of the lingering memory of the decision to accept the 1954 Geneva Conference settlement; the post-1973 deterioration in Sino-Vietnamese relations; and the ailing Mao's hope, expressed to Pol Pot in 1975, a year before his death, that his own country's embrace of less radical policies was only a temporary detour from the highway to Marxist perfection. One also gains a sense of Mao's individual role in the conduct of Chinese foreign policy, as the ultimate arbiter, a genial, discursive, and authoritative host who often sought—not always successfully—to moderate the tensions arising from visitors' earlier conversations with such subordinates as Zhou and Chen.

Conclusions

This volume's findings help to illuminate the interrelated topics of Cold War intra-alliance diplomacy, especially within the communist bloc, China's involvement in and policy toward the Vietnam conflict, and how the changes in big-power relations over Vietnam ultimately affected the course of the broader Cold War.

During the 1960s, the escalating war in Vietnam was facilitated by the Sino-Soviet split while intensifying and magnifying it. On the intra-alliance level, the war was in some ways an example of what the historian Tony Smith has termed "pericentrism," arguing that "junior members in the international system at times took actions that . . . played a key role in *expanding, intensifying, and prolonging* the struggle between East and West." This meant that, "on important occasions, the superpowers" were "as much played upon as players, as much pulled into situations not of their own devising as pushing themselves in on the basis of their overweening power and ambition."[82] Thomas Christensen likewise argues that throughout the 1960s, the disunity and competition the Sino-Soviet split caused within the international communist bloc permitted smaller powers, notably North Vietnam, to force the larger powers into measures hostile to the West that the Soviet Union, at least, might otherwise have preferred to avoid, and so ratcheted up international tensions.[83] Despite assorted efforts by North Vietnamese officials to heal the Sino-Soviet breach, at least at times the divisions among the larger communist big powers may have been advantageous for them, enabling them to force their somewhat reluctant patrons to use military and economic aid to engage in a bidding contest for Vietnamese loyalties, and playing an important part in the ultimate 1964–65 Soviet decision to back the escalating North Vietnamese struggle.[84]

Similar factors were at work in North Vietnam's involvement in Laos in the early 1960s, where Chinese backing allowed the Vietnamese to support the Pathet Lao in a manner the Soviets found highly irritating.[85] In 1962, Vietnam National Liberation Front representatives carefully told both Chinese and Soviet officials what each wished to hear.[86] Robert Brigham highlights the manner in which, once the subject of peace negotiations arose, the Vietnamese carefully tailored their message to their audience, with Northerners who were suffering from heavy American bombing assuring Soviet officials of their eagerness to open peace negotiations, while to the Chinese leadership Southern National Liberation Front functionaries affirmed their determination to fight on.[87] Christensen perceptively points out, though, that after the Sino-Soviet split intensified in the late 1960s, North Vietnam had far less leverage, as both China and the Soviet Union were determined to improve relations with the United States, if necessary by compromising North Vietnam's goals.[88] Intriguingly, by July 1974 Vietnamese leaders, notably Duan, apparently believed that by speeding up their timetable to reunite Vietnam, ideally to 1975 rather than, as they had originally projected, the fall of 1976 or even 1977, they would be able to put themselves in a stronger position to resist the spread of both Soviet and Chinese influence in Southeast Asia.[89]

Clearly, fraternal ideological solidarity by no means always implied harmonious political relations; indeed, the tensions generated by the wars in Indochina helped to exacerbate the Sino-Soviet split to the point of outright military clashes, and soured the relationships between both Chinese and Vietnamese communists and the communist parties of Vietnam and Cambodia to the point where, in the later 1970s, Vietnam invaded Cambodia and China attacked Vietnam. Morris goes so far as to suggest that the Sino-Soviet split was a major factor in breaking the former Comintern-led unity of the international communist movement, as "national political self-determination emerged as a new legitimizing concept in evaluating political relations between Marxist-Leninist states and revolutionary movements."[90]

As more data become available, the broad nature of communist intra-alliance relations and their evolution over time may well prove a fruitful new research direction. Much of the new Cold War scholarship highlights the once somewhat neglected role of ideology in international affairs during the twentieth century.[91] It is worth asking whether the almost theological nature of twentieth-century communism, effectively a nineteenth-century rationalist attempt to found a secular religion that would solve all socioeconomic problems, gave particular bitterness to disputes, both within and between communist states, and also caused all such divergence to be couched in terms of rival interpretations of a common faith, with dissenters treated much as the sixteenth-century Catholic Church dealt with heretics. The Western alliance of this time was certainly not lacking in tensions. Rather instructively, at the Hong Kong conference both Logevall and Thomas A. Schwartz dealt with the often contentious relationships between the United States and Charles de Gaulle in the 1960s, focusing respectively upon his decisions to recognize China and to withdraw France from NATO.[92]

Although acquiescing in these moves, the United States undoubtedly resented them as jeopardizing its broader European and international strategic objectives; yet American officials restrained from the perfervid criticism of an erstwhile ally that came to characterize Sino-Soviet relations in the late 1950s and early 1960s. One must wonder whether treating dissent within the communist camp as not merely mistaken, but as treachery to the one true faith, contributed to the profound bitterness that such differences frequently generated. More broadly, scholars might inquire whether the saliency of ideological factors was itself a major weakness within international communism, a characteristic differentiating the communist alliance substantially from its Western rival, and perhaps contributing to its eventual collapse.

It may be, too, that weaker communist states found particularly galling and infuriating the morally superior public posture larger communist powers tended to adopt, of justifying on purportedly impeccable ideological grounds decisions such as the 1954 partitioning of Vietnam and the great powers' implicit or explicit refusal to assist the North to reverse this. Other examples include China's efforts during the 1960s to limit the scope of the conflict in Vietnam so as to avoid a situation that might force itself to intervene, and the shifts in Chinese policy on peace negotiations between North Vietnam and the United States. On a smaller scale, one might cite the attitude of both Chinese and Vietnamese communists toward communist movements in both Laos and Cambodia.

One can advance perfectly rational justifications, on the strategic and geopolitical level, for such choices, and argue, as indeed several speakers did at the original conference on which this volume is based, that in the long run they actually proved advantageous to the North's efforts to win control of all Vietnam. Yet, as John Foster Dulles likewise discovered, in international affairs the combination of hypocrisy in pursuing one's own objectives with the ineffable assumption of surpassing virtue is one that allies in one's own camp tend to find particularly galling and unacceptable. However close the relationship may have been at times, particularly in the first twenty years after World War II, on the Vietnamese side the recurrent readiness of Chinese leaders to subordinate Vietnamese goals to their own country's objectives cannot but have left a legacy of distrust and suspicion, one only intensified by the lengthy history of Chinese invasions and unwelcome domination.

Important, too, was the specific manner in which China used ideology as a foreign policy tool. Steven I. Levine notes that "the protean concept of a united front . . . sanctioned enormous tactical flexibility with respect to coalition-building and alliance formation." In Levine's view,

> ideology provided a general framework within which CCP leaders could analyse foreign relations. But rather than providing a set of prescriptions they could follow blindly, or acting as a constraint, Marxist-Leninist ideology actually empowered them. It placed in their hands the responsibility for defining the current situation, provided them with a vocabulary and a set of concepts to use in doing so, and inspired them with confidence in their ability to act in accordance with the best interests of the Party.

According to Levine, over time, despite "the profound commitment of Mao and his supporters to the ideological propositions they defended," the demands of a complex international situation and the emergence of a cadre of party foreign affairs specialists made the conduct of Chinese foreign affairs "increasingly flexible." Concomitant with this, however, was a capacity in international crises "to accuse their opposite numbers of deviating from or violating the principles or norms that were supposed to govern international relations."[93] Such tendencies were poorly designed to inculcate fraternal communist solidarity and cooperation.

The antagonisms that came to characterize Sino-Soviet and Sino-Vietnamese relations have often been perceived as rooted primarily in nationalism, but this may be too simplistic. Morris, for example, points out that "the Vietnamese leaders held a subtle and evolving set of attitudes toward China, attitudes far more complicated than those allowed by the broad explanatory concept of 'Vietnamese nationalism,' subscribed to by most Western academic and journalistic analysts and commentators." He also suggests that in the mid-1970s such leaders did not seek an outright break with China, and that even though their actions effectively brought this about, such consequences were unintentional. In isolation, the strength of nationalist sentiment cannot explain why the nature of intracommunist relationships changed over time, nor why, especially at their beginning, compromise and cooperation were frequently attainable, but later such relationships tended to deteriorate. In part, this may have reflected the manner in which the very process of dealing with each other served to exacerbate existing tensions, establishing a vicious spiral in which, given the existing presumptions of malice, sometimes innocent episodes were interpreted as evidence of ill will and treachery, which in turn further heightened mutual suspicions. Sino-Soviet disputes, for example, intensified significantly during the 1960s as the result of the various types of friction generated by their joint commitment to Vietnam, while these difficulties probably also contributed to the increasing problems in Sino-Vietnamese relations.

Vietnam, meanwhile, sought to limit both Chinese and Soviet advisers to purely ancillary roles and to restrict both their influence upon broader military decisions and their access to the general Vietnamese population. Here political culture may have played an important part. Despite several decades of close contacts among the various communist powers, most notably China, the Soviet Union, and Vietnam, it seems that mutual incomprehension of each other's priorities and perspectives remained the rule, and that a common commitment to communism could not trump differences in political culture and style.[94]

The international diplomacy of the Vietnam War also tends to confirm Chen Jian's argument that after 1949 great differences characterized the respective international positions of the Soviet Union and China: that, whereas the Soviet Union had become "an insider of the big-power club, assuming the identity of a quasi-revolutionary country and a status quo power at the same time,"

> from its birth date, Mao's China challenged the Western powers in general and the United States in particular by questioning and, consequently, negating the legitimacy of the "norms of international relations," which, as Mao and his comrades viewed them, were of Western origins and inimical to revolutionary China. Thus Mao's China had its own language and theories, its own values and codes of behavior in regard to external policies.[95]

The contrasting attitudes Soviet and Chinese leaders took toward the Vietnam War between 1964 and the early 1970s made this very apparent. Although both communist big powers believed that heavy military and economic aid for the Vietnamese revolutionary struggle was essential to the maintenance of their credibility as leaders of international communism, a major Soviet preoccupation was how best to bring the conflict to a timely end, if possible, perhaps providing the United States with a face-saving exit route. Soviet officials apparently feared that the war, especially as waged by their often unpredictable and bellicose Vietnamese clients, might all too easily spiral into a major international confrontation, perhaps involving themselves, and might even bring permanently increased American influence in Southeast Asia. From 1964 onward, therefore, they favored and attempted to facilitate the opening of peace negotiations, even though fear of alienating their difficult Vietnamese partners precluded the exertion of heavy Soviet pressure upon them to this end.[96] While Soviet leaders welcomed the enhancement of the USSR's own influence in Indochina that aid to Vietnam brought, especially because this came at China's expense, as they effectively had since 1954, these leaders eschewed demands for complete American withdrawal and readily contemplated the division of Southeast Asia into de facto Soviet and U.S. spheres of influence.[97] Under Mao,

by contrast, China opposed negotiations and as late as 1969 seemed to favor the conflict's indefinite prolongation, an outlook the Soviets believed
might well reflect his desire for a plausible excuse to maintain martial law
and pursue the Cultural Revolution within China on the grounds that China
faced a serious external threat, as well as his hopes for a direct Soviet-
American military confrontation.[98]

Sufficient information on Chinese policy toward Vietnam is now available to draw some tentative conclusions on its broader significance in Chinese foreign policy. Foremost, perhaps, among those communist leaders,
Chinese or non-Chinese, who habitually combined political opportunism
with lofty rhetoric was Mao, whose towering figure for almost three decades
undoubtedly bestrode China and all its policies like a colossus. Whereas
Stalin tended to choose those courses he considered most advantageous to
Soviet strategic interests, Mao was more complex. Mao was probably at
least partly impelled by nationalist considerations, by a need to vindicate
his country's international stature and avenge a century of humiliation by
making China the leader of international communism, and also by his personal ambition to become the greatest communist intellectual theoretician
of all. By the middle to late 1950s, he had thought out a well-developed
theory of continuous revolution.[99] Chen Jian repeatedly emphasizes how
frequently Mao used the threat of international crisis as a means of generating domestic social mobilization in support of such objectives as the elimination of political rivals, the Hundred Flowers campaign, the Great Leap
Forward, and the Cultural Revolution. In Thomas Robinson's words: "Domestic politics thus reigned supreme over international relations during
Mao's time."[100]

This strategy, however, had its paradoxical aspects, one of which was
that, as several of this book's chapters suggest, it required the perception
rather than the reality of international crisis. Chen and Zhang demonstrate
convincingly that, during the Korean War, Mao overrode most of the Chinese Politburo in pushing for Chinese intervention.[101] Yet, despite or perhaps even because of his frequent invocation of external threats and dangers to justify domestic purification campaigns, once that conflict had
ended, in practice Mao was remarkably prudent in risking another such war,
and in particular to exacerbating the danger of any increase of the U.S. military presence in the region. It may even be that the Korean War experience
had a chastening impact upon Mao, diluting what Zhang terms the "military romanticism" that in 1950 impelled him to eagerly take on American
forces.[102] In the United States, the conflict gave rise to a "never again" club

of those officials who opposed any future American intervention in an Asian land war; it seems that in China this had its counterpart among those officials, led by Mao, who sought to avoid any subsequent U.S. military involvement adjacent to Chinese territory.

Biased though Duan undoubtedly was, there was some justice in his assessment of Mao as a coward. Largely due to Chinese backpedaling, the successive Taiwan Strait crises of 1954–55 and 1958 both fizzled out.[103] Indeed, as the second episode was winding down in March 1959, Mao specifically boasted to the journalist Anna Louise Strong that China had learned from John Foster Dulles how to employ the tactics of brinkmanship, and not go beyond the edge of nuclear war.[104] Several chapters of this volume demonstrate (as does Zhai Qiang's study of China and the Vietnam War), the anxiety of China, during the Geneva Conference and throughout the later 1950s and early 1960s, to give the United States no excuse to intervene directly with massive military force in Vietnam or elsewhere in Indochina. This became particularly apparent in the international negotiations on Laos at the 1962 Geneva Conference.

Moreover, when American intervention did occur, China reached an implicit understanding with the United States as to the limits that both would observe in the conduct of that war.[105] Chen Jian suggests that "Beijing's leaders resorted to force only when the confrontation was in one way or another related to China's territorial integrity and physical insecurity."[106] Perhaps it was Mao's surprise that American involvement actually occurred that led China—in what seems a somewhat ironical reprise of Stalin's eagerness in 1950 to encourage the Chinese to fight the United States in Korea while carefully refraining from actions that risked a direct U.S.-Soviet clash—to oppose the opening of peace negotiations in Vietnam, arguing that talks would not succeed until the United States had been forced uncompromisingly to recognize the futility of continuing the military struggle.

By the early 1970s, however, when Chinese leaders finally realized the eagerness of the United States to extricate itself from Vietnam, and the genuine opportunity that existed to remove American troops from a neighboring state, they quickly reversed course. One might indeed argue that from the mid-1950s Mao seems consistently to have underestimated the United States, especially its willingness to use force, refusing to acknowledge that the "paper tiger" whose tail he so blithely tweaked did indeed possess formidable claws and teeth. Indeed, his contemptuous characterizations of American reluctance to fight might at least as appropriately have referred to China under his own leadership.[107]

Mao's policies had serious consequences for China. Zhang argues that China's domestic economic weakness seriously limited its ability to project its power internationally, because China had neither the deep pockets nor the technologically advanced weaponry necessary to underpin an extensive foreign economic and military assistance program.[108] From 1964 onward, when their former difficulties with the Soviets had been healed, these inadequacies led Vietnam to turn increasingly to the Soviets for aid, which brought Soviet power and influence uncomfortably close to China's own southern border, causing Vietnam gradually to switch allegiance from China to the Soviet Union, while, as Shen Zhihua and Li Danhui demonstrate, disputes over the transport of Soviet supplies and personnel to Vietnam further exacerbated Sino-Soviet relations.[109] And, as he had done with the United States, Mao also underestimated his Soviet antagonist's determination. As he regained influence after the disastrous Great Leap Forward, from 1962 onward his flaming rhetoric regarding both Soviet betrayal of true Communist principles, and the Sino-Soviet border—on the latter Mao himself admitted his words were meant for show, and did not imply further action—increasingly infuriated the Soviet Union.

Yet as the Cultural Revolution damaged China's economy, ravaged the Foreign Ministry and bureaucracy, and attacked foreign diplomats, prominent observers abroad questioned the very rationality of China's conduct of overseas affairs—weakening still more its international credibility and ability to finance any external policy. When, in 1969, in another miscalculation of an opponent's response, Mao and his designated successor, Defense Minister Marshal Lin Biao, eventually provoked bloody clashes between Chinese and Soviet troops at Zhenbao Island, on the Ussuri River border, the Soviet Union responded by verbally threatening and even requesting American acquiescence in a preemptive strike on Chinese nuclear facilities. Though Gaiduk suggests that Soviet pronouncements on this subject, like Mao's earlier comments on the Sino-Soviet border, were purely rhetorical propaganda efforts, saber rattling intended as warnings to their opponent, and that by late 1969 tensions were much relieved, they nonetheless helped to drive China to seek a reconciliation with the United States, for more than twenty years its foremost enemy.[110] Historians have noted that, while adopting this policy, Mao never gave it the enthusiastic public support some of his earlier initiatives received, probably an indication that only force majeure made him resort to it.[111]

The non-Chinese observer may find somewhat baffling the tenacity of Mao's hold upon power and, even more, upon the loyalties of his associates. The editor well remembers chairing an exhilarating and heated session in 1991 at a conference in Beijing, where a young scholar who had the temerity to suggest that Mao's anti-Americanism of 1949–50 was unwise attracted severe criticism from many older commentators, some of whom were clearly shocked at what they still regarded as lèse-majesté. Recent works by Chen Jian, Shu Guang Zhang, Li Xiangqian, He Di, and Niu Jun, included or referred to in this volume, no longer hesitate to give what are often, either overtly or implicitly, highly critical assessments of Mao's policies. In November 1964, Moscow deeply offended a visiting delegation led by Zhou when Soviet defense minister Marshal Malinovsky openly suggested that Beijing might depose Mao, just as it had recently overthrown Khrushchev.[112]

It has been argued that the willingness of lesser Communist officials, many of them decidedly able and competent men, to tolerate Mao's vagaries and the damage, both domestic and international, his policies inflicted upon China, reflected a major difference in political culture between the twentieth-century West and the Asian Confucian tradition—namely, the continuing reverence, respect, and loyalty that a dominating leader could expect from his followers, even if many of them thought his policies mistaken.[113] In all probability, it was also a tribute to the enduring strength among them of the communist vision that, more than any other individual in China, Mao embodied and had inspired, and the lasting hold upon his associates that Mao's energy, determination, and conceptual and strategic abilities won for him well before 1949.

By the early 1970s, however, even Mao could no longer attract the same unquestioning deference. The reasons why Lin Biao, Mao's designated heir —who had fought at Mao's side since the Chinese Civil War and, during the Cultural Revolution, was perhaps more radical even than his leader— purportedly broke with Mao and tried to overthrow him are still unclear; though some have suggested that Lin may have deplored the opening to the United States, others argue that the prospect of obtaining novel American military technology intrigued the marshal, and that his attempted coup arose from his fear that rivals such as Zhou were about to supplant him.[114] Whatever the precise rationale driving Lin's behavior, Chen follows Teiwes in suggesting that one of this episode's ramifications was "a crisis of faith" in China, because, even according to the official account, one of Mao's close associates had tried to assassinate the formerly sacrosanct chairman. Chen argues that the consequent demoralization and disorientation of Chinese politics was one major reason for the disillusionment with and loss of confidence in communism and the radical leadership of the Gang of Four that became so apparent in 1976.[115]

Although there were many reasons why Chinese communism might well have lost credibility by the early 1970s, one might well argue that what brought ultimately such perceptions to a head were Mao's miscalculations in handling the Vietnam War and the whole complex of related issues, including the use of foreign affairs to promote domestic political upheaval, the deterioration due to economic weakness of China's ability to project power internationally, and provocative diplomatic policies that simultaneously attracted hostile Soviet and American military and political presences to China's borders. His habitual tactics finally backfired on him and, having repeatedly sowed the wind, Mao finally reaped not one but several whirlwinds.

Yet even this may be paradoxical. In the period 1964–65, the Sino-Soviet split, for which China and more particularly Mao was predominantly responsible, was a major factor impelling the Soviet Union to endorse North Vietnam's efforts to defy and match the escalating U.S. involvement in Indochina. North Vietnam's development of an alliance relationship with the Soviets, in turn, eventually poisoned the once amicable Sino-Vietnamese relationship, while growing Soviet influence in Indochina helped to preclude any hope of resolving corrosive Sino-Soviet differences. As Chinese relations with the Soviet Union deteriorated, Mao decided to turn to the United States, a move that altered the entire dynamics of the Cold War. A chastened China gradually developed a new understanding with Western powers, underpinning the dramatic social and economic changes launched by Deng while breaking the country's isolation and greatly enhancing its international standing. Throughout the 1960s, Soviet officials always displayed enormous fear of any potential rapprochement between China and the United States, something their own policies nonetheless helped to precipitate.[116] Chen goes so far as to argue that, when this reconciliation occurred: "As a result of having to confront the West and China simultaneously, the Soviet Union overextended its strength, which contributed significantly to the final collapse of the Soviet empire in the late 1980s and early 1990s."[117]

Breaking with those historians who have characterized the Vietnam War as a mere "sideshow" in a broader Cold War in which the United States was ultimately victorious, Gaiduk likewise suggests that, even though the Vietnam War greatly increased Soviet influence in Southeast Asia, winning Vietnam over from the Chinese to the Soviet camp, the communist victory in Vietnam also gave Soviet leaders an unwarranted sense of hubris, leading them to "adopt a more aggressive and rigid foreign policy, particularly in the third world," and causing "Soviet involvement in turmoil in Africa and the Middle East" and in Afghanistan, which contributed substantially to the eventual collapse and dissolution of the Soviet empire and Soviet Union.[118]

In the 1970s, the outcome of the Vietnam war was almost universally perceived as a major international humiliation for the United States. Yet, as we learn more about the various national actors in Vietnam, it seems at least plausible that, in the longer term, the Vietnam War and the reorientation of international politics that it engendered made a major contribution to what is currently perceived as the ultimate U.S. victory in the Cold War, by encouraging overextension on the part of the Soviet Union and a turn in China toward the United States that soon went hand in hand with modernization, economic reform, and the jettisoning of ideology, and also by intensifying existing fractures within the communist bloc until they reached the point of no repair.

Notes

1. See Lester H. Brune and Richard Dean Burns, *America and the Indochina Wars, 1945–1990: A Bibliographical Guide* (Claremont, Calif.: Regina Books, 1992); Richard Dean Burns and Milton Leitenberg, *The Wars in Vietnam, Cambodia, and Laos, 1945–1982: A Bibliographic Guide* (Santa Barbara, Calif.: ABC-Clio, 1992); James S. Olson, ed., *The Vietnam War: Handbook of the Literature and Research* (Westport, Conn.: Greenwood Press, 1993); Carl Singleton, *Vietnam Studies: An Annotated Bibliography* (Lanham, Md.: Scarecrow Press, 1997); John Newman, *Vietnam War Literature: An Annotated Bibliography of Imaginative Works about Americans Fighting in Vietnam* (Lanham, Md.: Scarecrow Press, 1997); Timothy J. Lomperis, *"Reading the Wind": The Literature of the Vietnam War—An Interpretive Critique* (Durham, N.C.: Duke University Press, 1987); Anton Legler and Kurt Hubinek, *Der Krieg in Vietnam: Bericht und Bibliographie,* 5 vols. (Frankfurt: Bernard & Graefe, 1969–79); Ronald Spector, *Researching the Vietnam Experience* (Washington, D.C.: Analysis Branch, U.S. Army Center of Military History, 1983); and Spencer C. Tucker, ed., *Encyclopedia of the Vietnam War: A Political, Social, and Military History,* 3 vols. (Santa Barbara, Calif.: ABC-Clio, 1998), 835–44. Also see John Hellmann, *American Myth and the Legacy of Vietnam* (New York: Columbia University Press, 1986). Because it is continuously updated, the most current compilation of books and articles is Edwin E. Moïse, *Vietnam War Bibliography* (http://hubcap.clemson.edu/~eemoise/bibliography.html).
2. Robert S. McNamara, with Brian VanDeMark, *In Retrospect: The Tragedy and Lessons of Vietnam* (New York: Random House, 1995). The controversy over the publication of his memoirs is described in Theodore Draper, "The Abuse of McNamara," *New York Review of Books,* May 25, 1995, 16 ff.; Sidney Blumenthal, "McNamara's Peace," *New Yorker,* May 8, 1995, 66 ff. On the film *The Fog of War,* see also the book compiled by the movie's academic advisers, James G. Blight and Janet M. Lang, eds., *The Fog of War: Lessons from the Life of Robert S. McNamara* (Lanham, Md.: Rowman & Littlefield, 2005). On the scholarly controversy generated by recent works suggesting that the U.S. could and should have won the Vietnam War, see Robert Buzzanco, "Fear and (Self-)Loathing in Lub-

bock, Texas, or How I Learned to Quit Worrying and Love Vietnam and Iraq," *Passport* 36, no. 3 (December 2005): 5–14. *The Newsletter of the Society for Historians of American Foreign Relations.*

3. One recent example is "Distortion of History Denounced: Asian Scholars Urge Japan to Use Historical Fact in Textbooks," *China Daily,* March 29, 2002. The protracted spring 2005 Chinese protests attracted extensive reportage in the international press, including the *New York Times* and the *Washington Post,* throughout April and the first half of May 2005.

4. "Viets Urged to Tone Down History Textbooks," *South China Morning Post,* March 18, 2002.

5. "UN and Cambodia Still Unable to Agree on Trials," *International Herald Tribune,* March 27, 2002.

6. Andreas W. Daum, Lloyd C. Gardner, and Wilfried Mausbach, eds., "Introduction: America's War and the World," in *America, the Vietnam War, and the World: Comparative and International Perspectives,* ed. Andreas W. Daum, Lloyd C. Gardner, and Wilfried Mausbach (Washington and Cambridge: German Historical Institute and Cambridge University Press, 2003), 5.

7. R. B. Smith, *An International History of the Vietnam War,* 3 vols. (New York: St. Martin's Press, 1983–91).

8. Fredrik Logevall, *Choosing War: The Lost Chance for Peace and the Escalation of War in Vietnam* (Berkeley: University of California Press, 1999).

9. Caroline Page, *U.S. Official Propaganda during the Vietnam War, 1965–1973: The Limits of Persuasion* (London: Leicester University Press, 1996).

10. See Peter Edwards, with Gregory Pemberton, *Crises and Commitments: The Strategy and Diplomacy of Australia's Involvement in Southeast Asian Conflicts, 1948–65* (Sydney: Allen & Unwin, 1992); and Peter Edwards, *A Nation at War: Australian Politics, Society and Diplomacy during the Vietnam War, 1965–75* (Sydney: Allen & Unwin, 1997). Also see Glen St. J. Barclay, *A Very Small Insurance Policy: The Politics of Australian Involvement in Vietnam, 1954–1967* (St. Lucia, Australia: Queensland University Press, 1988). On Canada, see Douglas A. Ross, *In the Interests of Peace: Canada and Vietnam, 1954–1973* (Toronto: University of Toronto Press, 1984); and Victor Levant, *Quiet Complicity: Canadian Involvement in the Vietnam War* (Toronto: Between the Lines, 1986).

11. Robert M. Blackburn, *Mercenaries and Lyndon Johnson's "More Flags": The Hiring of Korean, Filipino and Thai Soldiers in the Vietnam War* (Jefferson, N.C.: McFarland, 1994).

12. Thomas R. Havens, *Fire across the Sea: The Vietnam War and Japan* (Princeton, N.J.: Princeton University Press, 1987).

13. Thomas A. Schwartz, *Lyndon Johnson and Europe: In the Shadow of Vietnam* (Cambridge, Mass.: Harvard University Press, 2003); John Dumbrell, *President Lyndon Johnson and Soviet Communism* (Manchester: Manchester University Press, 2004).

14. Peter Lowe, ed., *The Vietnam War* (Basingstoke, U.K.: Macmillan, 1998).

15. Lloyd C. Gardner and Ted Gittinger, eds., *International Perspectives on Vietnam* (College Station: Texas A & M University Press, 2000).

16. Daum, Gardner, and Mausbach, eds., *America, the Vietnam War, and the World.*

17. Lloyd C. Gardner and Ted Gittinger, eds., *The Search for Peace in Vietnam, 1964–1968* (College Station: Texas A & M University Press, 2004).

18. See the assorted issues of the *Cold War International History Project Bulletin,* and various relevant working papers published by the Cold War International History Project (CWIHP).

19. Odd Arne Westad, Chen Jian, Stein Tønnesson, Nguyen Vu Tung, and James G. Hershberg, eds., *77 Conversations between Chinese and Foreign Leaders on the Wars in Indochina, 1964–1977*, CWIHP Working Paper 22 (Washington, D.C.: Woodrow Wilson International Center for Scholars, 1998).

20. See the accounts given in Ilya V. Gaiduk, *The Soviet Union and the Vietnam War* (Chicago: Ivan R. Dee, 1996), xii–xiv; and Mark Kramer, "Archival Research in Moscow: Progress and Pitfalls," *Cold War International History Project Bulletin* 3 (Fall 1993): 1, 18–39.

21. Ilya V. Gaiduk, *Confronting Vietnam: Soviet Policy toward the Indochina Conflict, 1954–1963* (Washington and Stanford, Calif.: Woodrow Wilson Center Press and Stanford University Press, 2003); Gaiduk, *Soviet Union and the Vietnam War;* Mari Olsen, *Solidarity and National Revolution: The Soviet Union and the Vietnamese Communists, 1954–1960* (Oslo: Institutt for Forsvarsstudier, 1997; Olsen, *The Soviet Union, Vietnam and China, 1949–64: Changing Alliances* (New York: Routledge, 2006). New evidence from Central and East European archives on such topics as the Korean and Vietnam Wars, the Sino-Soviet split, and Chinese foreign and domestic policy has been presented in the activities of the CWIHP and the George Washington University Cold War Group, e.g., a fall 2003 conference in Budapest, cosponsored by these groups. Selections from these presentations are scheduled for publication through the CWIHP; see, e.g., *CWHIP Bulletin,* nos. 14–15 (Winter 2003–Spring 2004): 25–137, 440–50.

22. On these trends and their positive and negative aspects, see David H. Shambaugh, "Appendix: A Bibliographical Essay on New Sources for the Study of China's Foreign Relations and National Security," in *Chinese Foreign Policy: Theory and Practice,* ed. Thomas W. Robinson and David Shambaugh (Oxford: Clarendon Press, 1994), 603–18; Michael H. Hunt, *The Genesis of Chinese Foreign Policy* (New York: Columbia University Press, 1996), 232–50; and Chen Jian, *Mao's China and the Cold War* (Chapel Hill: University of North Carolina Press, 2001), 373–75. In Western sources, the progress of such scholarship can be traced not only in the *CWIHP Bulletin* and Working Papers but also in such collections as Yuan Ming and Harry Harding, eds., *Sino-American Relations, 1945–1955: A Joint Reassessment of a Critical Decade* (Wilmington, Del.: Scholarly Resources, 1989); Priscilla Roberts, ed., *Sino-American Relations since 1900* (Hong Kong: Centre of Asian Studies, University of Hong Kong, 1991); Michael H. Hunt and Niu Jun, eds., *Toward a History of Chinese Communist Foreign Relations 1920–1960s: Personalities and Interpretive Approaches* (Washington, D.C.: Asia Program, Woodrow Wilson International Center for Scholars, 1994); Odd Arne Westad, ed., *Brothers in Arms: The Rise and Fall of the Sino-Soviet Alliance, 1945–1953* (Washington and Stanford, Calif.: Woodrow Wilson Center Press and Stanford University Press, 1998); and Robert S. Ross and Jiang Changbin, eds., *Re-examining the Cold War: U.S.-China Diplomacy, 1954–1973* (Cambridge, Mass.: Harvard University Asia Center, 2001). A recent encouraging, though still tentative, development is the opening in 2004 of the Chinese Foreign Ministry archives, although initial releases were fragmentary and limited to the first decade of the PRC's existence.

23. Apart from the appropriate essays in *Brothers in Arms,* ed. Westad, and *Re-examining the Cold War,* ed. Ross and Jiang, stimulating recent examples of works by three of the leading such historians are Chen, *Mao's China;* Qiang Zhai, *China & the Vietnam Wars, 1950–1975* (Chapel Hill: University of North Carolina Press, 2001); and Shu Guang Zhang, *Economic Cold War: America's Embargo against China and the Sino-Soviet Alliance, 1949–1963* (Washington and Stanford, Calif.: Woodrow Wilson Center Press and Stanford University Press, 2001). Comparable works by Russian scholars in-

clude the volumes by Gaiduk cited above and Vladislav Zubok and Constantine Ple-shakov, *Inside the Kremlin's Cold War: From Stalin to Khrushchev* (Cambridge, Mass.: Harvard University Press, 1996).

24. Apart from those works cited in the previous note, see especially chapters 7, 8, and 10 in this volume by, respectively, Shu Guang Zhang, Li Danhui, and Shen Zhihua.

25. One notable such instance is Military History Institute of Vietnam, *Victory in Vietnam: The Official History of the People's Army of Vietnam, 1954–1975,* trans. Merle L. Pribbenow (Lawrence: University Press of Kansas, 2002). The bibliography to Robert K. Brigham, *Guerrilla Diplomacy: The NLF's Foreign Relations and the Viet Nam War* (Ithaca, N.Y.: Cornell University Press, 1999), is an extremely useful guide to those Viet-namese sources currently available. See also Fredrik Logevall, "Bringing in the 'Other Side': New Scholarship on the Vietnam Wars," *Journal of Cold War Studies* 3, no. 3 (Fall 2001): 77–93; Ang Cheng Guan, *Ending the Vietnam War: The Vietnamese Communists' Perspective* (London: RoutledgeCurzon, 2004), 2–4; and Pierre Asselin, "New Evidence from Vietnam," *Passport: The Newsletter of the Society for Historians of American Foreign Relations* 35, no. 3 (December 2004): 39–41.

26. Douglas Pike pioneered the use of such sources, in Douglas Pike, *PAVN: People's Army of Vietnam* (Novato, Calif.: Presidio, 1986). One excellent recent example of such a study is Brigham, *Guerrilla Diplomacy.* Other works that make extensive use of archival resources from several countries, including Vietnam, include Mark Bradley, *Imagining Vietnam and America: The Making of Postcolonial Vietnam, 1919–1950* (Chapel Hill: University of North Carolina Press, 2000); Ang Chen Guan, *Vietnamese Communists' Relations with China and the Second Indochina Conflict, 1956–1962* (Jef-ferson, N.C.: McFarland, 1997); Ang Chen Guan, *The Vietnam War from the Other Side: The Vietnamese Communists' Perspective* (London: RoutledgeCurzon, 2002); Ang Chen Guan, *Ending the Vietnam War;* Stein Tønnesson, *The Vietnamese Revolution of 1945: Roosevelt, Ho Chi Minh and de Gaulle in a World at War* (Oslo: International Peace Re-search Institute, 1991); Christopher E. Goscha, *Vietnam or Indochina? Contesting Con-cepts of Space in Vietnamese Nationalism, 1887–1954* (Copenhagen: Nordic Institute of Asian Studies, 1995); Christopher E. Goscha, *Thailand and the Southeast Asian Networks of the Vietnamese Revolution, 1885–1954* (London: Curzon Press, 1999); Thomas En-gelbert and Christopher E. Goscha, *Falling Out of Touch: A Study of Vietnamese Com-munist Policy towards an Emerging Cambodian Communist Movement, 1930–1975* (Clayton, Australia: Centre of Southeast Asian Studies, Monash University, 1995); William J. Duiker, *The Communist Road to Power in Vietnam,* 2nd ed. (Boulder, Colo.: Westview Press, 1996); William J. Duiker, *Sacred War: Nationalism and Revolution in a Divided Vietnam* (New York: McGraw-Hill, 1995); William J. Duiker, *Ho Chi Minh: A Life* (New York: Hyperion, 2000); Jeffrey Kimball, *Nixon's Vietnam War* (Lawrence: Uni-versity Press of Kansas, 1998); and Jeffrey Kimball, *The Vietnam War Files: Uncovering the Secret History of Nixon-Era Strategy* (Lawrence: University Press of Kansas, 2004).

27. Jayne S. Werner and Luu Doan Huynh, eds., *The Vietnam War: Vietnamese and American Perspectives* (Armonk, N.Y.: M. E. Sharpe, 1993).

28. Selections from the transcripts of one such conference, juxtaposing the often as-sertively differing perspectives of Vietnamese and U.S. officials upon the entire history of the Indochina wars, were later published. For a description of this project, see Robert S. McNamara, James G. Blight, and Robert K. Brigham, with Thomas J. Biersteker and Col. Herbert Y. Schandler, *Argument without End: In Search of Answers to the Vietnam Tragedy* (New York: PublicAffairs, 1999), esp. 11–15, 459–62.

29. Selections from the papers delivered at two such earlier conferences, in Wash-

ington in 1992, and Hong Kong in 1996, have been published. See Hunt and Niu, *Toward a History of Chinese Communist Foreign Relations;* and Westad, *Brothers in Arms.* At least one other book-length publication based upon the 1996 Hong Kong conference is in progress, while many other papers from these conference have been published as *CWIHP Bulletin* articles and working papers.

30. On the respective roles of Mao Zedong and Zhou Enlai, see esp. Steven Goldstein, "Nationalism and Internationalism: Sino-Soviet Relations," in *Chinese Foreign Policy,* ed. Robinson and Shambaugh, 226–48; Thomas W. Robinson, "Chinese Foreign Policy from the 1940s to the 1990s," in *Chinese Foreign Policy,* ed. Robinson and Shambaugh, 555–67; Shu Guang Zhang, "In the Shadow of Mao: Zhou Enlai," in *The Diplomats, 1939–1979,* ed. Gordon A. Craig and Francis L. Loewenheim (Princeton, N.J.: Princeton University Press, 1994), 337–70; Niu Jun, "The Origins of Mao Zedong's Thinking on International Affairs (1916–1949)," in *Chinese Communist Foreign Relations,* ed. Hunt and Niu, 3–26; He Di, "The Most Respected Enemy: Mao Zedong's Perception of the United States," in *Chinese Communist Foreign Relations,* ed. Hunt and Niu, 27–66; Zhang Baijia, "Zhou Enlai: The Shaper and Founder of China's Diplomacy," in *Chinese Communist Foreign Relations,* ed. Hunt and Niu, 67–88; Zhang Baijia, "The Changing International Scene and Chinese Policy toward the United States, 1954–1970," in *Re-examining the Cold War,* ed. Ross and Jiang, 46–76; and Hunt, *Genesis of Chinese Communist Foreign Policy,* 204–12.

31. Other recent works by Yang include Chen Jian and Yang Kuisong, "Chinese Politics and the Collapse of the Sino-Soviet Alliance," in *Brothers in Arms,* ed. Westad, 226–45; and Yang Kuisong, "The Sino-Soviet Border Clash of 1969: From Zhenbao Island to Sino-American *Rapprochement," Cold War History* 1, no. 1 (August 2000): 21–52.

32. See Chen, *Mao's China,* 54–55, 117–23; Zhai, *China & the Vietnam Wars,* 9–26.

33. Odd Arne Westad, *Decisive Encounters: The Chinese Civil War, 1946–1950* (Stanford, Calif.: Stanford University Press, 2003), 301, 317.

34. On Mao's eagerness to enter the Korean War, see also Shu Guang Zhang, *Mao's Military Romanticism: China and the Korean War, 1950–1953* (Lawrence: University Press of Kansas, 1995); and Chen Jian, *China's Road to the Korean War: The Making of the Sino-American Confrontation* (New York: Columbia University Press, 1994). Westad, *Decisive Encounters,* 318–24, gives a more restrained interpretation of Mao's position on Korea.

35. On Wang Jiaxiang's preferred policies, which also included efforts to alleviate or at least to refrain from exacerbating Sino-Soviet tensions, see also Li Jie, "Changes in China's Domestic Situation in the 1960s and Sino-U.S. Relations," in *Re-examining the Cold War,* ed. Ross and Jiang, 301–6. Niu Jun argues that from 1959 until early 1962, Mao Zedong shared the preference of most of his colleagues for pragmatic foreign policies intended to alleviate Sino-Soviet tensions and explore the possibility of a Sino-American accommodation. Niu suggests that the Chinese sought a stable international atmosphere in which to recover from the Great Leap Forward's economic effect. Only in 1962, he argues, did Mao, for domestic political reasons turn to a harsher diplomatic stance. Niu Jun, *1962: The Eve of the Left Turn in China's Foreign Policy,* CWIHP Working Paper 48 (Washington, D.C.: Woodrow Wilson International Center for Scholars, 2005), 9–36.

36. Ilya V. Gaiduk, "From Berlin to Geneva: Soviet Views on the Settlement of the Indochina Conflict, January–April 1954," paper delivered at International Workshop, "New Evidence on China, Southeast Asia, and the Vietnam War," January 11–12, 2000, University of Hong Kong, Hong Kong. On Soviet policies from 1954 to 1963, see also Gaiduk, *Confronting Vietnam.*

37. Gaiduk, *Confronting Vietnam,* 184–86.

38. Kochavi elaborates these arguments in his recent book, *A Conflict Perpetuated: China Policy during the Kennedy Years* (New York: Greenwood Press, 2002). See also Gordon H. Chang, *Friends and Enemies: The United States, China, and the Soviet Union, 1948–1972* (Stanford, Calif.: Stanford University Press, 1990), chap. 8; and Evelyn Goh, *Constructing the U.S. Rapprochement with China, 1961–1974: From "Red Menace" to "Tacit Ally"* (Cambridge: Cambridge University Press, 2005), 21–38.

39. On Kennedy's image, see Thomas Brown, *JFK: History of an Image* (London: I. B. Tauris, 1989); and Burton I. Kaufman, "John F. Kennedy as World Leader: A Perspective on the Literature," *Diplomatic History,* 17, no. 3 (Summer 1993): 447–69.

40. Logevall, *Choosing War.*

41. Westad et al., *77 Conversations,* 9.

42. Ang, *Vietnam War from the Other Side,* 45–46, 64, 75; see also Niu, *1962,* 24–26.

43. See Chen, *Mao's China;* Chen and Yang, "Chinese Politics and the Collapse of the Sino-Soviet Alliance"; and also Zhai, *China & the Vietnam Wars,* 115–16; Eva-Maria Stolberg, "People's War versus Peaceful Coexistence: Vietnam and the Sino-Soviet Struggle for Ideological Supremacy," in *America, the Vietnam War, and the World,* ed. Daum, Gardner, and Mausbach, 247–48; Thomas J. Christensen, *Useful Adversaries: Grand Strategy, Domestic Mobilization, and Sino-American Conflict, 1947–1958* (Princeton, N.J.: Princeton University Press, 1997); and Jeremi Suri, *Power and Protest: Global Revolution and the Rise of Détente* (Cambridge, Mass.: Harvard University Press, 2003), esp. 61–87, 206–11. On the role of domestic factors in the broader making of Cold War foreign policy, see also Patrick M. Morgan and Keith L. Nelson, eds., *Re-Viewing the Cold War: Domestic Factors and Foreign Policy in the East-West Confrontation* (Westport, Conn.: Praeger, 2000).

44. On Mao's earlier belief in the late 1950s that the United States would not risk war in Southeast Asia, see Ang, *Vietnamese Communists' Relations with China,* 106–10.

45. On Mao's belief in 1959 that neither the United States nor China wished for outright war with each other, see Ang, *Vietnamese Communists' Relations with China,* 130.

46. Ang, *Vietnamese Communists' Relations with China,* 222; Kochavi, *Conflict Perpetuated,* 119–20.

47. Richard Crockatt, *The Fifty Years War: The United States and the Soviet Union in World Politics, 1941–1991* (London: Routledge, 1995), 246; Robert Litwak, *Détente and the Nixon Doctrine: American Foreign Policy and the Pursuit of Stability, 1969–1976* (Cambridge: Cambridge University Press, 1984), 40.

48. Qu Aiguo, "Chinese Military Assistance to North Vietnam's Effort to Resist United States Intervention during the Vietnam War," paper presented at International Workshop, "New Evidence on China, Southeast Asia, and the Vietnam War," January 11–12, 2000, University of Hong Kong, Hong Kong. See also Zhai, *China & the Vietnam Wars,* 134–35, 179–80.

49. Gaiduk, *Confronting Vietnam,* 90, 108–9, 115; Ang, *Vietnamese Communists' Relations with China,* 102–3.

50. Ang, *Vietnam War from the Other Side,* 46, 78; Niu, *1962,* 24–26.

51. John Prados, "The Mouse That Roared: State Department Intelligence in the Vietnam War," http://www.gwu.edu/~nsarchive/NSAEBB/NASEBB121/prados.htm.; W. Dean Howells, Dorothy Avery, and Fred Greene, "Vietnam 1961–1968: As Interpreted in INR's Production," http://www.gwu.edu/~nsarchive/NSAEBB/NASEBB121/index.htm. Other primary sources are the following compilations of declassified U.S. Central Intelligence Agency analyses: "Special National Intelligence Estimate Number

50-2-64: Probable Consequences of Certain US Actions with Respect to Vietnam and Laos," May 25, 1964; John Holmes, "Memorandum for the President: Subject: Probable Communist Reactions to US or US-Sponsored Courses of Action in Vietnam and Laos," July 28, 1964; "Special National Intelligence Estimate Number 10-2-64: Probable Communist Reactions to Certain Possible US/GVN Courses of Action," October 9, 1964; "Special National Intelligence Estimate Number 10-3-65: Communist Reactions to Possible US Actions," February 11, 1965; "Special National Intelligence Estimate 10-3/1-65: Communist Reactions to Possible US Courses of Action Against North Vietnam," February 18, 1965; "Special National Intelligence Estimate 10-4-65: Probable Communist Reactions to Deployment of an ROK Combat Division for Base Security Duty in South Vietnam," March 19, 1965; "United States Intelligence Board Memorandum: Recent Indications of Communist Intentions in South Vietnam," April 9, 1965; "Special National Intelligence Estimate 10-5-65: Communist Reactions to Certain US Actions," April 28, 1965. These documents were located at http://www.foia.cia.gov/ search.asp?pageNumber=9&freqReqRecord=nic%5Fvietnam%2Etxt&refinedText= undefined&freqSearchText=undefined&txtSearch=undefined&extractPhrase= undefined&allWords=undefined&anyWords=undefined&withoutWords=undefined& documentNumber=undefined&startCreatedMonth=&startCreatedDay=&startCreated Year=&endCreatedMonth=&endCreatedDay=&endCreatedYear=&startReleased Month=&startReleasedDay=&startReleasedYear=&endReleasedMonth=&endReleased Day=&endReleasedYear=0sortOrder=DESC. See also Goh, *Constructing the U.S. Rapprochement with China,* 38–45, 77–78.

52. See Gaiduk, *The Soviet Union and the Vietnam War;* also Zhang Xiaoming, "Communist Powers Divided: China, the Soviet Union, and the Vietnam War," in *International Perspectives on Vietnam,* ed. Gardner and Gittinger, 88–92.

53. Similar allegations were sometimes made about North Vietnam. In late 1961, the Soviet Union suspended air shipments via Hanoi of military equipment for the Pathet Lao, suspecting that the North Vietnamese were diverting this matériel to support their own struggle in South Vietnam. Gaiduk states that such allegations were eventually substantiated. Ang, *Vietnamese Communists' Relations with China,* 209; Gaiduk, *Confronting Vietnam,* 169–70.

54. Zhai, *China & the Vietnam Wars,* 150–51.

55. Ang, *Vietnam War from the Other Side,* 139; Ang, *Ending the Vietnam War,* 27–28, 32. On the deterioration in Sino-Vietnamese relations in mid-1968, see also Chris Connolly, "The American Factor: Sino-American Rapprochement and Chinese Attitudes to the Vietnam War, 1968–72," *Cold War History* 5, no. 4 (November 2005): 501–7.

56. Ang, *Ending the Vietnam War,* 28, 30, 31; Connolly, "American Factor," 509.

57. Zhai, *China & the Vietnam Wars,* 207; see also Goh, *Constructing the U.S. Rapprochement with China,* 179–82; Connolly, "American Factor," 509–10.

58. Ang, *Ending the Vietnam War,* 143; Westad et al., *77 Conversations,* 182–84, 186–91; Connolly, "American Factor," 511–14.

59. Other major works by Niu Jun include Hunt and Niu, eds., *Chinese Communist Foreign Relations, 1920s–1960s;* Niu, "Origins of the Sino-Soviet Alliance," in *Brothers in Arms,* ed. Westad, 47–89; and Niu, *1962.*

60. Persistent shortages of ammunition would indeed be a major concern for the Vietnamese military in the final 1974–75 campaign, and efforts to seize Southern artillery dumps played a substantial part in their strategy. Ang, *Ending the Vietnam War,* 154, 160–61, 163.

61. Engelbert and Goscha, *Falling Out of Touch,* chap. 3; Ang, *Ending the Vietnam War,* 43–48. Ang's account also cites allegations by the Vietnamese that, after Sihanouk's

1970 overthrow, the Chinese initially tried to reach an agreement with Lon Nol on the continuing transit of Vietnamese supplies via Cambodian territory. Chinese leaders apparently thought that, in exchange for such facilities, North Vietnam might be prepared to recognize Lon Nol's government. On tensions and eventual outright fighting between the Vietnamese and Cambodian communists after the Lon Nol coup, see also Ang, *Ending the Vietnam War*, 50, 71, 113, 141–42, 144, 163–64.

62. Stephen J. Morris, *Why Vietnam Invaded Cambodia: Political Culture and the Causes of War* (Stanford, Calif.: Stanford University Press, 1999).

63. Gaiduk's study of the Soviet role in Vietnam suggests that, despite frequent North Vietnamese demonstrations of independence from the Soviet Union, including reluctance to inform Soviet officials of Vietnamese military and diplomatic decisions and the isolation of Soviet personnel in Vietnam, this tilt had developed at least as early as 1968, when Vietnam endorsed the Soviet invasion of Czechoslovakia. Gaiduk, *The Soviet Union and the Vietnam War*, 174–77; also see Ang, *Ending the Vietnam War*, 143. Even so, as late as spring 1970, Soviet leaders were apparently still uncertain just where Hanoi's affiliations lay on the Sino-Soviet split. Ang, *Ending the Vietnam War*, 54.

64. Zhai, *China & the Vietnam Wars*, 86–88.

65. Gaiduk, *The Soviet Union and the Vietnam War*, 230–41.

66. Olsen, *Solidarity and National Revolution;* Gaiduk, *The Soviet Union and the Vietnam War*, 69–72, 215–16.

67. Ang, *Ending the Vietnam War*, 99. According to Dobrynin (pp. 107–8), as the negotiations progressed the Soviets continued to find the Americans more forthcoming with information than were the Vietnamese; Anatoly Dobrynin, *In Confidence: Moscow's Ambassador to America's Six Cold War Presidents* (New York: Times Books, 1995), 248.

68. For comparison, see the numerous comments and interjections by Prof. Huynh in McNamara et al., *Argument without End.*

69. Qu Xing and Wan Tailei, "China and the Two Indochina Wars."

70. Zhai, *China & the Vietnam Wars*, 177–78.

71. Westad et al., *77 Conversations*, 10.

72. Zhai, *China & the Vietnam Wars*, 198–99; also Ang, *Ending the V ietnam War*, 85; Connolly, "American Factor," 514–19.

73. Ang, *Ending the Vietnam War*, 88; Connolly, "American Factor," 519–21.

74. Zhai, *China & the Vietnam Wars*, 208–14.

75. Tao Wenzhao, "Containment and Counter-Containment: A Review of the Peaceful Resolution of the Indochina Wars at the Geneva Conference," paper presented at International Workshop, "New Evidence on China, Southeast Asia, and the Vietnam War," January 11–12, 2000, University of Hong Kong, Hong Kong. In a forthcoming essay, Chen Jian makes many of the same points, likewise stressing Zhou Enlai's central role in persuading the Viet Minh, in the interests of preventing a prolongation of the conflict and potential American military intervention, to accept a compromise settlement. Chen also highlights the benefits to China in terms of enhanced international acceptance and credibility and a new appreciation of the PRC as a potential responsible diplomatic partner, developments that also increased the regime's domestic authority. See Chen Jian, "China and the Indochina Settlement at the Geneva Conference of 1954," in *The First Indochina War: Nationalism, Colonialism, and the Cold War*, ed. Fredrik Logevall and Mark Lawrence (Cambridge, Mass.: Harvard University Press, forthcoming).

76. Westad et al., *77 Conversations*, 41. In conversations with Henry Kissinger in 1971, Zhou Enlai repeatedly brought up the Vietnamese "Geneva complex" and their resentment of the 1954 settlement as a reason why China could not once again pressure

North Vietnam to reach a peace agreement with the United States and South Vietnam. Winston Lord, "Memorandum for Henry Kissinger: Subject: Memcon of Your Conversations with Zhou Enlai, 29 July 1971," box 1033, folder China HAK Memcons, July 1971, Nixon Presidential Materials Project, National Archives II, Washington, D.C.; available at http://www.gwu.edu/~nsarchive/NSAEBB/NASEBB66/ch-34.pdf.

77. Chen, "China and the Indochina Settlement," 27; cf. Connolly, "American Factor," 523.

78. Westad, "Introduction," *Brothers in Arms,* 27; Chen and Yang, "Chinese Politics and the Collapse of the Sino-Soviet Alliance," 275–77; for a recent restatement of this view, see Dong Wang, *The Quarrelling Brothers: New Chinese Archives and a Reappraisal of the Sino-Soviet Split, 1959–1962,* CWIHP Working Paper 49 (Washington, D.C.: Woodrow Wilson International Center for Scholars, 2006).

79. Zhai, *China & the Vietnam Wars,* 153–54; Gaiduk, *The Soviet Union and the Vietnam War,* 228–29.

80. Priscilla Roberts, ed., *Window on the Forbidden City: The Beijing Diaries of David Bruce, 1973–1974* (Hong Kong: Center of Asian Studies, University of Hong Kong, 2001), 31–32.

81. To compare the flavor of the two, see the version of Mao Zedong's conversation of November 17, 1968, with Pham Van Dong, as published in the 1994 official collection *Mao Zedong waijiao wenxuan,* given in *77 Conversations,* ed. Westad et al., 154–56.

82. Tony Smith, "New Bottles for New Wine: A Pericentric Framework for the Study of the Cold War," *Diplomatic History* 24, no. 4 (Fall 2000): 567–91; the quotations are on 568 and 571.

83. Thomas S. Christensen, "Worse than a Monolith: Disorganization and Rivalry within Asian Communist Alliances and U.S. Containment Challenges, 1949–69," *Asian Security* 1, no. 1 (January 2005): 80–127.

84. See esp. the two works by Gaiduk, *Confronting Vietnam* and *The Soviet Union and the Vietnam War;* also Zhang, "Communist Powers Divided," 83–97; and Stolberg, "Sino-Soviet Struggle," 249–56.

85. Gaiduk, *Confronting Vietnam,* chaps. 7–8.

86. Gaiduk, *Confronting Vietnam,* 199.

87. Brigham, *Guerrilla Diplomacy,* 59–64; Brigham, "Vietnam at the Center: Patterns of Diplomacy and Resistance," in *International Perspectives on Vietnam,* ed. Gardner and Gittinger, 98–107.

88. Christensen, "Worse than a Monolith."

89. Ang, *Ending the Vietnam War,* 154–55.

90. Morris, *Why Vietnam Invaded Cambodia,* 5.

91. See, e.g., Chen, *Mao's China.*

92. See Schwartz, *Lyndon Johnson and Europe,* a book that expands on the themes of Schwartz's paper, which is not included in the present volume.

93. Steven I. Levine, "Perception and Ideology in Chinese Foreign Policy," in *Chinese Foreign Policy,* ed. Robinson and Shambaugh, 30–34; the quotations are on 35, 36, 40, and 39.

94. See, e.g., Zhang, *Economic Cold War,* 273–76.

95. Chen, *Mao's China,* 4.

96. See, e.g., James G. Hershberg, "Peace Probes and the Bombing Pause: Hungarian and Polish Diplomacy during the Vietnam War, December 1965–January 1966," *Journal of Cold War Studies* 5, no. 2 (Spring 2003): 32–67.

97. See the account given in Gaiduk, *The Soviet Union and the Vietnam War.*

98. Gaiduk, *The Soviet Union and the Vietnam War,* 169–70.

99. Chen, *Mao's China,* 4–15, 70–77. On Mao's thinking, see esp. Stuart Schram, *The Thought of Mao Tse-Tung* (Cambridge: Cambridge University Press, 1989).

100. This is one of the major themes pervading Chen, *Mao's China.* See also Chen and Yang, "Chinese Politics and the Collapse of the Sino-Soviet Alliance," 246–77; Robinson, "Chinese Foreign Policy," 557–58; Steven M. Goldstein, "Nationalism and Internationalism: Sino-Soviet Relations," in *Chinese Foreign Policy,* ed. Robinson and Shambaugh, 227, 237, 244–45, 250; Hunt, *Genesis of Chinese Communist Foreign Policy,* 228–30; and chapter 5 below by Li Xiangqian. Also see Chen and Yang, "Chinese Politics and the Collapse of the Sino-Soviet Alliance," 248, 254–56, 270–71, 276–77.

101. Chen, *China's Road to the Korean War;* Zhang, *Mao's Military Romanticism.*

102. Zhang, *Mao's Military Romanticism.*

103. Chen, *Mao's China,* 167–70, 175–204.

104. Ang, *Vietnamese Communists' Relations with China,* 109; cf. Zhang Baijia, "The Changing International Scene and Chinese Policy toward the United States, 1954–1970," in *Re-examining the Cold War,* ed. Ross and Changbin, 57.

105. See chapters 1 and 6 below by, respectively, Yang and Hershberg and Chen. Also see Zhai, *China & the Vietnam Wars,* esp. 49–64, 81–83, 105, 108, 111, 117–20, 133–35, 138–41, 155–56; Chen, *Mao's China,* 212–19; and Ang, *Vietnamese Communists' Relations with China,* 130.

106. Chen, *Mao's China,* 14.

107. See, e.g., Chen, *Mao's China,* 174, 187, 189–90, 213; Zhang, *Economic Cold War,* 205–11.

108. See Zhang's chapter 7 below.

109. Gaiduk, *The Soviet Union and the Vietnam War,* 58–72, 97, 109–10, 174–77, 215–18.

110. Gaiduk, *The Soviet Union and the Vietnam War,* 226; Goh, *Constructing the U.S. Rapprochement with China,* 131-42; Elizabeth Wishnick, *Mending Fences: The Evolution of Moscow's China Policy from Brezhnev to Yeltsin* (Seattle: University of Washington Press, 2001), 32-40.

111. Robinson, "Chinese Foreign Policy," 561.

112. Chen, *Mao's China,* 84.

113. Zhai, *China & the Vietnam Wars,* 145; Frederick Teiwes, *Leadership, Legitimacy, and Conflict in China: From a Charismatic Mao to the Politics of Succession* (Armonk, N.Y.: M. E. Sharpe, 1984), 43–71; Zhang, "In the Shadow of Mao," 365. In this context, the editor finds illuminating the shock and surprise expressed to her in the early 1990s by Chinese scholars, who were amazed and found it incomprehensible that the British Conservative Party could possibly jettison a leader with such a record of accomplishment as Margaret Thatcher.

114. Frederick C. Teiwes and Warren Sun, *The Tragedy of Lin Biao: Riding the Tiger during the Cultural Revolution, 1966–1971* (London: Hurst & Company, 1996); Jin Qiu, *The Culture of Power: The Lin Biao Incident in the Cultural Revolution* (Stanford, Calif.: Stanford University Press, 1999); Chen, *Mao's China,* 277, 369 nn. 145–46.

115. Teiwes, *Leadership, Legitimacy, and Conflict in China,* 71–76; Chen, *Mao's China,* 277.

116. Gaiduk, *The Soviet Union and the Vietnam War,* 111–12, 211–12, 227–29, 232.

117. Chen, *Mao's China,* 2.

118. Gaiduk, *The Soviet Union and the Vietnam War,* 249–50.

Part I

The Beginning: From Colonial Rule to Escalation

1

Mao Zedong and the Indochina Wars

Yang Kuisong

For most of the period from 1949 until his death in 1976, Mao Zedong dominated the direction of China's foreign relations. Most of those scholars who have investigated China's role in the Vietnam War have focused on the first half of the 1950s and the later 1960s.[1] Due to the limitations of sources, these writings have been unable to present a clear picture of how and why Mao's attitude toward the Indochina wars altered over time.[2]

Like China's overall foreign policies, the People's Republic of China's (PRC's) attitude toward the Indochina wars was heavily influenced both by Mao's increasingly radical revolutionary ideology and by the Sino-Soviet dispute and the dilemmas it generated in China's international position. Seeking to prevent communist expansion there, during the Cold War the United States became involved in a series of wars in Indochina, first assisting France and then, from the mid-1950s to the 1970s, intervening directly in internal conflicts in Vietnam, Laos, and Cambodia. These states were very close geographically to China, whereas Beijing viewed Washington as its number one enemy, causing Chinese leaders to view American intervention and expansion in Indochina as a serious threat to their country's security. They chose to counter the American threat by providing active support to the various Indochinese communist parties and by courting nationalist governments in other Southeast Asian countries.

In practice, Mao occupied a central and unique position in the formation of China's foreign policy in this period. Without a clear understanding of exactly how Mao's attitude toward the Indochina war shifted over time and the reasons underlying his changing perspectives, it remains very difficult to comprehend the evolution of China's policy toward the Vietnam War. National security and ideology were two major determinants of China's approach to the Indochina conflict. Because Mao placed varying emphases on these at different times, oscillating between them, China's policy toward Indochina was apparently inconsistent and sometimes even self-contradictory. Drawing on recently released documents from China, Vietnam, and Russia, this chapter depicts the development and modification of Mao's attitude toward the Vietnam War, thereby facilitating a deeper comprehension of why China's policy toward the Indochina conflict changed dramatically over time.

From Supporting Wars of Liberation in Indochina to Advocating Peace in Southeast Asia

During the Chinese Civil War, the Chinese Communist Party (CCP), guided by Mao's revolutionary theory, sought to seize power through armed struggle and revolutionary warfare. From the Yanan period to the creation of the PRC, Mao had always adhered to the view that "the central task and the highest form of revolution is to seize power through armed struggle and to solve problems through war. This is a revolutionary principle of Marxism-Leninism, and it is universally applicable both in China and in the rest of the world."[3] Simultaneously, as revolutionary Communists, CCP leaders believed in class struggle. Working from country bases, CCP forces surrounded cities and in 1949 established the PRC. Class interest and class struggle constituted the Chinese Communists' basic worldview. They had always believed that a ''world revolution" was in progress and that only when the bourgeois class was eliminated everywhere could the victory of socialism be consolidated. Therefore, they argued that "when you are making revolution, you need foreign aid; after you have achieved victory, you ought to support foreign revolution." This, they believed should be the CCP's unshakable principle of internationalism.[4]

Because of the CCP's advocacy of the use of armed struggle to seize power and its belief in internationalism and revolution, immediately after achieving victory in China it began to demonstrate sympathy and give concrete support to those Asian communist parties that were engaged in their own revolutionary struggles. To some extent, the decision to provide such aid reflected the CCP's geopolitical interests, but ideological considerations predominated, and in the PRC's early years the desire to promote revolution throughout Asia was very apparent. CCP leaders told other Asian communist parties that the methods of organizing a united front under communist party leadership, creating revolutionary base areas, and seizing power through armed struggle that had succeeded in the Chinese revolution should become "the basic approach for national liberation struggle in all other colonial and semi-colonial countries" with conditions comparable to China's.[5] In accordance with this tendency to support Asian revolution, the CCP offered assistance to the anti-French war led by the Vietnamese Communists.

In August 1945, the Vietnamese Communist Party (Viet Minh) under the leadership of Ho Chi Minh took advantage of Japan's sudden defeat to establish the Democratic Republic of Vietnam (DRV), a temporary government based on united front principles. Once World War II ended, however, France sought to restore its own colonial rule in Indochina, and Chinese Nationalist forces entered northern Vietnam to supervise Japan's surrender, developments hazardous to the DRV. Although Ho, seeking to preserve the DRV's position and his forces, downplayed the role of the Vietnamese Communist Party and declared that the DRV was a neutral country, he failed to dispel French hostility, and in December 1946 the Franco-Vietminh war began.

Ho's conciliatory approach before December 1946 clearly differed from that adopted by Mao in China after World War II, and some CCP leaders criticized his behavior. With the opening of the Franco-Vietminh War, however, Mao and other CCP leaders changed their views. In December 1949, Ho sent envoys to Beijing, requesting military advisers, weapons to equip three divisions, and financial aid of $10 million from the CCP. Because it was still engaged in the war to unify China and its financial resources were limited, at this time the CCP could not meet all Ho's demands, but CCP leaders did instruct their military units in southern China to give the Vietminh as much assistance as possible.

Mao, who was then visiting Moscow, devoted considerable attention to Ho's struggle and his request for Chinese aid. After learning that his colleagues in Beijing had not met Ho's demands in their entirety, Mao sent a cable to the CCP Central Committee, instructing the leadership to inform

Ho's envoys that China would provide certain quantities of weapons, munitions, and medical supplies immediately, so that the Vietminh could familiarize themselves with Chinese matériel, and the PRC would increase its aid in the future. Mao also told Liu Shaoqi to adopt a friendly and cooperative attitude toward the Vietnamese Communists, encourage their struggle, and refrain from criticizing them. Mao insisted that "we might raise the issue of the Vietnamese Communist Party's weaknesses when high-level cadres sent by Ho Chi Minh arrive in Beijing." Referring to Ho's conciliatory approach during the period 1945–46, Mao said: "Ho Chi Minh once disguised his party and declared that the DRV remained neutral. It is too early to say that these two policies were mistakes in principle because the Vietnamese struggle did not suffer as a result of their implementation."[6]

In mid-January 1950, the PRC and the DRV established diplomatic relations. Ho paid a secret visit to Beijing and then went on to Moscow to meet with Joseph Stalin and Mao. In Moscow, Ho discussed with Stalin and Mao such issues as the development of the Vietnamese Communist Party, the national united front, military affairs, and foreign relations. Both Mao and Stalin expressed themselves willing to support the DRV's struggle against the French. In accordance with the Sino-Soviet agreement concluded in 1949 when Liu Shaoqi visited the Soviet Union, the CCP would be primarily responsible for providing support for the Vietminh.[7] Shortly after the Moscow meeting, China began to send military advisers, weapons, munitions, and equipment to Ho's forces in Vietnam. Within China, the CCP also equipped and trained the People's Army of Vietnam's (PAVN's) 308th Division, 209th Regiment, and 174th Regiment.

During the next three years, China not only continued to supply weapons and munitions to the Vietminh but also helped them to organize a series of important military campaigns. Mao often directly reviewed battle plans and gave specific directions. To better fight the French and win victory throughout Indochina, the Chinese leadership even proposed expanding the war to Laos and Cambodia to liberate those two countries. Seeking to attain that objective, Chinese advisers entered Laos to help direct military operations.[8]

The anti-French war in Vietnam (1946–54) coincided with the Korean War (1950–53), a conflict that revealed the huge discrepancy between China and the United States in equipment, firepower, and naval and air forces. China had to rely on Soviet weapons to fight the Americans. This alerted many CCP leaders to the urgent need to accelerate China's industrialization and modernize its national defense. But the Korean War seriously undermined their efforts to concentrate the country's primary resources on economic reconstruction.[9] After the Korean War ended in an inconclusive armistice in July 1953, the United States began to direct more attention to the Indochina conflict even as the Soviet government sought a general reduction of international tensions. In 1953, China began to implement its First Five-Year Plan and carry out its program of socialist transformation of the economy. Given these domestic needs, Zhou Enlai and many other CCP leaders favored the promotion of a peaceful international environment. These international and domestic constraints moderated the impulse of international mission in Mao's thinking, leading Mao to begin to accord the advancement of national interests a higher priority than the propagation of revolution.

Shortly after the Korean War ended, the Chinese government began to cooperate with the Soviet Union in advocating the reduction of international tensions. The attainment of peace in Indochina became a shared propaganda slogan for the Soviet Union, China, and the DRV. In February 1954, a foreign ministers' conference was held in Berlin, attended by representatives of the United States, the Soviet Union, France, and the United Kingdom. At Soviet instigation, on February 19 the conference declared that in two months a conference of major powers, including China, would be held in Geneva to discuss the Korean and Indochinese conflicts. China and the DRV voiced support for this declaration.

What was Mao's attitude? Although he endorsed negotiations, he doubted that the Geneva Conference alone could bring peace to Indochina, and he still felt that military victory was crucial. French forces in Indochina were still quite strong, and France had just deployed more than ten thousand troops at the strategic location of Dien Bien Phu, posing a serious threat to the Vietnamese Communist headquarters in Viet Bac and the transit route to Laos. As the conference date approached, Mao therefore began to urge the Vietnamese Communists to fight harder. At this time "using war to promote peace" became a basic principle in the CCP's approach to any Indochina settlement.[10] Zhou, a strong advocate of peace, also shared Mao's desire to approach the peace negotiations from a strong military position, and he hoped the Vietminh would win several military victories before the Geneva Conference embarked on discussions on Indochina. Accordingly, in a cable to the Chinese military advisory team shortly after the CCP firmed up its plan to attend the Geneva Conference, Zhou suggested that "in order to win the diplomatic initiative, can we organize several successful campaigns in Vietnam as we did in Korea before the conclusion of the Korean armistice?"[11]

The Dien Bien Phu campaign thus became urgent. At this time, Mao was still pessimistic about the Geneva Conference and, although he had endorsed negotiations, he clearly had not abandoned military measures. While Zhou, together with Ho and other Vietnamese leaders, went to Moscow in early April for discussions with the Russians on how to achieve success at the Geneva Conference, on April 3 Mao urged the Chinese military advisory team to wrap up the Dien Bien Phu campaign. He urged the PAVN to occupy Dien Bien Phu quickly and then attack Luang Prabang in Laos so as to prepare the way to take Hanoi, attack Saigon, and unify all Vietnam. He specifically ordered the Chinese military to help the PAVN organize four additional artillery regiments and two engineering regiments, specifying that all instructors and advisers for these regiments should be recruited from those Chinese artillery units that had fought in the Korean War; that artillery pieces could be drawn from Chinese artillery units; and that training could be conducted either in northern Vietnam or in Guangxi Province, China.[12]

A few days later, however, Mao modified his policy of expanding the war in Indochina. He did so for two reasons. The first was the American threat to intervene in Indochina. On March 29 and April 5, U.S. secretary of state John Foster Dulles twice declared that, as it had done in Korea, the United States would organize united international action to intervene in Indochina, to prevent "Communist Russia and its ally, the Chinese Communist Party, from imposing their political system on Southeast Asia."

The second reason had to do with the decisions reached at the meeting of Soviet, Chinese, and Vietnamese representatives in Moscow in early April, where all three interested parties agreed to make every effort to ensure that the negotiations at Geneva were successful. Bearing in mind both the danger of another direct confrontation with the United States and the consensus on Indochinese peace achieved at the Moscow meeting, Mao was forced to abandon his ideas to expand the war in Indochina. On April 17, he told his generals that, given the possibility of a cease-fire in Vietnam, the previous policy of expanding the war in Indochina should be suspended and that it was no longer appropriate to train Vietnamese artillery regiments in China. Later, when the Vietminh defeated the French at Dien Bien Phu, thus opening the way to attack Laos and Hanoi, Mao still urged the Vietnamese to restrain and refrain from expanding the scale of their frontline war, to ensure the success of the Geneva negotiations.[13] Clearly Mao now favored seeking a cease-fire and peace in Indochina through negotiation and compromise.

The United States, far from enthusiastic about reaching a peace settlement in Indochina at the Geneva Conference, even tried to prevent the conclusion of any peace agreement. For China to succeed in bringing peace to Indochina, therefore, its most important need was to isolate the United States. To achieve that goal, Zhou worked enormously hard to win the sympathy and understanding of the British, French, Laotian, and Cambodian delegates. Another obstacle to an agreement during the Geneva negotiations was the attitude of the Vietnamese. Especially after their May 7 victory at Dien Bien Phu, when they wiped out 16,000 French troops and captured General Christian de Castries, the French commander, the Vietnamese delegates at Geneva supported Mao's previous military plan even more belligerently, insisting that either the French must withdraw completely from Vietnam, Laos, and Cambodia, or the DRV would forcibly implement unification within about three years. They contended that Vietnam, Laos, and Cambodia represented one single entity in Indochina and that the problems of all three countries should all be resolved simultaneously. Insisting that the PAVN units in Laos and Cambodia were not foreign troops, the Vietnamese representatives resisted the demand of the royal governments of Laos and Cambodia that both France and the DRV withdraw all military forces from their countries.

At the time of the Moscow meeting in early April, China had little knowledge of Laos and Cambodia. Influenced by the Vietnamese Communists, the Chinese leaders believed that, because all three Indochinese countries were included within the French colonies, Laotians and Cambodians were actually minorities of Vietnam, and that all issues relating to the three should therefore be settled together as a whole. After arriving in Geneva and exchanging views with other delegates, the Chinese negotiators realized that the DRV's policy of including the three Indochinese countries in one settlement would not bring any agreement. Zhou therefore quickly adjusted his position, arguing that the various problems of Vietnam, Laos, and Cambodia should be settled separately. Where Vietnam was concerned, he believed that even if the United States did not intervene, fighting there would continue for several years. Given that Communist forces in Laos and Cambodia were still very weak, Zhou asserted that to continue the war in those two countries would only lead their royal governments to turn to the United States and would give Washington and London further impetus to organize the Southeast Asia Treaty Organization (SEATO).

Under such circumstances, Zhou thought it very likely that the United States would intervene in Laos and Cambodia, and that once it did so, any settlement of the Indochina situation would become even more difficult.

These tactical considerations led Zhou to prefer peace to continued fighting. As a first step to a settlement in Vietnam, he contended, a cease-fire agreement should be reached by dividing the country into two parts and then "reunification could be pursued through elections." Given the prestige the Vietnamese Workers' Party enjoyed among the population, Zhou believed that by these means the party would be able to achieve peaceful reunification. As for Laos and Cambodia, Zhou argued that the resistance forces should make those concessions necessary to achieve either an on-the-spot cease-fire or a cease-fire by regrouping. The resistance forces, Zhou continued, should join the royal governments according to democratic principles and promote neutrality in the two countries. To persuade the Vietnamese delegates, Zhou exchanged numerous telegrams with Mao, who clearly concurred in his views. Mao stated that the situation in Indochina differed from that in Korea and that Indochina could affect all Southeast Asia (including Burma, Thailand, Malaya, Indonesia, and the Philippines), Pakistan, India, Australia, New Zealand, and Ceylon. "If we are not careful," Mao went on, "we will affect 600 million people in ten countries. We should make necessary concessions. We should adhere to those positions that cannot be compromised. In this way, we can isolate the minority (the United States), win over the majority," and reach a final agreement.[14]

With Mao's backing, in July 1954 Zhou successfully persuaded Ho and the Vietnamese party leadership to sign the Geneva Accords, which gave the DRV control of Vietnam north of the 17th parallel, with a population of 12 million. Disagreements remained, because some Vietnamese leaders still considered the agreement detrimental rather than advantageous to the DRV. Some top DRV officials felt that even before the cease-fire, the party had already controlled a population of no less than 12 million, and that neither the French forces nor the royal governments' troops could halt the PAVN attack in Laos and Cambodia. Those leaders who were regrouped to the north from the southern bases complained particularly forcefully, doubting whether Vietnamese reunification could be achieved through elections in two years in accordance with the Geneva Accords. Once the party withdrew from Laos and Cambodia, they believed, it would have handed over control of the fate of those two countries to the landlord and bourgeois class.

Mao undoubtedly knew of and perhaps sympathized with these sentiments. Throughout his life, he had hated people who refused to permit him to advance revolution, and had always resented the way that in 1945, after China's victory in the Anti-Japanese War, Stalin had forced him to negotiate with Jiang Jieshi (Chiang Kai-shek) rather than continue his revolutionary struggle. Given Mao's penchant for revolution and the fact that, in later years, he repeatedly criticized himself to Vietnamese party representatives for having urged them to make concessions at Geneva, it seems quite plausible that Mao had not acted on his real convictions when he prodded the DRV to compromise at the conference.

From Preferring Peaceful Coexistence
to Advocating Cold War Coexistence

Because he was influenced by the doctrines of world revolution, Mao always found satisfaction in waging class struggle. Proud of the triumph of the Chinese revolution, he did not restrict his lifetime goals to its mere consolidation. One of his foremost concerns was how to take up the mantle of Marx and Lenin and use the example of China to help the oppressed around the world, including the nations of Asia, to win liberation.

Why, then, did Mao agree to make concessions to colonialism and imperialism in Indochina? In later years, Mao several times cited Lenin in his own defense on this matter, quoting Lenin's saying that, when you encountered a robber, you either allowed yourself to be killed by him or you gave him your money and car. Lenin suggested that you give the robber your money and car, but later, when opportunity arose, you should kill the robber and recover your money and car.[15] In other words, Mao considered the concessions made at Geneva temporary and tactical, desirable because at that time his own regime still needed consolidation and the DRV was not strong enough to attain full victory.

To some extent, therefore, Mao's preoccupation with China's own security requirement of domestic reconstruction undermined his efforts to implement his revolutionary ideals and plans. In mid-1949, he made leaning toward the Soviet Union and anti-imperialism the basic principles of Chinese foreign policy. After the 1950–53 military confrontation with the United States, he came to agree with other CCP leaders that building up national power should be the highest priority.[16] In 1953, China began its First Five-Year Plan, emphasizing the development of heavy industry. Its implementation required a relatively peaceful international environment. In addition to relying on Soviet aid, China also needed to win sympathy and support from those nationalist countries in Asia that stood between the socialist and capitalist camps, and even to develop better relations with capitalist countries. Such dealings would be based on mutual concessions between states, conducive to making peace rather than revolution. China's conciliatory approach at the Geneva Conference and its embrace of the "Five Principles of Peaceful Coexistence"—mutual respect for territorial integrity and sovereignty, nonaggression, noninterference in each other's internal affairs, equality and mutual benefit, and peaceful coexistence—demonstrated a modification of Mao's attitude toward peace and revolution.

Following the Geneva Conference, the United States organized SEATO, a military alliance designed to prevent "Communist aggression" and openly aimed primarily at China. In defiance of the Geneva Accords' stipulation that Laos and Cambodia should remain neutral, SEATO openly treated South Vietnam, Laos, and Cambodia as its "protected areas."[17] SEATO represented a major setback for both the DRV and China, which were committed to attaining peace in Indochina through compromise. Despite this development, Mao's position on seeking peace in Indochina remained unchanged. In the aftermath of Geneva, he even publicly advocated peaceful coexistence among countries with different social systems, stating repeatedly that "it is good to have no war" and "it is better not to fight" while declaring that war would only harm capitalism and imperialism, because it would trigger revolution and produce more Soviet Unions and Chinas. Mao openly stated that because China was engaged in industrial development, a long-term process, it needed a peaceful environment and friends, and that should war break out, China's economic and cultural plans would be suspended and its industrialization delayed. Given his reputation, even today many might find it almost unimaginable that Mao, a revolutionary who had always called for the overthrow of imperialist rule, could have uttered these words.[18] His concern with domestic development led him to pledge publicly that he would not support antigovernment armed struggles waged by communist parties in Southeast Asia, a policy that applied not only to Laos and Cambodia but also to Burma, Thailand, and Malaya.

During the Geneva Conference in 1954, Zhou visited Burma and issued a joint declaration with Prime Minister U Nu, stating that the relationship between the two countries would be based on the Five Principles of Peaceful Coexistence, that China would not export revolution, and that each country had the right to choose its own system of government and its own way of life without interference from foreign countries. Several reasons underpinned China's decision to make such promises. In Burma, Communists and minority groups had launched antigovernment resistance movements. Because Burma shared a border with China, some rebels had taken shelter in Chinese territory, and at the time of Zhou's visit, more than a hundred armed rebels and Communists from Burma were operating in China. Zhou's declaration offered reassurance to the Burmese government.

A few months later, during a visit to China, U again raised the issue of antigovernment activities. Mao told him explicitly that the Five Principles of Peaceful Coexistence included noninterference in each other's internal affairs. Domestic disputes within a country, Mao continued, should be dealt with by that country alone, and other nations should neither intervene nor exploit those disputes. Other states should recognize any government chosen by a country's own people. Burma had recognized the PRC, and China had recognized U's government. Because China and Burma shared a lengthy border, it was very possible that opponents of their governments would cross the border in both directions. China would not use Burmese dissidents on its territory to harm the interests of the Burmese government or launch a military invasion against Burma, and China would not instigate antigovernment activities within Burma. As for the radical elements among overseas Chinese in Burma, Mao pledged, China would advise them to distance themselves from Burma's internal affairs, to abide by Burmese laws, and to avoid contact with political parties that used violence against the government. Communist organizations among the overseas Chinese had been disbanded.

As for the Burmese Communist Party, Mao asked U to open informal negotiations with them, stating that it would be ideal if such talks could reach a mutually acceptable agreement. Should such negotiations fail to do so, they should be temporarily suspended but reopened when a suitable opportunity arose. Mao cited China's treatment of Tibet as an example, explaining that China was prepared to hold lengthy negotiations with the local government in Tibet; and that there were certain issues China would not insist be handled according to its policy. On these issues, China would first talk with the Tibetans; if they agreed, China would carry out its policy; if they did not agree, China would refrain from doing so. Such methods, Mao concluded, made it easier to reach acceptable compromises.[19]

Burma was one of the first Southeast Asian countries to establish diplomatic relations with the PRC, whereas Thailand, by contrast, was one of the few Southeast Asian countries that had still not done so by the mid-1950s. Because Thailand, a member of SEATO, was the primary partner of the United States in Southeast Asia, Mao clearly hoped that he could persuade Thailand to change its policy toward China, or at least to remain neutral between China and the United States. He stated several times that although Thailand was not particularly friendly to China, he wished to establish relations. On several occasions, he asked leaders from Burma and other countries to help convey his message to Bangkok that China would not interfere in Thailand's internal affairs.

When a Thai delegation visited China in December 1955, Mao met with them and made the following pledges: China would not propagate communism in Thailand; China stood for peaceful coexistence and friendship; China wanted to conduct trade with Thailand; China would not instigate others to overthrow the Thai government; China would not encourage the Thai Communist Party to attack the Thai government; China would disband communist organizations among overseas Chinese to dispel the suspicions that the governments of those countries where they lived had of them; China was willing to have friendly relations with all countries in the world, especially nations that opposed imperialism; China would support its friends that opposed imperialism; and if Thailand found it difficult to choose China's side because of its relationship with the United States, it could follow the Indian example of remaining neutral.[20]

Mao's peace offensive also influenced the Malayan Communist Party (MCP). During World War II, the MCP organized a guerrilla war against Japan. When the war was over, it ceased its armed struggle and was banned and suppressed by the authorities, who executed some of its members. In 1948, the MCP resumed military resistance, and by 1954 it had a guerrilla force several hundred strong. It also sent envoys to request aid from China. After the 1954 Geneva Conference, Chinese and Soviet officials held a special meeting in Moscow to discuss the MCP's future development. The meeting produced a resolution stating that because Malaya had no shared border with any socialist country, it was difficult for the MCP to wage armed struggle, and that it should change its tactics and adopt a peaceful and democratic approach to develop its strength. Accepting the Chinese and Soviet suggestion, the MCP quickly stopped its guerrilla operations, laid down its arms, and opened negotiations with the Malayan government.[21]

Between 1954 and 1957, the Chinese government also made extensive diplomatic efforts to court countries in Asia, Africa, and Europe, initiatives Mao clearly supported. Chinese representatives attended the April 1955 Bandung Conference that founded the nonaligned movement, and Foreign Minister Zhou visited the DRV, Cambodia, India, Burma, Pakistan, Afghanistan, Nepal, and Ceylon. The opening of the Sino-American ambassadorial talks in August 1955 also benefited from Mao's enthusiasm at that time to reduce tensions between China and the United States.[22]

Mao's conciliatory attitude, however, was neither the logical result of his ideological beliefs nor the product of his revolutionary experiences, but rather a diplomatic tactic determined by realistic policy needs. Closer examination reveals that even though Mao emphasized compromise and peace, his fundamental views on revolution and war remained unchanged. At the time of the 1954 Geneva Conference, for instance, Harry Pollitt, the British Communist Party (BCP) secretary general, wrote a letter to the CCP, claiming that in his party's translation of the second volume of the *Selected Works of Mao Zedong,* it intended to delete the sentence: "The central task and highest form of revolution is to seize power by armed struggle and to resolve problems by war." Pollitt explained that this sentence provoked much trouble for his party and that it did not fit the program the BCP had adopted in 1951, which stated that the methods of violent revolution whereby the Soviet Communist Party had seized power did not apply to the United Kingdom. In its draft response, CCP Central Committee's Propaganda Department endorsed the BCP's position, but when Mao learned of this, he criticized the Propaganda Department.

In subsequent conversations with foreign Communist leaders, Mao referred to this incident several times, stressing that his statement on using armed struggle to seize power was relevant not only to China but also to foreign countries and remained accurate not just for the past but also for the present.[23] Given Mao's strong conviction of the correctness of his theories on war and revolution, rather predictably, his endorsement of compromise and peace in Southeast Asia began to waver once the international situation changed.

The incident propelling Mao to reemphasize the issue of war and revolution was Nikita Khrushchev's denunciation of Stalin at the February 1956 Twentieth Congress of the Communist Party of the Soviet Union, and his claim that capitalism could develop into socialism through "peaceful transition." After learning of Khrushchev's report, Mao expressed doubts about the Soviet leader's practice and theory.[24] The Hungarian Uprising of 1956 and China's Anti-Rightist Campaign of 1957 further alerted Mao to the primacy of class and class struggle.[25] At the Moscow Conference of Communist and Labor Parties in November 1957, Mao and Khrushchev quarreled over the issue of war and revolution. Although they compromised on the final conference resolution, Mao was undoubtedly more determined than ever to press the issue of war and revolution. In 1958, Mao used the Middle East crisis as an occasion to launch a bombardment of the Nationalist-held offshore islands of Jinmen and Mazu.[26] The next year, China had a border clash with India after the rebellion in Tibet. On both occasions, Mao's militancy contrasted with Khrushchev's advocacy of détente with the United States. In October 1959, a heated debate broke out between the Chinese and Soviet leaders over whether to intensify or to reduce tensions in the world.[27] Spurred by the Sino-Soviet dispute, Mao switched to a vigorous defense of Marxist-Leninist orthodoxy, calling for anti-imperialist struggle and once more highlighting the importance of war and revolution.

At the Supreme State Conference in September 1958, held against the backdrop of renewed Chinese shelling of the offshore islands, Mao made a speech discussing whether it was preferable to reduce or intensify international tensions, and he claimed to believe that such tensions were not detrimental to China. Although tensions had negative aspects, he said, they could be valuable as a means to mobilize people, especially social groups reluctant to join the revolution. China's shelling of Jinmen and Mazu in the Taiwan Strait had generated international tension, Mao continued, but people primarily blamed the United States for fomenting trouble throughout the world, proving that such tensions were more damaging to imperialism. Mao urged the CCP not to fear international crises, because otherwise, he warned, the cadres and masses would become discouraged, which would be dangerous.[28]

Mao's renewed emphasis on anti-imperialism did not, however, translate immediately into active support for revolution in Southeast Asia. Driven by his concern for China's national security, he remained cautious toward Indochina and Southeast Asia. In his talks with foreign communist parties, he tried to avoid giving the impression that China was supporting antigovernment struggles in Southeast Asia. Mao's restraint was clearly demonstrated in his conversations with the leaders of the Lao People's Party (LPP) in October 1959. At the 1954 Geneva Conference, the Pathet Lao forces had been regrouped to the northern provinces of Sam Neua and Phong Saly. In November 1957, the Pathet Lao joined the royal government by turning over its two provinces and integrating its forces into the royal army.

In February 1959, however, the United States announced that it would establish a military advisory mission in Laos, a move that enhanced the influence of right-wing forces in Laos. Some LPP leaders were placed under house arrest or imprisoned, while other party officials were forced to flee to the mountains or North Vietnam. Of the two Pathet Lao battalions that had been integrated into the royal army, one was disarmed, and the other fled to North Vietnam. Both China and the DRV publicly condemned these Royal Laotian government policies. In his meeting with LPP chairman Kaysone Phomvihane, who visited China secretly in October 1959, Mao expressed support for the LPP's efforts to renew armed struggle. Praising the Lao leaders for adopting a correct policy, Mao advised them to wage a protracted struggle, suggesting that at present the LPP should not over-expand its forces and should keep its activities at a moderate level, because anything more, he warned, might trigger an excessive reaction from their opponents. At that time, Mao continued, the United States was spreading rumors that China and the DRV were helping the Pathet Lao to fight. Warning that the United Nations had dispatched an investigative team into Laos to seek evidence of outside support for the Pathet Lao, Mao asked the LPP to ensure that the West obtained no such proof.[29]

Likewise, when the DRV decided in 1959 to renew armed struggle in South Vietnam, the Chinese leadership initially remained cautious, advising that because it was currently impossible to implement revolutionary changes in the south, the DRV should "conduct long-term underground work, accumulate strength, establish contact with the masses, and wait for opportunities" so that, when the situation changed, "South Vietnam can be liberated in one form or another."[30]

By the end of the 1950s, the Sino-Soviet dispute had intensified.[31] Although there were several reasons for this dispute, including historical grievances, nationalist sentiments, and conflicting national interests, what most irritated Mao was Soviet reluctance to wage revolution. For Mao, revolution—whether class struggle or anti-imperialism—was not only the focal point of his life experience but also the key to the success of the Chinese revolution. In his mind, the negation of revolution, particularly violent revolution, meant the negation of the universal applicability of the Chinese revolutionary model and the rejection of his own "unique contribution" to Marxism-Leninism. In 1958, Mao therefore ordered the distribution of quotations on continuous revolution by Marx, Engels, Lenin, and Stalin among high-level party cadres, whom he wished to comprehend the nature of the Sino-Soviet dispute. In 1959, he stated several times that Marxists should recognize that class struggle without war could not solve problems entirely, a fact that had been true throughout history.

The party did sometimes advocate peaceful means, Mao continued, but that was because the consciousness of the masses had not yet been awakened. Because the bourgeoisie used the fear of conflict to intimidate the masses, the party had to highlight peaceful methods in order to win over the latter. A state was an institution based upon violence, something true of slave countries, feudal countries, and capitalist countries alike. Without violence, there was no state. Without resort to war, the institution of violence controlled by the exploiting class could not be smashed. When celebrating the fortieth anniversary of the October Revolution in Moscow in November 1957, Mao had approved the slogans of "peaceful coexistence" and "peaceful competition," proposing that "the Five Principles of Peaceful Co-existence be adopted by socialist and capitalist countries."[32]

By 1960, however, Mao rejected the principles of "peaceful coexistence," which he declared were no longer applicable, pointing to guerrilla wars in Cuba, Algeria, the Philippines, and Paraguay. Between socialist and capi-talist countries, he proclaimed, there existed Cold War coexistence, not peaceful coexistence. It was utter nonsense to believe that socialist coun-tries could for any length of time coexist and compete in peace with capi-talist countries. Cold War coexistence, Mao concluded, was characterized by international and domestic struggle.[33]

Their ideological conflict with the Soviet Union led Chinese leaders to criticize the Vietnamese Workers' Party (VWP). On May 21, 1960, Mao and Zhou had a conversation with North Korean leader Kim Il Sung, in which Zhou stated "the DRV has a clear policy in terms of anti-imperial-ism, but it is equivocal on some other issues." Zhou was alluding to the VWP's attitude toward the Soviet Union and some tendencies in its policy, notably its reluctance to imitate the Chinese model of consolidating revo-lution. Mao, who had discovered a few years earlier that the VWP's atti-tude toward class struggle was ambivalent and that it was unwilling to fol-low the Chinese example of carrying out thorough land reform, clearly shared Zhou's views. After the Sino-Soviet dispute became apparent, Ho Chi Minh had attempted to play the role of mediator. Mao told Ho on Au-gust 10, 1960, that although the VWP had been correct in conducting an anti-imperialist struggle, it must recognize the importance of following proper theories, policies, and tactics in opposing the United States and re-actionary forces in other countries and be able to discern who was the most reactionary enemy. He asked Ho to make clear distinctions among reac-tionary forces in Laos, Thailand, Burma, India, and Indonesia, and to treat them accordingly. Ho and Mao were at variance in their thinking on this issue, a discrepancy reflected in a November 2, 1960, conversation be-tween them on the treatment of reactionaries.

During this meeting, Mao and other CCP leaders displayed great enthu-siasm for the armed struggle in Laos and South Vietnam, stressing that the VWP had done an excellent job in conducting armed struggle in Laos and South Vietnam and had promoted revolution throughout Southeast Asia. Mao commented that it was excellent that the reactionaries had used vio-lence and killed people, and that when Jiang Jieshi killed people, he was ac-tually promoting revolution in China. Ho disagreed with Mao's analysis, contending that it was inhumane to kill people. Mao retorted that if reactionaries could massacre revolutionaries, then revolutionaries could kill reactionaries and there was nothing inhumane in such tactics. Liu Shaoqi added that revolutionaries did not invoke humanitarianism when dealing with bourgeois reactionaries. Because humanitarianism rejected class struggle, Liu continued, it contradicted Marxism. Communist parties could not rely on U.S. president Dwight Eisenhower's rationality to safeguard peace because his rationality differed from that of communists.[34]

In the early 1960s, differences existed among CCP leaders on the future course of the conflict in Laos and South Vietnam. A conversation among Ho, Mao, and other CCP officials on November 14, 1961, illustrated this divergence. Though Chinese leaders agreed on the need to fight in Laos and South Vietnam, they differed on the scale of such fighting and the wisdom of establishing coalition governments. Deng Xiaoping and Zhou preferred to limit the scope of the war. Deng argued guerrilla warfare should be waged and maintained at a low level. Small-scale fighting, Deng went on, would not trigger American intervention, though a large-scale war aimed at occupying big cities such as Saigon and overthrowing the Ngo Dinh Diem regime would quite possibly provoke American involvement. Zhou pointed out that there were three options in Indochina: namely, small-scale fighting (guerrilla war), medium-level fighting (more extensive war within Laos and South Vietnam), and major war (war with American troops). Of the three alternatives, Zhou recommended the second. Mao, however, disagreed. Declaring that there was nothing to fear, Mao asserted that even if a coalition government was established, it would only be a temporary expedient and sooner or later war would erupt. With the ongoing Geneva Conference on Laos in mind, Ho asked whether the war would expand if fighting in Laos continued and PAVN troops remained in place there. Without hesitation, Mao replied that the PAVN troops should keep fighting in Laos, while the DRV should continue to pretend that it had no soldiers in that country.[35]

During 1961 and the first half of 1962, differing views on Chinese foreign policy were voiced within the CCP leadership, eventually precipitating an inner-party dispute over Mao's increasingly radical statements and actions since the emergence of the Sino-Soviet quarrel. In the spring of 1962, Wang Jiaxiang, the director of the CCP Central Committee's International Liaison Department, and other officials wrote to Zhou expressing concern over Mao's radical attitude. Their concrete foreign policy proposals embodied similar sentiments. Insisting on continued adherence to the diplomatic principle of peaceful coexistence, they argued that war was avoidable and that China should adopt policies designed to alleviate, rather than intensify, international tensions. On Indochina, they contended that China should forestall a Korean-style war and prevent the United States from focusing its attention on China. As for the Sino-Soviet split, they recommended a policy of reconciliation to prevent further escalation of that conflict. Seeking to break the deadlock on the Sino-Indian border issue, they asked the party leadership to adopt new political, diplomatic, and propaganda measures.[36]

The sharp expansion in China's foreign aid after 1960 alarmed Wang. In chapter 7 of the present volume, Shu Guang Zhang suggests that in the early 1960s Africa, rather than Vietnam, was China's first foreign aid priority, and that economic strictures restrained China from launching more ambitious aid programs. Yet even if these undertakings were relatively modest, by 1960 China had nonetheless provided $6.7 billion in foreign aid to other countries, $3.5 billion as grants and $3.2 billion as loans. In 1960, one-third of China's total foreign aid of $1.9 billion went to the DRV, another $133 million went to Cambodia, and $670,000 went to Laos. Overall, between 1950 and 1960, China on average allocated 1.18 percent of its total annual financial spending to foreign aid, a modest percentage.[37]

At the end of 1960, Mao promised Ho that China would send food and weapons to Laos and South Vietnam via the DRV. After the American introduction of "special warfare" in South Vietnam the following year, the CCP decided to provide the DRV, free of charge, with weapons to equip 230 battalions.[38] Given that the disastrous Great Leap Forward had left China in an extremely difficult economic situation, Wang and his associates suggested that, under existing circumstances, Beijing should move cautiously in providing foreign aid and refrain from commitments that would strain China's limited resources.[39] On July 21, 1962, the Geneva Conference reached an agreement on Laotian neutrality, whereby the royal government of Laos would adopt a policy of peace and neutrality, enter into no military alliances, and receive no protection from SEATO. Influenced by Wang and his supporters, Liu and Zhou, who directed the Central Committee's daily work, supported the peaceful settlement of the Laotian question at the Geneva Conference.

Wang's ideas, however, quickly attracted sharp criticism from Mao. In August 1962, the CCP held a Central Work Conference at Beidaihe, where the chairman dwelt on the issues of class struggle and capitalist restoration in socialist conditions, linking the struggle against international revisionism with domestic problems. At the CCP Central Committee's Tenth Plenum in September, Mao discussed both international and domestic class struggles, declaring that so long as imperialism, reactionary nationalism, and revisionism existed, the task of waging class struggle would never end. Urging the party to hold high the banner of anti-imperialism, he insisted that China must support the "excellent armed struggles" in South Vietnam and Laos unconditionally. At Mao's behest, the meeting's participants all advocated radical revolution and criticized international and domestic revisionism. Even Zhou proclaimed that "the struggle against revisionism has entered a new stage" and that "class struggle has become a fundamental issue in our relations with fraternal parties." "The truth of Marxism-Leninism and the center of the world revolution," Zhou continued, "has moved from Moscow to Beijing. We should be brave and not shrink from our responsibilities."[40]

The CCP claim that China occupied the center of world revolution pushed the Sino-Soviet dispute to an open break. Its escalation posed a dilemma for the Vietnamese Communist leaders, who needed both Chinese and Soviet support to realize their goal of unification, and left them puzzled, disconcerted, and mystified. The CCP leaders, however, resented the attitude of their Vietnamese colleagues. At this time the Soviet Union was secretly encouraging European communist parties to write open articles or letters criticizing the CCP. Mao now treated the Sino-Soviet conflict as a fundamental split over whether to promote world revolution and continuous revolution, to liberate humanity from bourgeois oppression, a dispute whose results would, he believed, determine the future of China, humanity, and the entire world revolution. He was convinced that the Chinese and Soviet parties differed at the level of basic doctrines and would soon break their political and organizational ties with each other.[41]

Mao and other CCP leaders sought VWP support in the escalating Sino-Soviet dispute, and they began to register their displeasure when Vietnamese officials displayed ambivalence. At the CCP Central Work Conference in early 1963, Liu Shaoqi criticized the VWP for not standing up to Khrushchev. Since the Twenty-Second Congress of the Soviet Communist Party, held from October 17 to 31, 1961, Liu pointed out, Khrushchev had openly condemned Albania and Stalin, and in doing so he was actually aiming at China. By advocating all-people countries and all-people parties, Liu continued, Khrushchev was actually rejecting class struggle. Genuine communist parties had not followed Khrushchev's line, Liu contended. The Korean Communist Party most firmly adhered to true Marxism-Leninism. Equally staunch were the communist parties of Indonesia, New Zealand, Cuba, Venezuela, Malaya, Burma, Thailand, and Japan. As to the VWP, Liu said that Ho had always been a rightist who had wavered in the struggle against revisionism. When China urged him to institute land reform, Liu recalled, Ho at first refused to do so. Ho did not even want to be the VWP's chairman, Liu continued, because he sought to remain outside the party so that he could become the leader of all the Vietnamese.

Liu then recalled how he persuaded Stalin during a meeting in Moscow to pressure Ho to carry out land reform. Under Stalin's prodding, Liu said, Ho finally agreed to implement a land reform program. According to Liu, when the First Indochina War ended, Ho could not decide whether to establish a bourgeois or proletarian republic in Vietnam, though at China's urging he finally decided to set up a socialist state. During the current Sino-Soviet dispute, Liu complained, the DRV initially published both Chinese and Soviet articles in its newspapers, but when the VWP received more than 60,000 letters from the Vietnamese public, expressing their wish to read Chinese articles, Ho ordered instead that publication of them cease.[42]

China's discontent with the VWP was further indicated when, with Mao's approval, on March 12, 1963, the *Renmin Ribao* (People's Daily) published without comment several Vietnamese documents urging the DRV to remain neutral in the Sino-Soviet split. Although the CCP leaders insisted in a subsequent instruction to party members that the VWP should be treated differently from revisionist parties, the contemporaneous publication of a joint declaration by the VWP and the Czech Communist Party calling for unity in the communist camp irritated Mao, who was preparing to release a major article on the Sino-Soviet dispute, "A Proposal on the General Line of the International Communist Movement." In May, Mao invited Kim Il Sung to China to discuss this document. In their conversations, Mao complained that the joint Vietnamese-Czech declaration was directed against China. The VWP, Mao continued, accused China of excessive criticism of Khrushchev's revisionism and suggested that the CCP use more sugar and less pepper when dealing with the Soviet Communist Party. Mao then told Kim that, contrary to Vietnamese allegations, in the past China had relied too heavily on sugar in its relations with the Soviet Union, and more pepper was now called for, because he did not wish China to be spineless.[43] Given Mao's increasingly strong conviction that the Sino-Soviet dispute was crucially significant, the VWP's efforts to mediate the conflict clearly exasperated and irritated him.

From Opposing DRV-U.S. Peace Talks to Aligning with Washington against Moscow

Both intellectual and pragmatic reasons impelled the VWP's efforts to prevent the breakdown of Sino-Soviet relations. Their extensive French education, which inclined them to accept Soviet analyses of certain issues, meant that some VWP leaders had long been influenced by European ideas. More significantly, the VWP sought Sino-Soviet unity to advance its goal of national unification. Encouraged by the Soviet-American tensions over Berlin and the 1962 Cuban missile crisis in 1962, a majority of VWP leaders believed that the Soviet Union was resuming its policy of confronting the United States. The Sino-Soviet split would, they feared, greatly weaken the socialist bloc's support for their struggle against the Americans, especially because they believed that, of all international communist countries, only the Soviet Union had the military capability to challenge the United States. Furthermore, they reasoned, because the Soviet Union enjoyed the support of many European communist countries and parties, if the DRV alienated the Soviet Union and relied solely on China, it would merely place itself in a very unfavorable position to resist the United States.

To the great disappointment of Ho and his colleagues, however, Khrushchev did not act in accordance with their hopes but chose instead to seek to reduce international tensions and pursue improved relations with the United States, while showing little enthusiasm to support the DRV. The Cuban missile crisis left Khrushchev even keener on compromise with Washington, whereupon he not only refused any public Soviet endorsement of the armed struggle in South Vietnam and Laos but also strictly limited Soviet military aid to the DRV, whereupon VWP resentment of the Soviet Union swelled rapidly.

About two weeks after Mao's May 1963 criticisms of the VWP to Kim, the VWP began to lean toward the CCP. In June 1963, Le Duan, the VWP secretary general, led a party and government delegation to China, where he unequivocally endorsed the CCP's intent to publish Mao's article "A Proposal on the General Line of the International Communist Movement" and strongly condemned the Soviet policy of discouraging armed struggle in South Vietnam and Laos. Mao, satisfied with Duan's statements, promised that if the Soviet Union created difficulties for the DRV, China would stand behind Hanoi. The DRV was carrying a heavy responsibility, Mao continued, shouldering not just the task of building North Vietnam but also the obligation to support the struggle in South Vietnam and Laos. There was, he said, no reason why China should not share some of these responsibilities. The DRV's support for China, Mao told Duan, was primary and China's assistance to the DRV was merely secondary because, in supporting the struggle in South Vietnam and Laos, China was merely providing weapons, whereas the DRV was standing in the forefront of the battle and sacrificing lives.[44]

During this period, in accordance with Mao's ideas, China began to establish schools and bases to give secret military training to communist operatives from Asia, Africa, and Latin America, to prepare them to wage armed struggle in their own nations. Mao met frequently with young trainees from foreign communist parties to encourage them to return to their countries for this purpose. Mao also introduced them to the Chinese revolutionary experience of surrounding cities from the countryside, and he even agreed to supply them with funds and weapons. He paid particular attention to the revolutionary struggle being waged by Southeast Asian communist parties, including the Indonesian Communist Party (PKI), which had more than a million members and exercised crucial influence in Indonesian domestic politics. On several occasions, he urged the PKI to prepare for armed struggle, claiming: "It is the duty of Marxists and Leninists to make revolution. If you are not making revolution, you are not a Communist party. In the eyes of the people, a Communist party that is not making revolution is indistinguishable from bourgeois parties, and there is no need for such a party to exist."

By now, Mao had even come to believe that his own position on Indochina during the later 1950s had been mistaken, and several times he now told VWP leaders that China had made errors on Indochina. At the 1954 Geneva Conference, Mao said, China had advised the VWP to conduct only political warfare and refrain from armed struggle; but when the VWP withdrew its troops from South Vietnam, Diem began to kill Communists. Later, Mao said, China adjusted its policy by urging the VWP to combine political and military struggles but to leave military operations at a low level—advice Mao also now admitted had been erroneous. Claiming that the behavior of American imperialists and Diem had enlightened and educated him, Mao stated that he now realized that the 1954 Geneva Agreement had been a failure, and that both the CCP and the VWP had made mistakes, which had cost 160,000 lives in South Vietnam.[45]

During the period 1963–64, the United States gradually escalated its military involvement and intervention in Vietnam, exerting increasingly heavy military and economic pressure against both the DRV and guerrilla warfare in South Vietnam. Given Soviet reluctance to aid the DRV, the VWP had to rely on Chinese support. Meanwhile, Mao considered how best to encourage closer unity and coordination among the Southeast Asian communist parties in order to promote revolution throughout the entire region. To this end, China organized joint meetings between the CCP, VWP, and LPP, and at this time the latter two parties echoed China's position on the Sino-Soviet dispute. On January 30, 1964, a VWP delegation led by Duan stopped in Beijing en route to the Soviet Union. Mao asked Duan whether he believed his trip to Moscow would produce results, and Duan replied that he expected little in the way of agreements from the visit. The DRV-Soviet relationship, Duan predicted, would not change greatly in the future, though it might alter either for the better or for the worse. Duan told Mao that the DRV hoped to maintain the status quo in its relations with the Soviet Union, but Mao retorted it would be better if DRV-Soviet relations changed for the worse.

Citing his own country as an example to emphasize the importance of a policy of self-reliance, Mao explained that if the Soviet Union had not withdrawn its experts, China would not have adopted such policies, and that it was more dependable to trust only to oneself. Duan told Mao that the VWP Central Committee plenum had concluded that if the CCP had not resisted revisionism, greater damage might have been inflicted on the international communist movement, and that both VWP members and the Vietnamese masses fully grasped the importance of this issue. Mao said that Albania, with a population of just over 1 million, had nonetheless stood up against encirclement by the Soviet Union, Yugoslavia, and capitalist countries. The DRV's population, Mao continued, was ten times greater than that of Albania, making it well positioned to resist Soviet pressure. Mao informed Duan that he had told comrades from North Korea, Japan, and Indonesia that one must exercise independent thinking and not follow the wind.[46] As it transpired, Duan's journey to the Soviet Union proved fruitless, and the two parties even quarreled with each other, because in talks with the Russians Duan criticized the Soviet Union for pursuing peaceful coexistence with the United States, failing to support national liberation movements, and favoring India in the Sino-Indian border conflict.

The ideological support Mao received from the VWP and other Southeast Asian Communist parties encouraged him. In 1963, Chinese and North Vietnamese military leaders began to discuss how to coordinate their military operations should the United States invade the DRV. On several occasions in 1964, Mao told DRV visitors that "ineffective and indecisive skirmishes will not solve problems, and only large and decisive battles can solve problems." If the Vietminh had not annihilated the main French forces at Dien Bien Phu, Mao asked, would France have been so willing to give up Vietnam? He urged the DRV to send more troops to South Vietnam and dispatch at least several thousand soldiers to Laos. Mao said of Laos that even though it had a population of over 2 million people and had been at war for several years, to date the fighting had proved inconclusive, which meant that a new approach was called for to the conflict there. One method might be to recruit three to four thousand soldiers, group them into six or seven battalions, and train them to be combat-ready fighters rather than believers in Buddhism. Otherwise, Mao contended, the war in Laos would never end. He asked the VWP not to fear American intervention.

The worst scenario, Mao said, would be another Korean-type war, for which the Chinese armed forces were ready, and should the United States invade North Vietnam, Chinese troops would enter the DRV. Chinese soldiers wanted to fight, something the Americans should bear in mind. The Chinese had legs, Mao warned, and if the United States could send troops to North Vietnam, could not the Chinese do likewise? It would require just one step for the Chinese to cross into the DRV. Mao pledged unconditional Chinese participation in the struggle against their common enemies.[47] With Mao's support, China and the DRV signed a military agreement in December 1964, whereby China would send 300,000 troops (five infantry divisions and five antiaircraft artillery divisions) to the northern provinces of the DRV, thereby freeing the PAVN to dispatch additional regiments to South Vietnam to fight the Americans.[48] This marked the beginning of direct Chinese involvement in the Vietnam War.

For China, the Soviet Union, and the United States alike, the second half of 1964 and 1965 saw a crucial escalation of their commitment in Vietnam —as is demonstrated by chapters 4 and 5 of the present volume and by the work of Ilya Gaiduk.[49] In early August 1964, North Vietnamese naval torpedo boats clashed with American destroyers in the Gulf of Tonkin, an incident that gave the United States a pretext to escalate the war in Vietnam and launch retaliatory bombing raids against the DRV. China and the Soviet Union reacted very differently to the Tonkin Gulf incident, with the Soviets maintaining a low profile and minimizing the encounter.[50] China, by contrast, organized countrywide mass demonstrations involving about 20 million people. Mao told Duan, who visited China shortly after the Tonkin Gulf incident, that China supported the VWP's decision not to provoke the Americans but was prepared for an American landing in North Vietnam.

China planned to deploy 300,000 to 500,000 troops in southern China, Mao continued, and to build one or two large airfields in the Mengzi region, Yunnan Province, facilities that Chinese aircraft could use as bases to fight in Vietnam's support should the DRV be attacked. He informed Duan that one North Vietnamese air squadron equipped with thirty-six aircraft had returned to the DRV after receiving training in China. Mao stated that he planned to send another air division to Nanning, half an air division to Kunming and Simao, and two antiaircraft artillery divisions to Nanning and Kunming. Duan proposed that, should war break out, revolution might be launched throughout Southeast Asia, because communist parties throughout the region had all laid extensive grassroots foundations that would assure them of success.

Mao's assessment of the situation was rather different; he believed that revolutionary developments had been uneven in different Southeast Asian countries and, while believing such efforts might well succeed in South Vietnam and Laos, he was less confident about Thailand and Burma. Mao showed particular interest in revolutionary prospects in Thailand, a country he considered the key to Southeast Asia, without whose help the United States would find it difficult to wage war, because Americans not only relied on bases in Thailand but also wished to employ Thai troops in any conflict in Indochina. In urging the DRV to help the Communist Party of Thailand develop its military forces, Mao hoped that in five or ten years a Thai revolution might be launched.[51]

To Mao's surprise, in October 1964 Khrushchev was overthrown in an internal Soviet coup. The new Kremlin leadership, headed by Leonid Brezhnev, took a totally different and more assertive line toward the Indochina War, breaking with the relatively restrained policy that, as Mari Olsen demonstrates in chapter 2 of this volume, it had followed virtually since the signing of the 1954 Geneva Accords. In November 1964, the Soviet Communist Party publicly announced that it would provide the DRV with all necessary support. In February 1965, Soviet premier Alexei Kosygin visited Hanoi, where he promised that the Soviet Union would supply the DRV free of charge with artillery pieces, tanks, and missiles, a decision reinforced by the simultaneous U.S. bombing of North Vietnam in response to attacks on American barracks in Pleiku and Qui Nhon.

Soon afterward, the Soviet Embassy in Beijing orally requested the Chinese government to permit the Soviet Union to move personnel and weapons to North Vietnam across Chinese territory. The Soviet decision to provide military aid to the DRV, especially the transit of Soviet supplies through China, presented Beijing with a dilemma.[52] On the one hand, given the tensions in Sino-Soviet relations, the transit of Soviet equipment and personnel might jeopardize China's national security. Because the Soviet Union had more advanced weaponry than China, increased Soviet aid to the DRV would simply cause heavier Vietnamese dependence on Moscow. On the other hand, should China decline to allow the Soviet Union to transport weapons through its territory, this would complicate China's relations with the DRV and also contradict its policy of supporting national liberation struggles.

Furthermore, even if Beijing refused to permit the movement of Soviet weapons and personnel through China, they could reach the DRV by sea, prompting Hanoi's alienation from China and generating closer DRV-Soviet relations. To safeguard China-DRV friendship and uphold his policy of supporting wars of national liberation, Mao therefore agreed to the Soviet request, informing Kosygin of his decision in February 1965, when the Soviet premier visited Beijing.[53] On March 30, 1965, the Chinese and Soviet governments signed an agreement whereby China agreed to help the Soviet Union transport materials to the DRV, after which Soviet weapons, including antiaircraft guns and fighter planes, began to travel to North Vietnam through China.[54]

In practice, however, the CCP leaders had concluded that the Soviet Communist Party was ideologically opposed to revolution and were therefore deeply suspicious of Soviet motives in assisting the DRV. As chapter 8 of this volume amply demonstrates, for the next eight years the Chinese and Soviet governments clashed frequently over the shipment of Russian weapons through China to the DRV, and in these circumstances even the slightest technical dispute had the potential to precipitate serious friction between Beijing and Moscow, each distrustful of the other's motives.[55] Because the DRV relied on sophisticated Soviet weaponry to fight the United States, no matter how great Beijing's efforts to preserve China-DRV friendship, the North Vietnamese drew closer to the Russians. The more often disputes arose between Beijing and Moscow over the transportation of Soviet weapons through China, the more perplexed the North Vietnamese became. The fiercer the criticisms Chinese leaders leveled at the Russians and the more forcefully they demanded that the VWP maintain its distance from the Soviet Union, the more estranged from China Vietnamese officials became. Suspecting that China sought to control the DRV, they therefore moved increasingly closer to the Soviet Union.

To Mao, the most disturbing aspect of Soviet involvement in the Indochina War was what he perceived as the Soviet "peace plot." On February 16, 1965, two days after Kosygin returned from his DRV trip, the Soviet government sent the DRV and China a proposal to convene an international conference on Indochina. Soon after, on the initiative of Yugoslavia, a country China viewed as the number one revisionist state, seventeen nonaligned countries publicly appealed for a peaceful settlement to the Indochina conflict. Paradoxically, in March 1965, the Soviet Union sponsored an international meeting in Moscow attended by representatives of nineteen communist parties, which declared support for the revolutionary struggle in Indochina and called for unity in supporting revolution and opposing imperialism. These developments puzzled Mao, who reasoned that, because the Soviet Union had become a revisionist state, its current championship of revolution must represent some kind of conspiracy. Considering the then-extensive U.S. bombing of North Vietnam and the American threat to attack Viet Cong sanctuaries outside South Vietnam's borders, Mao even suspected that the United States and the Soviet Union might be conspiring to launch a "joint attack on China" from both North and South. He eventually concluded that, because past Soviet efforts to prevent revolution in Indochina had proved unsuccessful, Soviet leaders had now changed their tactics and were using peace talks as bait to lure the DRV into a Soviet-American trap.[56]

To foil what they perceived as a Soviet "conspiracy," Chinese leaders did their utmost to oppose DRV-American peace talks.[57] To strengthen the VWP's determination to carry on fighting to the end, Mao approved a series of plans—described in more detail in chapter 7 of this volume—to provide extensive aid to the DRV. China sent support troops to North Vietnam, which helped the DRV resist American air attacks; build and repair railways, roads, airfields, communication installations, and defense works; and sweep mines off the coast. Beijing instructed Yunnan, Guangdong, Guangxi, and Hunan Provinces to assist economic development in seven North Vietnamese provinces. Between 1962 and 1966, China provided the DRV with 270,000 guns, 540 cannons, 200 million bullets, 900,000 artillery shells, 700 tons of explosives, 200,000 sets of uniforms, and 4 million meters of cloth, as well as large quantities of mosquito nets, rain boots, food, and communication materials. In April 1965, Duan led a DRV party and government delegation to China, requesting the dispatch of Chinese support troops to North Vietnam, and the two sides signed an agreement on the subject. In June 1965, the first group of such Chinese "support troops" entered the DRV, and between then and March 1968, 320,000 Chinese soldiers—including antiaircraft artillery units, railway units, defense work engineering units, and road-building units—operated in North Vietnam.[58]

Paradoxically, one can nonetheless see elements of caution in Mao's strategy. In chapter 7 of this volume, Shu Guang Zhang suggests that the very fact that China restricted its contribution to such aid and support roles reassured American officials that China did not contemplate full-scale military intervention. So too, perhaps, did roundabout Chinese diplomatic efforts in 1965 (amply documented by James Hershberg and Chen Jian in chapter 6 of this volume) to signal to the United States that, provided the Americans did not escalate their military involvement in Vietnam to a point China found intolerable, China would not enter the war as an outright combatant.

At this stage, however, China—unlike the Soviet Union—did not favor peace negotiations. Mao's rhetoric was perhaps more bellicose than his actual behavior. Under heavy pressure from the massive American bombing of the DRV known as "Operation Rolling Thunder," the VWP began to demonstrate interest in the Soviet peace talk proposal. Noting Hanoi's changing attitude, on several occasions Mao told DRV leaders that he opposed peace talks. During a conversation with Ho on June 5, 1965, for instance, Mao made clear his objections to negotiations. When Ho expressed fears that if the DRV did not show itself willing to begin talks, the United States might increase its troop deployments in South Vietnam to 100,000 soldiers and bomb DRV factories, Haiphong, and even Hanoi, Mao urged that Ho not be afraid. After reminding him that the Americans had claimed that they would bomb China, Mao declared that it would be good if the United States bombed Guangzhou, Nanning, Kunming, and Hainan Island and even better if it bombed China's atomic bomb facility in Xinjiang.[59]

When Mao met with a DRV party and government delegation on October 20, he said that he had paid no heed to the subject of DRV-American negotiations and his only interests were how the DRV fought the United States and how it could drive the United States out of Vietnam. Highlighting past negotiations with the Americans at the Geneva Conference in 1954, Mao reminded his Vietnamese visitors that after the Geneva negotiations the Americans had not kept their pledges. When the DRV adhered to the Geneva Accords by withdrawing its armed forces from South Vietnam, Mao continued, their enemies began to kill people, and the DRV had to resume military struggle. While claiming that he did not reject negotiations per se, Mao nonetheless insisted that the time was not ripe for talks, and that the ultimate solution reached in Vietnam would depend on the DRV's fighting ability.[60]

In 1966, Mao went so far as to ask fraternal communist parties to endorse China's position on the alleged Soviet "peace talk plot." In March 1966, a Japanese Communist Party (JCP) delegation led by Kenji Miyamoto visited China and held discussions with CCP leaders, in which the two sides agreed to issue a joint communiqué. When drafting this document, both sides agreed that it should include a condemnation of revisionism—though, given the new Soviet leadership's positive attitude toward supporting the Vietnamese struggle against the United States, the JCP suggested that when doing so the communiqué avoid any specific mention of the Soviet Union. Mao sought to revise the draft so that it would not only name the Soviet Union as a revisionist power but further charge that the Soviets were only assisting the DRV as a blind to disguise their real policy of betraying the Vietnamese people. Mao told Miyamoto that "in my view, my revision was beneficial to both you and us. We should not show flexibility to traitors and scabs. I am not comfortable with the draft communiqué that you and my comrades in Beijing have written because it is not sharp enough. When it mentions revisionism, it does not indicate who is practicing revisionism. The draft lacks courage. I must criticize you for showing lack of courage and fear of isolation and war."

Miyamoto explained that in the past the JCP had several times criticized "Soviet revisionism" and that it also believed that the Soviet Union had ulterior motives in aiding the DRV. Even so, he continued, the Soviet Union was providing large quantities of weapons to help the DRV fight the Americans, and Soviet-American contradictions should be exploited for the sake of promoting an anti-American united front. He concluded his remarks by saying that one should not ignore Soviet assistance to the DRV. Clearly unhappy with Miyamoto's words, Mao stated that he disagreed with the JCP's position, though the Soviet Union would welcome it.[61] In the end, all attempts to issue the JCP-CCP communiqué were scrapped, causing the estrangement of the two parties.

Mao's skeptical attitude inevitably affected CCP-VWP relations. During this period, Chinese and North Vietnamese leaders quarreled openly.[62] The Chinese leaders insisted that both imperialism and revisionism must be opposed, and that it was impossible to separate anti-imperialism and anti-revisionism. DRV officials rejected Chinese arguments that the Soviet Union was betraying North Vietnam. After failing to convince the Vietnamese of this, in April 1966 Zhou insisted that from then onward the DRV should not mention Soviet and Chinese assistance simultaneously, because putting them together constituted an insult to China. He also told the North Vietnamese that, if they suspected China of trying to control the DRV, China could immediately withdraw its troops from their country and pull back to interior areas its military units stationed along the Vietnamese border.[63]

Mao's intransigence was closely related to his worldview. He always approached international affairs from the perspective of Lenin's theory of imperialism, which regarded imperialism as the highest stage of capitalism. In the imperialist stage, war was inevitable, and this would inexorably lead to revolution. For Mao, the creation of the Soviet Union due to World War I, the CCP's post–World War II victory, the formation of the socialist camp, and the rise of national independence movements all provided most powerful testimony to the correctness of Lenin's prediction. This made it anathema to Mao when Khrushchev pursued détente with the United States, the leading imperialist power, and claimed that, together with the Americans, he could establish "a world where there is no weapons, no army, and no war." Because Mao believed Khrushchev's policies of avoiding war were likely to numb the international revolutionary will and prevent further revolutions, he therefore strongly condemned the Soviet leader as a revisionist.[64] Mao perceived the Indochina war as an excellent opportunity to expose the fallacies of Soviet revisionism and prove that Leninism still held good. He therefore feared that Soviet intervention in Indochina would actually prevent the attainment of revolution by promoting a peaceful settlement between the DRV and the United States. His insistence that the VWP and other fraternal parties publicly disassociate themselves ideologically from the Soviet Union reflected his profound fear of the expansion of Soviet revisionism.

In practice, given active Soviet assistance to the DRV, Mao found it extremely difficult to force other communist parties to endorse his ideological repudiation of the Soviet Union. Despite strong criticism from China, in May 1968 the VWP opened peace talks with the United States in Paris. Mao calculated that it would take revolution and war on an even larger scale to expose the fraudulent intent of Soviet aid to the DRV and the true Soviet objective of seeking to compromise with imperialism. From the mid-1960s onward, as the aging Mao's health deteriorated, he became increasingly impatient and disappointed over the nonoccurrence of a new world war and the consequent global revolution he had predicted. Although Mao often stated that "this situation of neither war nor revolution will not last long," he gradually came to realize that, once both the United States and the Soviet Union possessed nuclear weapons, the outbreak of a world war had become more problematic than in the past.

At a meeting with E. F. Hill, the chair of the Australian Communist Party (Marxist-Leninist) on November 11, 1968, Mao explained why there had been no new world war. Rhetorically, he asked how likely it was that the United States and the Soviet Union would launch a nuclear war to eliminate most of the globe's people to allow them to dominate the world. He then continued that such a move was unlikely because, given the limited populations of those two countries, their leaders feared that, rather than eliminating people in other countries, they would end up wiping out their own populations. Furthermore, Mao added, countries in the intermediate zone, such as the United Kingdom, France, West Germany, Japan, and Italy, also opposed war. Optimistically, Mao concluded that "eventually people in various countries will return to the path of Marxism by making their own revolutions and then getting united among themselves."[65]

Although Mao had pinned his hopes of waging revolution on communist parties in different countries, he was disappointed with the actual revolutionary situation. On several occasions he complained that, although Asia, Africa, and Latin America were supposedly cauldrons of revolution, revolution had not occurred at all in such states as Thailand; while in others—notably Malaya, Indonesia, the Philippines, and South Korea—revolutionary forces had not attained a high level of development. On September 30, 1965, a military coup occurred in Indonesia, during which the PKI was suppressed. Because Mao believed that it would force the PKI to resort to armed struggle, he welcomed this coup, in which hundreds of thousands of alleged Communists were killed and a pro-Western military government seized power. At a meeting with an LPP delegation on December 11, 1965, Mao urged the Lao Communists not to regard the Indonesian revolution as a disaster, telling them he was delighted that the PKI Central Committee had followed his advice and "gone to the mountains" to wage revolution.[66]

Eager to promote revolution in Southeast Asia, Mao actively urged the communist parties of Thailand, Burma, and Malaya to establish military forces. At this time, Mao showed particular interest in promoting revolution in Thailand, where American military bases were located. On several occasions, he asked the LPP to help the Communist Party of Thailand (CPT) wage armed struggle, arguing that the development of guerrilla warfare in Thailand was extremely important, and that ideally the LPP ought to expand the areas it had liberated to Thailand, because this, rather than Laos, was a primary area behind the enemy lines.

If the LPP transformed Thailand into a communist bastion, Mao continued, the United States would be trapped there. Advising the LPP to send troops to Thailand, Mao declared: "You should carry the war to Thailand." Because American aircraft used bases in Thailand to attack the Lao liberated areas, Mao explained, the LPP had every right to broaden the war to Thailand. He was elated when he learned that, with Chinese help, the CPT had established some guerrilla zones and pockets of base areas, telling CPT leaders that the growth of the Thai revolution was a major event because it had linked together the revolutions in Burma, Thailand, Vietnam, Cambodia, and Malaya.[67]

In November 1967, Mao told Thakin Ba Thein Tin, the vice chairman of the Communist Party of Burma (CPB) Central Committee, that the CPT had done a good job and had a bright future and great potential. After the outbreak of anti-Chinese riots in Burma that year, Mao permitted the CPB to operate openly in China and assisted a large group of CPB members, who had spent the previous seventeen years in China, together with Burmese minority militants, to return to their country to wage armed struggle and establish base areas. Mao even suggested to LPP and CPB leaders that they visit southern Chinese provinces near Laos and Burma to recruit members of minority groups. It was the international duty of Chinese minorities, Mao explained, to assist the revolutions in Laos and Burma, and China's border regions could serve as rear areas for the LPP and the CPB. To ensure that the CPB members, who had just completed training in China, would safely return to Burma, People's Liberation Army (PLA) units escorted them to Burma. Occasionally, these PLA units even clashed with Burmese government forces.[68]

For a while, Mao was delighted by the continued war in Indochina and the unfolding of armed struggle in other Southeast Asian countries, telling a Lao communist leader:

> In my opinion, people in many countries have been awakened, including people in imperialist countries. Some people are promoting peace movements, some are carrying out guerrilla war, and others are thinking about their countries' future. There are also many people who have not been awakened. When people in different countries rise up against imperialism, we call their uprisings revolution. Can you believe that revolution can only happen in Russia, China, Vietnam, and Laos but not in other places? No. If revolution fails to take place in other countries, then Marxism-Leninism will be out of date.[69]

Soon, however, events within the communist bloc led Mao to embrace a drastic change of policy not just in Indochina but also toward the United States, for more than two decades China's official archenemy—as chapters 9 and 10 of this volume describe in detail. In August 1968, the Soviet Union invaded Czechoslovakia. The following year, protracted Sino-Soviet border clashes led Moscow to threaten a preemptive nuclear strike against

China, and Mao began to fear that a Soviet invasion was imminent. During his long revolutionary career, the most important lesson he had imbibed was that, when making revolution, one must above all preserve one's revolutionary home base. In 1927, he had defied the CCP Central Committee's order to attack the city of Changsha and instead transferred his soldiers to the Jinggangshan Mountains to establish a revolutionary base area and preserve his forces. In the early 1930s, he had conducted guerrilla war in the Jiangxi Soviet, disregarding the party leadership's instruction to launch attacks on the Nationalist forces, causing him to be stigmatized as a "rightist." During the Long March, he insisted that the best way to preserve the Red Army was to move it to northern China, where his forces could obtain assistance from Mongolia and the Soviet Union, which led to criticism of him for practicing "escapism." During the anti-Japanese war, Mao incurred suspicion from the Soviet Union, the Guomindang, and even some CCP cadres because he refused to wage positional war against the Japanese and instead conducted guerrilla war.

All these examples reveal that, when Mao believed his fundamental revolutionary base was in jeopardy, he could be pragmatic and flexible. The Soviet threat forced him to begin domestic war preparations, instructing the party and the people to "dig deep tunnels, store food, and prepare for war." He therefore began to demonstrate declining interest in promoting world revolution.[70]

Because Mao sought to protect China's security and was determined to align with America to resist the Soviet Union, he approved high-level secret contacts with the United States.[71] Ironically, China's opening to the United States strained its relations with North Vietnam. Disturbed by the new Sino-American rapprochement, the Vietnamese Communists criticized China for sacrificing DRV interests. From 1970 on, Mao began to moderate his criticism of the DRV-U.S. peace talks. The American invasion of Cambodia in April 1970 temporarily acted as a brake on Mao's opening to the United States. In meetings with Henry Kissinger and Richard Nixon during the period 1971–72, Mao and Zhou urged the United States to withdraw from Vietnam and forcefully rejected the American request that China put pressure on the North Vietnamese to reach an acceptable peace settlement.

In talks with his Vietnamese comrades, however, Mao nonetheless asked them to conclude the war at an appropriate time and ensure that their negotiations with the Americans produced concrete results.[72] Mao told DRV leaders that if the Paris talks succeeded, then both the National Liberation

Front and North Vietnam could normalize relations with the United States. Mao and Zhou even apologized to the Vietnamese for having in the past criticized their negotiations with the Americans, admitting: "Your policy of fighting and talking since 1968 is correct. At first, when you began negotiations, some of our comrades thought that you had made an error. Now we can see that you have made a correct decision."[73]

On January 27, 1973, the DRV-U.S. Paris talks resulted in a peace agreement. Mao lauded the settlement, but his praise failed to improve China's relations with the DRV. Furthermore, Mao's endorsement of the Vietnamese-American peace talks alienated Albania, which until then had been China's staunchest ally in the fight against revisionism. The Labor Party of Albania, which had consistently opposed the DRV-U.S. peace negotiations and any policies that would allow America to disengage from Indochina, was most unhappy over Mao's changed attitude toward the Vietnam peace talks, and it not only objected to the DRV-U.S. compromise but also criticized Beijing's rapprochement with Washington. The Albanians represented the outlook of a group of extremist communist parties that, given the Soviet threat to China, Mao could no longer afford to conciliate.

To justify his current policy toward the United States, Mao once again cited Lenin's theory on how best to deal with robbers. Claiming that the center of world revolution was in Asia and the center of the Asian revolution was in Vietnam, he stated that, even though Albania did not wish it to do so, the United States wanted to withdraw from Vietnam. Turning to the Albanian accusation that those who opposed continued war in Vietnam were rightist opportunists, Mao declared that he would not care if he were branded a rightist opportunist, insisting that Marxism never dictated that in making revolution one could not make compromises.[74]

Conclusion

The evolution of Mao's attitude toward the Indochina War can be divided into four stages. During the first stage (1949–53), Mao supported the Vietnamese resistance against France and opposed compromises. During the second stage (1954–57), he endorsed peace and democracy and favored suspending armed struggle in Vietnam. In the third stage (1958–69), he supported the DRV's anti-American war and opposed peace talks between Hanoi and Washington. In the fourth stage (1970–73), he approved the DRV-U.S. peace talks and supported ending the war in Vietnam.

During the first stage, Mao's backing of the Vietminh's war was heavily influenced by his ideological beliefs and his own revolutionary experiences. In terms of ideology, he believed that it was the international obligation of those proletarians who had achieved victory to support world revolution. In terms of his own revolutionary experiences, he was convinced that emulating the victorious path of the Chinese armed struggle represented the only correct method whereby the VWP and other Asian communist parties could successfully attain their objective of national liberation. His support for revolution in Vietnam also served the strategic purpose of providing a measure of diversion for the United States from the Korean War. Given, however, that in Indochina the French were the principal enemy, the desire to reduce American pressure in Korea was not the primary motivation for Mao's decision to support the Vietnamese struggle.

For both external and internal reasons, in 1954 Mao switched his attitude toward the Indochina conflict. After Stalin's death, the Soviet Union urged a cease-fire in Korea and promoted a policy of peace. In China, the policy-making process within the CCP was still relatively democratic, as demonstrated in the internal party debate over China's entry into the Korean War in 1950.[75] This relatively democratic policymaking mechanism won greater influence for the views of pragmatic CCP leaders, who focused more upon the implementation of China's First Five-Year Plan and called for adjustments in the country's strategic priorities. Influenced by the views of these officials, at this time Mao was able to view China's international position realistically. He recognized that after the Korean War the United States had shifted its military focus in Asia southward to Indochina and that, if China decided to fight the United States in Vietnam, many factors would militate against it. Mao therefore favored the creation of a peaceful international environment for China by safeguarding the security of North Korea and North Vietnam but avoiding war with the United States in Southeast Asia.

One major factor impelling Mao to revert to support for armed struggle in Vietnam was the development of his nationalist sentiments of humiliation. During the hundred years since the mid–nineteenth century, China had been victimized by imperialist aggression. With the founding of the PRC in 1949, China had become fully independent. It had elevated its position in Asia by successfully resisting the United States in Korea and by achieving political stability and economic development at home. But the United States continued to be hostile toward the PRC on the issues of UN representation and Taiwan, while the Soviet Union's economic and scientific advantages encouraged its arrogant treatment of China.

All these developments triggered the rapid growth of Mao's nationalist sentiments. Most galling to Mao was the Soviet Communist Party's ambivalence on the issue of war and peace, because this directly contradicted what he perceived as his most important contribution to Marxism-Leninism, namely, the theory of "using the countryside to surround cities and seizing power through armed struggle." To validate the international significance of the Chinese way of making revolution, Mao launched an intellectual struggle against revisionism. Because he viewed the serious setbacks to the peaceable approach in Vietnam and the revival of armed struggle in the South as convincing proof of the correctness of his theories on war and revolution, it was very natural for him to choose war over peace after 1958.

Unquestionably, the imperatives of national interests and security brought Mao's return in 1969 to a foreign policy of flexibility. The border clashes that year between China and the Soviet Union pushed them to the brink of nuclear war, once again forcing Mao to focus on the issue of disparities in power. Under pressure from China's international isolation due to the Sino-Soviet confrontation, and frustrated by the ineffectiveness of his efforts over many years to export revolution, Mao sought to align with the United States against the Soviet Union, once more employing the united front tactic to exploit international contradictions and improve China's strategic position. Naturally enough, at this time the United States—needing China's help to extricate itself from the Vietnam war quagmire and counter the Soviet Union—was responsive to Mao's changed attitude.

To conclude, Mao, the leader of a revolutionary party, maintained his revolutionary impulses even after his party had seized power. With the progress in national unification, the restoration and reconstruction of the economy, and the stabilization of society, the sense of vulnerability and crisis that he had felt during the war years no longer afflicted him. China had vast territory and abundant resources, all of which greatly spurred his sense of political obligation and nationalist pride. His profound belief in the correctness of his revolutionary experiences, his determination to defend revolutionary ideas, and his desire to fulfill his revolutionary mission all contributed to the radicalization of his attitude toward the Indochina war. For most of the period from 1949 to 1973, he was willing to place support for revolution in Indochina above the needs of national security, economic development, and the improvement of living conditions in China. To defend the correctness of his ideology, he was prepared to alienate all his "fraternal friends."

In certain circumstances, however, Mao could sober up and heed the realities of power politics. This occurred twice, first during the period 1954–57, when Mao was eager to build China into a strong power, and then after the Sino-Soviet border war in 1969, when he realized that the danger of war with the Soviet Union threatened his regime's survival. When internal or external pressures became too intense, his own preferences notwithstanding, he placed his regime's survival above the realization of his country's perceived ideological mission. Whatever the vagaries of China's foreign policies, however, for more than a quarter century from October 1949, his was the dominant voice in their formulation.

Notes

1. The most notable works include Qiang Zhai, *China and the Vietnam Wars, 1950–1975* (Chapel Hill: University of North Carolina Press, 2000); Chen Jian, "China and the First Indo-China War, 1950–54," *China Quarterly* 133 (March 1993): 85–110; Chen Jian, "China's Involvement in the Vietnam War, 1964–69," *China Quarterly* 142 (June 1995): 356–87; Chen Jian, *Mao's China and the Cold War* (Chapel Hill: University of North Carolina Press, 2001); and Li Danhui, "Zhongsu guanxi yu Zhongguo de yuanyue kangmei" [Sino-Soviet relations and China's assistance to the DRV against the United States], *Dangdai Zhongguoshi yanjiu* [Contemporary Chinese history research], no. 3 (1998).

2. In their writings, scholars have used such primary sources as the CCP Central Documentary Research Department, ed., *Jianguo yilai Mao Zedong wengao* [Mao Zedong's manuscripts since the founding of the PRC], 13 vols. (Beijing: Central Press of Historical Documents, 1987–98); and such secondary sources as Diplomatic History Research Office of the PRC Foreign Ministry, *Zhou Enlai waijiao huodong dashiji, 1949–1975* [Important events in Zhou Enlai's diplomatic activities, 1949–1975] (Beijing: World Knowledge Press, 1993); Guo Ming, ed., *Zhongyue guanxi yanbian sishinian* [The evolution of Sino-Vietnamese relations over the last forty years] (Nanning: Guangxi People's Press, 1991); Editorial Group for the History of Chinese Military Advisers in Vietnam, eds., *Zhongguo junshi guwentuan yuanyue kangfa douzheng shishi* [Historical facts about the role of the Chinese Military Advisory Group in the struggle to aid Vietnam and resist France] (Beijing: PLA Press, 1990); and Li Lianqing, *Da waijiaojia Zhou Enlai* [Master diplomat Zhou Enlai], 4 vols. (Hong Kong: Cosmos Books, 1994–95). Among the existing publications, only Zhai, *China and the Vietnam Wars,* draws directly on the recently available Chinese archival materials.

3. *Mao Zedong xuanji* [Selected works of Mao Zedong], 5 vols. (Beijing: People's Press, 1964–77), vol. 1, 529.

4. Mao, concluding speech at the CCP Seventh Congress, May 31, 1945.

5. Liu Shaoqi, opening remarks at the Trade Union Conference of Asian and Aus-

tralasian Countries, November 16, 1949, in *Jianguo yilai Liu Shaoqi wengao* [Liu Shaoqi's manuscripts since the founding of the PRC], ed. CCP Central Documentary Research Department (Beijing: Central Press of Historical Documents, 1998), 134–35.

6. Cable, CCP Central Military Commission to Lin Biao, December 12, 1949; Liu Shaoqi, cable to Mao, December 24, 1949; Mao, cables to Liu Shaoqi, January 27, 31, 1950, in *Jianguo yilai Liu Shaoqi wengao,* 165, 186–88, 347.

7. In June 1949, Liu Shaoqi led a CCP delegation to Moscow, where he concluded an agreement with Stalin. According to the agreement, except for North Korea, where the Soviet Union dispatched an occupation force immediately after World War II, the CCP was responsible for contacting, advising, and supporting communist organizations in Asia. See Shi Zhe, *Zai lishi juren shenbian: Shi Zhe huiyilu* [At the side of historical giants: Memoirs of Shi Zhe] (Beijing: Central Press of Historical Documents, 1991), 412.

8. Mao, cables to Chen Geng, July 23, 26, 28, August 24, October 6, 10, 1950; Qian Jiang, *Zai shenmi de zhanzheng zhong: Zhongguo junshi guwentuan fu Yuenan zhengzhan ji* [In the secret war: A record of the Chinese military advisory team in Vietnam] (Zhengzhou: Henan People's Press, 1992), 72–74, 96–97; Editorial Group for the History of Chinese Military Advisers in Vietnam, *Zhongguo junshi guwentuan yuanyue kangfa douzheng shishi,* 21–22, 56, 60, 88–89; Wang Xiangen, *Yuanyue kangmei shilu* [A factual record of assistance to Vietnam against the United States] (Beijing: International Cultural Publishing House, 1990), 42.

9. In 1950, China allocated 52 percent of its total annual financial budget for defense spending, 60 percent of which went to support the war in Korea. In 1952, when the war was stalemated, defense spending still constituted 33 percent of the total national budget; again, the bulk of this was devoted to the Korean War. China spent a total of $10 billion on the Korean War. See Li Ping, *Kaiguo zongli Zhou Enlai* [First Premier Zhou Enlai] (Beijing: Central Party Material and History Press, 1994), 261; and Yao Xu, "Kangmei yuanchao de yingming juece" [The wise decision to aid Korea and resist the United States], *Dangshi yanjiu* [Studies on party history] 5 (1980).

10. Xu Yan, "Shilun jianguo hou Mao Zedong de zhanbei sixiang" [A tentative examination of Mao Zedong's thinking on war preparation after the founding of the PRC], in *Huanqiu tongci liangre: Yidai lingxiumen de guoji zhanlue sixiang* [Leading the global trend: The international strategic thinking of a generation of leaders], ed. International Institute of Strategic Studies (Beijing: Central Press of Historical Documents, 1993), 243–44.

11. Editorial Group for the History of Chinese Military Advisers in Vietnam, *Zhongguo junshi guwentuan yuanyue kangfa douzheng shishi,* 88–99; CCP Central Documentary Research Department, ed., *Zhou Enlai nianpu, 1949-1976* [A chronological record of Zhou Enlai, 1949–1976] (hereafter *Zhou Enlai nianpu*), 3 vols. (Beijing: Central Press of Historical Documents, 1997), vol. 1, 358.

12. Mao, letter to Peng Dehuai, April 3, 1954, in *Jianguo yilai Mao Zedong wengao,* ed. CCP Central Documentary Research Department, vol. 4, 474–75.

13. Mao, telegram to Huang Kecheng and Su Yu, April 17, 1954; CCP CC to Zhou Enlai, June 20, 1954, in *Jianguo yilai Mao Zedong wengao,* ed. CCP Central Documentary Research Department, vol. 4, 480, 509.

14. Records of the Sino-Vietnamese meetings in Liuzhou, July 3, 5, 1954, in *Zhou Enlai zhuan* [Biography of Zhou Enlai], 3 vols., ed. Jin Chongji et al. (Beijing: Central Press of Historical Documents, 1998), vol. 3, 1131–32.

15. Mao, conversation with Pham Van Dong, June 15, 1961; Mao, conversation with

Zhang Chunqiao and Wang Hongwen, July 4, 1973. Unless otherwise noted, all of Mao's conversations referred to in this chapter are cited from an internally circulated (*neibu*) collection of documents compiled between 1975 and 1976.

16. From the mid-1950s to 1960, Mao made repeated references to China's backwardness, attributing it to his country's inadequate industrialization. He believed that to solve this problem, China needed to narrow the discrepancy between itself and the United States in steel production. Therefore, he launched the Great Leap Forward, primarily to catch up with the United States and the United Kingdom in steel production in the shortest possible time and to implement China's industrialization.

17. See, e.g., *New York Herald Tribune,* August 8, 1954.

18. Mao, conversation with a British Labour Party delegation, August 24, 1954; Mao, conversations with Jawaharlal Nehru, October 19, 23, 1954.

19. Mao, conversations with U Nu, December 1, 11, 1954.

20. Mao, conversations with U Nu, December 1, 11, 1954; Mao, conversation with a Thai delegation, December 21, 1955.

21. In 1967, Mao had a conversation with Chin Peng, Secretary General of the Malayan Communist Party, during which meeting Chin Peng referred to the history of his party during this period. See Mao, conversation with Chin Peng, January 17, 1967.

22. After the Bandung Conference, Mao approved Zhou Enlai's proposal to open negotiations with the United States, which effectively marked the end of the first Taiwan Strait Crisis of 1954–55. See Mao, conversation with the Pakistani ambassador, April 27, 1955.

23. CCP Central Documentary Research Department, *Jianguo yilai Mao Zedong wengao,* vol. 4, 530–32; Mao, conversation with Truong Chinh, secretary general of the Vietnamese Workers Party (VWP), and Dipa Nusantara Aidit, secretary general of the Indonesian Communist Party (PKI), March 14, 1956; Mao, conversation with the British Communist Party delegation headed by Harry Pollitt, September 14, 1956.

24. For a detailed discussion of Mao's reaction to Khrushchev's report at the Twentieth Congress of the Soviet Communist Party, see Yang Kuisong, *Zouxiang polie: Mao Zedong yu mosike de enen yuanyuan* [The path to the split: Mao's relations with Moscow] (Hong Kong: Joint Publishing Company, 1999), chap. 13; Wu Lengxi, *Shinian lunzhan, 1956–1966: Zhongsu guanxi huiyilu* [Ten years of polemics, 1956–1966: Recollections of Sino-Soviet relations] (Beijing: Central Press of Historical Documents, 1999), 5.

25. Chen, *Mao's China.*

26. Chen, *Mao's China;* and *Cold War International History Project* [hereafter *CWIHP*] *Bulletin,* nos. 6–7 (Winter 1995–96).

27. See *CWIHP Bulletin,* nos. 12–13 (Fall–Winter 2001): 263–71; and David Wolff, *"One Finger's Worth of Historical Events": New Russian and Chinese Evidence on the Sino-Soviet Alliance and Split, 1948–1959,* CWIHP Working Paper 30 (Washington, D.C.: Woodrow Wilson International Center for Scholars, 2000).

28. Mao, speech on international affairs at the Supreme State Conference, September 5, 1958, in *Mao Zedong waijiao wenxun* [Selected diplomatic papers of Mao Zedong], ed. PRC Foreign Ministry and CCP Central Documentary Research Department (Beijing: Central Press of Historical Documents and World Knowledge Press, 1994), 341–47; see translation in *CWIHP Bulletin,* nos. 6–7 (Winter 1995–96): 216–18.

29. Mao, conversation with Kaysone Phomvihane, October 4, 1959.

30. Guo Ming, ed., *Zhongyue guanxi yanbian sishinian,* 66.

31. See Odd Arne Westad, ed., *Brothers in Arms: The Rise and Fall of the Sino-Soviet Alliance* (Washington, D.C., and Stanford, Calif.: Woodrow Wilson Center Press and Stanford University Press, 1999).

32. *Renmin Ribao* [People's Daily], November 7, 1957.

33. Mao, conversation with Lance Louis Sharkey, secretary general of the Australian Communist Party, October 26, 1959; Mao, conversation with Kim Il Sung, May 21, 1960; Mao, conversation with Antonio Delgado Lozano, chairman of the Venezuelan Leftist Revolutionary Movement, April 3, 1961.

34. Mao, conversation with Kim Il Sung, May 21, 1960; Mao, conversation with Ho Chi Minh, August 10, November 2, 1960.

35. Mao, conversation with Ho Chi Minh, November 14, 1961.

36. Letter from Wang Jiaxiang, Liu Ningyi, and Wu Xiuquan to Zhou Enlai, Deng Xiaoping, and Chen Yi, February 27, 1962; "Wang Jiaxiang's Proposal on Foreign Affairs, June 23, 1962," in *Wang Jiaxiang xuanji* [Selected works of Wang Jiaxiang] (Beijing: People's Press, 1989), 446–60.

37. Foreign Economic Liaison Bureau's report on foreign assistance and future tasks, September 1, 1961.

38. Han Nianlong, ed., *Dangdai zhongguo waijiao* [Contemporary Chinese diplomacy] (Beijing: Chinese Academy of Social Sciences Press, 1988), 159.

39. *Wang Jiaxiang xuanji,* 444–45.

40. Mao, speech at the Tenth Plenum, September 24, 1962; Zhou Enlai, speech at the Tenth Plenum, September 26, 1962.

41. CCP Central Documentary Research Department, *Jianguo yilai Mao Zedong wengao,* vol. 10, 247–48.

42. Liu, speech on antirevisionism, February 25, 1963.

43. *Renmin Ribao,* March 12, 1963; "The CCP Central Committee's Instruction on How to Handle Questions Concerning Vietnam during Contact with Foreigners," March 19, 1963; Mao, conversation with Kim Il Sung, May 29, 1963.

44. Mao, conversation with the DRV party and government delegation, June 4, 1963; Mao, conversation with Choi Yong Kun, vice chairman of the Central Committee of the Korean Workers' Party, June 16, 1966.

45. Mao, conversation with the DRV party and government delegation, June 4, 1963; Mao, conversation with the Brazilian Communist Party (New Party) delegation, March 6, 1963; Mao, conversation with the delegation of the Colombian "Workers Learn from Farmers Movement," December 5, 1963; Mao, conversation with representatives of the Peruvian Communist Party (Leftist), December 12, 1963; Mao, conversation with Ho Chi Minh, June 19, 1966.

46. Mao, conversation with the VWP delegation, January 30, 1964.

47. Mao, conversation with the VWP delegation, January 30, 1964; Mao, conversation with Van Tien Dung, June 24, 1964; Mao, conversation with Tran Tu Binh, July 27, 1964.

48. Ilya V. Gaiduk, *The Soviet Union and the Vietnam War* (Chicago: Ivan R. Dee, 1996), 16.

49. Gaiduk, *The Soviet Union and the Vietnam War.*

50. In its August 3 issue, *Pravda* only carried a brief report on the Tonkin Gulf Incident. The next day, Khrushchev sounded moderate in his statement on the subject. See U.S. Department of State, *Foreign Relations of the United States, 1964–1968,* vol. 1, *Vietnam, 1964* (Washington, D.C.: U.S. Government Printing Office, 1992), 637.

51. Mao, conversation with Le Duan, August 13, 1964.

52. When the Sino-Soviet relationship began to deteriorate, China had notified the DRV that it did not want to see Hanoi accept Soviet aid. Gaiduk, *The Soviet Union and the Vietnam War,* 16.

53. Mao, conversation with Alexei N. Kosygin, February 11, 1965.

54. Wang Taiping, chief ed., *Zhonghua renmin gongheguo waijiaoshi* [Diplomatic history of the People's Republic of China], 4 vols. (Beijing: World Knowledge Press, 1998), vol. 2, 265, 267.

55. Li Danhui, "Zhongsu zai yuanyue kangmei wenti shang de maodun yu chongtu, 1965–1972) [Sino-Soviet dispute over aid to North Vietnam's anti-U.S. War, 1965–1972], unpublished paper.

56. Mao, conversation with the leaders of the Malayan Communist Party, March 19, 1965.

57. See the reply of the Chinese government, March 10, 1965, to the proposal by the Soviet government of February 16, 1965, regarding the convening of an international conference on Indochina, in Wang, *Zhonghua renmin gongheguo waijiaoshi,* vol. 2, 265–66; Zhou Enlai, conversation with Algerian president Ben Bella, March 30, 1965; Zhou, conversation with Pakistani president Ayub Khan, April 2, 1965, in *Zhou Enlai waijiao huodong dashiji, 1949–1975,* 444, 445; for an English translation of the April 2, 1965 Zhou–Khan talk, see *77 Conversations between Chinese and Foreign Leaders on the Wars in Indochina, 1964–1977,* CWIHP Working Paper 22, ed. Odd Arne Westad, Chen Jian, Stein Tønnesson, Nguyen Vu Tung, and James G. Hershberg (Washington, D.C.: Woodrow Wilson International Center for Scholars, 1998), 79–85.

58. Wang, *Zhonghua renmin gongheguo waijiaoshi,* vol. 2, 35; Han Huaizhi and Tan Jingqiao, chief eds., *Dangdai zhongguo jundui de junshi gongzuo* [Contemporary military operations of the Chinese armed forces], 2 vols. (Beijing: Chinese Academy of Social Sciences Press, 1989), vol. 2, 514; Historical Research Department of the Military Science Academy, ed., *Zhongguo renmin jiefangjun liushinian dashiji* [A chronicle of the sixty years of the People's Liberation Army] (Beijing: Military Science Academy Press, 1988), 616.

59. Mao, conversation with Ho Chi Minh, June 5, 1965.

60. Mao, conversation with the DRV party and government delegation, October 20, 1965.

61. Mao, conversations with Kenji Miyamoto, March 28–29, 1966.

62. See Westad et al., *77 Conversations.*

63. Meetings of Zhou Enlai and Deng Xiaoping with Le Duan and Nguyen Duy Trinh, March 23, April 13, 1966.

64. *Jianguo yilai zhongyao wenxian xuanbian* [Selected important documents since the founding of the PRC] (Beijing: Central Press of Historical Documents, 1997), 450–81.

65. Mao, conversation with Hill, November 28, 1968. See *CWIHP Bulletin,* no. 11 (Winter 1998): 157–61.

66. Aidit was later captured and executed by the Indonesian military when he left his mountain base to hold talks with President Sukarno, whereupon Mao criticized the PKI for having taken an insufficiently strong stance on continuing armed struggle. See Mao, conversation with the LPP delegation, December 11, 1965.

67. Mao, conversation with the LPP delegation, November 30, 1967; Mao, conversation talk with Kaysone Phomvihane, July 7, 1970; Mao, conversation with the leaders of the CPT, November 9 1967.

68. Mao, conversation with Thakin Ba Thein Tin, November 26, 1967.

69. Mao, conversation with Kaysone Phomvihane, July 7, 1970.

70. On Mao's war preparations in the wake of the Sino-Soviet border clash in 1969, see Yang Kuisong, *Zouxiang polie,* chap. 18; Yang Kuisong, "The Sino-Soviet Border Clash of 1969: From Zhenbao Island to Sino-American Rapprochement," *Cold War History* 1, no. 1 (August 2000): 21–52.

71. See Chen Jian and David L. Wilson, ed., "'All under the Heaven Is Great Chaos': Beijing, the Sino-Soviet Border Clashes and the Turn toward Sino-American Rapprochement, 1968–69," *CWIHP Bulletin,* no. 11 (Winter 1998): 155–75.

72. William Burr, ed., *The Kissinger Transcripts: The Top Secret Talks with Beijing and Moscow* (New York: New Press, 1999), 30–31, 102–6.

73. Mao, conversation with Nguyen Thi Binh, December 19, 1972; Zhou Enlai, conversation with Le Duc Tho, July 12, 1972, translated in *77 Conversations,* ed. Westad et al., 182–84; and Mao, conversation Le Duc Tho, February 2, 1973, translated in *77 Conversations,* ed. Westad et al., 186.

74. Mao, conversation with Zhang Chunqiao and Wang Hongwen, July 4, 1973.

75. Yang Kuisong, *Zouxiang polie,* chap. 11.

2

Forging a New Relationship:
The Soviet Union and Vietnam, 1955

Mari Olsen

This chapter focuses primarily on the Soviet Union's initiatives and recommendations in its relations with the Democratic Republic of Vietnam
(DRV) in 1955. The research involved is based upon documents from the
Archives of Foreign Policy of the Russian Federation. It forms part of a
broader study of the relationship between the Soviet Union and the DRV
from August 1954 to December 1960. The study's objective is to determine
the extent of Soviet influence upon the policies of the Vietnamese communists, especially on the questions of reunification and the development of a
strategy toward the South Vietnamese state. It also discusses the degree to
which growing American involvement in the southern portion of Vietnam
influenced Soviet policy in that area.

From late December 1954, the Soviet-DRV relationship changed char-

This chapter was previously published as a part of the author's Philol. thesis "Solidarity and National Revolution: The Soviet Union and the Vietnamese Communists,
1954–1960," *Defence Studies* (Institute for Defence Studies, Oslo), no. 4 (1997).

acter. As opposed to the quiet months following the Geneva Conference, Moscow now seized the initiative and started advising Hanoi on how to deal with the southern zone—the State of Vietnam. Parallel to these initiatives, Moscow also played an important role in planning diplomatic moves to arrange consultations for elections scheduled for July 1955 and the general elections scheduled for July 1956.

This chapter focuses on both the Soviet recommendations to the North Vietnamese from late 1954 through 1955 and the diplomatic struggle to implement the Geneva Agreement. Its chief purpose is to discuss the extent of Soviet influence on the policies of the Lao Dong Party (Vietnamese Workers Party) during this period, with special emphasis on the question of reunification and the creation of a strategy toward the South. It also focuses on the role of external factors, such as the U.S. presence in South Vietnam and, even more significantly, the traditional Chinese influence in Vietnam. These themes are assessed both in relation to domestic concerns in Vietnam and in light of the international position of the Soviet Union. Finally, the chapter evaluates whether Soviet policy toward Vietnam from late 1954 through 1955 was consistent, or whether Moscow was in effect following a two-track policy.

Diplomatic Struggle: Moscow, Hanoi, and the International Control Commission

In the first period following the Geneva Conference, it was important for Moscow to reach a solution within the Geneva framework. Hence, implementation of the Geneva Agreement and the existence and work of the International Control Commissions (ICCs) in all three Indochinese countries played important roles in the planning of Soviet strategy in this area through the latter part of the 1950s. According to the provisions in the Final Declaration of the Geneva Agreement, general elections would be held for the whole of Vietnam in July 1956. The purpose of the elections was a reunification of the two zones under a government chosen by the Vietnamese people through free, democratic elections. Consultations for elections were scheduled to start on July 20, 1955, between competent representatives from both of the two zones.[1]

Throughout 1955, Moscow laid great emphasis on the diplomatic struggle to fulfill the Geneva Agreement. The Soviet leaders promoted the work of the ICC. They issued statements concerning its status and insisted in public that all efforts toward fulfillment of the agreement should be carried out through diplomatic channels and within the Geneva framework. In the early years after Geneva, as well as later, its main vehicle in this diplomatic campaign was the mechanism of the three ICCs.

The Hanoi government worked hard to initiate consultations; but in spite of its efforts, the elections were not to be held. Neither the Ngo Dinh Diem government nor its American ally were interested in arranging elections that could have resulted in a reunified Vietnam possibly led by a communist-dominated government. The prevailing assumption in both the North and the South was that the Communists would probably receive enough votes in both zones to secure posts in a future government. Therefore Diem was reluctant to enter into consultations, and subsequently elections, that could favor the Hanoi government.[2] Without Diem's consent, it would be impossible to hold the consultations. In the North, despite the unfavorable situation, the Lao Dong Party continued to fight for the implementation of the Geneva Agreement. To succeed, however, Hanoi was dependent upon full support from its communist allies.

The first months following Geneva were rather quiet ones in the Soviet-DRV relationship. The North Vietnamese had their hands full with the reconstruction process, so the emphasis at that time was on consolidating the state north of the 17th parallel, rather than on planning new adventures in the South. During these months, the contact between the two countries consisted mostly of official communiqués referring to the Soviet assistance to the DRV during the Geneva negotiations. The few appeals for assistance were made discreetly, and Moscow's assistance was kept at a low level. As long as the situation in Vietnam was calm, Moscow saw no need to interfere.[3]

In late December 1954, the situation changed. Events in Vietnam forced Moscow to play a more active role. In a note to Soviet foreign minister Vyacheslav Molotov, Kirill Novikov, the head of the Southeast Asia Department of the Soviet Foreign Ministry predicted that Hanoi's public treatment of the state and government in South Vietnam could threaten the chance for a full implementation of the Geneva Agreement, and provoke intrigues from the American side. Novikov underlined that "considering the possibilities of intrigues on the part of the United States, which is interested in a deterioration of the relationship between the DRV and South Vietnam, I believe it expedient to carefully recommend the government of the DRV not to use various kinds of labels with regard to Ngo Dinh Diem, as well as to the government he heads."[4]

This statement indicates that the sharp tone of North Vietnamese criticism of the Diem government in South Vietnam had begun to concern Soviet leaders. In late 1954 and early 1955, Moscow had no interest in encouraging the DRV to arrange a campaign against the South Vietnamese government, and the Soviets would certainly not have participated in such a campaign. There were several reasons for this Soviet attitude. The Soviet leaders feared that an aggressive state in the North could provoke the United States and lead to a deeper involvement on their side, something Soviet leaders wished to avoid. They believed that the United States should not be given the opportunity to exploit the situation and thereby complicate the relationship between the two zones before the elections. The incessant North Vietnamese criticism of South Vietnam might also destroy the possibilities of holding elections. The South Vietnamese authorities were very reluctant to enter into consultations with the DRV; and from the Soviet perspective, North Vietnamese public criticism of Diem could only further complicate the situation.

In general, the period from late December 1954 was characterized by increased Soviet interest in Vietnam. The initiative presented above was only the first in a series of recommendations the Soviets made to the North Vietnamese during the winter and spring of 1955.

In its official pronouncements, Moscow stood up for the Geneva Agreement. It defended the legal status of the agreement and insisted that its provisions should be followed. The Soviet Union also emphasized that all discussions concerning the agreement should be held with the participation of all the great powers, and not just some of them. In mid-March 1955, Soviet deputy foreign minister Vasilii Vasil'evich Kuznetsov expressed his misgivings concerning the plans of the United States, the United Kingdom, and France to discuss the Vietnamese general elections at the NATO meeting in Paris in April that year. According to Kuznetsov, it would be necessary to ask the United Kingdom and France for an explanation of this behavior because "such a measure would show the governments of France and Great Britain that the Soviet Union was on guard against their attempts to violate the Geneva Agreement."[5] In 1955 a solution within the Geneva framework was, from a Soviet point of view, the best possible solution. This episode illustrated the Soviet emphasis on reaching a diplomatic solution to the Vietnamese problem. In addition, it may also reveal that the Soviet leaders feared that other powers would take control over the situation and developments in the region.

The Soviet position as cochairman of the Geneva Conference sometimes seemed a liability rather than an advantage in the Soviet-DRV relationship. Legally, the cochairman position did not imply any binding obligations on the Soviet Union. As the historian R. F. Randle has remarked, being chairman "was largely a procedural task, however, with no obligation to enforce the provisions of the Geneva agreements or otherwise act collectively to preserve the political equilibrium in Indochina."[6]

Randle's argument is legally accurate. The Soviet leaders did not sign or agree to any documents making them more responsible for political developments in the region than any of the other states that had participated at the Geneva Conference. For the Soviet Union, however, another aspect also played an equally important role. The state created in the northern zone of Vietnam had proclaimed itself socialist, and the leader of the socialist camp could not completely ignore it. So whether or not the Soviets were legally bound by their role as participant and cochairman of the Geneva Conference, the role they had assumed would, inevitably, become an important factor in the coming years.

In situations where the interests of the DRV authorities and ICC representatives clashed, Soviet diplomats were eager to calm things down. Interestingly, on occasions of disagreement with the ICC, Hanoi turned to Moscow for advice, which Moscow was indeed willing to provide.[7] As long as the ICC was allowed to work under acceptable conditions, the Soviets felt there was a fair chance of achieving a lasting solution to the Indochinese problem within the framework of the Geneva Agreement. Moscow therefore continuously promoted a good relationship with the ICC in all three Indochinese states, and it aimed to improve the ICC's working conditions.

Of equal importance is the question of whether the Soviets trusted in diplomacy alone in this context, or whether their policy in Vietnam also included other instruments. As is demonstrated below, the Soviet leaders, while promoting a diplomatic solution to the Vietnamese problem, also had other measures in mind for the leadership in Hanoi.

The Start of a New Soviet Policy?

From the late spring of 1955, Soviet policies toward Vietnam began moving in a new direction. Though still emphasizing the importance of reaching a solution within the Geneva framework, Moscow also encouraged the North Vietnamese to increase their influence in South Vietnam through a number of offensive measures. In brief, Soviet suggestions can be divided into two interlinked parts: Hanoi should use all efforts to unmask the aggressive actions of the Americans in South Vietnam; and Hanoi should also work to increase its influence on the Southern population, preferably by establishing a mass organization.

During the spring of 1955, the Soviets were increasingly worried by the U.S. presence in South Vietnam, something reflected in Moscow's behavior at this time. The first sign came in a note to the Central Committee of the Communist Party of the Soviet Union from Foreign Minister Molotov in mid-May 1955, evaluating the current situation in Vietnam.[8] The note described the growing American presence in South Vietnam, referring to U.S. efforts to undermine the economic position of France and reduce French influence, especially within the army. According to Molotov, the Americans had also tried to take over the French advisory position, and they generally were seeking to increase their influence in the political sphere.[9] The growing tension between the Americans and the French, combined with the intensification of civil strife between different political groups in South Vietnam, created, according to Molotov, a favorable situation for the North Vietnamese, which, in his words, they should use to "strengthen those public forces in South Vietnam which are in favor of a reunification of the country on a democratic foundation and which hold an anti-imperialistic position and speak for the national sovereignty of the country."[10]

Molotov also underlined that at a meeting on April 1, 1955, the Central Committee of the Lao Dong Party had passed a resolution containing orders to the local party organization in South Vietnam.[11] However, referring to consultations with the Soviet ambassador to Hanoi, Aleksandr Andreevich Lavrishchev, and the Soviet ambassador to Beijing, Pavel Fedorovich Iudin, Molotov concluded that the North Vietnamese directive possessed several serious deficiencies. In his view, the "aggressive policy of the Americans had been badly and insufficiently unmasked," a situation that enabled the Americans to simultaneously "spread propaganda against Communism and against the Soviet Union and the People's Republic of China."[12]

Even though they agreed on the need to exploit the situation in South Vietnam, the Soviet leaders seemed rather dissatisfied with the handling of this opportunity by the North Vietnamese, charging that they were not exploiting its potential in the South, so that both the North Vietnamese and their allies were missing possibilities of gaining influence. In addition, according to the Soviets, the situation enabled the Americans to conduct a widespread campaign against both the Soviet Union and China, as well as against communism in general. The Soviets therefore perceived a need to instruct their Vietnamese friends how best to handle the situation. Molotov emphasized that "our friends in the DRV have not yet made good enough use of the situation in South Vietnam in order to conduct the necessary work in that part of the country, especially with regard to the forthcoming elections in July 1956."[13]

Molotov did not, however, simply criticize the Vietnamese but also gave advice on how to exploit the situation in a manner the Soviet Union would consider satisfactory. His explicit advice to the Vietnamese was "to lay more emphasis on the conduct of work in South Vietnam in order to activate and unite the patriotic and anti-imperialistic forces in this part of Vietnam."[14] Moscow was seriously concerned over the evolving situation in the South. Most communist cadres had left the South for the North, and Diem had severely impaired the remaining communist networks, meaning that these would have to be rebuilt to serve their cause in the South.[15]

As a follow-up to the foreign minister's evaluation of the situation, the Foreign Ministry presented the main contents of his note in telegrams to the Soviet ambassadors in Hanoi, Beijing, Paris, and Warsaw. The telegram sent to Hanoi was identical with parts of the note from Molotov to the Central Committee of the Communist Party of the Soviet Union in mid-May 1955. It contained direct orders to the Soviet ambassador, who was told to visit Ho Chi Minh and inform him first of the decisions made in Moscow, and then make him understand that it would be expedient to take better advantage of the developing situation in South Vietnam. The North Vietnamese should continue working to strengthen those portions of the population that already were, or could possibly become, sympathetic to the DRV. Moscow indicated its desire to assist Hanoi at that stage through a direct question to Ho about "which additional measures the Vietnamese friends considered necessary to carry out and whether they would require any assistance from our [the Soviet] side."[16]

The telegrams reveal that Molotov's policy suggestions were accepted in Moscow and subsequently put into practice by the Soviet ambassador to Hanoi. The interesting question is whether Moscow initiated the policy or whether Molotov's proposals were only a follow-up of policies already initiated in Vietnam by the Lao Dong Party. Returning to Molotov's note, he referred to the resolution passed by the Central Committee of the Lao Dong on April 1 that year. The relevant resolution was most likely one discussed at the Seventh Plenum of the Lao Dong Central Committee, held in March 1955. Discussion of a change of strategy in the South, or at least an intensification of parts of the strategy, had for some time been current within the

Lao Dong. In the spring of 1955, however, the plans for a new strategy, which among other things included a widening of the front and an intensification of work among the people of the South, was still only an idea. The fact that the strategy had not yet been specified in the form of concrete goals could be the "serious deficiencies" mentioned in Soviet comments on the resolution.[17]

Consultations for the general elections had been scheduled to start in July 1955. According to the provisions in the Final Declaration, they would "be held between the competent representative authorities of the two zones from July 20, onwards."[18] As Hanoi took the initiative to begin consultations with the Diem government in the early summer of 1955, the North Vietnamese confronted a regime in the South that was highly unwilling to participate. Likewise, the North Vietnamese also had to face the fact, that in the international climate prevailing in May 1955, there was every reason to expect that, despite the provisions in the Final Declaration, the partition of Vietnam would continue.

The similarities with postwar Germany and Korea were striking, and the pervasive optimism in international affairs, implying possibilities for general disengagement and détente, made it unlikely that any of the big powers would want to do anything to upset the status quo in Vietnam. Given both South Vietnamese and American reluctance to enter into consultations, insistence on these by the Soviet and North Vietnamese could endanger the status quo. In both Europe and Asia, the atmosphere was less tense than it had been for years. The allied occupation of West Germany had ended on May 5, 1955, and in June the first steps toward establishing diplomatic relations between Bonn and Moscow were taken. On May 14 the Warsaw Pact, the Eastern equivalent to NATO, was created. The day after, on May 15, the occupation of Austria ended and that state was declared neutral.[19]

The easing of tensions was evident both in East-West relations and also within the communist camp. In late May and early June 1955, the most prominent Soviet leaders left for Belgrade to visit Marshal Tito, the first meeting between Soviet and Yugoslav leaders since Yugoslavia had been expelled from the Cominform in 1948–49. The final event in the sphere of détente was the "Big Four" summit conference in Geneva in mid-July, which brought a further reduction in East-West tensions.[20]

Just before the deadline on May 16, 1955, the regrouping of forces on each side had been almost completed, which meant that the military terms of the cease-fire had been fully implemented. The next challenge for the governments of the two Vietnams was to prepare for nationwide elections in 1956. Hanoi was ready to open consultations with the Diem government, and on June 6 the DRV's prime minister and minister of foreign affairs, Pham Van Dong, expressed the DRV's willingness to hold a consultative conference. Yet the DRV initiatives were not welcome in the South. Diem and his American advisers were unwilling to enter into any negotiations, and they continued to ignore Hanoi's appeals for consultations.[21]

Ho Chi Minh in Moscow

From July 12 to 18, 1955, shortly before the stipulated deadline for consultations, Ho Chi Minh, the president and premier minister of the DRV, led a DRV governmental delegation to Moscow. Almost one year had passed since the conclusion of the Geneva Conference, yet this was the first time Ho was properly received in Moscow as the leader of a fellow socialist country. The aim of the visit was to discuss the international situation and to develop further political, economic, and cultural relations between the Soviet Union and the DRV.[22] From the North Vietnamese point of view, the trip had enormous symbolic significance, regardless of whether or not it succeeded in securing future assistance. By receiving Ho in the same manner as other socialist leaders, the Soviet Union signaled their acceptance of the DRV as a member of the socialist bloc. Such acceptance was imperative to the North Vietnamese because, at least in principle, it promised future backing in the international arena.

Ho's trip to Moscow had two main purposes: to secure economic assistance from the Soviet Union for reconstruction and to achieve Soviet backing for the DRV's policies on consultation.[23] In terms of economic assistance, the mission was a success. During Ho's stay in Moscow, the two countries signed their first formal economic assistance agreement, primarily an aid program whereby the Soviet Union promised to assist the North Vietnamese with numerous projects. The amount of aid and its role in the relationship are discussed below. However, if his trip's objective was also to secure support for an immediate challenge to the partition, by military means if necessary, Ho left Moscow unsatisfied.

Ho's 1955 visit formalized the relationship. A Soviet document titled "Instructions for Negotiations with the Government Delegation from the Democratic Republic of Vietnam" (hereafter, the "Instructions") shows that the question of economic aid was only one of the themes discussed during the visit.[24] The policy outlined in this document would become the basis for the Soviet engagement in Vietnam in subsequent years, and its main contents are discussed here. The instructions touched upon political, economic, military, and cultural relations between the Soviet Union and the DRV and outlined the Soviet position in most areas of the relationship through suggestions on how to respond to requests forwarded by Ho and his colleagues. In general terms, the Soviet negotiators had been given clear instructions that support would be given within the framework of the Geneva Agreement, and the Soviet Union would raise the question of political regulation in Vietnam at the next Big Four meeting in July 1955.

The document's introduction stated that the fundamental goal of the negotiations with the DRV delegation was to

> further develop the friendly political, economic and cultural cooperation between the USSR and the Democratic Republic of Vietnam. To give assistance to the Vietnamese friends, and with all the means at one's disposal strengthen the Democratic Republic of Vietnam and its international position. [To assist in] the reunification of Vietnam on a democratic foundation, and [to assist in] a full implementation of the Geneva agreements on Indo-China, and [to assist in] a fast recovery of the national economy of the Republic.[25]

Another aim of the negotiations was to assure comrade Ho that the Soviet government was also ready to provide, in cooperation with their Chinese friends, "the necessary support to the Democratic Republic of Vietnam in the struggle for independence and reunification of the country, as well as in the case of the economic and cultural construction of the Democratic Republic of Vietnam."[26]

On several issues, the Soviet negotiators had received very specific instructions. It is not clear to what extent these instructions were open for discussion. However, judging by the format of the document and the way the instructions had been formulated, Soviet leaders had made definite decisions on how to conduct policy toward Vietnam. The strength of the Soviet delegation that negotiated with the DRV representatives may also indicate the seriousness behind the recommendations made by the Soviets to the Vietnamese. An impressive group of Soviet officials conducted the negotiations with Ho's delegation, consisting of the top Soviet leadership, Prime Minister Nikolai Bulganin, Presidium Chairman Kliment Voroshilov, Presidium member Lazar Kaganovich, Deputy Premier Anastas Mikoyan, Foreign Minister Molotov, and Party Secretary Nikita Khrushchev.[27] As both the content of the "Instructions" and the Soviet representation indicated, there were many important questions to discuss.

Overall, the "Instructions" provide much information as to how the Soviets saw their future relationship with the DRV and what kind of policy the Soviets wanted the DRV leaders to follow toward South Vietnam and the question of reunification. At the next Big Four meeting, Soviet leaders promised to suggest more assistance from the great powers for political regulation in Vietnam, Laos, and Cambodia, in accordance with the Geneva Agreement.[28] The Soviets also received positively the DRV suggestion to establish a broader common front with the French and pro-French elements against the Americans in South Vietnam. It seems clear that, rather than letting the Americans in, the Soviets preferred that the North Vietnamese maintain a good relationship with the French.[29]

"To Counter the American Influence"—"to Broaden the Front and Create a Mass Organization"

Their earlier recommendations notwithstanding, in the summer of 1955, the Soviets were still dissatisfied with the North Vietnamese handling of the situation in South Vietnam. Moscow continued to advise Hanoi on how to prevent increased American influence in the South. In the "Instructions," the question was raised again, this time under the subtitle "On Opposition to the Plans of the United States with Regard to Indochina." The main argument followed up Molotov's suggestions from mid-May. In the "Instructions," however, the argument was even stronger. It was no longer merely a question of strengthening different groups within Southern society in order to activate and unite patriotic and anti-imperialistic forces in the Southern part of Vietnam. Propaganda work would now be aimed directly at the enemy. According to the Soviet government, the Vietnamese friends should direct all efforts "to activate the work among all sections of the population in South Vietnam in order to counter the American influence."[30] In other words, it was no longer a question of joining the democratic forces without a specific target. At this point, the Soviet leaders had outlined the target, namely, the rapidly growing American influence.

In the period preceding Ho's visit to the Soviet Union, there had been an increase in U.S. activity in South Vietnam. From late 1954 through the spring of 1955, the Americans gradually became more visible in South Vietnam. On December 13, 1954, the Ely–Lawton Collins Agreement on the U.S. role in training South Vietnamese armed forces was signed. In early February 1955, the Americans established a Training Relations and Instruction Mission in South Vietnam, whereafter they took over financial and training responsibilities in South Vietnam from France. In May the first U.S.-Cambodia military assistance agreement was signed, and in June the Military Assistance Advisory Group in Cambodia was inaugurated.[31] Moscow perceived the rapid increase in Washington's influence as the beginning of an American takeover of South Vietnam. To prevent the Diem government and its U.S. advisers from gaining complete control in the Southern region, the North Vietnamese would have to organize effective countermeasures.

The establishment of a mass organization was the solution. The documents reveal that in the summer of 1955, the negotiators were told to "underline the importance of broadening the Unified National Front at the expense of founding new organizations of this front, not only in the liberated areas, but also in South Vietnam."[32] The Soviets were positive about a broadening of the Lien Viet (Unified National Front), and the suggested organization was a follow-up of the strategy mentioned in Molotov's note, which emphasized increasing work among the population of South Vietnam. As to where and how such a mass organization should be organized, the Soviet recommendations were straightforward:

> Recommend comrade Ho Chi Minh to consider the question of the expediency and possibility of creating a mass organization for the fight to reunify Vietnam that could attract the wider patriotic and democratic forces in the South and the North, and that at the same time would not be formally associated with the Unified National Front (Lien Viet). From a tactical point of view it would be preferable if the initiative to create such an organization was developed in the South and if the first organizations of that kind originated in South Vietnam.[33]

From the summer of 1955, the question was no longer how to activate the people but how to coordinate their activities into a mass organization, which would originate in the South and have no official connection to the North. One might reasonably assume that, from the Soviet viewpoint, a Southern organization that was formally associated with the Communist Party leadership in Hanoi would not be equally effective in activating the Southern people.

There were several reasons why Moscow preferred a situation with no official connections between the organization developing in the South and the Lao Dong Party in the North. One reason was the South Vietnamese government's attitude toward those suspected of working for or sympathizing with the Lao Dong. The summer of 1955 marked the start of Diem's so-called Anti Communists Denunciation Campaign, which was designed to root out subversive elements throughout the country.[34] To announce *publicly* the formation of a Southern mass organization that cooperated with the North would only intensify the hunt for communist sympathizers in the South and still further complicate the founding of the organization.

Another important argument had more to do with the international image of the Soviet Union. The United States might well regard as provocative the creation of a larger organization in the South with formal ties to the Lao Dong in Hanoi, which would damage Soviet-American relations. North Vietnamese involvement in creating such an organization in South Vietnam was likely to be perceived as indirect Soviet involvement in the area, a move that would legitimize even deeper involvement on the part of the Americans. Both domestic Vietnamese and wider international reasons, therefore, underpinned the Soviet proposal to keep this organization's construction an ostensibly South Vietnamese project.

Turning to Hanoi, how were these suggestions received in the DRV capital? According to the historian R. B. Smith, "Ho Chi Minh's journey to Moscow and Beijing in July 1955 failed to secure support for any immediate challenge to the partition, leaving Hanoi only a limited range of options in the South."[35] But Smith also stresses that in the following period "an attempt was made to devise a strategy which would combine the continuing demand for 'implementation' of the political settlement with a series of political and (clandestine) military moves."[36] He claims that the period between the Eighth and Ninth Plenary Sessions of the Lao Dong Central Committee, from August 1955 to April 1956, stands out as a crucial time in strategic planning for the South, and that at the Eighth Plenum discussions took place on the possibility of broadening the Unified National Front (the Lien Viet) and renaming it the Vietnam Fatherland Front. As part of this, the Central Committee is also said to have approved use of 'tactical' violence in the South.[37]

In the summer of 1955, Moscow and Hanoi agreed on a strategy toward South Vietnam. The Lao Dong discussions over the creation of a broad organization originating in the South accorded closely with the Soviet suggestions of July. It is difficult, however, to discern from Soviet documents to what extent Moscow continuously followed the ongoing Lao Dong debate over a new strategy toward the South. It is also difficult to specify how

Moscow responded to the North Vietnamese determination to increase the level of violence. What the documents do indicate is support and interest from the Soviet side.

How familiar were Soviet leaders with the internal structure of Vietnamese organizations such as the Lien Viet? Contact with the mass organizations, and particularly the Lien Viet, was stressed in the 1954 instructions from Moscow to Ambassador Aleksandr Lavrishchev. Toward the end of January 1955, Leonid Ivanovich Sokolov, the adviser at the Soviet Embassy in Hanoi, discussed the Lien Viet with vice chairman of the Central Committee of the Lien Viet Front, Hoan Quok Viet. During the conversation, Sokolov received information regarding the front's history, organization, ideological foundation, its task in relation to the fulfillment of the cease-fire agreement, and the nature of its work.[38] This may indicate that already, at this early stage, Soviet leaders perceived the possibilities of this organization. When the North Vietnamese began discussing whether to broaden it, the Soviet Union backed the proposal. To create an organization consonant with its foreign policy strategy, Moscow gave the Lao Dong its own recommendations for how best to organize it.

When the Lao Dong Central Committee convened its Eighth Plenum from August 13 to 20, 1955, its major preoccupation was to set up a new united national front to lead the consolidation of the North and the political struggle in the South. The reasoning behind this strategy demonstrated, according to the historian Carlyle Thayer, a strong feeling among the Lao Dong leaders "that it was unlikely that the Geneva Agreements would be implemented within the time frame envisaged in July 1954."[39] In the following months, the Vietnamese continued to emphasize to the Soviets the importance of a reunified Vietnam. Even though the Vietnamese claimed to prefer a peaceful solution as the most desirable option, they did not omit to mention that they had used force before, though still without stating that they would be ready to use it again.[40]

The China Factor

From mid-1955, the Soviet Union both expanded and formalized its relationship with the DRV. As the "Instructions" reveal, the Soviet leaders used the year after Geneva to develop the foundations of the relationship. The document covers most areas of the relationship, from cultural collaboration to the more sensitive questions of cooperation with the Chinese, and activities to counter the growing American influence in the Southern part of Vietnam. The Soviet leaders used the year after Geneva to further elaborate policies toward Vietnam. By the summer of 1955, they were signaling their readiness to provide assistance to the North Vietnamese, but they were simultaneously wary of making too many promises or concessions.

In most respects, Moscow and Hanoi concurred on how to handle the situation. There were exceptions, however; one being the nature of the triangular relationship between Moscow, Hanoi, and Beijing, a recurrent problem in Soviet-DRV relations. If Ho raised the question of establishing a joint Sino-Soviet economic and military mission, he would be told that such a step would not be expedient as the practice of cooperation in these fields between the Vietnamese and Chinese was already established.[41] Nevertheless, this did not exclude the possibility of Soviet technical aid for the DRV. The question had also been raised earlier. In a telegram to Soviet deputy minister of foreign affairs V. A. Zorin in early June 1955, General Alexey Antonov, chief of the Soviet High Command, underlined the inexpediency of establishing a joint Sino-Soviet military mission to coordinate questions related to the development of People's Army of Vietnam (PAVN) armed forces in Hanoi.[42] His argument was rooted in the Chinese military presence. Antonov emphasized that "at present PAVN has Chinese military advisors. These advisors know the peculiarities of the country and its army. They have many years of experience in advising the Vietnamese friends on questions of constructing the armed forces, including the instruction and education of troops."[43] The military command in Moscow, unwilling to engage in Vietnamese military affairs, preferred to keep the military mission in Hanoi strictly Chinese, and it responded negatively when asked whether to promise military aid to the Vietnamese.

Despite General Antonov's words, the Vietnamese military leaders continued to meet with both Chinese and Soviet officials to discuss military matters. On June 27, 1955, a Vietnamese military delegation led by Vo Nguyen Giap secretly visited Beijing, where they discussed the reconstruction of the DRV's armed forces and future war plans with Chinese defense minister Peng Dehuai and General Petroshevskii, a senior Soviet military adviser in China. A similar trip, also led by Giap, occurred in mid-October 1955, on which occasion Giap likewise discussed the same questions with the Soviet general Nikolai Gushev, deputy chief of staff of the Warsaw Pact.[44]

As chapter 1 of the present volume indicates, even in the 1950s the Chinese played an important role in providing economic assistance to the DRV. They resumed their economic and practical aid to North Vietnam immediately after the conclusion of the Geneva Conference. A general adviser to the embassy, Fang Yi, directed a team of economic advisers and experts that would provide the DRV with necessary economic and financial advice.[45] Meanwhile, Soviet economic assistance to the DRV immediately after Geneva remained very low key, identical to that given to other members of the socialist bloc, and by no means more important. Soviet financial assistance to some nonsocialist developing countries may well have exceeded that to the DRV, even though the Hanoi leaders had eagerly committed themselves to the ideals of the socialist world.[46]

Although the Soviet Union viewed both economic and technical assistance to the DRV as important factors in the struggle for Vietnamese reunification, it had no intention of assisting the DRV without any backing from the rest of the socialist camp. In a note to Foreign Minister Molotov on January 11, 1955, Deputy Minister Vasily Kuznetsov voiced his concern over the uncertainty regarding the Chinese position on how and when the other socialist countries should provide assistance to the DRV, not least the question of whether specialists from countries other than China should be sent to the DRV.[47] Beijing, however, also shared his concern. Addressing Ho through his Chinese advisors on January 18, Zhou Enlai emphasized that China alone could not be responsible for all assistance to the DRV and that the Soviet Union and the Eastern European countries must also give aid.[48]

China was an influential factor in Soviet decisionmaking on Vietnam, and Moscow's often expectant attitude was a result of Chinese policies. Despite some reluctance by both the Soviets and Chinese to institutionalize economic and military cooperation in Vietnam, both sides concluded that the DRV needed assistance in most fields. Moreover, the leaders in both Moscow and Beijing understood that they must cooperate to provide the DRV with the necessary assistance. The Soviet Union had the economic power, whereas China had the local expertise. Some tension will always characterize an alliance between two large powers, and the Sino-Soviet relationship was no exception. However, during the later 1950s both Soviet and Chinese leaders were inclined to cooperate on Vietnam, notwithstanding the emerging differences between the two communist powers.

Although the economic relationship was fairly well established by the summer of 1955, the question of military relations between the two countries would become a much more delicate issue. China has a long tradition of wielding influence in Vietnam, and the country was, and remained, an important factor in the bilateral relationship between the Soviet Union and Vietnam.[49] With the growing ideological split between the Soviet Union and China in the later 1950s, and especially in the 1960s, China's significance in Soviet-Vietnamese relations increased rather than diminished.

The Soviet Union seemed ready to transfer the major part of the responsibility for military affairs to China. Why were Soviet leaders willing to yield influence to the Chinese in such an important field? One reason could be that at that time, despite the growing Soviet interest in the country's political affairs, Vietnam was not of primary interest to the Soviet Union with regard to active military engagement. The Soviets were far more concerned with the military situation in Eastern Europe.[50] By handing over much of the military responsibility to the Chinese, the Soviets would retain their control within the communist sphere without being directly responsible, while simultaneously avoiding the risk of becoming overly involved. Another reason may derive from the state of Sino-Soviet relations in Vietnam in 1955. Although it has been claimed that tension between the two had started to surface, the further record of Sino-Soviet cooperation in Vietnam indicates that, with regard to Vietnam, the relationship between Moscow and Beijing was still functioning well. The two powers agreed on the need to assist the DRV. Beijing had long military experience in Vietnam, and it was therefore natural for both the Soviet Union and China that the present arrangement should continue.[51]

In September 1955, the situation changed. Moscow received a report from the Soviet ambassador to Hanoi stating that the Central Committee of the Chinese Communist Party had decided to withdraw all Chinese political and economic advisers working in the DRV by the end of 1955. The Chinese decision—which confirms Yang Kuisong's thesis in chapter 1 above that, in the years immediately following the Geneva Conference, Mao Zedong sought to reduce international tensions in Southeast Asia by refraining from Chinese encouragement of revolutionary movements—alarmed both the North Vietnamese and the Soviets. Moscow turned to Beijing to prevent a total Chinese withdrawal from the DRV. However, the situation must have been seen as somewhat delicate, because the Soviets decided to present their discontent to Beijing in "a tactful way," and make the Chinese understand that the Soviets favored greater long-term assistance from China to the DRV.[52] In early December 1955, the Chinese ambassador to the DRV, Luo Guibo, informed the Soviets that the Chinese advisers would only be allowed to stay until the end of 1955.[53]

On December 24, 1955, the Chinese defense minister, Peng Dehuai, informed his Vietnamese counterpart, Vo Nguyen Giap, of the decision to recall the Chinese Military Advisory Group, which had been in Vietnam since

July 1950. By mid-March 1956, all its remaining members had returned to China.[54] Soviet attempts to delay the final Chinese military withdrawal from Vietnam seem to have had little effect on the Chinese. For Soviet officials, who relied on the Chinese political, economic, and military presence in Vietnam, a Chinese withdrawal in any of these fields would complicate the situation, while also depriving the DRV of much needed resources. Lacking the Chinese presence, the Soviets would be forced to engage themselves more deeply in Vietnam if they wished to maintain current developments and progress in that country.

Defining a New Strategy

Politically, the autumn of 1955 was characterized by continuous efforts by the DRV government to reach an understanding with the Ngo Dinh Diem government on both consultation and election issues. On July 19, Pham Van Dong sent a message to Diem requesting that he nominate representatives for the consultations but received no reply. In August, the Saigon government declared that free elections in the North were impossible. At this point, the North Vietnamese leaders turned to Moscow for advice. The Soviet leaders, who saw the importance of pushing for implementation of the provisions of the Geneva Agreement, recommended that Hanoi raise the issue at the level of the two cochairmen of the conference, which meant that the Soviet Union would discuss the matter with the United Kingdom.[55] Dong followed up with a letter to the Geneva cochairmen, seeking their intervention to secure the implementation of the political terms of the settlement.[56]

Why did the Soviet Union insist on going through the "Geneva channel" rather than acting on its own—that is, defending the rights of the DRV independently of the other states and the statutes of Geneva? By the fall of 1955, the DRV had already submitted several complaints to the ICC and also to the cochairmen of the Geneva Conference that Diem was unwilling to prepare for consultations. At that point, all depended upon Diem. Without his consent, there would be no consultations and most likely no elections. The Soviet Union was more ready to support the Vietnamese cause under the label of Geneva cochairman than as the leader of the socialist camp. As with the ICC, Soviet officials played safe, expressing their readiness to assist in fulfilling the Geneva Agreement and offering to raise the question at the next meeting of the four great powers. In other words, they were ready to work through diplomatic channels but not, apparently, to support a return to armed struggle.

The prospects for consultations and achievement of a solution through diplomatic means were, however, poor. The French were preparing to pull out completely, leaving no one in charge of implementing the agreed-on provisions. The Diem government, which was supposed to succeed the French and undertake their obligations with regard to the agreement, refused to participate, claiming that because South Vietnam was not a signatory of the Geneva Accords it had no obligations whatsoever. During the autumn of 1955, Diem further consolidated his power, gradually eliminating or reaching agreement with all his internal enemies, among them the three religious sects in South Vietnam that had all received French funding.[57] Both the North Vietnamese and the Soviets now clearly recognized that the Diem government would remain in power for some time.

In Hanoi, the party leaders still tried to achieve a solution within the framework of the Geneva Agreement. But despite all their efforts to arrange for consultations on elections, the DRV leaders had no success in approaching the South Vietnamese government on the subject. Before the two cochairmen had met to discuss the situation in Vietnam, Diem had gone one step further in his attempt to consolidate the state in the South. On October 23, 1955, he arranged a referendum in South Vietnam, whereby he dethroned the former emperor Bao Dai and had himself elected president. Shortly afterward, he broke off economic relations with France, left the French Union, and finally proclaimed the Republic of Vietnam on October 26, 1955.[58] The referendum provoked no major protests from either the Soviet Union or China, indicating that the two communist powers accepted the idea of a divided Vietnam. In other words, in the autumn of 1955, Hanoi was alone in protesting against both Diem's refusal to hold consultations and the referendum.

As has already been demonstrated above, parallel to its political and diplomatic efforts to secure a solution within the Geneva framework, Hanoi had started to plan a supplementary strategy that would increase North Vietnamese influence in the South and finally establish a mass organization in favor of the Northern regime. What was the Soviet role in this? To evaluate Soviet influence on the new strategy, one must again scrutinize Soviet moves during the spring and summer of 1955. In the final months of 1955, Soviet and Vietnamese officials did not discuss the new strategy and its implications in conversations. The Soviets seemed eager to promote a solution through diplomatic channels rather than to engage in support for any action inside South Vietnam. However, when looking back to the summer of 1955 and the suggestions that Moscow advanced during the July negotiations, the Soviets had at least a certain influence in preparing the new strategy. The fact that, in subsequent months, in the autumn of 1955, they insisted on using their role as a cochairman rather than following up their earlier suggestions reveals how they deliberately tried to avoid any official connection to the Lao Dong policy toward South Vietnam.

While the Lao Dong leadership continued to formulate their new strategy, the Soviet Union once again insisted on using the diplomatic channel. Consequently, the Vietnamese side's faith in solving the problem of reunification by political means was gradually diminishing, something also reflected in talks between Soviet and DRV officials. Following the referendum in October, the relationship between the Republic of Vietnam and its American advisers became gradually tighter. In early January 1956, the North Vietnamese submitted another request for assistance to the Soviets. Diem and the Americans had developed a series of policies, including extermination of the communists, the liquidation of the religious sects, provisions for both a new constitution and separate National Assembly elections for the South, and entrance into SEATO. Concerned by these measures, the North Vietnamese asked the Soviets to assist them in promoting their cause of unification in the West, especially in France.[59]

To counter the actions in the South, Hanoi suggested a new Geneva meeting with the same participants as in 1954, as well as the representatives of the ICC. The Soviet Union and China positively endorsed the suggestion, but the Soviets expressed genuine worry that other Geneva powers, especially the United Kingdom, would not welcome the proposal. Accordingly, the Soviet Union suggested that they themselves, the Chinese, and the Vietnamese should utilize any possible refusal to call a new meeting to unmask the policy of the Western powers to disrupt the Geneva Agreement and prolong the division of Vietnam.[60]

Had the North Vietnamese leaders lost faith in a diplomatic solution by early 1956? Hanoi knew that it had Beijing's support. The Chinese leaders had suggested a reconvention of the Geneva Conference to overcome Diem's disregard for the Agreement, and on February 14, 1956, Pham Van Dong sent another letter sounding the same theme to the Geneva cochairmen. About this time, a report from the Soviet Embassy in Hanoi to Moscow underlined that the fulfillment of the Geneva Agreement for the whole of Vietnam was seriously endangered. Its main argument was that "the events in Vietnam show that in the near future the fight around the fulfillment of the Geneva Agreement will be intensified."[61] On the North Vietnamese side, belief in a solution by diplomatic means was diminishing, if not already gone. In late February 1956, the secretary general of the Lao Dong, Truong Chinh, stated that because there had been no consultations before the elections, they would not be held, at least not within the time schedule set by the agreement.[62] Such a statement cannot be seen as anything but a confession by the DRV leaders that they had lost faith in a diplomatic solution, at least for the foreseeable future.

Conclusions: A Dual Policy?

From late 1954, there was a significant increase in Soviet interest in Vietnam. In contrast to the first months following the Geneva Conference, Moscow developed a more active policy toward Vietnam. This policy consisted of two different but still interlinked parts. On the one hand, it promoted Soviet diplomatic initiatives aimed at the full implementation of the Geneva Agreement; on the other, its emphasis was on Lao Dong work in the South aimed at increasing the level of North Vietnamese influence in the Southern part of the country.

The documentary sources often picture Moscow's policies toward Vietnam in 1955 as double-edged. Was that the aim of these policies? In its policymaking, the Soviet Union had many factors to consider, and policies toward Vietnam were part of a much larger picture, namely, Moscow's overall foreign policy. To evaluate Soviet policies toward Vietnam, one must differentiate between policies that concerned only the Soviet Union and the DRV, and those that were also directed toward the rest of the world. Soviet leaders had to relate to two different kinds of audiences: first, the international audience—the other great powers and world opinion at large; and second, the audience in Vietnam and the rest of the socialist camp, also taking into account the relationship with China. Soviet requests of 1954 that the North Vietnamese keep a low profile when referring to Diem and his government in both speeches and the press were a warning to the North Vietnamese designed to prevent them from upsetting the Americans, that is, a message in accordance with the Soviet Union's official policy. Soviet recommendations in the spring and summer of 1955, aimed at increasing North Vietnamese influence in the South, were directed toward the second audience, the socialist camp.

Within a short period of time, Moscow told the Vietnamese both to avoid strong criticisms of the South Vietnamese authorities in the press and also to extend their work among sections of the South Vietnamese people. From the outset, Moscow seems to have followed two different tracks. Did the Soviet leaders intentionally follow a double-edged policy, or was it circumstances that made their Vietnam policy appear inconsistent? It has been argued that in the Soviet period Moscow was "capable for the most part of distinguishing between propaganda and policy in its foreign relations, perceiving that its ideology and the national interest are not always synonymous."[63] In 1955, Soviet policies in Vietnam represented the conflict between the ideological dedication of the Soviet leaders and their understanding of what was in the best interest of the Soviet Union at that time. As we have seen, before recognition, contacts between Moscow and Hanoi were based on a shared ideology. As relations grew closer, political interests became more important. The duality in 1955 illustrated the difficulty for Soviet leaders of simultaneously emphasizing the ideals of their common ideology and the national interests of the Soviet Union.

Thus, this argument simultaneously promotes a realist view of Soviet foreign policies based on the notion that national governments act purposefully and respond in a calculating manner to perceived problems. In other words, all choices are made rationally given the nation's objectives.[64] But what if decisions were not made "rationally"? What if decisions were made by different constituencies within the Communist Party of the Soviet Union that had their own reasons for seeking to play to different audiences with regard to Vietnam? Considering that Soviet representation abroad consisted not only of diplomats but also of intelligence officers and party representatives, the potential for conflicting interests was tremendous. We do not yet have access to internal Soviet materials that might reveal whether competing factions existed within the Soviet bureaucracy, but the possibility of such a situation should remind us of the danger in simply rationalizing away the people within the foreign policy apparatus.

Epilogue

Between 1956 and the end of 1960, the Soviet-Vietnamese relationship was characterized by a few major developments outlined below, and the slow, gradual, but unstoppable alteration in Southern strategy evolving within the Lao Dong Party. There were two main features of Soviet policy during these years. First, despite their economic and political assistance to the DRV, Soviet officials appeared by no means always au fait with the developing situation in Vietnam; and second, Soviet officials felt little or no obligation to inform the Vietnamese in advance when Soviet policies were likely to have serious implications for Indochina as a whole and Vietnam in particular.

The first certain sign of differing Soviet and Vietnamese interests during these years was the February 1956 Twentieth Congress of the Communist Party of the Soviet Union. Like all other Soviet and foreign delegates attending, the Hanoi leaders were totally unprepared for the revelations at this meeting. Two months passed before the Lao Dong Party, after its extended Eleventh Plenum, officially stated that "the Plenum unanimously and warmly approved the decisions of the Twentieth Congress of the Communist Party of the Soviet Union."[65] Since the developments of the spring and summer of 1955, the Lao Dong had begun to reevaluate its Southern strategy, and factions within it had started to promote a new, more aggressive approach. In that respect, the resolutions of the Twentieth Congress and the new Soviet foreign policy line complicated the relationship between the two states. Soviet documents of this period convey the impression that the North Vietnamese gradually became increasingly reluctant to follow the new Soviet lead. The clash of interests generated by the change in Soviet policies increased the DRV's distrust of its Soviet allies, leading Ho Chi Minh to understand that he could not necessarily count on Soviet support to reunify Vietnam.

However, throughout the second half of the 1950s, the DRV continued to emphasize the need to hold consultations and conduct general elections, and it presented Soviet officials with several proposals designed to convince the South Vietnamese government to open consultations. All these were rejected by the Soviets, who argued that the proposals made too many concessions to the South.[66] Soviet officials still preferred to try to settle these matters through discussions between themselves and the United Kingdom, their fellow cochairman. This policy left the North Vietnamese in a rather hopeless position; and when the time appointed for elections came, they were not held. Neither of the two great communist powers, the Soviet Union and China, protested on behalf of the Vietnamese.

The first real test of sincerity in the Soviet-Vietnamese relationship after the failure to obtain elections in July 1956 came the following January. On January 23, 1957, the United States proposed the acceptance of both South Vietnam and South Korea as independent members of the United Nations. The American suggestion immediately provoked a Soviet counterproposal on January 24, to admit North Vietnam and North Korea as well. The Soviet counterproposal took the Hanoi leadership entirely by surprise, and Soviet materials confirm that no prior discussion of this subject took place between Soviet and Vietnamese officials. Clearly, too, the Soviet proposal left the DRV leadership deeply upset, and in subsequent days and weeks Soviet officials were repeatedly forced to defend their actions not only to the Vietnamese but also to the Chinese. The Soviets strongly denied Chinese allegations that the Soviet and DRV positions on the subject were seriously divergent, and the Soviet ambassador to Hanoi, M. V. Zimjanin, informed his Chinese counterpart that "there were no inconsistencies" between the two and that "the Soviet Union steadfastly defended the fundamental interests of the DRV."[67] The Soviets argued that admitting one of the two Vietnamese states as an independent member would have decreased the chances of any eventual reunification, whereas, according to them, the admission of both was compatible with the Geneva Accords. This UN episode generated renewed discussion of the Geneva Accords and related issues, and the North Vietnamese then once again unsuccessfully sought to implement the Geneva Accords. Ultimately, the United Nations admitted neither Vietnamese state.

During the years 1957–58, the Vietnamese gave numerous indications to Soviet officials in Hanoi of their intentions to change their reunification strategy. With some exceptions, most of these indications were made very discreetly. In conversations with Soviet officials, the North Vietnamese leaders repeatedly emphasized that changes in the Vietnamese situation required a new strategy to achieve reunification. The Soviet reaction to the Vietnamese attitude is far from clear. The archival documents indicate that Soviet embassy officials received enough information to discern a change of attitude within the Lao Dong leadership. One example is how Hanoi informed them of changes within the Politburo, which clearly indicated the ascendancy of individuals working in the South. The fact that Southerners increasingly gained power within the higher echelons of the party should have warned Moscow that changes were under way.[68]

The major strategic change in Hanoi's policy toward the South came in 1959 and 1960. Two significant political decisions were made during these years. The first, which approved in principle the resumption of armed revolt in the South, was made at the Fifteenth Plenum of the Lao Dong Central Committee held from December 1958 to February 1959, but not proclaimed officially until May that same year. The second decision, made at the Third Party Congress of the Lao Dong in September 1960, acknowledged the expansion of armed struggle in South Vietnam with the objective of overthrowing the Diem regime.[69]

The official communiqué giving the resolutions of the Fifteenth Plenum was not presented until May 13, 1959, nearly five months after the meeting itself. The communiqué did not specifically mention armed struggle, but it did outline a change in the course of the Southern struggle. Before the May announcement, Soviet diplomats had repeatedly asked Lao Dong leaders for information on the plenum resolutions. In January, during the plenum sessions, Ho Chi Minh told Soviet ambassador Leonid Ivanovich Sokolov that "the present situation in South Vietnam can be characterized as ripe for revolution."[70] In March, when the embassy once again requested materials from the plenum, the response was still negative. According to Nguyen Duy Trinh, this was because the final resolution had not yet been edited, and the main speaker at the plenum, Phan Hung, had left for Indonesia together with Ho.[71] Barely a month before the official announcement, on April 15, records show that Le Duan informed Sokolov of the subjects of discussion at the Fifteenth Plenum. However, Sokolov sought more than just vague information. He was most interested in those plenum decisions directly concerned with the basic problems of the development of the revolutionary movement in South Vietnam and the battle for the country's reunification.[72] Moscow received no clear answer to that question in April. Only after the official communiqué was released on May 13 was the Soviet embassy informed in some detail of the constituents of the new strategy.[73]

During their Third Party Congress in September 1960, the Lao Dong made a second major political decision that further expanded the Fifteenth Plenum's resolutions. The aim was now to "set the general policy of the 'liberation' of the South—that is, the overthrow of the Diem regime and the establishment of a coalition government favorably disposed toward reunification with Communist North Vietnam."[74] By contrast with the 1959 resolution, the decision made at the Third Congress had been discussed in advance with both the Soviets and the Chinese. From the fall of 1959, the Soviet leaders displayed a new interest in the situation in Vietnam. During a visit to Beijing in early October 1959, Nikita Khrushchev evidently discussed with Ho the future strategy in South Vietnam, because, although the actual contents of their talk are still unknown, Soviet files on China contain a note referring to this meeting.[75]

An analysis written by the Southeast Asia Department of the Soviet Foreign Ministry in 1961 may provide some enlightenment as to what was discussed at the meeting in Beijing. The report reveals that, in the spring of

1960, the Soviet Union and China jointly advised the Lao Dong on how to proceed with political preparations for the Third Congress. In May 1960, the Lao Dong Central Committee consulted in Moscow with the Central Committees of the Soviet and Chinese Communist Parties to discuss the thesis in the Lao Dong political account for the Third Congress. Of particular interest was the section of the thesis dedicated to the struggle for the reunification of Vietnam, indicating an intention to expand armed struggle in South Vietnam with the purpose of overthrowing the Diem regime and creating liberated areas governed by the people in the South. The Vietnamese side underlined that the new strategy was simply a continuation of the war of resistance (1946–54), and the creation of liberated areas was "the form of gradually accomplishing the reunification of the Mother country."[76]

Neither Soviet nor Chinese leaders agreed with the offensive strategy proposed by the Vietnamese Communists. In Moscow, the Vietnamese comrades were told that, given the developing situation in Vietnam, it would be inexpedient to repudiate the slogan of peaceful reunification of Vietnam on the basis of the Geneva Agreement. According to the Soviet report, "the friends agreed to this and the opening address of the Lao Dong CC [Central Committee] at the Third Congress set forth a position envisaging a peaceful reunification of the country."[77] To the Soviets, it now seemed that the Lao Dong had accepted Soviet and Chinese advice, as the party leaders set forth a policy promoting peaceful reunification of the country, the only form of Vietnamese reunification the Soviet Union would accept in 1960.

As chapter 12 of the present volume demonstrates, during the first half of the 1970s, the flow of information from the Vietnamese Communists to the Soviet Union was patchy, sporadic, and incomplete, and on the Vietnamese side the relationship between the two countries was marked by considerable suspicion, even antagonism. This was merely a continuation of the pattern established by the early 1960s, when the Vietnamese Communists, despite their public professions, felt no commitment to follow the Soviet line. They continued to build up their military forces in the South, and by 1961 the situation had changed significantly. The rapid escalation of the South Vietnamese struggle alarmed Soviet leaders, who feared that the situation, if not contained, "could lead to a significant complication of the political situation in the region and transform South Vietnam into a critical center of international tension."[78] Although international strategic considerations and Sino-Soviet competition would eventually, in late 1964, lead the Soviets to back the DRV's cause and provide extremely substantial military, economic, and technical support to the country's war effort, from the time the DRV government decided to resume armed struggle, its relationship with the Soviet Union was nonetheless consistently difficult and strained, fraught with unresolved and perhaps irresolvable tensions.

Notes

1. Robert F. Randle, *Geneva 1954: The Settlement of the Indochinese War* (Princeton, N.J.: Princeton University Press, 1969), 571. This work contains a thorough analysis of the legal aspects of the 1954 Geneva Agreement.

2. George M. Kahin, *Intervention: How America Became Involved in Vietnam* (New York: Alfred A. Knopf, 1986), 93.

3. For a detailed analysis of the Soviet-Vietnamese relationship during the first months after Geneva see Mari Olsen, "Solidarity and National Revolution: The Soviet Union and the Vietnamese Communists, 1954–1960," Philol. thesis, published in *Defence Studies* (Institute for Defence Studies, Oslo), no. 4 (1997): chap. 1.

4. "Note from Kirill Novikov, Head of the Southeast Asia Department, Soviet Foreign Ministry [MID], to Foreign Minister Vjateslav Molotov, December 29, 1954," archival reference: fond (f.) 079 (Referentura po V'etnamy) opis (op.) 9, papka (p.) 6, delo (d.) 8, list (l., i.e., page) 51, Archives of the Foreign Policy of the Russian Federation (AVP RF).

5. "Deputy foreign minister V. V. Kuznetsov to Molotov, March 19, 1955," f. 079, op. 10, p. 9, d. 8, l. 4, AVP RF.

6. Randle, *Geneva 1954,* 552.

7. "Record of conversation, Temporary Chargé d'Affaires Soviet Embassy in Hanoi, Leonid Ivanovich Sokolov and member of the Lao Dong Central Committee (CC), Spokesman of the High Command of the PAVN, in Charge of Questions on the Fulfillment of the Cease-Fire Agreement, Hoang Anh, September 5, 1955," f. 079, op. 10, p. 9, d. 5, l. 137, AVP RF.

8. "Note from Molotov to the CC CPSU, May 19, 1955," f. 06 (Foreign Minister Molotov's archival fond), op. 14, p. 12, d. 170, ll. 1–2, AVP RF.

9. Soviet intelligence reports on U.S. plans "to establish military, political, and economic control over Indochina, and to exclude the influence of France there in the interest of American monopolies" can be traced back to mid-1953. See Vladislav Zubok, *Soviet Intelligence and the Cold War: The 'Small' Committee of Information, 1952–1953,* Cold War International History Project Working Paper 4 (Washington D.C.: Woodrow Wilson International Center for Scholars, 1992), 24.

10. "Note from Molotov to the CC CPSU, May 19, 1955," f. 06, op. 14, p. 12, d. 170, l. 1, AVP RF.

11. The meeting referred to must be the 7th Plenum on the Lao Dong Central Committee held in March 1955; see Carlyle A. Thayer, *War by Other Means: National Liberation and Revolution in Viet-Nam 1954–1960* (Sydney: Allen & Unwin, 1989), 26–33.

12. "Note from Molotov to the CC CPSU, May 19, 1955."

13. "Note from Molotov to the CC CPSU, May 19, 1955."

14. "Note from Molotov to the CC CPSU, May 19, 1955." The background for this note can probably be found in the yearly report from the Soviet ambassador to MID. I have not had access to such reports for 1954–60.

15. William J. Duiker, *The Communist Road to Power in Vietnam* (Boulder, Colo.: Westview Press, 1981), 174.

16. "MID to the Soviet Ambassadors to Hanoi and Paris, May 18, 1955," f. 079, op. 10, p. 9, d. 8, ll.12, 14, AVP RF. The telegram to Hanoi contains a question from MID on whether the Vietnamese need any help from the Soviets in this matter.

17. "Note from Molotov to the CC CPSU, May 19, 1955."

18. "Final Declaration of the Geneva Agreement §7"; see Randle, *Geneva 1954*, 571.

19. Ralph B. Smith, *An International History of the Vietnam War, Volume I: Revolution versus Containment, 1955–61* (New York: St. Martin's Press, 1983), 20.

20. Smith, *International History of the Vietnam War,* vol. 1, 20–21.

21. David L. Anderson, *Trapped by Success: The Eisenhower Administration and Vietnam, 1953–61* (New York: Columbia University Press, 1991), 124–26.

22. *Diplomaticheskii Slovar'* 3 (1986): 128.

23. Thayer, *War by Other Means,* 35–36.

24. "Ukazaniya k peregovoram s pravitel'stvennoy delegatsiey Demokraticheskoy Respubliki V'etnam" [Instructions for negotiations with the governmental delegation from the Democratic Republic of Vietnam], June–July 1955, f. 022, op. 8, p. 117, d. 30, ll. 12–21, AVP RF (hereafter "Instructions June–July 1955").

25. "Instructions June–July 1955," 12.

26. "Instructions June–July 1955," 12.

27. "Note from Andrei A. Gromyko, I. Kabanov, G. Zhukov and K. Koval to the CC CPSU, June 27, 1955," f. 06, op. 14, p. 12, d. 172, l. 13, AVP RF.

28. "Instructions June–July 1955," 13.

29. "Instructions June–July 1955," 13–14; telegram from MID to the Soviet Ambassador to Beijing, May 1955, f. 079, op. 10, p. 9, d. 8, l. 28, AVP RF.

30. "Instructions June–July 1955," 14.

31. Smith, *International History of the Vietnam War,* vol. 1, 37.

32. "Instructions June–July 1955," 16. For the Vietnamese discussion see Thayer, *War by Other Means,* 27–32, 40–43, 46–48.

33. "Instructions June–July 1955," 16.

34. Thayer, *War by Other Means,* 49.

35. Smith, *International History of the Vietnam War,* vol. 1, 62.

36. Smith, *International History of the Vietnam War,* vol. 1, 62.

37. Smith, *International History of the Vietnam War,* vol. 1, 62–64.

38. "Record of Conversation, Adviser at the Soviet Embassy Leonid I. Sokolov and Vice Chairman of the Lien Viet CC Hoang Quoc Viet, January 30–31, 1955," f. 079, op. 10, p. 9, d. 5, ll.19-26, AVP RF.

39. Thayer, *War by Other Means,* 43.

40. "Record of Conversation, L. I. Sokolov and Hoang Ahn, September 5, 1955," f. 079, op. 10, p. 9, d. 5, ll. 135–38, AVP RF.

41. "Instructions June–July 1955," 12–21; by 1955 Chinese–North Vietnamese military cooperation was already well organized. When established on April 17, 1950, the Chinese Military Advisory Group (CMAG) consisted of advisers who could assist the PAVN headquarters, three full divisions, and finally an officers' training school. Altogether, the CMAG would number 281 people, of whom 79 were advisers and their assistants. See Qiang Zhai, *China and the Vietnam Wars, 1950–75* (Chapel Hill: University of North Carolina Press, 2000), 19.

42. "Telegram from General Antonov to Deputy Foreign Minister V.A. Zorin, June 10, 1955," f. 079, op. 10, p. 9, d. 8, l. 32, AVP RF.

43. Telegram from General Antonov to Deputy Foreign Minister V.A. Zorin, June 10, 1955.

44. Zhai, *China and the Vietnam Wars,* 74.

45. Zhai, *China and the Vietnam Wars,* 69–70.

46. For an estimate of Soviet assistance to India see Ramesh Thakur and Carlyle Thayer, *Soviet Relations with India and Vietnam* (London: Macmillan, 1992).

47. "Note from V. V. Kuznetsov to Molotov, January 11, 1955," f. 079, op. 10, p. 10, d. 15, ll. 1–2, AVP RF.

48. Zhai, *China and the Vietnam Wars,* 71.

49. Zhai, *China and the Vietnam Wars;* Chen Jian, *Mao's China and the Cold War* (Chapel Hill: University of North Carolina Press, 2001); Donald S. Zagoria, *Vietnam Triangle: Moscow, Peking, Hanoi* (New York: Pegasus, 1967).

50. Adam B. Ulam, *Expansion and Coexistence: Soviet Foreign Policy, 1917–1973* (Fort Worth: Holt, Rinehart and Winston, 1974), 558–60.

51. Zagoria, *Vietnam Triangle.*

52. "Note from V. A. Zorin to the CC CPSU, September 23, 1955," f. 079, op. 10, p. 9, d. 8, l. 57, AVP RF.

53. "Record of Conversation, L. I. Sokolov and Chinese Ambassador to the DRV, Luo Guibo, December 8, 1955," f. 079, op. 10, p. 9, d. 5, AVP RF.

54. Chen, *Mao's China and the Cold War,* 206; Zhai, *China and the Vietnam Wars,* 74.

55. "Note from Molotov to CC CPSU, August 10, 1955," f. 06, op.14, p. 12, d. 170, l. 16, AVP RF. "In the connection that the South Vietnamese government has not yet answered the suggestion from the DRV proposed on 19 July this year to start consultations for the elections in Vietnam, MID USSR thinks it expedient to and opportune for the DRV government to turn to the two co-chairmen with this question."

56. Smith, *International History of the Vietnam War,* vol. 1, 62.

57. Thayer, *War by Other Means,* 21–23, 37–40, 48–49.

58. Gabriel Kolko, *Anatomy of a War* (New York: Pantheon Books, 1985), 85; Anderson, *Trapped by Success,* 125–28; Thayer, *War by Other Means,* 48–49.

59. "Record of Conversation, Head of the SEAD in MID, Boris Mikailovich Volkov and Charge d'Affaires at the DRV Embassy in the USSR, to Kyang Day, January 19, 1956," f. 06, op. 15a, p. 28, d. 100, ll. 1–3, AVP RF.

60. "Note to the CC CPSU, January 31, 1956," f. 079, op. 11, p. 14, d. 16, ll. 27–29, AVP RF.

61. "Soviet Embassy in DRV to MID, February 10, 1956," f. 079, op. 11, p. 14, d. 16, ll. 41–50, AVP RF; the quotation is on page 49.

62. "Record of Conversation, V. V. Kuznetsov and Lao Dong General Secretary Truong Chinh, February 28, 1956," f. 079, op. 11, p. 13, d. 2, l. 3, AVP RF.

63. Ulam, *Expansion and Coexistence,* 9.

64. For an introduction to the realist approach to Soviet foreign policy, see Frederic J. Fleron and Erik P. Hoffmann, "Introduction," in *Soviet Foreign Policy: Classic and Contemporary Issues,* ed. Frederic J. Fleron et al. (New York: Aldine de Gruyter, 1991).

65. Record of conversation between Soviet Ambassador M.V. Zimyanin and Nguyen Duy Trinh, April 27, 1956, f. 079, op. 11, p. 13, d. 5, ll. 84-95, AVP RF.

66. "Record of Conversation between M. V. Zimyanin and Pham Hung, Ung Van

Khiem, and Than Hum Truong, April 20, 1956," f. 079, op, 11, p. 13, d. 5, ll. 75–77, AVP RF.

67. "Record of Conversation between Luo Guibo, the Chinese ambassador to Hanoi, and M. V. Zimjanin, the Soviet ambassador to Hanoi, January 30, 1957," f. 079 op. 12 p. 17 d. 5, l. 48, AVP RF.

68. On April 15, 1958, Pham Van Dong informed Soviet ambassador L. I. Sokolov that the party had appointed two additional deputy prime ministers to strengthen the government, Politburo members Truong Chinh and Pham Hung. Speaking of Pham Hung's appointment Dong said: "It has to be taken into account that the appointment of Pham Hung, who is a southerner, and has worked for a long time in South Vietnam, calls for certain political consequences in plans for the fight for a peaceful reunification of the country." See "Record of Conversation between Sokolov and Pham Van Dong, April 15, 1958," f. 079, op. 13, p. 20, d. 8, l. 95, AVP RF; and "Record of Conversations between Second Secretary at the Soviet Embassy G. Kadumov and Official from the DRV Ministry of State Security 'Thum,' April 4, 1958," f. 079, op. 13, p. 20, d. 10, ll. 202–3. "Thum" was most probably either an informant or a messenger. He might himself have been one of the regrouped Southerners who preferred armed struggle. The word "Thum" is not a Vietnamese name. The closest English translation of the Vietnamese word "thùm" is "stinking" or "smelling bad." (The ideas of Thum's possible role in this record of conversation originate from e-mail correspondence with the Vietnamese historian Nguyen Vu Tung on September 24, 1996.)

69. "K polozheniyo v Yoshnom V'etname" [On the situation in South Vietnam], an analysis by Acting Head of the Southeast Asia Department in MID Nikolai Moljakov, December 22, 1961, f. 079, op. 16, p. 32, d. 20, ll. 102–8, AVP RF (hereafter "On the Situation in South Vietnam"). On the last page of the document was added: "The report has been based on materials from MID, the General Staff of the Soviet Army, and KGB by the Council of Ministers"; for Hanoi's decisions in 1959–60, see King C. Chen, "Hanoi's Three Decisions and the Escalation of the Vietnam War," *Political Science Quarterly* 90, no. 2 (1975): 244–46.

70. "Record of Conversation between Ambassador Sokolov and Ho Chi Minh, January 16, 17, and 19, 1959," f. 079, op. 14, p. 23, d. 5, l. 24, AVP RF.

71. "Record of Conversation between Soviet Embassy Adviser A. M. Popov and Nguyen Duy Trinh, March 12, 1959," f. 070, op. 14, p. 24, d. 7, l. 168, AVP RF.

72. "Record of Conversation between Ambassador Sokolov and Le Duan, April 15, 1959," f. 079, op. 14, p. 23, d. 5, ll. 102–7, AVP RF.

73. "Record of Conversation between A. M. Popov and Truong Chinh, May 21, 1959," f. 079, op. 14, p. 24, d. 7, ll. 265–68, AVP RF.

74. Chen, "Hanoi's Three Decisions," 240.

75. "Note from Zimyanin to Malin, October 16, 1959," f. 0100 (China), op. 52, p. 442, d. 5, l. 52, AVP RF. The note confirms that a meeting between Khrushchev, Mao, Kim Il Sung, and Ho Chi Minh took place in Beijing on October 2, 1959, and that the discussion evolved around the future strategy in South Vietnam. See also *Pravda,* October 1, 1959.

76. "On the Situation in South Vietnam," 104.

77. "On the Situation in South Vietnam," 104.

78. "On the Situation in South Vietnam," 104.

3

Opportunities Lost?
Kennedy, China, and Vietnam

Noam Kochavi

The United States and China conducted an important relationship during the Kennedy years. The China factor figured significantly in John F. Kennedy's halting progress toward détente with the Soviet Union, in his quest for a nuclear test ban, and in his handling of Vietnam affairs. Moreover, the notion of a critical contest with the Chinese over developing-world allegiances both

This chapter, which summarizes the author's Ph.D. dissertation, could not have been completed without the encouragement and support he received from a number of people. First and foremost, he is grateful to his dissertation adviser, Ronald W. Pruessen of the University of Toronto, who supervised every stage of the writing with immense care and helped him clarify ideas and improve the writing and whose suggestions, criticism, advice, and encouragement were extremely valuable. The author also thanks Yitzhak Shichor and Ellis Joffe, who read parts of the manuscript, and Thomas P. Bernstein, Gordon Chang, Roderick MacFarquhar, Robert J. McMahon, Leopoldo Nuti, Gustav Schmidt, and Zhai Qiang, who all kindly shared materials and insights. A number of China watchers in the John F. Kennedy administration who consented to an interview or an exchange of letters complemented this; these include Roger Hilsman, James C. Thomson, and Allen S. Whiting.

127

fueled and colored official interest in the Asian and African arena.[1] For Beijing's part, as suggested in chapter 1 of the present volume, its perception that the United States was behaving imperiously reinforced Mao Zedong's hawkish predilections. In addition, Beijing almost certainly welcomed the opportunity to use friction with Washington to divert domestic attention away from the economic catastrophes that had befallen the country.[2] Until the appearance of my recent book, no full-length study, however, had made the Kennedy administration's China policy its principal focus.

The web of rashomonesque reminiscences and sharply competing interpretations surrounding Kennedy's performance enhances the value of inquiry into this topic. Writing on this subject has mirrored the familiar pattern of Kennedy historiography. As the historian Nancy B. Tucker notes, early eulogizers of Kennedy's "Camelot" insisted that, had the young president lived, he would have repaired relations with China in his second term.[3] This corresponded to the picture of an open-minded Kennedy who had proven himself extremely capable of "growing," learning from the recurring crises he experienced, and steering toward a more conciliatory stance in the handling of the Cold War.[4]

A later school of historians, conversely, posits a president who was more inclined to obsession than growth, in the China sphere as elsewhere. According to Thomas G. Paterson, Warren I. Cohen, James Fetzer, and particularly Gordon Chang, Kennedy rigidly "believed the Chinese to be fanatics and feared the atomic bomb that they were in the process of developing." To their mind, he epitomized an action-prone quest for victory, imbued with ethnocentricity and insensitive to the limits of American power.[5] Thus, utilizing newly available evidence to review Kennedy's China record may shed light on his overall performance as president.

Indeed, Camelot's troubled encounter with Beijing proves instructive in many ways. This chapter presents some principal themes of my study, starting with the primary policy shapers, expanding its focus to assess the administration's broad performance, and ending in an attempt to link an individual-level spotlight on Kennedy with a systemic-level appraisal of the conflict management strategies he employed. Finally, the chapter highlights the China dimension in the making of Vietnam policy during the Kennedy years.

Kennedy's Ambiguous Conduct

In keeping with other recent studies, the China–Vietnam policy sphere profiles a Kennedy more complex and ambiguous than either his hagiographers or his early critics have allowed. The president emerges as a man of many guises, whose disparate characteristics made for an unpredictable foreign policy personality.[6] On the one hand, he comes out as a shortsighted leader who often fell hostage to the Cold War and to the image of a uniformly predatory China. Inclined to obsession, he also slighted the obstacles to winning Asian (and by 1963, Soviet) support for an anti-Chinese crusade.

At times, however, the president rose to the challenge of astute statecraft. Showing clearer vision, he became quite aware of Washington's finite capacity to shape events on the Chinese mainland to its liking. With the possible exception of a preventive strike against China's budding nuclear installations, he was also reluctant to risk military confrontation with Beijing, overruling the advice of some of his more hawkish aides. Likewise, it is not impossible that on the eve of his assassination, Kennedy was converted to the notion of a China policy departure during his second term. Finally, in leadership style, a fragmentary and reactive pattern of policymaking pervaded both the conventional and the creative modes of his China conduct.

The record strongly suggests that, at least until his last months in office, Kennedy held firm to a stock of instincts and preconceptions about the China sphere. This was particularly the case with his view of the Chinese Communist regime as repugnant, unitarily bent on expansion, and posing an unacceptable challenge to the international order and the norms sustaining it. The Taiwan Strait crisis of the summer of 1962 triggered a demonstration of just how blind Kennedy was to evidence at odds with this image. Even as the two sides moved to defuse the crisis, and as the notion that China's cautious behavior belied its bluster gained ever increasing currency within the administration, a puzzled Kennedy wondered behind closed doors why Beijing accepted the Laos settlement, "since Communism traditionally pushed outward whenever it could."[7]

Partly consequent upon his belief in the domino theory, and partly a function of a certain ethnocentrism, Kennedy's grim assessment of the Chinese threat was also informed by twin and rather constant concerns: China's nuclear potential, and its standing as a source of both inspiration and support for wars of national liberation. The nuclear preoccupation almost certainly drove Kennedy to overestimate Moscow's willingness to participate, actively or passively, in strong measures to check China's nuclear progress.[8] In similar vein, the guerrilla concern contributed to a certain wishful thinking on his part as to the feasibility of establishing an anti-Chinese order in Asia and the Pacific.[9]

For Kennedy, another stimulus to project firmness derived from domestic politics: his perception of the China lobby's potency and of a public solidly adverse to changing the status quo on China. Given the narrow plurality of Kennedy's election, the difficulties he experienced in prevailing over Congress, and the still vivid memory of the Democratic Party's trials and tribulations generated by "who lost China" charges, one can understand Kennedy's propensity to tread cautiously on account of perceived domestic constraints. To understand is not to accept, however. As both Tucker and the political scientist Leonard Kusnitz suggest, after the Cuban missile crisis, Kennedy was probably unscrupulous enough to foster an image of a fearsome, irrational China as a means of satisfying his country's prevailing emotional xenophobia and thereby allowing Washington the freedom to seek working relations with what appeared more stable and constructive leaders in Moscow.[10] Still more disconcerting is the evidence that, more often than not, the public was more malleable to presidential leadership than Kennedy assessed it to be.[11]

These domestic constraints, whether real or imagined, evidently propelled Kennedy to give a secret guarantee to Jiang Jieshi (Chiang Kai-shek) to exercise the American veto pledge in the UN Security Council, if this were to prove essential to barring Communist China's admission to the United Nations. Not even John Foster Dulles, with all his fire and brimstone, had been willing to make such a commitment.[12]

Yet, with the possible exception of an antinuclear preemptive strike, Kennedy did not usually allow his combative impulses to govern his policy decisions. In particular, his endeavor to hold the fire-breathing Jiang at arm's length was even more unambiguous than Dwight D. Eisenhower's. Several deeply ingrained convictions underlay this disposition. Like most of his predecessors, Kennedy found objectionable the Guomindang's domestic American political clout. On the very day that he initiated the aforementioned veto pledge, for example, Kennedy wryly observed that "Adenauer, De Gaulle and Chiang Kai-shek seemed to want to operate as makers of U.S. policy and not as allies."[13]

Unlike some military officials, Kennedy also never toyed seriously with Jiang's contention that, together with the deepening Sino-Soviet rift, China's internal dislocation presented a golden opportunity for regaining the mainland.[14] During his tenure, Kennedy proved mindful of how failures to grasp the adversary's capabilities and intentions had figured in the outbreak of wars and international crises throughout the twentieth century.[15] More specifically, even before 1960, Kennedy had recognized the paucity of solid information on mainland conditions, and while in power he became acutely cognizant of this.[16] Palpably aware of this very factor's salience in the Bay of Pigs debacle, Kennedy joined other officials in citing this as one reason to adopt a circumspect approach toward China's economic predicament. Always careful to shore up his domestic fences, he was also not too proud to seek to turn to political advantage the gaps in the Chinese intelligence picture. Under his inspiration, American officials consistently challenged their Guomindang counterparts to produce solid intelligence to bear out the Chinese Nationalist theory that a mere spark would suffice to ignite a fire in the Chinese Communist hayrick.[17]

Prodding the Nationalists aside, through early 1962 at least, Kennedy significantly failed to translate these insights into a major initiative to improve intelligence coverage of Communist China. The China intelligence field—which was understaffed, underfunded, and impeded by a flimsy bureaucratic infrastructure—throughout 1961 suffered neglect, an omission for which Kennedy should shoulder much of the blame.[18] Decisionmakers have consistently played a much greater role throughout the intelligence process than is generally recognized; their oft-unspoken personal preferences help set the agenda for both collection and analysis. This may have been particularly true under Kennedy. Promoting a multiple-counsel system, he depended on conveying a sense of purpose to synthesize the system into a collegial and functioning whole.[19] Arguably, on the China intelligence front, Kennedy conversely offered little guidance. Hence, diversity within the policymaking community bred disintegration rather than constructive collaboration.

The reasons behind this lapse remain enigmatic, partly due to Kennedy's propensity to leave some of his closest aides ignorant of the coordinates of his China perspective.[20] But several preliminary and complementary explanations suggest themselves. First, when the internal crisis in China peaked, other items, like the Berlin crisis, crowded Kennedy's desk, won his attention, and sapped executive energies. Second, the evidence corroborates McGeorge Bundy's remark that, with the exception of such strategic considerations as China's nuclear potential or the state of Sino-Soviet relations, Chinese matters per se did not attract Kennedy's enthusiasm, a disposition that his perception of the domestic climate as restrictive evidently reinforced. Third, this tendency meshes with the observation of several Kennedy hands that he was prone to postpone decisions on major issues where results would not be immediately apparent.[21]

In fact, the intelligence lapse of 1961 furnished but the clearest example of the fragmented and reactive nature of overall China policymaking under Kennedy. This phenomenon requires elucidation, all the more so because it has recently surfaced as a hallmark of Kennedy's modus operandi in not just the Chinese but also the Italian context.[22]

Between 1961 and 1963, the charge that China policy lacked coherence and planning was a consistent theme among most "revisionist" officials, notably Undersecretary of State (until December 1961) Chester Bowles and Hong Kong consul general Marshall Green.[23] Bowles quite cogently pointed out one reason for this. In a late 1963 letter to Roger Hilsman, director of the Department of State's Bureau of Intelligence and Research, he lamented that "[the reactive style is] a built-up liability of democracies in general, i.e. the tendency to avoid forward planning because it is too controversial and leaks may cause embarrassment. As a result we react to events as they occur and then add all the reactions together and call it policy which henceforth must be defended against all comers."[24] Moreover, at least one study argues that this mode was not unique to the Kennedy era but rather was a standard feature of U.S.-China policy from Harry Truman through the Richard Nixon "shock."[25]

One still wonders what accounted for the Kennedy New Frontier's deep fragmentation on China policy. One cluster of explanations stresses linkage politics. Perceiving their domestic standing as precarious and obsessed with leaks, administration principals trod carefully and took extra pains to compartmentalize information, for example, through the establishment of "eyes only" communication channels—with Ambassador Jacob Beam in Warsaw in August 1961, with Central Intelligence Agency station chief Ray Cline in Taipei later in the year, and with Undersecretary of State for Political Affairs Averell W. Harriman in July 1963.[26] That procedure may well have facilitated diplomatic negotiations, but it only increased confusion outside the information loop. Another cluster emphasizes Kennedy's personal propensity to juggle contingencies and avoid choosing between policy alternatives, a characteristic illustrated by the protracted debates within the administration on Vietnam (see below).

Multilayered bureaucratic competition also obviously played a role. The year 1961, in particular, saw duels between outside talent and veteran Foreign Service officers, as well as a contest for the president's ear between Europeanists such as Undersecretary of State George Ball and Dean Acheson, and Asianists, among them Representative to the United Nations Adlai E. Stevenson, Bowles, and Deputy Special Assistant for National Security Affairs (until December 1961) Walt W. Rostow. State's malfunctioning during that year added fuel to these fires, contributing to the relative eclipse or elimination of most of these advisers.[27]

Blame also attaches to an apparent structural flaw in the American form of government—the lack of an effective method to transfer knowledge and experience from one administration to another. As Robert McNamara cogently observed in retrospect, "In parliamentary systems, a new government's ministers have usually served as opposition shadow ministers for several years before they take office. . . . The meeting between the Eisenhower and Kennedy teams was a poor substitute for such training."[28] A related contributory factor was the shaky transformation from Eisenhower's highly structured policymaking mechanisms to a more informal process heavily tilted toward the White House staff. Consequently, jurisdictional boundaries were often blurred and ill defined (e.g., Robert Komer of the National Security Council presided over too vast a geographical "empire of Darius").[29] Finally, Kennedy's "ad hoc" mechanism and his accent on brevity of expression, while a hedge against stifling conformity, lacked coordination and control, and emphasized current developments at the expense of planning.[30] The task of assigning relative importance to these factors awaits future research.

The remaining conclusions regarding Kennedy's style cover more familiar ground, and hence may be recounted more briefly. First, China policy provides a ringing case in point for political scientists' Levering and Kern's assertion that, contrary to conventional judgment and popular imagery, the president was more influenced by press opinion than a manipulative charmer of it.[31] Second, Kennedy tended to make some of his most important decisions "off the record."[32] Third, the related—and celebrated—Kennedy obsession with leaks was especially pronounced in the China sphere. According to Kennedy's secretary of state, Dean Rusk, the president capped their seminal (and unrecorded) May 1961 tête-à-tête in the White House with this admonition: "What's more, Mr. Secretary, I don't want to read in the *Washington Post* and the *New York Times* that the State Department is thinking about a change in China policy."[33]

The Policymaking Community

Himself a champion of confidentiality in diplomatic affairs,[34] Rusk implemented to the letter these cautionary words. Recently declassified documents corroborate Rusk's later inference that, under conditions of unbreakable secrecy, he was at certain points willing to engage in "hidden-hand" diplomacy to test China's motives and aims. He insisted on either extending the feeler himself or informing only his most trusted subordinates.[35]

On balance, Rusk seems indeed to have charted a more sophisticated and nuanced course than his "revisionist" critics have allowed.[36] His hostility toward the Chinese Communist leaders undoubtedly ran deep, not least because of the Korean War carnage. In June 1962, for instance, he confessed to the British that the administration felt "much closer to the East Germans than to the Chinese Communists."[37] Nonetheless, as a fascinated and quite informed student of modern China, he apparently came to power without a set agenda for China policy,[38] and thereafter he alternated between two divergent strategies prevalent within the State Department. In the summers of both 1961 and 1962, he endorsed discreet probes in the hope of nurturing moderate forces within Beijing's ruling circle. Other times saw him favoring the "pressure-wedge" logic, which prescribed the ostracizing of Beijing as a means of deepening the Sino-Soviet rift. The Rusk pendulum tilted most strongly in this latter direction for most of 1963, after the Cuban missile crisis and the Sino-Indian War discredited in official Washington the notion that China's moderate actions belied its rhetorical bluster.[39] The records leaves it unverifiable whether Rusk's hurried clearance of the Hilsman speech of December 1963 indicates his reversion to the more probing line.[40]

Yet a vexing puzzle regarding the Rusk–Kennedy dynamic casts doubt upon the validity of this analysis. Virtually all previous renditions of Rusk's concept of proper secretary of statesmanship have stressed his determination to publicly project solid alignment between himself and the president.[41] Thus, it is quite inconceivable that Rusk would have executed or authorized the various probes into China's intentions without Kennedy's knowledge. Lacking solid evidence, one may cautiously surmise that Kennedy and Rusk tacitly agreed on presidential plausible deniability—namely, that Kennedy would turn a blind eye to Rusk's discreet approaches and deny any knowledge of them if the issue surfaced to burn Rusk's fingers.

How well did their intelligence experts serve Kennedy and Rusk? The intelligence community registered a patently uneven record on China. Any attempt to draw up a balance sheet should acknowledge the formidable barriers China presented as an intelligence target: the cryptic nature of the Chinese media, Chinese disinformation efforts, the depth of cultural and ideological estrangement, and the impossibility of deriving insights from direct Sino-American communication.[42] Yet Washington's initial handling left much to be desired. Flimsy infrastructure combined with weak executive guidance and cognitive closure to hamper intelligence work.[43] The situation improved somewhat over time, with increased allocation of experienced personnel (and probably funds), and as intelligence doctrine veered away from the orthodox mode toward a greater sensitivity to the influence of American behavior on Chinese policy.

Intelligence performance varied markedly in different contexts. Chinese domestic affairs proved especially slippery terrain, despite some close calls on intraleadership trends. Most glaring was the failure to appreciate the scope of China's domestic dislocation. As for the task of imputing Chinese intentions, experts groped in the dark, falling victim to many of the pitfalls surrounding that difficult mission.[44] Moments of clearer vision did exist, however, not least because of fruitful collaboration with London. One conspicuous illustration was the sober advice producers offered on the limited scope of Beijing's autumn 1962 Himalayan thrust.[45] Moving to the strategic realm, China watchers scored an inadvertent success in predicting the timing of the Chinese nuclear detonation.[46] The most unblemished achievement was in monitoring the Sino-Soviet rift, largely the product of a dedicated effort by Ray Cline's task force (see below). Even here, however, producers conformed to the prevailing atmosphere at the apex of power and, until 1963, hesitated to declare the rift irreversible.[47]

The China intelligence theater also featured a wide array of engaging actors, both perceptive and opinionated. Cline in particular exhibited a fateful amalgam of these traits. On the one hand, he deserves much credit for sensitizing consumers to the undue neglect of the China intelligence scene and for timely and quite accurate coverage of Sino-Soviet trends. On the other, as a consequence of his stint in Taipei, Cline allowed himself to become a Guomindang apologist.[48] As for the directors of the Central Intelligence Agency, Allen Dulles was apparently too enamored of clandestine operations, too engrossed in the slew of recurrent crises of 1961, and too injured by the Bay of Pigs debacle to focus on either the Chinese scene or the tottering China intelligence effort. It fell to John McCone to implement some essential reforms. A strong "worst-case" bias, however, clouded McCone's judgment. Though he was attentive to compelling evidence that the People's Liberation Army's was weakening, he was still inclined, for example, to presume during the third Strait crisis that the Chinese Communists were bent on attacking Taiwan, and until well into 1963 he also doubted that the Sino-Soviet rift would endure.[49]

No such worst-case bias distorted the China outlook of Marshall Green. His competent guidance helped the Hong Kong Consulate outperform any other American intelligence organ during the latter part of Kennedy's tenure.[50]

This calm appraisal of China's capabilities and intentions constitutes the distinguishing feature of "revisionist" thinking during the Kennedy years.

Ebbing and flowing in currency within revisionist circles, this attitude peaked in the summer of 1962 and again in the administration's closing months. Having been predicated on the premise of China's relative weakness vis-à-vis the United States, it departed from the alarmist line that had previously dominated much American China policy from at least the Korean War onward. Beyond this unifying thread, one may discern three schools in the revisionist group, each evincing a markedly different tenor in its concept of Sino-American relations.

The first school is *visionary revisionism.* Epitomized in purest form by Walt W. Rostow, this strand had a rather expansive sense of China's susceptibility to American power and resolution. A certain hubris permeated this approach. Rostow evidently believed that the United States was exceptionally capable of exporting the gospel of economic and social progress. This belief contributed to what Nick Cullather has termed (albeit in the Philippine context) *Illusions of Influence.*[51] Rostow presumed, for example, that the Chinese Communists had been so demoralized as to shed their pride and acquiesce, as part of a food deal, in what amounted virtually to a Pax Americana in the Far East in general and in Southeast Asia in particular.[52] In July 1962, Rostow explicitly urged this point upon the president's military representative, Maxwell D. Taylor, a key figure in forging Southeast Asian policy: "The Chinese [domestic] situation should strengthen our will to pursue a policy which would deny South Vietnam, Thailand— and Laos, too—to the Communists over the indefinite future; and we should pursue this policy with inner confidence."[53]

The second school is *containment without isolation* (or *temperate revisionism*). This strand found articulate spokesmen in, for instance, Allen Whiting, James Thomson, ambassador to India John Galbraith, and ambassador to Japan Edwin O. Reischauer. Far more than Rostow, these China enthusiasts were alert to both the salience of fierce nationalist pride in Chinese Communist identity and the pervasive image among Asian elites of the United States as domineering.[54]

Arguably, the pertinent literature has thus far overlooked the degree to which this school of thought broke with established American practice. The historian Ronald W. Pruessen and others have persuasively demonstrated that, with all the complexity of its China posture, the Eisenhower administration consistently followed a zero-sum approach to Beijing, defying the People's Republic's quest for a place in the sun. Albeit to a limited degree, Eisenhower and Dulles could empathize with Soviet concerns over

German unification, for example, and attempt to assuage Moscow's anxieties in this regard. They never evinced any comparable respect for China's concerns and interests. As Pruessen argues, over and again the formulators of policy sought to "create a regional system in which American advantages would be maximized and China's role and opportunities would be drastically curtailed."[55]

Under Kennedy, Rostow—as well as such hard-liners as Cline and U.S. Air Force chief of staff General Curtis E. LeMay—perpetuated this tradition.[56] The temperate revisionists charted an alternative course, mixing deterrence with nonconfrontational modes of managing Sino-American relations. In fact, in its most sophisticated manifestations, this school of thought favored the very "beyond deterrence" strategies identified by the political scientists Richard N. Lebow and Janice G. Stein, namely, "reassurance through reciprocity"; "reassurance through self-restraint"; and "reassurance through the development of informal, even tacit, 'norms of competition.'"[57] In other words, the temperate revisionists conformed closely to the prescription for de-escalation proposed by the political scientist Robert Jervis:

> States should try to construct a policy of deterrence which will not set off spirals of hostility if existing political differences are in fact bridgeable; the policy should be designed to conciliate without running the risk that the other side, if it is aggressive, will be emboldened to attack. Such a policy requires the state to combine firmness, threats, and apparent willingness to fight with reassurances, promises, and a credible willingness to consider the other side's interests.[58]

The third school is *conditional containment without isolation* (or *educative revisionism*). The somewhat disjointed revisionist endeavor finally settled, in the summer of 1963, on a more coherent drive, informally dubbed the "Hilsman Project," which borrowed from both "visionary revisionism" and "temperate revisionism." Advocating most of the specific remedies championed by the "temperate" school, the Hilsman Project still contained a heavy dosage of an educative element. The notion that China would have to learn to behave before it could be rewarded and thereby become less isolated betokened the premise that Washington was entitled to set the norms and rules associated with the relationship. In short, the Hilsman Project, rather than reflecting a concept of equitable Sino-American relations, revealed a quest for primacy.[59]

Kennedy's Contradictory Legacy

In the absence of conclusive proof as to Kennedy's China posture on the eve of his assassination, at present it remains impossible to determine just how influential the revisionist effort ultimately was in terms of shaping the administration's China policy. Indubitably, however, the administration left a dual and contradictory legacy.

On the one hand, the concept of a China policy departure gained official legitimacy during the Kennedy years. Detailed blueprints took firm hold within a segment of the foreign policy bureaucracy. The Lyndon Johnson administration elaborated on these blueprints. It might have even built upon them to embark on bolder and more innovative policies—had the Vietnam War not so sapped Washington's energies and abilities, and had not the Chinese themselves plunged into the destructive Cultural Revolution.[60] Moreover, in a few isolated cases the Kennedy years saw the evolution of an incipient Sino-American capacity to reduce mutual tensions. An admixture of deterrence and tacit understandings proved conducive, for instance, to a precarious draw in Laos—an area, to be sure, Kennedy (and possibly the Chinese) deemed neither crucial nor suitable for a military showdown.[61] The Taiwan Strait provided the scene for a more lasting exercise in conflict management. Unambiguous signaling through the Warsaw channel, serving to overcome a multitude of hitherto mutually misperceived signals, helped deflate the third Strait crisis.[62] To a degree, then, this study affirms James Thomson's assertion that the seeds of the "Nixon shock" were sown in the Kennedy era.[63]

Examined from a shorter-range perspective, however, the Kennedy tenure only added fuel to the fire of Sino-American confrontation. In particular, the Hilsman speech evidently impressed Mao and his colleagues less than did the Test Ban Treaty, which accentuated the sense of encirclement and vulnerability afflicting Beijing's psyche. The clouds gathered most ominously in Vietnam.

Given this volume's focus, it seems imperative to elaborate briefly on how the China factor figured in the making of Vietnam policy during the Kennedy years. The last decade has witnessed both a massive declassification of pertinent documentation and a proliferation of studies touching on Kennedy's responsibility for America's growing involvement in the conflict. In the words of the historian Robert J. McMahon, "Most historians agree that Kennedy's decisions brought incremental, but not dramatic, escalation and that he left his successors with stronger, but still limited, ties to South Vietnam. They differ on almost all other critical questions."[64]

The scholarly controversy is especially pronounced regarding Kennedy's own performance. The disparate, often emotionally charged verdicts have depicted the president as a persistent Cold Warrior who was blinded principally by false confidence that he had understood the nature of Vietnamese insurgency; a schemer highly instrumental in establishing the ill-fated norms of "adhocracy," superficiality, and duplicity; and a consistent voice against committing ground troops to Vietnam, who played a Janus-faced game for the perceived sake of domestic political survival as the 1964 elections approached but would have opted for disengagement had he lived to win re-election.[65] Though not aspiring to tackle the Kennedy enigma in its totality, my study argues that China policy considerations shaped Kennedy's behavior to a greater extent than has hitherto been recognized.

Concerns over China played a major and complex role in Camelot's decisionmaking during the Vietnam War. On the one hand, fears of the influence of the revolutionary doctrines of Mao—grounded more in preconception than in solid evidence[66]—probably encouraged the New Frontiersmen to involve Washington more deeply in Vietnam than leaders would otherwise have considered worthwhile.[67] The desire to avert a replay of the electoral injuries wreaked on Truman and Acheson by "who lost China" charges worked in the same direction.[68] On the other hand, this very vision of a China poised to dominate the region injected some caution into the administration's conduct.[69] In particular, Kennedy's reluctance to introduce combat forces stemmed in large part from his concern lest Beijing be provoked to retaliate in kind, as it had done in the Korean War.[70]

Finally, despite his image of China's preponderant influence, Kennedy and most of his advisers did not consider the Middle Kingdom a legitimate partner for a negotiated regional settlement. In the summers of both 1961 and 1962, Washington did extend hesitant feelers to plumb Beijing's regional intentions. Yet, at the first signs of Chinese firmness, Kennedy reverted to a zero-sum conceptualization of the Sino-American position in Vietnam.[71] On this last score, it is not impossible that toward the very end of his tenure Kennedy entertained second thoughts. The evidence is inconclusive, but by November 1963, Kennedy may have so despaired of the Vietnam enterprise as to contemplate some modus vivendi with Beijing.[72] By that stage, however, China's leaders were themselves set on a con-

frontational course, not least because of Washington's heightened presence
in the area and Kennedy's previous rhetorical blasts.[73]

Clearly, Kennedy bears some responsibility for the Sino-American impasse, in Vietnam and elsewhere. Cultural arrogance colored the president's
double-edged anxiety over China's nuclear and guerrilla potential.[74] Most
important, at least until the autumn of 1963, Kennedy personified a deci-
sionmaker so obsessed with the objective of deterrence as to overlook the
"security dilemma," failing to appreciate the degree to which his deterrence
policies acquired the nature of a self-fulfilling mechanism, stoking apprehension and hostility on the Chinese side, and thus contributing to an escalatory spiral.[75]

Evidently, Kennedy evaded few if any of the pitfalls inherent in a spiral
condition. A preoccupation with credibility permeated his China policy.
Paying close attention to dramatic events and manifesting a worst-case bias,
he exaggerated Chinese hostility. Like many in Washington, for example,
he construed the Himalayan war of October-November 1962 as proof of
Beijing's bellicosity, even though some officials were not blind to both
Delhi's provocations and the limited nature of Beijing's thrust.[76] Moreover,
less dramatic developments, such as the dismantling of the "Great Leap Forward," suggesting the possibility of a shift away from radicalism, largely
escaped Kennedy's grasp.[77] Finally, Kennedy patently failed to empathize
with Mao; that is, he tended to pay insufficient attention to constraints and
pressures faced by the Chinese leadership, including those generated by
Washington's own actions, evincing little understanding, for example, of
Mao's fear of nuclear blackmail by the two superpowers.[78]

One feature of Kennedy's China record stands out as the most dysfunc-
tional of all. Throughout most of his thousand days, cognitive closure rendered him impervious to the image of a malleable China, restricting the
horizons of his China policymaking. To some degree, it also facilitated an
escalatory spiral, as the strident public posture of the administration frequently reflected Kennedy's view of a truculent China.

It is too easy, however, to fault Kennedy excessively, thus distorting the
historical record. First, whether Kennedy was in the autumn of 1963 won
over to the alternative image of China remains an open question meriting
close attention in future research. Second, one should not lose sight of the
broader canvass of history. In dealing with a spiral condition, Kennedy fared
no worse than the majority of statesmen, American and otherwise, and his
pattern of behavior was particularly common among post–World War II
American policymakers, the China sphere (at least through the Johnson

years) definitely included.[79] It may even be that Eisenhower, rather than Kennedy, carries the greatest burden of missing a genuine opportunity for rapprochement with the Chinese Communists. Recent research suggests that from the Bandung Conference of 1955 through the first half of 1956, the Chinese appear to have sought rapprochement with their American archrival. This trend, which was authorized by Mao in key party meetings,[80] matured into quite determined overtures but encountered no responsive chord in Washington.

Indeed, the most profound reason for an evenhanded verdict on Kennedy's responsibility for the perpetuation of Sino-American conflict, both in general and in Vietnam in particular, stems from a focus on the Chinese side. Kennedy's firmness may have contributed to the endurance of confrontation, but was almost certainly not its root cause. A transformation of relations required receptivity to accommodation in Beijing as well as in Washington. Much, unfortunately, is still obscure as to the dynamics of power within the Chinese Communist hierarchy. Some in Beijing did advocate easing tensions with the United States. Beijing's extension of a few cautious feelers—always at points incompatible with Washington's own feeble overtures regarding accommodation[81]—so indicates, as does Wang Jiaxiang's letter of February 1962.[82] But, as chapters 1 and 5 below confirm, Mao and other key leaders, clearly holding the upper hand, adamantly rejected this option. In light of Mao's determination to embark on a radical course at this early stage of Kennedy's tenure, it seems unlikely that even a subtle and sophisticated combination of deterrence and assurance on Washington's part could have diverted Mao, in particular, from pursuing a confrontational line.[83]

In sum, although the precise salience of Kennedy's rigidity in Beijing's own intransigence looms large on the agenda for future research, it seems that neither side was ready for a breakthrough. During the Kennedy years, the opportunity to transform Sino-American relations was apparently nonexistent.

Notes

1. See Gordon H. Chang, *Friends and Enemies: The United States, China, and the Soviet Union, 1948–1972* (Stanford, Calif.: Stanford University Press, 1990), 217–52; James Fetzer, "Clinging to Containment: China Policy," in *Kennedy's Quest for Victory: American Foreign Policy, 1961–1963,* ed. Thomas G. Paterson (New York: Oxford University Press, 1989), 196; "Notes on the NSC Meeting," November 15, 1961, U.S. De-

partment of State, *Foreign Relations of the United States, 1961–1963* (hereafter *FRUS*), vol. 1, *Vietnam 1961* (Washington, D.C.: U.S. Government Printing Office, 1988–), 607; and Dennis Merrill, *Bread and the Ballot: The United States and India's Economic Development* (Chapel Hill: University of North Carolina Press, 1990), 142–48.

2. Roderick MacFarquhar, *The Origins of the Cultural Revolution, Volume 3: The Coming of the Cataclysm* (Oxford: Oxford University Press, 1997), 270–81, 298, 325; Rosemary Foot, *The Practice of Power: US Relations with China since 1949* (Oxford: Clarendon Press, 1995), 263; Alfred D. Wilhelm Jr., *The Chinese at the Negotiating Table: Style and Characteristics* (Washington, D.C.: National Defense University Press, 1994), 214–15.

3. Nancy Bernkopf Tucker, "No Common Ground: American-Chinese-Soviet Relations, 1948–1972," *Diplomatic History* 16, no. 2 (Spring 1992): 321; Roger Hilsman, *To Move a Nation: The Politics of Foreign Policy in the Administration of John F. Kennedy* (Garden City, N.Y.: Doubleday, 1967), 347–48, 580–81; Hilsman letter to author, May 7, 1995; Theodore C. Sorensen, *Kennedy* (New York: Harper & Row, 1965), 665–66.

4. As historian Thomas Paterson explains, this concept of growth and unfulfilled promise, cultivated by many a Kennedy associate, has also been central to the interpretive framework of a number of historians. See Paterson, introduction to *Kennedy's Quest,* 6, 318–19 nn. 15, 16. The image achieved an enduring hold over the American popular mind, in good part due to the trauma of Kennedy's assassination. For general discussions of Kennedy historiography and myth making cf. Thomas Brown, *JFK: History of an Image* (London: I. B. Tauris, 1989); and Burton I. Kaufman, "John F. Kennedy as World Leader: A Perspective on the Literature," *Diplomatic History* 17, no. 3 (Summer 1993): 447–69. A good starting point for researching the Kennedy era is James N. Giglio, comp., *John F. Kennedy: A Bibliography* (Westport, Conn: Greenwood Press, 1995).

5. Fetzer, "Clinging to Containment," 178–97; Chang, *Friends and Enemies,* 217–52; Warren I. Cohen, "The United States and China since 1945," in *New Frontiers in American–East Asian Relations: Essays Presented to Dorothy Borg,* ed. Warren I. Cohen (New York: Columbia University Press, 1983), 160. The quotation is from Nancy B. Tucker, "Continuing Controversies in the Literature of U.S.-China Relations since 1945," in *Pacific Passage: The Study of American–East Asian Relations on the Eve of the Twenty-First Century,* ed. Warren I. Cohen (New York: Columbia University Press, 1996), 226.

6. This overview of the Kennedy literature draws on Kaufman, "John F. Kennedy as World Leader," esp. 463, 466, 469.

7. "Memcon Kennedy–Souvanna Phouma, July 27, 1962," in *FRUS, 1961–1963,* vol. 24 (1994), *Laos Crisis,* 876. The tensions over Laos furnish a promising test case of the New Frontier record in China. See Edmund F. Wehrle, "'A Good, Bad Deal': John F. Kennedy, W. Averell Harriman, and the Neutralization of Laos, 1961–1962," *Pacific Historical Review* 67, no. 3 (August 1998): 349–77; Noam Kochavi, "Limited Accommodation, Perpetuated Conflict: Kennedy, China, and the Laos Crisis, 1961–1963," *Diplomatic History* 26, no. 1 (Winter 2002): 95–135.

8. See "Memcon Kennedy–Macmillan, June 29, 1963," in *FRUS, 1961–1963,* vol. 7 (1995), *Arms Control And Disarmament,* 754; Michael R. Beschloss, *The Crisis Years: Kennedy and Khrushchev, 1960–1963* (New York: Edward Burlingame Books, 1991), 618. Gordon Chang argues that the specter of a nuclear China so haunted Kennedy that he approached the Soviets with suggestions of a joint military strike against Chinese research and development facilities, or at least Soviet acquiescence in such a feat. That as-

sertion has sparked a lively debate. Chang's contenders deem the evidence he marshaled too spotty and circumstantial to confirm his point. McGeorge Bundy, James Thomson, Roger Hilsman, and the historian Nancy Tucker argue further that Chang mistakes speculation on, and contingency planning of, such a preemptive strike for action. Compare: Gordon Chang, *Friends and Enemies,* chap. 8; James C. Thomson, "Whose Side Were They On?" *New York Times Book Review,* July 29, 1990; Thomson interview with the author, December 7, 1994, Boston; Hilsman letter to the author, May 7, 1995; Nancy B. Tucker, "No Common Ground," 321; and McGeorge Bundy, *Danger and Survival: Choices about the Bomb in the First Fifty Years* (New York: Vintage Books, 1988), 532. While the spotty record does not permit a final verdict on this point, the evidence suggests that a preemptive strike scenario probably reached a more advanced planning stage than either Thomson or Hilsman allow, but did not advance to the operational phase.

9. For misplaced optimism as to enlisting Japan, see "Memo Deputy Secretary of Defense (Gilpatric) to Kennedy, 8 February 1963," in *FRUS, 1961–1963,* vol. 22 (1996), *Northeast Asia,* 767; Michael Schaller, "Altered States: The United States and Japan During the 1960s," in *The Diplomacy of the Crucial Decade,* ed. Diane B. Kunz (New York: Columbia University Press, 1990), 270–72. Through late 1963, the same misconception undermined the New Frontier's policies toward the Indian subcontinent. See Robert J. McMahon, *The Cold War on the Periphery: The United States, India and Pakistan* (New York: Columbia University Press, 1994), esp. 274; "The President's Views on India as Expressed at 25 April Meeting," memo Bundy for record, May 26, 1963, folder: "NSC Meetings 1963, No. 514," NSF: M&M, box 314, John F. Kennedy Presidential Library, Columbia Point, Boston (hereafter cited as JFKL).

10. Nancy B. Tucker, "US-China Relations since 1945," in *Pacific Passage,* ed. Warren I. Cohen, 227; Leonard Kusnitz, *Public Opinion and Foreign Policy: America's China Policy, 1949–1979* (Westport, Conn.: Greenwood Press, 1984), 106. Given the scheming nature of such a stratagem, one would be hard-pressed to find conclusive traces of it in the documentary record. Shreds of oblique evidence, however, do exist to enhance the plausibility of the Tucker-Kusnitz hypothesis. According to one midlevel State Department officer, as early as mid-1962 the idea of magnifying the dimension of the Chinese enemy for domestic consumption appealed to movers and shakers. See: R. W. Barnett Paper, "Foreign Policy and China," April 25, 1962, folder: "General, 4/62-6/62," box 15, Thomson papers, JFKL.

11. Kusnitz, *Public Opinion,* 102, 123 n. 45; Foot, *Practice of Power,* 99.

12. Nancy B. Tucker, *Taiwan, Hong Kong, and the United States: Uncertain Friendships* (New York: Twayne, 1994), 49; "Message Bundy to Cline, October 11, 1961," in *FRUS, 1961–1963,* vol. 22 (1996), 154–55; "Cable Bundy to Cline, October 18, 1961" (not sent), folder: "China General CIA Cables 7/61–10/16/61," NSF Countries, box 22, JFKL.

13. "Krock Interview with Kennedy, October 11, 1961," book III, Arthur Krock Papers, Seeley Mudd Manuscript Library, Princeton, N.J., 343.

14. For officials inclined to "return-to-the mainland" schemes, see Elvis Stahr Oral History interview, JFKL, 51; Cline Oral History interview, May 31, 1983, Lyndon Baines Johnson Library, Austin (hereafter cited as LBJL); Ray S. Cline, *Secrets, Spies and Scholars: Blueprint of the Essential CIA* (Washington, D.C.: Acropolis Books, 1976), 192, 195; James Thomson interview with author, Boston, December 7, 1994; "Memo Bundy to JFK, July 7, 1961," in *FRUS, 1961–1963,* vol. 22 (1996), 89–91;

"Weekend Reading 4/20/62," Index of Weekend Reading, folder: General, 1/62–6/62, box 318, NSF: M&M, JFKL; "Meeting: The White House," Memo Hilsman, June 20, 1962, in *FRUS, 1961–1963,* vol. 22 (1996), 251–55.

15. "See Kennedy Press Conference in Paris, June 2, 1961, *Public Papers of the Presidents* (hereafter *PPP*), 1961, 436.

16. John F. Kennedy, "A Democrat Looks at Foreign Policy," *Foreign Affairs* 36, no. 1 (October 1957): 50; "United States–China Relations, Memcon China–U.S., August 1, 1961," in *FRUS, 1961–1963,* vol. 22 (1996), 110; "Memcon JFK–Chiang Ching-kuo, September 11, 1963," in *FRUS, 1961–1963,* vol. 22, 388; Kennedy Press Conference, May 23, 1962, *PPP,* 1962, 431.

17. See "410 Deptel Rusk to Taipei, January 8, 1962," folder: "China General Return to the Mainland," box 23, JFKL; "Memo for the Record on Meeting with Chiang Ching-kuo," memo Hilsman, March 22, 1962, folder: "China-Planning on Mainland Operations," box 1, Hilsman Papers, JFKL; "Memo for the Record Bundy, March 12, 1962," in *FRUS, 1961–1963,* vol. 22 (1996), 194.

18. Cline, *Secrets, Spies and Scholars,* 208.

19. Mark M. Lowenthal, "Tribal Tongues: Intelligence Consumers, Intelligence Producers," *Washington Quarterly* 15 (1992): 159, 167; Alexander L. George, "Presidential Management Styles and Models," in *Perspectives on American Foreign Policy,* ed. Charles W. Kegley Jr. and Eugene R. Wittkopf (New York: St. Martin's Press, 1983), 476–77.

20. "Using the Chen Ch'eng Visit, Memo Komer to Bundy, July 20, 1961," folder "China General 7/15/61–7/24/61," NSF:CO, box 22, JFKL; Michael V. Forrestal Oral History, JFKL.

21. U. Alexis Johnson, *The Right Hand of Power* (Englewood Cliffs, N.J.: Prentice-Hall, 1984), 326; George W. Ball, *The Past Has Another Pattern* (New York: W. W. Norton, 1982), 168; Moya Ann Ball, *Vietnam-on-the-Potomac* (New York: Praeger, 1992), 56–58.

22. The historian Leopoldo Nuti reported his largely parallel findings on Kennedy's Italian policy at a conference on "The United States, the Federal Republic of Germany, and 'Third Areas'—American-German Relations, 1955–1968," Bochum, Germany, May 1997. The discussion here benefits from his insights. See also Leopoldo Nuti, "L'administration Kennedy et sa politique italienne: Un 'test case' du processus de decision dans la politique etrangere des Etas-Unis," *Relations Internationales* 84 (Winter 1995): 485–500.

23. Cf. Bowles Address, "Africa, Asia, and Berlin," August 15, 1961, *Department of State Bulletin* 45 (September 18, 1961): 486–87; "Robert Blum memo on His Conversation with Marshall Green, December 27, 1963," folder "General Correspondence," Record of Groups Volume C, Council on Foreign Relations Records. New York; "Notes for the Tuesday Planning Session," memo Komer to Bundy and Rostow, March 6, 1961, folder "Komer 1/1/61–3/14/61," NSF: M&M, box 321, JFKL.

24. "Letter Bowles to Roger Hilsman, September 3, 1963," folder "Bowles, Chester," box 438, W. Averell Harriman Papers, Library of Congress Manuscript Division, Washington.

25. Richard Moorsteen and Morton Abramowitz, *Remaking China Policy: U.S.-China Relations and Government Decisionmaking* (Cambridge, Mass.: Harvard University Press, 1971), xxxvii, 60.

26. "Bundy to Kennedy, July 7, 1961," in *FRUS, 1961–1963,* vol. 22 (1996), 90;

"221 Deptel Rusk to Beam, August 13, 1961," in *FRUS, 1961–1963,* vol. 22, 118–20; memo U. Alexis Johnson to Rusk, August 13, 1961, in *FRUS, 1961–1963,* vol. 22, 118n.; Chang, *Friends and Enemies,* 329.

27. David L. Dileo, *George Ball, Vietnam, and the Rethinking of Containment* (Chapel Hill: University of North Carolina Press, 1991), 43; James C. Thomson, "On the Making of U.S. China Policy, 1961–1969: A Study in Bureaucratic Politics," *China Quarterly* 50 (April–June 1972): 222–23; Thomson interview with the author, Boston, December 7, 1994; Ball, *Past Has Another Pattern,* 171, 196–97. Bundy, McNamara, and Robert Kennedy were destined to enjoy greater rapport with Kennedy. Only when more work has been done on the general historical role of these figures can one attempt a considered assessment of their respective China policy impact.

28. Robert S. McNamara, *In Retrospect: The Tragedy and Lessons of Vietnam* (New York: Times Books, 1995), 35. Both Kennedy's and Eisenhower's personal prestige was apparently too engaged, in the context of inflated campaign rhetoric, to allow an effective meeting of their minds. I wish to thank Ronald W. Pruessen of the University of Toronto for sharing these insights.

29. Anna Kasten Nelson, "President Kennedy's National Security Policy: A Reconsideration," *Reviews in American History* 19, no. 1 (March 1991): 6; John Prados, *Keepers of the Keys: The History of the National Security Council from Truman to Bush* (New York: William Morrow, 1991), 97, 102, 105, 118–19; I. M. Destler, "The Rise of the National Security Assistant, 1961–1981," in *Perspectives on American Foreign Policy: Selected Readings,* ed. Charles W. Kegley Jr., and Eugene R. Wittkopf (New York: St. Martin's Press, 1983), 263–64.

30. For this point of criticism, see Mark M. Lowenthal, *US Intelligence: Evolution and Anatomy,* 2nd ed. (Westport, Conn.: Praeger, 1992), 31; and Ball, *Vietnam-on-the-Potomac,* 36–37, 56–58.

31. Ralph B. Levering and Montague Kern, "The News Management Issue and John F. Kennedy's Foreign Policy," in *John F. Kennedy: The Promise Revisited,* ed. Paul Harper and Joann P. Krieg (New York: Greenwood Press, 1988), 144. For Kennedy's "oversensitivity" to press criticism, see also Sorensen, *Kennedy,* 304.

32. Sorensen, *Kennedy,* 4–5. E.g., the political scientist and Kennedy China watcher Allen S. Whiting recalls one such telephone conversation, in May 1962, between Kennedy and Harriman. Harriman argued that the record of turning a blind eye to China's domestic catastrophe might one day haunt the United States. This consideration apparently figured in Kennedy's decision to use the ambassadorial channel in Warsaw to inform the Chinese that the United States could reconsider its present policy against selling food grains, if and when it became evident that Chinese Communist needs could not be met by purchases elsewhere. Whiting interview with the author, January 11, 1996.

33. Dean and Richard Rusk, *As I Saw It* (New York: Penguin Books, 1990), 282–83; Thomas J. Schoenbaum, *Waging Peace and War: Dean Rusk and the Truman, Kennedy, and Johnson Years* (New York: Simon & Schuster, 1988), 387–88; Warren I. Cohen, *Dean Rusk* (Totowa, N.J.: Cooper Square, 1980), 165. The meeting probably took place on May 5. "Editorial Note," in *FRUS, 1961–1963,* vol. 22 (1996), 55.

34. Rusk, *As I Saw It,* 11, 16–17; Cohen, "New Light on Dean Rusk? A Review Essay," *Political Science Quarterly* 106, no. 1 (1991): 125; William P. Snyder, "Dean Rusk to John Foster Dulles, May–June 1953: The Office, the First 100 Days, and Red China," *Diplomatic History* 7, no. 1 (Winter 1983): 83. Although far too sardonic, Rudy Abramson's phrase still rings true; Rusk, he argues, "made discretion and integrity a fetish."

Abramson, *Spanning the Century,* 614. Even U. Alexis Johnson, widely regarded as Rusk's closest subordinate, portrayed Rusk in such terms. Cohen, *Dean Rusk,* 99; Johnson, *Right Hand of Power,* 320–21.

35. Rusk, *As I Saw It,* 287; Rusk Oral History, Richard B. Russell Library, University of Georgia, Athens, "UUU" transcript, May 1985; "221 Deptel Rusk to Beam, August 13, 1961," in *FRUS, 1961–1963,* vol. 22, 118–20; "Memo U. Alexis Johnson to Rusk, August 13, 1961," in *FRUS, 1961–1963,* vol. 22, 118 n.

36. Special Assistant to the Under-Secretary James Thomson, Galbraith, Hilsman, and the historian Foster Rhea Dulles have been among the most strident critics of Rusk on this score. See Thomson, "On the Making," 233; "James Thomson Oral History, July 22, 1971," LBJL; "Hilsman Oral History, May 15, 1969," LBJL; Foster R. Dulles, *American Policy toward Communist China,* 192; John K. Galbraith, *A Life in Our Times* (Boston: Houghton Mifflin, 1981), 402–6, 428 n. 3. Warren Cohen and James Fetzer have conversely pinned the lion's share of responsibility on Kennedy. Fetzer, "Clinging to Containment," esp. 181; Cohen, "The United States and China since 1945," 160.

37. "Memcon Rusk-Home-Macmillan, June 24, 1962," in *FRUS, 1961–1963,* vol. 22 (1996), 277.

38. See: Chang, *Friends and Enemies,* 178–82; Rockefeller Brothers Fund, *Prospect for America: The Rockefeller Panel Reports* (Garden City, N.Y.: Doubleday, 1961), 46–47; "Rusk to Bowles, December 4, 1959," Chester Bowles Collection, box 215, Yale University, cited in Cohen, *Dean Rusk,* 86.

39. "Rusk News Conference, December 10, 1962," *Department of State Bulletin* 47 (December 31, 1962): 999; "Airgram 5667, November 22, 1962," in *FRUS, 1961–1963,* vol. 22 (1996), 350 n. 1; "Rusk Testimony, June 5, 1963," Committee on Foreign Relations, U.S. Senate, *Executive Sessions of the Senate Foreign Relations Committee* (Historical Series) (hereafter *Executive Sessions*) 15 (1963): 352.

40. Hilsman and James Thomson believe the speech passed inadvertently through the bureaucratic vetting process, by force of fortuitous circumstances. In particular, a harassed secretary of state had time only to glance at the text and give the green light once he had been assured that the speech did not call for French recognition of Beijing. The historian Nancy Tucker conversely depicts a secretary far more amenable to the Hilsman line. Compare Thomson, "On the Making," 230–31; Hilsman, *To Move a Nation,* 355; Hilsman Oral History, LBJL; and Nancy B. Tucker, "Threats, Opportunities, and Frustrations in East Asia," in *Lyndon Johnson Confronts the World,* ed. Warren I. Cohen and Nancy B. Tucker (Cambridge: Cambridge University Press, 1994), 102.

41. Cf. Cohen, *Dean Rusk,* 95–97.

42. See Noam Kochavi, "Mist across the Bamboo Curtain: China's Internal Crisis and the American Intelligence Process, 1961–1962," *Journal of American-East Asian Relations* 5, no. 2 (Summer 1996): esp. 141–42. For a general analysis of the formidable nature of this task, cf. Ernest R. May, "Conclusion," in *Knowing One's Enemies: Intelligence Assessment before the Two World Wars,* ed. Ernest R. May (Princeton, N.J.: Princeton University Press, 1985), esp. 530.

43. See Kochavi, "Mist across the Bamboo Curtain," 149–51.

44. For catalogues of the difficulties involved in imputing intentions, cf. Raymond L. Garthoff, "On Estimating and Imputing Intentions," *International Security* 2, no. 3 (Winter 1978): 22–32; and Richard K. Betts, "Analysis, War and Decision: Why Intelligence Failures Are Inevitable," *World Politics* 31, no. 1 (October 1978): 961–88.

45. William H. Sullivan, *Obbligato, 1939–1979: Notes on a Foreign Service Career* (New York: W. W. Norton, 1984), 172–73; John K. Galbraith, *Ambassador's Journal: A Personal Account of the Kennedy Years* (Boston: Houghton Mifflin, 1969), 378; "Galbraith Letter to Kennedy, November 13, 1962," reprinted in Galbraith, *Ambassador's Journal,* 411–14; and McGeorge Bundy's approving comments, November 17, 1962, folder "Index of Weekend Papers General 7/62–12/62," NSF: Bundy Correspondence, box 318, JFKL; "The Five-Fold Dilemma: The Implications of a Sino-Indian Conflict," memo Hilsman to Rusk, November 17, 1962, folder "India, Sino-Indian Border Clash 1962, Implications Analysis," box 1, Hilsman papers, JFKL; FO 371/164929, November 6, 1962, and November 12, 1962, Public Records Office, Kew, London.

46. "Briefing on Current Foreign Policy Problems," Rusk testimony, June 5, 1963, *Executive Sessions* 15 (1963): 340; SNIE 13-2-63, "Communist China's Advanced Weapons Program," July 24, 1963, folder: "National Intelligence Estimates," box 4, NSF, LBJL; Willis C. Armstrong, William Leonhart, William J. McCaffrey, and Herbert C. Rothenberg, "The Hazards of Single-Outcome Forecasting," in *Inside CIA's Private World,* ed. H. Bradford Westerfield (New Haven, Conn.: Yale University Press, 1995), 244–346; William Burr and Jeffrey T. Richelson, "A Chinese Puzzle," *Bulletin of the Atomic Scientists* 53, no. 4 (July–August 1997): 42–47.

47. See Noam Kochavi, "From Puzzled Prudence to Bold Experimentation: Washington's View of the Sino-Soviet Split, 1961–1963," *Intelligence and National Security* 15, no. 1 (Spring 2000): 50–79; and Harold P. Ford, "The CIA and Double Demonology: Calling the Sino-Soviet Split," *Studies in Intelligence* (Winter 1998–99): 57–71.

48. Cline Oral History, March 21, 1983, LBJL; Harold P. Ford, *Estimative Intelligence: The Purposes and Problems of National Intelligence Estimating* (Lanham, Md.: University Press of America, 1993), 92; Cline, *Secrets, Spies and Scholars,* 3, 172, 181; Hilsman, *To Move a Nation,* 314; "White House Meeting on GRC Plans," Hilsman Memo for the Record, March 31, 1962, in *FRUS, 1961–1963,* vol. 22 (1996), 204; Cline memo, "Sino-Soviet Relations," January 14, 1963, in *FRUS, 1961–1963,* vol. 22, 340; Chang, *Friends and Enemies,* 235–36.

49. "Appraisal of the Chinese Army Documents," memo McCone to Kennedy, January 9, 1962, folder "China Security 62-3 (19)," box 113a, POF, JFKL; memo Komer to Bundy, August 1, 1963, folder "China General 7/63-8/63," NSF:CO, box 24, JFKL; "Chinese Communist Intentions," Summary Record of the 516th Meeting of the NSC, July 31, 1963, in *FRUS, 1961–1963,* vol. 22 (1996), 373; "Briefing of General Eisenhower in Gettysburg," Forrestal memo for the record, June 21, 1962, in *FRUS, 1961–1963,* vol. 22, 256. See also "Memo for the record Hilsman, June 20, 1962," in *FRUS, 1961–1963,* vol. 22, 251.

50. "668 Green to Rusk, December 21, 1961," folder "Food For China 1961," James Thomson Papers, box 15, JFKL; "1525 Green to Rusk, June 22, 1962," in *FRUS, 1961–1963,* vol. 22 (1996), 272–73; "1503 Lacy to Rusk," in *FRUS, 1961–1963,* vol. 22, microfiche supplement, doc. 50.

51. See: Nick Cullather, *Illusions of Influence: The Political Economy of United States–Philippines Relations, 1942–1960* (Stanford, Calif.: Stanford University Press, 1994); and Robert J. McMahon, "The Cold War in Asia: The Elusive Synthesis" in *America in the World: The Historiography of American Foreign Relations since 1941,* ed. Michael J. Hogan (Cambridge: Cambridge University Press, 1996), 534. This "arrogance of power" permeated Rostow's policy toward Asia as a whole. Cf. Rostow and Richard W. Hatch, *An American Policy in Asia* (London: Chapman and Hall, 1955); Ros-

tow's speech at the U.S. Army Special Warfare School, Fort Bragg, N.C., June 28, 1961, *Department of State Bulletin* 45 (7 August 1961): 234–37; and "Letter Rostow to Taylor, July 31, 1962," in *FRUS, 1961–1963,* vol. 22 (1996), 299.

52. See Kochavi, "Mist across the Bamboo Curtain," 149.

53. "Letter Rostow to Taylor, July 31, 1962."

54. Cf. Foot, *Practice of Power,* 97; Comments by Ambassador Reischauer on S/P Study: "A U.S. Policy towards Communist China," December 5, 1962, folder "S/P Study: "A U.S. Policy towards Communist China," box 15, Thomson Papers; "Food for China," Rice memo to Rusk, May 24, 1962, folder "Food for China 3/62–5/62," box 15, Thomson Papers; "The Situation in India," Galbraith testimony, June 6, 1962, *Executive Sessions* 14 (1962): 521.

55. Ronald W. Pruessen, "Pondering the 'Evil Fact' in Asia: John Foster Dulles and China, 1953–1954," paper prepared for the Annual Meeting of the Society of Historians of American Foreign Relations, Annapolis, Md., June 1987, 16.

56. "Memcon on Laos, April 29, 1961," in *FRUS, 1961–1963,* vol. 24 (1998), 153.

57. Richard N. Lebow and Janice G. Stein, "Beyond Deterrence," *Journal of Social Issues* 43, no. 4 (Winter 1987): esp. 40–56.

58. Robert Jervis, "War and Misperception," *Journal of Interdisciplinary History* 18, no. 4 (Spring 1988): 686. Jervis goes on to note cogently that "the task is difficult, and neither decisionmakers nor academics have fully come to grips with it."

59. Representative documents include Hilsman Address, "United States Policy toward Communist China," December 13, 1963, *Department of State Bulletin* 50 (January 6, 1964): 12; "Letter Hilsman to Stevenson, December 19, 1963," in *FRUS, 1961–1963,* vol. 22 (1996), 411; FE paper, "FE—Office of Asian Communist Affairs," n.d., in *FRUS, 1961–1963,* vol. 22, 397–99; Memo Hilsman to Crockett of Organization, "Gearing FE to Do the Job Ahead," October 9, 1963, folder "Far East 5/8/63–2/25/64," box 5, Hilsman papers, JFKL. The history of the "Hilsman project" has thus far been told largely by its champions. See Hilsman, *To Move a Nation,* 346–52; James C. Thomson, "On the Making," 228–31; Marshall Green; John H. Holdridge; and William N. Stokes, *War and Peace with China: First-Hand Experiences in the Foreign Service of the United States* (Bethesda, Md.: Dacor-Bacon Press, 1994), 59–63. For more detached appraisals, see Chang, *Friends and Enemies,* 251; Rosemary Foot, "Redefinitions: The Domestic Context and America's China Policy in the 1960s," draft of a paper delivered at the conference on U.S.-China Relations in the 1960s, Beijing, October 28–30, 1996, 5. For a critique of the quest for hegemony or primacy in American foreign relations, see especially Stanley F. Hoffmann, *Primacy or World Order* (New York: McGraw-Hill, 1978).

60. See Tucker, "Threats, Opportunities, and Frustrations," 104–11; Foot, *Practice of Power,* 263.

61. The last decade has witnessed a revival of scholarly debates concerning the Kennedy record in Laos. See Wehrle, "'Good, Bad Deal,'; William J. Duiker, *U.S. Containment Policy and the Conflict in Indochina* (Stanford, Calif.: Stanford University Press, 1994), 253–60; Stephen W. Twing, *Myths, Models, and U.S. Foreign Policy: The Cultural Shaping of Three Cold Warriors* (Boulder, Colo.: Lynne Riener, 1998), 124-28; Timothy N. Castle, *At War in the Shadow of Vietnam: U.S. Military Aid to the Royal Lao Government, 1955–1975* (New York: Columbia University Press, 1993), esp. 128–37; and John Prados, *The Blood Road: The Ho Chi Minh Trail and the Vietnam War* (New York: John Wiley, 1999). These studies have not, however, assigned sufficient weight to

the China factor in the making of Laos policy during the Kennedy years. For a study of China's Laotian policies, see Qiang Zhai, *China and the Vietnam Wars, 1950–1975* (Chapel Hill: University of North Carolina Press), chap. 4.

62. For analysis of the 1962 straits crisis, see Allen S. Whiting, *The Chinese Calculus of Deterrence: India and Indochina* (Ann Arbor: University of Michigan Press, 1975), 63–70; Wang Bingnan, *Nine Years of Sino-American Talks in Retrospect: Memoirs of Wang Bingnan,* JPRS-CPS-85-069 (Washington, D.C.: Joint Publications Research Services, 1985).

63. Thomson, "On the Making," esp. 220–33.

64. Robert J. McMahon, "US-Vietnamese Relations: A Historiographical Survey," in *Pacific Passage,* ed. Cohen, 325. See also Kaufman, "John F. Kennedy as World Leader," 463–65.

65. Compare Lawrence J. Bassett and Stephen E. Pelz, "The Failed Search for Victory: Vietnam and the Politics of War," in *Kennedy's Quest for Victory: American Foreign Policy, 1961–1963,* ed. Thomas G. Paterson (New York: Oxford University Press, 1989), 223–52; Ball, *Vietnam-on-the-Potomac;* Fredrik Logevall, *Choosing War: The Lost Chance for Peace and the Escalation for War in Vietnam* (Berkeley: California University Press, 1999); and David Kaiser, *American Tragedy: Kennedy, Johnson and the Origins of the Vietnam War* (Cambridge, Mass.: Belknap Press, 2000).

66. The clearest—and most extreme—elucidation of this frame of mind came from Rostow's pen: "It is a moot point whether Peiping is directly responsible for Communist insurgency efforts in Southeast Asia . . . the force of circumstances, if nothing else, deeply engages Communist China's prestige, and perhaps even its confidence, in these efforts. A Communist triumph in South Vietnam, for example, will almost certainly do much to revive the dimmed hopes of the Chinese leadership and elite." Rostow, "A U.S. Policy Toward Communist China," draft State Paper, November 15, 1962, folder "A U.S. Policy Toward Communist China," box 15, Thomson papers, JFKL. For similar arguments, see "US Oversees Internal Defense Policy," State Paper in collaboration with other prepared in State in collaboration with other members of the Counter-Insurgency Special Group, August 13, 1962, folder "NSAM 182," M&M, box 338, JFKL.

67. Kennedy himself read Mao on guerrilla warfare and, in early 1961, went about urging others in the administration to do the same. See Michael D. Shafer, *Deadly Paradigms: The Failure of American Counterinsurgency Policy* (Princeton, N.J.: Princeton University Press, 1988), 20–21; Fetzer, "Clinging to Containment," 196; Sorensen, *Kennedy,* 631–32. During the period 1961–62, Kennedy paid little heed to the argument of several aides that China was too preoccupied with its domestic predicament to engage appreciably in Southeast Asia. See Bowles, "US Policies in the Far East," April 4, 1962, folder "Bowles, Chester 4/62," box WH-3a, Schlesinger Papers; Memo Harriman to Rusk, July 30, 1962, folder "Bowles, Chester," box 438, Harriman Papers; "3313 Embtel Galbraith to Harriman, April 19, 1962," in *FRUS, 1961–1963,* vol. 22 (1996), 336; "Letter Rostow to Taylor, July 31, 1962," in *FRUS, 1961–1963,* vol. 22, 299; "Memcon Kennedy–Souvanna Phouma, July 27, 1962," in *FRUS, 1961–1963,* vol. 24 (1998), 876.

68. See George C. Herring, *America's Longest War: The United States and Vietnam, 1950–1975,* 3rd ed. (New York: McGraw-Hill, 1996), 83.

69. The historian Robert Schulzinger has characterized the impact of China on *Johnson's* Vietnam policy in nearly identical terms, in "The Johnson Administration, China, and the Vietnam War," paper delivered at a workshop on Sino-American Relations, 1955–1971, sponsored by the Fairbank Center, Harvard University and the International

Strategic Research Center, Central Party School, Beijing, October 28–30, 1996. The continuity between the two administrations in this regard is striking.

70. "Notes on the NSC Meeting, Washington, November 15, 1961," in *FRUS, 1961–1963,* vol. 1 (1988), 607–8.

71. "Memo Harriman to Rusk, July 30, 1962," folder "Bowles, Chester," box 438, Harriman Papers; "913 Rusk Deptel to Delhi, September 5, 1962," in *FRUS, 1961–1963,* vol. 2 (1988), 614. For details on Harriman's July 1962 abortive attempt to negotiate with North Vietnamese delegates in Geneva, cf. Wehrle, "Good, Bad Deal," 372–73. As has been widely recognized in the literature, still more profoundly injurious to the neutralization bid was the firm belief, at that point in Kennedy's entourage, in the winnability of the Vietnam War, or rather, in the doctrine that the problems of Vietnam lent themselves to an American solution. Cf. Duiker, *U.S. Containment Policy,* 289–300.

72. For this debate, cf. Fetzer, "Clinging to Containment," esp. 197; Hilsman, *To Move,* 347–48; Hilsman Oral History, LBJL.

73. See Chen Jian, "China's Involvement in the Vietnam War, 1964–1969," *China Quarterly* 142 (June 1995): 362; Zhai, *China and the Vietnam Wars,* 114–20; MacFarquhar, *Coming of the Cataclysm,* 270–81, 298, 325.

74. See George F. Kennan, *Memoirs 1950–1963* (New York: Pantheon Books, 1972), 268; FO 371/170661, March 14, 1963, FO 371/170662, October 4, 1963, both in Public Records Office, Kew, London; Chang, *Friends and Enemies,* 170–71, 236.

75. For elucidations of the spiral model, its merits and shortcomings, cf. Robert Jervis, *Perception and Misperception in International Politics* (Princeton, N.J.: Princeton University Press, 1976), 58–113; Jervis, "War and Misperception," 685; Jervis, Richard N. Lebow, and Janice G. Stein, eds., *Psychology and Deterrence* (Baltimore: Johns Hopkins University Press, 1985), passim.

76. See Felix Greene, *A Curtain of Ignorance* (Garden City, N.Y.: Doubleday, 1964), 234; Cohen, *Dean Rusk,* 170; JFK, "Address at the Waldorf-Astoria Hotel, December 14, 1962," PPP, 1962, 887; "JFK Press Conference, December 17, 1962," *PPP,* 1962, 901–2; Robert J. McMahon, *The Cold War on the Periphery: The United States, India, and Pakistan* (New York: Columbia University Press, 1990), 287; and Sorensen, *Kennedy,* 747. This episode illustrates what the political scientist Richard Lebow terms the "way in which assumptions about adversaries can be confirmed tautologically." Lebow, conclusion to *Psychology and Deterrence,* ed. Jervis, Lebow, and Stein, 243.

77. See Kochavi, "Mist across the Bamboo Curtain," 139.

78. See Thomson, "Whose Side Were They On?" These pitfalls are cited in Jervis, "War and Misperception," esp. 690, 699.

79. Jervis, "War and Misperception," esp. 699; Jervis, "Political Psychology: Some Challenges and Opportunities," *Political Psychology* 10, no. 3 (1989): 488; Garthoff, "On Estimating and Imputing Intentions," 22–23; Moorsteen and Abramowitz, *Remaking China Policy,* xxii.

80. He Di, "The Most Respected Enemy: Mao Zedong's Perception of the United States," *China Quarterly* 137 (March 1994): 151; Robert D. Accinelli, *Crisis and Commitment: United States Policy toward Taiwan, 1950–1955* (Chapel Hill: University of North Carolina Press, 1996), 203–4; Ronald Pruessen, *To the Nuclear Brink for Asia* (forthcoming), chaps. 7–8.

81. See: "Confe 279, Harriman to Rusk, June 26, 1961," in *FRUS, 1961–1963,* vol. 24 (1998), 254 n. 2; "1934 Embtel Beam to DOS, June 30, 1961," in *FRUS, 1961–1963,* vol. 24, 87–89; "Wang Ping-nan's approach to Ambassador Beam," memo Hilsman to

McConaughy, July 7, 1961, folder "China General 7/15/61–7/24/61," NSF:CO, box 22, JFKL. This conforms to the more general pattern in Sino-American relations identified by Tucker in "Threats, Opportunities, and Frustrations," 104.

82. Wang Jiaxiang, head of the Chinese Communist Party's International Liaison Department, argued that China should not become involved in another Korean-style confrontation with the United States in Laos and Vietnam. He proposed to defuse tensions in China's international environment, Southeast Asia included, to facilitate economic recovery at home. Cf. Carol Lee Harmin, "Elite Politics and Foreign Relations," in *Chinese Foreign Policy: Theory and Practice,* ed. David Shambaugh (Oxford: Clarendon Press, 1994), 87; Zhai, *China and the Vietnam Wars,* 114–17; MacFarquhar, *Coming of the Cataclysm,* 270–81, 298, 325.

83. See: MacFarquhar, *Coming of the Cataclysm,* 270–81, 298, 325; Foot, *Practice of Power,* 263; Alfred D. Wilhelm Jr., *Chinese at the Negotiating Table,* 214–15. The political scientist Arthur Waldron makes much the same point—but less persuasively, because he has not consulted any of the new documentation on the question. See Waldron, "From Nonexistent to Almost Normal: U.S.-China Relations in the 1960s," in *The Diplomacy of the Crucial Decade,* ed. Diane B. Kunz (New York: Columbia University Press, 1994), esp. 230; Tucker, "Continuing Controversies," 242 n. 85.

4

The French Recognition of China and Its Implications for the Vietnam War

Fredrik Logevall

In January 1964, France extended diplomatic recognition to the People's Republic of China, following several months of talks between French and Chinese officials. French president Charles de Gaulle acted partly with Vietnam in mind when he opted for recognition, and leaders in Beijing also saw that movement toward normalization of Sino-French relations could have potentially major ramifications for the conflict in Indochina. American officials, when they learned in late 1963 of the French plans, likewise recognized immediately the problems that recognition could pose for their effort to win international support for the Saigon government in its struggle against the Hanoi-backed insurgency in South Vietnam. Hence the determined American effort to persuade de Gaulle to abort or at least delay his initiative. The effort failed, and on January 27, 1964, a joint statement issued simultaneously in Paris and Beijing announced that France and China

Portions of this chapter are drawn from the author's book, *Choosing War: The Lost Chance for Peace and the Escalation of War in Vietnam* (Berkeley: University of California Press, 1999).

had "decided to establish diplomatic relations" and therefore to exchange ambassadors within three months. This chapter examines the reasons for de Gaulle's initiative, the United States' response to his plan, and the implications of the Sino-French opening for the conflict in Vietnam.

The Path to French Recognition of China

The French decision did not come suddenly. Already in the early 1950s, de Gaulle's predecessors prepared the way. At the Geneva Conference in 1954, Pierre Mendès France met with Chinese prime minister Zhou Enlai, and their cooperation in reaching a peace settlement in Indochina suggested to some that recognition might come sooner rather than later. But for a long time, Chinese support for the Algerian rebels thwarted the process, as did warnings from Washington in the 1950s that Paris must expect to suffer repercussions if it initiated rapprochement with Beijing. For de Gaulle, there was also the Jiang Jieshi (Chiang Kai-shek) factor—the Frenchman was acutely aware of the common struggle waged against the authoritarian regimes in World War II, and he did not want to trample on the rights of the Chongqing regime that had resisted Japanese aggression.[1]

In 1957, a year before his return to power, General de Gaulle read *Le serpent et la tortue: Les problemes de la Chine populaire,* a book written by former French premier Edgar Faure that advocated the establishment of diplomatic relations between France and China.[2] Faure sent a copy of the book to de Gaulle, and the general responded that he was "entirely favorable to your point of view." In 1960, de Gaulle invited Faure to the Elysée Palace to talk about "the Chinese problem." The two men agreed on the need for recognition, but also on the need to delay any action until the Algerian conflict had been resolved. Beijing had extended recognition to the provisional Algerian government, and as long as the conflict in North Africa continued, no alteration in French official attitudes was possible.

By the early autumn of 1963, de Gaulle was ready to act. Not only had the Algerian War ended by then, but the Sino-Soviet split had deepened. The French government had been excluded from the Anglo-American negotiations with the USSR that year, and some Paris officials were concerned that by choosing to remain outside the Moscow negotiations on the test ban treaty, France had ensured that its role in future negotiations of similar importance would be a limited or subordinate one. A move on the China issue represented one dramatic way to demonstrate France's great-power status.

De Gaulle had other motives as well. On the most basic level, he considered it unrealistic to ignore the existence of a rising power in Asia. Jiang Jieshi's band of aging generals was, he knew, unlikely ever to set foot on the mainland again, and in opting for recognition he was simply following the path that the United Kingdom had pioneered more than a decade earlier. De Gaulle also felt strongly that the Chinese had adopted communism not out of ideological conviction but as a way of disciplining and organizing their vast country, and that the clear conflict between Beijing and Moscow guaranteed the independence of Chinese foreign policy. In addition, de Gaulle was undoubtedly motivated by the situation in Southeast Asia. China had to be part of any lasting settlement to the war, he believed, and he hoped that closer ties with Beijing, when combined with France's historic ties with both Vietnam and the United States, might allow Paris to play a mediating role in settling the conflict, in the process boosting French influence in Southeast Asia.[3]

Finally, and perhaps most important, de Gaulle saw in China an opportunity to further one of his chief aims since taking power in 1958: to distance his country from the American colossus and stake out a more independent French position within the Western Alliance. In 1963, de Gaulle assumed the role of leader of the actual or potential "third force" countries of Asia, Africa, and Latin America, and his name increasingly became one to reckon with in world affairs. Well aware that France and China were the only two great powers to refuse to sign the test ban treaty, the general saw in China a potential partner in his effort to prevent a division of the world between the U.S. and Soviet superpowers.

Chinese leaders did indeed share French concerns on this score, and as 1963 progressed their growing difficulties with the Soviets made French overtures still more welcome to them. For Beijing officials, moreover, a rapprochement with Paris had the benefit of causing embarrassment and humiliation to the United States, at a time of growing American involvement in East Asia. If other nations followed the French lead, so much the better, because this might have important ramifications for China's efforts to gain a United Nations seat and generally help increase Chinese influence in world affairs.

Little wonder that Sino-French contacts increased markedly in 1963, culminating with Edgar Faure's visit to Beijing as de Gaulle's representative in late October and early November.[4] Faure and Zhou Enlai drew up a draft protocol agreement, and Mao Zedong greeted Faure warmly. After his return to Paris, Faure called on de Gaulle on November 22, mere hours before John F. Kennedy's assassination. Upon learning of the killing, the two men agreed that action on recognition would have to wait until the slain president's successor, Lyndon Baines Johnson, had had a chance to assume control and guide the American nation through the difficult early weeks. January 1964 looked to de Gaulle to be the right moment.

American intelligence had known of increased Sino-French contacts for some months but had misjudged both the seriousness of these and their own ability to dissuade the French from going as far as recognition. As late as mid-December 1963, after U.S. secretary of state Dean Rusk met with de Gaulle in Paris, Washington officials professed to believe that French recognition of Beijing was unlikely until late 1964 at the earliest. De Gaulle gave no hint in the meeting that action was imminent, though he was circumspect when Rusk asked him whether recognition would occur in the near or more distant future. That was not up to France alone to decide, de Gaulle replied elliptically, but the United States could rest assured that it would be forewarned if Paris chose to follow London's course and establish diplomatic relations with Beijing.[5] If Rusk was mollified by that answer, the feeling did not last long; for in the days that followed, speculation increased that France was preparing to move, perhaps before the end of January.

The possibility made American policymakers shudder. Already alarmed by the level of Gaullist involvement in the Vietnam conflict—de Gaulle had caused great trepidation in Washington on August 29, 1963, when he called publicly for a Vietnam free of external involvement—they knew that the China initiative would likely raise it still further. U.S. officials perceived only too clearly what later historians have often missed: the significant influence that France retained in its former colony, even close to a decade after the end of the Franco-Vietminh War. It was not uncommon for foreign diplomats in both Saigon and Hanoi to remark on the powerful hold of the French language and culture on the country, and on how the passage of time appeared to have blunted the feelings of bitterness toward France engendered by the Franco-Vietminh War. ("Already a [North] Vietnamese Minister can talk of having fought the French with 'tenacity' but fighting the Americans with 'hatred,'" one British observer noted in May 1963.) The Vietnamese, according to this view, no longer feared France as a colonial power and were, after several generations of French education, more prepared to heed the French than any other Western people. It is noteworthy, in this regard, that French correspondents were among the few foreign journalists allowed in Hanoi.[6]

The French connection was particularly close in South Vietnam. In the autumn of 1963, some 17,500 French citizens lived there, about 6,000 of whom had been born in France. Thousands of Vietnamese children, including those of the ruling Ngo family, attended French-run primary schools and *lycées,* and when they fell ill they were often treated by French doctors in hospitals built by the French. Several of Ngo Dinh Diem's cabinet members had French wives. Meanwhile, France's economic presence in South Vietnam remained substantial, with French citizens in 1963 owning most of the public utilities, hotels, breweries, cigarette factories, and rubber plantations. France was also South Vietnam's best customer, buying 43.6 percent of its exports in 1962. There were also less tangible ties, unmistakable to any perceptive visitor. Bouillabaisse and *bifteck-pommes frites* were common in Saigon restaurants, along with Algerian *vin ordinaire.* For young urbanites, French was still the language to learn, not English; and Paris, not New York or San Francisco, was the city a student dreamt of. As a result, in late 1963 the French capital had a large South Vietnamese émigré population, much of which was clamoring to end the conflict through a diplomatic settlement.[7]

Equally important to Washington policymakers, French recognition of China would deliver a direct blow to their much-trumpeted rationale for standing tough in Vietnam: checking expansionist Chinese ambitions in Southeast Asia. Washington officials were not unaware of the mistrust that existed between Hanoi and Beijing; they understood that, helpful though it might be, Chinese material assistance and verbal support to North Vietnam was not yet instrumental. They also thought that Beijing would try to avoid a major confrontation with the West over Indochina. Nevertheless, most officials professed to believe that China had aggressive designs on its southern neighbors and that it would therefore seek to exploit any far-ranging and rapid change in the region's status quo. The notion of credibility played a key role here. Many in the Johnson administration argued that standing up to China was a test of American resolve, one that could decisively influence the attitudes of both friends and foes, in Asia and across the world.[8] French recognition of China would demonstrate to the world that de Gaulle disagreed. Recognition would signify a rejection of the contention that Beijing had expansionist aims in Southeast Asia, and the idea that South Vietnam was vital to Western security.

What American officials found particularly galling was the timing of de Gaulle's action. Rumors of endemic war-weariness and neutralist sentiment in Saigon had been gaining momentum for weeks in early January 1964, and U.S. decisionmakers did not doubt that a Paris-Beijing rapprochement would only strengthen the momentum for an early negotiated settlement. Moreover, it would inevitably increase speculation that the West's opposition to a China supportive of Hanoi was diminishing. The fact that 1964 was a U.S. presidential election year also made the timing poor from the administration's perspective. The Republican nominee might be able to make French action into a campaign issue—particularly, White House officials feared, if a sizable number of other countries followed France's example and thereby won China a United Nations seat.

The Johnson Administration's Response to French Recognition

Lyndon Johnson and his aides therefore launched a concerted effort to persuade de Gaulle to abandon his plan, or at least delay its implementation until the situation in Vietnam had stabilized. They moved on several fronts. On December 29, U.S. assistant secretary of state for far eastern affairs Roger Hilsman appeared on NBC Television's *Meet the Press* and, without directly mentioning France, said that the West needed to maintain a policy of firmness and dispassion with regard to Communist China. No credible evidence existed, Hilsman said, that Chinese leaders were about to become moderate and reasonable; if anything, they might take an "even tougher" stand in world affairs. When asked what scope for negotiations he believed might exist, Hilsman forcefully replied that he saw no prospects for early improvement in relations between China and the Western allies.

Four days later, on January 3, the State Department instructed Charles Bohlen, the U.S. ambassador in Paris, to seek an appointment with the French leader as soon as possible to convey American concerns and elicit a promise from him to discuss the issue with Washington before proceeding with recognition. De Gaulle, it turned out, was away from the capital, but Bohlen did meet with Foreign Minister Maurice Couve de Murville. He did not get the response he sought. Couve told him that no military victory was possible for the West in Indochina, and that France therefore supported the neutralization of the whole region, including possibly Thailand. The foreign minister did not object to American desires to keep Vietnam divided, but he said that any long-term partition could come only by way of negotiation, not by military force. French recognition of China, he insisted, would enhance the prospects for successful neutralization. A few days later, Bohlen encountered de Gaulle at a party at the Elysée Palace and told the general that France simply could not proceed with recognition in an American election year. When Soviet ambassador Sergei Vinogradov joined the group, he saved de Gaulle from having to respond.[9]

The French reaction was hardly the response Bohlen and policymakers in Washington had hoped to receive, and left them uncertain how to proceed. Some favored a letter from Johnson himself to de Gaulle, on the grounds that only direct presidential intervention could induce the general to reconsider. Rusk appeared to endorse this view, as did U.S. undersecretary of state for political affairs W. Averell Harriman, who told Rusk that de Gaulle simply had "to be faced up with the fact that if he recognizes Red China this year he will do so in direct opposition to the wishes of the President of the United States." But others, including Bohlen and National Security Adviser McGeorge Bundy, were uncertain that a presidential communication would do any good; experience had shown, they believed, that the French president did not respond to such pressure, and failure would reflect badly on Johnson. "You yourself will want to be in a position to shrug this off if it happens," Bundy counseled the president. Instead, the State Department should continue to press for a delay until 1965, and should "generate as many expressions of concern to Paris from other countries as possible."[10]

Bundy's argument won the day. The president evidently shared his concern that all efforts to persuade de Gaulle might fail, and that he should therefore avoid any personal involvement. This soon proved an accurate assessment—by the middle of the second week in January, despite continued State Department pressure against this, all signs pointed to a French announcement of recognition before the end of the month. On January 15, France's ambassador in Washington, Hervé Alphand, confirmed to Harriman that action was imminent. Harriman replied bitterly (with "extreme rudeness," Alphand later recalled) that the move would constitute a slap in Lyndon's Johnson's face during an election year, as well as a setback to free world interests. In Indochina, for example, pressure would increase for a neutralist settlement sure to be detrimental to the West.[11]

U.S. officials quickly shifted to a second objective: convincing allies and the Saigon government of Duong Van Minh that de Gaulle's China initiative would not alter American commitments in Vietnam. Key U.S. embassies were instructed to emphasize that the administration intended to stand firm, and that French thinking on the situation was mistaken. Undersecretary of State George Ball represented the administration strategy in a White House conversation with Canadian external affairs minister Paul

Martin on January 22. Ball said French recognition of China would "upset a few apple carts" and would provoke increased speculation in South Vietnam that neutralization was in the offing, but would not diminish U.S. determination to help the Vietnamese achieve a victory over communism. A neutralist solution was no solution at all, Ball maintained, and would effectively only serve to facilitate a takeover by China.[12]

Senior U.S. officials also took the same hard line in nondiplomatic venues. On January 22, Rusk told an audience at Barnard College that the United States was in Vietnam to fulfill its obligations in the struggle against communism and that "no new conference or agreement [on Vietnam] is needed. All that is needed is for the North Vietnamese to abandon their aggression." Five days later, Secretary of Defense Robert McNamara, appearing before the House Armed Services Committee, declared that the situation in South Vietnam "continues grave" but that "the survival of an independent Government in South Vietnam is so important to the security of all Southeast Asia and to the free world that I can conceive of no other alternative other than to take all necessary measures within our capability to prevent a communist victory."[13]

Rusk and McNamara understood only too well that none of these affirmations of American determination would mean anything unless the South Vietnamese themselves were persuaded that neutralization was disastrous and U.S. support for the war remained firm. Already uncertain over the Minh government's commitment to a military solution, the Johnson team worried about the impact that de Gaulle's China initiative might have on its thinking. By mid-January, Saigon was awash in rumors involving de Gaulle, Beijing, and Indochina. On January 18, an Agence France-Presse (AFP) article that was widely circulated in Saigon said that France planned to use its impending recognition of China to bring about a negotiated settlement in Indochina. The article equated American actions in the war with those of the Vietcong and North Vietnam, and it termed a cease-fire an essential first step on the road to peace.

An outraged Henry Cabot Lodge, the U.S. ambassador in Saigon, moved quickly "to repudiate French plans to recognize Peiping and the whole line of thought contained in the AFP article." On January 21, he met with top Saigon leaders, including Minh, Prime Minister Nguyen Ngo Tho, Foreign Minister Pham Dang Lam, and General Le Van Kim. President Johnson was committed to their struggle, the ambassador assured them, and had no interest in any solution proposed by Paris. Indeed, so determined was the president, Lodge pointed out, that he had approved "a plan for expanded operations against North Vietnam."[14]

Lodge appears to have been uncertain about the junta members' reaction to his comments, for he gave contradictory reports of the meeting. In the first, submitted the same day, he conceded that the South Vietnamese had criticized the rationale behind the plan for North Vietnam (most significantly, they rejected the notion that the proposed actions would demoralize the North). Still, he "had the sense" that the AFP article and de Gaulle's plans had disturbed Tho and Kim, and that Minh was "greatly reassured and relieved that we did not take the French maneuvers too seriously." In a second report, however, submitted some ten days later (after the junta had been ousted from power), the ambassador pondered uneasily the eagerness with which Minh and the others had sought to discuss de Gaulle and neutralization. General Kim, in particular, had been "obviously eager to discuss it," and Lodge now wondered whether this might be because Kim supported such a solution.[15]

U.S. Opposition to Neutralist Solutions in Vietnam

The incessant American concern over absence of will among the South Vietnamese and their leaders pointed to the fundamental problem the United States faced in Vietnam as 1964 began: finding a government committed to producing political stability in Saigon and to waging war against the Vietcong. As with the Diem regime before it, doubts over the Minh regime's determination on both counts had existed since it came to power. Now, some ten weeks later, a growing number of Americans in South Vietnam, particularly in the military, were convinced that any such commitment was missing and new leadership must be found.

In mid-January 1964, many of these officials believed they had found such leadership in the figure of General Nguyen Khanh, who was widely regarded as the most hawkish and pro-American military officer in the South. Ambitious and unscrupulous, Khanh had supported the coup against Diem but turned against the new government when Minh failed to appoint him to a key post in the ruling Military Revolutionary Council. Khanh saw an opportunity to advance his cause by spreading word around Saigon that Paris was behind a conspiracy to bring to power a procommunist South Vietnamese government that would implement de Gaulle's call for neutralization.

On January 28, one day after the French Foreign Office announced that France would establish diplomatic relations with China, he informed American officials that the key Vietnamese in this plot were Don and Kim, both of whom had served in French colonial administrations, and General Mai

Huu Xuan. Khanh charged that, together with Minh, they were "pro-French and pro-neutralist" and firmly supported de Gaulle's plans. As proof, he noted that Don had recently held a dinner for two Gaullist deputies from the French National Assembly and had invited Minh and Kim.[16]

Was there any substance to Khanh's charge? It is hard to say, but it seems doubtful; certainly, little hard evidence to support it has emerged over the years. At the time, though, the Central Intelligence Agency's (CIA's) Saigon station gave considerable credence to his assertions, as did Lodge. The ambassador made clear in cables to Washington on January 28 and 29 that he was sympathetic to a Khanh-led coup, and he chose not to inform the Minh government of the general's scheming. That silence may have been critical, for on January 30, in a hastily executed action, Khanh and a group of officers toppled the three-month-old government. Khanh and other sources in Saigon told American officials the same day that the coup was intended to save South Vietnam from a neutral settlement resembling that de Gaulle had suggested. The settlement, Khanh said, was to have coincided with France's recognition of China, and would have been announced by Minh on January 31 or in the first few days of February.[17]

In Paris, meanwhile, de Gaulle drew a direct link between his government's recognition of China and the war in Vietnam during a much-publicized news conference on January 31. "There is no political reality in Asia," he said, "which does not interest or touch China. Neither war nor peace is imaginable on that continent without China's becoming implicated. Thus it is absolutely inconceivable that without her participation there can be any accord on the eventual neutrality of Southeast Asia." With Beijing on board, however, the prospects for such a successful neutralization were excellent, de Gaulle insisted, provided that the agreement was guaranteed at the international level; that it outlawed "armed agitations" by the states involved; and that it excluded "the various forms of external intervention." Such an outcome, the general concluded, "seems, at the present time, to be the only situation compatible with the peaceful existence and progress of the peoples concerned."[18]

American analysts paid close attention to the French president's press conference and struggled to devise an effective response. When Johnson in a February 1 press conference appeared to give qualified endorsement to the notion of a neutralized Vietnam, aides became alarmed, even though he also said that de Gaulle was harming U.S. efforts in the region. The domestic and foreign press could, these aides feared, twist his remarks any number of ways to make it appear that the United States supported a neutral solution. Secretary of State Rusk immediately instructed subordinates to prepare a clarifying statement indicating that the administration had been and remained strongly opposed to the French position and was determined to press ahead with the war. He then instructed Lodge to issue the same clarification in Saigon. "It would be incorrect," Rusk emphasized, "to read any change in policy into the President's remarks."

Johnson himself took an unambiguous tone in a handwritten letter to Khanh the same day. "I am glad we see eye to eye on the necessity of stepping up the pace of military operations against the Vietcong," Johnson wrote. "We shall continue to be available to help you carry the war to the enemy and to increase the confidence of the Vietnamese people in their government." And Lodge, in early meetings with Khanh, assured him that U.S. policy was unchanged and warned that he would "rise or fall, as far as American opinion was concerned," on the results he obtained in the military effort against the Vietcong.[19]

This signified a categorical rejection of the notion of seeking a negotiated settlement of the type proposed by de Gaulle. Once again, as so often in the period 1963–69, American officials showed a remarkable ability to fret about the potential spread of the French president's ideas while steadfastly refusing to seriously consider those ideas on their merits. In subsequent months, they would continue to worry about the implications of de Gaulle's China initiative, even as they laid the groundwork for an expanded war.

The day after the coup, Johnson summed up his administration's thinking for Walker Stone, editor-in-chief of the Scripps-Howard newspapers. "This Khanh is the toughest one they got and the ablest one they got," Johnson declared. "And he said, 'Screw this neutrality, we ain't going to do business with the Communists, and get the goddamned hell out of here. I'm pro-American and I'm taking over.' Now it'll take him a little time to get his marbles in a row, just like it's taking me a little time. But it's de Gaulle's loss and the neutralists' loss, not the Americans' loss."[20]

Conclusions

How, then, to interpret de Gaulle's China initiative in 1964 and its relationship to the Vietnam conflict? In its direct impact, the connection was arguably minor. The fighting in South Vietnam continued, American involvement increased, and in 1965 a large-scale war erupted that would claim well more than a million lives and cause the destruction of vast areas of North Vietnam, South Vietnam, and neighboring Laos and Cambodia. De Gaulle's stated hope, that recognition of China could help promote a political settlement in Vietnam, never came close to being realized.[21]

Indeed, if the French leader's action had any immediate impact on the Vietnam conflict, it was in a way he did not intend. Nguyen Khanh, in justifying his coup d'état, said he had acted to head off a French-inspired neutralist deal. One can readily imagine the power-hungry Khanh making a grab for power even without de Gaulle's initiative, but the rumors swirling around Saigon in January about a Sino-French play for peace in Indochina undoubtedly helped his cause and made American officials yet more welcoming toward the coup.

This coup unquestionably proved momentous. Coming so soon after the overthrow of Diem, Khanh's ouster of the Minh junta has often been overlooked in the scholarly literature. This is regrettable, for as many contemporaneous observers immediately sensed, the second coup bore great historical importance in its own right. British, Australian, and French officials, for example, thought the coup was a disastrous development, not just because of the tumult it generated throughout South Vietnam's governmental structure but also because of what they considered Khanh's grave shortcomings as a leader. Those traits Americans had seen as negatives in Duong Van Minh—his determination to keep the United States at arm's length and to some degree to shift the struggle from the military to the political plane—such foreign observers tended to view as positives, while the attributes in Khanh the Johnson administration thought appealing they perceived as weaknesses.

"In General Khanh, the Americans appear to have found the kind of man whom they think they can understand and appreciate and who, so they believe, understands and appreciates them," the British ambassador in Saigon, Gordon Etherington-Smith, cabled London, describing Khanh's "bounce and fluency" and "no-nonsense" approach. "To us here," he said, "it seems increasingly probable that the very qualities which make Khanh attractive to American soldiers and politicians render him unpleasing to a very great many Vietnamese." The ambassador was convinced that the Johnson administration, even if it did not instigate the January coup, could and should have prevented it, telling the Foreign Office on February 12: "[The U.S.] failure to support Minh against Khanh has made many people draw bitter conclusions regarding American loyalty. U.S. prestige as a whole has suffered and, if the situation were to deteriorate further, the Americans might well find that the influence they can now exert on the Vietnamese is less than it was." The same viewpoint emerged at quadripartite talks in Washington early in the month, where officials from Australia, New Zealand, and the United Kingdom made clear their uneasiness about new developments and their skepticism toward Khanh.[22]

American policymakers, too, would become disenchanted with Khanh, but not until around mid-1964. Even then, he would retain power for several more months, until February 1965. Thus, for some twelve critical months, Khanh would lead the Government of Viet Nam (GVN), twelve months during which the Vietcong consolidated its hold on key areas of the South and war weariness and alienation from the GVN became rampant at all levels of South Vietnamese society. When Khanh lost favor with American officials, it was for failing in their eyes to prosecute the war sufficiently vigorously. Like the Diem regime and Minh junta before him, Khanh learned that his ability to win broad-based domestic support would be directly linked to his ability to preserve a degree of independence from the Americans.

More than anything, de Gaulle's China initiative should win attention from Vietnam War scholars for the light it sheds on both the nature of Western allied interaction at a key point in the conflict and the failure of diplomacy in the run-up to a major war. Washington proved spectacularly unsuccessful in its efforts to persuade friendly governments around the world to join in opposing de Gaulle's planned China initiative and convince him to reconsider. Few world leaders objected to the French action, and many welcomed it. In early October 1963, Eisaku Sato, a top Japanese official soon to become prime minister, told de Gaulle in Paris that Tokyo shared the French perspective and had worked hard to boost Japanese commercial relations with Beijing. The Americans, Sato said, lacked an accurate sense of the realities of the situation. In mid-January 1964, Canadian prime minister Lester Pearson told de Gaulle that Ottawa had no objection to French recognition of China. Canada indeed hoped to follow suit itself before too long, Pearson said, and he assured de Gaulle that Ottawa would not participate in any United States–sponsored anti-French action.[23] It was not coincidental that when, a year later, Washington used the supposed China threat to justify major escalation in Vietnam, Tokyo, Ottawa, and most other allied governments would express deep skepticism.

The lack of influence went both ways. These weeks in late 1963 and early 1964 displayed one of the central elements in U.S. decisionmaking on Vietnam under Kennedy and Johnson: the unalterable American opposition to an early negotiated settlement.[24] Washington planners would spend much time discussing the French leader's actions and ideas, but only in terms of how best to counter them. The substance of his argument was not closely examined, then or thereafter. Three decades later, McNamara would acknowledge as much, expressing regret over the "limited and shallow" nature of the arguments he and his associates made in early 1964 against neutralization or withdrawal.[25] But their arguments also revealed something else, namely, the continuing American fear that the momentum for such a settlement might become too great to stop. The neutralization proposals de Gaulle and others (notably Cambodian leader Norodom Sihanouk) advanced were vague, but Americans knew that was precisely why the concept might appeal to many in South Vietnam and elsewhere.

Undoubtedly, the fact that de Gaulle was making this pitch proved unhelpful. Washington strategists distrusted the French leader, and they were convinced that he had ulterior motives in opposing U.S. efforts in Vietnam. Many of them viewed his intervention as having little to do with Vietnam but a great deal with his longtime goal of winning greater independence for France within the Western alliance. In this formulation, his pronouncement was merely one more in a long line of specific policy decisions that flowed from that larger objective—others included his continuation of the nuclear weapons development program initiated by his predecessors in the Fourth Republic; his push for greater French influence over decisionmaking within NATO; and his rebuff of Anglo-American attempts to admit the United Kingdom into the European Common Market.

U.S. policymakers also reasoned that de Gaulle, embarrassed by the French defeat in the region, did not wish the United States to succeed where France had failed. They were, moreover, convinced that what they saw as de Gaulle's own negative view of the United States, dating back to his troubled relationship with Franklin Roosevelt during World War II, contributed to the French position. Many were certain that de Gaulle would automatically oppose *any* American initiative that was not immediately beneficial to France, and they often speculated that Franco-American friction would end once de Gaulle left office.[26]

Still, the real problem for the Johnson team was the message, not the messenger. The Frenchman's ideas would have been anathema coming from anyone. The U.S. administration was determined to avoid all negotiations on Vietnam until the war effort had been turned around and America was in a position to dictate terms. For Johnson, there was also another consideration: 1964 was an election year. Until voting day, he was determined to avoid dramatic moves on Vietnam in either direction, whether toward negotiated withdrawal or major escalation. To the extent possible, Vietnam should remain on the back burner. In those early post-Dallas months, in particular, he was loath to do anything that could be depicted, especially by Robert F. Kennedy, as marking a significant change from his slain predecessor's foreign policy.

The skeptical reader might wonder whether, in practice, this American posture made a major difference in historical terms. Could the kind of political settlement envisioned by de Gaulle genuinely have been reached in early 1964, if Washington had been willing to seriously attempt it? Like all counterfactual questions, this one resists conclusive answer. But as I have argued at some length elsewhere, the best answer is that it could have been. U.S. officials themselves thought so—the acute American concern over the prospect of early negotiations is in itself indirect but powerful additional evidence of their viability. Washington officials fretted over negotiations on Vietnam at the start of 1964 precisely because they recognized that diplomacy represented a workable—if from their perspective also odious—means to bring the conflict to an end.

The British, Canadian, and Japanese governments also saw opportunities for a negotiated solution during this period, particularly given the strong desire on the part of Hanoi and Beijing to prevent a major American intervention in the conflict, and they agreed that de Gaulle's China initiative substantially boosted the prospects for such an agreement. Even Australian diplomats, throughout the war the most hawkish among America's allies with respect to Vietnam, considered the French leader's analysis rational and plausible, even though they opposed his policy prescription. In the U.S. Senate, Democratic heavyweights such as Mike Mansfield and J. William Fulbright viewed a vigorous and imaginative attempt at a diplomatic solution as infinitely preferable to escalation. Senator and then vice president Hubert H. Humphrey felt likewise, as did such influential media voices as the *New York Times* and the columnist Walter Lippmann.

As for the North Vietnamese, Chinese, and Soviets, much remains to be learned about their decisionmaking on the conflict in these months. The available evidence, however, suggests strongly that these governments were neither anxious to start early negotiations nor actively opposed to them. In early February 1964, for example, Ho Chi Minh and Pham Van Dong told officials of the French *délegate-géneral* in Hanoi that they supported de Gaulle's position on the war and were prepared to let South Vietnam choose its own political system pending reunification. If the Americans chose to fight, however, Hanoi was ready. Dong concluded by urging France to continue its efforts for peace and said: "We don't want Americans in the South, but we are in no hurry, and we know how to wait. When the time comes, we will talk around a table. The reunification of the country presupposes a single government, but we will respect the interests of the South, sincerely, without any pressure."[27]

For the Soviets, meanwhile, an international conflagration over Vietnam would be the wrong war in the wrong place at the wrong time, particularly because it might result in increased Chinese influence in the region. And the Chinese, keen to preclude a large-scale American presence on their southern frontier, were—notwithstanding all Mao's bellicose rhetoric on the subject in the domestic context and when dealing with Vietnamese officials, as demonstrated in chapters 1 and 5 of the present volume—careful to avoid making specific pledges of support to Hanoi in the event of a major U.S. intervention. Indeed, chapter 6 below reveals the extraordinary diplomatic convolutions that the Chinese government subsequently undertook to ensure that distinct if undefined limits circumscribed both its own and the United States' involvement in Vietnam.

Ultimately, it is hard to argue against the assertions of numerous contemporaneous observers that Washington had wrongly closed itself off from a negotiated solution in Vietnam, and that de Gaulle now offered a way to rectify this mistake.[28] Decades later, McNamara and Bundy, two of the key architects of American intervention, would concede as much.[29] In early 1964, they and their colleagues were determined to press ahead with the war effort. That determination, combined with the unwillingness of the other key players in the world arena to work hard at starting negotiations, ensured that diplomacy would fail. It is no contradiction to say that de Gaulle's 1964 initiative constituted a missed opportunity, but one never close to realization, to prevent the tragedy that the Vietnam War became.

Notes

1. The background to the 1964 opening is very well treated in Inge Johnsen, "La reconnaissance de la République populaire de Chine par la France en 1964" [The recognition of the People's Republic of China by France in 1964], M.A. thesis in history, University of Oslo, 1999.

2. Edgar Faure, *Le serpent et la tortue: Les problèmes de la Chine populaire* [The snake and the tortoise: The problems of the People's Republic of China] (Paris: Julliard, 1957).

3. Paris to Foreign Office (FO), January 8, 1964, FO 371/175923, Public Record Office, Kew Gardens, England (hereafter PRO); Paris to FO, January 15, 1964, FO

371/175923, PRO. See also the meeting notes taken by Alain Peyrefitte during several French Cabinet meetings in November and December 1963 and January 1964, in Alain Peyrefitte, *C'était de Gaulle: La France reprend sa place dans le monde* [This was de Gaulle: France regains her place in the world] (Paris: Fayard, 1997), 480–94; and Maurice Vaïsse, *La grandeur: Politique étrangère du général de Gaulle 1958–1969* [Greatness: The foreign policy of General de Gaulle, 1958–1969] (Paris: Fayard, 1999), 514–21; Vaïsse, *L'établissement de relations diplomatiques entre la France et la Chine populaire (27 janvier 1964)* [The establishment of diplomatic relations between France and the People's Republic of China (27 January 1964)], Cahier 1, Cahiers de la Fondation Charles de Gaulle [Publications of the Charles de Gaulle Foundation] (Paris: Fondation Charles de Gaulle, 1995). According to Philippe Devillers, de Gaulle's talks with Johnson and Rusk at the time of Kennedy's funeral convinced him that U.S. Asian policy would henceforth be more unrealistic than ever, and that France must resume contact with Beijing as soon as possible. Philippe Devillers, "French Policy in the Second Vietnam War," *World Today* 23 (June 1967): 249–63. For French recognition of China, see also Jean Lacouture, *De Gaulle: Le Souverain, 1958–1969* (Paris: Seuil, 1986), 439–43; W. W. Kulski, *De Gaulle and the World: The Foreign Policy of the Fifth French Republic* (Syracuse, N.Y.: Syracuse University Press, 1966), 315–17; Edgar Faure, *Mémoires, II* (Paris: Plon, 1982), 673–74; and Charles G. Cogan, *Charles de Gaulle: A Brief Biography with Documents* (Boston: Bedford Books, 1996), 149–50.

4. "Instructions pour Edgar Faure, 26 septembre 1963," in *Lettres, Notes, et Carnets, 1961–1963,* by Charles de Gaulle (Paris: Plon, 1986), 374–75. See also Edgar Faure, "Reconnaissance de la Chine," *Espoir,* no. 1 (1972): esp. 24–25; Johnsen, "Reconnaisance," 164–66.

5. "Entretien de Gaulle–Rusk, 16 décembre 1963," Entretiens et Messages (hereafter EM), Ministère des Affaires Etrangères (hereafter MAE), Paris; CIA Report, "France Reassessing Policy toward Communist China?" September 6, 1963, box 72, National Security File, Country File (hereafter NSF CF), John F. Kennedy Library, Boston (hereafter JFKL); Bohlen to State, October 16, 1963, box 73, NSF CF, JFKL; CIA Memorandum for the Director, "Gaullist France and Communist China," October 23, 1963, box 73, NSF CF, JFKL; State to Bohlen, January 3, 1964, box 461, W. Averell Harriman Papers, Manuscripts Division, Library of Congress, Washington (hereafter Harriman Papers). See also Peyrefitte, *C'était de Gaulle,* 484; and "Entretien de Gaulle–Bohlen, 5 novembre 1963," EM, MAE.

6. Hanoi to FO, May 24, 1963, FO 371/170103, PRO; Hanoi to FO, January 14, 1963, FO 371/170103, PRO; Mieczyslaw Maneli, *War of the Vanquished* (New York: Harper & Row, 1971), 202–3.

7. *Newsweek,* September 16, 1963; *New York Times,* November 12, 1963; Jean Daniel, "De Gaulle's Vietnam," *New Republic,* September 14, 1963.

8. See "Talking Points for Douglas-Home Visit," February 4, 1964, box 212, National Security File, Country File (hereafter NSF CF), Lyndon Baines Johnson Library, Austin (hereafter LBJL). In January 1964, the JCS warned that an American failure to stand up to China in Vietnam would damage American credibility throughout Asia and have "a corresponding unfavorable effect upon our image in Africa and Latin America." CIA Memorandum, January 1964, box 1, NSF, Vietnam File (hereafter NSF VN), LBJL.

9. State to Bohlen, January 3, 1964, box 461, Harriman Papers; Bohlen to State, January 8, 1964, box 169, NSF CF, LBJL; Paris to FO, FO 371/175923, PRO.

10. Harriman to Rusk, January 8, 1964, box 454, Harriman Papers; McGeorge

Bundy to LBJ, January 8, 1964, box 1, NSF Memos to the President—Bundy, LBJL; Memcon, Tyler and Bohlen, January 7, 1964, box 1, NSF VN, LBJL; LBJ–McGeorge Bundy telcon, January 15, 1964, JT. Bohlen had initially favored intervention by LBJ. On December 30, 1963, he had even drafted a suggested letter from Johnson to de Gaulle. Bohlen to Harriman, December 30, 1963, box 454, Harriman Papers. The desire to be able to "shrug this off if it happens" also led the administration to reject a proposed meeting between Johnson and de Gaulle in Martinique.

11. LBJ–Russell telcon, January 15, 1964, Johnson Tapes of White House Telephone Conversations (hereafter JT); U.S. Department of State, *Foreign Relations of the United States, 1964–1968* (hereafter *FRUS*), vol. 1, 32; Hervé Alphand, *L'étonnement d'être: Journal, 1939–1973* (Paris: Fayard), 420–23. See also Harriman's comments to British officials, as reported in Washington to FO, January 18, 1964, FO 371/175923, PRO.

12. Most of Martin's comments in the conversation remain sanitized, but Ball's phraseology suggests considerable Canadian skepticism about U.S. policy. MemCon, Ball and Martin, January 22, 1964, box 167, NSF CF, LBJL. See also Entretien Couve-Martin, 15 janvier 1964, EM, MAE.

13. Rusk and McNamara statements are from "Chronology on Vietnam," November 1965, box 38, NSF NSC History, LBJL. On McNamara before the HASC, see also Deborah Shapley, *Promise and Power: The Life and Times of Robert McNamara* (Boston: Little, Brown, 1993), 295–96.

14. This was known as OPLAN 34A. Lodge to State, January 19, 1964, box 1, NSF, VN, LBJL; Lodge to State, January 21, 1964, box 1, NSF VN, LBJL. The State Department lauded Lodge for his comments. The United States, it said in a cable, was "180 degrees opposed" to the recommendations in the AFP article, believed the war could be won, and saw the "French approach as avenue of disaster which could lead to communist control of all Viet-Nam and Southeast Asia." State to Lodge, January 21, 1964, box 1, NSF VN, LBJL.

15. Lodge to State, January 21, 1964, box 1, NSF VN, LBJL; Lodge to State, February 1, 1964, box 1, NSF VN, LBJL.

16. *The Pentagon Papers: The Defense Department History of Decision-Making on Vietnam,* Senator Gravel edition, 5 vols. (Boston: Beacon Press, 1971–72), vol. 2, 308–9, and vol. 3, 37–38 (hereafter *PP*).

17. *PP,* vol. 3, 39. In his first press conference, Khanh justified his action on this ground, attacking those in the previous regime "who took a subservient attitude, paving the way for neutralization and thereby selling out the nation." *Le Monde,* January 31, 1964.

18. The de Gaulle quotation is in Press and Information Division, French Embassy, *Chronology of Charles de Gaulle's Press Conferences, 1958–1966* (New York: French Embassy, 1968), 89. A State Department statement issued the day of the announcement described the French action as an "unfortunate step, particularly at a time when the Chinese communists are actively promoting aggression and subversion in Southeast Asia and elsewhere." *New York Times,* January 31, 1964.

19. Rusk–Manning telcon, February 1, 1964, *FRUS, 1964–1968,* vol. 1, 57–58; State to Saigon, February 1, 1964, box 2, NSF VN, LBJL; LBJ to Khanh, February 2, 1964, box 2, NSF VN, LBJL; Lodge to State, January 31, 1964, box 1, NSF VN, LBJL. The emphasis on continuity extended to the potentially prickly recognition issue. On January 31, the administration announced that the United States was "continuing rela-

tions with the new leaders of the Government of the Republic of Vietnam," and that "accordingly no question of recognition" was involved.

20. LBJ–Stone telcon, January 31, 1964, JT. Johnson used similar language in another telephone conversation the same day. See LBJ–Marshall McNeil telcon, January 31, 1964, JT.

21. This was the case at least in the short term. Richard Nixon and Henry Kissinger would later say that French recognition of China in 1964 helped pave the way for the American opening to Beijing seven years later, and to the extent that that opening helped bring about the Paris Peace Accords of 1973, de Gaulle's hope can be said to have been at least partially realized. See Lacouture, *De Gaulle,* 443.

22. Saigon to FO, February 6, 1964, FO 371/175468, PRO; Saigon to FO, March 16, 1964, FO 371/175495, PRO; Saigon to FO, April 8, 1964, FO 371/175495, PRO; Saigon to FO, February 12, 1964, FO 371/175493, PRO; Record of Meeting, Washington, February 10, 1964, FO 371/175090, PRO.

23. "Entretien Eisaku Sato–de Gaulle, 4–5 octobre 1963," EM, MAE; Paris to FO, January 17, 1964, FO 371/175923, PRO.

24. This is one of the main themes in my book, *Choosing War: The Lost Chance for Peace and the Escalation of War in Vietnam* (Berkeley: University of California Press, 1999).

25. Robert McNamara, with Brian VanDeMark, *In Retrospect: The Tragedy and Lessons of Vietnam* (New York: Times Books, 1995), 106–7.

26. Responding to such speculation, one administration official who was convinced that de Gaulle had widespread support for his policy said: "[The] U.S. should not assume that everything which de Gaulle stands for is merely a product of his peculiar outlook and state of mind; that if it weren't for de Gaulle, France would be a docile and reasonable ally." William Tyler to McGeorge Bundy, March 3, 1964, box 169, NSF CF, LBJL. Similarly, Marianna Sullivan has demonstrated that most political leaders and journalists in France agreed with de Gaulle's analysis of Vietnam and supported his policy. Marianna P. Sullivan, *France's Vietnam Policy: A Study in French-American Relations* (Westport, Conn.: Greenwood Press, 1978), 75–79.

27. Hanoi to Paris, February 11, 1964, "Visite au président Ho Chi Minh et au premier Pham Van Dong," RDVN, #78, MAE.

28. See, e.g., Walter Lippmann's columns in the *Washington Post,* February 4 and 11, 1964; Mike Mansfield to LBJ, January 6, 1964, box 1, NSF VN, LBJL; *New York Times,* December 8, 1963, and January 31, 1964. See also McGeorge Bundy's comment on the "soft" editorial page of the *Times* in Bundy–LBJ telcon, February 6, 1964, JT.

29. McNamara, *In Retrospect;* McGeorge Bundy, interview with the author, New York City, March 15, 1994.

5

The Economic and Political Impact of the Vietnam War on China in 1964

Li Xiangqian

Broadly speaking, there is little argument that the Vietnam War had substantial economic and political effects upon China, but it remains difficult to assess just how great was its role and how significant its impact upon China's development. Historians may well have been tempted to stress unduly its domestic influence upon China, while ignoring the degree to which Chinese leaders, especially Mao Zedong, were able to take advantage of the war as a pretext or excuse for promoting domestic policies they considered desirable, and thereby consolidating their own political position. In the mid-1960s, the Vietnam War was only one of various factors that may have substantially influenced the political and economic evolution of China, and one should neither underestimate nor exaggerate its impact. As a rule, the greater the application of external force, the stronger the internal reaction; conversely, the less the outside pressure, the weaker the reaction from within. A detailed study of the actual economic and political effects of the Vietnam War on China will enhance our understanding of the causes and patterns of Chinese domestic development as affected by outside forces

173

originating in the international arena; and it will further illuminate the roles that both China and the broader Cold War played in each other's history, along with the interplay between Chinese domestic policies and the Vietnam War.

Mao Zedong's 1964 Policy Shift on Vietnam

The years from 1962 to 1965 were a period of domestic economic rehabilitation in China. Political considerations and human psychology alike suggested following the course of encouraging economic and political stability, because both the troubled domestic economy, severely damaged by the Great Leap Forward and the political wounds inflicted by the Anti-Rightist movements of late 1959, required aggressive treatment and rehabilitation. Yet, in practice, history rarely develops as human plans anticipate. As 1964 opened, China began to experience economic and political changes that were at least superficially related to the escalating Vietnam War and the tense situation along the Chinese border.

If one seeks a simple cause-and-effect relationship, the war in Vietnam and rising tensions in the border regions contributed to a shift in China's basic developmental structure, which Chinese leaders had agreed upon and set forth in the Third Five-Year Plan, from emphasizing the development of economic sectors providing food, clothing, and consumer goods, to stressing the prevention of war and the defense program. The construction and management of the Three Lines (Third Front) Projects was a prime example of the new approach. Such a major switch had a profound impact on Chinese society. Not only was the already limited long-term investment in basic infrastructure redirected toward military preparations, but to a great extent these efforts also absorbed the capital that would otherwise have been devoted to economic rehabilitation in the interests of the people. Socially, the increasing emphasis on war generated new tensions. From the broader backdrop of the progress of China's modernization, although the Three Lines Projects generated relatively large-scale industrial development in various regions of China, they also inflicted much long-term damage on the Chinese economy.

Previous studies that have sought to explain the reasons for this strategic shift have tended to rely on traditional interpretations and accepted beliefs, and have therefore been of limited interpretive value. They have tended to follow the popular belief that, as one historian puts it, "in 1964 a tense situation developed in China's border areas, in which it was expected 'all winds and storms would break loose.' It was feared that at any moment China might face military invasion from overseas. On August 5, 1964, two months before China successfully tested its first nuclear bomb, the U.S. Navy launched attacks on the Democratic Republic of Vietnam, bearing the fires of war and aggression all the way north to China's southern borders and directly threatening Chinese national security. In China's north, the border clashes with the Soviet Union that began in 1964 escalated continuously. In China's southwest, tensions on the Chinese-Indian borders were still not completely settled."[1] The prevailing popular interpretation therefore argues that domestically China was left with no alternative but to initiate a strategic readjustment toward war preparations.

Yet it is not enough to rely simply on popular beliefs, rather than seeking evidence to validate or disprove such theories. For example, the Tonkin Gulf incident occurred on August 5, 1964, yet at least two months earlier Mao had first raised the possibility of changing the Third Five-Year Plan. Likewise, Mao rather suddenly suggested to the first line leadership of the Chinese Communist Party (CCP) Central Committee that China should swiftly adjust its strategic direction, even though the accepted working program was already under way.

Why did Mao move so unexpectedly and without warning to disrupt the established plan? Did other factors, such as the escalating ideological disputes between the Chinese and Soviet Communist Parties, or the sudden increased awareness of class struggle in China, play any role in this? If one regards the Vietnam War as the primary external factor in altering Chinese economic and political development, then is it true that, given the probable scope and impact of such a war, Mao and other Chinese leaders felt such alarmingly heightened concern for China's national security that they were forced to retract the plan they had already announced to focus economic development on meeting the basic needs of the people?

In reality, it seems that Mao abruptly changed the direction of the Third Five-Year Plan in mid-1964 because by then, in strategic terms, he had already begun to perceive growing cause for alarm. It was Mao himself who originally stated, in August 1963, that "1963, 1964, and 1965 will be years of rehabilitation."[2] More important, Mao raised his new suggestion with the CCP Central Committee at a time when heated arguments over whether or not any such adjustment should be made were in progress. Mao had not originally intended to reallocate any capital investment within the Chinese domestic economy, nor had he considered the possibility that China would enter a period of war preparation. Given how intensely China had suffered from the recent failure of the Great Leap Forward, it was reasonable to anticipate that the maintenance of stable economic development would be the highest priority. Moreover, at this time the scarcity of material resources, quite apart from any other human or emotional factors, severely limited the scope for any significant national economic or political shift.

Investigation reveals, however, that well before mid-1964 officials in the State Planning Commission already had some second thoughts regarding the Third Five-Year Plan. For example, in 1962 Li Fuchun wrote to Mao, suggesting that the next plan should emphasize the improvement of living standards among the people, with agricultural development the country's first priority, and further industrialization resting on a firm foundation of agricultural development.[3] Clearly, his preliminary suggestion served as the prototype for the subsequent Food, Clothing, and Goods Plan. In early 1963, the Third Five-Year Plan was formally submitted to the CCP Central Committee for discussion in the form of a report written by Li, "Main Points in the Task of Making Long Term Plans," which stated that the central goal of the Third Five-Year Plan would be to concentrate all resources on solving the problem of providing the people with food, clothing, and consumer goods.[4] The CCP Central Committee endorsed the major points of this report, and in September 1963 it gave official approval to the Third Five-Year Plan by affirming an economic program of "solving the problems of food, clothing, and consumer goods, enhancing heavy industries while taking care of the defense industry, and pursuing high-technology breakthroughs."[5]

There were two reasons why planning officials took a positive attitude toward the proposed five-year plan. First, they believed that the failure of the Great Leap Forward had been largely due to excessively rapid alterations in economic plans, to the extent that one might even characterize the Chinese economy as arbitrarily run without any planning whatever, tendencies that eventually inflicted great suffering on the entire population.[6] Second, the Great Leap Forward seriously retarded agricultural development and even brought famine, so that for several years China did not even have enough food to feed all its population. A consensus therefore existed that any program must have the overall objective of providing sufficient "food, clothing, and consumer goods." At a meeting of the CCP Central Committee in September 1963, in what may be regarded as a coda to the move to strengthen production of basic necessities, Deng Xiaoping put forward a scheme to bring under cultivation 500 million mu of high-yielding farmland, equivalent to one-third of the total existing cultivated land in China.[7]

Mao's Three Lines policy, however, interrupted this reasonable, commonsense approach. In May 1964, just before the CCP Central Committee met to finalize the Third Five-Year Plan, Mao suggested the Three Lines Projects. On May 10 and 11, 1964, he added several important riders when the leaders of the State Planning Committee reported to him. Two of these comments significantly modified the approach adopted by the State Planning Commission officials. First, when the report discussed railroad development during the Third Five-Year Plan, Mao said: "The steel factories in Juquan and Panzhihua still demand development. If not, what will I do if a war breaks out?" Second, when officials reported that heavy industrial development was still poorly coordinated with the development of the transportation system, Mao stated: "You will fall down if you do not stand on a firm footing. I see two fists—one is agriculture, the other the defense industries—and one backside, heavy industry. All of these must be improved. Above all, heavy industry must be improved; the rest should not be overemphasized."[8] Obviously, any improvement in heavy industry would come at the expense of light industry. In 1963, Li Fuchun had told a State Council national conference on transportation that "leaders at all levels must avoid the mistake of focusing solely on the industrial sectors," and "agricultural development must come first."[9] But now Mao's comments, which came as a complete surprise to those Chinese officials present, placed the defense industries and agriculture on an equal footing.

One must consider whether any evidence exists to suggest a direct causal relationship between the escalating Vietnam War and Mao's sudden proposal to alter the already almost finalized five-year plan to favor defense preparations and the Three Lines Projects. Close research—in particular, the fact that Mao made these suggestions well before the Tonkin Gulf incident of August 5, 1964, which led to full-scale American air strikes on North Vietnam and marked the escalation of the Vietnam War from local conflicts to a full-scale war—suggests the contrary, which further implies that purely strategic motives by no means fully accounted for his advocacy of such changes.

From May 10 and 11 onward, Mao's remarks on war and the need to prepare for it grew steadily more strident, climaxing on June 16, 1964, when Mao spoke at the Shisanling Reservoir. Besides those already quoted, on May 10 and 11 Mao made such remarks as: "I still rely on soldiers to fight wars.

One should have nuclear bombs—not too many, just a few to scare off enemies. But yellow gun powder and artillery are still very useful. The imperialists were most afraid of artillery."[10] When Mao discussed the Three Lines policy in Sichuan on May 27, 1964, he warned: "We should make preparations now. If we do not start now and further delays occur, this will not be good for the future. Conventional weapons will still be needed for the duration of the Third Five-Year Plan, and may even be needed during the Fourth and Fifth Five-Year Plans. In order to make the imperialist aggressors think twice before starting any war, we still need high-technology weaponry."[11] On June 6, 1964, Mao told a CCP Central Committee meeting:

> As long as the imperialists exist, there will be danger of war. We are not the commanders-in-chief for the imperialists. Thus, we have no way of knowing when they plan to start a war. The determining factor in winning eventual victory is not the nuclear bomb. It is conventional weapons. The program for the Three Lines Projects should include some industrial defense projects in the First and Second Lines. Defense industries should exist in every province, producing their own weapons and ammunition. As long as we have these, we can rest in peace. Unless Panzhihua Steel Plant is fully developed, I cannot go to sleep at night. If there is no Panzhihua Steel Plant, I will have to ride on a donkey to get to meetings. If we do not have enough money, use the royalty payments on my writings.[12]

Shifts in Chinese Strategic Thinking

When Mao discussed Chinese strategic thinking at the Shisanling Reservoir on June 16, 1964, he overturned the existing defense strategy of "defending the north and relinquishing the south," stating: "If our enemies wish to come, they may come from anywhere. We should be prepared and on high alert everywhere. We should make our strategic plans according to where our enemies come from."[13] He also stated that "the party chiefs of major areas should be responsible for those army units there. They will need guns as well as money."[14]

This evidence strongly suggests that, when discussing defense policies or developing the Three Lines, Mao did not focus solely on the Vietnam situation and its strategic implications. On the contrary, he believed enemies might assail China from any direction and therefore China should prepare itself on all fronts.

The suggestion that enemies might come from anywhere, and preparations should be made everywhere, conveyed a superficial sense of urgency, but in reality was even more ambiguous than the strategy of "defending the north and relinquishing the south." Zhou Enlai gave a definitive explanation of the Three Lines as follows: "Except for Panzhihua, all the provinces on China's borders and coasts belong to our Front Line. On the east coast, Fujian is at the forefront, and the provinces in the southeast also belong to our First Line. Toward Southeast Asia, China's south is our Front Line. Opposing imperialism, the northwestern and northeastern provinces are our Front Lines. If trouble with India begins in Xizang [Tibet], the entire interior will be our Third Line. Our real Third Lines are Qinghai, Hunan, Yunnan, and Panzhihua."[15]

Zhou surveyed China's strategic situation in all four directions, and his assessment of the dangers confronting China in the south—that is, China's defenses bordered on neighboring Vietnam—resembled his view of those from other directions. Contrary to popular belief that by then "the battle flames had reached China's door step," at this time Chinese leaders did not perceive a threat sufficiently grave to place China on full alert for war. The changes in the program for the Third Five-Year Plan and the proposal of the Three Lines did not, therefore, result from the urgent pressure of war, but rather from a broad overall sense that unspecified dangers existed.

One might more accurately argue that, rather than assigning highest significance to the pressure of war from the south, Chinese leaders focused primarily on the north. When Li Fuchun gave his report, "A Few Suggestions on the Plans," on May 18, 1964, the largest project in the original Third Five-Year Plan was the construction of the Jiuquan Jintieshan Steel Plant in Gansu Province, whose first phase was to be completed between 1972 and 1973, providing an annual production capacity of one to 1.5 million tons.[16] After Mao spoke to officials in Sichuan on May 27, 1964, however, the strategic importance of the Jiuquan Jintieshan plant decreased. As Li explained: "We have two home bases. One is in the southwest. The other is in the northwest. Currently, the southwest base is the most reliable one."[17] Deng also gave his thoughts on this issue: "Jiuquan used to be our home base, just like the southwest. Now, the situation has changed. It is now our second line."[18] Although Deng placed Jiuquan in the Second Line, otherwise their statements clearly resembled Zhou's remarks, that "when opposing imperialism, the northwest and the northeast are our

Front Line." By "imperialism," Zhou obviously meant the forces of the Soviet Union.

From the time of their first border clash in Xinjiang, initiated by the Soviet Union in August 1960, the Sino-Soviet borders became unstable. In 1962, larger clashes occurred at Yili and Daqing, and between August 1960 and October 1964, there were more than a thousand such military flare-ups along the Sino-Soviet border.[19] These conflicts disrupted normal diplomatic relations between China and the Soviet Union and led both sides to re-examine the history of a series of unequal treaties China and Czarist Russia had negotiated in the nineteenth century. On March 8, 1963, the *People's Daily* openly stated that the Aihui, Peking, and Yili Treaties were all unequal agreements forced upon China by the czarist government, and continued: "If the Soviet Union insists on the precedents established by the cases of Hong Kong and Macau [treaties between China and Western powers which the Soviet Union claimed were invalid], does that mean that all the unequal treaties remaining from the past should be re-examined together?" On September 27, 1963, the Chinese Foreign Ministry presented to the Soviet government a memorandum formally raising issues concerning the unequal treaties. On November 19, 1963, the Chinese foreign minister further stated that "many issues regarding the borders between China and the Soviet Union need to be discussed."[20]

Its lengthy Russian history and traditions clearly heavily affected the international outlook of the Soviet Union, leading to intense Soviet emphasis on security relations with those countries on its borders. The Soviet Union viewed matters relating to historical border disputes far more seriously than other, related issues (e.g., undecided boundaries), largely because historical border disputes and their resolution had the potential to precipitate significant frontier adjustments. As the ideological differences between China and the Soviet Union peaked in the 1960s, historical border issues became commensurately sensitive. When Mao met in July 1964 with Suzuki Mosaburo, a leader of the Japanese Socialist Party, he repeatedly emphasized: "Not until less than one hundred years ago did the area to the east of Lake Baikal become Russian territory. Because of this, Haishenwai, Khabarovsk, and Kamchatka all became the territory of the Soviet Union. We have left these debts alone so far."[21]

Nikita Khrushchev, the Soviet general secretary, reacted strongly to Mao's remarks, and on September 15, 1964, told members of the Japanese Diet: "The territory of the Soviet Union was created by history. The borders of the Soviet Union are sacred. Any one who wants to take Soviet territory would encounter strong attacks from the Soviet people."[22] In practice, Mao did not wish to reverse these historical agreements, nor did China seek to regain territory from the Soviet Union. To quote Mao himself, his remarks were merely "offensive tactics" and "empty words," designed to unnerve Khrushchev.[23]

In Mao's thinking, there was a dialectical relationship between the states of tension and relaxation. To enjoy a period in which one could afford to relax, it was sometimes necessary to generate a certain degree of tension, meaning that one might sometimes create tensions to moderate conflicts or shift their focus. Mao often recounted stories about being unafraid, illustrating his favorite point: The more one feared a ghost, the more likely it was to appear; whereas if one remained unafraid, one could instead frighten away the ghost.

Even though Sino-Soviet ideological warfare peaked in 1964, no evidence suggested that the Soviet Union planned to take military action against China. Although their border disputes became a heated issue in Sino-Soviet relations, by comparison with the ideological controversies dividing them, these disputes were in a sense only marginal. When the Soviet Communist Party Central Committee replied on March 7, 1964, to a request the CCP Central Committee had made the previous November that they both address issues related to the border disputes, the Soviet response did not even mention the subject.[24] At that time, the CCP Central Committee, when assessing the Soviet situation, believed that Khrushchev had managed to transform the Soviet Communist Party into a primarily industrial and agricultural party, but the fruits of this policy had been largely unsuccessful, generating intellectual confusion within the Soviet Union and growing discontent within the Soviet Communist Party. Mao even correctly predicted that Khrushchev might soon fall from power.[25] Speaking of Sino-Soviet relations, Mao stated: "We have now entered the phase of offense and we have the ability to take over the world and destroy all the rules and regulations they [the Soviets] have set for us."[26]

Other key figures on the CCP Central Committee shared this view of Khrushchev and believed that, if China acted more forcefully, Khrushchev would yield, whereas if China showed any sign of weakness, Khrushchev would opportunistically exploit this to take advantage of China.[27] In numerous meetings with foreign visitors in 1964, Mao asked whether the Soviet Union was good at fighting wars. The fundamental Chinese internal assessment of the Soviets was: "Even if the Soviet Union deploys all the tricks it knows," such as joining forces with the United States, breaking off diplomatic relations, abrogating the Sino-Soviet Treaty of Friendship and Alliance, or deploying troops against China, it would be impossible for the Soviet Union to send large forces there or wage a full-scale war against China. It was, however, entirely possible that the Soviets would provoke some small-scale conflicts or border clashes.[28] If this judgment was correct, then China needed to make limited defense preparations, but it would be unnecessary, unreasonable, and premature to significantly readjust its entire domestic economic program to accommodate the need for strategic defense against nuclear attack.

Mao Zedong's View of the U.S. Threat in 1964

From the subjective perspective, even in the South, the possible threat arising from U.S. actions in Vietnam had not yet reached the level at which war was inevitable. On July 1, 1964, in discussions with military officials in Tianjin, Liu Shaoqi, the president of China, stated: "Chairman Mao Zedong recently discussed military issues at a CCP Central Committee working meeting. He discussed several possible scenarios for enemy attacks. You should be prepared for the worst case scenario but strive for the best. So far there has been no sign of an attack by the imperialists. However, you must be prepared and be constantly conscious of the enemy's existence."[29] In this context, by "imperialists" Liu clearly meant the Americans, and was not suggesting the possibility of an emerging Soviet threat to China. The two key phrases Liu used, "be prepared" and "be constantly conscious of the enemy's existence," merely suggested the possibility, not the urgent likelihood, that enemy attacks were imminent, phrases resembling those used in the 1962 Taiwan Strait crisis. It seems that, when he suggested that to date the American imperialists "had not wanted a war," Liu correctly glossed Mao's remarks at the Shisanling Reservoir. When he conveyed this understanding to military officials, it profoundly influenced their interpretation of current trends in world affairs.

Mao's own assessment of the situation was even more dramatic. On August 13, 1964, ten days after the Tonkin Gulf incident, Mao and Le Duan, North Vietnam's Communist Party secretary, discussed whether or not the United States was determined to cross the dividing line of the 17th parallel north and attack North Vietnam itself. In Mao's view: "It appears neither China, the United States, nor Vietnam wants a war. Therefore, a war will not take place." He endorsed the strategically brilliant approach the Vietnamese leaders adopted during the war, and also the Vietnamese Communist Party Central Committee's decision not to irritate the United States unnecessarily and thereby provoke its antagonist into waging full-scale war.[30] Mao further stated: "The imperialists would indeed be realists if the United States regards the Soviet Union as an immediate enemy and China as a long-term adversary. However, long-term vision is not important to the Americans, because it is too far away for them to see. Therefore, they prefer to ignore the long-term adversary."

Mao said that, historically, the United States had always entered global conflicts at the last possible moment. The United States was an unlikely candidate to initiate a major global war, especially at the current time, when it had stretched its hands too far. "The ten fingers are trying to press down ten fleas. At the end, it cannot catch even one."[31] Mao argued that it would be very difficult for the United States to find the resources to wage a war against China. "The United States has learned from the French. The French had fought for three years in Vietnam but could not win. They could not continue to fight and had to leave." Bearing in mind the experience Mao had gained through direct confrontations with the United States during the Korean War and the 1958 Taiwan Strait crisis, as well as the message the United States had conveyed in 1962 when it stated that the United States would neither support an attack by Taiwan or the mainland nor involve itself in the Taiwan Strait crisis, Mao's judgment that the United States would not seek a forcible confrontation with China was reasonable.

If, therefore, one seeks to cite the People's Liberation Army report of April 25, 1964, "Preparing for Sudden Enemy Attacks,"[32] as evidence that war was imminent, or to argue that the anticipation of war lay behind the significant shift in the Third Five-Year Plan, one must also address these seemingly contradictory statements by Mao and Li, that war was not likely. If these statements cannot be reconciled, then the popular beliefs mentioned above must be questioned.

Another flaw in these popular beliefs is that they completely ignore another series of historical events that took place concurrently in China, and they instead focus solely on the theory that a war was considered imminent. The expanded debates on the subjects of class and class struggles within China significantly affected Chinese politics and national security policies. Ever since the Tenth Meeting of the Eighth CCP Congress had reemphasized class struggle, internal politics and the domestic economy had begun to develop in two different directions: Economic rehabilitation proceeded, while politics continued to move leftward. When the issues of class and

class struggle were overemphasized, politically the nation became extremely tense, making it only natural to conclude that "the enemy was approaching." Enemies, whether foreign or domestic, were all perceived as
quite capable of overthrowing the government. In practice, in the 1960s it
would have been impossible for the domestic economy to diverge for very
long from politics, as ultimately internal politics would "lead" the economy.
The claim that "war is imminent" was the strongest, and perhaps the most
convenient, factor that could be used to force the economy out of its independent course and back into accord with politics.

As a rule, when war approaches, a nation responds by maintaining political stability while putting its economic machinery into overdrive, to mobilize industrially for war. In the mid-1960s in China, however, a diametri-
cally opposite pattern prevailed. By normal standards of political logic, it is
impossible to understand why China would launch such full-scale domestic chaos as that caused the Cultural Revolution, even as the Vietnam War
escalated dramatically after the Tonkin Gulf incident and military pressure
on the northern border also intensified.

It has often been said that, on no less than three occasions from the late
1950s to the 1970s, Mao was prepared to start a war even while ferocious
internecine CCP struggles were in progress. The first such time was during
the second meeting of the Eighth Party Congress in May 1958, and the third
during a Politburo meeting in December 1973. The second and subsequently the most heavily analyzed such episode occurred in May and June
1964.

On March 17, 1964, at a Politburo meeting at his residence, Mao proclaimed themes that became important in justifying his subsequent decisions, stating: "For the past year I have mainly concentrated on the struggles against Khrushchev. Now it is time to return my focus to domestic
issues, especially to the issues of preventing and encountering revisionism."[33] In 1964, a vigorous Cleansing Four movement sprang up within
China; its objective was to fight those persons demonstrating "four kinds of
ambiguity." Shortly afterward, this was renamed the Socialist Education
movement; its targets were now "persons of authority within the party who
were on the road to capitalism."

Preventing and countering revisionism within China was a logical progression from Mao's efforts to do the same worldwide. The publication of
nine articles by the CCP Central Committee, which criticized the open letter recently sent to them by the Soviet Communist Party Central Committee, provided an intellectual framework for the prevention and countering

of revisionism in the socialist state already constructed in China. This framework was the theory that socialist society would endure for a prolonged time span, during which classes and class struggle would still exist, as would conflicts between socialism and capitalism. Socialist revolution must occur not just in the economic arena but also on the front lines of politics and ideology; otherwise, in as few as ten or as many as several dozen years, China would "change color." When Mao depicted fearsome, if somewhat fanciful, future prospects for China's national security and international position, he did so to promote his own interests in political struggles within China.

One major reason why Chinese were prepared at that time to accept the theory of revision was because internationally the concept of equality embedded in socialism had deteriorated, due to the emergence in the Soviet Union of a "high salary class" and "the self-motivated in the country side." Judging by results, Chinese officials argued, the Soviet "special classes were frightened of war and sought peace from the Kennedy administration." Moreover, they warned: "If China does not resolve this issue, in about twenty years, revisionism would grow in China as well."[34] The different approaches China and the Soviet Union adopted toward issues of war and peace therefore became the central focus of Sino-Soviet contention. Closely related to this point was the vanishing of revolutionary instincts. Mao told the visiting Albanian defense minister, Beqir Ballaku: "Revisionism inevitably appears during peace time. We are now confronting this issue again. The party is no longer pure. The enemy has taken over parts of the party structure. If, therefore, we do not take counter revisionist measures, China will see the emergence of revisionism."[35]

The bulk of Mao's June 16, 1964, remarks at the Shisanling Reservoir were devoted to the issue of the "next generation of leadership," who would take over their seniors' tasks in the name of communism. Mao proposed various conditions that suitable candidates for this new generation must meet. The nine articles criticizing the open letter from the Soviet Communist Party Central Committee quoted extensively from Mao's statements on the subject, which profoundly influenced all subsequent Chinese political development. The topic of the next generation of leaders was closely linked to the larger issue of countering revisionism; it was also connected to new discussions then under way at the ongoing working meeting of the CCP Central Committee. Mao believed that revisionism had attained power in the Soviet Union because, after Khrushchev deceived Stalin and thereby won his trust, Khrushchev was named leader of the next generation, a progression he believed carried serious lessons for other communists around the world.

Mao also noted that Khrushchev was a leader who frequently changed his mind and, after he took office, modified his views significantly at least five times, on each occasion ousting those whose opinions differed from his. Mao believed this, too, was an equally important cautionary tale for the Chinese.[36] Following this train of thought, to the surprise of many present, Mao suddenly asked at a CCP Central Committee meeting: "What would we do if Khrushchev existed in China? Should a Khrushchev controlled revisionist central committee appear in China, the party committees in each province must resist it." This was why, at the beginning of his Shisanling speech of June 16, 1964, Mao stated that "the party chiefs of major areas should be responsible for those army units there. They will need guns as well as money." From this perspective, one can easily discern the undeniable correlation between military and political preparedness.

The 1964 defense preparations, therefore, which interrupted the routine progression of the Third Five-Year Plan, had a complex political background. At the very least, it was not simply a reaction to international military pressure, but rather the product of the tense environment generated by internal Chinese class struggles, combined with the international counter-revisionist movement. Indeed, because the need to prepare for war preempted the possibility of domestic economic rehabilitation, it contributed greatly to the sharpening internal situation and international ideological rivalries.

Undoubtedly, one cannot ignore either the pressures the Vietnam War imposed on China in the 1960s or, equally important, China's need to ready itself for conventional warfare. Yet there were actions China could have taken to neutralize these external factors. There was, for example, scope to seek solutions to neutralize both the military pressure the U.S. presence in Indochina exerted on China, and the tense situation near the Sino-Soviet border. It was irrational for China to renounce any effort to reach such solutions and, instead, to generate internal tensions whose force surpassed these outside pressures—behavior that effectively deprived the Chinese domestic economy of any basis for rehabilitation.

At this time, Mao accurately claimed: "The more nuclear weapons that are produced, the less likely is it that a nuclear war will begin."[37] The absence of nuclear war meant that the industrial bases built up under the Three Lines Projects to enable China to survive such a conflict eventually modified their strategic and industrial functions. Indeed, as early as the 1950s and 1960s, some Chinese officials had pointed out that the distinctive characteristics of an era of peace and development had already emerged.[38] Even so, China carried the burden of its history well into the 1970s, as domestic political struggles continued until 1976.

Two historical points deserve some comment. First, in 1965, when the Vietnam War escalated and China's efforts to assist Vietnam's resistance against the United States peaked, Mao remained surprisingly calm, pointing out that there might be two possible outcomes: Either the war might begin or it might never do so. Mao's confidence is easier to understand in the light of the revelations given by James Hershberg and Chen Jian in chapter 6 below that in 1965 China secretly conveyed messages to U.S. officials implicitly suggesting that, provided the United States did not escalate the war in Vietnam unduly, China would not undertake full-scale military intervention. As Shu Guang Zhang points out in chapter 7 below, in practice China limited its contributions to economic and military assistance and support troops, sedulously avoiding direct involvement in ground combat situations. Second, in 1965 the "stupidity" of the State Planning Commission alienated Mao, who then established his own working group to consider "strategic issues" and soon afterward dismantled all party and governmental structures and with great aspirations and ambitions launched his own revolution.

This chapter reveals that the impact of the Vietnam War on China's domestic political and economic development was limited—it was neither as direct nor as strong as many believed. At the very least, China's domestic political and economic evolution was determined by a combination of complex factors, whose ultimate determinant was the logical connections and causal relationships among issues related to Chinese internal affairs. In chapter 1 above, Yang Kuisong points out the role that both Mao's commitment to international revolution and his readiness to follow pragmatic if opportunistic policies when events dictated played in the making of his policies on Vietnam. Nonetheless, as Hershberg and Chen note in chapter 6, one should not therefore ignore the salient contribution of domestic political factors to the making of Chinese foreign policy. As a rule, in the middle to late 1960s, the role of domestic ideology in China's political and economic development was greater than has often been supposed. This was the reason why political, ideological, or strategic "accidents" repeatedly modified realistic policies, objectives, and plans, up to and including even China's state developmental plans. To some extent, of course, international factors determined such "accidents." Yet, from the perspective of Cold War international history, one should exaggerate the influence neither of the outside world on China, nor of China on the outside world. Within China, changes were mostly determined by internal Chinese events, whereas China's ability to affect the outside world was limited. In the past, China had used harsh words but only fired empty cannons. As one later scholar pointed out,[39] only by changing its own tactics could China change the world.

Notes

1. Jin Chongji, ed., *Zhou Enlai zhuan* [A biography of Zhou Enlai], 2 vols. (Beijing: Central Press of Historical Documents, 1998), vol. 2, 809.

2. Bo Yibo, "On the 1964 Plans," *Dangde Wenxian* [Archives of the Communist Party] 4 (1998): 5–6.

3. Li Fuchun, "Letter to Mao Zedong on the Ten Year Plan, December 31, 1962," in *Li Fuchun xuanji* [Selected works of Li Fuchun] (Beijing: China Planning Press, 1992), 302–4.

4. Bo Yibo, *Ruogan zhongda juece yu shijian de huigu* [Recollections of certain important decisions and events], 2 vols. (Beijing: Chinese Communist Party Central Committee Press, 1993), vol. 2, 1194.

5. Bo, *Ruogan zhongda juece yu shijian de huigu,* vol. 2, 1195.

6. Bo, *Ruogan zhongda juece yu shijian de huigu,* vol. 2, 1193.

7. Yang Maorong, "A Major Reform in China's Strategic Economic Planning in the 1960s," *Dangde Wenxian* 3 (1996): 27.

8. "Mao Zedong's Additions to the Report by the State Planning Commission on Plans for the Third Five-Year Plan," May 10, 11, 1964, *Dangde Wenxian* 3 (1996): 27.

9. Bo, *Ruogan zhongda juece yu shijian de huigu,* vol. 2, 195.

10. See Li Fuchun, "Remarks at a Working Meeting of the Chinese Communist Party Central Committee, May 18, 1964," *Dangde Wenxian* 3 (1996): 12. When quoting Mao Zedong's statements to this effect, Li Fuchun introduced them with the words: "The chairman recently said." The context suggests that Mao Zedong made these comments on either May 10 or 11, 1964.

11. Zhou Enlai, "Several Issues Concerning the Third Five-Year Plan," *Dangde Wenxian* 3 (1996): 15–19, 19–20.

12. Bo, *Ruogan zhongda juece yu shijian de huigu,* vol. 2, 1199–1200.

13. Chen Xiaolu, "Chen Yi Zhongguo waijiao" [Chen Yi and Chinese diplomacy], in *Huanqiu tongci liangre: Yidai lingxiumen de guoji zhanlue sixiang* [Leading the global trend: The international strategic thinking of a generation of leaders], ed. Institute for International Strategic Studies (Beijing: Central Press of Historical Documents, 1993), 152; see also Huang Yao and Zhang Mingzhe, *Luo Ruiqing zhuan* [Biography of Luo Ruiqing] (Beijing: Contemporary China Press, 1996), 472, 477–78.

14. Huang and Zhang, *Luo Ruiqing,* 472.

15. Jin, *Zhou Enlai zhuan,* 811.

16. Li Fuchun, "Remarks at a Working Meeting of the Chinese Communist Party Central Committee, May 18, 1964," *Dangde Wenxian* 3 (1996): 21.

17. Li, "Remarks at a Working Meeting."

18. Li, "Remarks at a Working Meeting."

19. *Renmin Ribao* [People's Daily], May 25, 1969.

20. Li Danhui, "1969 nian zhongsu bianjie chongtu: yuanyi he jieguo" [The border clashes between China and the Soviet Union in 1969: Courses and results], *Dangdai Zhongguoshi yanjiu* [Contemporary Chinese history studies] 5 (1996): 42.

21. Li, "1969 nian zhongsu bianjie chongtu," 42. On September 10, 1964, a slightly more conciliatory Mao Zedong again raised the issue with French guests, but added: "This was not to say that we wanted the Soviet Union to return the territories. We wanted to make it clear that these are unequal treaties. Many similar problems still remain unresolved."

22. Li, "1969 nian zhongsu bianjie chongtu," 42.

23. Li, "1969 nian zhongsu bianjie chongtu," 43.

24. Wu Lengxi, *Shinian lunzhan, 1956–1966: Zhongsu guanxi huiyilu* [A decade of polemical debate, 1956–1966: A memoir of Sino-Soviet relations] (Beijing: Central Press of Historical Documents, 1999), 725.

25. Wu, *Shinian lunzhan,* 734.

26. Wu, *Shinian lunzhan,* 734.

27. People's Republic of China Foreign Ministry and Chinese Communist Party Central Documentary Research Department, *Mao Zedong waijiao wenxuan* [Selected diplomatic works of Mao Zedong] (Beijing: World Knowledge Press, 1994), 516.

28. Wu, *Shinian lunzhan,* 675–76.

29. Chinese Communist Party Central Documentary Research Department, *Liu Shaoqi nianpu, 1898–1969* [A chronological record of Liu Shaoqi, 1898–1969], 2 vols. (Beijing: Central Press of Historical Documents, 1996), vol. 2, 594.

30. Li, "1969 nian zhongsu bianjie chongtu," 44.

31. Official collection *Mao Zedong waijiao wenxuan,* given in *77 Conversations between Chinese and Foreign Leaders on the Wars in Indochina, 1964–1977,* Cold War International History Project Working Paper 22, ed. Odd Arne Westad, Chen Jian, Stein Tønnesson, Nguyen Vu Tung, and James G. Hershberg (Washington, D.C.:, Woodrow Wilson International Center for Scholars, 1998), 513.

32. People's Liberation Army, "Preparing for Sudden Enemy Attacks," *Dangde Wenxian* 3 (1996): 34–35.

33. Wu, *Shinian lunzhan,* 733.

34. Deng Zihui, "Report Delivered at the Advanced Party School, July 1, 1962," in *Quisuo Zhongguo: Wenge qianshi nianshi* [Looking for China: The history of the ten years before the Great Cultural Revolution], 2 vols., ed. Xiao Donglian (Beijing: Red Flag Press, 1999), vol. 2, 995.

35. Deng Zihui, "Report Delivered at the Advanced Party School," 1012.

36. Wu, *Shinian lunzhan,* 779.

37. *Mao Zedong waijiao wenxuan,* 476.

38. He Fang, "Lun Deng Xiaoping lilun deshi daibeijing" [The historical background to Deng Xiaoping's thought], *Dangdai Shejie Shehui Zhuyi* [Contemporary World Socialism] 2 (1999): 77.

39. Zhang Baijia, "Congli shibian dongkan Zhongguo" [Exploring China from the Angle of Changing History]," *Shijie Zhishi* [World Affairs] 24 (1991): 3.

Part II

The Widening War

6

Informing the Enemy: Sino-American "Signaling" and the Vietnam War, 1965

James G. Hershberg and Chen Jian

Early in 1965, the Vietnam War reached a critical juncture. When Washington began to dispatch more combat troops to South Vietnam and, by executing "Operation Rolling Thunder," inaugurated the massive and continuous bombardment of North Vietnam, Beijing repeatedly warned that if the United States continued to escalate its military involvement, the People's

The authors would like to thank a number of institutions and individuals for helpful support and advice in the research, writing, and revision of this chapter, and they apologize for any omissions: the National Security Archive (Tom Blanton, Malcolm Byrne, and William Burr); the Cold War International History Project (Christian Ostermann); the George Washington University Cold War Group (Jim Goldgeier and Hope Harrison) and Elliott School of International Affairs (Harry Harding); the Miller Center of Public Affairs at the University of Virginia; the staff of the Lyndon B. Johnson Library; the British Public Record Office; the National Archives of Canada; and the U.S. National Archives II; and F. S. Aijazuddin, James Blight, janet M. Lang, Robert Jervis, Melvyn Leffler, Li Danhui, Fredrik Logevall, Luu Doan Huynh, Priscilla Roberts, Shen Zhihua, Odd Arne Westad, David Wolff, and Zhai Qiang.

Republic of China (PRC) would do everything necessary, even at the risk of a major confrontation, to "assist Vietnam and resist America."[1] It seemed that once again, as had happened during the Korean War fifteen years before, China and the United States were on a collision course, approaching a military showdown that would resemble—yet might be even more costly than—the Sino-American war in Korea that had lasted from the fall of 1950 to the summer of 1953.

It was against this background that, in the spring of 1965, the PRC "signaled" the United States through a variety of channels regarding the military situation in Vietnam and the grave danger involved in the war's escalation. From the beginning, both Beijing and Washington balanced twin goals in their signaling: on the one hand, to demonstrate determination and preparedness to support their respective rival Vietnamese allies; and on the other, to make it clear that they hoped to avoid another direct Sino-American military clash. In dealing with each other—as chapters 1, 5, and 7 of this volume also demonstrate—both sides combined highly aggressive and charged rhetoric with pronounced caution in military actions. In actuality, policymakers in Beijing and Washington tried very hard to understand the "signals" emitted by the other side, always taking into account the adversary's possible responses as crucial factors in making their own key strategic or military decisions. Consequently, although the Vietnam War escalated dramatically after the spring of 1965, with both the United States and the PRC providing extensive military support (in both personnel and supplies) to their respective allies, a Korea-style Sino-American confrontation did not occur.

In retrospect, the Sino-American signaling in 1965 merits close attention for three main reasons. First, it represents a crucial, yet inadequately researched, episode in the history of the Cold War in general and of the Vietnam War in particular. Indeed, as the successful signaling between Beijing and Washington might have averted turning the Vietnam War into a Sino-American war, it could also have dramatically altered the evolution of the Cold War. From an American perspective, a thorough investigation of this episode will help refine our understanding of the pivotal deliberations by President Lyndon B. Johnson (LBJ) and his administration that led to the major decisions made in the summer of 1965 to increase U.S. ground forces in South Vietnam while eschewing options to bring the ground war to North Vietnam or the air war to China. Most American scholars of the Vietnam War, though having long recognized these decisions as a landmark crossing of the Rubicon on the path to a full-scale American war in Vietnam, have paid relatively little attention to the importance of Washington's concerns regarding Beijing's potential intervention, let alone the significance of the Sino-American signaling.[2]

Second, the absence of a second Sino-American war—or, to put it another way, the successful steps taken by both sides to avoid one—marked a subtle yet perhaps significant evolution in Sino-American relations. Among other effects, it may have helped instill between these two hostile ideological and geopolitical enemies a degree of mutual caution—and, as a result, mutual confidence—that would help pave the way for both sides just a few years later to begin moving toward a more dramatic improvement in their relations even as the Vietnam War continued to rage. Thus this event constitutes an important turn on the path from confrontation to rapprochement between Beijing and Washington.

Third, the story holds critical implications for international relations theory, particularly concerning conflict control, interbelligerent communications, and the value of "learning from history" and using historical analogies.[3] It demonstrates that effective communications between belligerents (or potential belligerents) lacking diplomatic relations can help reduce the danger that a potential conflict between them might occur through miscalculation, misjudgment, or inadvertence. It also reveals that, by acutely recalling how miscommunication or misperception had led to disaster in the past, conflicting actors might earnestly seek to avoid a repetition without appearing "weak" or sacrificing their key foreign policy interests.[4]

In a sense, the previous lack of in-depth study on this important subject epitomizes the extreme difficulties scholars face in gaining access to source materials (particularly in China) on decisionmaking in and interactions between Washington and Beijing in the spring of 1965, and how decisions, actions, and statements by each side were perceived by the other and, in turn, influenced further decisionmaking by both. The situation has improved in recent years with the declassification and release of substantial new documentation and materials from the U.S., Chinese, and British archives (as well as a far more limited amount of Vietnamese sources and oral history accounts), allowing scholars to construct a more comprehensive, if still far from complete, account of the Sino-American signaling on Vietnam in 1965. Moreover, this enhanced account puts analysts in a better position to compare the 1965 episode with the failure of the Sino-

American signaling regarding Korea in 1950, and thereby to reevaluate its historical significance within the context of conclusions reached by previous studies and findings from international relations theories and analyses.

With the support of insights gained from new American, Chinese, and British sources, this chapter first briefly reviews Washington's misreading of Beijing's intentions in Korea in October 1950 and recapitulates the evolution of Beijing's and Washington's efforts to "get to know the enemy" through the decade of crises that followed the Korean armistice. It then discusses how Washington intended to escalate the Vietnam War after the August 1964 Gulf of Tonkin incident and how Beijing perceived and prepared to deal with this increasingly dangerous situation. The chapter further explores how and why Beijing decided to send a series of warning signals to Washington to restrict the scale of the Vietnam War, and how the signaling may have influenced Washington's decisionmaking. It concludes with a discussion of why the Sino-American signaling about restricting the escalation of the Vietnam War worked in 1965 by comparing it with the failure of Sino-American signaling in 1950, thus reaching some more general conclusions on lessons gained from history.

Korea in 1950: How Washington
Misperceived Beijing's Intentions

To explain the background of the Sino-American signaling regarding Vietnam in 1965, it is essential first to review how Washington misread Beijing's warnings concerning Chinese intentions in Korea in October 1950. This failure not only resulted in a major military conflict between the United States and the PRC that ultimately prolonged the Korean War for several years but also drove the two countries into a state of bitter confrontation that would last for more than two decades.

The outbreak of the Korean War in June 1950 turned Northeast Asia into a main battlefield of the Cold War. During the early stage of the war, the North Korean Communists stormed southward across the 38th parallel to seize almost the entire Korean peninsula, leaving only the "Pusan Perimeter" under the control of U.S./UN forces, which came to the rescue of Syngman Rhee's South Korean (Republic of Korea, ROK) regime. However, the successful American landing at Inchon on September 15, 1950, completely changed the course of the war. By the end of September, the North Korean resistance neared total collapse, and a final victory by the U.S./ UN/ROK forces seemed only a matter of time. It was at this juncture that the question of whether or not the PRC would intervene on behalf of the North Korean Communists emerged as a serious question for American policymakers and military planners.

As revealed by newly available Chinese and Russian documentation, Beijing had been preparing for possible intervention in Korea since shortly after the war's outbreak. On July 13, 1950, after a series of consultations with Moscow, Beijing formally established the "Northeast Border Defense Army," assigning it the task of preparing for military intervention in Korea in case the war turned against North Korea.[5] After more than a quarter million Chinese troops had taken up positions along the Chinese–North Korean border, on August 18, Mao Zedong set the end of September as the deadline for these troops to complete preparations for military operations in Korea.[6] When Beijing's leaders made these decisions, they certainly were concerned with safeguarding China's physical security—even though at that point, before Inchon, the North Koreans were still fighting well south of the 38th parallel. But the Chinese Communist Party (CCP) leaders, and Mao in particular, also hoped that a policy of active intervention would help transform the challenge and threat posed by the Korean crisis into new dynamics to mobilize ordinary Chinese citizens in Mao's "continuous revolution" at home, while promoting revolutionary China's prestige and influence on the international scene.[7]

When the U.S./UN/ROK forces crossed the 38th parallel at the end of September and in the first week of October 1950, Beijing's leaders were under great pressure—including a forceful personal appeal from Stalin to Mao—to make a crucial decision on whether or not to intervene in Korea.[8] Though Mao favored sending PRC troops to Korea, many top Chinese leaders had reservations. When members of the CCP Central Secretariat met on October 2 to discuss the Korean crisis, over some resistance Mao pushed for a preliminary decision to enter the war.[9] On that day (though it is unclear at exactly what point in the deliberations), Mao personally drafted a telegram to Stalin to inform the Soviet leader that Beijing had decided "to send a portion of our troops" (under the guise of "volunteers") to Korea. He emphasized that even though China's intervention might provoke a Sino-American war, this action was necessary for the sake of the Korean and Eastern revolutions. He also made it clear that to defeat the U.S. troops in

Korea, China needed substantial Soviet military support, especially air cover for Chinese troops in Korea.[10]

However, probably because Mao hoped to see CCP leaders reach a wider and deeper consensus on intervention, as well as to strengthen China's bargaining position in getting Soviet air support, he evidently did not dispatch this telegram to Stalin.[11] Instead, he sent a different message to Stalin, through the Soviet ambassador to China, N. V. Roshchin, informing him that because direct military intervention in Korea "may entail extremely serious consequences," including "provoking an open conflict between the United States and China" that might drag in the Soviet Union, many leaders in Beijing believed that China should "show caution." Therefore, Mao informed Stalin that despite the disappointment this would cause (both in Pyongyang and Moscow), the CCP had tentatively decided *not* to send troops to Korea.[12]

Yet Mao's heart was with intervention. When the CCP Politburo met on October 4 and 5, he used both his political skill and authority to push his colleagues to endorse the decision to enter the war.[13] On October 6, Stalin dispatched a telegram to Mao, again urging him to come to North Korea's rescue, even at the risk of igniting World War III. The Russian leader argued that the PRC and USSR occupied a stronger position than that of the United States and the United Kingdom at that time, whereas in a few years a rearmed Japan and West Germany would be able to contribute to the enemy's military cause. "If a war is inevitable," Stalin reasoned, "then let it be waged now, and not in a few years when Japanese militarism will be restored as an ally of the United States and when the USA and Japan will have a ready-made bridgehead on the continent in the form of an entire Korea run by Syngman Rhee."[14] Stalin's pressure further reinforced the CCP chairman's position on intervention.[15] On October 8, Mao formally issued the order for the "Chinese People's Volunteers" to enter the Korean War.[16]

Within the above context, two major concerns—how to further legitimize the war decision at home and abroad, and how to delay the U.S./UN/ROK forces' offensive across the 38th parallel so that the Chinese troops would gain valuable time to get better prepared for military operations—dominated the minds of Mao and his comrades. It was against this background that Beijing issued a series of warnings to Washington. As early as September 30, Premier Zhou Enlai declared at a mass rally that "the Chinese people will absolutely not tolerate foreign aggression, nor will they supinely tolerate seeing their neighbors being savagely invaded by the imperialists."[17] Shortly after midnight on the night of October 2–3, when top CCP leaders had already inconclusively discussed the question of sending troops to Korea, Zhou arranged an emergency meeting with Indian ambassador K. M. Panikkar, asking him to convey a message to the Americans:

> The American forces are trying to cross the 38th parallel and to expand the war. If they really want to do this, we will not sit still without doing anything. We will be forced to intervene [*women yao guan*].[18]

From Beijing's perspective, the message, though composed in explicit language, probably was not designed to halt the U.S./UN/ROK forces' northward march across the 38th parallel—indeed, it appears inconceivable that, under the circumstances that South Korean troops had already crossed the parallel and North Korea's resistance had virtually collapsed, that Beijing would have assigned the message such a daunting task; rather, it had two important purposes in tactical and strategic senses: If the message indeed was to play a role of deterrence, thus reducing the scope and/or speed of the enemy forces' northward advance, Beijing would gain much-needed space and time for the Chinese troops to complete mobilization and preparation for entering the war; and if Washington reacted by ignoring the warnings and continuing to push the war toward the Sino-Korean frontier, the PRC leadership would gain a vital justification before the Chinese people and world opinion for its argument that Beijing's intervention in Korea was a just one necessitated by a severe threat to China's own physical safety. In the final analysis, therefore, Chinese leaders saw little prospect that their message had a plausible chance of heading off a direct military confrontation in Korea with the United States.[19]

Before dawn on October 3 (Washington time), U.S. State Department officials learned of Zhou's warning, transmitted by the Indians via the British Foreign Office in London.[20] However, from the beginning, the Americans gave scant credibility to the message. First of all, the messenger used by the Chinese to convey the warning generated suspicion in Washington. In line with prevailing Cold War attitudes, which meant that New Delhi's "neutrality" was regarded with distaste, State Department officials considered Panikkar to be "emotional, unstable, and strongly biased in favor of Mao's regime."[21] In appraising Panikkar's report of the conversation with Zhou, Central Intelligence Agency (CIA) analysts immediately suspected the Indian diplomat of gullibility or worse. Panikkar's "reliability and accuracy" were "open to question," the CIA told policymakers in Washington, and it was "entirely possible that he is being used by the Chinese Communists to plant this information in an effort to influence US and UK policy."[22]

Furthermore, U.S. officials widely regarded Beijing's warnings as no more than "bluffing." In Tokyo, British diplomats rushed to show General Douglas MacArthur cables describing Panikkar's report of his conversation with Zhou, only to hear the American commander dismiss the warning as "pure bluff" and "blackmail." If the Chinese were "foolish" enough to jump into the fray, the general boasted, he had plenty of troops to handle them, and "would immediately unleash his air force against towns in Manchuria and North China including Peking."[23] When the State Department learned of Zhou's statements, Secretary of State Dean Acheson commented that "we should not be unduly frightened at what was probably a Chinese Communist bluff." Although recognizing that allowing American forces to march north beyond the 38th parallel entailed some danger, he emphasized that "a greater risk would be incurred by showing hesitation and timidity."[24] Continuing in this dismissive vein, the CIA further speculated that Zhou's "intimation that Communist China is now prepared to rush to its neighbor's assistance was probably an attempt to bluff the UN into not crossing the 38th Parallel, rather than a forewarning of Chinese intervention."[25] Simply put, policymakers in Washington refused to take Beijing's warnings seriously.

Several assumptions underlay this approach. First, U.S. officials were inclined to believe that after Inchon the best time for China's intervention in Korea had passed.[26] Second, they believed that Beijing's leaders had to focus on daunting domestic challenges, especially rebuilding after decades of war, and thus would be unlikely to embroil China in a conflict with a military and technological superpower, the United States, over Korea.[27] Third, American analysts also believed that China's entry into the Korean War would make it even more dependent on Soviet support while minimizing Beijing's opportunity to take China's seat at the United Nations.[28] Finally, U.S. intelligence experts doubted that either Moscow or Beijing would risk provoking a third world war by directly intervening in Korea (a consideration that, we now know, was directly raised, and pooh-poohed, by Stalin in his communications with Mao).[29]

Underlying these assumptions, it appears, rested a deep-rooted sense of American superiority toward a backward China, and a stubborn contempt toward Beijing's Communist leaders because they were Chinese. Recent history reinforced these cultural and even racial sentiments, because U.S.

officials had come to disdain Chinese military prowess during their frustrating, often exasperating, efforts during World War II to encourage the Chinese Nationalists led by Jiang Jieshi (Chiang Kai-shek) to undertake offensive operations against the Japanese. Indeed, American policymakers simply could not imagine that Beijing might gain anything by involving China in a major confrontation with the United States. A consistent belief among policymakers in Washington was that even if the Chinese Communists did intervene in the Korean War, America's military and technological superiority would easily guarantee a victory over them. Thus, while assessing Moscow's and Beijing's possible reaction to America's "rollback" policy, Washington's eyes were fixed on Moscow. Once U.S. policymakers became convinced that direct Soviet military involvement in the Korean fighting was unlikely, they quickly jumped to the conclusion that a Chinese intervention was even less probable. Because intelligence analysts and policymakers in Washington were influenced by this mentality, they blithely ignored clues regarding Beijing's military redeployment and political mobilization for entering the war.

Not surprisingly, the CIA concluded as late as October 12, four days after Mao issued the formal orders to send Chinese troops to Korea: "Despite statements by Chou [Zhou] Enlai, troops movements to Manchuria, and propaganda charges of atrocities and border violations, there are no convincing indications of an actual Chinese Communist intention to resort to full-scale intervention in Korea."[30] Even when Chinese troops began to stream into Korea in late October 1950, both policymakers in Washington and, in particular, General MacArthur, again misjudged the military situation. Despite indications that the Chinese had already entered the war, MacArthur decided to initiate a new "end the war offensive" in late November 1950, which led to what the political scientist Jonathan Pollack has termed "the most infamous retreat in American military history."[31] It seems evident that what was involved here was more than a simple intelligence failure.

The direct Chinese-American military confrontation that began in late October 1950 would not end until July 1953. And the pervasive enmity between China and the United States would endure for the next two decades, until the early 1970s. As we shall see, during that period policymakers in Beijing and Washington did not forget this Korean War episode, and they would try to understand why and how Beijing's warning signals had been so egregiously misconstrued in Washington. This, as it turned out, would play an important role in shaping the Sino-American signaling regarding Vietnam in 1965.

Getting to Know the Enemy:
Sino-American Crises, 1954–62

There was a cease-fire for the Korean War in July 1953, but the Sino-American confrontation persisted, particularly in the Taiwan Strait. In 1954–55 and 1958, crises in the strait twice threatened to escalate into, yet halted just short of, direct military conflict between China and the United States. Beginning in 1955, the two sides conducted sporadic talks at the ambassadorial level, first in Geneva and then in Warsaw, yet this channel of communication quickly degenerated into a forum for rhetorical mutual animosity.[32]

In the absence of normal diplomatic exchanges, ironically, Beijing's and Washington's management of the crises in the Taiwan Strait evolved into mutual probing exercises and a de facto dialogue that provided the two sides with unusual opportunities to learn more of the other's patterns of behavior, tactics, and priorities. Consequently, both countries accumulated valuable knowledge and experience and, as a result, a unique form of mutual confidence that would influence their leaders' perceptions and styles of crisis management when they again approached a collision course in Vietnam in the mid-1960s.

The implicit and gradual shift in Beijing's and Washington's ways of managing their confrontational relationship first surfaced in the 1954–55 Taiwan Strait crisis, when the Chinese People's Liberation Army (PLA) conducted a series of offensive operations against several Nationalist-controlled offshore islands, including shelling Mazu and Jinmen (Matsu and Quemoy) off the Fujian coast in September 1954 and attacking and occupying Dachen and Yijiangshan off Zhejiang Province in early 1955. In ordering these operations, Mao certainly hoped that they would help strengthen the PRC's coastal safety and, in particular, secure its coastal transportation lines north of Fujian; in the meantime, he also intended to use the operations to "highlight" the Taiwan issue in international politics, while driving a wedge between Washington and Taipei. In a deeper sense, though, the Chinese chairman also meant to use the tension created by the crisis "to raise the political consciousness and political alertness of the people of the whole country and to stir up our people's revolutionary enthusiasm, thus promoting our nation's socialist reconstruction."[33]

But Beijing's bellicose behavior provoked strong reactions from Washington. President Dwight D. Eisenhower and his secretary of state, John Foster Dulles, publicly declared their determination to defend the Nationalist-controlled islands against attack—even at the risk of being compelled to use nuclear weapons against the far larger conventional Chinese forces. In December 1954, Washington and Taipei signed a treaty of mutual defense, thus making the U.S.-Taiwan relationship closer than ever in a strategic sense and pushing Mao's goal of reunifying Taiwan with the mainland even further into the future.

In this tense context, both Beijing and Washington refrained from taking dramatic actions that might drive the potentially explosive crisis out of control. When Chinese Communist forces were preparing for a major joint amphibious operation aimed at taking over the Yijiangshan and Dachen Islands, Beijing's leaders clearly instructed PLA commanders that in no circumstances should they provoke a direct confrontation with the Americans.[34] Policymakers in Washington, despite their promise to use U.S. forces to defend Taiwan in the event of Communist invasion, never extended the same commitment to all of the Nationalist-held offshore islands. In January 1955, when the PLA conducted a full-scale landing operation in Yijiangshan and Dachen, U.S. forces, except for helping the Nationalist troops to withdraw from these islands, did not intervene. The absence of a direct Chinese-American military conflict, in turn, created the necessary precondition for Zhou to announce in Bandung, Indonesia, in late April 1955 that Beijing was willing to negotiate with Washington to "reduce the tension in the Far East"—an offer the Eisenhower administration promptly accepted—thus bringing the first Taiwan Strait crisis to an end.[35]

The same pattern, in which Beijing and Washington refrained from a military showdown despite their bellicose rhetoric, reemerged in the two nations' management of the Taiwan Strait crisis of 1958. When Mao ordered the PLA to initiate large-scale shelling of Jinmen beginning on August 23, he argued that this operation would once again draw the international community's attention to the Taiwan issue, and that it would make it difficult for Washington to concentrate on dealing with the crisis in the Middle East at the same time. In the final analysis, however, the emphasis of Mao's deliberation fell on the operation's mobilization effects at home, especially on creating new momentum for the promotion of China's "continuous revolution," which in 1958 was experiencing one of its most critical (and ultimately disastrous) episodes—the "Great Leap Forward." In the Chinese chairman's own words, in the midst of the crisis: "Besides its disadvantageous side, a tense [international] situation can mobilize the population, can particularly mobilize the backward people, can mobilize the people in the middle, and can therefore promote the Great Leap Forward in economic construction."[36] From the beginning, Beijing's management of the crisis

combined provocative language with nonprovocative actions, especially toward the United States. At almost every juncture of the crisis's development,
Mao made it very clear to his commanders that they should do everything
possible to avoid provoking direct military clashes with the U.S. forces.[37]

Washington's reactions were also very cautious. Fearing that the shelling
presaged a military assault not only on the small offshore islands but possibly also on Taiwan itself, President Eisenhower, after much deliberation,
decided in early September to use the Seventh Fleet to help escort Chinese
Nationalist supply vessels to Jinmen. In the meantime, however, he also ordered American commanders that they should stay at least three miles offshore to avoid exchanges with the Chinese shore batteries.[38] Consequently
the Chinese and U.S. forces never engaged in direct fighting during the 1958
crisis.

As far as the essence of Sino-American relations is concerned, Beijing
and Washington remained bitter enemies during the two Taiwan Strait crises,
as they had been during the Korean War. But the Chinese and American leaders' handling of the 1954–55 and 1958 confrontations demonstrated two interesting yet important features in comparison with their experience during
the Korean War. First, in October 1950 neither Beijing nor Washington took
the avoidance of a direct military conflict with the other as a top priority for
their strategies toward Korea. Beijing's warning message, as discussed
above, was designed primarily further to legitimate the war decision as well
as creating better conditions for entering the war, whereas U.S. policymakers and military planners were unwilling to regard China as a qualified chal-
lenger to America's strategic interests in the Far East.

The situation had changed during the two Taiwan Strait crises. In formulating an overall strategy for crisis management, both Beijing and Washington placed great emphasis upon avoiding a large-scale direct Chinese-
American military confrontation. For Beijing, this was necessary because
otherwise Mao would not be able to concentrate the nation's valuable scarce
resources on carrying out the "socialist revolution and socialist construction" at home. No matter how much Mao desired to use international tension to promote domestic mobilization, he would not allow the crisis to escalate into a direct military showdown with the United States. Indeed, as
has been pointed out by the political scientist Thomas Christensen, what
was ideal for Mao was a "conflict short of war."[39] For Washington, the challenges from Beijing had to be dealt with, but U.S. policymakers and military planners also understood completely that America's primary Cold War
enemy was not China but the Soviet Union. Therefore, engaging in a major

war with Communist China was not in the best strategic interests of the United States.

Moreover, in the practical process of crisis management, both Beijing and Washington demonstrated a willingness and, as a result, an enhanced ability to distinguish between the other side's rhetoric and its actions. Although both Beijing and Washington, out of domestic political considerations and confined by the Cold War international environment, frequently adopted provocative language in public statements during the crises, they were very cautious in dealing with specific situations that might result in uncontrollable military conflicts. And once it was apparent that such a conflict could occur, they were more than willing to make tactical compromises. Consequently, a specific yet critical form of "mutual confidence" gradually penetrated Beijing's and Washington's strategic thinking: Without yielding to the other side's policy goals or their underpinning ideology—and certainly without accepting their legitimacy—both sides nevertheless developed a conviction of the other side's willingness and capacity to pursue a limited and pragmatic course of action in accordance with its own rationale, logic, and perceived interests.

During the 1958 Taiwan Strait crisis, Beijing and Washington decided to resume the Sino-American ambassadorial talks in Warsaw. Although the talks failed to produce a solution to the dispute that was acceptable to both sides, this channel remained open after 1958. An incident in 1962, when U.S.-Chinese animosity ran as deep as ever, revealed that an unusual sense of mutual confidence indeed had emerged between the two enemies. That summer, Beijing's leaders were alarmed by the intelligence reports that the Taiwan regime was preparing to conduct large-scale landing operations in the mainland's coastal area. Wang Bingnan, the Chinese ambassador to Poland, was instructed to meet the American ambassador, John M. Cabot. He informed the American side that Jiang was planning to attack the mainland, and that if Washington supported Jiang's actions it would cause "the most severe consequence" and the United States "would certainly be held responsible for it." Cabot replied that the United States "had no intentions of supporting [an] attack on Mainland under existing circumstances," and that if Jiang's forces "invaded Mainland it would be contrary to their commitments to us." The American ambassador further stated that he "did not believe they [Jiang's forces] would do it." Beijing later found that indeed the Americans had acted in accordance with what Cabot had promised in Warsaw.[40]

All the above formed the context in which, in 1964–65, Sino-American relations again encountered extreme tension because of the escalation of the

Vietnam War. When policymakers in Beijing and Washington had to make critical policy choices that would determine whether the two countries would engage in another bloody war, over their deliberations—as we shall discuss in the following pages—there always loomed the heavy shadow of memories of the failure of the Sino-American signaling in October 1950. Furthermore, the specific "mutual confidence"—one in which each party perceived the other as both willing and able to impose constraints on its aims as well as to adhere to its own rationale in its actions—had prepared a crucial condition for the two sides to conduct more effective signaling when dealing with the possibility that they might be dragged into another costly and unwanted direct military confrontation.

After the Gulf of Tonkin: Washington's Decision to Escalate the War in Vietnam

The August 1964 Gulf of Tonkin incident brought both the Vietnam conflict and Washington's strategy toward it to a critical juncture. After much internal debate, President Johnson and his close advisers became convinced that to prevent South Vietnam from falling to increasing Communist pressure, it was necessary for the United States to play a larger military role. By early 1965—after Congress, by passing the Gulf of Tonkin Resolution, gave the president a virtual free hand to pursue a more aggressive strategy in Southeast Asia—senior Johnson administration officials, such as Defense Secretary Robert S. McNamara and National Security Adviser McGeorge Bundy, were ready to take major steps to escalate the Vietnam War by dispatching more ground forces to the South and conducting air raids against the North. They secretly recommended a sharp increase in military action against the North—"to use our military power in the Far East and to force a change of Communist policy," as Bundy put it in his famous January 27 "fork in the road" memorandum.[41]

It was at this juncture that the National Liberation Front (NLF) attacked U.S. military personnel at Pleiku and Qui Nhon on February 7 and 10, the first of these raids occurring during Bundy's trip to Saigon. Recent Vietnamese oral history testimony suggests that these attacks most likely stemmed from the initiative of local Vietnamese Communist commanders acting without Hanoi's specific authorization, and that "*NLF forces at Pleiku were unaware that U.S. personnel were present at the time of the attack!*" However, U.S. policymakers "had little doubt that Hanoi had ordered the attack at Pleiku specifically to send a signal of its own to the United States while the Bundy team was visiting Saigon," and even suspected that it had been timed to coincide with the presence in the North Vietnamese capital of Soviet Premier Alexei Kosygin.[42] To Washington, already convinced that it faced the unpalatable alternative of watching the Saigon government go down the drain (necessitating a humiliating American extraction), the Pleiku assault seemed precisely to fit the bill for a suitable provocation to justify the envisioned more aggressive policy. Accordingly, after a series of limited reprisal raids in mid-February ("Operation Flaming Dart"), on March 2 Washington launched Operation Rolling Thunder, the campaign of "sustained" and "graduated" bombing of North Vietnam—intended simultaneously to retaliate for the recent attacks, punish the North for its support of the guerrilla insurgency in the South, and bolster the sagging morale of the Saigon regime in the hopes that this would produce a more robust military effort on its part.

To supplement this tougher aerial bombing campaign, the Johnson administration also went forward with the highly publicized landing of 3,500 U.S. Marines near Danang, abandoning the pretense that the United States had only advisers, not combat personnel, in Vietnam. Ostensibly their mission was defined as guarding air bases from which the bombing missions would be staged, but this was widely seen as a harbinger of a far larger and more aggressive ground force. By late March, nearly 30,000 U.S. troops had already reached Vietnam, and by the summer 45,000 to 50,000 more American soldiers arrived as Johnson administration officials contemplated plans for an even larger deployment in line with the new strategy of using American military pressure to try to force an acceptable political settlement in Vietnam that would include the North's relinquishing of the armed struggle to overthrow the Saigon government. Consequently, President Johnson announced on July 28 that he would immediately increase U.S. military forces in South Vietnam from 75,000 to 125,000, with additional troop deployments anticipated as requested by military commanders. In the history of American involvement in the Vietnam War, this became a milestone that led by the end of 1965 to the commitment of roughly 184,300 American military personnel to the war, a total that within two years would grow to almost half a million.[43]

From the beginning of their deliberations in early 1965 over the escalation of the U.S. war effort in Vietnam, Johnson and his top advisers carefully scrutinized China's reactions. They were fully aware that only a few months earlier, on October 16, 1964, the PRC had exploded its first nuclear device—an event long dreaded in Washington (and perhaps in Moscow) and one that implied a tougher PRC military posture.[44] As one historian notes, the blast at the Lop Nur testing site in the Taklamakan Desert fanned U.S. officials' fears of Chinese belligerence and expansionism while "raising new strategic concerns."[45] In a somewhat contradictory analysis that reflected Washington's apprehension and confusion, a July 1963 Special National Intelligence Estimate had doubted that Beijing's prospective nuclear capabilities would produce "major changes" in Chinese foreign policy, yet it also surmised that Chinese leaders (much like Harry Truman, who felt "tremendously pepped up" and possessed of "an entirely new feeling of confidence" at Potsdam in July 1945 upon learning of the successful atomic test at Alamogordo[46]) "would feel very much stronger and this mood would doubtless be reflected in their approach to conflicts on their periphery. They would probably feel that the U.S. would be more reluctant to intervene on the Asian mainland and thus the tone of Chinese policy would probably become more assertive."[47] In line with this prediction, U.S. policymakers noticed that since the Gulf of Tonkin incident, Beijing had vociferously backed Hanoi's stand in favor of "armed struggle" to overthrow the Southern government and unify the country under communist rule.

From the beginning, U.S. leaders, including Johnson himself, acutely recalled what had transpired between the PRC and America fifteen years before in Korea, causing some Johnson administration officials to worry that the two countries might once again be veering toward a catastrophic encounter. When the CIA director, John McCone, added his voice in early February to those recommending military action against North Vietnam, Johnson immediately asked whether this would not risk "bringing the Chinese Communists in the air or on the ground," only to receive McCone's not completely reassuring answer that "we had to face this contingency," especially of a ground intervention, but it was merely a "possibility" rather than a "probability."[48] "Have we faced—and has the President faced—the full shape of the risk of Chinese intervention?" wondered the National Security Council staff member and China specialist James C. Thomson Jr. on the eve of Rolling Thunder operations. "Are we willing—and is the President willing—to face a ground war in Southeast Asia against the combined armies of North Vietnam and China?" Leery of the "systematic reprisal track," Thomson (who later resigned to protest the war) warned that it would be "folly for the sheer momentum of events (or of actions taken to bolster the morale of our friends in Saigon) to lead us into a land war with China in which our air and naval power would be relatively ineffective."[49] Undersecretary of State George Ball, a consistent skeptic on the efficacy of military escalation, likewise cautioned that pressures to "take out" air bases used by Chinese MiGs might set the United States "on a course that would escalate into all-out conflict with China."[50] With the lessons of Korea lingering in their minds—at one point in the discussions over whether China would intervene, LBJ noted that Douglas MacArthur, shortly before his death the year before, had "passionately warned him against the use of American ground troops in Asia"[51]—top U.S. policymakers had to take the "China factor" seriously when they considered expanding American war involvement in Vietnam.

In the months immediately after the Tonkin Gulf incident, Johnson administration officials appeared relieved that Beijing seemed to have confined its initial reactions to the U.S. escalation to an intensification of the harsh rhetoric it had used to denounce America's "aggressive behavior." But when the Rolling Thunder bombings and landings of American Marines began, Washington noticed that Beijing strengthened a note in its propaganda reminiscent of the language it had employed fifteen years earlier as the U.S./UN/ROK forces crossed the 38th parallel in Korea. Indeed, although falling short of specifying any concrete or definite vows to intervene in Vietnam, Chinese public statements pledged that the PRC would not "stand idly by" or "look on with folded arms" while the U.S. imperialists committed aggression against North Vietnam, expressing a willingness to send weapons and people to help defeat the aggressors and likening the relationship between the PRC and the Democratic Republic of Vietnam (DRV) to that between "the lips and the teeth."[52] Beijing similarly roundly denounced Johnson's peace gestures during this period—for example, his April 7 Johns Hopkins University speech expressing a willingness to engage in "unconditional discussions" and a five-day bombing "pause" in May—as a "swindle pure and simple" and a "fraud."[53]

In the meantime, U.S. intelligence analysts noticed that augmenting these open Chinese statements, but largely hidden from public view, Beijing authorities also undertook a series of military mobilization and deployment measures in late 1964 and early 1965, which they interpreted as constituting measures to prepare for a potential conflict in Vietnam and/or signals aimed at deterring Washington from taking aggressive steps that might imperil Chinese interests. Allen S. Whiting, the head of the Far East division of the State Department's Bureau of Intelligence and Research (INR) from 1962 to 1966, has pointed out that they included a "systematic reinforcement of its air power," particularly in the southern Chinese border region adjacent to North Vietnam—and including the construction of three new air bases just north of the frontier (implying their availability as a refuge for planes engaged in operations over North Vietnam), joint PRC-DRV air exercises in January 1965, the limited deployment of Chinese MiG fighters to North Vietnam, and sharp Chinese reactions to U.S. and Nationalist Chinese overflights of the PRC border by intelligence and military aircraft.[54] In addition to these specific observable military actions, Beijing also organized massive protests and at the same time began constructing a "third front" by moving key industries away from coastal cities to inland locations, a further indication that Beijing was preparing for a possible U.S. bombing campaign or blockade in the event of a full-scale Sino-American war.[55]

Although much of the intelligence data (e.g., electronic intercepts and satellite and aerial reconnaissance photographs) that might clarify the Johnson administration's perception of China's actions remains secret, the recent declassification of a massive internal INR study of its Vietnam-related analyses permits a fuller reconstruction of how the State Department's intelligence branch perceived Beijing's involvement, and the risk of its greater intervention, in the mounting Vietnam crisis.[56] The study confirms that in late 1964 and early 1965, more than other government intelligence agencies, INR consistently warned policymakers of the danger of Chinese intervention in response to U.S. military escalation in Vietnam, a policy option under constant consideration. In May 1964, INR went along with a U.S. Intelligence Board estimate that stressed "Peking's caution in risking open hostilities with the United States and, with a confidence never seen again, concluded that there 'would probably not be [a] high risk of Chinese Communist ground intervention unless *major* US/GVN [Government of Viet Nam] ground units had moved *well* into the DRV or Communist-held areas of northern Laos, or *possibly,* the Chinese had committed their air [force] and had subsequently suffered attack on CCAF [Chinese Communist Air Force] bases in China.'"[57]

From then on, however, while emphasizing Hanoi's willingness to sustain its struggle even in the face of an intensifying U.S. military attack, INR expressed concern that Beijing had made "an actual commitment" to North Vietnam to assist the DRV should Washington deepen its military involvement. As early as July 1964, INR interpreted "the escalating Chinese verbal threat" as "an effort to deter the United States by raising the likelihood of Chinese involvement in response to US action against the North, while at the same time avoiding a commitment to a specific course of action."[58]

Taken by surprise by the Tonkin Gulf events in August, INR incorrectly suspected that China had urged Hanoi to take the deliberately provocative step of staging a second attack on U.S. ships on August 4 (two days after an initial raid two days earlier) in defiance of American warnings.[59] (Later evidence raised considerable doubts that the second attack had actually occurred, let alone that China had advocated launching it.[60]) If Washington were to retaliate by bombing North Vietnam, INR correctly predicted that Beijing would respond by sending North Vietnamese jet aircraft, ground antiaircraft equipment, and advisers, and "communicate evidence of mobilizing moves within China" to stimulate U.S. "concern over the threat of ground intervention."[61]

During the rest of 1964, INR discerned "tentative indications" of possible Chinese preparations for "greater involvement" in North Vietnam despite their "typically imprecise" warnings. These signs included "the dispatch of Chinese fighters with training personnel for North Vietnamese use," joint PRC-DRV air defense exercises, more aggressive pursuit of U.S. reconnaissance flights along China's periphery, and a rapid improvement of fighter capabilities, landing strips, radar facilities, and air bases in southern China near the Vietnamese border.[62] An October 1964 U.S. Intelligence Board estimate forecast that if the United States launched aggressive air attacks against North Vietnam, China would "probably" send "limited numbers" of ground troops (though not air force units) "both to prepare for further escalation and to make clear Peking's commitment to assist the North Vietnamese." (It doubted a large-scale ground intervention unless "major US/GVN ground units" actually invaded North Vietnam or Communist-held areas of Laos.)

The following month—in response to a major Johnson administration internal review of plans for escalation in Vietnam undertaken by the assistant secretary of state for far eastern affairs, William P. Bundy, and the assistant secretary of defense for international security affairs, John T. McNaughton—INR reaffirmed the warning of potential Chinese ground intervention in North Vietnam in response to U.S. attacks.[63] In addition to citing earlier warnings and military preparations, the new assessment drew on fresh "ominous" intelligence that the Chinese were constructing "on a priority basis" an airfield at Ningming only a few miles from the Sino-Vietnamese frontier to conclude that Beijing "may be preparing to provide air defense for the Hanoi-Haiphong area against possible US air attacks."[64]

Throughout the Johnson administration's escalation in Vietnam both in the air and on the ground in the first half of 1965, INR continued to insist that policymakers take seriously—more seriously—the danger of Chinese intervention. In February, INR criticized McGeorge Bundy's recommendation for air strikes against North Vietnam following Pleiku for failing to take potential Chinese reaction into consideration.[65] Later that month, INR dissented from intelligence community assessments by predicting that if U.S. bombing inflicted "severe damage" on North Vietnam, China might intervene with large-scale ground forces and "would probably" send fighters from PRC air bases into the fray.[66] Unlike other agencies, INR stressed that the Chinese had committed "their prestige to a more vigorous response to any future escalation" and could not easily back away from its promises.[67]

Continuing to dissent from predictions that enhanced U.S. bombing would elicit North Vietnamese concessions, INR in March and April repeatedly underlined the likelihood that China would insert itself directly into the fray. Once the United States threatened "vital" DRV targets, it estimated, the intervention, more for political than military impact, "would entail a 'visible, physical Chinese involvement,' as 'volunteers' at airfields, with MiG squadrons as 'volunteer' units, the shadowing of American attack aircraft from Chinese bases, or even engagement of US planes in defense of the Hanoi-Haiphong complex."[68] Beijing's vocal public vows to fight alongside NLF forces in South Vietnam brought it "closer to the point of no return in its obligation to support Hanoi should US escalation persist."[69] Noting China's public campaign to rouse its populace for war, INR observed that "'the more specific those statements are the more difficult it will be not to back them up with deeds' if the United States is not deterred."[70] More than other intelligence agencies, INR believed China would make a "major military response" to non-nuclear U.S. strikes on Chinese territory aimed at convincing Beijing to curb its support for Hanoi.[71]

Other U.S. intelligence agencies tended to emphasize more reassuring portents regarding Beijing's intentions, so long as the United States did not directly attack Chinese territory or launch a massive ground invasion of North Vietnam. According to a recently declassified CIA report, in early February China made a point of "privately indicating (to Washington through a third party) that PLA were *not* massed on the southern border." CIA analysts interpreted the message as a "not so bold move to disarm a pre-emptive American air strike on bases in south China."[72] Repeatedly, in estimates produced in February and June 1965, the CIA disagreed with INR's contention that bombing northern North Vietnam would likely prompt Chinese aircraft to take to the skies to counter the American attacks.[73]

Such mixed intelligence left senior Johnson administration officials to try to fathom China's intentions as they considered plans for bombing North Vietnam and escalating the U.S. military presence in the South. "Throughout all of the strategy debate in early 1965 ran a common thread—the concern with possible intervention in the conflict by elements of the North Vietnamese Army or the Communist Chinese Army or both," *The Pentagon Papers'* authors noted. Though the Joint Chiefs of Staff viewed the danger as simply a justification for additional deployments and the National Intelligence Board "consistently discounted the possibility of such intervention,"[74] the nightmare of a massive Chinese entry into the conflict clearly influenced President Johnson to limit the pace and appearance of escalation to as gradual and low-key a process as possible.[75] As described by journalists, Johnson used a characteristically earthy analogy to a congressional delegation in late March to explain his restraint in Rolling Thunder operations:

> To illustrate his caution, he showed critics the map of North Vietnam and pointed out the targets he had approved for attack, and to the many more targets he had disapproved. As for Communist China, he was watching for every possible sign of reaction. Employing a vivid sexual analogy, the President explained to friends and critics one day that the slow escalation of the air war in the North and the increasing pressure on Ho Chi Minh was seduction, not rape. If China should suddenly react to slow escalation, as a woman might react to attempted seduction, by threatening to retaliate (a slap in the face, to continue the metaphor), the United States would have plenty of time to ease off the bombing. On the other hand, if the United States were to unleash an all-out, total assault on the North—rape rather than seduction—there could be no turning back, and Chinese reaction might be instant and total.[76]

Thus we have encountered a series of crucial questions: How did Beijing's leaders perceive the Tonkin Gulf incident and, on the basis of the perception, formulate China's strategies to deal with the escalating Vietnam War? What were the real meanings of Beijing's aggressive public statements? To what extent and in which senses did Beijing's leaders learn from the lessons they drew from the Korean War while forming their responses to the situation in Vietnam in late 1964 and early 1965? The answers to these questions will allow us to comprehend better the process of the Sino-American signaling in the spring of 1965.

Beijing's Perception and Strategy
after the Gulf of Tonkin Incident

If the danger of Chinese intervention aroused serious concerns in Washington, the converse was at least as true: the dramatic expansion of U.S. military intervention in Vietnam, both in the air and on the ground, clearly provoked intense apprehension both in Hanoi and Beijing, and mutual consultations between the North Vietnamese leadership and, separately, Hanoi's two major communist patrons, the Soviet Union and PRC, which, despite their own acrimonious rivalry, expressed solidarity with the DRV. The Soviet-DRV exchanges are beyond the purview of this chapter, although it is clear that the U.S. initiation of bombing North Vietnam in February 1965 during Kosygin's visit to Hanoi only hardened Moscow's position that it had no alternative but to back the DRV.[77] As for Sino-Vietnamese consultations in late 1964 and early 1965 on how to perceive Washington's intentions and how to respond in the event of a major American intervention, newly available Chinese and Vietnamese sources, though still somewhat fragmentary, have placed scholars in a position to go beyond previous knowledge to ask new questions and provide new answers.[78]

According to these sources, immediately after the Tonkin Gulf events in August 1964, Chinese and North Vietnamese leaders intensively discussed the changing situation in Vietnam, paying special attention to potential courses of action in the event that the United States undertook to convert the struggle in South Vietnam from a "special" (i.e., antiguerrilla or "counterinsurgency") war into a "limited" or "local" war involving substantial American ground troops or—more closely resembling the Korean War scenario—even a U.S. invasion of North Vietnam. On August 5, Chinese premier Zhou Enlai and People's Liberation Army chief of staff Luo Ruiqing cabled North Vietnamese president Ho Chi Minh, premier Pham Van Dong, and People's Army of Vietnam chief of staff Van Tien Dung, advising them to "investigate and clarify the situation, discuss and formulate proper strategies and policies, and be ready to take action."[79]

To coordinate Chinese and Vietnamese strategies toward the new situation precipitated by the Gulf of Tonkin incident, Le Duan, the Vietnamese Workers' Party first secretary, secretly visited Beijing in mid-August and had a two-hour meeting with Mao on August 13 at Beidaihe. The two leaders exchanged intelligence information on the Gulf of Tonkin incident. Duan confirmed to Mao that the incident of August 2 was the result of a decision made by the Vietnamese commander at the site, and Mao told Duan that, according to Beijing's intelligence sources, the incident of August 4 was "not an intentional attack by the Americans," but was caused by "mistaken judgment" as the result of wrong information. While discussing the prospect for the war to be expanded into North Vietnam, Mao pointed out: "It seems that the Americans do not want to fight a war, you do not want to fight a war, and we do not necessarily want to fight a war. As none of the three sides wants to fight a war, the war will not happen." When a member of Duan's delegation mentioned that "the enemy is now making outcries to attack North Vietnam," Mao responded: "If the United States attacks the North, they will have to remember that the Chinese also have legs, and legs are used for walking." The Chinese leader also vowed to make some visible military deployments to indicate Beijing's support. "We will move another air division and a half airborne division to Kunming and Simao," both located in Yunnan Province close to the Vietnamese frontier, Mao vowed, "and we will make this open." He also promised to deploy two antiaircraft artillery divisions to the southern cities of Kunming and Nanning, as well as to move 300,000 to 500,000 troops to those southern provinces, "but not more than that as we will need to take care of Tianjin, Beijing, Shanghai, and Fujian, and we cannot deploy too many troops in those places either."[80]

U.S. intelligence soon began to detect Chinese actions evidently intended to signal Beijing's commitment to Hanoi and to respond to the threat of further American aerial attacks on North Vietnam. According to Whiting, American surveillance noted a prompt Chinese deployment of a squadron of MiG-17s to Hanoi following the Tonkin Gulf incident, followed that fall by the beginning of work on new airfields in areas of southern China near the Vietnamese frontier, at a time of "relative inactivity [in air defense construction] elsewhere on the mainland." U.S. analysts interpreted these moves as clearly designed to provide air support for North Vietnam in the event of American attacks, possibly including sanctuary and alternative bases for DRV airplanes, and, in combination with increased air strength on Hainan Island, "added protection to the North Vietnamese heartland, the Red River Delta, with its industry, dikes and population centers."[81]

Chinese and North Vietnamese leaders, however, still clearly hoped to minimize the extent of American intervention. On October 5, 1964, Mao met with Pham Van Dong in Beijing. The DRV premier told the Chinese chairman that Hanoi would strive to keep the conflict limited to a "special" war, remaining "cautious" to avoid provoking Washington.[82] While encouraging Hanoi to "eliminate" the South Vietnamese forces, Mao agreed heartily on the need to avoid a frontal confrontation with U.S. forces, and while he dispensed military advice to visitors in the event that the Americans "dare to take the risk to bring the war to the North," there is no indication of any explicit discussion of Chinese direct military intervention were that invasion to occur.[83] Similarly, in a January 1965 conversation, Zhou exhorted a Vietnamese military delegation to attack the enemy's "main forces" and its "strategic hamlets" by the end of the year, optimistically predicting that such efforts, combined with the Saigon regime's "political bankruptcy," might produce victory "even sooner than our original expectation."[84]

With both Beijing and Hanoi hoping to score a quick triumph in the South to capitalize on the Saigon regime's disarray and forestall any massive U.S. intervention, the American actions in February and March—to launch a sustained bombing campaign against North Vietnam and deploy a large and growing ground force in South Vietnam—evidently came as an unpleasant surprise to North Vietnamese and Chinese leaders. Mao and his comrades now had to reconsider the implications of U.S. actions in Vietnam and formulate new Chinese strategies to deal with the escalating crisis. While doing so, the thinking of Beijing's leaders appears to have been influenced not only by the lessons of the Korean War but also by the assumption that the Americans too would learn from their experience in Korea.

In March and April of 1965, top Beijing leaders held a series of discussions of the situation in Vietnam, putting special emphasis on whether Washington would further expand the war by bringing the ground war to North Vietnam and air and ground war to China. Deng Xiaoping's speech at a CCP Politburo meeting of April 12, which was also attended by Liu Shaoqi and Zhou, revealed some of the basic considerations of top Beijing leaders:

It seems that the [American] bombardment will continue. The first step of the U.S. imperialists was fighting a special war. According to the judgment of the Vietnamese comrades, the [American] special war has reached a new stage. Our view is that the special war has failed, and the war will be expanded. The American air bombardment has penetrated into the air space only twelve kilometers south of Hanoi, and, if the bombardment continues, it is inevitable that even Hanoi, Hai Phong and Thai Nguyen will become the targets. If this will not [allow them to reach their goals], it is even possible for them, under the excuse of chasing after Vietnamese planes, to invade our airspace. . . . If this is allowed to continue, they will come to Yunnan and Guangxi. Then the war will expand to part of China, and then, to the whole China.[85]

In discussing potential prospects for the escalation of the Vietnam War, Deng mentioned that there existed four scenarios: "First, the war will be fought in South Vietnam; second, the war will be fought both in South and North Vietnam, and will be linked to the war in Laos; third, the war will be fought in our provinces neighboring Vietnam; and, fourth, the U.S. imperialists will fight a larger regional war with us, even including Korea."[86] Liu, Zhou, and Deng all emphasized at the meeting that all of China had to be immediately mobilized to deal with a possible worst-case scenario.

Although both Liu and Deng mentioned in their speeches that China should not be afraid of "being dragged into the expanding Vietnam War," and that it was China's "duty of proletarian internationalism" to provide the Vietnamese comrades with all possible support, they also made it clear that it would be in the fundamental interests of both the Chinese and Vietnamese people for China not to become involved in a direct Sino-American confrontation. Zhou particularly argued that China should "try to gain mastery by striking the enemy only after he has struck first," and that therefore Beijing should not immediately introduce the slogan of "assisting Vietnam, resisting U.S. Imperialists."[87]

These discussions among top CCP leaders illuminate the complexity involved in Beijing's approach toward the Vietnam crisis. As is well known, in 1964–65, Mao already was planning to push China toward the highest stage of his "continuous revolution"—the "Great Proletarian Cultural Revolution." In the face of American escalation in Vietnam, Mao certainly saw an increasing threat to China's security interests. In the meantime, informed by his past experiences (e.g., his handling of the Korean crisis in 1950 and the Taiwan Strait crisis of 1958), he also realized that the intensifying Vietnam crisis provided him with a convenient pretext to mobilize the Chinese population. This helps explain why Beijing's rhetoric toward U.S. escalation of the Vietnam War was from the outset extremely militant. Indeed, Beijing's belligerent statements on the war in Vietnam were not aimed only at both Hanoi and Washington; in the final analysis, their targets also included ordinary Chinese.

Considerations along the above lines determined that Beijing's strategic aims were also complicated: Mao and his comrades certainly hoped that the Vietnamese revolutionaries would eventually defeat the U.S. imperialists and their Saigon "lackeys," and it was thus necessary for Beijing to support their struggle; but it would be against Mao's interests if such support indeed led to a direct Chinese-American military showdown, thus sabotaging his efforts to implement the Cultural Revolution at home. So, by April 1965,

Beijing's leaders had decided on three basic principles in formulating China's strategy toward Vietnam. First, if the Americans went beyond bombing the North and used land forces to invade North Vietnam, China would have to send military forces. Second, China would give explicit warnings—clear in some respects, deliberately ambiguous in others—to the Americans, so that they would not feel free to expand military operations into the North, let alone to bring the war to China. Third, China would avoid direct military confrontation with the United States as long as possible; but if necessary, it would not shrink from such a clash.[88] These principles formed the foundation for Beijing to send a series of warning signals to Washington beginning in late March 1965.

The Signaling

With the continuous escalation of the Vietnam War, both U.S. and Chinese leaders perceived the danger of a Korea-like clash to be increasing. However, it was no easy matter to compose and convey a subtle mixed message that would blend resolve—and readiness for military confrontation—with limited objectives that would at least preclude an unnecessary clash brought on by misunderstanding, misperception, or miscommunication. And compounding the difficulty of relaying this crucial mixed message in an effective and nuanced manner, Beijing also had to transcend ideological, cultural, and linguistic barriers, in addition to the lack of formal diplomatic relations, all exacerbated by nearly two decades of troubled history characterized by accumulating mutual hostility, distrust, and other negative emotions, including fear. To do so, China's leaders formulated a four-point message (three-point in some instances) for U.S. leaders in April and May 1965. This message reconfigured, in a sharper and more concrete yet still partly ambiguous form, many of the same elements that had characterized Chinese public statements of support for North Vietnam for months. But it also included new elements that seemed specifically designed to influence U.S. decisionmaking on military escalation in the fluid context of that spring, because Johnson was known to be considering a range of options.

The first instance of such signaling was delivered in a more traditional and general form on March 25, when the official *Renmin Ribao* (People's Daily) announced in an editorial that China would offer "the heroic Vietnamese people any necessary material support, including the supply of weapons and all kinds of military materials," and that, if necessary, China was also ready "to send its personnel to fight together with the Vietnamese people to annihilate the American aggressors."[89] Four days later, on March 29, Zhou made the same open announcement at a mass rally in Tirana, the capital of Albania, where he was making a formal visit.[90]

U.S. officials indeed caught the hardening of tone. Before a secret top-level White House meeting on April 1, National Security Adviser McGeorge Bundy advised Johnson that "Peiping has stiffened its position within the last week. We still believe that attacks near Hanoi might substantially raise the odds of Peiping coming in with air."[91] Though Johnson sounded undeterred about escalating U.S. attacks—"we got to find 'em and kill 'em"—U.S. officials ordered renewed intelligence attention on the question of Beijing's likely responses to alternative scenarios for increasing the American ground presence in Vietnam. "*How to make pressure* [on North Vietnam] w/o reaching flash point" was how Secretary of State Dean Rusk summarized the dilemma facing American policymakers.[92]

Clearly aware that their U.S. counterparts were urgently considering decisions on increased military involvement in Vietnam, Chinese leaders decided that private as well as public communications were needed to produce the desired influence. Beijing's first serious effort to signal the Americans occurred on April 2, when Zhou, visiting Karachi, asked Mohammad Ayub Khan, Pakistan's president, to convey the following points to President Johnson during a visit to Washington scheduled for later that month:[93] (1) "China would not take the initiative to provoke a war against the United States"; (2) "the Chinese mean what they say, and China will honor whatever international obligations it has undertaken"; and (3) "China is prepared." In this conversation, the Chinese premier also mentioned that "if the United States expands the war to China, it will really suffer." But he did not, as Beijing later did in delivering several similar warnings, present this as a clearly defined fourth point.[94]

According to the detailed (and apparently contemporaneous) Chinese record of their conversation, Zhou provided a gloss on each of these points for the Pakistanis to use in relating the PRC position. To support his first statement—that China would not initiate or provoke a war with the United States—Zhou pointed to Beijing's restraint in handling the Taiwan issue. Despite having "every right to recover" the island, he noted, Beijing had "never used armed force" to do so (evidently considering the shelling of the offshore islands too trivial to fit that description) and had been conducting talks with the Americans in Warsaw despite the continued presence of the U.S. Navy's Seventh Fleet in the Taiwan Strait. By placing this point first,

Zhou and the Chinese leadership wanted to emphasize that, despite Beijing's often bellicose revolutionary rhetoric, the PRC did not seek to expand its power or to spread communist rule throughout Asia while the United States was being expelled (as some U.S. analysts believed was the case[95]).

Zhou's commentary on the second point—"The Chinese mean what they say"—is particularly interesting because it explicitly links Beijing's efforts to signal Washington in the spring of 1965 to its understanding of the circumstances surrounding China's entry into the Korean War in the fall of 1950. The premier recounted to Ayub the well-known story of his warning to the Americans not to cross the 38th parallel or otherwise China would be forced to intervene, a message conveyed via Panikkar, the Indian ambassador to the PRC, just after midnight on October 2–3, 1950. "But the United States would not listen, not believing that China would support [North] Korea," Zhou recalled. "When Your Excellency visits the United States, please convey these points to them. Maybe they will again not believe us. Maybe, as Your Excellency has predicted, they will believe us. Both possibilities exist."[96]

Some U.S. intelligence analysts believed that the power and relevance of the Korean analogy for Chinese efforts to deter American escalation in Vietnam had already eroded due to the fact that despite repeated allusions to its Korean War actions in public statements, Beijing had failed to respond forcefully (either in terms of military actions or concrete threats to intervene) to Washington's initiation of repeated bombing raids against the North on several occasions in February and then continuously since early March.[97] The Chinese probably did not recognize these considerations in Washington. However, the fact that Zhou put great emphasis on recalling the lessons of the Korean War demonstrated that Beijing's leaders certainly understood that every senior U.S. official, including Johnson, had lived through the trauma of the Chinese intervention in Korea—which had inflicted the greatest U.S. military setback since World War II—and could hardly once again blithely disregard a loud "no trespassing" warning from China.

Zhou was also well aware that some commentators had judged that one reason for U.S. leaders and analysts to have erroneously dismissed his October 1950 warning as a "bluff" was distrust of the intermediary, Panikkar, whom American officials regarded as anti-American and unreliable. "However," Zhou told Ayub, "our friend has changed this time, it is not India but Pakistan."[98] Though it is true that one reason for switching intermediaries might have been the fact that since the late 1950s Sino-Indian relations had greatly deteriorated, Zhou and the Beijing leadership also understood that the Pakistani leader enjoyed far closer ties with Washington, at the level of head of state, and thus could more credibly convey the Chinese message to the highest American levels than the Indian envoy had been able to.

Like his second point, Zhou's third point—"China is prepared"—was directly related to the issue of credibility. "The United States says that China has not made war preparations, using this to deceive its people," Zhou told Ayub, noting that the Pakistani leader had publicly called China a "peace-loving country" and had witnessed "no signs of war preparations" during a visit just weeks earlier to Beijing and Shanghai. Yet, the Chinese premier stressed, "in a military sense, we cannot but make due preparations. If the United States brings the war flame to our side, we have to extinguish it. . . . If the United States expands the war, the war will gradually be expanded to China. We are prepared both materially and spiritually."[99]

Perhaps as a deliberate step to enhance the credibility of Zhou's warning, one week after Zhou's talks with Ayub, Beijing launched a new policy of responding more firmly to American overflights of PRC territory. On April 9, an air battle reportedly occurred between Chinese and U.S. fighters over Hainan Island. An official Chinese announcement stated: "Eight U.S. military planes in two groups intruded over China's Hainan Island. Panicking when Chinese planes took off to meet them, the U.S. planes fired two air-to-air missiles at random and fled. In the confusion, one U.S. plane was hit by a missile fired by another and crashed in the area of Hainan."

Whiting has commented that the reported incident and China's handling of it may have constituted a carefully calibrated message that combined both toughness and restraint. "The decision to scramble MiG fighters under circumstances that did not otherwise presage an American attack carried the risk of provoking an engagement, but it also offered an opportunity to communicate an important signal," Whiting wrote in *The Chinese Calculus of Deterrence.* "Peking's prompt announcement of the incident and its careful explanation of the shootdown indicated its sensitivity to the provocative implications and its desire to deny Washington an excuse to retaliate."[100] Missing from Whiting's analysis is the fact that the Hainan incident occurred precisely as Beijing was attempting to send a crucial politico-military message to Washington that Zhou believed was already on its way, and the incident thus probably indicated Beijing's determination to demonstrate to Washington that it was ready and able to honor its warnings.[101]

Zhou's last point, which he initially simply appended as an analysis in addition to his three-point message—"If the United States expands the war

to China, it will really suffer"—was ominous but vague. Zhou strongly implied, but did not explicitly state, that U.S. attempts to limit an expansion of
the war to the territory of Vietnam would inevitably bring China in: "The
United States believes that if it does not expand the war in Vietnam to China,
China will not support Vietnam. Our position is that even if the war is not
expanded to China, still China will support Vietnam, so long as the DRV requests it, so long as the NLF [National Liberation Front] in South Vietnam
requests it. When the war expands, it is impossible to draw a line."[102] More
specifically, in language that in some respects inverted John Foster Dulles'
1954 "massive retaliation" speech (vowing that America would reserve the
right to retaliate against Soviet aggression "at places and with means of its
own choosing"), Zhou noted that the United States might attack from the air,
but China might respond "using other strategy, everywhere on the ground.
If the United States is to carry out an extensive bombing in China, that is
war, and a war has no boundaries."[103] Left to the imagination of American
officials were the possible scenarios for a massive conventional Chinese
riposte—not only in Vietnam itself, but perhaps in other sensitive Cold War
Asian flashpoints bordering China, such as Laos, Taiwan, or South Korea—
any one of which might force Washington to fight a two-front war, escalate
to the use of nuclear weapons, or suffer a humiliating military defeat.

It should be emphasized that to a considerable extent, each aspect of
Zhou's warnings had been previously stated or at least implied in open Chinese statements. However, Beijing's leaders evidently calculated that a less
polemical, more cogent version, mingling elements of moderation, firmness,
and ambiguity, carrying the premier's authoritative and personal stamp,
would receive more serious credence and attention when delivered personally to a senior American personage, presumably Johnson himself, by the
head of a major Asian nation known for its close ties to both the PRC and
the United States. (Or, to use the phrase employed by Zhou when five years
later a top-level Pakistani channel—this time Ayub's successor, Yahya
Khan—was again used to communicate an important message between the
United States and China, this time to him from U.S. president Richard Nixon,
"From a Head [of state/government], through a Head, to a Head!"[104]) In this
regard, we also see how Beijing's leaders had learned from the Korean experience—to make the warnings work better, it too important to present them
in the right format and deliver them through the right channels.

The Pakistani leader, for his part, who after visiting China in early March
and hosting Zhou on April 2 then journeyed to Moscow in a further display
of what he termed his "triangular tightrope" balancing act between East and

West, undoubtedly welcomed the opportunity to deliver such an important message to Washington. He could clearly sense that by helping to contain the escalating Vietnam conflict and serving as a top-level messenger between the United States and its most belligerent communist rival, his efforts to forge a new friendship with Beijing—an initiative he knew infuriated the Americans—would be fully justified. Furthermore, he could use this opportunity to boost his country's stature as an independent, albeit smaller, power, while simultaneously enhancing his own prestige as a competent participant in high-stakes big power diplomacy.[105]

However, neither Ayub nor Zhou could have foreseen that in mid-April, Johnson would suddenly postpone indefinitely the planned visit to Washington by Ayub (as well as one planned for shortly thereafter by his Indian counterpart, Prime Minister Lal Bahadur Shastri), thus leaving Beijing uncertain when, if, and how the Pakistani leader would be able to convey the important message Zhou had given him. Johnson's precise reasons for canceling the India-Pakistan summit in Washington have never been made entirely clear, but most observers blamed it on his resentment of the two leaders' criticism of U.S. policy in Vietnam (and his ire over another foreign leader, Canadian prime minister Lester Pearson, for calling for peace negotiations rather than bombing in an April 2 speech at Temple University, an act that earned him an angry tongue lashing and lapel grabbing from LBJ at Camp David).[106]

Ironically, Johnson informed Ayub that one reason for deferring the visit (aside from the press of legislative business) had been concern that the Pakistani's recent trip to Beijing and talks with high-level PRC officials would attract unfavorable publicity in Washington (given the deep American animosity toward the Communist Chinese) that could endanger congressional support for U.S. military and economic aid programs to Pakistan.[107] In any event, Johnson inadvertently and unwittingly passed up an opportunity to receive a firsthand account of a senior PRC leader's communication, at precisely the moment when deciphering Chinese intentions in Vietnam was a matter of paramount concern. Although, according to British records, the Pakistanis apparently did transmit the message to Washington in some form via either diplomatic or intelligence channels, such transmission did not carry the strength the message that it would have had, had it been delivered directly by Ayub to Johnson.[108]

With the fate of Zhou's message in limbo, and indications of imminent U.S. military escalation continuing to mount, Beijing's leaders appear to have concluded, perhaps with some anxiety, that it was necessary and prudent to employ other channels besides Ayub to communicate the message to Washington. Burma's Ne Win and Cambodia's Prince Norodom Sihanouk are among those to whom Zhou was reported to have passed comparable warnings at different points in April, although no evidence has emerged that these leaders relayed Beijing's messages to senior levels in Washington.[109] On April 20, Zhou repeated the four-point message in a speech to leaders of the Non-Aligned Movement in Bogor, Indonesia, at a gathering marking the tenth anniversary of the Bandung Conference.[110] Over the next month or so, Zhou repeated the four sentences to "many foreign friends," as he told Indonesian foreign minister Subandrio at a meeting in Guangzhou on May 28. When Subandrio asked him point-blank what Beijing would do if the United States bombarded China from the air, Zhou repeated his message, implying strongly that such an action would provoke a sharp response:

(1) China will not take the initiative to provoke a war against the United States. We have conducted negotiations with the United States for over ten years on the Taiwan issue, which can be taken as evidence. (2) China will honor what is said. The Korean War can be taken as evidence. (3) China is prepared. At present, our whole country is under mobilization. (4) If the United States bombs China, that means bringing the war to China. The war has no boundary. This has two meanings: First, you cannot say that only an air war on your part is allowed, and the land war on my part is not allowed. Second, not only you may invade our territory, we may also fight a war abroad.

Compared with the warnings Zhou had given via Ayub, this time he further clarified the fourth point, particularly stressing that if the United States brought the air war to China, the PRC would retaliate. In the meantime, the Chinese premier again cited the Korean experience as evidence to enhance the warning's credibility.

Beijing's repeated warnings were not just issued to influence the Americans; they were also meant for use with Vietnamese comrades as reassuring evidence of China's solidarity. On May 16, Zhou told a visiting NLF delegation at the Great Hall of the People in Beijing of his conversation with Ayub, describing the four-point warning for relay to the Americans (evidently for the first time to his visitors, though presumably Hanoi had been previously informed), with some slightly different twists in the commentary. In noting China's vow to "never launch a war against the United States" and citing Taiwan as a "case in point," Zhou admitted a need to "render self-criticism to our shortcomings," because the Taiwanese people had not risen up as had the South Vietnamese. Regarding point two, the congruence of China's words and deeds, Zhou added: "We will go to Vietnam if Vietnam is in need, as we did in Korea." On Beijing's preparedness for war, point three, Zhou declared that the DRV could see that the Chinese "bordering provinces" were ready and vowed, "The whole of China is also ready." Finally, Zhou's formulation of point four went: "The war will have no limits if the US expands it to Chinese territory. The US can fight an air war. Yet, China also can fight a ground war."[111]

It is interesting to note that Beijing did *not* use the Sino-American ambassadorial talks in Warsaw as a channel to communicate its critical signals to Washington. Since 1955, the PRC and United States had engaged in a direct dialogue despite the absence of normal diplomatic relations through the ambassadorial talks, first in Geneva and then, after 1958, in Warsaw. In the summer of 1962, as discussed above, the Kennedy administration had used the Warsaw talks to reassure Beijing that Washington would not support a Taiwanese attack on the mainland "under existing circumstances."[112] In 1965, the two sides were represented by Chinese ambassador Wang Guoquan (Wang Kuo-ch'uan) and U.S. ambassador John M. Cabot, and, according to American records, Vietnam issues indeed dominated the 124th ambassadorial meeting, held on February 24, and the 125th session, on April 21.[113]

The latter meeting, in particular, came precisely as Chinese leaders were seeking to transmit the four-point message to Washington via various intermediaries. As in previous talks, on April 21 Wang reiterated contempt for America's "aggression" in Vietnam, stock phrases about Sino-Vietnamese solidarity, and predictions of ultimate certain defeat for Washington's "imperialistic" policies. He also cited Zhou's statements to the effect that the "Chinese would send South Vietnamese people all their needs, including arms, and would send [its] own men when South Vietnamese people want them."[114] Yet Wang did not pass along the authoritative and specific four-point warning as delivered by Zhou to Ayub and others.

Beijing's failure to employ the Warsaw channel to signal stands as a puzzle: Perhaps the ambassadorial talks had so long before degenerated into empty propaganda exchanges that Chinese leaders decided that Washington would not pay attention should a genuinely important statement be made; perhaps Beijing judged that Wang would be seen as insufficiently authoritative, or that Cabot was too low-level for such an important communication, or both, preferring a method certain to reach Johnson personally; or perhaps Beijing's leaders worried that the conciliatory side of the message might be taken as a sign of weakness if made in a direct Sino-American conversation.

After receiving through diplomatic channels the four-part "signal" described here, some U.S. officials were "not inclined to take these noises from Peking very seriously," because the Warsaw conversations remained "totally sterile." It seemed "very doubtful that [the] first dove of peace would fly out of that particular nest," William P. Bundy told a Canadian diplomat after reporting the latest bleak exchanges.[115] For whatever reason, the Sino-American ambassadorial talks continued to be a forum for mutual attack, rather than a serious channel of bilateral communication. Not until a year later, when Beijing had already publicly issued the four-part warning through a Pakistani journalist, did China's representative in the Warsaw talks relay the message to his American counterpart.[116]

By the end of May, Beijing's leaders had apparently grown so concerned about the danger that their message had failed to reach top policymakers in Washington that they decided to take a highly unusual step. Though still disdaining a direct channel such as the Warsaw ambassadorial talks, Beijing opted for the next best thing: turning to America's closest ally as an intermediary (another sign that the PRC had learned a lesson from the problems that had stemmed from using a figure or country distrusted in Washington, e.g., India's Panikkar). On the morning of May 31, 1965, the senior British diplomat in China, chargé d'affaires Donald Charles Hopson, customarily isolated in the capital and ignored by top-level officials, received a rare summons to a meeting with Foreign Minister Chen Yi.[117]

Although the PRC had frequently and harshly criticized British policy in Vietnam as subservient to American imperialism, and had only recently contemptuously refused to receive a peace envoy dispatched by London, Chen was "courteous" and "in good humour" throughout a meeting that lasted more than an hour, Hopson reported afterward. The purpose of the audience, the Briton had discovered, was the Chinese foreign minister's "very long exposition" of China's position on the Vietnam situation—summed up in the four-point message:

(I)   China will not provoke war with United States;

(II)   What China says counts;

(III) China is prepared; and,

(IV) If United States bombs China that would mean war and there would be no limits to the war.

Chen explained the background to Hopson: Zhou had originally given the message to Ayub Khan but given the Pakistani's failure to go to Washington, Beijing would be "grateful" if the British government would instead relay it to Washington. Somewhat tempering the urgency of the danger of Chinese intervention, however, Chen noted that North Vietnamese prime minister Pham Van Dong had recently declared in Bandung (evidently at the tenth anniversary commemorations in late April) "that the Vietnamese people would continue the struggle against the Americans to the bitter end whatever happened" and (rather disingenuously given the Beijing-Hanoi exchanges cited above) that the "Vietnamese did not at present need material assistance but only moral and political support from China.[118]

During the talks, Chen systematically delineated the PRC's anti-American stand on the Vietnam issue. Particularly interesting, in the context of the Korean analogy, was his response to arguments that the "Soviet Union was behind China then [in 1950] and not now, and therefore Chinese would not be as resolute." In fact, the foreign minister argued, this claim was "fundamentally mistaken" because the PRC had actually intervened in Korea precisely "*because* Russia had refused to do so" (emphasis added). As one U.S. analyst noted upon seeing the British report of the conversation, this claim was "the first time the Chinese have made this charge to our knowledge"[119]—and one, incidentally, that has been buttressed by recent disclosures from Russian archives.[120] Chen also made a case that Zhou had perhaps not felt it necessary to lay out to Ayub, that contrary to the American tendency to attribute North Vietnam's actions and other revolutions in the developing world to the aggressive machinations of the "Sino-Soviet bloc," these "national-liberation movements" arose and acted independently, in this case in response to U.S. policy, and were not directed by China, any more than they were engineered by the Soviet Union (as Washington charged) before the adoption of its "revisionist line" in 1956.

Having made one argument probably framed for British ears—which were generally more skeptical of U.S. warnings of the "domino theory" and better attuned to intracommunist rivalries than their American counterparts—Chen also complimented London for being "sensible" during the last stages of the Chinese Civil War by recognizing reality and accepting the PRC's establishment even as Washington clung to the lost cause of Jiang Jieshi's Nationalists, and he lamented that there was no need for London to follow its ally to disaster in Vietnam, either. Perhaps recalling Anthony Eden's avid enthusiasm for his role as cochair, alongside Soviet foreign minister V. M. Molotov, of the 1954 Geneva Conference, in trying to bring

peace to Indochina (as well as British prime minister Harold Wilson's recent criticism of LBJ's bombing decisions), Chen even dangled the notion
of some sort of Sino-British collusion to bring their warring allies to the
peace table and to their senses.

From Beijing's perspective, the Chen-Hopson meeting constituted the
Chinese leaders' most serious and, as they hoped, most effective effort to
communicate to Washington what the PRC *would do* and *would not do* if
the Vietnam War escalated further. All of this took place as Beijing's top
leaders and military planners reached the final stage, by working together
with their North Vietnamese counterparts, of formulating the details of
China's strategies toward the war. According to Chinese documentary
sources, Hanoi's chief of staff, Van Tien Dung, building on a series of visits by top Vietnamese leaders (including Ho Chi Minh and Duan) to China
in previous months, visited Beijing in early June 1965. His meetings with
Luo Ruiqing finalized the guiding principles and concrete details of China's
support to North Vietnam under different scenarios. If the war remained in
its current status—that is, if the United States were directly involved in military operations in the South while using only aerial force to bombard the
North—the Vietnamese would fight the war by themselves, and China
would offer military and material support in ways chosen by the Vietnamese. If the Americans used their naval and air forces to support a South
Vietnamese invasion of the North, China would send its air and naval forces
to support North Vietnam operations. If American land forces were directly
involved in invading the North, China would use its land forces as strategic
reserves for the Vietnamese, and carry on operational tasks whenever necessary. Dung and Luo also had detailed discussions about the actual form
China's military involvement would take in different situations. If the Chinese air force were to enter the war, the first option would be to use Chinese
volunteer pilots and Vietnamese planes in operations; the second option
would be to station Chinese pilots and planes on Vietnamese air fields, and
enter operations there; and the third would be to adopt the "Andong
model,"[121] that is, when engaging in military operations over Vietnam, Chinese pilots and planes would take off from and return to bases in China. If
Chinese land forces were to be used in operations in Vietnam, they would
basically serve as a reserve force; but if necessary, Chinese troops would
participate in fighting.[122] It is apparent that Beijing's signaling efforts, especially the one through the British channel, were related to its strategic
planning during the same period, and Beijing's leaders obviously hoped that

the signaling, if successful, would preclude the need for China to have to face the "worst-case scenario."

The delicate Sino-Vietnamese consultations over potential scenarios for Chinese aid also help explain the deliberately cryptic and ambiguous aspects of Beijing's signaling to Washington. For example, while making clear that U.S. bombing of Chinese territory would provoke a sharp response, the warnings were far less clear concerning Beijing's reaction should the United States invade North Vietnam—despite the fact that the 17th parallel constituted an obvious "parallel" to the role played by the 38th parallel in triggering Chinese intervention in the Korean conflict. While making general assertions of solidarity with Vietnam, they did not explicitly vow that China would intervene militarily with its own forces if American forces entered the DRV, nor did they distinguish between various scenarios ranging from a limited invasion of the region just north of the Demilitarized Zone to a full-scale invasion.

There are two obvious reasons why it made sense for China to stay ambiguous on this matter. First, it appears that Beijing and Hanoi themselves had not agreed in advance on precisely what sort of U.S. land invasion would require direct Chinese military intervention in response. Rather than issuing a predated invitation, North Vietnamese leaders would naturally have preferred to await a concrete situation before resorting, as a desperate, last-ditch measure, to such an invitation to their giant northern neighbor and traditional rival. ("We wanted the advantages of Chinese deterrence," one North Vietnamese official later recalled, "without having to suffer the consequences if they actually had to carry out their threat" to intervene.[123]) Second, being precise about what minimal action would provoke a Chinese response risked undermining the signal's deterrent value, because it would implicitly give a green light to any and all American military actions up to that point. Far better, instead, to produce maximum uncertainty, and thus caution, among Washington's decisionmakers when they considered even those escalatory steps short of attacking China.

Message Delivered

We do not know how—or even if—the previous Chinese signaling had reached top U.S. policymakers. We do know now, thanks to British archives, that London quickly delivered Chen Yi's message to Washington.

As early as March 1965, British prime minister Harold Wilson had publicly expressed misgivings over Johnson's decision to bomb North Vietnam.
Beijing's decision to turn to the United Kingdom as a reliable channel of
communication delighted U.K. officials (and presumably Wilson in particular), who were already assiduously seeking prestige, relevance, and credit
in Washington and other world capitals by playing a role in bringing peace
in Vietnam. They also hoped the encounter might presage an improvement
in Sino-British relations, then confined to consular representatives, particularly because Chen seemed to have expressed the same willingness.[124]
British officials made sure that Beijing's message promptly reached Washington. They shared Hopson's cables with the U.S. Embassy in London and
transmitted copies of the telegrams to the British Embassy in Washington
for delivery to the State Department, along with instructions to "emphasize
that leakage would prejudice prospects of further access to Chen Yi and that
in consequence we must ask them to safeguard this material."[125]

To help the Americans better understand the Chinese message, Foreign
Office aides added their own view of the conversation in Beijing, commenting that the "main interest" of Chen's presentation was its emphasis on
the confrontation between Washington and Hanoi "(no mention of Viet
Cong), and his efforts to disclaim Chinese responsibility for or control over
Hanoi." The London officials interpreted these and other statements as un-
derlining Chen's first point—"that China's present intention is not to intervene militarily while war is conducted broadly within present limits, and
probably not unless China were directly attacked." This seeming equanim-
ity also fit with the foreign minister's "confidence" in a North Vietnamese
military victory "without direct external assistance," an assessment that explained his "disinterest" at present in negotiations.[126] As a supporting Foreign Office analysis observed, the Chinese foreign minister had been "at
pains to emphasise that China will only intervene militarily if directly attacked," in line not only with published statements, "common prudence,"
and the PRC's favorable assessment of the military prospects in Vietnam,
but also "to avoid an unnecessary Sino-U.S. confrontation either through
carelessness on the part of the Americans, or through an extension to China
of the U.S. philosophy of retaliatory bombing." Chen, analyst C. M.
MacLehose commented, was "realist enough to know how weak"—"weak
and bombastic"—were the three points threatening retaliation if attacked,
since "the Chinese have no military answer to U.S. military power, if the
Americans are really prepared to use it." From conversations in Washington, the Foreign Office analyst had gleaned the impression that U.S. offi-

cials were not only "determined to avoid a clash with the Chinese" but also "inclined if anything to over-estimate the possibility of Chinese intervention rather than to treat it too lightly." MacLehose also threw cold water on the notion that the conversation reflected any enhanced Chinese appreciation of the United Kingdom's role as a potential mediator or peace channel, because he noted that plenty of more sympathetic intermediaries would be available should the Chinese or North Vietnamese desire to open negotiations, and Chen's hint about Beijing and London influencing their respective allies "was probably thrown out to whet the appetite the Chinese believe us to have for a mediatory role, in the mild hope of detaching us from the Americans."[127]

On June 2, the British diplomat Michael N. F. Stewart duly relayed Hopson's cables to William Bundy, who noted that Washington had received "a somewhat similar message through the Pakistanis but in less clear terms and without the amplifications" that Chen had given Hopson.[128] At a more senior level, on the afternoon of June 3, Ambassador Sir Patrick Dean took up the Chinese message personally with U.S. secretary of state Rusk. Rusk thanked the British for providing the record of the Hopson–Chen Yi conversation, "which at first sight they were not disposed to regard as at all alarming or threatening," but which the Americans "were studying with the greatest of care."[129] In addition—in what William Bundy described to Rusk as a regrettable "mistake"—the British intelligence liaison in Washington also disclosed the Chen approach to the CIA, which included a somewhat general account in its Current Intelligence Brief that went straight to the president.[130]

An initial U.S. analysis of the message found Chen's comments "not surprising" and evidently intended—as State Department analyst Lindsey Grant wrote William Bundy on June 3—"to pry the UK away from us, to give added currency to the assumption that the Chinese Communists are not directly involved in the Vietnamese situation, and to warn the U.S. to avoid actions against China." In fact, Grant found the message "surprisingly mild." Chen had explicitly threatened intervention only if Washington directly attacked China, he noted, and had "failed to take the opportunity to warn that U.S. escalation (the bombing of Hanoi, for instance) would lead to retaliation." Instead, the PRC foreign minister had confined himself to a "nebulous" warning against introducing other countries' troops (and even here had not mentioned specifically the possible use of Nationalist Chinese forces, an action that administration advisers felt would provoke Beijing's wrath). Grant also found it "less than likely" that Beijing would provide air support to North Vietnam from Chinese bases, though he could "not dismiss" the danger. He judged their failure to threaten such action in response to U.S. bombing of the DRV to be in line with "several indications"— including guided tours for foreign correspondents of southwest China in February to show the lack of any troop buildup near the border, the cautious handling of the "Hainan fighter scrap" in April, and a "recent apparent message to us" that the PRC opposed Soviet overflights of China in April due to concern that the United States might intercept them—"of extreme Chinese sensitivity to the possibility that we will misread their actions and thereby precipitate a direct Sino-U.S. conflict." Grant conceded that Beijing's descriptions of what the PRC and DRV would do if necessary in response to American escalation "accurately reflect their estimate and their position," although he, like MacLehose, took with a grain of salt Chen's "casual" and "lightly delivered" crack about China and the United Kingdom being able to render "good advice" to their respective allies in Hanoi and Washington, a comment that, the analyst noted, "fits into a standard Chinese Communist tactic of offering a vague hope in exchange for concrete action."[131]

Despite Grant's general skepticism as to the message's import or freshness, the British cables quickly attracted the attention of Johnson's national security adviser, McGeorge Bundy, who recognized them as sufficiently significant to bring them to LBJ's personal attention with the following cover note:

1. The CIA daily brief last night had a very important annex on Chinese Communist policy toward Vietnam, but they did not make it wholly clear that this account was part of a direct effort to send a message from Chou En-lai to the U.S. Government. This is so interesting that I think you will want to read it yourself in the British telegrams which have been provided to us. The first two pages of the attached gives a brief summary, and there follows a long reporting telegram which is worth reading in full.

2. Dean Rusk's first impression is that this is a relatively defensive message. My own feeling is more mixed. The basic trouble with the message is that it does not tell us at all at what point the Chinese might move in Vietnam itself in a way which would force us to act against China. And that of course is the $64 question.[132]

Ironically, only a day earlier Johnson had been voicing concern to congressional leaders that bombing Hanoi or other escalatory measures being proposed might "bring China into the struggle,"[133] so one must presume that LBJ devoured the British reports with extreme interest. On June 4—even as Zhou, in Dar-es-Salaam, repeated the message to Tanzanian president Julius Nyerere for him to convey to the Americans[134]—William Bundy told the British that they could inform Beijing that Washington had indeed received the Chen message, and took measures to see that knowledge of the Chinese message via the Hopson channel be kept as restricted as possible lest public exposure dissuade Beijing from using it again. After Johnson presumably read the British telegrams, a special weekend White House lunch meeting was held on Saturday, June 5, attended by LBJ, McGeorge Bundy, Rusk, McNamara, and Ball, to discuss the Vietnam situation and "the appropriate shape of an answer to the Chinese."[135]

No record of the discussion has been found, but senior U.S. officials evidently found both the content of Chen's message and his method for sending it to Washington to be highly interesting, even if, as Bundy noted to Johnson, it remained blurry on what U.S. actions would set off an escalatory action-reaction sequence with China. On the evening of June 5, after the high-level discussion, Bundy forwarded to Johnson what he called a "rather cooler assessment" by a "bright guy" in the State Department Bureau of Intelligence and Research, whose view contrasted with the "importance which some of us" had attached to the message.[136] The INR analyst, George C. Denney Jr., stressed that Chen's message "contains no element or idea which has not for months been part of the standard Chinese Communist presentations" and pooh-poohed the idea that it represented a "special Chinese effort to open channels of communication with the US" as Chen had recounted Zhou's earlier abortive attempt to use Ayub instead. Denney also underlined its "fuzzy" failure to clarify Beijing's reactions to prospective U.S. escalation short of attacking China itself. Though the expressed determination and readiness to resist American aggression "might bolster Peking's deterrence posture," Denney argued that they "provided no real clarification of the limits to which China is prepared to go in support of Hanoi or, conversely, the extent to which China is prepared to acquiesce in US attacks against North Vietnam. If Ch'en's motivation was to create further ambiguity in these areas, he succeeded." Like MacLehose, Denney also viewed the message as a transparent effort to "split" London from Washington on the Vietnam issue.[137]

McGeorge Bundy's verdict on Denney's memo was that it was "well written and persuasive, except that I think the actual transmission of the message has a little more meaning than he gives it."[138] Similarly, the other

Bundy brother, William, judged that despite the familiar content, "the repetition of a specific message, allegedly sent once through Ayub though not
clearly conveyed to us through that channel, plus the length of the discussion, does indicate Peiping wants a channel and has perhaps chosen this one
at least for the time being." Agreeing with Grant's analysis, William Bundy
characterized Chen Yi as "(a) tough about DRV resolve; (b) mild in the sense
that he appeared to be saying China would not come in unless China itself
were attacked; (c) tough as to China going all the way if it did come in."[139]

Meanwhile, in Beijing, the British had gained some possible insight into
Chen Yi's perspective when Hopson discovered from the Soviet ambassador to the PRC that the Chinese foreign minister had also met with *him* on
May 31, and had said (according to Hopson's paraphrase of the Soviet's report of Chen Yi's words) "not only that the United States Government knew
that China would not (repeat not) provoke a war with the Americans but
also that the Chinese knew that the Americans would not (repeat not) attack
them."[140] London had markedly less success, however, in translating the
Hopson–Chen Yi meeting into an ongoing channel or a palpable improvement in Sino-British relations.

When, during a June 7 "courtesy call" on the director of the PRC Foreign Ministry's West European Department, Hopson informed Chinese officials that Chen's message had been delivered to Rusk, he found that the
Chinese had returned to the familiar harsh language they had previously
used to denounce British policy, "treat[ing] [Hopson] to a long discourse on
how to deal with burglars and aggressors," and accusing London of collusion in Washington's phony peace offer (which he described as a "trick").
Hopson felt compelled to deny vehemently that "Her Majesty's Government" would ever "be party to such a thing."[141] Nor did subsequent months
see any warming trend between China and the United Kingdom—not surprisingly, given Beijing's descent toward the revolutionary chaos of the
Cultural Revolution.

For their part, when they knew for certain that China's warning signals
had reached Washington, Beijing's leaders became more confident that the
danger of a direct Sino-American military confrontation had receded. Chen
specifically discussed this issue in an internal speech on the "current international situation" on November 23, 1965. "A question we must answer,"
said the Chinese foreign minister, "is whether or not the Americans will
attack China." He stressed that "now we are of the opinion that the Americans do not have the strength, and that they dare not to make a decision in
that direction." He further explained that this conclusion was reached by

"putting ourselves into the shoes of the Americans, and we have made every consideration for the Americans—for America's president, for its Joint Chiefs of Staff, and for its monopoly capitalist cliques. Finally we say that the Americans dare not to attack us."

Then, Chen asked an interesting question: "Since we were of the opinion that the Americans would not attack us now, why did we still issue those [warning] statements? Were those warnings empty cannons?" In answering his own question, Chen contended that "it is exactly because we knew that America would not attack us, we then had to issue the [warning] statements. By doing so we were able to put this issue in front of the Chinese people, the people of the whole world, and the people of the Soviet Union, so that the Chinese people, the people of the world and the people of the Soviet Union would be mentally mobilized." "In the final analysis," argued the Chinese foreign minister, "the less one is scared by the ghost the less possibility that the ghost will appear, and the more one is scared by the ghost the more likely that the ghost will come."[142] Chen's discussion, in spite of its exaggerated tone, clearly indicated that Beijing's leaders now believed that the signaling had fulfilled its mission.

The Message's Afterlife

But the story did not end here. Beijing's four-part signal itself, after being secretly conveyed through the British channel to Washington in the spring of 1965, went on to an interesting afterlife. In May 1966, as the Vietnam conflict continued to escalate and China verged on the "Great Proletarian Cultural Revolution," Beijing suddenly opted to go public with the message. This time, again, it employed a Pakistani channel. In an April 10, 1966, interview with a correspondent, Ejaz Husain, from the newspaper *Dawn*, Islamabad's semiofficial mouthpiece, Zhou authoritatively—and in a more bombastic style than in private—issued his four-part warning, which would be openly announced by China's own media and published in newspapers throughout the country one month later:

1. China will not take the initiative to provoke a war with the United States. China has not sent any troops to Hawaii; it is the United States that has occupied China's territory of Taiwan Province. Nevertheless, China has been making efforts in demanding, through negotiations, that the United States withdraw all its armed forces from Taiwan

Province and the Taiwan Strait, and it has held talks with the United States for more than ten years, first in Geneva and then in Warsaw, on this question of principle, which admits of no concession whatsoever. All serves as very good proof.

2. The Chinese mean what they say. In other words, if any country in Asia, Africa, or elsewhere meets with aggression by the imperialists headed by the United States, the Chinese government and people definitely will give it support and help. Should such just action bring on U.S. aggression against China, we will unhesitatingly rise in resistance and fight to the end.

3. China is prepared. Should the United States impose a war on China, it can be said with certainty that, once in China, the United States will not be able to pull out, however many men it may send over and whatever weapons it may use, nuclear weapons included. Since the 14 million people in Southern Vietnam can cope with over 200,000 U.S. troops, the 650 million people in China undoubtedly can cope with 10 million of them. No matter how many U.S. aggressor troops may come, they will certainly be annihilated in China.

4. Once the war breaks out, it will have no boundaries. Some U.S. strategists want to bombard China by relying on their air and naval superiority and avoid a ground war. This is wishful thinking. One the war gets started with air or sea action, it will not be for the United States alone to decide how the war will continue. If you can come from the sky, why can't we fight back on the ground? That is why we say the war will have no boundaries once it breaks out.[143]

Although the message still contained the same four basic topic sentences as in the secret messages that had been conveyed to Washington one year earlier, there were several noticeable differences. First, in a language that Beijing had used continuously in its anti-American propaganda (especially with a domestic audience as the target), Zhou highlighted the Taiwan issue, emphasizing that China had not sent troops to Hawaii, but that the United States had occupied China's Taiwan Province. Furthermore, Zhou contended that China was willing to negotiate with the United States, but it was the United States that had refused to adopt a constructive attitude in the negotiation. By doing so, Zhou meant to make it clear—especially to China's own people—that if a Chinese-American war were to break out again, the United States would be fully responsible.

Second, Zhou significantly expanded the scope that the warning message would cover. Instead of concentrating on Vietnam, he contended that China would render "support and help" "if any country in Asia, Africa, or elsewhere meets with aggression by the imperialists headed by the United States," and that China would fight to the end if such "just action" caused "U.S. aggression against China." This feature of "going beyond Vietnam" clearly indicated that this message was not exclusively designed to restrict U.S. intervention in the Vietnam War. It was more compatible with the belligerent language of anti–United States imperialism prevailing in Chinese propaganda on the eve of the Cultural Revolution.

Third, in explaining what Beijing might do "should the United States impose a war on China," Zhou demonstrated a passion that had been absent in the secret messages. When he announced that "since the 14 million people in Southern Vietnam can cope with over 200,000 U.S. troops, the 650 million people in China undoubtedly can cope with 10 million of them," one is reminded of the zealous language that Defense Minister Marshal Lin Biao had used in his famous article, "Long Live the Victory of the People's War," which had exhorted "the Chinese people and the oppressed peoples of the world" to join "the struggles that would finally bury imperialism, revisionism, and all reactionary forces."[144] Bearing all these considerations in mind, we have strong reason to believe that the primary purpose of Zhou's open statement was not to signal Washington (although the Chinese premier certainly understood that in any case the statement itself would be read in Washington as another strong warning from Beijing); instead, the statement targeted China's ordinary populace as its main audience, and, most likely, it was designed primarily to enhance the widespread mass mobilization that would quickly sweep across China's cities and countryside, leading the whole nation to the Cultural Revolution.

Beijing also reaffirmed the four-point message to Washington via private channels. On May 25, 1966, Ambassador Wang Guoquan, the Chinese representative at the Warsaw talks, read the complete text of Zhou's statement to his U.S. counterpart, Ambassador John A. Gronouski. Wang particularly emphasized that "whatever policies of hostility US may adopt, China will never make slightest change in its solemn position."[145] Two weeks later, on June 9, Chen Yi once more called in the British chargé Hopson (through whom he had relayed the message a year earlier), asking him to convey the four-point statement Zhou made on April 10 to Washington. But in contrast to the situation a year before, this time Chen did not make delivery of the message to U.S. policymakers a top priority. Instead, he concentrated on opposing the search for a solution to the Vietnam War through negotiations or by convening another Geneva conference, arguing that the only way to achieve peace was that "the US must immediately withdraw from Vietnam."[146] Chen was clearly more concerned to demonstrate Beijing's firm stand on the Vietnam issue rather than, as before, to use the channel to send a crucial message to the Americans. This again indicates that Beijing's leaders were already convinced that China would not face the prospect of a direct military confrontation with the United States over Vietnam.[147]

There is also some fresh evidence that, due to underlying Sino-Vietnamese suspicions, Beijing now had less reason to expect a North Vietnamese invitation to intervene on their behalf. Newly released Albanian documents disclose that in late June, during a visit to Tirana, Zhou vowed that China would make "all possible attempts" to help Hanoi if it remained steadfast, but he confessed that "we are also facing some difficulties, because the Vietnamese, being under the influence of the SU [Soviet Union], are very afraid of our help and especially of the intervention of Chinese troops into Vietnam to enter the war against the American imperialism. Why is it so? It is because the Soviets are scaring the Vietnamese, telling them that when the solemn meeting to celebrate the victory is called, Vietnam will not exist anymore, because all the Vietnamese will have perished."[148]

Intriguingly, as the Chinese went public with their four-part signal in spring 1966, the intermediaries they used also conveyed titillating intimations that Beijing might wish to explore the possibility of a rapprochement in the future. Once America withdrew from Vietnam, Chen told Hopson on June 9, "there would be hope of improving Sino-U.S. relations."[149] Given the unlikelihood of that happening any time soon, Chen's comment was easily overwhelmed by his strongly anti-American rhetoric in the conversation. However, a Pakistani approach implied a more concrete Chinese interest in a high-level dialogue. In late March 1966, a senior PRC delegation (including Liu Shaoqi and Chen Yi) visited Pakistan.[150] On the evening of April 21—after Zhou had given his *Dawn* interview but before it had been publicized—Pakistani foreign minister Zulfikar Ali Bhutto discussed China with U.S. secretary of state Rusk when the two met in Ankara. According to the unpublished secret U.S. cable describing their talk, Bhutto "repeatedly turned to two subjects: could Formosa [Taiwan] be frozen as an issue between US and Chicoms and would Secretary be interested in private secret talks with Chen Yi, if Paks arrange? Paks have impression Chen Yi more forthcoming than other Chicom[s]." Rusk, however, responded diffidently, even sourly, to Bhutto's offer—"Secretary said Paks should not take any initiative; we shall keep in touch"—and steered the conversation back to a virtual admonition to Pakistan not to warm up too closely to the Chinese lest it endanger U.S.-Pakistan relations.[151] Despite Rusk's tepid reaction, Johnson administration officials in spring 1966 actually did briefly flirt with the idea of proposing a foreign ministers' meeting to the Chinese (which Beijing itself had suggested years earlier), with LBJ purportedly "fascinated" by the notion, but put the idea "on ice" on the grounds that given the situation in Vietnam it would "only be construed as a sign of weakness by Peiping."[152]

It is, indeed, difficult to conjure up the image of the stolid, cautious Rusk clinking glasses of mao-tai and wandering through the Forbidden City, forging in 1966 the clandestine diplomatic breakthrough that the more wily and adventurous Henry A. Kissinger accomplished five years later. For that matter, was Chairman Mao already really "thinking the unthinkable"? In early 1966, the Chinese leadership indeed had incentive to seek a strategic counterweight to what Mao regarded (or at least depicted) as a looming Soviet threat: tensions between Beijing and Moscow were more acute than ever (despite their common support for Hanoi), evidenced by ongoing disputes—described in chapter 7 and more fully in chapter 8 of this volume—over the transfer of Soviet bloc aid to North Vietnam through Chinese territory, and the signing in January of a Soviet-Mongolian treaty that paved the way for a major USSR troop movement to the Sino-Mongolian border.

Conversely, at this same time Mao was making every effort to radicalize China's political and social life, and the full-scale outbreak of the Cultural Revolution was only a few months away. Thus it is hard to imagine how the rapid revolutionization of Chinese domestic politics would have squared with a shocking public conciliation with the ultimate class enemy and imperialist aggressor. It appears at least as plausible that Bhutto (interested in improving ties with Washington and justifying Pakistan's controversial policy of cultivating China) may have been testing the waters on his own, intending to approach Chen had Rusk responded positively.

Further Pakistani and Chinese evidence must emerge before a firm judgment may be rendered as to whether a genuine opportunity existed in the spring of 1966 for a Sino-American détente via Pakistan. But the episode testifies to Islamabad's readiness, even eagerness, to play this role, setting the stage for what occurred in the period 1969–71. After Richard M. Nixon succeeded Johnson and Soviet-Chinese polemics exploded into violent border clashes, Pakistan did indeed play the role it relished: The government of Yahya Khan, who had toppled Ayub Khan, conveyed messages between Beijing and a U.S. president who now welcomed, rather than disdained,

Pakistan's friendly ties with Communist China for the opportunity these afforded to open a high-level back channel and strategic dialogue even as the Vietnam War continued.[153]

Conclusion

This chapter has narrated a story that has been missing from past accounts of Washington's 1965 decisionmaking on Vietnam. It was not mentioned by Herring, Berman, Kahin, Khong, or VanDeMark;[154] and the most influential study of Chinese efforts to deter U.S. escalation in Vietnam, Whiting's *The Chinese Calculus of Deterrence,* refers only to the four-point message that was publicly delivered by Zhou in April 1966 and mentions nothing about the secret signaling between Beijing and Washington through diplomatic intermediaries a full year earlier.[155] It appears, too, that the original four-part warning was a tightly kept secret within the U.S. government—at least as tightly held as possible. William Bundy noted at the time that knowledge of the Chen Yi approach was "confined to the UKG [U.K. government] and USG [U.S. government] among allies" and "held very close when first received" although due to the British intelligence "mistake" of informing the CIA that a report of it had made it into the Current Intelligence Brief. "Thus," Bundy concluded, "it is more widely known within the USG than it should be, but I hope we do not have a leak problem."[156]

Indeed, neither in Washington nor London, let alone Beijing, did it leak to the public.[157] And the absence of Chen's 1965 warning from Whiting's study suggests that due to its high classification he, too, was left in ignorance of the signaling. More surprisingly, a secret CIA intelligence study titled "The Sino-Vietnamese Effort to Limit American Actions in the Vietnam War," dated June 9, 1965, and closely scrutinizing Chinese public and private statements gathered from various sources refers neither to the Chen message via Hopson nor to any other version of the four-point warning Zhou had been disseminating to various figures since April. With the support of access to new Chinese and U.S. sources, we are now in a position to integrate this previously little known episode into the larger narratives of the Vietnam War as well as the international Cold War.

Precisely what impact, if any, Chen's May 31, 1965, warning had on Johnson's own attitude toward the Vietnam decisions in the summer of 1965 remains uncertain. It seems highly likely, as Fredrik Logevall has noted, that President Johnson had already decided to embark on a course of trying to use military force, including a sharp rise in combat troops, to try to force a victory on the ground in Vietnam. But the Chinese message may nevertheless have influenced the pace, scale, and presentation of those decisions. It probably strengthened Johnson's caution about taking any action that risked precipitating Chinese entry into the war—such as some of the escalatory measures being proposed by military leaders and right-wing political figures (e.g., bombing airbases and rail lines in southern China or along the Sino-Vietnamese frontier, or a land invasion of North Vietnam)—and the danger of either sparking World War III, facing a resort to the use of nuclear weapons, or accepting a military defeat or disaster as had happened in the fall of 1950. Without referring to the signaling episode described in this chapter, Herring has written in his standard account of the war that in the late July 1965 decisions, "[Johnson] and his civilian advisers continued to fear that a direct, full-scale attack on North Vietnam might provoke Chinese intervention."[158]

According to George McT. Kahin, who closely scrutinizes the spring-summer 1965 decisions in his *Intervention: How America Became Involved in Vietnam,* the risk of a major Chinese intervention "was taken very seriously. . . . The record shows not only that the administration was deeply concerned about so provoking Peking [if it invaded North Vietnam], but that in fact it had very good reason to be."[159] Therefore, there is little doubt that the Sino-American signaling played an important role in limiting the scale of the escalation of the Vietnam War, thus preventing the PRC and the United States from stumbling into another direct confrontation.

Throughout the process of the Sino-American signaling in 1965, the Korean analogy served as an important precedent influencing both Beijing's and Washington's policymaking.[160] When Chinese leaders considered how to compose the messages that were to be delivered to Washington, and when they were selecting appropriate channels to convey them, they had in their minds the lessons derived from the Korean War. The PRC's specific four-point warning drew clear lines between what was tolerable and what was unacceptable to the PRC in terms of various scenarios that might arise from American war actions in Vietnam, thus leaving little doubt that if Washington should cross the lines, a Sino-American war would follow. While doing so, Beijing repeatedly cited Korea to highlight the credibility of its warnings, reminding Washington that failure to pay serious attention to similar warnings fifteen years before had led to disaster. Without the support of the Korean analogy, those warnings would have been far less powerful and credible; indeed, Beijing would even have lost the basic condition to conduct the signaling.

Conversely, the message's credibility was enhanced by the mutual confidence that the two sides had achieved through the experience of managing the Taiwan crises in the previous decade. With policymakers in Washington accepting this as evidence of Beijing's rationality, pragmatism, patience, limited aims, and willingness to avoid all-out confrontation despite rhetorical and ideological extremism, another important condition for the Korean analogy to work had been created.

The lessons of the Korean War had also produced a profound impact upon policymakers in Washington. Although the materials now available do not provide us with sufficient information concerning exactly how Johnson administration officials interpreted each Chinese signaling effort, it is certain that as U.S. policymakers and military planners formulated strategies toward the escalating Vietnam War, they understood that *this time* they must treat Beijing seriously. Influenced and reinforced by the Chinese warnings, the Johnson administration reached and adhered to the key decisions that the Vietnam War should be limited to Vietnam (confining the ground war to the South and the air war to the North). While doing so, their clearly defined limit was that no American military action should cross the lines drawn by the Chinese, and that every precaution should be taken in order to avert a direct Sino-American military confrontation. In this sense, the Sino-American signaling certainly should be regarded as a success. (Indeed, the apparent impact of the four-point "signal" on the Americans so pleased the Chinese leaders that they used the same message, and the same messenger, Pakistan, to communicate with Moscow during the Sino-Soviet border clashes and breakdown of normal bilateral diplomatic channels in 1969.[161]) Consequently, we must also conclude that, under specific conditions, policymakers may learn useful lessons from history instead of repeating its errors—and did so in this case.[162]

The episode's consequences for Sino-American relations also appear noteworthy. It reveals that differences in ideology and culture need not lead to military confrontation between rival nations. In the 1950s and 1960s, China and the United States were two different types of international actors: Whereas the United States was a Western power occupying a central position in the existing international system and international regime, the PRC was a "revolutionary country" that took the destruction of the existing international order as one of its key state policy goals. Sharp differences in ideology and, related to it, perception and definition of national interests indeed separated China and the United States, and the difficulty in managing relations between them was further exacerbated by each country's domestic politics.

Yet all such considerations notwithstanding, by transcending bitter ideological hostility and divergent cultural perspectives, the two sides found ways to collaborate in a delicate mutual effort to limit the Vietnam War's potentially lethal impact on their already hostile and tenuous relationship at a time of increasing fluidity and multipolarity in the Cold War. The avoidance of a United States–PRC war over, or in, Vietnam in the mid-1960s, in turn, marked an important and necessary, though generally unrecognized,[163] step toward and precondition for the dramatic breakthrough in their relationship that would take place only half a decade later.

Finally, this story is not without relevance for contemporary and prospective Chinese-American relations. In the decade following the end of the Cold War and the disappearance of the Soviet Union—against whom Beijing and Washington had tacitly cooperated for nearly two decades—Sino-American relations have encountered new problems and challenges. Friction over human rights, espionage scandals, charges of interference in political campaigns, Taiwan, trade, missile defense, and other subjects even began to produce dangerous incidents—such as Chinese military maneuvers in the Taiwan Strait in 1996, the protests over the June 1999 U.S. bombing of the PRC Embassy in Belgrade during the Kosovo war, and the April 2001 standoff over the crew of a U.S. reconnaissance plane that made an emergency landing on Hainan Island after colliding with a Chinese jet, killing the pilot—that bred mutual suspicion, acrimony, misunderstanding, and fears that the two countries may be heading for another major confrontation. Chinese media whip up nationalist passions and charge Washington with plotting to deny China its rightful place in the world, and American bookstores offer alarmist titles highlighting "the China threat" and the danger of "the coming war with China." Pentagon planners talk of China as a looming "strategic competitor" in Asia, and, on one occasion, an American president warns that the United States will do "whatever it takes" to defend Taiwan if it is attacked from the mainland. American analysts have been debating whether China is bent on expansionism and domination in Asia, prone to ideological and nationalistic militancy, or can be relied upon to act cautiously and pragmatically.

Against such a background, a clear understanding as to how and why China and the United States have, in the past, either slipped into war or avoided it, may be vital if they are to surmount and survive future tensions and crises—and understand each other's signals correctly—without making errors that might lead to catastrophe. Indeed, the implication of this story should generate cautious optimism for the prospect of a peaceful development of Sino-American relations in the twenty-first century: If China and the United States were able to avoid direct military confrontation through effective communication when they were still bitter enemies in the heyday of the Cold War, why should they not—with enhanced interdependence and widespread shared interests between them in the post–Cold War and especially the post–September 11, 2001, age—be able to manage the differences separating them in peaceful and constructive ways?

Notes

1. See, e.g., *Renmin Ribao* (People's Daily), March 30, 1965, 1.

2. Fredrik Logevall, *Choosing War: The Lost Chance for Peace and the Escalation of War in Vietnam* (Berkeley: University of California Press, 1999), argues that Johnson had already essentially decided in favor of a massive escalation of U.S. ground forces in Vietnam by March 1965, and that the summer deliberations essentially ratified a policy decision reached months earlier. We find much merit in the argument, but note that even if a fundamental decision to escalate U.S. military involvement had already been reached, the scale, timing, and nature of U.S. military actions and deployments remained to be determined, and thus may have been influenced by consideration of the possible Chinese response and the "signaling" process described in this chapter.

3. For an assessment of the relevance of the Korean analogy for U.S. Vietnam decisionmaking in 1965 (but which does not include the Sino-American "signaling" episode described here), see Yuen Foong Khong, *Analogies at War: Korea, Munich, Dien Bien Phu, and the Vietnam Decisions of 1965* (Princeton, N.J.: Princeton University Press, 1992); and Yuen Foong Khong, "The Lessons of Korea and the Vietnam Decisions of 1965," in *Learning in U.S. and Soviet Foreign Policy,* ed. George Breslauer and Philip Tetlock (Boulder, Colo.: Westview Press, 1991), 302–49. For more general evaluations of policymakers' use of history that include the Vietnam decisions, see Ernest R. May, *"Lessons" of the Past: The Use and Misuse of History in American Foreign Policy* (New York: Oxford University Press, 1973); and Richard Neustadt and Ernest May, *Thinking in Time: The Uses of History for Decision-Makers* (New York: Free Press, 1986).

4. Of particular relevance, in this context, are the works of Allen S. Whiting, a leading China specialist and former State Department intelligence analyst who has published influential studies on both the Korean and Vietnamese cases utilizing public sources as well as internal U.S. government materials, but lacking access to internal documentation on Chinese decisionmaking or exchanges with other communist governments. See Allen S. Whiting, *China Crosses the Yalu: The Decision to Enter the Korean War* (New York: Macmillan, 1960); Whiting, "How We Almost Went to War with China," *Look,* April 29, 1969, 76–79; Whiting, *The Chinese Calculus of Deterrence: India and Indochina* (Ann Arbor: University of Michigan Press, 1975), esp. chap. 6; and Whiting, "China's Role

in the Vietnam War," in *The American War in Vietnam,* ed. Jayne Werner and David Hunt (Ithaca, N.Y.: Southeast Asia Program, Cornell University, 1993), 71–76.

5. "Letter, Mao Zedong to Nie Rongzhen, July 7, 1950," in *Jianguo yilai Mao Zedong wengao* [Mao Zedong's manuscripts since the founding of the People's Republic] (Beijing: Zhongyang Wenxian, 1987), vol. 1, 428; see also Han Huanzhi and Tai Jinqiao et al., *Dangdai zhongguo jundui de junshi gongzuo* [Military affairs of contemporary Chinese armed forces] (Beijing: Chinese Academy of Social Sciences Publishing House, 1988), vol. 1, 449–50.

6. "Telegram, Mao Zedong to Gao Gang, August 18, 1950," in *Jianguo yilai Mao Zedong wengao,* vol. 1, 499; see also "Telegram, Mao Zedong to Gao Gang, August 5, 1950," in *Jianguo yilai Mao Zedong wengao,* vol. 1, 454.

7. For a more detailed discussion, see Chen Jian, *China's Road to the Korean War: The Making of the Sino-American Confrontation* (New York: Columbia University Press, 1994), chap. 5.

8. For Stalin's October 1, 1950, appeal to Mao, found in the Russian Presidential Archives in Moscow, see *Cold War International History Project Bulletin* (hereafter *CWIHPB*), nos. 6–7 (Winter 1995–96): 114.

9. For top CCP leaders' discussion of the Korean crisis on October 2, 1950, see Zhang Xi, "Peng Dehuai and China's Entry into the Korean War," trans. Chen Jian, *Chinese Historians,* 6 (Spring 1993): 6–8; see also Chen Jian, *China's Road to the Korean War,* 173–75.

10. "Telegram [Draft], Mao Zedong to Stalin, October 2, 1950," in *Jianguo yilai Mao Zedong wengao,* vol. 1, 539–40.

11. For a more detailed discussion on why Mao drafted one telegram and sent a different message to Stalin, see Shen Zhihua (trans. Chen Jian), "The Discrepancy between the Russian and Chinese Versions of Mao's 2 October 1950 Message to Stalin on Chinese Entry into the Korean War: A Chinese Scholar's Reply," *CWIHPB,* nos. 8–9 (Winter 1996–97): 237–42.

12. "Ciphered Telegram, Roshchin to Stalin, 3 October 1950, conveying Mao to Stalin, 2 October 1950," *CWIHPB,* nos. 6–7 (Winter 1995–96): 114–16.

13. For a more detailed discussion, see Chen Jian, *China's Road to the Korean War,* 181–86.

14. For Russian documentation on the October 1950 Mao-Stalin exchanges, see Alexander Mansourov, "Stalin, Mao, Kim, and China's Decision to Enter the Korean War, Sept. 16–Oct. 15, 1950: New Evidence from Russian Archives" (article and documents), *CWIHPB,* nos. 6–7 (Winter 1995–96): 94–119 (Stalin's message to Mao quoted here is on 116–17).

15. Receiving the message from Roshchin, Mao told the Russian ambassador that Stalin's opinion mirrored his own analysis to the CCP Politburo. In the meantime, he pointed out that the PRC would require massive technical aid and air support from Moscow. Telegram, Roshchin to Stalin, October 7, 1950 (reporting on his talk with Mao on the evening of October 6), in "Russian Documents on the Korean War," intro. James G. Hershberg, trans. Vladislav M. Zubok, *CWIHPB,* nos. 14–15 (Winter 2003–Spring 2004): 377–78; for Stalin's reasoning, see also Kathryn Weathersby, *"Should We Fear This?" Stalin and the Danger of War with America,* CWIHP Working Paper 39 (Washington, D.C.: Woodrow Wilson International Center for Scholars, 2002), 18–19.

16. Mao Zedong, "Order to Establish the Chinese People's Volunteers, October 8, 1950," in *Jianguo yilai Mao Zedong wengao,* vol. 1, 543–44.

17. Zhou Enlai, speech on September 30, 1950, at the convention celebrating the first anniversary of the establishment of the PRC, *Renmin Ribao,* October 1, 1950.

18. Minute, Zhou Enlai's talks with K. M. Panikkar, October 3, 1950, *Zhou Enlai waijiao wenxuan* [Selected diplomatic documents of Zhou Enlai] (Beijing: Central Press of Historical Documents, 1990), 25–27. For an English translation, see Sergei N. Goncharov, John W. Lewis, and Xue Litai, *Uncertain Partners: Stalin, Mao, and the Korean War* (Stanford, Calif.: Stanford University Press, 1993), 276–78; for Panikkar's account, see his *In Two Chinas: Memoir of a Diplomat* (London: Allen & Unwin, 1955), 109–11; and his *An Autobiography,* trans. K. Krishnamurthy (Madras: Oxford University Press, 1977), 235. According to the recollections of Pu Shouchang, Zhou's English language interpreter, Zhou carefully discussed with him how to find an accurate English term for "*yao guan,*" which in other circumstances could be translated as "to be concerned" or "to take care of." Zhou, however, believed that "intervene" was a more proper term to express what he meant. See Pei Jianzhang et al., *Xinzhongguo waijiao fengyun* [New China's diplomatic experiences] (Beijing: World Knowledge Press, 1990), 97.

19. Even in the unlikely scenario that Washington heeded Zhou's warning and halted the offensive either at the 38th parallel or somewhat north of it, Beijing might well still have eventually dispatched troops to Korea—assuming Kim Il Sung's invitation remained in effect. In that case, as Mao himself later explained, Chinese forces would "set up two to three defensive lines in the areas north of the Pyongyang-Wonsan line" for six months, and would then launch an offensive when "our troops have been fully equipped and trained, as well as have achieved an overwhelming air and land superiority over the enemy's troops." "Telegram, Mao Zedong to Zhou Enlai, October 14, 1950," in *Jianguo yilai Mao Zedong wengao,* vol. 1, 560.

20. "Chargé in the United Kingdom (Holmes) to the Secretary of State, October 3, 1950 (rec'd 5:35 a.m.)," in *Foreign Relations of the United States* [hereafter *FRUS*], *1950,* U.S. Department of State (Washington, D.C.: U.S. Government Printing Office, 1976), vol. 7, 868–69.

21. State Department report dated October 12, 1950, cited in Rosemary Foot, *The Wrong War: American Policy and the Dimensions of the Korean Conflict, 1950–1953* (Ithaca, N.Y.: Cornell University Press, 1985), 79.

22. "Daily Summary Excerpt, 3 October 1950," in *Assessing the Soviet Threat: The Early Cold War Years,* ed. Woodrow J. Kuhns (Washington, D.C.: Center for the Study of Intelligence, U.S. Central Intelligence Agency, 1997), 445.

23. "Tokyo (Sir A. Gascoigne) to Foreign Office, 3 October 1950," no. 1371, FO 371/84099, Public Record Office, Kew Gardens, England (hereafter cited as PRO).

24. "Memorandum of Conversation by Allison, 4 October 1950," in *FRUS,* vol. 7 (1950), 868–69.

25. See "Weekly Summary Excerpt, 6 October 1950," in *Assessing the Soviet Threat,* ed. Kuhns, 446–48.

26. A CIA report of September 28 alleged that the Chinese had missed the opportunity to turn the tide of the war at an early point, and "like the USSR, [China] will not openly intervene in North Korea." Alan Kirk, U.S. ambassador to Moscow, predicted that the threat of Chinese intervention had receded because the most favorable time for China's intervention "was logically when UN forces were desperately defending the small area of Taegu-Pusan, when the influx of overwhelming numbers of Chinese ground forces would have proved the decisive factor." The CIA concluded on October 12 that "from a military standpoint the most favorable time for [Chinese] intervention

in Korea has passed." Bruce Cumings, *The Origins of the Korean War,* vol. 2, *The Roaring of the Cataract* (Princeton, N.J.: Princeton University Press, 1990), 734–35; Foot, *Wrong War,* 80; "Memorandum by the CIA (ORE 58-50), 12 October 1950," in *FRUS,* vol. 7 (1950), 934; and Kuhns, *Assessing the Soviet Threat,* 450–51.

27. The CIA observed on October 12 that the Chinese Communists faced tremendous domestic problems. If the CCP led China into a military conflict with the United States, "the regime's entire domestic program and economy would be jeopardized" and "anti-Communist forces would be encouraged and the regime's very existence would be endangered." Acheson was more than ready to accept such a view, stating that "it would be sheer madness" for the Chinese to enter the Korean conflict given their internal predicament. "CIA Memorandum, 12 October 1950," in *FRUS,* vol. 7 (1950), 934; Gaddis Smith, *Dean Acheson* (New York: Cooper Square Publishers, 1972), 201.

28. "CIA Memorandum, 12 October 1950," 934.

29. "CIA Memorandum, 12 October 1950," 934.

30. "CIA Memorandum, 12 October 1950," 933–34.

31. Jonathan D. Pollack, "The Korean War and the Sino-American Relations," in *Sino-American Relations, 1945–1955,* ed. Harry Harding and Yuan Ming (Wilmington, Del.: Scholarly Resources, 1989), 224.

32. For a informative summary of the Sino-American ambassadorial talks, see Steven M. Goldstein, "Dialogue of the Deaf? The Sino-American Ambassadorial-Level Talks, 1955–1970," in *Reexamining the Cold War: U.S.-China Diplomacy, 1954–1973,* ed. Robert S. Ross and Jiang Changbin (Cambridge, Mass.: Harvard University Asian Center, 2001), 200–37; for a study reflecting a Chinese view of the talks, see Zhang Baijia and Jia Qingguo, "Steering Wheel, Shock Absorber, and Diplomatic Probe in Confrontations: Sino-American Ambassadorial Talks Seen from the Chinese Perspective," in *Reexamining the Cold War,* ed. Ross and Jiang, 173–99.

33. "Telegram, CCP Central Committee to Zhou Enlai, 27 July 1954," in *Zhou Enlai nianpu, 1949–1976* [A chronology of Zhou Enlai] (hereafter *Zhou Enlai nianpu*) (Beijing: Central Press of Historical Documents, 1998), vol. 1, 405.

34. Han Huaizhi et al., *Dangdai zhongguo jundui de junshi gongzuo,* vol. 1, 256–57.

35. Xue Mouhong et al., *Dangdai zhongguo waijiao* [Contemporary Chinese diplomacy] (Beijing: Chinese Academy of Social Sciences Publishing House, 1987), 76–78. The resolution of the crisis came at a fortuitous moment; only days earlier, John Foster Dulles had secretly gained Eisenhower's support for a plan to combine a pullout from the perilously exposed offshore islands with a long-term blockade of mainland Chinese ports that, it appears, might have vastly extended and expanded the conflict. Though Jiang vetoed any evacuation from Mazu and Jinmen, the American proposal demonstrated the inherent danger of even a limited military confrontation between two rival nations that understood each other so poorly. See Gordon H. Chang, "To the Nuclear Brink: Eisenhower, Dulles, and the Quemoy-Matsu Crisis," *International Security* 12, no. 4 (Spring 1988): 96–123; and Gordon H. Chang and He Di, "The Absence of War in the U.S.-China Confrontation over Quemoy and Matsu in 1954–1955: Contingency, Luck, Deterrence?" *American Historical Review* 98, no. 5 (December 1993): 1500–24.

36. "Mao Zedong's Speech to the Supreme State Council, 5 September 1958," in *Jianguo yilai Mao Zedong wengao,* vol. 7, 386. For an English translation, see *CWIHPB,* nos. 6–7 (Winter 1995–96): 214–16.

37. See Ye Fei, *Ye Fei huiyilu* [Ye Fei's memoirs] (Beijing: PLA Press, 1988), 654–55, 659–60; see also discussions in Chen Jian, *Mao's China and the Cold War* (Chapel Hill: University of North Carolina Press, 2001), 181, 191.

38. Dwight D. Eisenhower, *The White House Years: Waging Peace, 1957–1961* (Garden City, N.Y.: Doubleday, 1965), 302; see also Ye Fei, *Ye Fei huiyilu*, 660.

39. Thomas J. Christensen, *Useful Adversaries: Grand Strategy, Domestic Mobilization, and Sino-American Conflict* (Princeton, N.J.: Princeton University Press, 1996), 219.

40. Wang Bingnan, *Zhongmei huitan jiunian huigu* [Recalling the nine-year Chinese American talks] (Beijing: World Knowledge Press, 1985), 86–90; "Telegram, Cabot to State Department, 23 June 1962," in *FRUS*, vol. 22 (1961–63), 273–75; see also Noam Kochavi, *A Conflict Perpetuated: China Policy during the Kennedy Years* (Westport, Conn.: Praeger, 2002), 95–97.

41. "Memorandum from the President's Special Assistant for National Security Affairs (Bundy) to President Johnson, Washington, 27 January 1965," in *FRUS*, vol. 2 (1964–68), 95–97.

42. Robert S. McNamara, James G. Blight, and Robert K. Brigham, with Thomas J. Biersteker and Col. Herbert Y. Schlander (ret.), *Argument without End: In Search of Answers to the Vietnam Tragedy* (New York: PublicAffairs, 1999), 173 (emphasis in original), 212. At a June 1997 oral history conference in Hanoi organized by James G. Blight and janet M. Lang of Brown University's Watson Institute and attended by former senior U.S. and (North) Vietnamese civilian and military officials, a former North Vietnamese military officer recounted that the Pleiku attack had not been specifically ordered from Hanoi and was undertaken without reference to the visits then taking place by Bundy to Saigon and Kosygin to Hanoi (contrary to U.S. interpretations that it constituted a deliberate "mousetrap" to provoke an American reprisal during the Soviet leader's visit in order to pressure Moscow into providing additional military support to the DRV). See, for references to the "mousetrap" argument, comments at White House meetings on February 6 and 8, in *FRUS*, vol. 2 (1964–68), 159, 188.

43. Important studies focusing on this decision include Larry Berman, *Planning a Tragedy: The Americanization of the War in Vietnam* (New York: W. W. Norton, 1982); and Brian VanDeMark, *Into the Quagmire: Lyndon Johnson and the Escalation of the Vietnam War* (New York: Oxford University Press, 1991).

44. See William Burr and Jeffrey T. Richelson, "Whether to 'Strangle the Baby in the Cradle': The United States and the Chinese Nuclear Program," *International Security* 25, no. 3 (Winter 2000–1): 54–99; see also Gordon H. Chang, *Friends and Enemies: The United States, China, and the Soviet Union, 1948–1972* (Stanford, Calif.: Stanford University Press, 1990), esp. 228–52.

45. VanDeMark, *Into the Quagmire*, 24–25.

46. Henry L. Stimson diary, July 21, 1945, Sterling Memorial Library, Yale University, quoted in Martin J. Sherwin, *A World Destroyed: The Atomic Bomb and the Grand Alliance* (New York: Alfred A. Knopf, 1975), 223–24.

47. Director of Central Intelligence, SNIE 13-2-63, "Communist China's Advanced Weapons Program," July 24, 1963, quoted in Burr and Richelson, "Whether to 'Strangle the Baby,'" 66.

48. See McCone memorandum for the record, "Discussion with the President re South Vietnam, 3 February 1965," in *FRUS*, vol. 2 (1964–68), 129–31.

49. "Memorandum from Thomson to NSC staff member Chester Cooper, Washington, 10 February 1965," in *FRUS,* vol. 2 (1964–68), 228–29.

50. Ball comment at White House meeting, February 10, 1965, cited in *FRUS,* vol. 2 (1964–68), 222.

51. See David K. E. Bruce diary entry, February 10, 1965, in *FRUS,* vol. 2 (1964–68), 212–13.

52. See quotations from *Renmin Ribao* and other public sources cited in Whiting, *Chinese Calculus of Deterrence,* 173–75, 178; and in CIA Directorate of Intelligence, "The Sino-Vietnamese Effort to Limit American Actions in the Vietnam War (POLO XX)," June 9, 1965, RSS 0008/65, National Security Files-Country Files (NSF-CO), Vietnam, box 19, folder "Vietnam Memos (D) Vol. XXXV 6/16-30/65, Lyndon B. Johnson Library (LBJL), Austin. To compare with Beijing's rhetoric prior to its intervention in Korea, see, e.g., Whiting, *China Crosses the Yalu,* esp. chap. 6.

53. *The Pentagon Papers: The Defense Department History of United States Decisionmaking on Vietnam,* Senator Gravel Edition (Boston: Beacon Press, 1971), vol. 3, 277, 354.

54. See Whiting, *Chinese Calculus of Deterrence,* 175–79. The initial sighting of PRC MiGs in North Vietnam was made public, but Whiting cites "intelligence data" and "information available to the author from official data" for the data concerning the airfields' construction and the PRC-DRV joint exercises.

55. See Barry Naughton, "The Third Front: Defense Industrialization in the Chinese Interior," *China Quarterly,* no. 115 (September 1988): 351–86; see also Chen Jian, "China's Involvement in the Vietnam War," *China Quarterly,* no. 142 (July 1995): 365–66; Zhai Qiang, "Beijing and the Vietnam Conflict, 1964–1965: New Chinese Evidence," *CWIHPB,* nos. 6–7 (Winter 1995–96): 233–50, esp. 237–38.

56. *Vietnam 1961–1968 as Interpreted in INR's Production,* by W. Dean Howells, Dorothy Avery, and Fred Greene, declassified Nov. 2002, accessed on the National Security Archive Web site (http://www.nsarchive.org). Hereafter, INR Study.

57. SNIE 50-2-64, "Probable Consequences of Certain US Actions with Respect to Vietnam and Laos," May 1964, quoted in INR Study, chap. A-IV ("Time of Decision: November 1963–March 1965"), 32.

58. Memo to the Acting Secretary, "Peiping Strengthens Implicit Commitment to Defend North Vietnam," July 9, 1964, quoted in INR Study, chap. A-IV, 33-34.

59. RM, RFE-56, "Peiping and Hanoi: Motivations in Gulf of Tonkin Crisis," August 6, 1964, INR Study, chap. A-IV, 35.

60. See Edwin E. Moise, *Tonkin Gulf and the Escalation of the Vietnam War* (Chapel Hill: University of North Carolina Press, 1996). esp. chaps. 6–8.

61. Memorandum for the Secretary, "Probable Foreign Reactions to the US Strike," August 4, 1964, INR Study, chap. A-IV, 35-36.

62. INR Study, chap. A-IV, 37; and "Chinese Military Activity, September 1964–January 1965," INR Study, special annex III, p. E3-1.

63. INR Study, chap. A-IV, 39–40.

64. MM-RFE-64-257, "New Chinese Communist Airfield Near North Vietnam," November 28, 1964, INR Study, chap. A-IV, 43.

65. INR Study, chap. IV, 45.

66. SNIE 10-3-65, "Communist Reactions to Possible US Actions," February 11, 1965; and SNIE 10.3/1-65, "Communist Reactions to Possible US Course of Action

Against NV," February 18, 1965, INR Study, chap. IV, 45–47; *FRUS,* vol. 2 (1964–68), 244–50, 320–25.

67. IN, "Tough Chinese Communist Posture on Vietnam," February 19, 1965, INR Study, chap. IV, 47.

68. "Asian Communist Reactions to U.S. Escalation in Vietnam," March 20, 1965, in INR Study, chap. V ("Trial by Force: March 1965–February 1966"), 29.

69. IN, "Peiping Promptly Endorses Viet Cong Statement, Expresses Readiness to Send Men," March 26, 1965, INR Study, chap. V, 29–30.

70. MM-RFE-65-102, "The Threat of Foreign Volunteers to Aid the Viet Cong," April 6, 1965, INR Study, chap. V, 30.

71. SNIE 10-5-65, "Communist Reactions to Certain US Action," April 28, 1965, in INR Study, chap. V, 31.

72. CIA Directorate of Intelligence, "Sino-Vietnamese Effort to Limit American Actions in the Vietnam War," 22; emphasis added.

73. See briefing paper by CIA Office of National Estimates, "NIE's and SNIE's on South Vietnam," June 11, 1965, in *FRUS,* vol. 2 (1964–68), 768–69.

74. *Pentagon Papers,* vol. 3, 397. CIA director John McCone consistently rated the Chinese as "not yet ready to get into the fight," despite providing aid to Hanoi; see, e.g., McCone's comments at a White House meeting, February 10, 1965, and at an NSC meeting, March 26, 1965, in *FRUS,* vol. 2 (1964–68), 223, 482.

75. Important voices within the administration warning of the "great" risks of Chinese intervention (including the possibility of a U.S.-Soviet confrontation, pressure to resort to the use of nuclear weapons, or both) as a response to a major U.S. commitment of ground forces to Vietnam included George Ball and Llewellyn Thompson. While supporting air strikes and a "program of gradually increasing military pressure," they cautioned LBJ to be "prepared and alerted—whenever it appears that military conflict may have reached the level of intensity where Chinese ground intervention seems likely—to accept a cease-fire under international auspices short of the achievement of our total political objectives." See Ball memorandum, "Subject: Vietnam," February 13, 1965, in *FRUS,* vol. 2 (1964–68), 252–61.

76. Evans and Novak column, n.d., quoted in *Pentagon Papers,* vol. 3, 354.

77. Only a limited portion of Russian archives on the Vietnam War have been opened (or *remained* opened), but for the best account of Soviet involvement to emerge so far, see Ilya V. Gaiduk, *The Soviet Union and the Vietnam War* (Chicago: Ivan R. Dee, 1996).

78. Some of these materials on Sino-DRV exchanges have been compiled and published in *77 Conversations between Chinese and Foreign Leaders on the Wars in Indochina, 1964–1977,* CWIHP Working Paper 22, ed. Odd Arne Westad, Chen Jian, Stein Tønnesson, Nguyen Vu Tung, and James G. Hershberg (Washington, D.C.: Woodrow Wilson International Center for Scholars, 1998). Among the other important studies of Sino-Vietnamese exchanges regarding the war during this period utilizing newly available Chinese sources are Chen Jian, "China's Involvement in the Vietnam War, 1964–1969"; and Chen Jian, *Mao's China and the Cold War,* chap. 8; various articles by Zhai Qiang—including "Beijing and the Vietnam Conflict, 1964–1965: New Chinese Evidence"; "Opposing Negotiations: China and Vietnam Peace Talks," *Pacific Historical Review* 68, no. 1 (February 1999): 21–49; and *Beijing and the Vietnam Peace Talks, 1965–1968,* CWIHP Working Paper 18 (Washington, D.C.: Woodrow Wilson International Center for Scholars, 1997)—culminating in his monograph, *China and the Vietnam Wars, 1950–1975* (Chapel Hill: University of North Carolina Press, 2000); and

Yang Kuisong, *Changes in Mao Zedong's Attitude toward the Indochina War, 1949–1973,* CWIHP Working Paper 34 (Washington, D.C.: Woodrow Wilson International Center for Scholars, 2002).

79. Li Ke and Hao Shengzheng, *Wenhua dageming zhong de jiefangjun* [The People's Liberation Army in the Cultural Revolution] (Beijing: CCP Central Party Material and History Press, 1989), 408; Qu Aiguo, "Chinese Military Assistance to North Vietnam's Effort to Resist United States Intervention during the Vietnam War," paper presented at International Workshop, "New Evidence on China, Southeast Asia, and the Vietnam War," January 11–12, 2000, University of Hong Kong, Hong Kong, p. 40; and *Beijing Review,* November 30, 1979, 14. The same day, as a precautionary measure, the Central Military Commission and the General Staff in Beijing ordered the Military Regions in Kunming and Guangzhou (the two military regions adjacent to Vietnam) and the air force and naval units stationed in southern and southwestern China to enter a state of combat readiness, ordering them to "pay close attention to the movement of American forces, and be ready to cope with any possible sudden attack." See Wang Dinglie et al., *Dangdai zhongguo kongjun* [Contemporary Chinese Air Force] (Beijing: Chinese Academy of Social Sciences Publishing House, 1989), 384.

80. Transcript, Mao Zedong's conversations with Le Duan, 16:00–18:00, August 13, 1964, Chinese Communist Party Central Archives (hereafter CCA). On the Chinese side, participants at this meeting included Deng Xiaoping, Peng Zhen, Kang Sheng, and Wu Xiuquan. It is not clear, from the existing record, whether the redeployment of 300,000 to 500,000 troops to the Nanning-Kunming area actually took place.

81. Whiting, "How We Almost Went to War with China," 76–77.

82. The strategy, however, obviously failed, and was dropped, or was poorly executed given the subsequent attacks at Pleiku and Qui Nhon.

83. See discussion between Mao Zedong and Pham Van Dong, Hoang Van Hoan, Beijing, October 5, 1964, in *77 Conversations,* ed. Westad et al., 74–77.

84. See excerpt from conversation between Zhou Enlai and Vietnamese military delegation, January 22, 1965, in *77 Conversations,* ed. Westad et al., 75 n. 118.

85. Minutes, Deng Xiaoping's speech at the Politburo meeting, April 12, 1965, CCA; see also Li Ke and Hao Shengzheng, *Wenhua dageming zhong de jiefangjun,* 104.

86. Minutes, Deng Xiaoping's speech at the Politburo meeting, April 12, 1965, CCA; see also Li Ke and Hao Shengzheng, *Wenhua dageming zhong de jiefangjun,* 104.

87. Minutes, Zhou Enlai's speech at the Politburo meeting, April 12, 1965, CCA; see also *Zhou Enlai nianpu,* vol. 2, 724.

88. Minutes, CCP Politburo meeting, April 12, 1965, CCA.

89. *Renmin Ribao,* March 25, 1965.

90. *Renmin Ribao,* March 30, 1965.

91. McGeorge Bundy memorandum, "Key Elements for Discussion," April 1, 1965, in *Pentagon Papers,* vol. 3, 346–47; also in *FRUS,* vol. 2 (1964–68), 506–10.

92. LBJ's and Rusk's comments are from McGeorge Bundy, personal notes of a meeting with President Johnson, April 1, 1965, in *FRUS,* vol. 2 (1964–68), 511.

93. Johnson had invited Ayub Khan to come to Washington in mid-April, and Indian Prime Minister Lal Bahadur Shastri to follow him in early June, in an effort to mediate between them on the Kashmir dispute.

94. Record of Zhou Enlai's conversation with Ayub Khan, 2 April 1965, in *77 Conversations,* ed. Westad et al., 79–85.

95. See, e.g., "Communist China's Foreign Policy," National Intelligence Estimate,

NIE 13-9-65, Washington, May 5, 1965, which judged that Beijing's "principal aims" over the next few years were "(a) to eject the West, especially the US, from Asia and to diminish US and Western influence throughout the world; (b) to increase the influence of Communist China in Asia; (c) to increase the influence of Communist China throughout the underdeveloped areas of the world; and (d) to supplant the influence of the USSR in the world at large, especially in the presently disunited Communist movement"; in *FRUS*, vol. 30 (1964–68), 168–70 (quotation on 169); for the full text, see NSF–National Intelligence Estimates, box 4, folder "13-61 to 13-65, Communist China," LBJL. Interestingly, this U.S. estimate, and the Sino-American signaling episode described in this chapter, coincided in the winter and spring of 1965 with a lengthy and vociferous secret dispute among British Government analysts—touched off by a report (dated February 26, 1965, and titled "Is China Dangerous?") from London's chargé d'affaires in Beijing—over China's foreign policy objectives, essentially pitting those who viewed the PRC as motivated by traditional, limited Chinese sphere-of-influence aims vs. a prevalent camp which attributed the dominant influence to communist ideological expansionist considerations. The present authors plan to describe the debate more fully in a future version of this study, using Foreign Office materials from the FO 371 files at the Public Record Office (PRO).

96. Record of conversation between Zhou Enlai and Ayub Khan, Karachi, April 2, 1965, in *77 Conversations,* ed. Westad et al., 82.

97. See CIA Directorate of Intelligence, "Sino-Vietnamese Effort to Limit American Actions in the Vietnam War," 23–24.

98. Record of meeting between Zhou Enlai and Ayub Khan, Karachi, April 2, 1965, in *77 Conversations,* ed. Westad et al., 82.

99. Record of meeting between Zhou Enlai and Ayub Khan, 83.

100. Whiting, *Chinese Calculus of Deterrence,* 178–79.

101. We now know that on April 9, the PLA's deputy chief of staff Yang Chengwu reported these two incidents to Zhou Enlai and Mao Zedong, suggesting that the Chinese air force should "give a firm strike" to American planes invading China's airspace. That afternoon, Mao ordered that the air force and the navy should send their best units to southern China and the South China Sea, unify their command system, and strike the Americans firmly if they invaded China's airspace. The deterrence implication of this decision is evident. See Yang Chengwu's report to Zhou Enlai and the CCP Central Committee, April 9, 1965, and Mao Zedong's remarks on Yang Chengwu's report, April 9, 1965, in *Mao Zedong junshi wenji* [A collection of Mao Zedong's military papers] (Beijing: Military Science Press, 1993), vol. 6, 403.

102. Record of meeting between Zhou Enlai and Ayub Khan, Karachi, April 2, 1965, in *77 Conversations,* ed. Westad et al., 83. In his conversation with Ayub, Zhou noted that his private statements accorded with earlier public statements, such as the March 25 *Renmin Ribao* editorial, subsequently confirmed by Foreign Minister Chen Yi to the North Vietnamese foreign minister, declaring that China would "support the people in South Vietnam to win victory [and is] preparing to offer all kinds of support, including weapons, to the people in South Vietnam. When the people in South Vietnam are in need, China will send its personnel to fight together with the people in South Vietnam."

103. Record of meeting between Zhou Enlai and Ayub Khan, 84.

104. F. S. Aijazuddin, *From a Head, Through a Head, To a Head: The Secret Channel between the US and China through Pakistan* (Karachi: Oxford University Press, 2000).

105. Although Pakistani archival records for this period are unfortunately not avail-

able, several sources offer useful information on Ayub Khan's actions at this juncture, though they do not mention his role in the secret Sino-U.S. "signaling" described here. See, e.g., Altaf Gaulhar, *Ayub Khan: Pakistan's First Military Ruler* (Lahore: Sang-e-Meel Publications, 1993), esp. 289–303, and Dennis Kux, *The United States and Pakistan, 1947–2000: Disenchanted Allies* (Washington, D.C., and Baltimore: Woodrow Wilson Center Press and Johns Hopkins University Press, 2001), 153–54, quoting ("triangular tightrope") Ayub Khan, *Friends Not Masters* (London: Oxford University Press, 1967), 119.

106. On the cancellation of the Ayub Khan and Shastri visits, see Richard N. Goodwin, *Remembering America: A Voice from the Sixties* (New York: Harper & Row Perennial, 1989), 394–95; Robert J. McMahon, *The Cold War on the Periphery* (New York: Columbia University Press, 1996), 318–24; Dennis Kux, *India and the United States: Estranged Democracies* (Washington, D.C.: National Defense University Press, 1993), 232–33; Chester Bowles, *Promises to Keep: My Years in Public Life, 1941–1969* (New York: Harper & Row, 1971), 498–500; David Kaiser, *American Tragedy: Kennedy, Johnson, and the Origins of the Vietnam War* (Cambridge, Mass.: Belknap Press of Harvard University Press, 2000), 427; and H. W. Brands, *The Wages of Globalism: Lyndon Johnson and the Limits of American Power* (New York: Oxford University Press, 1995), 131–33. On the Pearson episode, see Andrew Preston, "Missions Impossible: Canadian Secret Diplomacy and the Quest for Peace in Vietnam," in *The Search for Peace in Vietnam, 1964–1968,* ed. Lloyd C. Gardner and Ted Gittinger (College Station: Texas A & M University Press, 2004), 117–43. Sander Vanocur, in an interview in Santa Barbara, Calif., January 16, 1999, surmised that LBJ also acted due to his pique over Ayub Khan's closeness to the Kennedys.

107. See Johnson to Ayub, 14 April 1965, in NSF–Memos to the President, Box 3, folder "McG Bundy, vol. 10 [2 of 2], 4/15–5/31/65," LBJL.

108. A British diplomat in Washington cited a comment from Assistant Secretary of State for Far Eastern Affairs William P. Bundy indicating that Pakistan did relay a communication about China's position in Vietnam. See Washington (Sir P. Dean) to FO, no. 1466, priority/confidential, June 4, 1965, FO 371/180996, PRO.

109. See Roderick MacFarquhar, *The Origins of the Cultural Revolution, 3: The Coming of the Cataclysm, 1961–1966* (New York: Oxford University Press and Columbia University Press, 1997), 617, fn. 176.

110. See *77 Conversations,* ed. Westad et al., 88 n. 131.

111. Meeting of Zhou Enlai and Nguyen Van Hieu, Nguyen Thi Binh, Beijing (Great Hall of the People), May 16, 1965, in *77 Conversations,* ed. Westad et al., 86. It is important to note that Zhou again limited Beijing's vow of retaliation to the contingency of the United States actually attacking "Chinese territory"—leaving unclear whether a U.S. invasion or other military action against North Vietnam would be sufficient to prompt such an action.

112. Wang Bingnan, *Zhongmei huitan jiunian huigu,* 86–90; see also *FRUS,* vol. 22 (1961–63), 273–75.

113. Summaries of the Cabot-Wang talks relayed by Cabot to the State Department after the February 24 and April 21 sessions can be found in *FRUS,* vol. 30 (1964–68), 148–51, 165–68; the nearly verbatim minutes have been declassified and can be found in the NSF-CO files (boxes 200-202) at LBJL.

114. Apparently an allusion to Zhou's March 29 statement in Tirana, essentially reaffirming the *Renmin Ribao* editorial four days earlier (see citations above).

115. "washdc (Ritchie) to external ott, no. 2203, Subject: vietnam, 9 July 1965," in Department of External Affairs, Record Group 25, vol. 3096, file 20-VIET (pt. 1), National Archives of Canada, Ottawa.

116. See telegram from U.S. Embassy in Poland on Gronouski–Wang talks, May 25, 1966, in *FRUS,* vol. 30 (1964–68), 315.

117. China's decision ultimately to turn to the British to transmit the four-part signal is missing from the otherwise well-informed account in MacFarquhar, *Origins of the Cultural Revolution, 3: Coming of the Cataclysm,* 369–75, 616–17, esp. fn. 176.

118. Peking (Mr. Hopson) to FO, No. 720, Priority/Confidential, 31 May 1965, FO 371/180996, PRO.

119. INR-George C. Denney Jr. to the Secretary [Rusk], "Subject: Ch'en Yi Message to US on Vietnam," June 4, 1965, NSF-CO, Vietnam, box 18, folder Vietnam Memos (B), Vol. XXXV, 6/1-6/15/65, LBJL.

120. See Mansourov, "Stalin, Mao, Kim, and China's Decision to Enter the Korean War," *CWIHPB,* nos. 6–7 (Winter 1995–96): 94–119.

121. Andong is a city on the Chinese side of the Yalu River marking the Sino-North Korean frontier. During the Korean War, Chinese and Soviet air forces used bases on the Chinese side of the Sino-Korean border to fight the American air force over northern Korea. This was known as the "Andong model."

122. Li Ke and Hao Shengzhang, *Wenhua dageming zhong de jiefangjun,* 417. Whiting reports that Vietnamese scholars state that the Chinese informed Hanoi in June 1965 that "it would be unable to defend the North against US air attack" (Whiting, "China's Role in the Vietnam War," 73). The Chinese sources cited here clearly contradict this assertion.

123. Comment by a former DRV Foreign Ministry official in conversation during an oral history conference in Hanoi, June 1997.

124. Peking (Mr. Hopson) to FO, no. 721, priority/confidential, May 31, 1965, FO 371/180996, PRO.

125. FO to Washington, no. 4546, priority/confidential, June 1, 1965 (d. 0240, 2 June 1965), FO 371/180996, PRO.

126. FO to Washington, No. 4589, priority/secret, June 3, 1965, FO 371/180996, PRO.

127. C.M. MacLehose, "Note on Mr. Hopson's Interview with Chen Yi," 3 June 1965, confidential, FO 371/180996, PRO.

128. Washington (Sir P. Dean) to FO, no. 1466, 4 June 1965, FO 371/180996, PRO. A U.S. State Department analyst assessing Chen Yi's four-point message via Hopson noted that he had "no record that Ayub delivered it to us in such specific form, though SOA [South Asian Affairs] tells me that they have reason to think that the Pak Ambassador here [in Washington] sometimes fails to convey the full substance of what he is instructed to pass to us." ACA-Lindsey Grant to FE-Mr. [William P.] Bundy, "Subject: The Chen Yi-Hopson Interview of May 31—information memorandum," June 3, 1965, NSF-CO, box 238, LBJL.

129. Washington (Sir P. Dean) to FO, no. 1460, priority/confidential, June 4, 1965, FO 371/180996, PRO. No U.S. documentation of this meeting has been located.

130. Memorandum from the assistant secretary of state for far eastern affairs (Bundy) to Secretary of State Rusk, "Subject: Negotiating Developments re South Viet-Nam," Secret, June 5, 1965, declassified in 1997 (case NLJ 86-296, document 300) and kindly provided to the author by William Burr of the National Security Archive, Wash-

ington; the passage regarding the British intelligence liaison "mistake" in revealing the Chen Yi approach is deleted from the version of the memorandum printed in *FRUS,* vol. 2 (1964–68), 728–29.

131. ACA-Lindsey Grant to FE-Mr. [William P.] Bundy, "Subject: The Chen Yi-Hopson Interview of May 31—INFORMATION MEMORANDUM," June 3, 1965, NSF-CO, box 238, LBJL.

132. Memorandum from Bundy to President Johnson, Washington, June 4, 1965, in *FRUS,* vol. 30 (1964–68), 173–74.

133. Memorandum of Senator Mike Mansfield, June 3, 1965, in *FRUS,* vol. 2 (1964–68), 709.

134. On July 9, 1965, William Bundy told the Canadian ambassador to the United States that the "Finns had received another nibble from [the] Chinese similar to message transmitted via Nyerere. Their persistent theme was that they did not want war and would not stir it up unless attacked." In response, Bundy reported, Washington had communicated to Nyerere a response similar to the stand taken in the ongoing Sino-American ambassadorial talks in Warsaw, "emphasizing peaceful objectives of USA." See WASHDC (Ritchie) to EXTERNAL OTT, no. 2203, Subject: VIETNAM, July 9, 1965, in Department of External Affairs, Record Group 25, vol. 3096, file 20-VIET (pt. 1), National Archives of Canada, Ottawa. The June 4 date for the Zhou–Nyerere conversation in Dar-es-Salaam is from *77 Conversations,* ed. Westad et al., 88–89.

135. See "Editorial Note," in *FRUS,* vol. 2 (1964–68), 700–1.

136. McGeorge Bundy, Memorandum to the President, "Subject: Ch'en Yi message on Vietnam," Saturday, June 5, 1965, 6:50 p.m., NSF-CO, Vietnam, box 18, folder "Vietnam Memos (B), Vol. XXXV, 6/1-6/15/65," LBJL.

137. INR–George C. Denney Jr. to the Secretary [Rusk], "Subject: Ch'en Yi Message to US on Vietnam," June 4, 1965, NSF-CO, Vietnam, box 18, folder "Vietnam Memos (B), Vol. XXXV, 6/1-6/15/65," LBJL.

138. McGeorge Bundy, Memorandum to the President, "Subject: Ch'en Yi message on Vietnam," Saturday, 5 June 1965, 6:50 p.m., NSF-CO, Vietnam, box 18, folder "Vietnam Memos (B), Vol. XXXV, 6/1-6/15/65," LBJL.

139. Memorandum from William P. Bundy to Rusk, June 5, 1965, in *FRUS,* vol. 2 (1964–68), 728–29.

140. Peking (Mr. Hopson) to FO, no. 750, confidential, June 8, 1965, FO 371/180996, PRO.

141. Peking (Mr. Hopson) to FO, No. 746, confidential, June 7, 1965, FO 371/180996, PRO.

142. "Comrade Chen Yi's Speech on the Current International Situation," November 23, 1965, Quanzong 101, Mulu 12, Juanzhong 101, 16–17, Fujian Provincial Archive, Fuzhou, China.

143. *Zhou Enlai waijiao wenxuan,* 460–61; the interview with Zhou's public warning was circulated by the Chinese news agency on May 9, 1966, published in *Renmin Ribao* on May 10, and printed in *Foreign Broadcast Information Service* [FBIS] 90 (Far East), May 10, 1966, p. BBB-1.

144. For related discussions, see Roderick MacFarquhar and John K. Fairbank, eds., *The Cambridge History of China* (Cambridge: Cambridge University Press, 1991), vol. 15, 226–27; and Maurice Meisner, *Mao's China and After* (New York: Free Press, 1986), 356.

145. Telegram from U.S. Embassy in Poland on Gronouski–Wang talks, May 25, 1966, in *FRUS,* vol. 30 (1964–68), 315.

146. See telegram from State Department to Consulate General in Hong Kong, June 16, 1966, relaying an account of a June 9, 1966, Hopson–Chen Yi conversation, in *FRUS,* vol. 30 (1964–68), 321–23. See also telegrams from the Department of State to the Embassy in Poland, May 23, 1966, in *FRUS,* vol. 30 (1964–68), 308–13. Rusk anticipated that the Chinese side would refer to the four points Zhou gave in his interview with *Dawn,* and, it is interesting to note, instructed Gronouski to inform the Chinese side that "we do not intend to provoke war" and that "we have acted with restraint and care in the past and we are doing so today" (p. 310).

147. This analysis, using fresh Chinese and U.S. sources, is consistent with deductions made by some contemporary analysts. E.g., Harold C. Hinton observed that in the spring of 1966 "Chinese fear of an American attack, at least in the near future, seemed to diminish." See Hinton, "China and Vietnam," in *China in Crisis,* vol. 2: *China's Policies in Asia and America's Alternatives,* ed. Tang Tsou (Chicago: University of Chicago Press, 1968), 201–24 (quotation on 214).

148. See the record of the conversation between Zhou Enlai and Enver Hoxha, Tirana, June 27, 1966, Albanian State Archives (AQPPSH-MPKK-V1966-D13, list 18, folder 13), Tirana, obtained by Christian Ostermann, James Hershberg, and Ana Lalaj, translation by Enkel Daljani courtesy of Cold War International History Project.

149. *FRUS,* vol. 30 (1964–68), 323.

150. On that visit, see Gauhar, *Ayub Khan,* 404–5; Sultan M. Khan, *Memories & Reflections of a Pakistani Diplomat* (London: London Centre for Pakistan Studies, 1997), 161–64; and Kux, *United States and Pakistan,* 169–70.

151. Telegram from Ankara, secret, secstate priority 1334, April 22, 1966, in folder "POL-POLITICAL AFF. & REL. CHICOM-PAK 1/1/64," Central Foreign Policy Files, 1964-66, RG 59, NA II.

152. See *FRUS,* vol. 30 (1964–68), 285, 299–300, 307. LBJ would indeed approve limited "bridge-building" measures toward Beijing in an effort to reduce China's isolation in the context of avoiding a direct clash over Vietnam, but he consistently rejected suggestions for a more dramatic policy reversal. See Michael Lumbers, "The Irony of Vietnam: The Johnson Administration's Tentative Bridge-Building to China, 1965–1966," *Journal of Cold War Studies* 6, no. 3 (Summer 2004): 68–114; and Evelyn Goh, *Constructing the U.S. Rapprochement with China, 1961–1974: From "Red Menace" to "Tacit Ally"* (Cambridge: Cambridge University Press, 2005), esp. 88–89, 92–98.

153. On Pakistan's role in the Sino-U.S. opening, see Aijazuddin, *From a Head,* and F. S. Aijazuddin, ed., *The White House & Pakistan: Secret Declassified Documents, 1969–1974* (Oxford: Oxford University Press, 2002).

154. David Kaiser briefly notes the Chinese warning in *American Tragedy,* 439–40.

155. Whiting, *Chinese Calculus of Deterrence,* 193–94.

156. Memorandum from Bundy to Rusk, "Subject: Negotiating Developments re South Viet-Nam."

157. The U.S. consul in Hong Kong, America's chief watching post for China, learned of the Hopson–Chen Yi interview from an "allied source" two weeks after the fact and immediately complained with some irritation to Washington that his station's reporting would "likely lose contact with reality" were it not informed of such developments. Hong Kong to SecState (for Bundy from Rice), no. 1897, Secret/Exdis, June 15, 1965, NSF-CO, box 238, folder "China Cables Vol. III 4/65-6/65," LBJL.

158. George C. Herring, *America's Longest War: The United States and Vietnam, 1950–1975,* 3rd ed. (New York: McGraw-Hill, 1996), 152–53.

159. George McT. Kahin, *Intervention: How America Became Involved in Vietnam* (New York: Alfred A. Knopf, 1986), 338–41.

160. The fullest previous scholarly analysis of the impact of the Korean analogy on U.S. Vietnam decisionmaking in 1965 can be found in Khong, *Analogies at War.* Our analysis is generally consistent with Khong's, but it goes beyond it in several respects. First, Khong deals only with U.S. decisionmaking, whereas we show that the common historical experience influenced *both* sides. Second, the story of the Chinese signal shows how the Korean experience concretely influenced how Beijing's leaders communicated their intent to Washington, rather than simply resting in the background of their deliberations. Third, it shows how in their messages to U.S. leaders the Chinese explicitly used the historical analogy of Korea (and, to a lesser extent, Taiwan) to reinforce their credibility. Fourth, it links the Chinese signal—not mentioned in *Analogies at War*—to the Johnson administration's top-level decisionmaking process and LBJ's concern about provoking Chinese intervention in the summer of 1965.

161. Zhou Enlai disclosed this information to Richard Nixon and Henry Kissinger during their February 1972 visit to China, according to recently declassified U.S. records. "Our attitude toward the Soviet Union at the present time still consists of these four points," Zhou stated. Nixon and Kissinger, however, appeared unfamiliar with the earlier Sino-American signaling. See Memorandum of Conversation, Friday, February 25, 1972, 5:45–6:45 p.m., President's Guest House, Peking, pp. 2–3, top secret/sensitive/exclusively eyes only, courtesy of National Security Archive, Washington.

162. This tentative conclusion regarding this particular episode by no means contradicts the view that other analysts (including May, *"Lessons" of History,* and Khong, *Analogies at War*) have reached that policymakers have frequently egregiously abused historical analogies, in particular in their belief in and justification for the necessity of U.S. military intervention in Vietnam in the first place.

163. Surveys of U.S.-China relations tend, understandably, to race past the Johnson administration, viewing it as a period of unremitting mutual hostility and intellectual inertia (despite growing awareness of the depth of the Sino-Soviet split) among U.S. officials before the Nixon-Kissinger movement toward improvement in 1969–71. Ignoring the learning process that actually took place as both sides tacitly agreed to limit their confrontation over Vietnam, one analyst writes that the Johnson administration's policy toward China remained "remained virtually frozen" as its "fears of hostile and aggressive Chinese intentions increased." Banning N. Garrett, "The Strategic Basis of Learning in U.S. Policy Toward China, 1949–1988," in *Learning in U.S. and Soviet Foreign Policy,* ed. George Breslauer and Philip Tatlock (Boulder, Colo.: Westview Press, 1991), 208–63 (quotation on 220).

7

Beijing's Aid to Hanoi and the United States–China Confrontations, 1964–1968

Shu Guang Zhang

Economic aid in pursuit of foreign policy objectives was an integral part of great-power politics during the Cold War. Economic and technological aid, comprising both "butter and guns," was offered in exchange for political leverage and moral influence over recipient governments. The exercise of "positive" economic diplomacy invariably caused the targeted adversary to worry about an external threat and the recipient country to resent unfavorable leverage. Several well-documented studies exist on how the superpowers, the United States and the Soviet Union, employed economic weapons to confront one another.[1] Yet few diplomatic historians have seriously examined how China, a second-rate power, managed its foreign aid policy in general—and how, in particular, Beijing's aid to Hanoi shaped bigpower politics during America's Vietnam War. Hence this chapter.

China's Strategic Position in the Early 1960s

From 1960 onward, China's strategic position underwent drastic changes. The Beijing/Moscow rift hopelessly divided the two great communist powers, and the American threat seemed heightened, especially in Indochina and the Taiwan Strait. In response, the Chinese Communist Party (CCP) re-oriented its foreign policy, of which foreign economic aid became a major component.[2]

One of the most serious challenges the CCP faced was the sudden break in Sino-Soviet economic cooperation. On July 16, 1960, Moscow notified Beijing that all Soviet advisers and experts in China would be withdrawn. Without giving China any chance to reply, on July 25 the Kremlin in-structed all the Soviet advisers and experts to leave China no later than September 1. Simultaneously, Moscow stopped the dispatch of more than 900 experts whom it had previously agreed to send to China. Within one month, as many as 1,390 Soviet technical personnel departed, and Moscow terminated the implementation of 12 agreements on economic and technological aid and abrogated more than 200 cooperative scientific and technological projects.[3]

Chinese leaders were shocked and furious. The total Soviet withdrawal of advisers and experts and abrogation of all aid projects inflicted huge dam-age on China: Many important projects came to a halt only half-completed. Specifically, Zhou Enlai reported to an emergency CCP Central Committee meeting on July 31, projects related to "economic construction, technolog-ical cooperation, special defense technology, and nuclear energy" would be worst affected. Moreover, China's cooperation with Eastern European countries in such areas as "technology transfer, dispatch of students, polit-ical propaganda, attending international conferences, diplomatic inter-course, and foreign trade" would be seriously jeopardized.[4] To minimize the anticipated damage, in its first response to Moscow on July 31 Beijing sought to persuade the Kremlin to reconsider its decision, or at least to let those experts in situ remain until their contracts expired. On August 4, vice premier and foreign minister Chen Yi called an emergency meeting with Stepan Chervonenko, the Soviet ambassador to China. Chen pointed out that, because the Soviet Union had already inflicted financial damage on China, Moscow must stop "hurting the friendship between the two coun-tries." Although the two parties could continue their polemics on different interpretations of basic theories of Marxism-Leninism and international is-sues, Chen urged that "the mutual [economic] relations [at governmental level] should by no means be severed."[5] To the CCP's disappointment, how-ever, the Kremlin refused to reconsider its decision.

After the withdrawal of Soviet technicians from China, in the first half of the 1960s the Sino-Soviet split slowly but surely became a reality. There is some reason to suppose that the breakup of the Sino-Soviet bloc came as a surprise to both parties. Neither Moscow or Beijing initially anticipated that the difficulties caused by their ideological quarrels and private bickering would go so far as to cause their economic cooperation to fall apart, a development that inevitably left the CCP somewhat isolated within the communist bloc.

Concurrent with the Sino-Soviet break came a perceived intensification of the U.S. threat. Speaking to a group of "democratic" leaders on September 28, 1961, Zhou recalled a prediction Mao Zedong had made "ten years ago," that the imperialist bloc would, "to some extent," maintain a defensive posture toward the socialist camp as long as the latter stayed united; but "once the socialist camp breaks up and weakens itself, the imperialists will seize and exploit the opportunity and may become offensive [toward us]." This was why, in Mao's characterization, the United States had persistently attempted to "calcify our socialist camp." Should the United States switch from defense to offense, the "intermediate zone" consisting of the underdeveloped and ex-colonial countries in Asia, Africa, and Latin America would still be the primary battleground. The John F. Kennedy administration, Zhou pointed out, was already acting according to this scenario. By abandoning the policy of "brinkmanship," Kennedy had "taken a bigger step than [John Foster] Dulles by adopting a limited war policy" in dealing with Cuba, Laos, and probably Vietnam. In Zhou's judgment, the danger of limited war, particularly in the intermediate zone, had drastically increased.[6]

Beijing soon reoriented its defense and foreign policy to meet the perceived danger. In addition to its focus on "war preparation [*beizhan*]" and the construction of "the third line [*sanxian*],"[7] as described by Li Xiangqian in chapter 5 of the present volume, the CCP made the expansion of foreign economic aid a diplomatic priority. In early October 1962, Zhou directed the State Administration of Foreign Economic Contacts, the Ministry of Trade, and the Office of Foreign Affairs of the State Council to conduct a joint study on how China could enhance its economic aid to "socialist countries and independent national states." Zhou particularly expected this interagency study to identify the principal areas where China's aid could be most effective in achieving political objectives.[8] These agencies rapidly formulated principles to guide the People's Republic of China's foreign economic aid. The outcome, "Eight Guidelines on Foreign Economic and Technological Aid," was initially mentioned by Zhou at the fourth plenary session of the Second National People's Congress on December 2, 1963, and published early in 1964.[9] These principles included:

First, on the basis of "equality and mutual benefit," China would never bestow its aid as a "unilateral favor"; second, China would always "strictly respect recipient countries' sovereignty, attaching no special requirements nor any request for special rights"; third, China's aid would always be in the form of "no-interest or low-interest loans" and China would be "willing to defer payment if needed so as to reduce the recipient countries' burden"; fourth, instead of forging a dependent relationship, China's aid aimed only to "help the recipient countries to become independent and acquire the capability to develop their economies on their own"; fifth, China would guarantee that its aid projects would be "the most cost-effective" so as to insure increases in the recipient governments' revenue; sixth, although promising to provide its best equipment, technology and material at acceptable international prices, China would guarantee to accept returns of these materials, if they proved unsatisfactory; seventh, China would share its technological knowledge completely with recipient countries; and eighth, all Chinese specialists and technicians would have no "special rights" nor require any "special treatment" from recipient governments.[10]

The underlying tone of these eight policy principles suggested the CCP's twofold covert agenda. To break its isolation within the communist bloc, the CCP tried to differentiate itself from the Soviet Union when providing economic and technological assistance. Accusing Moscow of being chauvinistic, selfish, and exploitative in its economic relations with its socialist brothers, the CCP intended to project a fair, humble, and benevolent image, enabling it to take the moral high ground. Addressing a high-ranking delegation from Albania in late December 1961, Zhou pointed out that all the socialist countries had "an international responsibility" to help others, and any one that declined that responsibility, especially when it possessed the ability to do so, should by no means be considered a "true Marxist." Despite the "enormous difficulty deriving from the three-year natural disaster and the withdrawal of the Soviet technicians," Zhou assured the Albanian leaders, China would still shoulder its responsibility to aid all fraternal states, even though "our aid might not come in as large a quantity, fast a fashion, or good quality as expected."[11]

Simultaneously, Beijing tried to differentiate its economic aid policy from that of the United States, hoping to diminish American influence on developing and newly independent nations. To determine whether a country's aid aimed at "colony building" or not, Zhou explained to the Swedish ambassador to China on April 5, 1961, one had to apply three "dividing lines": first, "whether or not it demands special rights and privileges and exercises control"; second, "whether or not it truly intends to help the backward countries to build an independent economy"; and third, "whether or not it actually assists the recipient countries to advance faster than otherwise." Zhou claimed that, whereas the United States would fail each of these tests, China by contrast was willing to be tested in every one of these areas, for China only intended its foreign aid policy to "contribute to the courses of world peace and human progress."[12]

Whether or not economic aid could render a contribution, however, would depend largely on the donor's economic resources. In practice, China could not afford to offer much. Indeed, by mid-1960 the Chinese leadership was feeling serious effects from its delusive "Great Leap Forward" economic program as the country began to suffer its most devastating economic crisis. A countrywide famine unfolded in the spring, and national revenues declined drastically in the months of July and August. With no effective means to remedy its problems, the nation's economy went from bad to worse by the end of 1960: Although gross national product increased by 5.4 percent, it only reached 69.3 percent of the central government's projected target; agriculture yielded about 287 million tons of grain, 26.4 percent less than in 1957, its best year; and the state budget showed an overall 818 million yuan deficit.[13]

More troubling were the social and political ramifications of the nationwide food shortage. As the number of deaths due to hunger and malnutrition skyrocketed (even today, definitive statistics on the number of deaths have not been made available), large numbers of peasants began to migrate to cities and towns, and cases were reported of furious farmers forcibly abolishing the communes and violently assaulting CCP authorities at the village level.[14] Conflict intensified when, in May 1961, the CCP Central Committee decided to lay off as many as 10 million employees of state-owned enterprises by the end of that year and another 10 million over the next two years, who would be forced to relocate permanently in the countryside. Although a desirable measure to reduce the budgetary deficit, this policy caused widespread discontent, disillusionment, and anger with the CCP.[15]

There can be little doubt that the nation's economic problems were deeply embedded in the Communist system, with the CCP's relentless imitation of the Soviet model of industrialization, unrealistic anxiety to "catch up with" the Western powers, and self-righteous aspirations for the Great Leap Forward primary contributory factors.[16] Slowly but certainly, the CCP leadership came to recognize the gravity of the catastrophe. Instead of re-straining its international outreach, however, it tended to expand the im-plementation of its economic diplomatic initiative. On July 18, 1964, Zhou told the departmental heads of the State Council that, because the current international situation offered "a great opportunity" for China to increase its influence, especially among the Asian and African nations, "we must seize the moment and take a firm grasp of the central issue [of our economic foreign policy]." To guarantee the delivery of foreign aid, Zhou directed, many domestic economic projects must yield priority to overseas assistance efforts.[17]

To this end, a budgetary guarantee for China's economic aid program was mandated at the central level. On July 31, 1964, at a meeting with Vice Premier Li Xiannian, who was in charge of economic affairs, Zhou urged every department responsible for economic construction to "change its view by paying attention to foreign [economic] aid, . . . [and] by, in partic-ular, focusing its support to the Central Commission on Foreign Economic Contacts." He then specifically instructed that "foreign aid programs should be at least 3 percent of the total annual state budget." Moreover, he asked Li to come up with a percentage figure on how much hard currency should also be set aside for foreign aid programs.[18] Then, in early August, when considering a report from the Central Commission on Foreign Economic Contacts on how China's international economic and technological aid could be expanded, Zhou made it very clear that he would "like to see" 3 percent of the annual state budget and 3 percent of total foreign exchange revenues earmarked for foreign aid.[19]

The CCP's resolve to challenge the perceived U.S. threat, compete with the Soviet Union for moral leadership, and expand its influence among de-veloping countries set the tone for China's aid diplomacy toward Indochina. Although Beijing had never expected to focus on that area, as the conflict unfolded in the mid-1960s, China ended up committing itself to large-scale, extremely costly, and almost bottomless aid diplomacy toward Vietnam.

Chinese Aid to North Vietnam

The People's Republic of China had a long history of supplying North Viet-nam, as described in chapter 1 of the present volume. Although its Vietnam aid in the period 1950–54 totaled 1 million Chinese yuan, it consisted largely of weapons and military equipment. Not until the mid-1950s did

Beijing begin to provide economic assistance. In August 1954, Beijing dispatched 145 economic advisers to North Vietnam, who were to help the North Vietnamese with urban management, the restoration of production, economic planning, and the administration of trade, financial, and monetary matters.[20] During his trip to Beijing the following July, Ho Chi Minh was promised a total of 800 million Chinese yuan in direct assistance, which was to "aid the Vietnamese people with their economic reconstruction and growth" for the years 1955–57.[21]

Throughout the late 1950s, China's economic aid centered on three areas. First, Beijing supported Hanoi's economic relief programs in major cities, especially Hanoi and Hai Phong. Chinese goods for everyday use, in particular, helped the Vietnamese to stabilize the urban market, reduce the pressures of famine, and restore the production of handicrafts and light industries.

Second, China helped to repair and rebuild North Vietnam's transportation infrastructure. In late 1954, numerous Chinese railroad technicians and laborers crossed the Sino-Vietnamese border, as did equipment and material. They first repaired the badly crippled railway Hanoi and Mo Nam Pass, to establish a connection between the Chinese and Vietnamese railways, and then rebuilt the railways linking Hanoi with Lao Cai and Nam Dinh, in all 523 kilometers (317 miles) in length. Chinese technicians and laborers also participated in the reconstruction of sea and river ports, highways, and major bridges.

Third, China played a major part in Hanoi's economic planning and personnel training. Three high-ranking technological advisory groups—led respectively by Wang Guangwei (a senior official from the state planning commission), Lu Zhengcao (later minister of railway engineering), and Qian Zhengying (later minister of hydraulic engineering)—spent more than a year in North Vietnam designing railway and water irrigation projects. A total of nineteen advisory groups went to Hanoi in 1955–56 to assist in the construction of various new textile factories, electric power stations, paper mills, postal services, radio communications, printing shops, and match manufacturing plants. Simultaneously, as many as 750 Vietnamese students went to China to study handicrafts, machinery, agriculture, forestry, fishing, electric power, transportation, banking, and film production.[22]

From the outset, however, the CCP attached to its economic and technological aid to North Vietnam political expectations that became ever more institutionalized. In late 1956, Beijing set up an office of economic representation in Hanoi and appointed Fang Yi the first chief representative. Fang devoted extensive efforts to studying how China's aid to North Vietnam could best promote a close relationship between the two governments. In a series of reports to the central leadership in 1957, he proposed that, first, China's aid projects should all make political sense, especially in ensuring a significant Chinese impact on the Vietnamese economy and finance; second, China's aid should differ from its Soviet counterpart by always taking into account the "actual situation" in Vietnam so as to avoid "blind pursuit of modernization or advanced technology"; and third, China should conduct more "on-the-spot" training of Vietnamese specialists and technicians so as to build solid "teacher-student" relations.[23]

Beijing, in endorsing Fang's suggestions, early in 1958 approved a long-term economic aid commitment to North Vietnam. Under a March 31 Sino-Vietnamese agreement, China bound itself to build eighteen industrial projects between 1958 and 1961, including an electrical power plant, a chemical factory, a paper mill, a chromium mine, a sugar plant, and cigarette, soap, and toothpaste manufacturing facilities. Later, to speed up the construction, Beijing offered to finance some of the projects for free.[24]

Interestingly, however, China's economic aid to North Vietnam did not increase dramatically between 1961 and 1965. Though Hanoi kept pressing for more assistance to its First Five-Year Plan, Beijing actually dissuaded the Vietnamese from expecting too much from China. Battling its own economic problems resulting from the Great Leap Forward and the disruption of Sino-Soviet economic relations, the CCP prioritized Africa in its aid diplomacy.[25] Speaking to a Vietnamese vice premier on January 31, 1961, Zhou warned that Hanoi should not adopt any ambitious plans for industrial buildup, because, "according to the CCP experience, any grand industrial plan will surely require a large number of laborers and consequently detract from agricultural production and, since agriculture is the base for almost all of our socialist countries, one cannot have a healthy and sustainable industry if the base is destabilized."[26]

When Zhou met with a group of Vietnamese hydraulic engineers on July 4, 1961, he again urged the Vietnamese to move more slowly in building large water irrigation systems, implying that China could not spare any more resources for such purposes. On August 5, he further pointed out to high-ranking Vietnamese officials Hoang Van Hoan and Xuan Thuy that, in its economic buildup, "any nation has no other choice but to rely on its people; since foreign aid is by nature secondary and complementary, one has to adopt the principle of self-reliance, not to depend too much on foreign aid." His message was loud and clear: that Hanoi should not have overly high expectations of China's economic aid.[27]

Beijing's participation in North Vietnam's industrial buildup remained limited during this period. In 1961, Beijing provided two long-term, no-interest loans to cover the cost of building eight factories—iron and steel works, shipyards, nitrogenous fertilizer plants, and printing and dyeing mills—all regarded as Hanoi's premium projects.[28] In addition to one iron and one limestone mine near the Vietnam-China border, Chinese technicians and specialists contributed extensively to constructing an iron and steel plant in Thai Nguyen. This plant was the very first large foreign aid project on which, up to this point, China had ever embarked. Breaking ground in 1961, the factory was all set for production by 1965, with an annual yield of 150,000 tons of iron, 100,000 tons of steel, and 81,000 tons of rolled steel. Very soon, Thai Nguyen became the primary base for iron and steel production in North Vietnam.[29] Instead of providing substantial free economic aid, however, China expanded its trade with North Vietnam, with two commercial and maritime transportation agreements signed into effect on December 5, 1962.[30]

When the Gulf of Tonkin incident occurred in early August 1964, Beijing moved to high alert. When a Burmese leader inquired early in July what China would do if the United States were to attack North Vietnam, Zhou stated that the Chinese government could not "sit idly and remain indifferent [*zuoshi buguan*]" and would have to prepare for "a Korean-type war."[31] Speaking to the leftist American writer Han Suyin on September 10, Zhou again said that China would consider a U.S. attack on North Vietnam as "a hostile act toward China and we are fully prepared for this eventuality." It would be unwise, Zhou believed, for Washington to "lose its cool head" by expanding its military involvement in Southeast Asia, because "the Americans cannot win this war given the many disadvantages [the United States] suffers in the area of rear and logistical services, and given the opposition of the American people [to such a war]."[32]

From the summer of 1964 onward, the CCP leadership seriously debated how best to respond to the Vietnam conflict. Early in July, Mao began to "study the strategic issues" and, in a conversation with Zhou, Peng Zhen, He Long, Yang Chengwu, and Wu Xiuquan, urged them to enhance the level of combat readiness immediately in case the United States attacked China's southwestern borders or eastern coast.[33] When Zhou met soon afterward with the leaders of the CCP Southwestern Bureau, he demanded that the southwestern provinces should focus on the construction of a "third [de-fensive] line" along the Sino-Vietnamese border.[34] The U.S. air strikes on North Vietnam in February 1965 further alarmed the CCP leaders. At a Cen-tral Military Commission combat preparation meeting in mid-May, Zhou drew military commanders' attention to the need to prepare for a general and not necessarily limited war. He nonetheless explained that this precau-tionary measure did not imply "imminent danger," and he stated that China still "has time to prepare for the worst possibility."[35]

To win more time for China to prepare itself soon became a top CCP pri-ority. In chapter 6 of the present volume, James Hershberg and Chen Jian document the manner in which, in 1965, through circuitous secret "signal-ing" Chinese leaders sought to persuade the United States to limit its in-volvement in Vietnam to a level that would not provoke retaliatory Chinese full-scale intervention. At an enlarged Politburo meeting on April 12, 1965, Zhou cautioned that it would be advisable for China to adhere to the prin-ciple of "gaining mastery by striking only after the enemy has struck [*hou fazhi ren*] and leaving some leeway [*liu you yudi*]," because there was a need "to link the task of war preparation with [our] long-term [economic] plans." China would place itself in an advantageous position if "we do not raise the banner of 'Resisting America and Aiding Vietnam and Resisting America [Yuan Yue Gangmei]' now and wait till later." The best strategy, he believed, was to leave North Vietnam to "assume the primary responsibility" in com-bat, with China "only assisting Vietnam's struggle against the U.S." The Politburo endorsed Zhou's proposition.[36]

The CCP leadership clearly regarded its policy of aiding Hanoi as one of immense strategic importance: China would even subordinate its own eco-nomic development to the priority of furnishing aid to North Vietnam. A CCP Central Committee "Instruction on Strengthening the Work of War Preparation," dated April 12, 1965, urged the entire Party to prepare itself not merely for "a worst contingency" but also for every possible sacrifice to be made to assist the Vietnamese people.[37] At a May 11 CCP Politburo meeting called to consider adjustments to the economic and budgetary plans for 1965, Mao and Zhou advocated a drastic reduction of central govern-ment expenditures on China's own industrial projects, "especially those with no vital significance and of no immediate use." This budgetary modi-fication was designed to ensure sufficient financial support for foreign aid, war preparations, and "third line" construction.[38]

When Fang Yi, now chairman of the State Commission on Foreign Eco-nomic Contacts, reported that some material and goods designated as aid to

North Vietnam were priced too high by local manufacturers, Zhou immediately instructed that all the "Aiding Vietnam" projects be reviewed to ascertain how widespread such overpricing practices were. Any unfair pric-
ing of the foreign aid material, he urged, would have to be remedied,
because economic profit must invariably take second place to political interests.[39] So long as China's aid would sustain the Vietnamese "fighting
spirit," Zhou told the North Vietnamese vice premier on July 13, 1965,
China would not mind making economic sacrifices.[40]

A significant portion of China's aid consisted of supplies given directly
to the National Liberation Front (NLF) in South Vietnam. "Whatever materials the South request, so long as we are capable of giving these," Mao
directed the State Council in 1965, "should be provided by us unconditionally; some materials, including mosquito nets, umbrellas and raincoats,
medicines, first-aid dressings and kits, or even ship's biscuit which the Vietnamese side has not requested but we are able to provide should also be offered by us." China's assistance, he explained, must take into account the
fact that "life [for the NLF in] the South is very harsh and difficult" and the
Chinese supplies received would therefore have a real impact.[41]

Late that year, Mao again instructed the People's Liberation Army Department of the General Staff to add supplies such as ship's biscuits, dried
meat floss, canned pork, salt fish, egg flour, raincoats, and mosquito nets to
the list of materials to be shipped to the NLF.[42] Concurring with Mao, Zhou
urged that more attention be given to storing materials in South Vietnam,
because "the situation in the South changes very rapidly, and we must therefore take the opportunity now to ship in more materials in case transportation thereafter may be made very difficult by the enemy's blockade or sanc-
tions." He also required that all aid packages to South Vietnam "must be
easy to use, carry, disguise, and transport." Because a large proportion of
these packages would be hand-carried by women, he specifically requested
that no package should weigh more than 30 kilograms.[43]

Comprehensive statistics on the exact amount of Chinese supplies to the
NLF have yet to appear. However, an agreement signed on June 11, 1967,
by the deputy minister of logistics of the People's Liberation Army's Kunming Military Command, Liao Kaifeng, and Doan Khue, a Vietnamese rear-
service representative, does demonstrate the scope and nature of Chinese
aid. The agreement stipulated that for 1967 the Kunming Military District
would equip 2,200 NLF men with supplies of 687 items. These supplies
were intended to ensure that every NLF soldier would have 3 suits of clothes
and 3 pairs of shoes every year, along with a daily ration of 800 grams of

rice, 30 grams of salt, 80 grams of meat, 30 grams of fish, 30 grams of peanuts or sesame seeds, 30 grams of beans, 30 grams of lard, 10 grams of soy sauce, and 30 grams of sugar. In addition, China was to provide "daily office use" supplies, including 8,000 toothbrushes, 11,100 cases of toothpaste (Liunan Fragrance, the best brand in China), 24,700 cakes of soap, 10,600 cakes of toilet soap, and 109,000 cartons of cigarettes. Interestingly, many "luxury" items, such as necklaces, bracelets, and sports equipment, were also on the supply list.[44]

While supplying the NLF directly, Beijing took as its primary responsibility the effort to maintain and expand those North Vietnamese land transportation routes linked to China. Meeting with Mao in Changsha (Hunan Province) in mid-May 1965, Ho Chi Minh explicitly requested Chinese assistance for the ongoing construction of six vehicle roads intended to link the NLF rear bases in the South with the Chinese border. With China's takeover of the construction, Ho stressed, roughly 30,000 Vietnamese laborers and personnel who now were tied up on these projects could be freed for dispatch to the South. Viewing this as an effort to sustain the NLF fight in South Vietnam, Mao immediately agreed to Ho's request.[45] The CCP Central Committee soon put the Central-South China Bureau in charge, with four provinces (Guangdong, Guangxi, Yunnan, and Hunan) under its supervision. These four provinces, which were responsible for mobilizing and organizing personnel, equipment, and matériel for the task—as Tao Zhu, the first secretary of the Central–South China Bureau, told Ho on April 13—would constitute the first rear-base line for Vietnam.[46]

China's participation in North Vietnam's construction and repair of transportation soon expanded as the U.S. bombing of North Vietnam intensified. In December 1970, Zhou sent the vice minister of foreign trade, Li Qiang, to assess the damage to transportation. To obtain firsthand information, Li was even instructed to journey along the Ho Chi Minh Trail.[47] Upon Li's return, China dispatched to North Vietnam and Laos more than a thousand road and railroad engineers and technicians and several thousand laborers, with complete sets of machinery, materials, and equipment. Over the years, they repaired as many as seven highways, their total length amounting to 1,234 kilometers (748 miles), and built nine new vehicle roads in North Vietnam, providing a further 1,229 kilometers (745 miles) of highway, and seven roads in Laos, totaling 825 kilometers (500 miles). Many truck drivers and their trucks used these roads to transport Chinese goods for the war.[48] Chinese railway engineers and laborers assumed the main responsibility for repairing, upgrading, and constructing several major railroads vital to Sino-Vietnamese transportation, totaling 883.39 kilometers (535 miles).[49] Despite growing tensions with Moscow, Beijing allowed Soviet and East European goods to pass through China and even provided free internal transportation for them.[50]

Beijing also made it a priority to stabilize North Vietnam's supplies of daily necessities so as to offset pressures caused by shortages of food and other goods. Besides shipping goods directly from China, in 1968 and 1969, respectively, Beijing helped to construct two sugar refineries capable of producing 30 tons a day, and various small grain mills, rice flour mills, bean curd plants, and monosodium glutamate factories.[51] As its industrial centers endured constant U.S. air strikes, in 1970 North Vietnam's continued war effort met its most serious challenge. At Hanoi's request, Zhou sent Fang Yi across the border on a fact-finding mission. After on-the-spot investigation, Fang proposed to reorient China's economic assistance toward recovery, asserting that thenceforth China "ought to focus on restoring those factories built by us but severely crippled by the U.S. air assaults as quickly as we could." China should also "be more proactive and receptive toward some of [North] Vietnam's requests to build new plants," provided these were needed immediately. He suggested, moreover, "doubling our assistance effort for road repair and construction and providing, in particular, complete sets of machinery and equipment." These, he believed, were the areas where China's aid could make an immediate difference.[52]

Table 7.1, drawn from an official Chinese source, provides a sketch of China's overall economic aid to Hanoi. According to official Chinese calculations, between 1965 and 1970, aid to North Vietnam made up 57.6 percent of China's total foreign aid, most of which was donated without charge; between 1971 and 1975, China's aid to North Vietnam, Cambodia, and Laos made up 43.4 percent of the total, of which 93.1 percent went to Hanoi.[53]

It would have been impossible to provide such huge amounts of economic aid without a central control system and the participation of local—provincial and prefectural—governments. The General Bureau of Foreign Economic Contacts (GBFEC), established in January 1961, acted as the single central agency to supervise foreign economic and technological aid projects. Primarily to meet the demands of aiding Vietnam, however, in 1965 a centralized "goods-delivery" structure was created, to assess Vietnamese needs, something it accomplished largely through the office of economic affairs at the Chinese Embassy in Hanoi and by sending advisory groups and ad hoc

Table 7.1. China's Economic Aid to Hanoi during the Vietnam War

Category	1965–70	1970–75	Subtotal
Hard currency (millions of dollars)	$254.62	$380	$634.62
Grain (tons)	2,435,600	2,961,000	5,396,600
Cotton (tons)	26,000	34,000	60,000
Cotton yarn (tons)	30,600	37,000	67,600
Cotton cloth (millions of meters)	75	194.6	269.6
Cotton blankets (millions of pieces)	1.9	2.15	4.05
Chemicals (tons)	70,600	540,000	610,600
Fertilizer	—	—	—
Rolled steel (tons)	185,100	416,000	601,100
Coal (tons)	100,000	1,810,000	1,910,000
Asphalt (tons)	40,000	144,400	184,400
Gasoline (tons)	95,500	1,800,000	1,895,500
Paper (tons)	41,000	49,200	90,200
Trucks	4,200	30,835	35,035
Vessels	334	352	686
Tractors	2,430	2,300	4,730
Road construction (pieces)	1,238	4,135	5,373
Machinery	—	—	—
Locomotives (pieces)	107	20	127
Railroad cars (pieces)	2,200	1,090	3,290
Bicycles	477,000	380,000	857,000

Note: A dash in a cell means that the amount was negligible.
Source: Dangdai zhongguo de duiwai jinji hezuo [China today: Economic cooperation with foreign countries] (Beijing: Chinese Academy of Social Sciences Press, 1989), 52, 57–58.

investigation teams to the field; to establish affiliations and distribute contracts through its department of affiliates; and to oversee quality control and the delivery of goods through its department for that purpose.[54]

Moreover, four southern and southwestern provinces—Guangdong, Guangxi, Yunnan, and Hunan—each formed a partner relationship with one of the North Vietnamese provinces along the Sino-Vietnamese border, with responsibilities ranging from providing goods for daily use to participating in the planning and supervision of production.[55] This structure functioned until the end of 1970. To improve central-local cooperation, in 1972 the practice of "[local] assumption of production [*chengjian zhi*]" was adopted, under which the GBFEC assigned production tasks to each affiliated ministry (ministries of light industry, machinery, commerce, textiles, etc.), which in turn would divide them among all the individual manufacturers or research institutes under its supervision and inform the local governments of these arrangements. Within the local governments, specialized agencies (bureaus of light industry, commerce, etc.) would then take charge of production, inspection, and transportation.[56]

It is important to remember that even while China itself experienced the chaotic political campaign of the Cultural Revolution, the CCP ensured continuous large-scale economic aid to North Vietnam. An important incentive for doing so was China's desire to compete with the Soviet Union for influence and, more important, for moral leadership in Indochina. In a conversation with Cambodia's Prince Sihanouk shortly after the Gulf of Tonkin crisis began, Mao accused Moscow of "making friends with the Americans." So far as international aid to Vietnam was concerned, he believed, the Soviet Union, although a socialist state, would be less reliable than Cambodia, even though the latter was under a noncommunist government.[57] Zhou echoed Mao's harsh criticisms of Moscow. Speaking to Pakistani president Ayub Khan in early April, Zhou made it very clear that the Soviet Union could not be trusted to support any national liberation struggle, and China would therefore never expect any Soviet support or cooperation in meeting its commitment to the Vietnamese war against the Americans; meanwhile, Beijing would prove to the African and Asian countries that China was their only reliable and dependable supporter.[58]

As chapters 1, 8, and 9 of the present volume all demonstrate, Sino-Soviet tensions heightened as Moscow became increasingly involved in the Vietnam War. After Soviet prime minister Aleksei Kosygin visited Beijing and Hanoi from February 4 to 11, 1965, the CCP strongly opposed the Soviet proposal that all the socialist countries participate in issuing "a joint statement in support of Vietnam" and, more specifically, it rejected Moscow's offer of forty-five Soviet planes to airlift weapons and equipment from Russia to the Sino-Vietnamese border areas. On March 1, Zhou explained to Ho that, while the former measure would signal Soviet primacy in aiding Vietnam, the latter would arouse Chinese concern over potential "Soviet subversive activities."[59] Soviet aid, the CCP tried to persuade the North Vietnamese, would always come with an "evil motive" attached; in this case, the objective was to drive a wedge between China and Vietnam. When "[Nikita] Khrushchev held power," Zhou told Pham Van Dong on October 9, "the Soviets could not divide us because Khrushchev gave you little help"; current Soviet assistance to Hanoi had now placed the Soviets in a better position than ever before to do so.[60] "To win your trust in a deceitful way," Zhou more explicitly explained to Le Duan on March 23,

1966, Moscow intended to "cast a shadow over the relationship between Vietnam and China, to split Vietnam and China, with a view to further controlling Vietnam so as to improve [its] relations with the United States and obstruct the struggle and revolution of the Vietnamese people."[61] Conveying the same message to Ho earlier that year, the CCP Central Committee's general secretary, Deng Xiaoping, went so far as to suggest that "if Vietnam finds it inconvenient to expose the fact [that the Soviet aid was given to serve its own purposes], let us do it on your behalf."[62]

One central issue, covered in greater detail by Li Danhui in chapter 8 below, was the transshipment of Soviet supplies to Vietnam via China. In 1965, Beijing agreed to allow a monthly 10,000 tons of Soviet equipment to be transported via China's land and coastal routes. Early in April 1967, however, the Soviets requested an increase of the quota from 10,000 to 30,000 tons, and they proposed sending their own locomotives to haul these materials, while China should reserve for this effort two or three of its southern ports, which Russia could use to ship supplies directly to Vietnam.[63] The CCP leadership firmly rejected the Soviet proposal. At a meeting with Dong on April 10, Zhou not only argued that there was no immediate need for the Soviets to increase their aid to Vietnam or use Chinese ports for direct shipment but also asserted that the Soviet proposition was made "for other ulterior motives."[64]

On May 13, 1967, when Moscow asked Beijing for permission to transport 24 MiG aircraft via air over China to North Vietnam, Chinese deputy foreign minister Qiao Guanhua called in Ngo Minh Loan, the Vietnamese ambassador to Beijing, to state the CCP's stance: that the Soviet proposal entailed "bad intentions and is a conspiracy," which ought to be opposed. Qiao believed that, because this undertaking might enable Moscow to brag about its "large-scale aid to Vietnam" in its propaganda, "by doing so, the Soviets [want to] reveal military secrets to the U.S."[65] The CCP was indeed determined to minimize Soviet influence in Indochina; on April 11, Zhou had explained to his associates and some Vietnamese leaders that "the closer to victory your struggle is, the fiercer our struggle with the Soviet Union will be."[66]

China's aid to North Vietnam entailed various policy implications, which were far more wide ranging than simply the outcome of the Vietnam War. It drastically complicated Sino-Soviet competition within the communist bloc and strained the Beijing-Hanoi relationship. By the same token, it seriously affected Washington's "incremental" response to the military conflict, clearing a new battleground for United States–China confrontations.

American Assessments of Chinese Aid
to North Vietnam

American officials closely monitored China's involvement in the Vietnam conflict. They naturally assumed that Beijing was responsible for the escalation of the crisis in Vietnam and therefore remained alert for prospective armed Chinese intervention.[67] When Washington realized that Beijing was restricting its "aiding Vietnam" policy to the provision of economic and military supplies, however, it decided to try at least restraining Chinese aid to that level. During his visit to Taiwan in mid-April 1964, U.S. secretary of state Dean Rusk dissuaded Jiang Jieshi (Chiang Kai-shek) from undertaking any offensive actions against the mainland. "It may be that Southeast Asia cannot be made secure unless the Chinese Communists are hurt and hurt badly," Rusk explained to Jiang; but according to U.S. intelligence, "no Chinese Communist personnel had ever been found in South Vietnam. There was not even evidence of large numbers of Chinese Communist military or technicians in North Vietnam." And the United States was "not prepared to move too far or too fast in the direction of precipitating" a war with the "large masses of men on the Asia mainland."[68]

To this end, on October 28, U.S. National Security Council staff member James C. Thomson suggested to President Lyndon Johnson's special assistant for national security affairs, McGeorge Bundy, that the administration should not simply assume that Beijing dominated Hanoi, because he did not believe that "this tail belongs to that particular dog."[69] It soon became a matter of consensus in Washington that any action that would lead to "provoking or at least providing a public excuse for Chinese Communist intervention in Vietnam" must be avoided.[70]

American officials seemed to have understood that China's commitment to supplying North Vietnam was a part of Beijing's new diplomatic initiative. The CCP, a National Intelligence Estimate (NIE 13-9-65) asserted on May 5, 1965, was waging "an international guerrilla struggle which attempts to wear down the enemy's strength by attacking the weak point." Having "chosen the underdeveloped, ex-colonial world as its most advantageous arena of conflict," Beijing clearly expected Southeast Asia to feel "the greatest impact" of its new policy and, the NIE stated, "the theater of primary interest is Indochina, where Peiping is seeking a decisive and humiliating defeat of the US." But, so long as U.S. actions did not threaten "China's vital security interests," Beijing would adhere to its existing policy of economic aid and moral and political support, rather than armed intervention, in Vietnam.[71] This assessment was further confirmed by a high-level China Confrontational Study Group's report in July that, "while the Chinese are utterly opposed to the U.S. presence in Southeast Asia, they expect to use subversion and infiltration of supplies to achieve their objectives, and not direct military force unless their immediate lines of defense are threatened."[72]

Washington officials—who were concerned much less about China's aid to Vietnam than about the possibility of its armed intervention there—believed that, by trying to meet Hanoi's material needs, Beijing was placing itself in a disadvantageous position. China's economy was far from adequate to support and sustain its aid diplomacy. Although the Vietnam conflict "has not yet added serious strains to the Chinese economy," an NIE of January 13, 1966, predicted that "a sustained increase in the level of fighting in Vietnam, if accompanied by a comparable rise in Chinese assistance as well as significant defensive measures within China itself, would add [so] greatly to China's economic problem" that China might eventually be compelled to reduce or even terminate its aid to Vietnam.[73]

More specifically, a special joint State Department–Defense Department study explained in June that "Chinese economic growth is weighed down by the failure of the regime thus far to resolve the problem of expanding agricultural output faster than population," partly because of the CCP's "heavy commitment of scarce engineering and scientific manpower" and resources to foreign economic aid and military production programs. This "prolonged semi-failure" in the economic field would inevitably have "adverse effects on the morale of the cadres and on the people's responsiveness to exhortations for continued [sacrificial] effort." Given "China's size, huge population, cultural conservatism and limited natural resources," the report calculated, it was scarcely imaginable that any leadership could successfully implement a financially costly and politically unpopular foreign aid policy. Beijing's chances of success would be even slimmer in a competition with the United States, the mightiest economic power in the world. Through its own economic aid, the special paper posited, the United States could easily demonstrate "the lack of relevance of Chinese experience to much of the underdeveloped world, the limited ability of the Chinese to provide useful assistance, and the threat to the integrity of new and weak nations posed by Chinese-supported subversion and insurgency."[74]

U.S. officials also believed that China's aid policy toward North Vietnam would exacerbate the Sino-Soviet split. An NIE of May 5, 1965, pointed out that the Soviet Union "has come increasingly to rival the United States as a dominant problem for Chinese foreign policy." Through its new foreign policy initiatives, Beijing aimed as much to "dilute or supplant Soviet influence and to win over or split Communist parties and front movements" as to "erode US strength."[75] It was therefore unlikely that Moscow would not respond vigorously to the CCP challenge. At a State Department–Defense Department joint meeting on China on August 27, Rusk stressed the possibility that "the Soviets may not prefer to see a settlement in Southeast Asia, . . . [for] the struggle with Peiping is very deep rooted and as a result may force the Soviets to take a stronger position than would otherwise be the case."[76]

In early March 1965, a special "China Study" reiterated that Moscow had already declared its support for "the concept of wars of national liberation" and made a public commitment to "defend the interests of North Vietnam," whereas "the Chinese did not intend nor have they been in the past the principal supporters of the doctrine of national liberation." Fierce Sino-Soviet competition over prestige and influence in Vietnam would probably intensify. Sino-Soviet cooperation, the report claimed, would be possible only in the event of an open armed clash between China and the United States either in Vietnam or in South China, because the Soviets might feel "compelled to provide the ChiComs [Chinese Communists], after some period of delay, with military equipment, e.g., advanced fighters and missiles" first, and to "become involved militarily to a highly dangerous degree" should "the existence of a Communist regime in Peiping" be threatened. But, provided Beijing continued its aid policy, without directly or openly involving its armed forces in the war—a measure that might force the United States to retaliate by attacking the mainland and thereby escalate the conflict—the two communist rivals would probably end up at one another's throats.[77] Meanwhile, as chapter 6 above indicates, by late 1965 top American officials had concrete reason to believe that, provided the United States did not escalate its Vietnam commitment excessively, China would not embark on a full-scale military intervention in the conflict.

As the war in Vietnam continued, the Sino-Soviet rift seemed to widen. An NIE of December 1, 1966, noted the intensification of Sino-Soviet quarrels over Vietnam. Perceiving the conflict as "a prime example of a 'people's war' waged against their main enemy, US imperialism," the NIE argued, the Chinese hoped for an outcome "which would support their claim that this Maoist strategy is essential to revolutionary advance and at the same time diminish Soviet claims to give authoritative guidance to the revolutionary struggle." The Soviets, conversely, "increasingly sought to use the Vietnamese War as an issue against China." In particular, they "employed their aid to North Vietnam as a means to increase their influence in Hanoi at Chinese expense, and in this they have apparently had some success." The NIE report thus saw Sino-Soviet hostility reaching "new levels of intensity," given "the hints from both capitals [Beijing and Moscow] of growing difficulties over the transshipment of Soviet supplies to North Vietnam" across China, and also Moscow's public accusation that Beijing's "failure to cooperate [in diplomatic talks] had prolonged the war by preventing a 'quick end' to U.S. 'outrages.'"[78]

Although American officials were convinced that China was in a difficult position to fulfill its aid commitments to Hanoi, they believed that China had reason to believe that it could win eventually in Vietnam "by applying patience, pressure, and the principles of indirect aggression." Although the United States had "created something close to a stalemate around the whole periphery of Chinese power from Korea to India," the U.S. assistant secretary of state for international organization affairs, J. Harlan Cleveland, asserted in late October 1964, that "the Viet Nam salient of that stalemate is precarious in the extreme."[79] National Security Council staff member Thomson concurred, stating in a letter of October 28 to McGeorge Bundy that the U.S. containment policy "actually serves Peking's interests": Though Beijing had "no intention of 'shaping up' in terms of taking tension-relieving initiatives" with the United States in Southeast Asia, it was "seriously intent on isolating us—while we, in turn, are generally blamed for trying (unsuccessfully) to isolate Peking." He therefore urged Bundy to "try [a strategy of] modified containment" involving "the careful use of free world goods, people, and ideals—instruments which have proven their long-term corrosive value in our relations with other totalitarian societies."[80]

An immediate action area, the U.S. assistant secretary of state for Far Eastern affairs, William P. Bundy, suggested to Rusk on June 16, 1965, would be to ease restrictions on travel to China by American scholars and representatives of humanitarian organizations. Because Beijing would probably not respond favorably to such an overture, Bundy argued, the United States would then "have an unusual opportunity here to put the Chinese Communists on the defensive and nullify domestic criticism of both the right and the left."[81] Thomson, however, pushed for "a multiple strategy." Along with "traditional military containment . . . as in Vietnam," he wrote to Jack Valenti, Johnson's special assistant, on March 1, 1966, the administration ought to consider providing "generous assistance to the fragile societies on

China's perimeter in the process of nation-building," and undertaking "systematic efforts to help erode the Chinese totalitarian state, to influence Chinese behavior, and to combat Chinese ignorance and fear of the outside world." A comprehensive package would include:

1. unilateral termination of the present travel ban to Communist China (we now bar all Americans except bona fide journalists and, since December, specialists in medicine and public health);
2. a renewed invitation to Chinese journalists, scholars, artists, etc., to visit the U.S.;
3. licensing of commercial sales of medicines and foodstuffs to China;
4. eventual further modification of the present trade embargo to permit trade in non-strategic goods, as with the USSR;
5. inclusion of China in disarmament talks;
6. a shift in our UN strategy from exclusion of Peking to inclusion of Taipei; and
7. [a] proposal that the now sterile Warsaw dialogue be reinvigorated through transfer of these talks to a major European or Asian capital (Paris?).

Thomson believed that such favorable diplomatic overtures could "most easily" be implemented "at a time when our toughness and firmness in opposition to Chinese Communists aggressiveness is manifested in Southeast Asia as never before."[82]

High-level discussions of the feasibility of such a multiple strategy continued until the end of 1968 but brought no major change in U.S. policy toward China.[83] One major obstacle was the perceived long-term conflict of interest between the United States and China. It was true, a Central Intelligence Agency estimate of September 23, 1966, argued, that "caution is being shown in [Beijing's] foreign affairs, specially on Vietnam; . . . it was unlikely that the Chinese would intervene with their own forces in the Vietnam War."[84] Another NIE, dated May 25, 1967, also admitted that, because China's Cultural Revolution not only caused domestic chaos within the regime but also damaged Chinese prestige abroad, it was very likely that "internal changes in the direction of moderation . . . will create more favorable conditions for reappraising foreign policy and perhaps for introducing elements of greater moderation."[85] The Johnson administration, however, found it hard to take any step toward a Chinese-American rapprochement because, a special State-Defense study had asserted in June

1966, "the Chinese regime's objectives of regional hegemony and world revolution *clash with our own fundamental interests* in preventing domination of Asia by any single power and in developing a peaceful and open world society of free nations" (emphasis added).[86]

Triangular Washington-Moscow-Beijing politics also made it difficult for the United States to move toward reconciliation with China. Since the Sino-Soviet split, the Kremlin had worried about a less confrontational U.S.-China relationship. At the end of 1968, the Soviets were even "concerned over the possibility of a U.S.-China alliance," as Boris Davydov, the second secretary of the Soviet Embassy in Washington, explained on December 21 to Daniel I. Davidson, a senior State Department staff member. The Soviet leadership, Davydov stated, would regard as "extremely dangerous" any attempt to form a U.S.-China alliance. In response, in Asia the USSR would "attempt to counter a U.S. move toward China by increased efforts to induce Japan to give up its American alliance," and in Europe, Russia "could not rule out the possibility of Soviet use of military force"—most likely in Germany. At the very least, Davydov stressed, the Soviet Union would ensure that "any hope of progress in U.S.-Soviet relations would be completely impossible." On behalf of his government, the Soviet diplomat warned Washington not to "play the dangerous game of U.S.-Chinese reconciliation."[87]

The Johnson administration remained more cautious but no less purposeful through the end of its second term. "Since our firm position in Asia generally remains crucial," Secretary of State Rusk explained to Johnson on February 22, 1968, "any significant 'concessions' to Communist China would be seriously misunderstood in key quarters, not to mention the Congress"; and more important, he reminded Johnson, "we must keep Communist China always in mind in our choice of military actions in Viet-Nam and elsewhere."[88]

Conclusions

In the early 1960s, China joined the big-power league in the field of economic diplomacy. The use of economic aid in pursuit of foreign policy objectives did not seem alien to the CCP leaders. China had indeed practiced tributary diplomacy for centuries. It clung to the fond, if fictitious, notion that China, as the Middle Kingdom on Earth, was the center of the known civilized world and that all countries desiring relations with it must accept their tributary status. It was no accident that Beijing slowly but definitely switched from alliance politics and militant belligerency to economic diplomacy as its first line of defense.

China's aid policy toward the Vietnam conflict happened to become a major part of the CCP's new diplomatic thrust. Although the CCP leaders initially made Africa their highest foreign aid priority, shortly after the Gulf of Tonkin incident, they quickly focused their attention and resources on Vietnam. China's Vietnam aid was intended partly to enhance the country's border security, because it seemed "rational" to assist their neighbor in fighting a potential enemy, without necessarily becoming directly or overtly involved. Simultaneously, by providing aid to an Asian communist country that was fighting for "national liberation," Beijing expected to win moral leadership in its rivalry with Moscow, both among the Asian and African nations and within the communist bloc.

In practice, however, China's Vietnam aid brought mixed results. Without China's aid, Hanoi could not have sustained the burden of fighting a guerrilla war that was, in some sense, a war of attrition with the United States. While making an all-out effort to supply both the NLF and North Vietnam, China itself was passing through an immensely difficult time of unprecedented economic and political chaos. National security and international imperatives clearly trumped pressing economic and nationalist needs. Nor, competing with the Soviets, did the Chinese emerge victorious. As chapters 8, 9, and 10 will demonstrate in greater detail, while the Sino-Soviet rift widened further, Beijing merely managed to establish a very weak leverage over Hanoi, which proved too fragile to prevent the two from waging a large-scale border war from 1979 to 1989. Gradually and reluctantly, Beijing learned that without a sound economic base, a country's foreign policy was only built on sand.

No less significant was the impact of China's Vietnam aid on U.S. intervention in Indochina. Although meant to deter Washington from escalating the war, Beijing's initial response of providing only economic support for Hanoi in the conflict signaled Washington that China was not yet ready to fight a Korean type of war in Vietnam. American officials were indeed initially puzzled but then relieved that China would weaken itself by engaging in economic warfare with the United States. Concurrently, as chapter 6 likewise suggests, the sight of a militarily less belligerent but diplomatically more "mature" Beijing intrigued those within the Johnson administration

advocating a "normal" relationship between the United States and China—
a policy that, though not implemented, effectively paved the way for the triangular politics to come in the early 1970s.

Notes

1. See, e.g., Diane B. Kunz, *Butter and Guns: America's Cold War Economic
Diplomacy* (New York: Free Press, 1997); Burton I. Kaufman, *Trade and Aid: Eisen-
hower's Foreign Economic Policy, 1953–1961* (Baltimore: Johns Hopkins University
Press, 1982); and William H. Becker and Samuel F. Wells Jr., eds. *Economics and World
Power: An Assessment of American Diplomacy since 1789* (New York: Columbia University Press, 1984), 333–458. In my recent book, *Economic Cold War: America's Embargo against China and the Sino-Soviet Alliance, 1949-1963* (Washington, D.C., and
Stanford, Calif.: Woodrow Wilson Center Press and Stanford University Press, 2001), I
touch upon some policy aspects of Soviet aid diplomacy toward China.

2. Very little has been written in English on this topic. Recently, however, some official Chinese explanations have appeared. See "A Historical Review of China's Foreign
Aid Efforts," in *Dangdai zhongguo de duiwai jingji hezuo* [China today: Economic cooperation with foreign countries] (Beijing: Chinese Academy of Social Sciences Press,
1989), 32–4, 64–5; and "The Deterioration of Sino-Vietnamese Relations," *Dangdai
zhongguo waijiao* [China today: Diplomacy] (Beijing: Chinese Academy of Social Sciences Press, 1988), 268–1. Although providing limited aid to North Korea and North
Vietnam in the 1950s, Beijing did not have a general policy toward or a central government agency to implement "foreign economic aid" programs. Not until early 1961 was
"foreign economic aid" clearly conceived as a foreign policy instrument and incorporated into the foreign policy system. See *Dangdai zhongguo duiwai jingji hezuo,* 31.

3. *Dangdai zhongguo waijiao,* 117–18. Unfortunately, documents as to why
Khrushchev chose to adopt a policy of economic blackmail against China have not yet
become available.

4. Zhou Enlai, speech at a Central Committee meeting at Beidaihe (a summer resort for Mao and his associates), July 31, 1960, in *Zhou Enlai nianpu, 1949–1976* [A
chronological record of Zhou Enlai, 1949–1976] (hereafter *Zhou Enlai nianpu*), 3 vols.,
ed. CCP Central Documentary Research Department (Beijing: Central Press of Historical Documents, 1997), vol. 2, 336.

5. *Dangdai zhongguo waijiao,* 117–18.

6. Zhou Enlai, speech, "The Characteristics of Current World Situations," September 28, 1961, *Zhou Enlai waijiao wenxian* [Selected diplomatic works of Zhou En-
lai], ed. Ministry of Foreign Affairs and Central Division of Archives and Manuscripts
(Beijing: Central Press of Historical Documents, 1990), 316–21.

7. On the CCP's "war preparations" and "third-line" building focus, see Mao's instructions enclosed in the excerpts of CCP Central Committee's "Working Meetings,"
May 15–June 17, 1964, *Zhou Enlai nianpu,* vol. 2, 643; Mao's instructions to Zhou Enlai, Peng Zhen, He Long, Wu Xiuquan, and Yang Chengwu, July 2, 1964, *Zhou Enlai
nianpu,* vol. 2, 644.

8. Zhou Enlai, instruction on the State Administration of Foreign Economic Con-

tacts' report, "On Supplying Korea with Complete Sets of Machinery," October 5, 1962, *Zhou Enlai nianpu,* vol. 2, 500.

9. Zhou Enlai, report (excerpt) at the 4th plenary session of the Second National People's Congress, December 2, 1963, *Zhou Enlai nianpu,* vol. 2, 597–98; Zhou Enlai, interview with a Ghanaian news agency, January 15, 1964, *Zhou Enlai nianpu,* vol. 2, 611–12.

10. "Eight Guidelines on Foreign Economic and Technological Aid," January 15, 1964, *Zhou Enlai waijiao wenxuan,* 388–99.

11. Zhou Enlai, conversation with a high-ranking Albanian delegation, December 31, 1961, *Zhou Enlai nianpu,* vol. 2, 447–48; minutes (excerpt) of conversation between Zhou Enlai and Pham Van Dong, June 12–16, 1961, *Zhou Enlai nianpu,* vol. 2, 416–17.

12. Minutes of conversation (excerpt) between Zhou Enlai and the Swedish ambassador to China, April 5, 1961, *Zhou Enlai nianpu,* vol. 2, 402–3.

13. Li Cheng, ed., *Shangxia qiusuo, 1957–1965: Gonghe guo shiji* [To pursue from up and down: Historical records of the People's Republic of China], 2 vols. (Changchun: Jilin People's Press, 1996), vol. 2, 421.

14. See CCP Zhejiang Provincial Committee, report to the Central Committee, August 26, 1960, enclosed in note 1, *Jianguo yilai Mao Zedong wengao* [Mao's manuscripts since the founding of the People's Republic of China], ed. CCP Central Documentary Research Department, 13 vols. (Beijing: Central Press of Historical Documents, 1996), vol. 9, 362–63; CCP Sichuan Provincial Committee, report to Mao and the Central Committee, November 20, 1960, enclosed in note 2, *Jianguo yilai Mao Zedong wengao,* vol. 9, 360–61; Hebei working committee, report to the General Office of the Central Committee, December 15, 1960, enclosed in note 1, *Jianguo yilai Mao Zedong wengao,* vol. 9, 390.

15. Central Committee, resolution (excerpt), May 21–June 12, 1961, in *Shangxia qiusuo,* ed. Li Cheng, vol. 2, 632–33; and CCP Ministry of United Front Affairs, report, November 25, 1960, enclosed in *Jianguo yilai Mao Zedong wengao,* vol. 9, 374–75.

16. Zhou Enlai, instruction at the Enlarged Central Committee Meeting, January 19–22, 1961, *Zhou Enlai nianpu,* vol. 2, 452–53; Zhou Enlai, speech at the Central Committee's Leading Group on Finance and Economy, March 8, 1961, *Zhou Enlai nianpu,* vol. 2, 462–63; Zhou Enlai, speech at the 18th Supreme State Affairs meeting of the State Council, March 21, 1961, *Zhou Enlai nianpu,* vol. 2, 464–65.

17. Zhou Enlai, conversation with departmental heads of the State Council, July 18, 1964, *Zhou Enlai nianpu,* vol. 2, 657.

18. Zhou Enlai, conversation with Vice Premier Li Xiannian, July 31, 1964, *Zhou Enlai nianpu,* vol. 2, 660.

19. Zhou Enlai, instruction on a Central Commission on Foreign Economic Contacts report, "On the Basic Situation Concerning [Our] Foreign Economic and Technological Aid and Suggestions for the Future Work," August 7, 1964, *Zhou Enlai nianpu,* vol. 2, 663.

20. See *Dangdai Zhongguo de duiwai jinji hezuo,* 26–27.

21. "The Communiqué of the Chinese and Vietnamese Governments," July 7, 1955, *Renmin Ribao* [People's Daily], 1.

22. *Dangdai Zhongguo de duiwai jinji hezuo,* 28–29. See also "Work Report on the 'Aid-Vietnam' Projects for 1956," Bureau of Foreign Trade, Guangdong Provincial Government, August 7, 1956, Quanzhong [Record Group] 302, Juanzhong [box] 01, Anjuan [file] 50–56, Guangdong Provincial Archives, Guangzhou, China.

23. *Dangdai Zhongguo de duiwai jinji hezuo,* 30.

24. Bureau of Textile Industry, Shanghai Municipal Government, "Report on Our Bureau's 'Aid-Vietnam' Projects," [undated] January 1961, Quanzhong B134, Juanzhong 01, Anjuan 1187, Shanghai Municipal Archives, Shanghai, China; and Bureau of Textile Industry, Shanghai Municipal Government, correspondence over the issue of technology transfer to Vietnam, [undated] January-December 1961, Quanzhong B134, Juanzhong 01, Anjuan 1203, Shanghai Municipal Archives, Shanghai, China; also see, *Dangdai Zhongguo de duiwai jinji hezuo,* 32.

25. Zhou Enlai, speech, July 18, 1964, at the executive meeting of the State Council, *Zhou Enlai nianpu,* vol. 2, 657.

26. Zhou Enlai, minutes (excerpt) of conversation with a Vietnamese delegation, January 31, 1961, *Zhou Enlai nianpu,* vol. 2, 388–89.

27. Zhou Enlai, minutes (excerpt) of conversation with a Vietnamese delegation of hydraulic engineers, July 4, 1961, *Zhou Enlai nianpu,* vol. 2, 421–22; Zhou Enlai, minutes (excerpt) of conversation with Hoang Van Hoan and Xuan Thuy, August 5, 1961, *Zhou Enlai nianpu,* vol. 2, 426.

28. *Dangdai zhongguo de duiwai jinji hezuo,* 32–33. See also Ministry of Textiles, "On the Plan to Help Vietnam Build Four Textile-Dyeing Factories," December 1958, Quanzhong B134, Juanzhong 01, Anjuan 525, Shanghai Municipal Archives, Shanghai.

29. *Dangdai zhongguo de duiwai jinji hezuo,* 171–72.

30. Agreements between China and Vietnam on trade and maritime transportation, December 5, 1962, *Renmin Ribao,* 1; Bureau of Foreign Trade, Guangdong Provincial Government, "Summary of Trade between Vietnam and Guangdong in 1963," December 1963, Quanzhong 302, Juanzhong 01, Anjuan 34–63, Guangdong Provincial Archives, Guangzhou, China.

31. Zhou Enlai, minutes (excerpt) of a conversation with a Burmese leader, July 10, 1964, *Zhou Enlai nianpu,* vol. 2, 655.

32. Zhou Enlai, minutes (excerpt) of a conversation with Han Suyin, September 10, 1964, *Zhou Enlai nianpu,* vol. 2, 657.

33. Mao Zedong, minutes (excerpt) of conversation, with Zhou Enlai, Peng Zhen, He Long, Yang Chengwu, and Wu Xiuquan, July 2, 1964, *Zhou Enlai nianpu,* vol. 2, 654; see also Mao Zedong, instruction on the minutes of conversation between Lin Biao and Yang Chengwu, July 15, 1964, *Jianguo yilai Mao Zedong wengao,* vol. 11, 103–4.

34. Zhou Enlai, minutes (excerpt) of a conversation with the leaders of CCP Southwestern Bureau, July 9, 1964, *Zhou Enlai nianpu,* vol. 2, 655.

35. Zhou Enlai, minutes (excerpt) of a conversation with the participants at the Central Military Commission combat preparation meeting, May 19, 1965, *Zhou Enlai nianpu,* vol. 2, 731.

36. Zhou Enlai, speech (excerpt) at the enlarged Politburo meeting, April 12, 1965, *Zhou Enlai nianpu,* vol. 2, 724.

37. CCP Central Committee, "Instruction on Strengthening the Work of War Preparations," April 12, 1965, cited in Li Ke and Hao Shenzhang, *Wenhua dageming zhong de renmin jiefangjun* [The People's Liberation Army during the "Cultural Revolution"] (Beijing: CCP Party Material and History Press, 1989), 408; and see also Zhou Enlai, speech at a welcoming ceremony in Albania, March 29, 1965, *Zhou Enlai nianpu,* vol. 2, 721–22. The CCP soon launched a nationwide campaign to mobilize the people's support to aid Vietnam, which is reflected in the Second Bureau of Commerce, Shanghai Municipal Government, "Summary of the Resisting America and Aiding Vietnam Mo-

bilization Campaign," August 21, 1965, Quanzhong b98, Juanzhong 04, Anjuan 2147, 1–36, Shanghai Municipal Archives.

38. Zhou Enlai, speech (excerpt) at the CCP Politburo meeting, May 11, 1965, *Zhou Enlai nianpu,* vol. 2, 729–30.

39. Zhou Enlai, instruction on a report by Fang Yin on some problems concerning the foreign aid projects, May 15, 1965, *Zhou Enlai nianpu,* vol. 2, 730.

40. Zhou Enlai, minutes (excerpt) of meeting with Le Thanh Nghi, Vietnamese vice premier, July 13, 1965, *Zhou Enlai nianpu,* vol. 2, 743.

41. Mao's instruction to the State Council is cited in State Council's Instruction to Guangdong, Beijing, Shanghai, and Tianjin CCP authorities, November 15, 1967, B29, 2-1385, Shanghai Municipal Archives, Shanghai.

42. Mao Zedong, instruction, November 1965, *Jianguo yilai Mao Zedong wengao,* January 1964–December 1965, vol. 11, 478–89.

43. Zhou's instruction is enclosed in the State Council, instruction, "Requirements on Food Supplies to Vietnam," November 6, 1968, Quanzhong b98, Juanzhong 02, Anjuan 138, Shanghai Municipal Archives, Shanghai.

44. Supply agreement between the Kunming Military Command of China and the Northwestern Military Command of Vietnam, June 11, 1967, cited in Li Ke and Hao Shengzhang, *Wenhua dageming zhong de renmin jiefangjun,* 410–11.

45. Minutes of conversation (excerpt), Mao Zedong and Ho Chi Minh, May 16, 1965, in *77 Conversations between Chinese and Foreign Leaders on the Wars in Indochina, 1964–1977,* Cold War International History Project Working Paper 22, ed. Odd Arne Westad, Chen Jian, Stein Tønnesson, Nguyen Vu Tung, and James G. Hershberg (Washington, D.C.: Woodrow Wilson International Center for Scholars, 1998), 86–87.

46. Minutes of conversation (excerpt), Tao Zhu and Ho Chi Minh, April 13, 1965, in *77 Conversations,* ed. Westad et al., 87 n. 128.

47. Minutes of meeting between Zhou Enlai and Li Qiang, December 1970, as partially cited in *Dangdai zhongguo de duiwai jinji hezuo,* 51–52.

48. *Dangdai zhongguo de duiwai jinji hezuo,* 49, 192–93.

49. Guo Ming ed., *Zhong yue guanxi yanbian sishinian* [The evolution of Sino-Vietnamese relations over the last forty years] (Nanning: Guangxi People's Press, 1991), 71. See also *Dangdai zhongguo de duiwai jinji hezuo,* 199.

50. *Dangdai zhongguo de duiwai jinji hezuo,* 50.

51. Central Commission on Foreign Economy and Trade and the Ministry of Public Health, instructions, "On the Task of Aiding Vietnam with Machinery," May 29, 1967, Quanzhong b29, Juanzhong 02, Anjuan 1385, Shanghai Municipal Archives; and State Council, "On the Assignments of 'Aid-Vietnam' Program for Guangdong, Beijing, Shanghai, and Tianjin," November 15, 1967, Quanzhong b29, Juanzhong 02, Anjuan 1385, Shanghai Municipal Archives, Shanghai. See also *Dangdai zhongguo de duiwai jinji hezuo,* 163, 165.

52. Fang Yi, report to Zhou Enlai and the Central Committee, [undated] 1970, cited in *Dangdai zhongguo de duiwai jinji hezuo,* 51.

53. *Dangdai zhongguo de duiwai jinji hezuo,* 52, 57–58.

54. *Dangdai zhongguo de duiwai jinji hezuo,* 85–86.

55. *Dangdai zhongguo de duiwai jinji hezuo,* 50, 58–59.

56. *Dangdai zhongguo de duiwai jinji hezuo,* 86.

57. Minutes of conversation between Mao and Sihanouk, September 28, 1964, in *77 Conversations,* ed. Westad et al., 71.

58. Minutes of conversation between Zhou Enlai and Ayub Khan, April 2, 1965, in *77 Conversations,* ed. Westad et al., 84.

59. Minutes of conversation between Zhou Enlai and Ho Chi Minh, March 1, 1965, in *77 Conversations,* ed. Westad et al., 77–78.

60. Minutes of conversation between Zhou Enlai and Pham Van Dong, October 9, 1965, in *77 Conversations,* ed. Westad et al., 89.

61. Minutes of conversation between Zhou Enlai and Le Duan, March 23, 1966, in *77 Conversations,* ed. Westad et al., 93.

62. Minutes of conversation between Zhou Enlai, Deng Xiaoping and Ho Chi Minh, May 17, 1965, in *77 Conversations,* ed. Westad et al., 87.

63. Minutes of conversation between Zhou Enlai and Pham Van Dong, April 7, 1967, in *77 Conversations,* ed. Westad et al., 99.

64. Minutes of conversation between Zhou Enlai and Pham Van Dong, April 10, 1967, in *77 Conversations,* ed. Westad et al., 101.

65. Minutes of conversation between Qiao Guanhua and Ngo Minh Loan, May 13, 1967, in *77 Conversations,* ed. Westad et al., 121–23.

66. Minutes of conversation between Zhou Enlai and Vietnamese and Chinese delegations, April 11, 1967, in *77 Conversations,* ed. Westad et al., 107.

67. James C. Thomson Jr., National Security Council staff member, to McGeorge Bundy, the President's Special Assistant for National Security Affairs, October 28, 1964, U.S. Department of State, *Foreign Relations of the United States 1964–1968* (hereafter *FRUS*) (Washington, D.C.: U.S. Government Printing Office, 1998), vol. 30, 117. Thomson expressed his concern over the "danger in pushing too far the thesis of Peking's responsibility for the South Vietnam crisis."

68. Minutes of conversation between Dean Rusk and Chiang Kai-shek, 4–6 P.M., April 16, 1964, lot 66, D 110, CF2384/E, record group 59, Department of State Records, National Archives II, College Park, Md.

69. Thomson to Bundy, October 28, 1964, in *FRUS,* vol. 30, 117.

70. This consensus is reflected in Ray S. Cline, CIA deputy director to CIA director John McCone, December 6, 1965, in *FRUS,* vol. 30, 231.

71. NIE 13-9-65, "Communist China's Foreign Policy," May 5, 1965, in *FRUS,* vol. 30, 169–70.

72. "Critical Policy Problems," March 8, 1965, enclosed in Acting Deputy Under Secretary of State for Political Affairs Thompson to Rusk, July 15, 1965, in *FRUS,* vol. 30, 186.

73. NIE 13-5-66, "Communist China's Economic Prospect," January 13, 1966, in *FRUS,* vol. 30, 241–42.

74. Special State-Defense Study Group's report, "Communist China: Long Range Study," June 1966, in *FRUS,* vol. 30, 332–43.

75. NIE 13-9-65, "Communist China's Foreign Policy," May 5, 1965, in *FRUS,* vol. 30, 169.

76. Minutes of conversation, State–Defense joint meeting, August 27, 1965, in *FRUS,* vol. 30, 197.

77. "Critical Policy Problems," March 8, 1965, enclosed in Acting Deputy Under Secretary of State for Political Affairs Thompson to Rusk, July 15, 1965, in *FRUS,* vol. 30, 185–86.

78. NIE 1-12-66, "The Outlook for Sino-Soviet Relations," December 1, 1966, in *FRUS,* vol. 30, 479–89.

79. Policy paper, "The Taming of the Shrew: Communist China and the United Nations," drafted by Assistant Secretary of State J. Harlan Cleveland, October 31, 1964, UN 6 CHICOM, Central Files, Department of State, Record Group 59, National Archives II, College Park, Md.

80. James C. Thomson Jr., National Security Council staff member, to the President's Special Assistant for National Security Affairs Bundy, October 28, 1964, in *FRUS,* vol. 30, 118.

81. Bundy to Rusk, June 16, 1965, in *FRUS,* vol. 30, 174–75.

82. Thomson to Valenti, March 1, 1966, in *FRUS,* vol. 30, 262–64.

83. See Edward E. Rice, the consul general at Hong Kong, to Lyndon B. Johnson's special assistant Walt W. Rostow, April 15, 1966, in *FRUS,* vol. 30, 282–84; W. Averell Harriman, ambassador at large, to Johnson's special assistant William B. Moyers, June 3, 1966, in *FRUS,* vol. 30, 318–89; policy study paper, "Communist China: Long Range Study," prepared by special State–Defense study group, June 1966, in *FRUS,* vol. 30, 332–41; Rostow to Johnson, February 24, 1968, in *FRUS,* vol. 30, 662–65; William P. Bundy to Rusk, March 6, 1968, in *FRUS,* vol. 30, 666–69; and "Further Thoughts on China," paper prepared by Alfred Jenkins of National Security Council staff, October 9, 1968, in *FRUS,* vol. 30, 709–18.

84. Memorandum by the Board of National Estimate, CIA, "The China Tangle," September 23, 1966, in *FRUS,* vol. 30, 399–402.

85. NIE 13-7-67, "The Chinese Cultural Revolution," May 25, 1967, in *FRUS,* vol. 30, 573–74.

86. "Communist China: Long Range Study," prepared by special State–Defense study group, June 1966, in *FRUS,* vol. 30, 332–60.

87. Memorandum of conversation, Daniel I. Davidson, December 21, 1968, in *FRUS,* vol. 30, 726–78.

88. Rusk to Johnson, February 22, 1968, in *FRUS,* vol. 30, 645–6.

8

The Sino-Soviet Dispute over Assistance for Vietnam's Anti-American War, 1965–1972

Li Danhui

For the United States, Vietnam, China, and the Soviet Union alike, 1965 to 1972 were eventful years. The United States sent troops to South Vietnam, expanded its bombing of North Vietnam, escalated its invasion of Vietnam from "special warfare" to "local warfare," and then adopted the policy of "Vietnamization of the war." These were also the years when the armed liberation forces of North Vietnam and South Vietnam waged a total military and political contest with the United States. During the same period, the Soviet Union shifted its Vietnam policy from one of "staying away," as described above in chapter 2 of the present volume, to "lending a hand," and continuously increased its aid to Vietnam, boosting its military assistance in particular. Because the Soviet Union mostly supplied advanced weaponry still beyond China's capacity to produce, at least in bulk, at that time, Soviet prestige rose greatly in Vietnam, and the relationship between the two countries became much closer.

Meanwhile, as shown in chapters 9 and 10 below, the transition in the Soviet leadership from Nikita Khrushchev to Leonid Brezhnev did nothing to improve Sino-Soviet or Sino-Vietnamese relations. The new Soviet regime took a more uncompromising stance on China's policy toward the Soviet Union. The relationship between the two countries consequently remained tense, and for some time in 1969 war appeared imminent. In the 1970s, Sino-Soviet relations gradually moved from hostility to outright confrontation. Because the Soviet factor predominated in Mao Zedong's assessment of the international situation and China's external strategy, China overestimated the severity of the threat posed by the Soviet Union. And because China was faced with the prospect of growing closeness between Vietnam and the Soviet Union, even as it sent its neighbor massive amounts of aid, it became increasingly anxious and wary of Vietnam, and a rift began to develop between the two countries.

Unquestionably, had China and the Soviet Union been prepared to collaborate in supporting Vietnam, this would have represented the most beneficial strategy for the Vietnamese people's war to resist the United States and save their motherland. As documented in chapters 1 and 7 above, however, Chinese efforts to persuade Vietnam to decline Soviet aid proved unavailing, while China scornfully rejected several Vietnamese attempts to encourage Sino-Soviet reconciliation. From the Soviet perspective, however, the primary goal was to infiltrate politically and thus win control over the strategically important Southeast Asian region, and Vietnam presented the best avenue whereby this objective might be achieved. As the Sino-Soviet relationship continued to deteriorate, the Soviet Union felt compelled to use all possible means to win over Vietnam as an ally, to bring about China's complete strategic encirclement, and preclude excessive vulnerability on its own part should a reconciliation between China and the United States occur.

From the Chinese viewpoint, to guarantee that Vietnam, an important regional power, would always remain aligned with China, the Soviet Union could not be allowed to gain the advantage in winning over the Vietnamese. Fearing China would face a Soviet threat on its southern border, which would complete their country's encirclement, Chinese officials did not want the Soviet Union to incorporate Vietnam into its strategic sphere of influence and fill the gap left once the United States withdrew its troops from the country.[1] Although the Vietnamese had by the late 1960s already decided to conclude a formal alliance with the Soviets,[2] they were reluctant to lose the substantial quantity of aid they received from China, which generally arrived more directly and promptly than its Soviet equivalent, and so sought to continue to appear at least superficially neutral in the Sino-Soviet confrontation.

These assorted considerations made it impossible for the Soviet Union and China to collaborate and join forces to assist Vietnam. Even worse, the conflict of interests they provoked led the two powers to engage in a contest of will and compete for Vietnam's favor. Consequently, China and the Soviet Union, while both aiding Vietnam, experienced constant friction with each other, and sometimes even intense confrontational clashes. This chapter, which is based on relevant archival materials, divides this period into two stages, 1965–69 and 1970–72, to present a historical review of these Sino-Soviet conflicts and confrontations and to trace their development and evolution.[3]

The 1965–69 Period

Between 1965 and 1969, the relationship between the Soviet Union and China gradually moved toward hostility. During this period, the relationship between the Soviet and Chinese communist parties broke down and that between the two nations continued to deteriorate. In March 1969, large-scale Sino-Soviet military clashes occurred on Zhenbao Island. In August, the Soviet Union took retaliatory actions in the Tielieketi area of Yunming County in China's Xinjiang Province, causing serious bloodshed. China and the Soviet Union reached their highest point of tension and entered the stage of outright antagonism. Simultaneously, with the continuous augmentation of Soviet military and economic aid to Vietnam, the relationship between Vietnam and the Soviet Union began warming.

Against this background, during this period there emerged two notable issues related to China's support for Vietnam against the United States. First, in the time up to Ho Chi Minh's death in September 1969, China made various subtle changes in some areas of its Vietnam policy, without altering the premise of its general principle. For instance, China began to emphasize to Vietnam that it should not depend too heavily on military support from other countries but should instead follow a strict policy of independence and self-reliance, and utilize its domestic human and material resources more efficiently. China had not yet provided all of the hundred aid items it had promised to deliver in 1968, and had only supplied 31.4 percent of the aid it had agreed to give during the first six months of 1969. By the end of 1970, various Chinese import and export corporations under the Ministry of Foreign Trade still owed Vietnam some aid supplies without strings pledged for 1967.[4] The primary underlying reason for these subtle signals of Chinese displeasure lay in China's resentment of the ever in-creasing closeness between Vietnam and the Soviet Union; they were in-tended to exert pressure on Vietnam and did not signify a change in China's overall Vietnam policy.

Second, China and the Soviet Union engaged in a series of hostile and sometimes even fierce confrontations. These manifested themselves in well-publicized disputes over Soviet military aid action plans, the dispatch of Soviet volunteers to Vietnam, and the delivery and transshipment of Soviet aid.

The Sino-Soviet Dispute over Soviet Military Aid Action Plans

After the visit of Soviet premier Aleksei Kosygin to Vietnam in February 1965, the Soviet Union drew up a new military aid action plan. In accor-dance with this plan, on February 25 the Soviet Central Communist Party and the Soviet government submitted three verbal requests through the Soviet embassy in China: first, that a brigade of combat troops and other ar-mored personnel, numbering 4,000 in all, would be dispatched to Vietnam over Chinese railroads; second, that China reserve one or two air bases, Kunming Airfield, for example, for use by Soviet MiG-21 interceptors, and also allow 500 active Soviet military personnel to be stationed there to se-cure the airfields; and third, that the Soviet Union would open an air route over Chinese territorial airspace for shipping Soviet airplanes and other supplies required by Soviet military personnel in Vietnam. To further em-phasize the emergency nature of these three requests, on February 27 the Soviet Union, through its Embassy in Beijing, demanded that, because the Vietnamese urgently needed Russian help, China should permit them to fly forty-five airplanes through Chinese airspace to deliver eighteen antiaircraft guns and seventy-five antiaircraft machine guns to Vietnam.[5]

On March 10, the Chinese government responded officially, through diplomatic channels, to the Soviet government's three verbal requests of February 25, declaring that the military actions the Soviet Union proposed went beyond the normal scope of military aid. China rejected the first Soviet request, arguing that Vietnam itself did not favor the entry and stationing of Soviet combat troops in Vietnam. China declined the request to establish an air force combat base, pointing out that using Chinese airfields would mean a long flight time for Soviet airplanes and would not achieve the objective of protecting Vietnam's airspace. As for the third request, for passage through China's airspace, China had already responded on February 28 that large-scale air shipments were incompatible with the principle of absolute secrecy advocated by the Soviet Union, and it suggested relying instead on land shipments.

At this time, China reiterated its argument that whatever limited weaponry and combat supplies the Soviet Union was giving to Vietnam would prove inadequate to intimidate the enemy into retreating, whereas repeated flights of Soviet airplanes to and from China would speedily alert the enemy to the Soviet presence. The Chinese also pointed out that to launch such major operations without prior negotiations among Vietnam, China, and the Soviet Union would constitute an imposition on China, which was therefore quite unable to assent to the Soviet military action plan. The Chinese reply also claimed that the Soviet requests would effectively place China, the Soviet Union, and North Vietnam in the immediate position of waging open warfare against the United States, thereby complicating the existing ongoing anti–United States struggle of the Vietnamese people.

To sum up, from the Chinese government's perspective, the Soviet Union's request proved its ulterior motives. For instance, the Soviet Union requested the emergency shipping of antiaircraft weapons to Vietnam, but it waited until March 8 to hand these over to the Chinese, who then completed their delivery to Vietnam within two days. China queried why, if the matter was so urgent, the Soviet Union waited eight days to hand these over.[6] The Soviet Union's behavior provoked numerous misgivings among Chinese leaders, who felt that, in the current state of Sino-Soviet relations, such requests constituted an invasion of China's sovereignty and threatened Chinese national security.

Moscow used China's discouraging response to launch unbridled propaganda attacks against China, alleging that it sought to block Soviet aid to Vietnam. During the Moscow conference in March 1965, Soviet leaders again announced that, because it was of the utmost importance to shield northern Vietnamese cities as soon as possible against attack from the U.S. Air Force, they were requesting China to allow Soviet transport planes carrying military technology and essential military experts to overfly Chinese airspace. China once more rejected this request, arguing that Soviet airplanes passing over China ran the risk of discovery by the enemy and "suffering unnecessary losses."

A few days later, Chinese leaders put forward another, extremely im-
plausible, justification, namely, that they viewed the Soviet request to transport air force personnel and supplies through Chinese airspace as purely an
attempt to "control China and Vietnam." Chinese officials advanced this
speculation unblushingly, despite the absurdity of the suggestion that a few
hundred men on China's border with the Vietnamese Democratic Republic
"could control" China, a nation of 650 million people. The Soviet Union in
turn riposted that, due to China's attitude, although the United States was
intensifying its invasion of Vietnam, the military technology and equipment, primarily antiaircraft equipment, which the Soviet Union provided to
Vietnam had to be transported far more slowly overland. Even so, thanks to
Soviet efforts, some of this equipment did make its way to Vietnam.[7]

When considering its response, the Chinese Foreign Ministry believed
that, although the present was not an appropriate moment for public refuta-
tion, Chinese officials must inform interested parties of their country's position. They asked Chinese foreign affairs personnel to clarify the facts in
their conversations with overseas leftists and middle elements, and to explain that the Soviet Union, since its "divisive Moscow Conference," had
"set off a rumor mongering campaign, accusing China of blocking its aid
efforts to Vietnam and instigating anti-China sentiments among people who
did not know the true picture." But the only basis for this rumor was a disagreement over eighteen antiaircraft guns and seventy-five antiaircraft machine guns, which China believed it was neither necessary nor desirable to
transport by air, and so had naturally suggested shipping overland instead.
Moreover, China had spared no effort to help Vietnam obtain whatever it
needed and the Soviet Union was prepared to provide; it had followed this
policy in the past and would continue to do so in the future. The Vietnamese
comrades knew this, as did the Soviet comrades, and these facts could not
be disputed. But the Soviet Union had twisted these facts and, in a pre-
meditated anti-Chinese move, falsely accused China of obstructing Soviet
aid to Vietnam.[8]

In May 1967, the Soviet Union again reopened this earlier dispute, by
asking to transport twelve M-17 and twelve M-21 airplanes through Chinese airspace, a request the Chinese naturally once more rejected. China
believed that the Soviet suggestion of allowing these planes to overfly Chinese territory was a deliberate scheme to disclose secret military information to the enemy and implicate China in the Vietnam conflict. China resented the fact that the Soviet Union sought to force it to acquiesce in such
a large military operation without proper consultation, believing that this

displayed outright great-power chauvinism. Calculating that China would probably not agree to this proposal, North Vietnam, while relaying the Soviet message, alternatively proposed transporting the airplanes by rail, which the Chinese accepted.[9]

China's Reaction to the Dispatch
of Soviet Aid Volunteers to Vietnam

On March 23, 1965, Soviet general secretary Brezhnev spoke at the mass victory rally for Soviet pilots on Moscow's Red Square, and for the first time he mentioned that the central government had received numerous letters from Soviet citizens, expressing their readiness to join the Vietnamese people's struggle for freedom and independence, and that the Soviet government greatly appreciated the fraternal solidarity and sentiments of proletarian internationalism displayed by the Soviet people. Subsequently, on April 17, the Soviet Union publicly announced, in the joint communiqué published following the visit to Moscow by Vietnamese Communist Party and government delegates, headed by party secretary Le Duan, that if the United States intensified its invasion of the Vietnamese Democratic Republic, the Soviet Union would agree to send Soviet citizens to Vietnam, should circumstances warrant this and Vietnam request it.[10]

In practice, Brezhnev's remarks were only intended to state the Soviet position with regard to the call for aid (including volunteers) from socialist countries issued by the South Vietnam People's Liberation Front on March 22. At this time, Vietnam had no intention of making any substantive request for Soviet volunteers. On March 26, during a meeting with Ilia S. Scherbakov, the Soviet ambassador to Vietnam, Vietnamese deputy foreign minister Hoang Van Loi disclosed that, while the South Vietnam People's Liberation Front expressed its gratitude for the Soviet offer of volunteers, as yet it did not need any, though it would request them later if this became necessary.[11] Hence, the Soviet government's declaration was nothing more than political posturing. The rhetoric about sending volunteers served mainly as a propaganda tool designed to exert pressure on the United States; its political significance outweighed its military importance.

Nonetheless, the Soviet Union's position annoyed China. Chinese leaders communicated China's dissatisfaction when the Vietnamese side expressed gratitude for the Soviet offer of volunteers. In October 1965, Zhou Enlai, meeting with Pham Van Dong, North Vietnam's premier, stated that he did not support the idea of sending Soviet volunteers to Vietnam, and

Chinese Politburo member Peng Zhen and Luo Ruiqing, the People's Liberation Army chief of staff, shared his view. In March 1966, while discussing with Duan Vietnam's request that socialist countries send volunteer pilots, Zhou specifically warned that the Soviet Union might reveal this secret to the enemy, and he suggested that whatever little help Vietnam might gain from Soviet pilots would not suffice to compensate for the losses they caused. In August, using the excuse that Chinese aid personnel in Vietnam were regular military forces, Zhou officially told Dong that China had a right to reject the request of other nations to send volunteers to Vietnam.[12]

Sino-Soviet Disputes over the Passage of Aid Supplies

Because the most convenient and practical route to ship aid supplies from other socialist nations to the Vietnamese Democratic Republic was across Chinese territory, throughout the entire period in which China was supporting Vietnam against the United States, Chinese railroads became an important conduit for transporting to Vietnam, free of charge, equipment sent by the Soviet Union, North Korea, Mongolia, Eastern European countries, and other socialist nations.[13] During this time, the Soviet Union and China battled fiercely over transporting Soviet supplies along Chinese rails, disputes whose complexity demonstrated only too well the conflicts between China and the Soviet Union over the issue of aid to Vietnam.

In February 1965, Soviet premier Kosygin twice passed through China on his way to Vietnam, and he told Zhou that, now that the United States was bombing northern Vietnam, the Soviet Union could move boldly ahead with aid to Vietnam, and it would provide cannons, tanks, and surface-to-air missiles free of charge. Zhou expressed his hope that the Soviet Union would deliver these weapons speedily, and he stated that China would help to ship them along Chinese railroads. Mao, meeting with Kosygin on February 11, also promised that China would assist the Soviet Union to transport Soviet military equipment to Vietnam expeditiously.

Later, on March 30, 1965, China and the Soviet Union concluded and signed an agreement governing the transit of special supplies from the Soviet government to the Vietnamese Democratic Republic. China subsequently made the issue of transit its top priority, and it set up a special team to handle this task.[14] In July, Chinese and Vietnamese transportation delegates convened meetings in Beijing, initialing a summary of their meetings on July 26. They agreed that, during the second half of 1965, China would transport a projected 148,500 tons of aid supplies from the Soviet Union and other East European nations, of which 55,000 tons would be military equipment and 75,000 tons nonmilitary commodities.[15]

According to Chinese records, in March 1965 China shipped to Vietnam more than 150 truckloads of supplies specified on Soviet shipping lists. From April to October 1965, the Soviet Union planned to transship about forty trainloads of military equipment. On May 26, the Soviet Union and Vietnam reached another agreement in Moscow, committing the Soviet Union to deliver various supplemental supplies to Vietnam, with whose transit China was asked to assist. Between 1965 and 1968 a total of 179 trains, comprising 5,750 cars of aid supplies, traveled along Chinese railroads to Vietnam. The Chinese believed that, from the very beginning right to the end, they loyally fulfilled their commitments, followed the agreements strictly, and organized full, timely, and safe deliveries of Soviet aid.[16]

Yet, even in early July 1965, in a letter addressed to the Central Chinese Communist Party, the Soviet government accused China of failing to transport Soviet aid supplies expeditiously. In response, the Chinese government sent the Soviets a letter refuting the accusation. The Soviet government, however, continued to allege that the Chinese government had broken Comrade Mao's promise and, ever since the Soviet Union began to ship military resources to Vietnam, had begun to make trouble. Moreover, they charged, Chinese government representatives blocked the transportation of Soviet supplies to Vietnam after the Soviet Union and the Vietnamese Democratic Republic had agreed to increase consignments of military equipment and to accelerate their shipment.[17]

What were the facts of the matter? Indeed, is it even possible to distinguish between facts and accusations? When dealing with the issue of transporting aid supplies from the Soviet Union and other countries to Vietnam, China followed a consistent pattern. Once a donor nation initiated a request for transshipment, China would first consult with the recipient nation, namely, Vietnam, and coordinate shipping plans with it, and then reach a corresponding agreement with the donor nation. On August 26, 1965, the Soviet Union submitted to China's Overseas Economic Liaison Committee a request for the transit of additional military aid supplies to Vietnam over the period 1965–67. The Chinese side followed its usual practice, whereby on September 2 the Chinese ambassador to Vietnam informed Vietnam's Foreign Ministry of the Soviet request, and repeatedly, on September 17, September 27, and October 7, urged Vietnam to respond.

Meanwhile, between September 18 and October 18, 1965, officials of China's Overseas Economic Liaison Committee explained five times to

Soviet Overseas Economic Liaison Committee representatives and military attachés that, once China received Vietnam's response, they would initiate discussions to finalize an agreement with the Soviet Union. By early November, Vietnam had still not responded. China then temporarily set aside the Soviet request. In response to a request for a speedy agreement that Soviet Overseas Economic Liaison Committee representatives submitted on October 7 to their Chinese counterparts, China declared that it would not accept these Soviet military materials for transit until it had a chance to find out "which among this batch of the Soviet military equipment were needed first by Vietnam, what time frame Vietnam had in mind, and what technological capabilities were required to accept the technological equipment." Accordingly, China announced to the Soviet representatives that it would deny passage to a series of transport vehicles carrying Soviet military equipment. This affected the movement of ten aircraft repair trucks and forty antiaircraft guns.[18]

Before long, however, China became more accommodating in response to special circumstances. With Vietnamese concurrence, on October 12, 1965, Chinese officials contacted Soviet military attachés and proposed that China and the Soviet Union exchange letters with each other dealing specifically with the passage of these two categories of items, repair trucks and antiaircraft guns, so that these could be shipped to Vietnam even before the supplemental agreement was signed. China followed up with repeated requests for a response, but after lengthy discussions the Soviet Union submitted none. When questioned as to their government's intentions, the military attachés and other Soviet representatives indicated that they themselves were ignorant of these. In a letter of October 21 to the Chinese government, the Soviet Union accused China of "deliberately delaying the signing" of the agreement and denying transit to the aforementioned supplies. Replying on November 5, China stated that it was as clear as daylight that the Soviet Union was solely to blame for the delay in transporting these particular items. China counterattacked further, claiming that the Soviet Union purposely "made trouble out of nothing, insisted on deliberate slandering," and intentionally turned things upside down, all with the intent of manufacturing malicious gossip that could be used for anti-Chinese propaganda.[19]

Additionally, in the actual process of transporting Soviet supplies, China insisted on strictly following the agreement and was unwilling to change its own shipping plans to accommodate the Soviet Union. The Soviet side, by contrast, emphasized that because this was an unusual time, the aid operation need not be conducted according to the strict letter of the agreement but could be handled more flexibly. Therefore, the Soviet Union frequently violated the various Sino-Soviet transit agreements. Sometimes it failed to deliver projected shipments on time; sometimes it failed to dispatch trains as agreed; and sometimes unscheduled Soviet trains even showed up at stations within China's borders without any notice. The Chinese felt this pattern not only totally disrupted their plans but also made it impossible for them to coordinate their transit plans with Vietnam. Such behavior violated their agreements and seriously hampered the smooth transmission of aid supplies.

On September 2, 1965, Li Qiang, the deputy director of China's Overseas Economic Liaison Committee, met with representatives from the Soviet side and pointed out that Soviet conduct was designed to create a situation in which, if China accepted supplies transported in violation of the agreement, the Soviet Union would feel free to disrupt the transit schedules China and Vietnam had arranged. Conversely, if China refused to acquiesce, the Soviet Union would spread rumors that China was attempting to block the passage of Soviet materials. Li declared that China firmly opposed such conduct. The Soviet representatives gave their word that from then onward, they would take effective measures to conduct business in accordance with the agreement.

The problem was that, after this exchange, the situation remained unchanged. Even in September 1965, trains dispatched without prior scheduling or in disregard of established arrangements made up 72 percent of the total. Between September 18 and October 23, China therefore contacted the Soviet embassy on ten occasions, stating that, if this problem was not resolved, the Soviet Union would have to take full responsibility for all delays in shipping. The Soviet representatives thanked China for "showing immense patience in the face of work obstacles created by Soviet errors," and it promised to get to the root of the problem and prevent further disruptions occurring on their side. They also earnestly requested China "not to give up hope on the Soviet Union."[20]

Unfortunately, however, such incidents continued to recur. On November 25, 1965, for instance, a batch of explosives and demolition equipment from the Soviet Union and Poland that China was to store for Vietnam arrived in China ahead of schedule, creating operational difficulties for China's Foreign Trade Corporation. In early April 1966, another consignment of explosives and detonators arrived from Poland; because Soviet officials had mishandled the paperwork as the shipment passed through their country, the inventory and contents did not tally. Fortunately, the errors were discovered sufficiently early enough for adjustments to be made; otherwise, the discrepancies would have added another chapter to the saga of Sino-Soviet disputes.[21]

While visiting Hungary toward the end of April 1966, Soviet defense minister Rodion Malinovski commented that, because the Soviet Union and Vietnam shared no common border, Soviet aid materials had to pass through China, and Soviet assistance would have been more effective if China had not tried to block the transit of Soviet aid materials. On May 4, the spokesperson for China's Foreign Affairs Ministry publicized China's counterdenunciation, proclaiming that China had given all military resources from the Soviet Union priority and swift and free shipping, and by the end of 1965 had transported more than 40,000 tons of such supplies from the Soviet Union to Vietnam.

The Chinese statement also pointed out that, in quality and quantity, Soviet military aid was unworthy of its national might; not only were the amounts small, but all the weapons were outdated and some even damaged. For the first quarter of 1966, the Soviet Union had asked China to prepare a shipping capacity of 1,730 cars, to which China agreed and made the necessary arrangements; but in practice Soviet supplies only filled 556 cars. And the Chinese queried why—although the Soviet Union likewise had no shared border with Cuba, and in fact the distance between them was greater than that from the Soviet Union to Vietnam—the Soviets found it possible to ship rockets and nuclear weapons to and from Cuba, yet could not even complete the shipping of conventional weapons the relatively short distance to Vietnam. Again, the Soviet Union and India had no common border, but the Soviet Union managed to shift massive amounts of equipment by sea to support India in its conflict with China. Why, then, could it not move its aid supplies by ship to help the Vietnamese people fight the American imperialists?[22]

In early July 1966, the *People's Daily* published a special editorial, exposing the alleged lies circulated by Soviet revisionists and declaring:

China has agreed to help transport and has never tried to block military aid supplies accepted by the Vietnamese. As soon as Soviet aid materials arrive at the Chinese border, the Chinese railroad system transports them right away, using express military transportation. China has never stalled for time, nor did it ever keep materials too long in storage. Moreover, the Chinese railroad system has provided all the shipping free of charge. We have never sought a rouble, a dollar or half a gram of gold from the Soviet government, let alone military goods such as land-to-air missiles.[23]

China and the Soviet Union indulged in frequent verbal bickering over the transit of Soviet aid materials over Chinese rails. This placed the Vietnamese, who eagerly sought obtain massive quantities of such supplies, in a dilemma. To ensure that military resources would be transported to Vietnam as a first priority, Vietnam took two measures. First, in early 1966, the Vietnamese government informed China that Vietnam had concluded an agreement with the Soviet Union and other Eastern European nations to arrange direct shipment to Vietnam's harbors of the bulk of their economic assistance and equipment.[24]

Second, while bearing in mind that it must not offend the Soviet Union, on which it was so heavily dependent, Vietnam also tried to defend China. On June 19, 1966, Vietnam's central news agency received permission to publish a statement deflecting the spearhead of criticism upon the West: "China has always made great efforts to help transport military materials from the Soviet Union and other nations as scheduled. Western media organizations have broadcast the so-called news that 'transit materials have experienced blockages.' This is pure fabrication, and an extremely despicable conspiracy to instigate discord." On February 28, 1967, Vietnam again declared that China had "transported properly and according to schedule all aid materials from the Soviet Union and other nations to Vietnam."[25]

Since Chinese railroads continued to carry the bulk of Soviet military aid supplies, on February 10, 1968, China and the Soviet Union reached a new agreement on this specific issue. Its implementation, however, still remained highly problematic. In early 1969, the Soviet Union accused China of refusing to transport military vehicles that the Soviet Union had made available for Vietnam's use, between January and March forcing the Soviets to defer repeatedly the dispatch of trains carrying missile technology equipment. According to Soviet records, more than 500 trucks for transporting missile weapons were periodically reloaded and dispatched to the Sino-Soviet border, only to be returned to their place of origin. The Soviet Foreign Ministry reported that, in early March, representatives of the Soviet Overseas Economic Committee repeatedly requested meetings with appropriate Chinese personnel so as to announce that, under the agreement, a fresh military train had been dispatched. The Chinese side initially cited busy schedules as an excuse to defer such a meeting, and when they even-

tually met flatly refused to accept the shipment, giving the reason that the
notification had come too late. Moreover, the Chinese representatives were
verbally crude and passionately anti-Soviet in sentiment.

The Soviet report also charged that China, in violation of the new agreement, had again begun to present obstacles to the transit of military materials from the Soviet Union and other socialist countries. Vietnam itself, the
report stated, was quite concerned over the results of negotiations between
China and Vietnam on the transit of military materials from the Soviet
Union and other socialist countries during 1969, and once even emphati-
cally pointed out to the Soviet Union that the reason China was making difficulties over the movement of aid materials was that it wished Vietnam to
break away from the Soviet Union. The transportation of military materials
would likewise also face hurdles. That same year, as China and the Soviet
Union drew ever closer to war, China halted its overland transshipments of
Soviet aid supplies to Vietnam.[26] For a while, the Soviet Union relied exclusively on the sea lanes to transport aid materials to Vietnam, though that
same year it opened alternative air shipping routes over Laos, Burma, and
India.

Besides the railroads, Chinese ports also played some part in transferring
Soviet aid materials. In practice, however, Sino-Soviet disputes over rail
transportation and the encouragement of Vietnam-U.S. peace talks interfered
with the concrete process of transporting supplies from Chinese harbors, so
most freight the Soviet Union shipped by sea went directly to North Vietnam.
Where "ocean shipping" was concerned, the summary of talks initialed in
July 1965 by Chinese and Vietnamese transportation delegations specified
that, when the Vietnamese railroads lacked the capability to carry all the aid
materials and normal commercial products in transit through China, Vietnam
would coordinate with the relevant receiving department to switch these to
ocean shipping, and China would do its best to provide the necessary shipping and dispatch such goods in a timely manner.[27]

Not long after the agreement was signed, however, when refuting Soviet
propaganda that "China was blocking the border transit of Soviet aid materials," China asked the Soviet Union why the latter could not utilize its numerous oceangoing freighters to carry its own military materials to Vietnam:
"Why have you not yet supplied the warships, which you promised our Vietnamese comrades last February, directly to their naval harbors, rather than
trying to hand them over to our Vietnamese comrades by way of Chinese
ports?" China considered simply untruthful the Soviet explanation that, because the United States had sealed off Vietnam from the Soviet Union and

Vietnam had no common border, passage through Chinese territory was the "only realistic way." According to China, it was common knowledge that ships of all nations, including many Chinese vessels and some Soviet ones, managed to enter and exit Vietnamese ports; the only difficulty was that the Soviet Union feared the United States and therefore would not use its own ships to transport military aid equipment to the Vietnamese people.[28]

In retrospect, the Chinese criticism was rather far-fetched. Moving military equipment by rail was undoubtedly faster and safer than ocean freight. In addition, the Soviet Union proposed using Chinese railroads to transport military supplies because the Vietnamese urgently requested that such materials be given priority and delivered as fast as possible. Moreover, the Soviet Union did not rely entirely on China's land and water shipping facilities. Military equipment aside, for the second half of 1965 the Soviet Union and Eastern European nations scheduled shipments of 592,000 tons of nonmilitary goods, 447,900 of which went directly to Vietnam by sea without passing through China. This represented six times the quantity of nonmilitary goods (75,000 tons) and eight times that of military supplies (55,000 tons) concurrently scheduled to travel over Chinese railroads, and it constituted a substantial proportion of overall Soviet shipments to Vietnam.[29] In practice, had it not been for the existing friction between China and the Soviet Union, neither rail nor ocean transfers of Soviet aid materials would have caused any problems.

Until 1966, the Soviet Union never suspended the dispatch of ships loaded with goods and materials from Soviet ports to Vietnam, and about twenty ships were constantly engaged in transporting supplies to Vietnam. By July 18, 1966, those materials scheduled for shipping, in the process of shipping, or already shipped totaled more than 110,000 tons. According to reports from the Soviet Ocean Transportation Department, the problem was that Vietnamese naval functionaries deliberately delayed the unloading of Soviet ships, believing that the more Soviet ships there were moored within coastal defense areas, the safer the port would be. Moreover, Vietnamese pilots would guide Chinese ships to avoid areas of dangerous water, but they quite specifically directed Soviet ships through these to check whether they held any concealed deep-water mines.[30] The Soviets therefore hoped that the Chinese would take over more ocean shipping.

In April 1967, while meeting with Zhou Enlai, Pham Van Dong conveyed the following suggestions from the Soviet Union: first, that China increase the amount of aid materials it shipped, from 10,000 to 30,000 tons per month; and second, that China open two or three ports to load and unload

Soviet supplies. Replying to the first request, China replied that it could not commit itself to such a policy without first undertaking a full analysis of the situation. As to the second, China clearly responded that, because Vietnamese coastal defense ports had not to date been bombed, it was therefore unnecessary to utilize Chinese ports, and China expressed suspicions that the Soviet request to use Chinese harbors had ulterior motives beyond facilitating the transfer of aid supplies.[31]

The 1970–72 Period

From 1970 to 1972, the Sino-Soviet relationship began a metamorphosis from hostility to outright political and military confrontation. During this period, China focused on shifting its diplomatic strategies, seeking to modify its vulnerable position of facing enemies on both sides—the Soviet Union and the United States—by instigating a reconciliation with the United States that would enable the two to take joint action against the Soviet Union, their common chief enemy.

Against this background, the evolution of China's support for Vietnam's anti–United States war during this period displayed two prominent features. The first was that, by comparison with the 1960s, for several reasons China greatly increased the amount of its material aid to Vietnam, a development also described in chapter 10 below. First, after the death of Ho Chi Minh in September 1969, pro-Soviet forces totally controlled Vietnam's Communist Party leadership. Because of the prevailing tense relationship between China and the Soviet Union, the area of Indochina appeared particularly crucial to China's national security. Hence, China found the development of the Soviet-Vietnamese relationship even more sensitive, and it hoped to retain Vietnam's favor through intensified aid efforts, thereby preventing Vietnam falling within the Soviet sphere.

Second, as peace negotiations continued, in preparation for what they anticipated would be a subsequent North Vietnamese war to conquer and unify South Vietnam, both China and Vietnam wished to rush more weapons to the southern part of the country before the war ended and international scrutiny was imposed.[32] Third, China needed to support the spring 1973 Easter Offensive strategy that Vietnam launched against the United States on the southern battlefields in the hope of facilitating a greater military victory, which would impel the United States to extricate itself swiftly from enmirement in the Vietnam War. Simultaneously, China was persuading

Vietnam to compromise at the negotiating table, in the hope of ending the war as expeditiously as possible, so that continuing hostilities would not delay the early realization of China's strategic goal of aligning itself with the United States against the Soviet Union.[33]

As soon as late September 1969, therefore, after Mao's discussion with Dong on the possibility of using some Chinese provinces as aid bases for Vietnam, four Chinese provinces—Guangdong, Guangxi, Yunnan, and Hunan—quickly established Vietnam aid leadership teams and began negotiating with those Vietnamese provinces receiving aid to determine their requirements.[34] In September 1970, Zhou promised Vietnam's leaders that China was determined to satisfy Vietnam's overall needs and was committed to bending all its energies to help Vietnam. Even more specifically, Mao emphasized to Dong that all those who said China had its difficulties and should not help Vietnam were reactionaries, and, in November, authorized raising the monetary value of aid supplies to Vietnam from 2 to 5 million renminbi. The Ministry of Foreign Trade sent a notice to all import and export companies, requesting them to check whether they still had any outstanding orders related to Chinese aid donated to Vietnam since 1967 and stating that, if so, they should make every effort to complete these in the near future.[35]

In March 1971, the Chinese government affirmed its policy of further boosting Vietnam aid efforts.[36] From 1971 to 1973, China sent Vietnam the greatest quantity of such supplies, in a massive scale aid program. During this period, China agreed to provide a total of 90 billion renminbi worth of such assistance, and in the final two years donated more military aid than in the entire two previous decades.[37]

Simultaneously, though, China also actively encouraged Vietnam to obtain more supplies from the Soviet Union.[38] China's Marshal Ye Jianying, a member of the Politburo's Central Committee and vice chairman of the Central Military Commission, told Le Ban and others, for instance, that Vietnam should ask the Soviet Union to send weapons, food, useful supplies, indeed everything, the more the better, which could be stored in China even if they could not be transferred immediately. Li Qiang also discussed with Vietnamese officials whether the latter should request the Soviet Union to dispatch more weapons and munitions. When Truong Chinh visited China, Zhou also advised him that Vietnam should obtain more trucks and other goods from the Soviet Union.[39] Although China adopted this policy to alleviate its own burdens, it also intended to use this opportunity to create conflict between the Soviet Union and Vietnam. China hoped that Vietnam, unhappy with the Soviet Union's inability to meet its requests, would develop a grudge against the Soviets, thereby instigating increasing dissension and discord within the Soviet camp.

Concurrently, another significant change occurred in the process of China's efforts to assist Vietnam; namely, China adjusted its attitude and policy toward the Soviet Union's intensified aid to Vietnam, and in particular on the transfer of Soviet aid supplies through China. Disputes, tensions, and conflicts between China and the Soviet Union over large-scale aid operations consequently moderated somewhat, a change particularly noticeable after the South Vietnamese Liberation armed forces launched a full-scale military offensive in March 1972.

During this period, China not only allowed the passage of large quantities of Soviet military supplies through China but also—in four ways—took the initiative in advising Vietnam to pressure the Soviet Union to accelerate their shipping. First, in January, March, and April 1972, China signed agreements covering the transportation to Vietnam during 1972 of special materials from the Soviet Union, East Germany, Bulgaria, Romania, and other socialist nations; thereafter, the Chinese encouraged Vietnamese officials to persuade the Soviets to expedite these shipments.[40] Soon afterward, on the night of May 20, when meeting with Le Duan and Ngo Thuyen, Vietnam's ambassador to China, Zhou proposed that Vietnam should urge the Soviet Union and other Eastern European nations to accelerate moving those materials already pledged that Vietnam still required, to which China was prepared to offer free shipment. In late August, China again asked Vietnam to press the Soviet Union to rush-ship by rail 50,000 tons of flour that had originally been scheduled for ocean shipment that month but had not yet arrived.[41] In addition, China actively sought ways and means to accelerate the shipping of Soviet and Eastern European aid supplies, advising Vietnam, for example, to open up more highways and add more routes. China also suggested that missiles from China itself and military supplies in transit from elsewhere should travel by separate routes, and that some materials could be shipped directly, using through transportation.[42]

Second, China agreed to allow experts in "special materials" escorting such train shipments to pass through China and, moreover, during a period of less than six months, increased the maximum number of such personnel permitted in China at any one time from forty-six to sixty. On one occasion, with Zhou's permission, 400 unarmed Soviet military personnel passed through China accompanying aid supplies.[43]

Third, on June 18, 1972, Zhou told Le Duc Tho that China would allow freight ships from the Soviet Union, Cuba, and Eastern European countries to unload their contents at Chinese ports, reopening to the Soviet Union the door to ocean transportation of aid supplies. The Vietnamese government was profoundly grateful, considering this one of the highest examples of support given to the Vietnamese people's war of resistance to preserve their motherland from the United States. Shortly afterward, on July 10, China and Vietnam signed an agreement specifying that such materials as grains, steel, oil, sugar, and bagged chemical fertilizers shipped by sea from the Soviet Union to China would be transshipped either by land or by sea.[44] In early August, Li Qiang told Vietnam that, except for a very few categories (e.g., yellow iron minerals, potato seeds, and perishable goods), China was willing without exception to accept all goods, even chicken incubators.[45] In reality, these were no longer urgent war requirements. At this time, China not only permitted Soviet ships to unload in Chinese ports but even allowed the shipment of Soviet helicopter parts to the port of Zhanjiang, where they were assembled and test flown at Zhanjiang Airport.[46] Anxiety over the "air corridor," so pronounced in the mid-1960s, had apparently greatly declined.

Fourth, China again began storing aid materials sent from the Soviet Union and other nations and designated for Vietnam.[47] The United States resumed bombing the southern portions of the Democratic Republic of Vietnam in April 1972, and in May it sealed off Vietnamese ports with mines. Worried that the Soviet Union and Eastern European nations would not negotiate aid agreements for 1973 because the 1972 Vietnamese aid agreements were not yet completely implemented, in June 1972 Le Thanh Nghi specifically directed Le Ban to consult with Li Qiang and also to seek Li Xiannian's permission and agreement that China would transport and store within China urgently needed aid supplies from the Soviet Union and other Eastern European nations. Le made it clear that China should feel free to use these goods (mainly guns, steel, and oil) initially, and in turn substitute its own supplies when Vietnam could receive these. In addition, Vietnam asked China to reinstate its past practice of 1966 and 1967, of providing storage warehouses for Soviet military equipment. China agreed to all these requests, submitting to Vietnam a preliminary version of the exchange of letters on the storage of materials, which Vietnam approved.[48]

When Vietnam instructed China to proceed to use the aid supplies stored in China, this was primarily because Vietnam was concerned whether the Soviets could provide these materials in a timely fashion. Vietnam, for instance, hoped that all 260,000 tons of Soviet grain would arrive in China during the three months from September to November, 1972. Unless this grain were shipped as early as possible, bad harvests might mean that the Soviet Union was left unable to deliver. More than 1 million tons of aid supplies were scheduled for shipment from the Soviet Union; but six months later, 1 million tons had still not arrived. Vietnam therefore asked China to initially consume those portions that Vietnam could not utilize immediately, believing that these goods, "while still in the Soviet Union belonged to the Soviet Union, but once shipped to and stored in China, would belong to Vietnam."[49]

Another Vietnamese concern was that China might be reluctant to store these goods, so the offer of such a bonus might induce China to accept this request. China thus consumed quite substantial quantities of Soviet aid supplies (e.g., grain, oil, chemical fertilizers, and other supplies), promising to replace them with similar or substitute goods.[50] Shortly afterward, China decided to use up those aid materials it had determined that Vietnam did not need urgently, but that China could use and replace later. Whatever China did not utilize or could not subsequently replace would be stored in warehouses in central China, and Vietnam would no longer be consulted as to the details.[51]

This account indicates that, although the process of transporting Soviet aid supplies through China became a little smoother during this period, it represented only a reduction in degree. Disputes and conflicts on this issue still remained, as five examples demonstrate. First, China deeply resented and reacted fiercely to some of the Soviet propaganda statements on Vietnam aid, considering them posturing intended to impress the United States and exert pressure on China. In early May 1972, for instance, Kosygin wrote to Zhou, requesting that Russian aid supplies be unloaded at Chinese ports and transported to Vietnam on Chinese railroads. Xuan Thuy, who headed the North Vietnamese government delegation at the Paris peace talks, and Hanoi both conveyed messages or sent notes to China, expressing hope that China and the Soviet Union would reach agreement on this matter.

This issue might well have been resolved amicably if the Soviet Tass news agency had not reported that the Chinese ambassador to the Soviet Union had gone to Moscow airport to speed Thuy on his way to Beijing. When Zhou met Thuy on May 14, the premier sharply pointed out that the Soviet Union sought to create an atmosphere in which it would be believed that, but for Chinese intransigence, the agreement might already have been signed and Soviet supplies could have entered Vietnam without running risks from American mines. What, he inquired, was the Soviet motive in doing so? If this information was correct, would not the Soviet Union be inviting the United States to bomb the railroads? If it was untruthful, would not the Soviet Union be seeking to pressure China into accepting this agreement? Did the Soviet Union intend serious negotiations, or simply to create a certain atmosphere? China therefore refused to reopen Chinese ports to Soviet vessels bearing Vietnam aid supplies. On May 20, Zhou reemphasized to Le Ban that China still refused to accept Soviet ships.[52] Only after repeated requests from Vietnam did China agree to allow Soviet ships to enter Chinese ports.

In June 1972, moreover, Soviet missiles earmarked for Vietnam arrived in China. These were covered with blankets, which were torn by the time the weapons arrived in China, rather than the usual tarpaulins. The Soviet Union asked China to cover the missiles with tarpaulins, and China in turn inquired why the Soviet Union had not done so when they were first shipped. China pointed out that the busier the Pingxiang Railroad became, the more supplies the Soviet Union tried to ship. Whenever the railroad was too busy to do so, the Soviet Union also spread rumors that it wished to provide additional aid supplies to Vietnam, including missiles, for which they sought transit. When the Soviets failed to cover missiles with sturdy tarpaulins, they wished not only to demonstrate to China what they were sending Vietnam but, even more, they "wanted the Americans to see, because American satellites over the earth could see everything."[53]

Second, China disliked Soviet involvement in the negotiation and arrangement of transit shipping for Vietnam aid materials. On July 27, 1972, when the Soviet deputy minister of ocean transportation asked to fly from Hanoi to Beijing to discuss this issue, Li Qiang stated firmly that, to put it briefly, China would only talk with the Vietnamese. On Vietnam's behalf, China was prepared to receive Soviet supplies at Chinese ports, but the matter of how these would be transported once they were in China did not concern the Soviet Union. Li also told Le Duan that all future discussions on transit of supplies would be held in Beijing, and the Chinese Embassy in Hanoi would no longer handle these.[54] China thereby placed negotiating power firmly under the sole control of the central government, thereby preventing the Soviet Union and Vietnam from reaching any private agreements.

China also proposed adopting the procedure of arranging through shipping with North Vietnam to handle aid supplies in transit from the Soviet Union and other Eastern European nations, so that donors would not need to take any further action on these supplies once their ships had docked at Chinese ports. From that point onward, China and Vietnam would handle these goods, and China would determine the destination to which supplies would be sent. North Vietnam understood and agreed with this procedure, stating that once the designated ships had reached Chinese ports, "there is nothing left for these countries to do. They do not need to inquire whether the materials arrived in Vietnam, and how much arrived, etc. Vietnam will be responsible for all fees, losses, and transportation after these countries deliver their materials at Chinese ports. . . . Only we need to know about this between us, and we are not telling them."[55] Such preventive measures allowed China to exclude the Soviet Union completely from these matters, denying it any right to inquire as to such details as transfer time, storage sites, and destinations.

Third, the Soviet Union was also guarded and cautious in its dealings. In August 1972, Vietnam informed China that, in the case of four shipments of military goods China had already agreed to receive, the Soviet side was unwilling to follow the cross border transit protocols established for the transfer of military supplies, and that the Soviet Union would prefer to have Vietnamese personnel come to Vladivostok. Alternatively, the Soviet Union suggested that Soviet and Vietnamese officials might complete the transaction in the Chinese port of Huanan. This request demonstrated that the Soviet Union did not entirely trust China. The Chinese replied, "More studies would be needed on this issue. If they were so afraid of the Chinese and did not wish to come ashore, how could the Chinese handle matters in the future, when missiles were being transported?"[56]

Fourth, China actively opposed Soviet officials' involvement in cross-border transfers of aid supplies. In November 1972, after China had agreed to transport 400 Soviet personnel across the frontier, the Soviet Union asked that it might take charge of all six trains involved, and suggested that the only Chinese officials accompanying them be those needed to facilitate communications. China considered these requests unreasonable, replying: "China would not allow Soviet trains full of military equipment to pass through Chinese territory without inspection or supervision." China also refused to allow Soviet embassy staff to accompany these trains. In response to a Soviet request to send embassy staff to Zhanjiang to receive ships carrying missiles bound for Vietnam, China not only issued a negative reply but also did so after the missile ships had already left the Chinese port.[57]

Fifth, in the early stages of assistance, when China transshipped some aid supplies to Vietnam by sea, China set tight limitations on the types of equipment thus shipped, placing restrictions on all goods except food, steel, fuel, and sugar. On June 27, 1972, Vietnam requested that, in addition to 600,000 tons of these commodities, China permit the shipping of 300,000 tons of minerals, a request the Chinese side immediately refused. Zhou told Le Duc Tho that, though China would consider increasing the quantities of the original four commodities, others would have to wait.[58] Even the first four, China would only agree to unload after Vietnam provided full plans for their distribution, an extremely time-consuming process, which meant that the unloading of various shipments from Poland, Czechoslovakia, and Hungary was consequently delayed.

The Soviets and East Europeans blamed China for these delays. China, on the one hand, accused the Soviet Union of using mere rumors to fabricate disputes; on the other hand, it was forced to remove the restrictions on the types of supplies it would accept for onward shipment. From that point on, no matter what commodities were delivered, or whether or not Vietnam urgently needed these, China accepted all arriving shipments.[59] There are at least three possible reasons why these disputes may have initially arisen. First, Vietnam always believed the more aid the better, and did not restrict its requests to those goods it most urgently needed. Second, China did not wish goods to stay in China long enough to place pressure upon limited storage facilities. Third, the Soviet Union and Eastern European countries were reluctant to follow the rules set by China. The first two reasons given appear to have been the most significant factors.

A Brief Synopsis

During the Vietnam War, from 1965 until the end of 1972, China and the Soviet Union supported Vietnam in its war against the United States, in the midst of a deterioration in Sino-Soviet relations that evolved from conflict to full-scale confrontation. Over time, the intertwinings of the Soviet-Vietnamese and Chinese-Vietnamese relationships made this process even more complex. Three main conclusions can be drawn:

First, from the middle to late 1960s, China and the Soviet Union cooperated passively in providing support to Vietnam, with incessant sharp conflicts and constant disputes between the two big powers, whose communication with each other was always poor. China emphasized the importance of observing agreed-on plans and schedules when it shipped aid to Vietnam, whereas the Soviet Union maintained that unusual circumstances required unconventional solutions. Various factors—including China's strong anti-Soviet feeling, the inefficiencies of the Soviet bureaucracy, Soviet dissatisfaction with China, Soviet efforts to win North Vietnam's loyalties away from China, and China's attempts to prevent Vietnam leaning toward the Soviet Union—gave rise to arguments between China and the Soviet Union.

Soviet behavior on this matter undoubtedly had a negative impact on China's plans to ship supplies to Vietnam. But if the relationship between the two countries had been fundamentally good, such effects would have been minimized; they only became significant as Sino-Soviet relations deteriorated. Whether or not they initially intended to do so, both China and the Soviet Union seized any opportunity to oppose and spar with the other. Even so, in these years their quarrels did not seriously affect or interfere with both countries' support for Vietnam and opposition to American imperialism.

Second, in the early 1970s, China gradually implemented a major realignment of its foreign policies and international strategy. As the war intensified, China now helped North Vietnam to transport those supplies it required to the South and upgraded its efforts to support the North, in the hope of ending the war as soon as possible, which would help China attain its new strategic objectives. Noting that, in the triangular relations between the Soviet Union, Vietnam, and China, the Chinese position was disadvantageous, China's leaders sought not to generate needless animosity with Vietnam. In addition, China and the Soviet Union had opened border negotiations, so the conflicts between them were less intense than in the middle and late 1960s. Although disputes still occasionally occurred between them, China and the Soviet Union generally followed the principle of cooperating to provide assistance to Vietnam.

Third, gauging the success of the efforts of both China and the Soviet Union to assist Vietnam against the United States between 1965 and 1972, even though there were constant disputes between them over matters relating to the actual transportation of material aid to Vietnam, both countries made significant efforts to provide such assistance and both achieved significant success in delivering it. No matter what conflicts existed between the Soviet Union and China or how intense such disputes became, Vietnam continued to benefit from their joint efforts to supply and deliver material aid.

In sum, during the Vietnam War, against the larger background of the international Cold War, the policies and actions of both China and the Soviet Union were limited, not only by both powers' preoccupation with the image they projected within the international communist movement but also by the need to protect their own interests, factors that facilitated the relatively smooth provision of assistance to Vietnam. From the Chinese perspective of its own national interests and its regional geopolitical stake, the Soviet Union, viewing China's intransigent attitude toward itself as potentially threatening, had therefore decided to enter the Vietnam War. From this point on, Soviet-Vietnamese relations improved, while Chinese-Vietnamese relations steadily deteriorated, until the Soviet Union finally moved in to fill the void left after the United States withdrew from the war and abandoned the country. A Chinese proverb accurately described the situation China then faced: "Enemy at the front gate and thieves at the backdoor." As Soviet support encouraged the expansion of Vietnam's hegemonism, China would be forced to confront a new and hazardous regional environment, which within a few years would propel it into outright war against its former Vietnamese ally.

Notes

1. On April 29, 1968, Zhou Enlai commented: "Now the Soviet Union is also encircling China. The circle is getting complete, except [the part of] Vietnam." Minutes of meeting between Zhou Enlai and Pham Van Dong, April 29, 1968, in *77 Conversations between Chinese and Foreign Leaders on the Wars in Indochina, 1964–1977,* Cold War International History Project Working Paper 22, ed. Odd Arne Westad, Chen Jian, Stein Tønnesson, Nguyen Vu Tung, and James G. Hershberg, Cold War International History Project Working Paper 22 (Washington, D.C.:, Woodrow Wilson International Center for Scholars, 1998), 130.

2. According to the recollection of Truong Nhu Tang, minister of justice of the Provisional Republican Revolutionary Government of South Vietnam: "I know the Party had long ago decided to form an alliance with the Soviet Union. The movement in this direction started way back in 1969, and the passing away of Ho Chi Minh paved the way for officially making the decision. However, there was no open declaration, because Chinese assistance was still needed." Truong Nhu Tang, with David Chanoff and Doan Van Toai, *Parting Company with Hanoi,* Chinese ed. (Beijing: World Knowledge Press, 1989), 229.

3. During the entire period when China and the Soviet Union assisted Vietnam against the United States, disagreements and conflicts also arose between them over another important issue, that of peace negotiations between Vietnam and the United States. I propose to analyze these in another essay, and in this one to focus on the relationship between China and the Soviet Union during the period in which they provided material support to Vietnam.

4. "Minutes of Meeting of April 12, 1969, among Zhou Enlai, Kang Sheng, and Pham Van Dong," in *77 Conversations,* ed. Westad et al., 156–58; "Minutes of Meetings of Li Qiang and Le Ban," August 1 and 14 and April 23, International Liaison Division Records, Ministry of Railway Administration Archives, Beijing (hereafter Railway Archives), vol. 379 (1968), 31, 29, 15; Ministry of Foreign Trade, "Notice," November 14, Foreign Aid Division Records, Railway Archives, vol. 23 (1970), 3; report by P. Ivashutin, director, Intelligence Bureau, Soviet General Staff Headquarters, August 15,

1969, SD01840 (personal classification system for Li Danhui / Shen Zhihua collection of Soviet records). For further details on this question and changes in Sino-Vietnamese relations, see Li Danhui, "Zhongsu guanxi yu Zhongguo de yuanyue kangmei" [Sino-Soviet relations and China's policy of resisting American aggression and aiding Vietnam], *Dangdai Zhongguoshi yanjiu* [Contemporary Chinese history research] 3 (1998): 111–26.

5. Chinese Foreign Ministry, "Report of Meeting on 'China's Blocking of Soviet Aid to Vietnam,'" April 1, 1965, Jilin Archives, 77-11-7, p. 38, Changchun; Wang Taiping, ed., *Zhonghua renmin gongheguo waijiaoshi, 1957–1969* [Diplomatic history of the People's Republic of China, 1957–1969], 4 vols. (Beijing: World Knowledge Press, 1998), vol. 2, 265, 267.

6. See the references cited in the previous note.

7. Summary report by Mikhail Suslov regarding the Communist Party and the Workers' Party negotiating conference, March 26, 1965, SD08116, Li/Shen Collection.

8. Chinese Foreign Ministry, "Report of Meeting on 'China's Blocking of Soviet Aid to Vietnam.'"

9. "Minutes of Meeting between Qiao Guanhua and Ngo Minh Loan, Vietnam's Ambassador to China, May 13, 1967," in *77 Conversations,* ed. Westad et al., 121–23.

10. Records regarding the issue of sending Soviet volunteers to Vietnam, Southeast Asia Division, Soviet Foreign Ministry Archives, SD06764, Li/Shen Collection.

11. "Memorandum of Conversation between Ilia S. Scherbakov and Hoang Van Loi, March 26, 1965," SCCD, fond (f.) 5, opis'(op.) 50, delo (d.) 721, list (l., i.e., page) 117, quoted in Ilya V. Gaiduk, *The Soviet Union and the Vietnam War* (Chicago: Ivan R. Dee, 1996), 38.

12. "Minutes of Meetings between Zhou Enlai and Pham Van Dong, October 9 and August 23, 1965," and "Minutes of Meeting between Zhou Enlai and Le Duan, March 23, 1966," in *77 Conversations,* ed. Westad et al., 89–90, 93, 99.

13. China stipulated that it would not charge shipping fees for transporting supplies from these nations, and domestically accounts would be settled between the Railway Bureau and the Foreign Ministry. See Ministry of Railway Administration, "Shipping Procedures and Fee Settlement for Transporting Aid Materials from the Soviet Union, Eastern Europe, Korea and Other Nations to Vietnam through Our Country," September 30, 1965, International Liaison Division Records, Railway Archives, vol. 665 (1965), no page no.

14. Chinese Foreign Ministry, "Report of Meeting on 'China's Blocking of Soviet Aid to Vietnam,'" 37–38; Soviet Communist Party, letter to the Chinese Communist Party, October 21, 1965, Jilin Archives, 1, 1-21-135, p. 7; Wang, *Zhonghua renmin gongheguo waijiaoshi,* vol. 2, 265, 267.

15. The supplies China agreed to send also included 18,500 tons of Vietnam's normal commercial imports. Foreign Trade Bureau, "Minutes of Meeting between Chinese and Vietnamese Transportation Delegates," July 26, 1965, Materials Division Records, Railway Archives, vol. 409 (1965), 2, 7, 3.

16. Wang, *Zhonghua renmin gongheguo waijiaoshi,* vol. 2, 265–68; Han Huaizhi and Tan Jingqiao, eds., *Dangdai Zhongguo jundui de junshi gongzuo* [Contemporary military operations of the Chinese Armed Forces] (Beijing: Chinese Academy of Social Sciences Publishing House, 1989), 540; Shi Lin, ed., *Dangdai Zhongguo de duiwai peihe jingji* [Foreign economic cooperation in contemporary China] (Beijing: Chinese Academy of Social Sciences Publishing House, 1989), 50; Jilin Archives, 1, 1-21-135, p. 2.

17. Wang, *Zhonghua renmin gongheguo waijiaoshi,* vol. 2, 268; Jilin Archives, 1, 1-21-135, p. 2.

18. Soviet government to Chinese government, letter of October 21, 1965, and China's reply of November 5, 1965, Jilin Archives, 1, 1-21-135, pp. 6, 3, 2.

19. Soviet government, letter of October 21, 1965, to Chinese government, and China's reply, November 5, 1965, Jilin Archives, 1, 1-21-135, pp. 3, 6.

20. Jilin Archives, 1, 1-21-135, p. 4.

21. "Notice from Foreign Trade Transportation Corporation of Consignee and Arrival Station Regarding Explosives and Detonators to Be Stored," November 25, 1965, International Liaison Division Records, Railway Archives, vol. 64 (1965), 33; "Status Report Regarding Storage and Shipping," May 3, 1966, International Liaison Division Records, Railway Archives, vol. 680 (1966), no page no.

22. Wang, *Zhonghua renmin gongheguo waijiaoshi,* vol. 2, 268, 269; see also Jilin Archives, 1, 1-21,135, pp. 2, 4, 5.

23. *Renmin Ribao* [People's Daily], July 7, 1966. The author has not seen any Soviet or Chinese documents that verify whether or not China ever asked the Soviet Union for shipping fees or military supplies, or whether the Soviet Union ever spread rumors to this effect.

24. "Notice from the Ministry of Foreign Trade," March 24, 1966, International Liaison Office Records, Railway Archives, vol. 680 (1966), no page no.

25. Quoted in Guo Ming, ed., *Zhongyue guanxi yanbian sishinian* [The evolution of Sino-Vietnamese relations over the last forty years] (Nanning: Guangxi People's Publishing House, 1991), 76.

26. Status report from the Soviet government to the East German Communist Party, cited in "Appendix: Documents Nos. 1, 2," to "The Sino-Soviet Border Clashes of 1969: New Evidence from the SED Archives," by Christian F. Ostermann, paper delivered at conference on "New Evidence on the Cold War in Asia," January 1996, Hong Kong.

27. Ministry of Foreign Trade, "Summary of Talks between Chinese and Vietnamese Transportation Delegations," July 26, 1965, Materials Division Records, Railway Archives, vol. 409 (1965), 3.

28. Chinese government, reply to the Soviet government, November 5, 1965, Jilin Archives, 1, 1-21-135, pp. 4, 5.

29. Ministry of Foreign Trade, "Summary of Talks between Chinese and Vietnamese Transportation Delegations," 7.

30. Soviet Ocean Transportation Department, report to the central Soviet government, July 18, 1966, SD06763, Li/Shen Collection.

31. "Minutes of Meetings between Zhou Enlai and Pham Van Dong, April 7, 10, 1967," in *77 Conversations,* ed. Westad et al., 99, 101.

32. On October 16, 1972, in his reply to Vietnam's request, conveyed by Le Ban, Vietnam's deputy minister of foreign trade, that China send military aid and equipment, Li Qiang proposed that China would first transport those materials needed in the South, and would wait until later to ship those materials going to other parts of Vietnam. On November 13, Le Ban conveyed to Li Qiang a message from Le Thanh Nghi, Vietnam's vice premier, to the effect that Vietnam hoped China would transport heavy weapons. Because heavy weapons took longer to produce, Vietnam suggested that China first borrow these items from various departments to deliver to Vietnam, and once the inventory of goods for Vietnam aid was replenished return items from it to the appropriate departments as substitutes to replace them. Otherwise, once the war ended and an inter-

national control regime was in place, it would be very difficult to move heavy weapons to the South. They therefore required immediate rush shipment, because as yet there was no international control regime and it was the dry season. Li Qiang mentioned that Vietnam was not ready to receive deliveries and many trains were already spoken for and loaded, but he agreed that efforts should be made to transport more weapons and munitions and rush these to the South before international control took hold. "Minutes of Meetings between Li Qiang and Le Ban," October 16 and November 13, 1972, Office Records, Railway Archives, vol. 53 (1972), 144, 147, 149–50.

33. "Talk between Zhou Enlai and Le Duc Tho, July 12, 1972," and "Talk between Mao Zedong and Nguyen Thi Binh, December 19, 1972," in *77 Conversations,* ed. Westad et al., 182–85.

34. Yun Shui, *Chushi qiguo jishi: jiangjun dashi Wang Youping* [Record of diplomatic missions to seven nations: General Ambassador Wang Youping] (Beijing: World Knowledge Press, 1996), 127–28.

35. "Talk between Zhou Enlai and Pham Van Dong, September 17, 1970," and "Talk between Mao Zedong and Pham Van Dong, September 23, 1970," in *77 Conversations,* ed. Westad et al., 175, 178; Mao Zedong's written comments on Foreign Affairs Ministry, "Request and Report on the Issue of Increasing Aid Materials to Five South Vietnamese Provinces," Jilin Archives, 1, 1-23-21, p. 67; "Mao Zedong's Written Comments Regarding International Publicity Work and Foreign Affairs, 1967–1971," Aid Office Records, Railway Archives, vol. 23 (1971), 3.

36. CCP Central Documentary Research Department, *Zhou Enlai nianpu, 1949–1976* [A chronological record of Zhou Enlai, 1949–1976], 3 vols. (Beijing: Central Press of Historical Documents, 1997), vol. 3, 441.

37. Xue Mouhong and Pei Jianzhang, eds., *Dangdai Zhongguo waijiao* [Contemporary Chinese diplomacy] (Beijing: Chinese Academy of Social Sciences Press, 1988), 162; Yu Qiuli, speech at a Vietnam aid mobilization meeting, May 19, 1972, National Planning Committee Archives, 20-0149. For further details, see Li Danhui, "Zhongsu guanxi yu Zhongguo de yuanyue kangmei," 111–26. According to Soviet estimates, in 1972 China gave Vietnam aid worth $500,000. USSR Foreign Ministry, "Vietnam-China Relations" (memorandum), July 4, 1973, SSCD, f. 5, op. 66. d. 71, l. 88, quoted in Gaiduk, *The Soviet Union and the Vietnam War,* 231.

38. The Vietnam aid policy and strategy affirmed in 1965 by the central Chinese government contained a clause "encouraging Vietnam to demand from the Soviet Union." The Overseas Economic Committee directed all relevant departments to stick to this strategy so as "to reveal the true color of the Soviet revisionists who were pretending to support Vietnam, but in reality selling Vietnam out." Overseas Economic Committee, "Preliminary Summary of Sino-Vietnamese Economic Conference and Future Operations," International Liaison Division Records, Railway Archives, vol. 293 (1965), 51–53.

39. "Minutes of Meeting of Ye Jianying, Li Xiannian, and Le Ban," June 28, 1972, "Minutes of Meeting of Li Qiang and Le Ban," November 13, 1972, and "Minutes of Meeting of Li Qiang, Ngo Thuyen, and Le Ban," December 25, 1972, Office Records, Railway Archives, vol. 53 (1972), 78, 151, 165.

40. The term "special materials" referred to military goods. Letters from the Chinese government to the Soviet Union, East Germany, Bulgaria, and Romania, confirming these agreements, June 6, May 27, and June 2 and 10, 1972, Office Records, Railway Archives, vol. 85 (1972), 38–39, 34–37, 40–41.

41. Transportation Ministry, "Bulletin on Foreign Affairs Activities," May 22, 1972, no. 10, "Minutes of Meeting of Li Qiang, Le Ban, and Ngo Thuyen," August 22, 1972, and "Minutes of Meeting with Ngo Thuyen," August 26, 1972, Office Records, Railway Archives, vol. 52 (1972), 53, and vol. 53 (1972), 126–27, 131.

42. "Minutes of Meetings between Li Qiang and Le Ban," June 25 and August 16, 1972, and "Minutes of Meeting of Li Qiang, Le Ban, and Ngo Thuyen," August 22, 1972, Office Records, Railway Archives, vol. 53 (1972), 95–96, 117, 126.

43. "Chinese Letter to Soviet Overseas Economic Liaison Committee Confirming Sino-Soviet Agreements," June 6, 1972, Office Files, Railway Archives, vol. 85 (1972), 38, 42, 1–2.

44. "Minutes of Meeting between Zhou Enlai and Le Duc Tho," June 18, 1972, "Minutes of Meeting of Ye Jiangying, Li Xiannian, and Le Ban," June 28, 1972, and "Minutes of Meeting of Li Qiang and Le Ban," July 10, 1972, Office Records, Railway Archives, vol. 52 (1972), 19, 21–22, and vol. 53 (1972), 78, 99, 98–99.

45. China had a dual purpose in doing so: The first was not to disrupt unloading at the ports; second, China itself could use these goods. Li Qiang told Le Ban: "We can use first whatever you can not ship. We hope you can ship as much as possible and as fast as possible, but we can use up whatever is left. Of course, whatever we use will be returned later on." "Minutes of Meeting between Li Qiang and Le Ban," Office Records, Railway Archives, vol. 53 (August 2, 1972), 115–16,.

46. "Minutes of Meeting between Li Qiang and Le Ban," October 16, 1972, Office Records, Railway Archives, vol. 53 (1972), 145.

47. The history of materials storage during the 1960s was that, in June 1965, Li Xiannian assented to Vietnam's request that China should store aid supplies from the Soviet Union and other nations. In July 1965, Vietnamese and Chinese transportation delegations held meetings and agreed to designate four warehouses, the materials to be coded as "869" and the warehouses as "869-1." They also established concrete procedures for such matters as transportation, storage, and final accounting. In March 1966, Vietnam officially informed China that it had concluded an agreement with the Soviet Union that in future most aid materials would go directly to Vietnamese ports. In addition, improvements to the railroad system greatly increased Vietnam's capacity to transfer goods, so for the time being "869" materials were no longer stored in China. From then until 1967, China only stored Soviet military materials. See "Vietnam's Request to China to Store Materials from the Soviet Union and Eastern European Nations," June 21, 1965, and "Li Xiannian's Written Instructions," June 22, 1965, Office Records, Railway Archives, vol. 664 (1965), 41–42, 45; "Minutes of Meeting between Chinese and Vietnamese Transportation Delegations, July 26, 1965, Materials Division Records, 1965, Railway Archives, vol. 409 (1965), 4–5; Ministry of Foreign Trade, "Notice Regarding Vietnam's Return of the Four Storage Warehouses to China and the Withdrawal of Personnel Stationed There," March 24, 1966, International Liaison Division, Railway Archives, vol. 680 (1966), no page no.; and "Minutes of Meeting between Li Qiang and Le Ban," June 16, 1972, Office Files, Railway Archives, vol. 53 (1972), 69.

48. "Minutes of Meeting between Li Qiang and Le Ban," June 16, 1972, Office Records, Railway Archives, vol. 53 (1972), 63–64, 69; "Minutes of Meeting between Zhou Enlai and Le Duc Tho," June 18, 1972, Office Records, Railway Archives, vol. 52 (1972), 19, 21, 23; "Minutes of Meeting between Li Qiang and Le Ban," August 16, 1972, Office Records, Railway Archives, vol. 53 (1972), 117.

49. "Minutes of Meetings between Li Qiang and Le Ban," August 16 and June 16, 1972, Office Records, Railway Archives vol. 53 (1972), 118, 64.

50. "Minutes of Meetings between Li Qiang and Le Ban," June 25 and July 1 and 6, 1972, Office Records, Railway Archives, vol. 53 (1972), 91–92, 82, 86–87.

51. "Minutes of Meeting between Li Qiang and Le Ban," July 24, 1972, Office Records, Railway Archives, vol. 53 (1972), 107.

52. Office Records, Railway Archives, vol. 53 (1972), 4–6, and vol. 52 (1972), 54.

53. "Minutes of Meetings between Li Qiang and Le Ban," August 16 and June 16, 1972, Office Records, Railway Archives vol. 53 (1972), 118, 64.

54. "Minutes of Meeting between Li Qiang and Le Ban," July 27, 1972, Office Records, Railway Archives, vol. 53 (1972), 111, 110.

55. "Minutes of Meeting between Li Qiang and Le Ban," July 1, 1972, Office Records, Railway Archives, vol. 53 (1972), 80–81.

56. "Minutes of Meeting of Li Qiang, Le Ban, and Ngo Thuyen," August 20, 1972, Office Records, Railway Archives, vol. 53 (1972), 124.

57. "Report to Zhou Enlai Concerning the Transport of 400 Soviet Personnel," November 28 and 29, 1972, Office Records, Railway Archives, vol. 85 (1972), 1–2; and "Minutes of Meeting between Li Qiang and Le Ban," November 30, 1972, Office Records, Railway Archives, vol. 53 (1972), 153–54.

58. "Minutes of Meetings between Li Qiang and Le Ban," July 6 and 1, 1972, Office Records, Railway Archives, vol. 53 (1972), 84–86, 81.

59. "Minutes of Meeting between Li Qiang and Le Ban," July 24, 1972, Office Records, Railway Archives, vol. 53 (1972), 106–7.

9

The Background to the Shift in Chinese Policy toward the United States in the Late 1960s

Niu Jun

In recent years, much Chinese historical research has focused on the process and stages of changing Chinese policy toward the United States in the late 1960s. By comparison, works on the background to this policy shift seem rather weak. Although some studies have touched on several related aspects from various angles, these provide no detailed and systematic analysis of how these assorted aspects were connected either to the changes in Chinese foreign policy toward the United States or to each other.[1] The goal of this chapter is to fill the void currently left by other studies and provide a systematic description of the historical background and characteristics of the shift in China's policy toward the United States, through discussion of the various changes in, as well as the correlations among, Chinese security strategy, foreign policy, and Chinese-Vietnamese relations from the mid-1960s to 1968.

The Shift in China's Security Strategy

In the mid-1960s, China's security environment deteriorated rapidly, a deterioration characterized by simultaneous military pressure from both north

319

and south, exerted upon China by the Soviet Union and the United States, respectively. In the early 1960s, renewed disorder broke out in Indochina. After the second Geneva Conference of 1961–62, most Chinese leaders nonetheless believed that the possibility of a direct American attack on North Vietnam was slim.[2]

Then, on August 3, 1964, the Tonkin Gulf incident suddenly occurred, and American troops launched air strikes against targets in North Vietnam. Shortly afterward, both houses of the U.S. Congress passed the Tonkin Gulf Resolution, proclaiming that "the Congress approves and supports the determination of the President, as Commander in Chief, to take all necessary measures to repel any armed attack against the forces of the United States and to prevent further aggression." It authorized the United States president to "take all necessary steps, including the use of armed force, to assist any member countries or protocol state of the Southeast Asia Collective Defense Treaty requesting assistance in defense of its freedom."[3] Almost simultaneously, the U.S. Air Force began sending auto-piloted air planes into Chinese airspace on repeated military-intelligence-gathering missions.

The Chinese leadership followed U.S. military actions with serious concern. Chapters 1, 5, and 6 of the present volume all agree that, shortly before the Tonkin Gulf incident, Chinese leaders had already begun to respond to the threatened American attacks against North Vietnam. From May 15 to June 17, 1964, the Chinese Communist Party (CCP) Central Committee held several meetings to discuss China's Third Five-Year Plan, during which Mao Zedong began to shift the stated goal of the planned domestic economy from solving the problems of supplying "food, clothing, and consumer goods" to the construction of the so-called Three Lines projects, whereby he ordered all Chinese provinces to develop defense industries.[4] After the meetings had ended, Mao reemphasized the importance and urgency of building up a strong industrial defense sector. He even asked major cities, such as Beijing and Tianjin, to make military preparations to withstand a war.[5] On July 27, Mao received a delegation of officials from North Vietnam. He said that while the Chinese would continue to make every effort to help the North Vietnamese resist American attack, China would also prepare for war itself, and he even suggested that China conceivably might enter the war in Vietnam.[6]

In the first half of August 1964, clearly affected by continuing American air strikes on North Vietnam, Mao and other Chinese leaders paid closer attention to the threat of war with the United States. On August 5, when the United States began to attack targets in North Vietnam, the Central Military

Committee of China's People's Liberation Army (PLA) ordered all troops and divisions placed on defense alert. Mao even chose to cancel a scheduled speech the next day because "a war was about to break out."[7]

During the CCP Central Committee Secretariat meeting in mid-August, Mao repeatedly emphasized that Chinese should concentrate all their time and efforts on preparations to counter a war of aggression by the United States. He even said that the issues of whether or not China should implement the construction of the Three Lines projects resembled those that had arisen during the China's revolutionary struggles, particularly the questions of whether or not to go to the countryside, or whether to wage revolution.[8] In October, in a document addressed to President Liu Shaoqi and Premier Zhou Enlai, Mao said that building the Three Lines was "a matter of long-term strategy. If no action [was] taken, it would be too late to regret it in the future."[9] Mao's decision rapidly became the accepted consensus among Chinese policymakers, and his decision was quickly implemented.[10]

On March 2, 1965, U.S. troops launched Operation Rolling Thunder, conducting continuous air raids on North Vietnam. In the name of protecting U.S. Air Force bases, American ground troops engaged in direct military confrontations with the forces of the Vietnamese People's Army in Vietnam. The first batch of U.S. Marine troops landed in April at Da Nang in South Vietnam. In May, the United States began operations in the area north of the 20th parallel demarcation line, extending its air strikes across all North Vietnam's territory. In addition, carrier-based U.S. naval aviation forces intensified their activities over Chinese airspace, and U.S. naval vessels frequently patrolled along China's coastline on the South China Sea, breaching Chinese airspace. American war planes even attacked Chinese commercial shipping and fishing boats.

U.S. escalation of military actions in Vietnam and increased incursions upon China's airspace posed serious threats to Chinese security in the southern border area. To counter American aggression, in early 1965 Chinese aviation forces were sent to bases on Hainan Island. At the beginning of April, the PLA's Central Military Committee decided to lift the restriction permitting the PLA's Air Force only to "monitor" American planes invading Chinese air space, and replace it with policy instructions that "resolute actions should be taken to attack any enemy planes that enter the air space above China's mainland as well as above Hainan Island."[11] The PLA Air Force developed plans to repel the U.S. Air Force, as well as plans to counterattack U.S. war planes near the southern Chinese border area.[12]

China was obviously very sensitive to the possibility of a U.S. air strike.

Zhou asked visiting foreign diplomats to convey a message to the United States: "If the United States launches a full-scale air attack on China, it would be the beginning of a war. A war has no limit."[13] On April 12, the CCP Central Committee's Politburo held an extended meeting, which discussed and passed "The Resolution on Enhanced Defense Efforts," stating that U.S. escalation of the Vietnam War had "seriously threatened" China's national security. "China will be prepared to repulse the battle flames that the American imperialists will push to China," this document proclaimed; "China will be fully prepared to counter the enemy's air attacks," and "China will be prepared to fight a small-scale or medium-scale war, as well as a large-scale one."[14]

While China readied itself for war with the United States, Chinese leaders also tried to use diplomatic channels to express China's grave concern over American escalation of the war in Vietnam. As described in greater detail in chapter 6 above, China sought to make its bottom line clear in order to avoid any misunderstanding that might precipitate direct military conflict with the United States. On April 2, Zhou took the opportunity of a visit to Pakistan to explain to Pakistan's president, Ayub Khan, who was about to visit the United States, three important Chinese principles: "1. China will not initiate a war against the United States without provocation. 2. The words of Chinese people count. 3. China is prepared." He also clearly defined what would constitute a war waged by the United States against China: Even if the United States limited attacks against China to airstrikes, China would considered this as the opening of war.[15] Because Ayub Khan postponed his trip to the United States, during a visit to Tanzania Zhou took another opportunity to ask Julius Nyerere, that country's president, to relay China's message to the United States.[16] On August 20, Zhou again restated China's position, as described above, to an official delegation from Zambia.[17]

One important measure China took to safeguard China's national security was to lend support insofar as possible to Vietnam's war of resistance against American intervention. Bearing recent history much in mind, Chinese leaders would never tolerate a situation in which a hostile power took forcible action in an area bordering so closely on China, and indeed considered the very act of escalating the war in Vietnam as a hostile action aimed at China. After the Tonkin Gulf incident, North Vietnamese leaders informed Chinese officials that they planned to act cautiously and would try to negotiate with the United States to prevent a direct U.S. attack on North Vietnam. It is a strong possibility that, thinking likewise, Chinese leaders concurred in North Vietnam's precautionary strategy, including their plans to attempt to open peaceful negotiations.[18]

Starting in the spring of 1965, however, when the United States increased its air strikes on North Vietnam and also sent ground troops to participate in the Vietnam War directly, Chinese leaders began to oppose North Vietnam's position on peaceful negotiations with the United States. In chapter 1 of this volume, Yang Kuisong suggests that Chinese opposition to peace moves in Vietnam may have sprung from the fact that the Soviet Union, China's ideological rival, supported these, an outlook Mao believed sprang from covert Soviet opposition to the international revolutionary policies he himself favored. In early April, Le Duan, the first secretary of the ruling Viet Minh Party, visited Beijing to request that China send support troops to North Vietnam. The two sides signed a series of agreements covering Chinese military assistance and economic aid to North Vietnam.

Toward the end of May, a delegation of Vietnamese military officials visited China to discuss specific arrangements for Chinese assistance and to coordinate their war strategies. From June 1965 onward, Chinese PLA support troops entered Vietnam, to assist in antiaircraft operations and the construction of military facilities and railways, and to provide auxiliary support. Between then and July 1970, as chapters 7 and 8 of the present volume describe in greater detail, China sent a succession of 320,000 antiaircraft defense, railway, engineering, and auxiliary troops to Vietnam, on occasion as many as 170,000 troops within a single year.[19]

Clearly, losing the military support its alliance with the Soviet Union had previously provided severely vitiated China's capacity to counter U.S. attacks, especially its ability to coordinate air and naval power. Therefore, the threats both the escalating Vietnam War and U.S. incursions upon Chinese airspace and territorial waters posed to Chinese national security also increased commensurately. China had no option but to take strong emergency counter measures, which in turn undoubtedly increased the possibility of direct military confrontations between China and the United States.

During the same period, the deterioration of China's security environment also became apparent in its continuous border disputes with the Soviet Union. At that time, China and the Soviet Union shared the longest inland frontiers in the world. Long before the border clashes of the 1960s, territorial and border disputes had existed between China and the Soviet Union, a situation rooted in complex historical and current events. After the establishment of the People's Republic of China in 1949, given the overall strategic environment, China needed to maintain its alliance with the Soviet Union; and bearing in mind the historical aspects of these border disputes, China was prepared to agree to define the entire border between China and the Soviet Union according to the many unequal treaties left over from various periods of history. After the bilateral relationship deteriorated, both sides began to focus on boundary issues, to increase the forces stationed along them, and to accuse each other of initiating conflicts along their common frontier. From a historical perspective, border disputes did indeed serve as a barometer of increased hostility between China and the Soviet Union, as well as a tool both sides used to resolve mutual conflicts. Especially for the Soviet Union, border disputes also became a method of exerting political and military pressure on China.

From the time the first such border clash took place in China's Xinjiang Province in August 1960, there was no peace along the Soviet-Chinese border. According to statistics published by the Chinese, between August 1960 and October 1964, there were more than 1,000 such border confrontations.[20] During that time, not only did the Soviet Union provoke military clashes on its borders with China, but Soviet leaders also used China's territorial disputes with other countries, especially those with India, to criticize China's foreign policy and discredit China's internationally.[21]

In response to these Soviet attacks, on March 8, 1963, the *People's Daily* published an editorial, "On the Declaration of the American Communist Party," which for the first time openly brought up those unequal treaties that had been used to settle Chinese and Russian territorial questions. The article sharply queried the Soviet Union: "If the Soviet Union is now so keen to raise the historical issue of unequal treaties [between China and other countries], does the Soviet Union seek to discuss all the unequal treaties?"[22]

In July 1963, the Soviet Union and the People's Republic of Mongolia signed an Accord to Enhance Soviet Assistance for the Defense of the Mongolian Borders, and Soviet troops began entering Mongolia. The People's Republic of Mongolia had previously declared that, because it was situated between two giant socialist countries, Mongolia had no reason to maintain a regular defense force. As a result, all Soviet troops previously stationed there withdrew entirely in the 1950s.[23] Soviet troops now entered Mongolia and were deployed near the Chinese-Mongolian border, clear evidence of the Soviet intention to increase its military pressure on China.

From February to August 1964, China and the Soviet Union held border talks in Beijing, but the two sides failed to reach any agreement or understanding. Responding to the Soviet attitudes and views demonstrated in these talks, on July 10 Mao told Suzuki Mosaburo, a Japanese Socialist Party representative then visiting China: "Czarist Russia occupied a large portion of Chinese territory by force. We have not yet settled those debts."[24] When Mao's remarks became public in early September, the Soviets accused Chinese leaders of "advancing expansionist plans with complicated motives." Possibly seeking to clarify the original meaning of his remarks to the international community, in September Mao took the opportunity of a meeting with French visitors to explain that China did not intend to ask for the return of 150 square kilometers of territory currently belonging to the Soviet Union. According to Mao, he only sought to state that these disputes arose from unequal treaties and therefore wished to "take offensive measures" to put the Soviet Union "on notice."[25]

Soviet leaders were nonetheless unwilling to ignore the episode. On September 15, 1964, the Soviet general secretary, Nikita Khrushchev, when meeting Japanese Diet members, warned: "Those who dared to sabotage the sacred borders of the Soviet Union would be met with resolute counter attacks."[26] After the unsuccessful border talks between China and the Soviet Union, the Soviet Union decided to send additional troops to the region along the Chinese-Soviet border, a move that converted the border disputes into heated military conflicts. Chinese leaders paid special heed to both Khrushchev's remarks and the new military installations along their Soviet border.

On October 7 and 9, 1964, Mao met with leaders from North Korea and Albania respectively, on both occasions stating that China should be prepared for Khrushchev to take potential military action against China.[27] When Mao discussed the defense arrangements in major cities in northern China, he emphasized that "attention should be paid both to the south and to the north. All must be ready."[28]

On May 21, 1965, Zhou spoke at the strategy session of the PLA's Central Committee, warning that China must gird itself for an early and major war. Zhou said: "We will take on both imperialism and revisionism simultaneously. We will fight a nuclear war. . . . We will be prepared to fight a war in both directions."[29] His remarks on that occasion were the most direct and demonstrative public statements of the Chinese government to date that, if necessary, China contemplated waging war against the Soviet Union.

Mainly because of the American pressure afflicting China in the South— even though the country was on high alert for potential Soviet military action against China after the unsuccessful conclusion of the Soviet-Chinese border talks—China handled the border issues cautiously and with restraint, and it effectively froze its border disputes with other nations. Although China undoubtedly strongly assailed the Soviet Union's foreign policy during this period, such attacks remained purely verbal. To quote Mao, the arguments dividing China and the Soviet Union were "wars fought with brush and ink" and "would not cause death."[30] The Chinese leadership maintained that the Soviet threat was fundamentally different from the menace of a U.S. escalation of the war in Vietnam, because only American aggression and expansionism constituted direct global threats.

On October 14, 1964, Khrushchev suddenly fell from power. Chinese leaders were determined to use this opportunity to attempt to improve their relationship with the Soviet Union.[31] In November, Zhou led a delegation of Chinese government and party officials to Moscow. Although this visit clearly failed to accomplish its goal of improving Soviet-Chinese relations, Chinese leaders made further efforts to this end.

In February 1965, Mao received Soviet prime minister Aleksei Kosygin, who was on his way to visit North Vietnam. Zhou also had several talks with Kosygin and presented him with a six-point proposal of suggested measures to improve bilateral relations.[32] In Zhou's judgment, the meeting between Mao and Kosygin "naturally contributed positively" to Soviet-Chinese relations, because, even though such a meeting might produce no concrete results, it could "lay the foundation" for future talks. When Zhou subsequently met with the Soviet ambassador to China, Stepan Chervonenko, Zhou reiterated to him the six-point proposal he had offered Kosygin in February, adding: "The words of the Chinese government count."[33] Clearly, Chinese leaders still sought to stabilize the bilateral Sino-Soviet relationship.

From March 1 to 5, 1965, despite repeated objections from the CCP Central Committee, the Soviet Communist Party Central Committee called an international conference of communist parties and labor parties from various countries, which issued a joint declaration. On March 23, the *People's Daily* and *Red Flag* (Hong Qi) jointly published an editorial, "Assessing the March Conference in Moscow." The CCP Central Committee publicly broke with the Soviet Communist Party Central Committee by condemning the latter's efforts to continue Khrushchev's revisionism.[34] In June, the *People's Daily* and *Red Flag* again jointly published another editorial, "Carrying through the Struggles against Khrushchev's Revisionism to the End," its theme that if China were to combat American imperialism this policy was essential.[35]

On September 6, India launched military attacks on Pakistan, as their dispute over Kashmir brought a full-scale war between these two countries.

The Chinese government immediately issued a statement, condemning the "naked acts of invasions" by the Indian troops.[36] In addition, China increased its pressure on the Indian government over Chinese-Indian border issues. On the same day, China issued a statement condemning India's invasion of Pakistan, and the Chinese government presented a statement to the Indian Embassy in Beijing strongly protesting Indian troops' action in crossing China's Xizang (Tibetan) border and entering Chinese territory along the western reaches of the Chinese-Indian border so as to conduct military activities.[37]

China's strong reaction to conflict between Pakistan and India directly reflected the state of Chinese-Soviet relations. When the Chinese government pointedly characterized the military actions taken by India as an act of aggression, it emphasized that the United States was not the sole supporter of India's invasion of Pakistan; the Soviet Union had also "provided strong backing to the aggressors." China's government characterized Soviet efforts to support India as "the same trick" as the policy the Soviet Union followed during border clashes with China in 1959 and 1962, "aimed at generating world wide anti-Chinese sentiment."[38]

In January 1966, the Soviet Union and Mongolia signed a friendship treaty resembling a defensive alliance treaty. The Soviet Union also increased the number of its troops along the Chinese-Mongolian border, to which Chinese leaders reacted strongly. On March 28, when Mao received a Japanese Communist Party delegation, he fiercely accused the Soviet Union of attempting to invade China's northeast and Xinjiang, as well as joining forces with the United States to divide China.[39]

Chinese leaders' consciousness of and reaction to the anti-Chinese sentiment fomented by the Soviet Union, together with the ever escalating border disputes between the Soviet Union and China, were the main reasons why Chinese leaders were unyielding on the frontier conflicts. According to statistics provided by the Chinese government, between October 1964 and March 1969, 4,189 such clashes occurred along the Chinese-Soviet border, a frequency three times that in the early 1960s.[40] Even if one assumes that this figure was inflated, the growing number of clashes nonetheless indicated the increasing seriousness of the situation.

It was against this background that, in January 1968, Chinese decision-makers decided to launch retaliatory military attacks along the eastern sector of the Chinese-Soviet border. The Central Military Commission asked PLA troops in the Shenyang and Beijing Military Districts to make all necessary preparations to "facilitate diplomatic efforts with military actions."

The Central Military Commission also authorized border troops to fire in self-defense if their warnings were ignored or Chinese soldiers were killed.[41]

On August 21, 1968, Soviet troops entered Czechoslovakia, a crucial event in persuading the Chinese leadership to consider the Soviet threat from the perspective of their comprehensive national security strategy. On August 23, Mao held an emergency meeting at his residence in Zhongnan-hai, attended by all Chinese political and military leaders except Lin Biao.[42] The meeting discussed the world situation after the Soviet invasion of Czechoslovakia, and those present decided that measures must be taken to condemn the Soviet action. On the same day, the *People's Daily* published an editorial condemning the Soviet Union as a "socialist imperialist country" and the Soviet invasion of Czechoslovakia as "a result of a joint attempt by the United States and the Soviet Union to repartition the world."[43]

On October 31, 1968, the public statement authorized by the Twelfth Plenum of the Eighth Central Committee of CCP confirmed the judgment that "the United States and the Soviet Union had attempted to redivide the world."[44] During this period, Mao also repeatedly warned visiting foreign diplomats that a world war must now be considered a serious possibility. "There appears to be a war. The state of no war and no revolution should not last very long."[45]

These facts prove that a significant shift in China's security strategy occurred during the period between 1964, when the border talks between China and the Soviet Union failed, and October 1968, when Soviet troops invaded Czechoslovakia. Its main feature was the alteration from emphasizing "the south (i.e., the United States)" to emphasizing both "the north and the south (i.e., the United States and the Soviet Union)," at a time when China faced threats from both directions. Subsequent events, including the peace talks between Vietnam and the United States and the Zhenbao Dao incident, caused China to readjust its security strategy from "protecting the south (from the United States)" to "protecting the north (from the Soviet Union)."

The Evolution of Chinese Foreign Policy and the Rebuilding of the Decisionmaking System

As China's national security policy evolved over time, China's foreign policy and decisionmaking structure also underwent subtle changes during the chaos generated by the Cultural Revolution. In the late 1950s, under the influence of the Great Leap Forward campaign and revisionist thinking in the international communist movement, leftist tendencies appeared in China's foreign policy. In the early 1960s, serious difficulties in China's domestic economy forced China to adjust its national economic policies significantly.

There appeared to be signs that corresponding changes might also be under way in China's foreign policy. One of the more obvious phenomena was a systematic reevaluation and critique of China's foreign policy and its guiding principles over time, conducted by Wang Jiaxiang, the minister for external relations of the CCP Central Committee.[46] Judging from the fact that Wang was relieved of his duties in the second half of 1962, these efforts to correct the leftist emphases in China's foreign policy proved unavailing. After 1963, the ever intensifying disputes between China and the Soviet Union contributed to the growing strength of leftist perspectives among the guiding principles of Chinese foreign policy. In terms of the theoretical concepts directing Chinese foreign policy, including prevailing trends and international developments, war and peace, world revolution, peaceful coexistence, nuclear warfare, reductions in military forces, national independence, and peace movements, the thinking of Chinese leaders became to all appearances increasingly one-sided and absolutist.

During 1965, following the March publication of "Assessing the March Moscow Conference" in the *People's Daily* and *Red Flag,* which announced the breakup of the socialist camp, in June the *People's Daily* and *Red Flag* reprinted "Carrying the Struggles against Khrushchev's Revisionism to the End," charging that the "sinister principle" of Soviet foreign policy was to pursue cooperation with the United States. The article also mentioned for the first time that "countering imperialism required countering revisionism," marking the beginning of the phase of "fighting with two fists" in China's foreign policy.[47]

On September 3, 1965, the *People's Daily* published a lengthy article titled "Ten Thousand Years: The People's War!" under the byline of China's defense minister, Lin Biao. This article emphasized the commonality and relevance to all countries of Mao's guiding memory of wars of the masses in the international revolutionary movement, claiming that the time had arrived for world capitalism and imperialism to expire, opening an era of success for socialism and communism. The international political arena, it argued, was "a city of the world" and "countryside of the world," and "the world revolution also takes on the form of surrounding cities from the countryside"; finally, using extreme propagandist language, the article stated that "China is the home base of world revolution."[48] Within China, this article provoked strong reactions, and the views it articulated became the main tenets of the theory that "China is the center of world revolution," which guided thinking during the early Cultural Revolution, for which Lin's article effectively provided the leftist intellectual foundation.

The CCP Central Committee's Eleventh Meeting, held in August 1966, endorsed Lin's article, characterizing it as a "scientific Marxist-Leninist analysis of a series of important issues in contemporary world revolution." The meeting approved a report that significantly affected the making of Chinese foreign policy, a document further emphasizing that "in a new era of world revolution, several forces are experiencing significant changes and transformation." In these circumstances, "the highest guiding principle in Chinese foreign policy" was "proletarian internationalism."[49]

First, China's foreign policy propaganda became ever more extreme and strident. On the one hand, China proclaimed that "the new era of world revolution has come," that this "era is guided by the great banner of Mao thought," and "it is the great era in which the stage of a final match between the Proletarians and the Capitalists has been set world wide."[50] On the other hand, China proclaimed itself "the focal point of world conflicts and the storm center of global revolution," as well as the "revolutionary center of the world."[51] One must bear in mind that such propaganda programs were intended to encourage as many people as possible to actively participate in the Cultural Revolution. Therefore, this propaganda described domestic political struggles against revisionism in great detail as battles for "the future of world revolution and the realization of beautiful human ideals," proclaiming that "the future of China will determine the future of the global proletarian revolution . . . and a global proletarian revolution is a top priority throughout the world."[52] However, such descriptions of the prevailing world revolutionary trends, as well as China's self-proclaimed significance to the world, inevitably vitiated the ability of some Chinese leaders to understand international affairs and distorted their judgment when conducting foreign affairs.

By that time, the Cultural Revolution had already begun, and China's domestic political situation was becoming ever more chaotic. Fanned by such propaganda as described above, there was a feverish outpouring of extreme and radical sentiments, a phenomenon that derailed Chinese foreign policy. Chinese diplomatic missions abroad suffered severely. Soon after the Cultural Revolution began, the Chinese government eventually recalled all its ambassadors, except for Huang Hua, who was then the ambassador to Egypt, a policy that undoubtedly generated problems in China's bilateral relations with other countries.

On September 8, 1966, the External Affairs Secretariat of the State Council published the document, "A Brief Report on External Affairs during the Cultural Revolution." The Interim Secretariat of the Cultural Revolution Coordination Committee of the Communist Youth League Central Committee also published the article, "A Letter from a Tanzanian Citizen Criticizing Bourgeois Behavior among Chinese Diplomats at Foreign Mission Posts." Both were sent to Mao, who commented the next day: "This letter of criticism was well written. All foreign mission posts should pay attention. We need a complete revolution."[53]

From then on, chaos reigned in Chinese foreign diplomatic missions, because all their efforts and undertakings had to be directly related to the revolution at home. As China's domestic political climate hardened, spreading Mao's thought throughout the world became the central mission of every Chinese embassy. Some diplomats indiscriminately distributed propaganda material on Mao's thought and circulated flyers and posters publicizing China's Cultural Revolution whenever an opportunity arose, while others made inappropriate remarks at diplomatic functions.

Shortly after chaos engulfed Chinese missions overseas, the tempests of the Cultural Revolution also seriously affected the foreign affairs bureaucracy back home. On January 11, 1967, the *People's Daily* published an editorial urging the rebels to "take over power" nationwide.[54] A massive wave of struggles for power quickly spread throughout the foreign policy bureaucracy. From Foreign Minister Chen Yi to each ambassador and minister counselor, everyone was criticized and paraded through the streets. Virtually no bureau within the foreign policy infrastructure could function normally.

On August 7, 1967, Wang Li, a member of the Chinese Cultural Revolution Central Committee, addressed the rebel group inside the Chinese Foreign Ministry, encouraging them to oust Foreign Minister Chen and to seize power within the Foreign Ministry.[55] Such support from the Central Committee emboldened the dissident group within the Foreign Ministry to heighten its activities. The group took over the political office of the ministry, sealed off the party secretary's office, and in the name of the Foreign Ministry issued orders to Chinese diplomatic missions around the world. With the authority to make foreign policy left to this band of rebels, diplomatic activities fell into a state of anarchy.

While the Chinese foreign policy system lapsed into chaos, mass movements and vicious political storms also affected foreign diplomatic missions in China. In January 1967, some Chinese students returning from college in

Europe stopped in Moscow on their journey home. Gathering before the tombs of Lenin and Stalin, they recited the words of Mao. Soviet police quickly surrounded and beat up the students, and when news of this reached China, many Chinese people went to the Soviet Embassy in Beijing to protest. Further protests in front of the Indian, Indonesian, and Burmese embassies followed this demonstration. Between May and August 1967, assorted conflicts arose between China and a dozen African, Asian, and European nations with which it had established formal diplomatic ties.[56] The most serious incident took place on the evening of August 22, when more than ten thousand people surrounded and attacked the office of the British chargé d'affaires in Beijing, burning down an office building and parading the British chargé through the streets.

The destruction of the British Consulate in Beijing not only marked the high watermark of the chaos in Chinese foreign affairs during the Cultural Revolution but also offered a window of opportunity to readjust Chinese foreign relations. The disorder in various foreign diplomatic missions quickly attracted the attention of those Chinese leaders who directed foreign affairs. In January 1967, Zhou sent Chen to the Great Hall of the People to announce that "the authority vested in the foreign affairs system cannot be taken away."[57] On February 6, responding to the total confusion in Chinese diplomatic missions abroad, Chen ordered his secretary to draft a telegram prohibiting so-called Big Four activities in Chinese embassies around the world. The draft telegram was sent to Zhou, who in turn passed it along to Mao, who approved the telegram the followed day. When subsequently editing this draft further, Zhou added that within Chinese embassies "exchanges of revolutionary experience" activities and "revolutionary fighting teams" were strictly prohibited, dispatching the telegram as an order on February 7.[58] On March 3, the CCP Central Committee, the People's Republic of China State Council, and the PLA Central Military Commission jointly issued a document, *Notice Discouraging Members of the Red Guard and Other Revolutionary Masses from Offering Voluntary Assistance to Vietnamese Efforts against the United States,* forbidding Red Guards and other youths from entering Vietnam illegally.[59]

These measures were clearly inadequate to eliminate all the disorder afflicting the foreign affairs bureaucracy. After his defeat in the subsequent February Resistance War, Chen lost control over the Foreign Ministry, and Zhou was repeatedly forced to tackle the situation himself. On August 8, Zhou read the "August 7 Speech" of Wang Li in a newsletter circulated by the Red Guards, and he immediately summoned Wang and Kang Sheng, head of the Chinese secret police, to a meeting, an invitation they both turned down. Quite possibly, Zhou had hoped that at this meeting they would be able to reach a consensus on how to control the situation, but he then realized that even his power had become severely limited.[60] Several subsequent confrontations with rebels within the Foreign Ministry made it clear to Zhou that he could no longer rely solely on his reputation and prestige to prevent the situation from deteriorating further.

Facing these difficulties, Zhou was determined to use the opportunity provided by the burning of the British mission to turn the situation around. On August 25, he met with General Yang Chengwu alone, and he asked him to report on the succession of recent events, including the contents of Wang's "August 7th Speech," to Mao, who was away on an inspection tour. On August 26, Mao condemned Wang's remarks as "the worst type" of sentiments, and he decreed that Zhou must take charge and arrest Wang and his followers.[61] Acting on Mao's instructions, the CCP Central Committee ordered an investigation of Wang and his associates. On October 3, during a meeting with foreign diplomats to which Zhou accompanied Mao, Mao again offered his support to Zhou, saying that "it was wrong" for the Red Guards to try to oust Zhou and Chen.[62]

Mao's statements marked a turning point in the readjustment of Chinese foreign affairs, and their dual significance quickly became apparent. First, they ended the chaos afflicting the foreign affairs bureaucracy, enabling Zhou to regain at least partial control. The reason Mao sought to support Zhou and stabilize the foreign affairs apparatus was because he did not wish the system to suffer genuine complete paralysis. From Mao's perspective, serious dangers still menaced Chinese national security, and China continued to bear the burden of its responsibilities to assist other countries to counter both revisionism and American imperialist expansion. On several occasions, from the summer of 1967 until right before the Ninth Party Congress, Mao issued instructions on China's external affairs, criticizing individuals who were self-centered or who forced their wills on others.[63]

Although, given the background of the overheating Cultural Revolution, Mao's limited remarks could not fundamentally remedy the misguided leftist policies imposed on the foreign affairs apparatus, his moves against Wang and his condemnation of Wang's August 7 speech undoubtedly struck down Wang's supporters within the Cultural Revolution Central Committee in the battle to control the making of Chinese foreign policy. More crucially, even though the latitude won was extremely limited, Mao did provide some room for Zhou to maneuver, as he sought to restore a functional foreign affairs structure and to normalize its operations.

Moreover, in the process of dealing with Wang and his associates, a decisionmaking structure composed of Mao and Zhou was instituted—or rather, indeed, reaffirmed. At the beginning of the Cultural Revolution, domestic political struggles and changes in personnel broke up the established structure of decisionmaking on Chinese foreign affairs. Most major players in the foreign policy arena, such as Liu Shaoqi and vice premier Deng Xiaoping, found it impossible to continue to function, reducing the diplomatic apparatus to near breakdown. Those who gained power at the beginning of the Cultural Revolution undoubtedly coveted control over foreign affairs, but the radical sentiments they fanned eventually led to such disruptive incidents as the burning of the British consulate, and they lacked the ability to devise plans to manage the consequences.

Zhou, in sharp contrast, demonstrated the wits, clear vision, and skills required to run China's foreign policy. When Mao accepted Zhou's suggestion and vested him with the authority to arrest Wang and his associates, he effectively eliminated any possibility that the leftists would win control of foreign affairs and reaffirmed Zhou's authority to make and implement China's diplomatic policies. The subsequent history of the realignment of China's international position would demonstrate the significance of the establishment in August 1967 of a foreign policy decisionmaking system centered on Mao and Zhou.

Changes in Chinese-Vietnamese Relations

Changes in Chinese-Vietnamese relations were critically important factors affecting the evolution of Chinese-American relations in this period, a point frequently overlooked in earlier studies. After the establishment of the People's Republic of China, many Chinese leaders made repeated statements demonstrating their belief that the Sino-American relationship was characterized by conflicts and confrontations at three levels: those of global strategy, bilateral relations, and regional problems.

At the level of bilateral relations, such conflicts and confrontations were primarily related to U.S. interference in China's internal affairs and American policies detrimental to China's national unification and territorial integrity, with Taiwan the sharpest and most serious point of difference. At the regional level, the principal issues were forcible American interventions in countries and areas along China's borders, especially U.S. military involvement in Vietnam, which directly threatened China's national security. At the level of global strategy, the United States sought to be the sole superpower and hoped that the Soviet Union would join it in suppressing revolutionary activities in China and in other countries.

In the mid-1960s, the Sino-American confrontation on the battlefield in Vietnam also reflected ongoing conflicts and struggles between China and the United States on both the regional and global strategic levels. In other words, as long as the United States continued to escalate the war in Vietnam, China had no choice but to enhance its political and military relations with North Vietnam and assume the responsibility to support and aid North Vietnam. So long as this situation prevailed, therefore, it would be difficult for China to realign its security strategy or foreign policy toward the United States. In 1968, a historic opportunity presented itself when important changes occurred in the China-Vietnam relationship.

After the United States escalated its level of intervention in Vietnam in the spring of 1965, China resolutely decided to intensify its backing for North Vietnam, and it sent support troops directly to Vietnam. China actively assisted North Vietnam's efforts to resist the American invasion, bringing an unprecedented strengthening and development of the bilateral relationship between China and Vietnam. Yet, viewing the relationship from another angle, at best the close military and political ties between China and North Vietnam only papered over differences between the two countries, which had the potential to become increasingly inflamed.

First, historical and regional political factors generated friction within this bilateral relationship. Even while China voluntarily mobilized almost all the resources at its command to help North Vietnam resist the United States, newspapers and magazines in North Vietnam periodically published articles on past aggression against Vietnam by Chinese emperors. Likewise, even though Vietnamese troops were receiving military aid from China, leaders of the Vietnamese armed forces were wary of China, and they did not wish to share sensitive information on the progress of the conflict or the numbers of Vietnamese troops. The Vietnamese military sought the right to issue orders to Chinese antiaircraft batteries, while in the name of maintaining national sovereignty the port authorities in North Vietnam sometimes refused even to admit Chinese ships.

The most egregious instance of this outlook occurred when, while China was most resolutely and actively helping Vietnam to repel the American invasion, some North Vietnamese openly discussed "the threat from the North [namely, China]." Chinese leaders repeatedly condemned such rhetoric.[64] On April 13, 1966, during a meeting of Chinese and Vietnamese leaders, Deng Xiaoping clearly demonstrated both China's anger and the pressure to which North Vietnam felt it was subjected when he told the Vietnamese: "I remember Comrade Mao criticizing us . . . for having 'too much enthusiasm' in the Vietnam question. . . . Are you suspicious that China helps Vietnam for our own intentions? . . . The problem will be easily solved. We will withdraw our military men at once."[65] As the war progressed, the friction and distance such incidents generated became ever more apparent.

Second, after Soviet Communist Party secretary Leonid Brezhnev took office in Moscow in October 1964, a drastic modification occurred in Soviet policy, from passive opposition to the Vietnam War, as described in chapter 2 of the present volume, to active Soviet involvement. One indication of the changed attitude was a Soviet statement of November 27, 1964, to the effect that the Soviet Union "was willing to provide necessary aid" to Vietnam.[66] In February 1965, when Soviet Prime Minister Aleksei Kosygin visited Hanoi, the Soviet Union and North Vietnam made a joint declaration, in which the Soviet Union stated that it would not "sit by and watch" when Vietnam needed a security guarantee.[67] From April 10 to 17, the first secretary of the Vietnamese Communist Party, Le Duan, was in Moscow; and in this visit's Soviet-Vietnamese joint communiqué, the Soviet Union claimed that it would send troops to Vietnam to participate in the war if the situation demanded this action or if Vietnam asked it to do so.[68] The Soviet Union's active participation and the massive quantities of military and economic assistance it provided to North Vietnam brought these two countries closer than ever before, clearly enhancing Soviet influence within North Vietnam.

Almost as soon as the Soviet Union expressed its readiness to become involved in the Vietnam War, disputes on various matters began to arise between China and the Soviet Union. In February 1965, Soviet prime minister Kosygin visited Beijing and made two rather different requests. The first was that China and the Soviet Union should coordinate their efforts to offer support to Vietnam and that the leaders of all socialist countries should issue a joint statement backing Vietnam's resistance efforts against the United States. Second, they should institute efforts to resolve the Vietnam question peacefully and to "find a way out for the United States in Vietnam." Even though such measures would have removed the American threat from their southern border, the Chinese leaders clearly lacked any interest in cooperating with the Soviet Union on Vietnam; they rejected both these suggestions and only discussed issues in bilateral Sino-Soviet relations with Kosygin.[69]

After the Moscow March Conference, China's criticism of Soviet policy in Indochina became increasingly pointed, with repeated statements that China opposed not only any Soviet suggestions for the peaceful resolution of the Vietnam question but also any "joint actions" with the Soviet Union.[70] The report of the Eleventh Meeting of the Eighth CCP Congress clearly stated: "The global alliance against the United States could not possibly include the Soviet Union"; "a line between the alliance and the Soviet Union must be clearly drawn"; "the truth about these scabs must be openly revealed"; and "it is impossible to conduct joint activities with the Soviets."[71]

The CCP Central Committee's principle of noncooperation with the Soviet Union was reflected at the level of policy. As chapter 8 above explains at length, soon after Kosygin's February 1965 visit to China, the Soviet Union sought permission from the Chinese government to use Chinese railroads to transport Soviet troops to North Vietnam. The Soviet Union also requested that China open its airspace to Soviet military aircraft en route to North Vietnam and allow these to use Chinese military air bases. China refused all these Soviet requests.[72] The Chinese leaders insisted that if the Soviet Union planned to transport material aid to Vietnam via China, it must observe their existing agreements on the subject, a pretext they employed to deny the Soviet Union the use of Chinese ports.[73] They repeatedly informed North Vietnam's leaders that China resolutely opposed the deployment of Soviet volunteer troops in the Vietnam War.[74]

Although rooted in what was then China's dominant foreign policy perspective, China's opposition both to Soviet involvement in Vietnam and to Soviet efforts to exploit the situation in Vietnam elicited a bitter North Vietnamese response. For North Vietnam's leaders, the primary issue was how to prevent the United States from escalating the war, and their overriding objective was nothing less than national survival. Vietnam needed any assistance it could find, and it therefore could not acquiesce in Chinese policies to block or limit the transportation of Soviet assistance. In addition, some North Vietnamese leaders had always rather distrusted China.

It might therefore be anticipated that Chinese pressure would have adverse results. Faced with Chinese demands that they reject Chinese aid—as described in chapters 1, 7, and 8 of this volume—the North Vietnamese leaders told their Chinese counterparts outright that they believed the Soviet Union was "partly sincere" in offering aid, and they did not believe that the

Soviet Union was selling out Vietnam's interests. They stated that adherence to internationalist principles should be the standard whereby one socialist country should judge another, and that this should be especially true of North Vietnam.[75] This Vietnamese stance revealed that the fundamental objective of North Vietnam's policy toward the Soviet Union was to win Soviet assistance, and it was therefore clear that, whatever the Chinese intent might be, North Vietnam would resent China's refusal either to cooperate with the Soviet Union or to allow it to transport aid for Vietnam through China.

Third, dissension—far sharper than that over the previous two issues, whose impact on Sino-Vietnamese relations was much less far reaching— also existed between China and North Vietnam on the subject of peace negotiations with the United States. China's decision to assist Vietnam was based largely on considerations of Chinese national security and the need to support the Vietnamese revolution. But China took the subject of peace negotiations much more seriously than either of these two matters, and from the strategic perspective regarded them as the most critical issue for both China and the United States.

As chapter 1 above also demonstrates, from about the spring of 1965, China began to oppose peace talks between the United States and North Vietnam. China's reasons for doing so were extremely complex; some were related to the widening of the war in Vietnam, and others to on-going Chinese struggles against Soviet revisionism. As soon as the Soviet Union became involved in Vietnamese affairs, there were signs that it sought a peaceful resolution of the Vietnam conflict. In addition, in the perfervid climate of the Cultural Revolution, the North Vietnamese struggle against the United States won "double billing," for resisting American imperialism on the front line and simultaneously brandishing high the waving banner of international revolution.[76] One must also remember that, no matter how complex the factors influencing Chinese policies at various stages were, the goal of China's policy in backing North Vietnam remained consistent and accorded with that of both North Vietnam itself and its southern National Liberation Front: to halt U.S. military intervention and support the national reunification of the Democratic Republic of Vietnam.

On March 22, 1965, the Central Committee of the National Liberation Front in South Vietnam issued a declaration stating five major points regarding Vietnam's war of independence against the United States, together with two preconditions for any peace talks: first, all American troops, military equipment, and installations must be entirely withdrawn from Vietnam; and second, the National Liberation Front must have the power of ultimate decision upon any political solution.[77]

In a report Pham Van Dong presented to the Second Meeting of the Third North Vietnamese Party Congress on April 8, he outlined four salient points of North Vietnam's position for peace talks: First, the United States must remove all its military forces and equipment and halt its military aggression in the South and air strikes against the North. Second, until the reunification of Vietnam came about, the United States must strictly observe the Geneva Accords. Third, in the South, the Vietnamese people must determine and resolve their own affairs according to the principles the National Liberation Front represented. And fourth, the people of both North and South must resolve the reunification of Vietnam free from foreign intervention.[78] The Chinese government immediately issued a statement declaring its support for the North Vietnamese position.

From 1965 onward, China and Vietnam repeatedly discussed the subject of potential peace negotiations between Vietnam and the United States, focusing primarily upon whether to implement and how best to achieve the goals that both North Vietnam and the National Liberation Front had enunciated. At that time, China did not support opening immediate negotiations between North Vietnam and the United States; it was more concerned that two factors—namely, Soviet pressure on Vietnam to make concessions to the United States, or the timing of negotiations—might effectively force North Vietnam to renounce its goals before attaining ultimate military victory against the United States.

On numerous diplomatic occasions, Chinese leaders explained how, during the Chinese Civil War, the Soviet Union had made concessions to the United States, and even attempted to prevent the PLA from crossing the Long River at the crucial last moment, just before China's final revolutionary victory. Chinese leaders viewed the American proposal for peace talks as a mere ploy to eliminate revolutionary forces in Vietnam, and they charged that, by acquiescing in the American proposal, the Soviet Union was prepared to leave the Vietnamese popular revolution unfinished.[79]

With regard to the timing of negotiations, judging by their own dealings with the United States, the Chinese leaders believed that the country would genuinely seek to negotiate and withdraw from Vietnam only after Vietnamese troops inflicted major casualties on the American forces in Vietnam and achieved military success on the battlefield.[80] Chinese officials asserted all these arguments even more strongly in 1967.[81] At that time, Vietnam's leaders agreed with them, in part because they believed there was a distinct possibility that the United States might lose and be forced to withdraw from Vietnam in 1968.[82]

Early in 1968, Vietnamese forces launched the Tet Offensive against American troops, a wave of attacks that achieved a major political triumph and caused huge shock waves in the United States, as the American people finally realized that, despite their commitment of enormous human and economic resources to Vietnam, and the significant casualties American forces had sustained, the United States could not suppress the determination or ability of the Vietnamese people to continue fighting. Under heavy pressure from an unprecedented public backlash against the war, the official will of the United States to continue the war in Vietnam was about to crumble. Even so, from the purely military perspective, Vietnam's armed forces suffered severe losses, heavily damaging their continuing fighting capabilities. The local structure of the National Liberation Front also absorbed grave damage, leaving its morale low, as large numbers of soldiers were killed and numerous cadres arrested.[83] In these circumstances, on March 31, 1968, U.S. president Lyndon B. Johnson gave a nationwide television address, announcing that he would halt all air strikes in the areas north of the 20th parallel, and on April 3 North Vietnam agreed to open talks with the United States.

As soon as the Chinese learned of North Vietnam's decision to hold these talks, they expressed resolute opposition to any negotiations with the United States at that time. In many meetings with North Vietnamese officials, Chinese leaders maintained that North Vietnam's decision to open peace talks with the United States was inconsistent with its previously announced goals, and that the timing of these talks would be detrimental to North Vietnam. China insisted that, by swiftly accepting the American suggestion to conduct such discussions, North Vietnam had abandoned an advantageous position for one of passive acquiescence.[84] The disputes between China and Vietnam over the timing of these talks also led the two countries to make divergent assessments of Soviet policy.[85]

These differences, together with North Vietnam's failure to consult China before announcing its decision to hold talks with the United States, seriously damaged their bilateral relationship. On November 14, 1968, after listening to a report by Zhou on his meetings with North Vietnamese leaders, Mao said: "Let's leave everything to them to decide."[86] On June 9, 1969, when Mao met with a visiting delegation of Romanian government and party officials, he openly explained China's new policy of making a clear separation between the respective interests and policies of China and Vietnam.[87]

From the perspective of the subsequent realignment of Chinese foreign policy, China's decision to maintain and increase its distance from North Vietnam did indeed provide it with a historic opportunity. One cannot imagine how China could have shifted the focus of its foreign policy northward had its relationship with North Vietnam not soured due to the latter's decision to hold peace talks with the United States. In addition—given a background in which, ever since the Eleventh Meeting of the Chinese Communist Eighth Party Congress, "proletarian internationalism" had become the "highest principle" of Chinese foreign policy—if China had continued to maintain a close relationship with North Vietnam and to bear the related political and military burdens, or if North Vietnam had not initiated a new stage in its relationship with the United States, at the very least it would have been far more difficult for Chinese leaders to reach their decision to normalize diplomatic relations with the United States.

This chapter has demonstrated that, well before the Zhenbao Dao Island incident of March 1969, China's strategic thinking on national security, its international outlook, its foreign policy apparatus, and its relations with Vietnam had all undergone significant modifications, which took place at various levels affecting different aspects of Chinese foreign policy. Not all of these, by any means, were deliberately instigated by Chinese leaders to facilitate the normalization of Sino-American relations. On the contrary, in many ways the Sino-American rapprochement was a response to international developments—including ever more antagonistic and openly hostile Sino-Soviet relations, the growth of Soviet influence in Vietnam, and Soviet assertion of the Brezhnev Doctrine—that China resented and in some cases had tried to prevent. Yet one may easily trace the mutually interacting effects and correlations among these changes, which formed a grand backdrop against which a significant shift occurred in China's policy toward the United States—one that, notwithstanding the extremely chaotic conditions created by the Cultural Revolution, ultimately enabled Mao and Zhou to consummate a strategic realignment in Chinese foreign relations.

Notes

1. Standard works in this field include Li Danhui, "1969 nian zhongsu bianjie chongtu: Yuanyi he jieguo" [The border clashes between China and the Soviet Union in 1969: Courses and results], *Dangdai Zhongguoshi Yanjiu* [Contemporary Chinese History Studies] 5 (1996): 39–51; and Li Jie, "Liushi niandai zhongguo guonei jushi de bianhua yu zhongmei guanxi" [Changes in China's domestic situation in the 1960s and

Sino-U.S. relations], in *1955–1971 nian de zhongmei guanxi: Huanhe zhiqian-lengzhan chongtu yu kezhi de zai tantao* [Sino-American relations, 1955–1971: A re-examination of cold war conflict and restraint before bilateral détente], ed. Jiang Changbin and Robert Ross (Beijing: World Knowledge Press, 1998), 256–97—published in English as *Reexamining the Cold War: U.S.-China Diplomacy, 1954–1973* (Cambridge, Mass.: Harvard University Press, 2001), 288–320.

2. See Li Jie, "Liushi niandai zhongguo guonei jushi de bianhua yu zhongmei guanxi," 265.

3. Shi Yinhong, *Meiguo zai yuenan de ganshe he zhanzheng* [U.S. intervention and war in Vietnam] (Beijing: World Knowledge Press, 1993), 174–75.

4. See Sun Dongsheng, "Woguo jingji jianshe buju de da zhuanbian" [The great transformation in the strategic planning of our country's economic construction: A brief description of the decision making on the construction of the third front], *Dangde Wenxian* [Archives of the Chinese Communist Party] 3 (1995): 44.

5. CCP Central Documentary Research Department, *Zhou Enlai nianpu, 1949–1976* [A chronological record of Zhou Enlai, 1949–1976] (hereafter *Zhou Enlai nianpu*), 3 vols. (Beijing: Central Press of Historical Documents, 1997), vol. 2, 654.

6. "Mao Zedong jiejian yuenan minzhu gongheguo daibiaotuan de tanhua" [Remarks to the Delegation from the Democratic Republic of Vietnam], July 27, 1964, Chinese Central Archives, Beijing.

7. Mao Zedong, "Dui zhongguo zhengfu kangyi meiguo qinfanyuenan de shengmingao de piyu" [Comments on the statement by the Chinese government protesting against the U.S. invasion of Vietnam], August 6, 1964, in *Jianguo yilai Mao Zedong wengao* [Mao Zedong's manuscripts since the founding of the People's Republic of China], 13 vols. (Beijing: Central Press of Historical Documents, 1996), vol. 11, 120.

8. See Lu Lihua and Guo Bing, "Mao Zedong jiakuai sanxian jianshe pingxi" [An analysis of Mao Zedong's efforts to speed up construction of the three lines], *Guoshi Yanjiu Cankao Ziliao* [Reference Materials for the Study of PRC History], 3 (1993): 38.

9. Mao Zedong, "Dui guangdong shenwei guanyu guofang gongye he sanxian gongzuo baogao de piyu" [Comments on the progress report submitted by the Party Committee of Guangdong Province on defense industry and three lines preparatory work]," *Jianguo yilai Mao Zedong wengao*, vol. 11, 196.

10. Zhou Enlai, "Jiaqiang yixian, erxian de houfang jianshe he zhanbei gongzuo" [Enhancing the construction of the first and second line bases and preparations for war], October 29, 1964, "Jiakua sanxian jianshe" [Enhancing the construction of the three lines], March 2, 1965, in *Zhou Enlai junshi wenxuan* [Selected military writings of Zhou Enlai], 4 vols, ed. CCP Central Documentary Research Department and PLA Military Science Academy (Beijing: People's Press, 1997), vol., 4, 490–93, 504–7; Li Fuchun, Bo Yibo, and Luo Ruiqing, "Guanyu guojia jingji jianshe ruhe fangbei diren turan xiji de baogao" [Report on how to defend against sudden enemy attacks and domestic economic construction], August 19, 1964; Liu Shaoqi, "Zai jiejian junwei zuozhan hui quanti tongzhi shi de jianghua" [Speech to all comrades at the military central commission meeting], May 19, 1965, *Dangde Wenxian* 5 (1995): 33–34, 41.

11. *Zhou Enlai nianpu*, vol. 2, 724; Wang Dinglie and Lin Hu, eds., *Dangdai Zhongguo kongjun* [The contemporary Chinese air force] (Beijing: Chinese Academy of Social Sciences Press, 1989), 385.

12. Wang and Lin, *Dangdai Zhongguo kongjun,* 385.

13. *Zhou Enlai junshi wenxuan,* vol. 4, 514.

14. *Jianguo yilai Mao Zedong wengao,* vol. 11, 359–60.

15. *Zhou Enlai junshi wenxuan,* vol. 4, 508–15.

16. *Zhou Enlai nianpu,* vol. 2, 736.

17. Diplomatic History Research Office of the PRC Foreign Ministry, ed., *Zhou Enlai weijiao huodong dashi ji, 1949–1975* [Important events in Zhou Enlai's diplomatic activities, 1949–1975] (Beijing: World Knowledge Press, 1993), 474.

18. Niu Jun, "1969 nian zhongsu bianjie chongtu yu zhongguo waijiao zhanlue de tiaozheng" [The Shift in Chinese diplomatic strategies and the border clashes with the Soviet Union in 1969], *Dangdai Zhongguoshi Yanjiu* 1 (1999): 69–70.

19. *Zhou Enlai junshi wenxuan,* vol. 4, 529; PLA Military Science Academy, *Zhongguo renmin jiefangjun dashji* [Major events of the People's Liberation Army] (Beijing: PLA Press, 1983), 376.

20. *Renmin Ribao* [People's Daily], May 25, 1969.

21. See Zhou Wen, *Teshu re fuza de keti-gongchan guoji, sulian he zhongguo gongchandang guanxi biannian shi* [Special and complex tasks: A history of international communism and the relations between the Chinese and Soviet communist parties, 1919–1991] (Wuhan: Hubei People's Press, 1993), 534.

22. "Ping meiguo gongchandang shengming" [On the declaration of the American Communist Party], *Renmin Ribao,* March 8, 1963.

23. For details, see Xu Yan, "1969 nian zhongsu bianjie de wuzhuang chongtu" [The 1969 military conflicts on the Sino-Soviet borders], *Dangshi Yanjiu Ziliao* [Party History Reference Material], 5 (1994): 3–4.

24. Yang Kuisong, "Cong zhenbao dao dao zhongmei guanxi huanhe" [From the Zhenbao Dao incident to Sino-American détente], *Dangshi Yanjiu Ziliao* 12 (1997): 6; Li, "1969 nian zhongsu bianjie chongtu," 42.

25. "Mao Zedong jiejian faguo jihshu zhanlan hui fuzeren ji faguo dashi de tanhua" [Remarks by Mao Zedong during the meeting with head of the French technology delegation and the French ambassador], September 10, 1964, Chinese Central Archives.

26. Zhou Wen, *Teshu re fuza de keti-gongchan guoji,* 541.

27. Li Danhui, "1969 nian zhongsu bianjie chongtu: yuanyi he jieguo," 45; Yang Kuisong, "Cong zhenbao dao dao zhongmei guanxi huanhe," 7.

28. *Zhou Enlai nianpu,* vol. 2, 654.

29. Zhou Enlai, "Women jiang yingde jinbu, yingde heping" [We will achieve progress and we will win peace], May 21, 1965, *Zhou Enlai junshi wenxuan,* vol. 4, 287.

30. Li Fenglin, "Mosike ershi nian [Twenty years in Moscow], in *Dangdai zhongguo shijie waijiao shengya* [Diplomatic careers of contemporary Chinese diplomats], 5 vols., ed. Diplomatic History Research Office of the PRC Foreign Ministry (Beijing: World Knowledge Press, 1995–1997), vol. 4, 287.

31. Yu Zhan, "Yici bu xunchang de shiming: Yi Zhou Enlai zuihou yici fangwen sulian" [An unusual mission: Zhou Enlai's last visit to the Soviet Union remembered], in *Xin zhongguo waijiao fengyun* [New China's turbulent diplomacy], 4 vols., ed. Diplomatic History Research Office of the PRC Foreign Ministry (Beijing: World Knowledge Press, 1990–96), vol. 3, 19.

32. PRC Foreign Ministry and CCP Central Documentary Research Department, *Zhou Enlai waijiao wenxian* [Selected diplomatic works of Zhou Enlai] (Beijing: Central Press of Historical Documents, 1990), 445–47; *Zhou Enlai waijiao huodong dashiji,* 436.

33. *Zhou Enlai nianpu,* vol. 2, 731.

34. *Xinhua yuebao,* 1965, no. 4.

35. *Renmin Ribao,* June 14, 1965.

36. "Zhonghua renmin gongheguo zhengfu shengming" [Statements by the government of the People's Republic of China], September 7, 1965, *Renmin Ribao,* September 8, 1965.

37. *Renmin Ribao,* September 9, 1965.

38. "Shui zai gei yindu qinluezhe chengyao" [Who are the supporters of India?], *Renmin Ribao,* September 18, 1965.

39. Masaru Kojima, ed., *Minutes of Meetings between the Japanese Communist Party and the Chinese Communist Party* (Tokyo: Central Committee of the Japanese Communist Party, 1980), 206–7.

40. "Zhongguo zhengfu guanyu zhongsu bianjie wenti de shengmin" [Statement by the government of the People's Republic of China on issues related to the Chinese–Soviet borders], *Renmin Ribao,* May 25, 1969. According to statistics published by the Soviet government, in 1962 over 5,000 disputes occurred. See Roderick MacFarquhar and John K. Fairbank, eds., *Cambridge History of the People's Republic of China, Volume 14: 1949–1965,* Chinese trans. (Beijing: Chinese Academy of Social Sciences Press, 1990), 559.

41. Li Ke and Hao Shengzhang, *Wenge qijian de zhongguo renmin jiefangjun* [The People's Liberation Army during the Cultural Revolution] (Beijing: Central Party Material and History Press, 1989), 318; Xu, "1969 nian zhongsu bianjie de wuzhuang chongtu," 5.

42. *Zhou Enlai nianpu* recorded a meeting between Zhou Enlai and Lin Biao after the Zhongnanhai meeting, and it seems likely that at this time Zhou Enlai briefed Lin Biao on what had transpired during the Zhongnanhai meeting. See *Zhou Enlai nianpu,* vol. 2, 51.

43. "Sulian xiandai xiuzheng zhuyi de zong pochan" [The complete failure of contemporary Soviet revisionism], *Renmin Ribao,* August 23, 1968.

44. "Zhongguo gongchangdang diba jie kuoda de zhongyang weiyuanhui di shierci quanti huiyi gongbao" [Public statement by the Twelfth Meeting of the Eighth Chinese Communist Party Congress], October 31, 1968, in *Renmin Ribao,* November 1, 1968.

45. "Mao Zedong huijian Aerbniya guofang Ba Luku de tanhua" [Remarks by Mao Zedong during a meeting with Albanian defense minister Beqir Balluku], October 1, 1968; and "Mao Zedong huijian Australian gongchandang (malie) zhuxi Xier de tanhua" [Remarks by Mao Zedong during a meeting with Australian Communist Party chairman Ted Hill], November 28, 1968, Chinese Central Archives.

46. Wang Jiaxiang, "Shishi qiushi, liangli erxing" [Seeking truth from facts, acting according to capacity], March 31, 1962, "Luetan dui mouxie guoji wenti de kanfa"[Brief remarks on a few international issues], June 29, 1962, both in Editorial Group of the Works of the Selected Works of Wang Jiaxiang, *Wang Jiaxiang juanxi* [Selected works of Wang Jiaxiang] (Beijing: Beijing People's Press, 1989), 444–45, 446–58; Zhang Tunsheng, "Nanneng de tansuo, kegui de nuli" [Difficult discovery valuable effort], in *Leading the Global Trend: The International Strategic Thinking of a Generation of Leaders,* ed. Institute of International Strategic Studies (Beijing: Central Press of Historical Documents, 1993), 171.

47. *Renmin Ribao,* June 14, 1965.

48. *Renmin Ribao,* September 3, 1965. The article implied that "China was the home base of world revolution." In a speech on November 6, 1967, Lin Biao explicitly said

that the goal was to build up China as "a stronger home base for world revolution." See Lin Biao, "Zai shoudu renmin jinian shiyu geming wushi zhounian dahui shang de jianghua" [Remarks at the Capital Conference Commemorating the 50th Anniversary of the October Revolution], November 6, 1967, in *Renmin Ribao,* November 7, 1967.

49. "Zhongguo gongchandang bajie zhongyang weiyuanhui shiyici quanti huiyi de gongbao" [Report by the 11th Meeting of the 8th Chinese Communist Party Congress], *Renmin Ribao,* August 14, 1966.

50. See Wang Li, "Proletarian Dictatorship and the Great Proletarian Cultural Revolution," *Hong Qi* [The Red Flag], no. 15 (1966); "Zhongguo de da geming he sulian de da beiju"[The great revolution in China and the great tragedy in the Soviet Union], *Renmin Ribao,* June 4, 1967; Lin Biao, "Zai shoudu renmin jinian shiyu geming wushi zhounian dahui shang de jianghua," November 6, 1967, in *Renmin Ribao,* November 7, 1967.

51. "Zou shehui zhuyi daolu? haishi zou ziben zhuyi daolu" [Road to revolution or road to capitalism?], *Renmin Ribao,* August 15, 1967; Lin Biao, "Zai shoudu renmin jinian shiyu geming wushi zhounian dahui shang de jianghua," *Renmin ribao,* November 7, 1967.

52. "Zhongguo gongchandang zhongyang weiyuanhui tongzhi" [Notice of the Chinese Communist Party Central Committee], May 16, 1966, *Renmin Ribao,* May 17, 1966; "Zou shehui zhuyi daolu? haishi zou ziben zhuyi daolu," *Renmin Ribao,* August 15, 1967.

53. Mao Zedong, "Guanyu zai zhuwai jiguan lai yige geminghua de piyu" [Comments on "A Complete Revolution], September 9, 1966, *Jianguo yilai Mao Zedong wengao,* vol. 12, 128–29.

54. "Wuchan jieji gemingpai da linahe, duo zou ziben zhuyi daolu dangquanpai de quan!" [Unite, proletarian revolutionists, take power over the capitalist authority], *Renmin Ribao,* January 22, 1967.

55. *Zhou Enlai nianpu,* vol. 2, 177.

56. Jin Zhongji, ed., *Zhou Enlai zhuan* [A biography of Zhou Enlai], 2 vols.(Beijing: Central Press of Historical Documents, 1998), vol. 2, 963.

57. Jin, *Zhou Enlai zhuan,* vol. 2, 963.

58. See Jin, *Zhou Enlai zhuan,* vol. 2, 123; Hu Shiyan et. al., *Chen Yi zhuan* (Beijing: Contemporary China Press, 1991), 608; Du Yi, *Daxue ya qingsong: Wenge zhong de Chen Yi* [Snow on pine trees: Chen Yi in the Cultural Revolution] (Beijing: World Knowledge Press, 1997), 117–18.

59. National Defense University Party History Office, ed., *Zhonggong dangshi jiaoxue cankao ziliao* [Reference materials for the teaching and study of party history], 28 vols. (Beijing: National Defense University Party History Office, n.d.), 25:329.

60. *Zhou Enlai nianpu,* vol. 2, 177.

61. *Zhou Enlai nianpu,* vol. 2, 182–83. Also see Chen Yangyong, *Kucheng weiju: Zhou Enlai zai 1967* [Managing the crisis: Zhou Enlai in 1967] (Beijing: Central Press of Historical Documents, 1999), 364–65.

62. *Zhou Enlai nianpu,* vol. 2, 194.

63. "Mao Zedong guanyu duiwai xuanchuan gongzuo de zhishi, 1967 Nian 3 Yue–1971 Nian 3 Yue" [Mao Zedong's instructions on external affairs, March 1967 to March 1971], *Zhonggong dangshi jiaoxue cankao ziliao,* vol. 26, 513–16.

64. Conversation among Zhou Enlai, Deng Xiao Ping, Kang Sheng, Le Duan, and Nguyen Duy Trinh, Beijing, April 13, 1966, conversation among Zhou Enlai, Pham Van

Dong, and Hoang Tung, Beijing, August 23, 1966, conversation between Deng Xiaoping and Le Duan, Beijing, September 29, 1975, in *77 Conversations between Chinese and Foreign Leaders on the Wars in Indochina, 1964–1977*, Cold War International History Project Working Paper 22, ed. Odd Arne Westad, Chen Jian, Stein Tønnesson, Nguyen Vu Tung, and James G. Hershberg (Washington, D.C.:, Woodrow Wilson International Center for Scholars, 1998), 94–101, 194–95.

65. Conversation among Zhou Enlai, Deng Xiao Ping, Kang Sheng, Le Duan, and Nguyen Duy Trinh, Beijing, April 13, 1966, in *77 Conversations,* ed. Westad et al., 94–98.

66. Xie Yishan, *Zhongsu guanxi liushiwu nian* [Sixty-five years of Soviet foreign relations] (Beijing: World Knowledge Press, 1987), 9.

67. Xie, *Zhongsu guanxi liushiwu nian,* 18.

68. Xie, *Zhongsu guanxi liushiwu nian,* 25.

69. Central Party School Research Institute, *Qishi niandai sulian duiwai guanxi dashiji* [Major events in Soviet foreign relations in the 1970s] (Beijing: Central Party School Research Institute Press, 1985),1–2; also see *Zhou Enlai nianpu,* vol. 2, 247.

70. "Bo sulian xin lingdao suowei de lianhe xingdong" [Denouncing the so-called joint action of the new Soviet Communist leadership], *Renmin Ribao* and *Hong Qi,* November 11, 1965; "Sulian lingdao tongshui linahe xingdong?" [With whom do Soviet leaders conduct joint activities?], *Renmin Ribao,* February 2, 1966.

71. *Renmin Ribao,* August 14, 1966.

72. Central Party School Research Institute, *Qishi niandai sulian duiwai guanxi dashiji,* 2; Li Danhui, "Zhongsu guanxi yu Zhongguo de yuanyue kangmei" [Sino-Soviet relations and China's policy of resisting American aggression and aiding Vietnam], *Dangdai Zhongguoshi Yanjiu* 3 (1998): 8.

73. *Zhou Enlai nianpu,* vol. 2, 74; Conversation between Zhou Enlai and Pham Van Dong, Beijing, April 10, 1967, in *77 Conversations,* ed. Westad et al., 103–5.

74. Conversation between Zhou Enlai and Pham Van Dong, Beijing, October 9, 1965, in *77 Conversations,* ed. Westad et al., 92–93; Conversation between Zhou Enlai and Le Duan, Beijing, March 23, 1966, in *77 Conversations,* ed. Westad et al., 17.

75. Conversation among Zhou Enlai, Deng Xiaoping, Kang Sheng, Le Duan, and Nguyen Duy Trinh, Beijing, April 13, 1966, in *77 Conversations,* ed. Westad et al., 94–98; Conversation among Zhou Enlai, Kang Sheng and Pham Van Dong, Beijing, April 29, 1968, in *77 Conversations,* ed. Westad et al., 129–34.

76. "Quan shijie renmin tuanjie qilai, yuanzhu yuenan renmin dabai meiguo qinluezhe" [The people of the world united, help Vietnam defeat American invaders], *Renmin Ribao,* March 25, 1965; "Mao Zedong zhuhe yuenan minzhu gongheguo chengli 22 zhounian de dianbao" [Congratulatory telegram from Mao Zedong to the Democratic Republic of Vietnam on the occasion of the 22nd anniversary of the founding of the Democratic Republic of Vietnam], September 1, 1967, *Jianguo yilai Mao Zedong wengao,* vol. 12, 407–8.

77. *Renmin Ribao,* March 25, 1965.

78. *Renmin Ribao,* April 14, 1965.

79. *Zhou Enlai nianpu,* vol. 2, 143; *Zhou Enlai waijiao huodong dashiji,* 451–52.

80. *Zhou Enlai nianpu,* vol. 2, 143; *Zhou Enlai waijiao huodong dashiji,* 510, 524; *Zhou Enlai waijiao wenxian,* 448–57.

81. The meeting between the Vietnam's delegation and Chinese delegation, April 11, 1967, in *77 Conversations,* ed. Westad et al., 113–19.

82. Conversation between Zhou Enlai and Pham Van Dong, Beijing, April 10, 1967, in *77 Conversations,* ed. Westad et al., 108–10.

83. Shi, *Meiguo zai yuenan de ganshe he zhanzheng,* 256–62.

84. *Zhou Enlai waijiao huodong dashiji,* 524; Conversation between Zhou Enlai and Pham Van Dong, Beijing, April 13, 1968, in *77 Conversations,* ed. Westad et al., 123–25; Conversation between Zhou Enlai and Pham Van Dong, Beijing, April 19, 1968, in *77 Conversations,* ed. Westad et al., 125–28; Conversation between Zhou Enlai and Pham Van Dong, Beijing, June 29, 1968, in *77 Conversations,* ed. Westad et al., 135–36; Conversation between Chen Yi and Le Duc Tho, Beijing, October 17, 1968, in *77 Conversations,* ed. Westad et al., 136–37.

85. Conversation among Zhou Enlai, Kang Sheng and Pham Van Dong, Beijing, April 29, 1968, in *77 Conversations,* ed. Westad et al., 129–35.

86. *Zhou Enlai nianpu,* vol. 2, 266.

87. *Zhou Enlai waijiao huodong dashiji,* 539.

10

Sino-U.S. Reconciliation and China's Vietnam Policy

Shen Zhihua

In the early 1970s, the international setting of the Cold War underwent important changes. In April 1971, the "ping pong diplomacy" initiated by Mao Zedong and Zhou Enlai created a global sensation. The thawing in Sino-U.S. relations, which had begun in 1968, reached a breakthrough. Finally, the publication of the 1972 Shanghai Communiqué signified that the United States and China had reached a reconciliation. Less than a year later, the lengthy Vietnam war came to an end when, following strenuous negotiations between North Vietnam and the United States, the Paris Peace Accords were signed. In what ways were these events related?

Hanoi later concluded that the Sino-U.S. reconciliation represented a "betrayal" and "abandonment" of Vietnam, in that China sought to prevent Vietnam's unification and to force North Vietnam "to acknowledge the southern puppet regime," thereby selling out Vietnamese interests to the United States.[1] Subsequent research and studies appear to have confirmed this conclusion.[2] Yet this view still seems rather distorted, and history presents a rather more complicated picture. Unquestionably, between the late

1960s and the early 1970s, for China to enable itself to cope with an environment of total international isolation—most specifically its vulnerability to being trapped between the United States and the Soviet Union—it shifted its foreign policy from "idealistic diplomacy" to "pragmatic diplomacy."

Nonetheless, as chapter 1 of the present volume also demonstrates, due to an ideological outlook evolved over many years, together with political struggles within their own power structures, the Chinese Communist Party and the Chinese government never ceased to support world revolutions in general, and in particular, the diplomatic concept of supporting peoples' revolutions in the developing world. It was on the basis of this fundamental assumption that, after China entered the United Nations, Mao gradually evolved his thesis of differentiating between three worlds. Realism forced China to become reconciled with the United States, whereas ideology required China to support Vietnam's anti-American struggle.

While confronting the concrete diplomatic issue of how to deal with Vietnam, China simultaneously had to contend with a tug of war between two interlocking triangles, the China–United States–Soviet Union relationship, and its China–Soviet Union–Vietnam counterpart.[3] As the China-U.S. relationship steadily improved, China became increasingly embroiled in a series of dilemmas over Vietnam. First, China needed to adjust its diplomatic strategies to the reality of the political power contest, yet it could not renounce the internationalist rhetoric it had consistently employed to support national liberation movements around the world. Second, China needed to continue to support and assist the Vietnamese in their struggle to save their nation and repel American aggression, but it also had to ensure that this would not raise obstacles to the reconciliation process between China and the United States. Third, China sought to achieve and safeguard the security of its southern border once the United States pulled its troops out of Vietnam, but it conversely had to prevent the Soviet Union from taking advantage of its precarious situation by presenting a new threat on that front. In summary, China was required not only to develop a relationship with the United States but also to support North Vietnam, the direct enemy of the United States.

The Initial Sino-American Rapprochement of 1971 and Its Impact on Vietnam

As described in chapters 1 and 9 above, from the time the United States began to escalate the Vietnam War, China consistently and steadfastly opposed peace negotiations and encouraged Vietnam to carry on its war of resistance to the bitter end. Even after the Paris peace talks began, the Chinese leadership still concluded that the conflict's final resolution would occur on the battlefield, not at the negotiating table. In May 1970, Mao said: "You may negotiate [with the Americans]. I am not saying that you cannot negotiate, but your main energy should be put on fighting."[4] Although China's principal antagonist on this issue was still the Soviet Union, its stance was also opposed to that of the United States. In the course of America's pursuit of normalization of relations with the People's Republic of China, the issue of how to resolve the Vietnam War was unquestionably a major factor.

On the one hand, to maintain the American strategic position in East Asia and to counterbalance Soviet power—which, within the triangular structure of states, would in turn attract China toward the United States—the Richard Nixon administration had to resolve the Vietnam issue with dignity. On the other hand, Washington also expected that the reconciliation between China and the United States would offer it some diplomatic opportunities to persuade the Soviet Union, or perhaps even China itself, to pressure Vietnam to compromise, so that the United States could withdraw speedily from the Vietnam War. Yet only when Henry Kissinger, Nixon's national security adviser, visited China in 1971, did Beijing seem seriously to consider the link between China-U.S. reconciliation and the Vietnam War.

At a Politburo meeting on March 3, 1971, China confirmed its policy of enhanced support for Vietnam. Zhou pointed out that, to provide full backing to the people of Vietnam in their war against the United States, the Chinese people were willing to endure the utmost sacrifices.[5] Zhou subsequently visited Vietnam, where he spoke at a popular rally, stating: "Our supreme leader Chairman Mao Zedong, under the lofty principle of Proletarian internationalism, has taught us that those among us who advocate that we should not assist the people of Vietnam to save their homeland against the American invasion, those people are in fact betraying us and are betraying the cause of revolution."[6] That same month, Le Thanh Nghi, the vice-premier of North Vietnam, visited China and requested that China increase its assistance by twelve complete projects, at a total cost of 150 million renminbi. China's Foreign Ministry and Ministry for Foreign Trade concluded that, "under the guidance of the Central Committee's full commitment to support the Vietnamese people in their effort to save their country against the United States, China agrees in principle to satisfy Vietnam's requests for an additional twelve projects, pending further discussion of a few items."[7]

A Chinese Politburo Central Committee report on the Sino-American negotiations, dated May 29, 1971, reflected the adjustments China had to make in its basic diplomatic principles. After reviewing the progress of Sino-American reconciliation efforts over the past several years, the report set out eight counterdemands that should be made during the forthcoming visits by Kissinger and Nixon. First, the United States should withdraw all its military forces and close all its military installations in Taiwan Province and the neighboring Taiwan Strait, a requirement that was crucial to the normalization of relations between China and the United States.

Second, the United States should recognize Taiwan as the territory of the People's Republic of China and its liberation as purely an internal matter for the People's Republic of China, one in which China would not tolerate interference by foreign forces, and would be particularly vigilant against the activities of Japanese militarism. Third, China would diligently endeavor to liberate Taiwan by peaceful means and to conduct Taiwan affairs cautiously. Fourth, China would resolutely oppose any activity that might lead to "two Chinas," or "one China, one Taiwan."

Fifth, in the event that the first three requirements were not met, China and the United States would not establish diplomatic relations, but both sides could establish liaison offices in each other's capitals. Sixth, China would not be the first to raise issues related to the United Nations. Seventh, China would not take the initiative to open the subject of bilateral trade. Eighth, to maintain peace in Asia, China contended that the United States should withdraw all its forces from Indochina, Korea, Japan, and Southeast Asian nations. Bearing in mind the influence of the opposition (Democratic) party in the United States, the report concluded that, "even if none of the above can be successfully negotiated, and even if our disagreements make Nixon's China visit impossible, this does not harm our position at all."

Toward the end of the report, one section discussed whether the Sino-American negotiations would impede progress in the Paris talks or other ongoing discussions on the war in Indochina. According to the report:

There might be occasional interruptions. . . . However clearly stating our position on such issues would eventually help the anti-invasion war in Indochina and help the Paris talks, because Nixon had already reached the conclusion that the main points of conflict between the United States and the Soviet Union lie in the Middle East and Europe, not Asia. If progress occurred in the Sino-American negotiations, this could only encourage America's withdrawal from Indochina and assist the Paris talks. Even though the causal relationship among these events was not yet clear, the talks would help the anti-invasion struggle in Indochina.

The report further contended that, so long as the peoples of the three Indochinese nations planned to continue fighting on a long-term basis, ultimately they would win victory.[8] Clearly the Chinese government, in managing its relations with the United States, assigned the foremost importance to Taiwan. The Chinese government concluded that, even if the subject of Vietnam came up during the Sino-American negotiations, reconciliation with the United States would benefit—and certainly not be detrimental to—Vietnam.

The agenda for Kissinger's secret July 1971 visit to China, in addition to reiterating the strategic basis for a reconciliation between China and the United States, included another important item: the war in Indochina. During his talks with Zhou, Kissinger devoted more time to explaining U.S. policy toward Indochina than to any other issue, and he obviously hoped that Beijing would persuade North Vietnam to speed up the peace negotiations. Seeking to link China's wish to solve the Taiwan problem with the American desire to end the Vietnam War as quickly as possible, Kissinger informed Chinese leaders that, once the Vietnam War had ended, within a short period of time the United States would prepared to withdraw two-thirds of its military forces from Taiwan. Responding to Kissinger's proposal, however, Zhou feigned ignorance, and he avoided the topic of Vietnam altogether, neither promising to encourage North Vietnam to modify its negotiating position, nor showing any interest in Kissinger's request that Hanoi alter its policy on American prisoners of war. When Kissinger subsequently reported on his trip to Nixon, he said: "Profound differences and years of isolation yawn between us and the Chinese. They will be tough before and during the summit [Nixon's first visit to China] on the question of Taiwan and other major issues."[9]

Seeking to avoid arousing any suspicions in Hanoi, the day after he said farewell to Kissinger, Zhou suggested that he himself make a secret visit to North Vietnam. On July 13 and 14, he held conversations with Vietnam's premier and foreign minister, Le Duan and Pham Van Dong, to whom he furnished information on the ongoing Sino-American negotiations. Referring to a covert reference by Hanoi to these negotiations in an editorial in the Vietnamese *People* newspaper, Zhou told his Chinese Foreign Ministry colleagues Zhang Chunqiao and Yao Wenyuan: "The editorial shows the Vietnamese comrades' worry and appraisal. I think it can be published in its entirety. There is no need for a summary. We need to show that we have nothing to hide." He then added: "The course of events will prove that China, as led by Chairman Mao, consistently supports the continuing efforts by the three countries of Indochina to resist foreign invasion."[10]

Soon afterward, Zhou spoke repeatedly to the international press, further clarifying China's position. He emphasized that, to reduce world tension, the United States must withdraw its military forces completely from Asia, especially from the three countries of Indochina, and allow the peoples of those nations to solve their respective problems independently. China viewed this as a matter of principle. Zhou said that the subjects under discussion in the Sino-American negotiations were only bilateral issues, involving no third party. Because the United States and China had different political systems and broad disagreements on matters of principle, it would be difficult for them to solve all the contentious issues dividing them. The Chinese people resolutely supported the Indochinese people in their struggle for independence against the United States, and China would provide such support until the very end, when victory was finally attained. It was the sovereign right of the peoples of the three countries of Indochina to solve their own conflicts, in which no other party had the right to interfere. Where the Vietnam War was concerned, North Vietnam's representatives must deal directly with their American counterparts. Unlike the Soviet Union, which publicly claimed no role but was prepared to make a private deal with the United States, China had betrayed none of its principles.[11]

The Joint Communiqué that China and Vietnam signed on November 25, 1971, demonstrated that China's support for the Indochinese people in their war against the United States was an "unquestionable and established policy," and that China would consistently "fulfill her own international obligations." It continued: "The Vietnamese people, together with all the peoples of the countries of Indochina, are determined to fight until the end. The Chinese people are determined to support such efforts until the end. In order to assist the peoples of Vietnam and of Indochina, the Chinese people are prepared on every front; they are prepared to accept all the consequences of their uttermost sacrifice." China's fundamental position on the resolution of the Indochinese conflicts remained unchanged: It supported the people of Vietnam, and the United States must withdraw its troops completely and renounce its backing of the Southern Vietnamese regime.[12]

Simultaneously, as also described in chapter 8 above, China continuously increased its material aid to Vietnam. On September 27, 1971, the Chinese and North Vietnamese governments signed an agreement in Hanoi that China would provide Vietnam with economic and military assistance throughout 1972. Including this agreement, in 1971 alone China had agreed to send Vietnam seven assistance packages, outright aid with no strings attached, totaling 3.614 billion renminbi, or 48.67 percent of China's total foreign aid for that year.[13] Bearing in mind China's increased obligations to developing countries after it joined the United Nations, the amount of support Vietnam received unquestionably proved that China assigned the highest significance to its assistance program for Vietnam.[14] In military supplies alone, the amount China donated to Vietnam in 1971 and 1972 surpassed the total quantity it had given during the previous twenty years.[15]

Chinese Aid to Vietnam in 1972

Nixon's trip to China marked a significant milestone in the evolution of Sino-American relations. Before and after his visit, the United States initiated two rounds of diplomatic maneuvers, to try to persuade Beijing to acquiesce in Washington's policy of pressuring Vietnam through additional military initiatives. Though Beijing was preoccupied with preparations for Nixon's visit, it also had to maintain friendly relations with Hanoi. Beijing therefore adopted the circumspect course of neither supporting nor opposing Washington's policy.

In December 1971, facing the largest assemblage of enemy military forces it had yet encountered in South Vietnam, the Nixon administration, ignoring public opinion and angry protests from the U.S. Congress, launched a two-day bombing campaign against the Vietnamese auxiliary base south of the 22nd parallel. Simultaneously, Washington sent one of its strongest warnings to Moscow and Beijing, that any retaliation by North Vietnam would only provoke even more severe attacks. The United States sought to protect its position in the forthcoming high-level talks with Hanoi's allies. China made no immediate response.[16]

In January 1972, when the American advance team preparing for Nixon's visit, led by Alexander Haig, arrived in Beijing, Zhou reiterated Beijing's moral support for Hanoi, urging a speedy end to the Vietnam War to reduce Soviet influence in Indochina. Speaking of Nixon's forthcoming trip, Zhou stated that China would do all in its power to ensure that this high-level visit brought successful and positive results. Zhou also pointed out that fundamental differences over Vietnam still separated China and the United States, and he added that the continued implementation of the existing U.S. policy toward Vietnam would involve "undesirable factors" in Nixon's visit.[17]

In a public address on January 25, 1972, Nixon urged North Vietnam to resume peace talks. He also contacted Moscow and Beijing, warning that the United States had reached the limit of the compromises it was willing to make, and that if Hanoi launched a military attack, the United States would respond strongly. Zhou "returned a tart reply," stating that China was unfamiliar with Hanoi's internal affairs, while accusing the United States of trying to embroil China in Vietnam's problems. In addition, this letter tacitly implied that though China had never asked the United States to make any commitments on Vietnam, China itself had likewise made no pledges thereon.[18]

The meeting between Nixon and Mao was more relaxed than the president's earlier meetings with Soviet leaders in Moscow. Whereas the highest U.S. and Soviet officials argued constantly over specific issues, Mao showed an unusual interest in lecturing Nixon on broad philosophy. Where substantive issues were involved, Mao preferred to limit his contributions to the enunciation of principles.[19] During Nixon's visit, however, his talks with Zhou, as well as those between Kissinger and Qiao Guanhua, China's vice foreign minister, both touched upon Vietnam. From the American perspective, China still maintained its position of preferring to hold aloof from the talks between the United States and North Vietnam. China repeatedly stressed that it would continue to provide moral and material support to North Vietnam, not for ideological reasons nor to further China's national interests, but because from the historical viewpoint it felt obliged to do so. The Chinese government maintained that the Paris peace talks concerned only the United States and North Vietnam, and China therefore proposed to have no opinion upon them. Kissinger observed that, although China urged the United States to withdraw its troops, it did not really insist upon the full official line as propounded by Hanoi. Moreover, China issued no warning against any potential action the United States might take.[20]

In late March 1972, North Vietnamese troops finally launched a full-scale, carefully planned assault on the South. From Hanoi's viewpoint, "winning a military victory on the battle field would have decisive and strategic significance," and this round of attacks would determine the war's outcome. Hanoi therefore concentrated all available troops on the advance into the South.[21] The United States had anticipated these moves, and it responded with large-scale air strikes and the planting of mines. Simultaneously, Washington also exerted pressure on Beijing and Moscow, hoping the two big powers could and would force Hanoi to return to the negotiating table. American officials threatened that, unless the Soviets did so, they would break off high-level talks with Moscow. After intense debates and deliberations, the Soviets decided to continue with their preparations to receive Nixon. Finally, the Soviet Union not only considered and agreed to relay to Vietnam the "constructive" suggestions made by the United States but also itself suggested that the North Vietnamese should unconditionally resume the negotiations.[22]

By contrast, China expressed continuing support for Vietnam, but it continued to hold aloof from the peace talks. On April 3, Kissinger sent a secret letter to China, explaining that it was of the utmost importance to his government that the United States undertake military action to force a peaceful resolution of the Vietnam War. Kissinger also reminded Beijing that, if the United States were humiliated in Indochina, this would not be in China's long-term interests. In response, the Chinese government deployed its Foreign Ministry to criticize publicly the air strikes on Hanoi. Through secret back channels, China also replied to the United States, expressing support for North Vietnam and warning America against becoming ever more deeply embroiled in Vietnam. Kissinger noted, however, that China's reply contained no threats and, in addition, at the message's end Beijing reiterated its desire to normalize relations with Washington.[23] On the same day that China dispatched this communication to the United States, Zhou received Nguyen Tien, the North Vietnamese deputy chief of mission in Beijing, and stated that in supporting North Vietnam's efforts to carry the war to victory the Chinese government and people were backing a just cause.[24]

At this time, China initiated a large-scale campaign to aid North Vietnam. On May 9 and 10, Chinese Foreign Ministry officials and Politburo members held several meetings to devise measures to counter Nixon's public announcement that the United States would impose a blockade and launch combined air and naval assaults against North Vietnam's coast.[25] On May 13 and 14, Zhou met with Xuan Thuy to discuss transport congestion problems caused by the American air strikes. Although he refused one new request, that China should open its ports to Soviet ships, Zhou agreed to provide assistance to rebuild railroads, open protected ocean routes, increase transfers of military hardware, and donate food and fuel, and also to sweep and disarm mines laid around Vietnamese ports.[26]

From May 18 to 22, 1972, China's Ministry of Planning and the Office of Defense Industry held a national conference in Beijing, bringing together officials from twenty-six provinces in charge of industrial transportation and defense industries and 224 representatives from state-owned enterprises, along with members of the State Council and People's Liberation Army auxiliary staff. The conference carefully considered Vietnam's requests for increased or expedited assistance, and it fully implemented 98 of the 133 existing projects and 92 of those additional projects Vietnam had requested.[27] The conference also decided that whatever material each factory needed, the Chinese central government would itself supply directly. When raw materials were urgently needed, those units responsible could purchase or borrow these to meet production needs, and the central government would either reimburse them or pay the costs directly. Factories with insufficient output to meet current needs were ordered to upgrade their technology, double or multiply workers' shifts, and otherwise improve productivity. The central government also ordered that, when North Vietnam critically required specific items, Vietnam's needs would have the highest priority.[28] At this conference, vice premier Yu Qiuli stated that increasing production to assist Vietnam against the United States was an urgent task: "We must find all possible avenues to satisfy their needs. . . . The task of providing aid to Vietnam is an honorable, important, and long-term endeavor. There is no room for compromise. This work must be completed."[29]

According to Chinese sources, between May 18 and August 22, China and North Vietnam held bilateral talks during which they discussed and resolved a series of concrete issues concerning aid to Vietnam. On May 18, it was decided that two additional field oil pipes would be laid between Pingxiang and Hanoi, and 200 tons of steel plates that Vietnam had purchased in Hong Kong would be rush shipped to Vietnam. Talks on May 20 agreed that the Chinese navy would assist with mine sweeping, and that China would promptly deliver 200 trucks, transfer equipment for emergency bridge repair, and dispatch army missile specialists to Vietnam, who would serve under Vietnamese command. On June 8, the two sides decided to open up a concealed sea route. Besides agreeing to supply 100 50-ton freight ships the Vietnamese had requested in their shipping list, China provided an additional 50 vessels, and volunteered to supply them with the food, water, and fuel they needed for their delivery runs, to repair any ships that broke down, and also to supply salvage equipment for sunken ships.

On June 16, it was decided that China would immediately dispatch highway transportation specialist delegations to Vietnam, who would begin to open up road transportation. On June 18, Zhou replied to Le Duc Tho, agreeing that China would temporarily store the 1.4 million tons of aid supplies that the Soviet Union and other East European countries had promised North Vietnam under their 1972 aid agreement, but which had not yet been delivered, a measure designed to facilitate the signing of the 1973 aid agreement between Vietnam and these Soviet bloc countries. At Vietnam's request, it was decided that, although two divisions of the Chinese corps of railroad engineers that had been assigned to Vietnam for emergency railroad and bridge repair could not make this trip, China would transport all the necessary repair equipment and materials to the Vietnamese. On July 6, China informed Vietnam that it had assembled a delegation of forty experts, whom the Vietnamese had invited over to undertake emergency railroad repairs, and within ten days they would be ready to leave for Vietnam. On August 16, Vietnam agreed to open up additional highway transportation facilities, while China agreed to provide 3,000 additional freight trucks Vietnam had requested, and promised to make every effort to deliver these before the year ended.[30]

During this period, the greatest assistance China rendered Vietnam was the removal of mines from coastal defense harbors. Sea transportation was the primary channel whereby aid supplies entered Vietnam. According to American estimates, as much as seven times as many such goods entered North Vietnam through defense harbors as were delivered by rail.[31] One may readily imagine, therefore, the difficulties that North Vietnam faced when the United States sealed off all the seaports and river outlets along Vietnam's northern coast with 7,963 mines.[32] In response, Vietnam asked China for emergency help with mine clearance. After consultation, the Chinese Navy dispatched its mine-sweeping team, consisting of 318 persons, 12 mine-sweepers, and 4 escort battleships, which began to arrive in Vietnam from May 28 onward.

The mine-sweeping team worked in Vietnam for a year, during which time it performed 586 missions, accumulated over 27,800 sea miles, and one by one managed to dredge all the sea routes in northern Vietnam.[33] Due to China's help, in 1972 almost twice as many aid supplies were shipped into Vietnam or transported from the North to the South as in 1971.[34] As the Vietnamese negotiating representative Le Ban stated, the Vietnamese Communist Party and government were highly satisfied both with China's supplementary assistance and by its all-out efforts to "meet all Vietnam's needs for basic commodities."[35]

Chinese Support for a Vietnamese Peace Settlement, 1972–1973

In 1972, as military operations in the Vietnam War and the peace talks both entered their most intensified and critical phase, Nixon's visit to Moscow and the signature of the Strategic Arms Limitation Treaty disturbed Beijing.

The rapprochement between Washington and Moscow unquestionably threatened China's diplomatic strategy and the developing Sino-American relationship. Simultaneously, China also hoped that the United States would speedily withdraw from Vietnam, and thereby encourage Soviet-American conflicts in other areas to intensify. Subtle changes occurred in Beijing's policy toward Vietnam, especially in Beijing's attitude toward the Paris peace talks. On the one hand, China condemned the heavy military operations the United States launched in North Vietnam; on the other, its bilateral ties with the United States continued to develop until March 1973, when both sides agreed to establish liaison offices in each other's capitals. Simultaneously, while Beijing satisfied all North Vietnam's requests for material assistance, it also maintained that when opportunity offered North Vietnam should end the war.

After the Soviet-American summit, between June 19 and 23, Kissinger paid another visit to Beijing. Even though the United States had made little progress with China on Vietnam, Kissinger sensed that Zhou had become increasingly interested in implementing a cease-fire there.[36] Kissinger's perception was accurate. During this meeting, Zhou did not change China's principles or stance on Vietnam, but in subsequent dealings with the North Vietnamese he made slight adjustments in the Chinese position. Before the Soviet-American summit, Zhou had reassured Hanoi that China would not interfere in the Paris peace negotiations, would support North Vietnam's continuation of the war, and favored ousting Nguyen van Thieu, the South Vietnamese president.[37]

After the summit, however, China hinted that Vietnam should return to the negotiating table. On July 6, 1972, Zhou met Xuan Thuy and pointed out that the following four months would be critical in deciding the outcome of the Vietnam War and could bring either the continuation of the war or a softening of the U.S. position.[38] A few days later, Zhou told North Vietnam's peace negotiator, Le Duc Tho, "the strategy that you have adopted since 1968, of simultaneously fighting while talking, is the correct one. When you first started peace talks, some of our comrades thought you had taken the wrong approach. However, it turned out you had made the right decision."[39] Zhou shared with Tho China's own experiences in negotiations during the Chinese Civil War and proposed that North Vietnam talk with the leaders of other nations. He also suggested that Hanoi should open direct discussions with Thieu and his representatives, since Thieu spoke for the conservative right, and no one could replace him.[40] Given that at this time North Vietnam had withdrawn from the peace talks and was mounting large-scale military operations, China's emphasis on the merits of peace negotiations was clearly intended to persuade North Vietnam to resume talks. Because Vietnam had requested that, as one condition of a cease-fire, the United States should remove Thieu, Zhou's words clearly implied that on this matter Beijing did not support Hanoi's position.

The peace talks continued to be delayed, as North Vietnam attempted to take advantage of the American presidential elections to pressure the United States into further compromises, while Washington had not yet ironed out its differences with the Saigon government. In the face of this situation, Nixon decided to gamble and stake everything on a final assault on North Vietnam. On December 18, the United States issued an ultimatum to the North, and simultaneously began mass bombing strikes on Hanoi, the North Vietnamese coastal defense line, and all of North Vietnam, mobilizing its air forces on an unprecedented scale and utilizing, among other planes, several hundred B-52 bombers.

Unable to withstand further heavy bombardment, North Vietnam yielded to American demands. Only to save face did the North, citing Tho's ill health as an excuse, delay the resumption of negotiations from January 3, 1973, the date suggested by the United States, to January 8. Meanwhile, North Vietnam "appealed to the Soviet Union to use all its prestige and influence to exert pressure on the United States to prevent the latter from further escalating the war, to persuade the Americans to return immediately to the state of affairs existing before December 18, 1972, and through serious negotiations to resolve the remaining issues dividing them so as to reach an early agreement."[41]

China, unwilling to risk another setback on Vietnam, urged the Vietnamese representatives participating in the Paris peace talks to work diligently to reach a successful agreement. On December 29, while meeting Madam Nguyen Thi Binh, North Vietnam's foreign minister and chief negotiator at the Paris peace talks, Mao stated that, if successful, the peace agreement would mean that not only Southern Vietnam, but also, to a large extent the North, would normalize its relationship with the United States.[42] On December 31, Zhou told Truong Chinh, chairman of the Standing Committee of North Vietnam's National Assembly, that because Nixon genuinely wished to withdraw from Vietnam, this time the peace talks must be conducted with all sincerity and they must succeed.[43]

One must, however, remember that Beijing's intention was not to force Vietnam to yield, but to achieve a cease-fire at the earliest date possible, so that the Vietnamese situation would not block China's broader objective of aligning itself with the United States against the Soviet Union. At that time, China regarded the Soviet Union as its greatest enemy, and it considered Soviet socialist imperialism "more deceptive, and hence more dangerous, than old line imperialism."[44] Even as it urged compromise on Vietnam, China was therefore also simultaneously pressuring the United States. After the Paris talks resumed, Huang Hua, China's ambassador to the United Nations, in an October 25 message to his U.S. counterpart, explicitly condemned Saigon for making trouble, expressed China's belief in Washington's sincerity, and urged the United States "to seize this 'extremely opportune time to end the Vietnam War.'"

When objections from Saigon led the United States to postpone signing the cease-fire agreement, China again vehemently condemned the South Vietnamese government and asked the United States to resolutely oppose Saigon's actions. Simultaneously, China reminded the Nixon administration that, if it were to prolong the war and delay negotiations, "then how are people to view the U.S. statements about its preparedness to make efforts for the relaxation of tensions in the Far East?" Therefore, when Kissinger entertained Qiao Guanhua on November 13 and again asked Beijing to persuade North Vietnam to yield, Qiao advised the United States to make concessions instead, arguing that a great country could afford to adopt a more generous attitude: "One should not lose the whole world just to gain South Vietnam."[45]

Besides, China's desire to end the war soon by no means implied that it intended to leave the Saigon regime intact. From the perspective of Chinese leaders, ending the war should not affect the North Vietnamese government's objective of unification. On January 3, 1973, Zhou pointed out to Tho, "Nixon has many international and domestic issues to deal with. It seems that the United States is still willing to get out from Vietnam and Indochina. You should persist in principles while demonstrating flexibility during the negotiations. The most important [thing] is to let the Americans leave. The situation will change in six months or one year."[46] Mao's words of February 2, 1973, to Tho expressed China's position more clearly: "After the Paris Agreements have been signed you need at least six months to stabilize the situation in South Vietnam [and] to strengthen your forces."[47]

The war ended on January 27, 1973, when the Paris Peace Accords were signed. Mao believed that China could now continue its strategy of "joining with the United States against the Soviet Union." During a conversation with Kissinger on February 17, Mao expressed satisfaction with the way the relationship between China and the United States was developing. He also emphasized that a present and growing Soviet threat did indeed exist. Mao hoped that China and the United States could cooperate to contain the Soviet Union and that the United States would take bolder initiatives to prevent the global spread of Soviet power, especially in Europe, the Middle East, and Asia.[48] At this time, however, the relationship between China and North Vietnam began to deteriorate. Only six months after concluding the 1973 agreement for Chinese aid to North Vietnam, Pham Van Dong and Le Duc Tho returned to Beijing, asking that China provide a new aid package for 1974, a gigantic request that overall totaled 8 billion renminbi. Zhou considered it unrealistic for China to agree to such a huge package, which surpassed its financial capabilities, but accepted a more modest aid package amounting to 2.5 billion renminbi.[49]

In practice, although China and the United States greatly improved their bilateral relations between 1971 and 1973, this was also the period when China provided the most substantial aid to Vietnam, worth a total of 9 billion renminbi. During the heaviest period of U.S. bombing, there were 58 groups, comprising 719 Chinese experts, in Vietnam.[50] If one compares the aid packages China provided to North Vietnam between 1971 and 1975 with their counterparts in the period 1965 to 1970, it is clearly apparent that, far from China reducing its aid after the Sino-American reconciliation took place, the amount actually rose. To give specific examples, the quantity of textiles increased by 160 percent, steel by 125 percent, coal by 1,710 percent, fuel by 1,785 percent, and automobiles by 643 percent.[51] The effort of providing such assistance to the cause of world revolution, especially in Vietnam, nonetheless inflicted a heavy toll on Chinese economic strength. From the early 1970s, the detrimental economic impact of the Cultural Revolution also became increasingly apparent, leaving China genuinely unable to satisfy Vietnam's growing appetite for aid.[52]

Seeking to recruit that country and retain its loyalties, in the same years the Soviet Union likewise increased its own stake in North Vietnam. In April 1971, the Twenty-Fourth Soviet Party Congress passed a resolution claiming that Indochina could prove crucial to its entry into Southeast Asia. According to this resolution, Soviet assistance to Vietnam would switch from an ad hoc and transitional to a planned and long-term cooperative basis.[53] Diplomatic cooperation between the Soviet Union and North Vietnam also intensified. For example, during the Paris peace talks, on July 12, 1971, the Soviet Union preapproved and supported a proposal by the North Vietnamese representatives to link U.S. troop withdrawals to the removal of South Vietnam's president Thieu.[54] North Vietnam even turned over to the

Soviet Union a confidential report from its central military committee to the Vietnamese Politburo, which contained many top secrets, including a status report on the assassination of leaders in Saigon by Hanoi's defense and intelligence agents, and a full list of the numbers and conditions of American prisoners of war.[55] Soviet aid to Vietnam continued to increase, surpassing Chinese aid by a large margin.[56] North Vietnam believed that it could capitalize on and maximize its gains from the conflict between China and the Soviet Union.

For this reason, therefore, only one month after Beijing turned down its request for additional assistance, the Vietnamese sought—and received— aid from the Soviet Union. The Soviet Union decided to convert its previous assistance to Vietnam from loans into outright aid, thereby eliminating Vietnam's obligation to repay this funding, and it agreed to offer Vietnam additional assistance amounting to $1.07 billion in 1975.[57] In practice, as chapter 12 below confirms, serious conflicts also existed between the Soviet Union and Vietnam, and Hanoi did not trust the Soviet Union. For instance, North Vietnam's leaders resented the development of détente between the United States and the Soviet Union, and Nixon's visit to Moscow infuriated them. The Soviet Union also disliked North Vietnam's attitude—that all outstanding issues must be resolved by military conflict.[58] Even so, tempted by the substantial financial benefits that might accrue to it, Vietnam calculatingly leaned toward the Soviet Union.

Despite or even because of their shared ideological outlook, throughout the Vietnam War, relations among North Vietnam and its two communist patrons, China and the Soviet Union, were perennially difficult, as each state pursued what it saw as its own best interests, while seeking to present itself as an exemplar of communist ideological purity and international solidarity. Sino-Soviet antagonisms, suspicions, and eventually military clashes were additional factors impelling China toward the United States.

The research undertaken for this chapter reveals that, although China did not take extreme measures to reduce American military pressure on Vietnam, because this might have damaged the ongoing process of Sino-American reconciliation, neither did it do anything detrimental to the interests of its ally, North Vietnam. China pursued a consistent foreign policy of providing moral and material support to Vietnam. The Nixon administration understood this attitude, and their differences over Vietnam did not affect the reconciliation between Beijing and Washington. While the United States looked to North Vietnam's allies to pressure that country into ending the war, its primary focus was on the Soviet Union rather than China. China's limited economic and military strength, together with the unfavorable regional political environment, made it impossible for the Chinese leadership to satisfy all of North Vietnam's demands while reorienting their own foreign policies, and so prevented the Chinese government from maximizing either its global or regional position.

In sum, in the late 1960s and early 1970s, the realigned Chinese foreign policy achieved its fundamental goal of normalizing relations with the United States. This new orientation meant that the Chinese government could no longer maintain friendly relations with its Vietnamese "comrades and brothers." As Vietnam gradually moved into the Soviet camp, China had to face a new challenge from the south. Throughout the 1970s, antagonism between China and Vietnam gradually intensified, eventually—after Vietnam invaded Cambodia and overthrew China's client there—resulting in the brief 1979 Sino-Vietnamese War, which marked the beginning of more than a decade during which China and Vietnam regarded each other as strategic enemies and targeted their military preparations at each other.

Notes

1. Memorandum of conversation between Li Xiannian and Pham Van Dong, September 10, 1977, *Renmin Ribao* [People's Daily], March 23, 1979; Roderick MacFarquhar and John K. Fairbank, eds., *The Cambridge History of China, Volume 15: 1966–1982,* Chinese ed. (Hainan: Hainan Publishing House, 1992), 432.

2. B. T. Kulik, "Sino-Soviet Conflict in the Cold War," paper prepared for the conference, "The Cold War and Sino-Soviet Relations," Beijing, October 1997; MacFarquhar and Fairbank, *Cambridge History of China,* 432.

3. In an article which focuses on analyzing the smaller, Chinese-Soviet-Vietnamese triangle, Li Danhui elaborates on the Chinese-Soviet-Vietnamese relationship. See Li Danhui, "Zhongsu guanxi yu Zhongguo de yuanyue kangmei" [Sino-Soviet relations and China's policy of resisting American aggression and aiding Vietnam], *Dangdai Zhongguoshi yanjiu* [Contemporary Chinese history research] 3 (1998): 111–26.

4. Meeting minute of Mao Zedong, May 11, 1970, in *77 Conversations between Chinese and Foreign Leaders on the Wars in Indochina, 1964–1977,* Cold War International History Project Working Paper 22, ed. Odd Arne Westad, Chen Jian, Stein Tønnesson, Nguyen Vu Tung, and James G. Hershberg (Washington, D.C.: Woodrow Wilson International Center for Scholars, 1998), 163–69.

5. Chinese Communist Party Central Documentary Research Department, *Zhou Enlai nianpu, 1949–1976* [A chronological record of Zhou Enlai, 1949–1976], 3 vols. (Beijing: Central Press of Historical Documents, 1997), vol. 3, 441.

6. Zhou Enlai, speech at welcoming ceremony in Hanoi, March 6, 1971, Fujian Archives, 244-1-77, p. 19, Fuzhou, China.

7. Aid Records, Ministry of Railway Administration Archives, Beijing (hereafter Railway Archives), vol. 7 (1971), 4–7.

8. Report of the Chinese Communist Party Politburo Central Committee, May 29, 1971, source not currently identifiable.

9. Henry A. Kissinger, *The White House Years,* 4 vols., Chinese ed. (Beijing: World Knowledge Press, 1980), vol. 3, 23–30; Xue Mouhong and Pei Jianzhang, eds., *Dangdai Zhongguo waijiao* [Contemporary Chinese diplomacy] (Beijing: Chinese Academy of Social Sciences Press, 1990), 221–22; Robert Ross, *Negotiating Cooperation: The United States and China, 1969–1989,* Chinese ed. (Beijing: World Knowledge Press, 1998), 51–54.

10. *Zhou Enlai nianpu,* vol. 3, 469–70. Despite Zhou's advice, due to Zhang Chunqiao's opposition this article was not published.

11. *Zhou Enlai,* interview with James Reston of the *New York Times,* August 5, 1971; interview with *Asahi Shimbun,* October 28, 1971; and interview with Neville Maxwell, British author and journalist, November 20, 1971, 244-1-77, pp. 48–49, 52–54, Fujian Archives.

12. *Renmin Ribao* [People's Daily], November 27, 1971.

13. Fang Weizhong, ed., *Zhonghua Renmin Gongheguo Jingji Dashiji (1949–1980)* [A Record of the Major Economic Events of the People's Republic of China, 1949–1980] (Beijing: Chinese Academy of Social Sciences Press, 1984), 484. The exact percentage has been calculated by this chapter's author.

14. The number of nations to which China provided assistance at this time totaled sixty-six, twice the number in the previous year. Shi Lin, ed., *Dangdai Zhongguo de duiwai peihe jingji* [Foreign economic cooperation in contemporary China] (Beijing: Chinese Academy of Social Sciences Press, 1989), 57.

15. Yu Qiuli, speech, May 19, 1972, file 20-0149, National Planning Committee Archives, Beijing.

16. Kissinger, *White House Years,* vol. 3, 401. Kissinger believed Zhou Enlai's words implied that China would remain uninvolved in this.

17. Kissinger, *White House Years,* vol. 4, 3. See also *Zhou Enlai nianpu,* vol. 3, 506–7.

18. Kissinger, *White House Years,* vol. 4, 5–6, 65–68.

19. China, to date, has only published portions of the records of these meetings. The U.S. version of these records has been published in William Burr, ed., *The Kissinger Transcripts* (New York: New Press, 1998), 59–66.

20. Kissinger, *White House Years,* vol. 4, 28–30, 45–47.

21. Military History Academy of the Department of Defense Vietnam, *History of the People's Army of Vietnam,* Chinese ed., 2 vols. (Nanning: Guangxi People's Press, 1991), vol. 2, 282; Anatoly Dobrynin, *Trust,* Chinese ed. (Beijing: World Knowledge Press, 1997), 285–90.

22. Kissinger, *White House Years,* vol. 4, 78–82, 86–87, 121–22, 183–84; Dobrynin, *Trust,* 285–86. Some scholars have argued, in this author's view unconvincingly, that U.S. diplomatic pressure on the Soviet Union had little effect. See Ni Xiaoquang and Robert Ross, eds., *Zhongsumei sanlian guanxi* [The triangular relationship among the United States, China, and the Soviet Union] (Beijing: People's Press, 1993), 230–33.

23. Kissinger, *White House Years,* vol. 4, 78–80, 84–85, 90.

24. *Zhou Enlai nianpu,* vol. 3, 519; Westad et al., *77 Conversations,* 181–82.

25. *Zhou Enlai nianpu,* vol. 3, 524.

26. "Conversations between Zhou Enlai and Xuan Thuy," May 13 and 14, 1972, Office Records, Railway Archives, vol. 52 (1972), 2–10.

27. Summary of meeting, May 25, 1972, no. 12 (122), National Planning Committee Archives, pp. 2–8.

28. Summary of meeting, May 25, 1972, National Planning Committee Archives.

29. Yu Qiuli, speech, May 19, 1972, File 20-0149, National Planning Committee Archives.

30. Minutes of the various meetings that took place between May 18 and August 22, 1972, Office Records, Railway Archives, vol. 53 (1972), 16–21, 48–53, 63–67, 84–89, 117–20, 125–27, and vol. 52 (1972), 37–51, 19–36.

31. Kissinger, *White House Years,* vol. 4, 164–65.

32. Military History Academy of the Department of Defense of Vietnam, *History of the People's Army of Vietnam,* vol. 4, 289.

33. Han Huaizhi and Tan Jingqiao, eds., *Dangdai Zhongguo jundui de junshi gongzuo* [Contemporary military operations of the Chinese armed forces], 2 vols. (Beijing: Chinese Academy of Social Sciences Press, 1989), vol. 1, 553–55.

34. Military History Academy of the Department of Defense of Vietnam, *History of the People's Army of Vietnam,* vol. 2, 292.

35. "Minutes of Meeting of Ye Jianying, Li Xiannian, Le Ban, and Others," June 28, 1972, Office Records, Railway Archives, vol. 53 (1972), 73–79.

36. Kissinger, *White House Years,* vol. 4, 322–23; Dobrynin, *Trust,* 296–97.

37. "Minutes of Meeting between Zhou Enlai and Le Duc Tho," June 18, 1972, Office Records, Railway Archives, vol. 52 (1972), 19–36.

38. *Zhou Enlai nianpu,* vol. 3, 535.

39. *Zhou Enlai nianpu,* vol. 3, 535.

40. "Minutes of meeting between Zhou Enlai and Le Duc Tho, July 12, 1972," in *77 Conversations,* ed. Westad et al., 182–84.

41. Minutes of meeting between Ilia S. Scherbakov and Hoang Van Loi, December 27, 1972, SD06768 (personal classification system for Li Danhui / Shen Zhihua collection of Soviet records).

42. "Meeting between Mao Zedong and Nguyen Thi Binh, December 19, 1972," in *77 Conversations,* ed. Westad et al., 180–85.

43. *Zhou Enlai nianpu,* vol. 3, 569.

44. Editorials, *Zhongguo Renmin Jiefangjun Ribao* [People's Liberation Army Daily] and *Hong Qi* [Red Flag Journal], October 1, 1972.

45. Kissinger, *White House Years,* vol. 4, 439–41, 449, 462–63.

46. *Zhou Enlai nianpu,* vol. 3, 571; Westad et al., *77 Conversations,* 186.

47. "Meeting between Mao Zedong and Le Duc Tho, February 2, 1973," in *77 Conversations,* ed. Westad et al., 186.

48. Burr, *Kissinger Transcripts,* 86–101.

49. Fang Weizhong, ed., *Zhonghua Renmin Gongheguo Jingji Dashiji (1949–1980)* [A Record of the Major Economic Events of the People's Republic of China] (Beijing: Chinese Academy of Social Sciences Press, 1984), 512; *Zhou Enlai nianpu,* vol. 3, 598.

50. Yun Shui, *Chushi qiguo jishi: jiangjun dashi Wang Youping* [Record of diplomatic missions to seven countries: Ambassador General Wang Youping] (Beijing: World Knowledge Press, 1996), 201.

51. Shi, *Dangdai Zhongguo de duiwai peihe jingji,* 58, percentage increases calculated by the author of this chapter.

52. During this period, most aid supplies were gathered together by "tapping into the inventory of warehouses," a movement in which the author participated during his youth.

53. Ilia S. Scherbakov, Political Report, May 21, 1971, SD01829, Li/Shen Collection.

54. Minutes of meeting between Scherbakov and Nguyen Gai Thi, July 1, 1971, SD01826, Li/Shen Collection; summary of meeting between Valerian A. Zorin and Xuan Thuy, July 15, 1971, SD01827, Li/Shen Collection.

55. Pyotr Ivashutin, chief of Soviet military intelligence, report to Central Soviet Party membership, November 11, 1972, SD01835, Li/Shen Collection.

56. Li, "Zhongsu guanxi yu Zhongguo de yuanyue kangmei"; Dobrynin, *Trust,* 280; Kissinger, *White House Years,* 4:59. During the spring offensive of 1972, 90 percent of the military equipment used by the North Vietnamese armed forces was of Soviet origin, with all tanks and up-to-date artillery supplied directly by the Soviet Union.

57. Guo Ming, ed., *Zhongyue guanxi yanbian sishinian* [The evolution of Sino-Vietnamese relations over the last forty years] (Nanning: Guangxi People's Press, 1992), 103.

58. Dobrynin, *Trust,* 282–83; Scherbakov, political report, May 21, 1971, SD01829, Li/Shen Collection.

11

China and the Cambodian Conflict, 1970–1975

Zhai Qiang

The twentieth century proved tragic for many countries, but hardly any place on Earth suffered as long, as much, and as pointlessly as Cambodia. From the time North Vietnam resumed armed struggle to unify the South in 1959, Cambodia lived in the shadow of the Vietnam War. Hanoi used Cambodian territory to send troops and supplies to South Vietnam to wage revolutionary war. To end North Vietnamese penetration into the South, the Richard Nixon administration initiated secret bombing of Vietnamese sanctuaries in Cambodia in 1969. The right-wing coup against Prince Norodom Sihanouk in 1970 and U.S. support for the Lon Nol regime drove Sihanouk into the arms of the Khmer Rouge led by Pol Pot. In 1975, Pol Pot assumed power in Phnom Penh, the beginning of a long national nightmare for Cambodia.

Much scholarly attention has been devoted to the role of the United States in destabilizing Cambodia in the period 1969–70 and paving the way for the rise of Pol Pot. China's response to the Cambodian crisis, by contrast, has received relatively little study. Drawing upon recently released Chinese and American sources, this chapter examines the complex relationship between China, Sihanouk, and the Khmer Rouge during the period 1970–75, focusing on how Beijing's competition with the Moscow and Hanoi affected its policy toward Phnom Penh.

China's Relations with Sihanouk before 1970

From the mid-1950s to the eve of the Cultural Revolution in 1966, Beijing maintained cordial relations with Phnom Penh. The Chinese leaders befriended Prince Norodom Sihanouk to advance two goals. Their first and primary motivation was that, by encouraging Cambodia to abjure any alliance with the United States, they sought to frustrate the American policy of containment against China. Second, Mao Zedong undoubtedly intended to use Sihanouk, a proud and ardent nationalist, as an instrument to limit Vietnamese influence in Cambodia.

China's friendship with Sihanouk began at the 1955 Bandung Conference, where Premier Zhou Enlai pledged support for Cambodian neutralism. He warned Sihanouk against the dangers implicit in U.S. policy and urged him, rather than using American advisers, to employ French military advisers to train his troops. He also invited Sihanouk to visit China. The Cambodian leader assured Zhou that he would not join any military bloc and would not provide military bases to the United States.[1]

During Sihanouk's February 13–21, 1956, visit to China, Mao flatteringly praised his stance of peace and neutrality, declaring that such a policy had a great global impact. Zhou stressed the principle of equality between states in international affairs, regardless of their size. In the joint declaration issued at the end of Sihanouk's trip, the two countries endorsed the Five Principles of Peaceful Coexistence as guidelines for Sino-Cambodian relations. In the wake of Sihanouk's visit, China agreed to provide Cambodia with free economic aid equivalent to £8 million. Cambodia would use this aid to build textile, cement, and paper factories; construct roads, bridges, and irrigation systems; and establish schools and hospitals.[2] Cambodia was the first nonsocialist country to receive free economic aid from China.

In November 1956, Zhou paid a state visit to Phnom Penh, where he reaffirmed China's respect for Cambodian neutrality. The Chinese premier also sought to allay Sihanouk's fears that China would seek to dominate Cambodia indirectly through the influence of the country's Chinese population, numbering about 400,000 and including many business leaders and merchants, by urging them to pledge loyalty to Cambodia. On behalf of the Chinese government, Zhou donated medical equipment and a grant to build an arts school to Cambodia.[3]

During this period, there undoubtedly was friction between China and Cambodia. Beijing deplored Sihanouk's acceptance of American military aid. Sihanouk, for his part, preoccupied with protecting his country's borders from the irredentist demands of South Vietnam and Thailand, criticized China's reluctance to give a blanket guarantee of Cambodian territorial integrity.[4] Yet despite these differences, Chinese-Cambodian relations remained largely friendly.

The Chinese leaders' endorsement of neutralism in the mid-1950s was a significant departure from their previous adherence to the rigid "two-camp" theory. In 1949, Mao had lashed out at the "illusion of a third road," while Liu Shaoqi had ridiculed such neutral statesmen as Jawaharlal Nehru, U Nu, and Sukarno as "stooges of imperialism" and urged communist groups in those neutral states to wage armed struggle on the Chinese model. By the mid-1950s, however, a more pragmatic and moderate policy of peaceful coexistence with Asian countries possessing different political systems ousted this radical approach.[5]

As chapter 1 of the present volume by Yang Kuisong demonstrates, in an attempt to discredit Soviet leader Nikita Khrushchev's advocacy of peaceful coexistence with the United States, Mao began in 1958 to reemphasize support for national liberation struggles. Despite the radical turn in their foreign policy, the Chinese leaders continued to woo Sihanouk, considering his neutrality policy advantageous to their efforts to break the American isolation of China. In June 1958, tensions between Cambodia and South Vietnam rose due to a border dispute. On June 30, Chinese foreign minister Chen Yi declared that China supported Cambodia in its conflict with South Vietnam. On July 19, China and Cambodia established diplomatic relations.[6] The timing of Sihanouk's decision to open diplomatic ties with Beijing indicated the close links between his China policy and his relations with South Vietnam and Thailand. He held the U.S. government, especially the Central Intelligence Agency, responsible for actions launched by Saigon and Bangkok. Cambodia's recognition of the People's Republic of China (PRC) represented a setback for U.S. containment policies in Southeast Asia, demonstrating that U.S. policymakers, preoccupied with Cold War confrontations, had paid little attention to the traditional long-standing rivalries among the regional players in mainland Southeast Asia.[7]

On August 15, 1958, Sihanouk arrived in Beijing for a state visit, as Mao's communist euphoria was reaching its apogee. That summer, Mao launched China on the Great Leap Forward, which he believed could be accomplished by the "mass movement" of the people. With a stroke of his ink brush, the Chinese leader hurled the vast rural population into communes, with all land owned by the state and worked in common. The peasants relinquished all property, even their shovels and hoes. Communal dining halls and laundries released women from household duties to work in the fields, while men learned to build backyard steel furnaces to supplement China's iron and steel output in the urban mills. On August 17, Zhou took Sihanouk to the Beijing Steel Plant, the showcase of Mao's effort to develop China's steel industry, and the two men discussed how best to enhance steel production. Advising the prince to build steel plants in Cambodia, the Chinese premier stressed that once a country began to make steel, it would no longer be vulnerable to outside aggression. When China produced no steel in the past, Zhou explained, it had been bullied by foreign powers. After expressing his readiness to help Cambodia build its steel industry, Zhou said that he hoped that all countries in the East possessed steel-making capabilities. On August 21, Zhou escorted Sihanouk to a rice-producing village in Wuqing County, Hebei Province.[8] Though Sihanouk's impressions of Mao's grand enterprise of the Great Leap Forward remain unclear, the warm welcome he received in China undoubtedly impressed him.

U.S. officials were very alarmed by Sihanouk's visit to China, fearing that he might accept military aid from Beijing. U.S. ambassador Carl Strom was relieved that, although China had offered both economic and military assistance to Cambodia, Sihanouk rejected any military help on the grounds that he found that provided by the United States and France sufficient for his needs. Sihanouk told Strom that his visit to China would cause no changes in Cambodian policy, though Strom retorted that Cambodia's announcement of support for PRC admission to the United Nations represented a definite modification. Sihanouk also informed Strom that he had discussed relations with the United States with Zhou, who had remarked that the real problem dividing China and the United States was Taiwan.[9] Sihanouk's rejection of proffered Chinese military assistance reflected his continuing policy of delicate balancing and carefully orchestrated maneuvers. Having drawn closer to China, Sihanouk was anxious not to overstep the mark and alienate the United States.[10]

Chinese-Cambodian cooperation continued into the 1960s. In 1960, Sihanouk sent three sons to study in China, created a Cambodia-China Friendship Association, and endorsed Zhou's proposal for a "zone of peace" in Indochina.[11] Toward the end of that year, Sihanouk visited Beijing, and the two countries signed a Treaty of Friendship and Non-Aggression, stipulating that both countries follow policies of nonaggression against each other and neither side would join a military bloc aimed against the other signatory.[12] China successfully prevented Cambodia from accepting the "protection" of the Southeast Asia Treaty Organization (SEATO).

In 1962, both Cambodia and China became embroiled in border disputes with their neighbors, and both sought support from each other. When tensions between Cambodia and Thailand increased due to their border conflicts, Sihanouk called for an international conference to guarantee his country's sovereignty and maintain its borders inviolate, a proposal China supported.[13] As Sino-Indian relations deteriorated following escalating tensions along their border, Beijing sought sympathy and support from Asian nations, including Cambodia. On June 4, Zhou explained China's position on the Sino-Indian border dispute to Penn Nouth, the first minister of the Royal Government of Cambodia, who was visiting China. Zhou said that China would follow two principles in settling the dispute: first, to maintain the status quo at the border; and second, to resolve the problem through negotiations. Because China had settled its border problems with Burma and Nepal through peaceful discussions and had begun border talks with Pakistan, Zhou asked, why could not China and India resolve their border differences likewise?[14]

In May 1963, Liu Shaoqi, the PRC's chairman, toured Cambodia, stressing the principle of equality between nations in international affairs and endorsing Sihanouk's call for an expanded Geneva conference to guarantee Cambodia's neutrality. Sihanouk commemorated Liu's visit by naming a Cambodian street after him.[15] Liu visited Cambodia at a time when Sihanouk was heightening his persecution of Khmer Rouge members (the Cambodian Communists), who were now forced to retreat to the countryside. As American involvement in South Vietnam escalated, both Beijing and Hanoi courted Sihanouk to check American expansion of the conflict through Cambodia. North Vietnam recognized Cambodia's rights over islands claimed by the Saigon government in the Gulf of Thailand. The communist states of China and North Vietnam were more interested in keeping Sihanouk friendly than in backing a Cambodian Communist revolt against his rule.[16]

In 1964, China continued to support Sihanouk's call for a Geneva conference to guarantee Cambodia's neutrality. Meeting the Cambodian ambassador to China on February 7, Vice Premier Deng Xiaoping complimented Sihanouk for adopting an independent foreign policy and praised him for resisting American pressure, reiterating China's endorsement of Sihanouk's call for an international conference on Cambodia.[17]

Sihanouk reciprocated China's goodwill and support by echoing Beijing on several international issues. In August 1963, he supported Beijing's position on the Partial Nuclear Test Ban Treaty and endorsed China's call for the total banning and complete destruction of nuclear weapons. On various occasions, Zhou expressed appreciation for Sihanouk's support.[18]

In 1965, the Chinese leaders showed less interest in supporting Sihanouk's plan for a Geneva conference on Cambodia, primarily because they feared that the United States and the Soviet Union might use such a meeting to discuss a negotiated settlement in Vietnam. In April, Sihanouk heeded China's advice by withdrawing his call for a Geneva conference on Cambodia.[19] When Sihanouk broke diplomatic relations with the United States in May, Zhou sent him a telegram, applauding his decision and pledging that if the United States extended the war to Cambodia, "China will not sit still."[20] In a conversation with Sihanouk in Beijing on September 29, Mao expressed his satisfaction with Cambodia's policy of standing up to the United States, Thailand, and South Vietnam, terming Sihanouk's international line a "popular" policy.[21]

When the Communist insurgency escalated in South Vietnam, Sihanouk allowed China to operate a transportation conduit through Cambodia to funnel weapons, munitions, food, and medical supplies to the National Liberation Front (NLF) in South Vietnam.[22] Between 1965 and 1967, Chinese weapons for 50,000 soldiers arrived by ship via Sihanoukville.[23] Some of the Chinese arms went to equip the Cambodian army.[24]

Mao's Cultural Revolution, however, seriously damaged Sino-Cambodian relations. In Phnom Penh, overseas Chinese, inspired by the radical frenzy in China, proclaimed their allegiance to Mao. In early 1967, Sino-Khmers held demonstrations outside the Soviet Embassy. Chinese instructors working with the Cambodian army distributed Mao badges among the Cambodian soldiers. Khmer leftists openly endorsed the Khmer-Chinese Friendship Association, which was active in the Chinese-language schools in eulogizing Mao.[25]

Sihanouk, greatly disturbed and alarmed by the Chinese Cultural Revolution, told Australian prime minister Harold Holt, who visited Cambodia in March 1967, that he could not understood what was going on in China, and expressed apprehension that Mao, its chairman, was apparently becoming senile while his wife was emerging as the real leader.[26] In August, Sihanouk sent his foreign minister, Prince Norodom Phurissara, to Beijing to ascertain China's official position. Phurissara arrived when ultra-leftist influence in the Foreign Ministry was at its peak, for some time drastically restricting Zhou's ability to direct Chinese foreign policy. On August 17 and 19, Zhou met with Phurissara.[27] According to Western sources, Zhou offered soothing remarks but claimed that Chinese should "be permitted to display their pride of the cultural revolution and their love for Chairman Mao."[28]

An angry Sihanouk reacted by closing the Cambodia-China Friendship Association, shutting down the five Chinese-language newspapers, and announcing the withdrawal of diplomats from the Cambodian Embassy in Beijing. Much alarmed by these setbacks in Sino-Cambodian relations and also the general disruption of Chinese foreign policy resulting from the ultra-leftist seizure of the Foreign Ministry, in late August Zhou moved to limit ultra-leftist influence over foreign policy and reassert his own control within the Foreign Ministry. He first condemned the ultra-leftists for making foreign policy decisions without consulting him. He then asked Yang Chengwu, the deputy chief of staff of the People's Liberation Army, to fly to Shanghai to see Mao and alert him to the negative consequences of the ultra-leftists' interference in the Foreign Ministry. Sharing Zhou's concerns, on August 26 Mao ordered the arrest of the ultra-leftist representatives in the Foreign Ministry.[29] Mao's intervention effectively ended radical control of Chinese foreign policy. On September 14 and October 26, Zhou met twice with the Cambodian ambassador to China, apologizing to him for Beijing's policy, whereupon Sihanouk rescinded his decision to withdraw Cambodian diplomats from China.[30]

Beijing–Khmer Rouge Ties from 1965 to 1970

Our information on Beijing's pre-1969 relations with the Khmer Rouge is still extremely limited. To date, little Chinese evidence has emerged to illuminate this subject. In 1965, Pol Pot decided to push for armed resistance in Cambodia. According to the *Black Paper* and Western sources, in the summer of 1965 Pol Pot visited Hanoi to meet with Vietnamese Communist leaders, but they turned down his request to launch a military struggle in Cambodia.[31] After visiting Hanoi, Pol Pot proceeded to China, where he spent several months, including some time working with Deng Xiaoping, the secretary general of the Chinese Communist Party (CCP).[32] According to David Chandler, Pol Pot was in China during the early phase of the Cul-

tural Revolution and was befriended by Kang Sheng, a senior Chinese official who headed Mao's secret police.[33] No Chinese evidence has yet confirmed the report of Pol Pot's 1966 visit to China, but it seems unlikely that
the Chinese leaders endorsed his plans to conduct an armed struggle in
Cambodia.

The tensions in Cambodia exploded early in 1967 with the outbreak of
an antigovernment uprising near Samlaut in western Battambang. This upheaval greatly disturbed the Chinese leaders, who found themselves in a
dilemma over Cambodia. On the one hand, they preferred Sihanouk's neutral policy because this served their purposes of preventing the expansion
of the Indochina conflict and restricting Hanoi's influence. Any overthrow
of Sihanouk threatened to escalate the war; raise Hanoi's profile within the
Cambodian revolutionary movement; and, given the Democratic Republic
of Vietnam's (DRV's) heavy reliance on sophisticated Soviet weapons, increase Moscow's influence in the region. On the other hand, because the
Chinese leaders believed that the Communist Party of Kampuchea (CPK,
the new name Pol Pot gave his party in 1966) had organized the Samlaut rebellion, any failure to endorse the revolt would compromise China's revolutionary image, making opposition difficult and embarrassing.[34]

To resolve this dilemma, Zhou devised the theory of "revolution through
stages" as he attempted to persuade Cambodian Communists to refrain from
revolution against Sihanouk. According to Zhou's formula, the anti-Nguyen
Van Thieu struggle in South Vietnam should take priority over the development of revolutionary forces in Cambodia. The Chinese premier explained this theory to Pham Van Dong and Vo Nguyen Giap during conversations in Beijing between April 7 and 12, 1967.

In the April 10 discussion, Zhou raised the question of Cambodia, emphasizing the importance of "winning Sihanouk's sympathy" because he had
been helpful in transporting materials to the NLF. When Dong asked the Chinese their opinions of Lon Nol, Zhou replied that the Cambodian general
was "not trustworthy," while Chen claimed he was "pro-American." Zhou
nonetheless believed that Lon Nol could be utilized to help support the war
in South Vietnam: "Lon Nol once visited China, and he made some impression. If we spend money on him, he can be exploited for some time."[35]

Meeting with Dong the next day, Zhou continued to stress the need to
work with Sihanouk and Lon Nol. Expressing his disapproval of the Samlaut revolt, Zhou reaffirmed China's preference for concentrating on the war
in South Vietnam and seeking a united front with the Cambodian government. "At this moment," Zhou asserted,

Vietnam's victory is the first priority. If the Vietnam-Cambodian border areas are blockaded, armed forces in South Vietnam will face difficulties, [and] then the Cambodian revolutionary forces will not proceed. The struggle of Vietnam is in the common interest of the Indochinese and Southeast Asian peoples, and the victory of this struggle is of a decisive nature. In this situation, the Cambodian struggle . . . has limited objectives. . . . One has to know how to place the overall interest above the limited ones.

Zhou urged the North Vietnamese to explain this "logic" to the Cambodian Communists. Dong admitted that Hanoi had instructed its Central Office for South Vietnam (COSVN) to contact the "people's faction" in Cambodia.[36] Zhou's remarks indicated that at this time Beijing did not have direct contacts with the CPK, whereas his assumption that the CPK controlled the situation in Battambang suggests he was ignorant of the actual situation in rural Cambodia.

As the revolutionary war in South Vietnam intensified, Hanoi also attached great strategic importance to Cambodia. Appreciating Sihanouk's acquiescence in the presence of sanctuaries and in shipments of weapons across Cambodia from Sihanoukville, the Vietnamese Workers' Party leadership pressed the Cambodian Communists not to wage armed resistance against the government. From 1967 on, fear of a U.S. invasion of the North Vietnamese bases in Cambodia preoccupied policymakers in Hanoi. Sihanouk's significance for them was closely linked to his highly publicized objection to any American incursion into Cambodia. Any change in his attitude would have represented a serious setback to Hanoi's war effort.[37]

China and the DRV thus adopted parallel approaches to Cambodia, but their policies, though similar, were based on divergent motives and goals. Beijing sought to encourage the emergence of a group of independent states in postwar Indochina and so forestall Vietnamese domination of the region. Hanoi wished to encourage Indochinese strategic unity to withstand American pressure and also to create a sphere of influence in Indochina that would guarantee Vietnam's postwar security. The shared interest of Beijing and Hanoi in Indochinese solidarity against the United States, one scholar rightly observed, "masked an emergent rivalry that stemmed from their divergent visions of an acceptable regional postwar pattern of power."[38]

In January 1968, the CPK decided to begin an armed struggle.[39] This decision coincided with Hanoi's buildup in eastern Cambodia for the Tet Offensive. The increased Communist pressure triggered a harsh response from

Sihanouk. In late January, the Cambodian government arrested several young Communists in Phnom Penh for distributing pamphlets criticizing the Yugoslavian head of state, Joseph Broz Tito, who was scheduled to visit Cambodia shortly. In March, Sihanouk sent the Air Force to attack suspected areas of CPK influence across Cambodia.[40]

The Chinese leaders' uneasiness over developments in Cambodia was clearly reflected when Zhou met with Pham Hung, the secretary of the COSVN, in Beijing on June 19, 1968. After mentioning the military operations conducted by the CPK in eastern Cambodia, Zhou asked Hung whether North Vietnamese troops in Cambodia had distributed Chinese weapons to the Cambodian Communists (the transcript does not give Hung's reply). Insisting that China maintained no direct ties with the CPK, Zhou said that, due to that country's complicated internal situation, Beijing did not want its embassy in Cambodia to establish relations with the Cambodian Communists. Zhou also raised the issue of Vietnamese chauvinism toward the Cambodians. Citing reports of North Vietnamese cadres' "improper attitudes in dealing with Khmer comrades," Zhou asked Hung to urge his lower-level officers to "show attitudes of equality" toward the Cambodian Communists.[41]

Zhou then proceeded again to stress the importance of concentrating first on the defeat of the United States in Vietnam before developing revolution in Cambodia: "The Cambodian comrades wish to develop the armed struggle. Sihanouk will oppress them, and you can no longer go through Cambodia. . . . If the whole of Indochina joins the efforts to drive the U.S. out of Vietnam, then the Lao and Cambodian revolutions will be successful, although not as fast as expected." Zhou asked Hung to discuss with the Khmer Communists "how to join efforts to fight the Americans first and then fight the reactionary forces in Cambodia." As for the North Vietnamese troops in Cambodia, Zhou urged Hung to remind them of "the overall context" of the Indochina struggle: "You should make them understand the international approach and understand that one cannot fight many enemies at the same time." At the close of the conversation, Zhou asked Hung about the background of Pol Pot: "I heard from Comrade Pham Van Dong that the present General Secretary of the Khmer Communist Party graduated from France and used to travel to Hanoi."[42] This last statement suggests that China's knowledge of Pol Pot was limited.[43]

During 1968 and 1969, the Communist insurrection in Cambodia pushed Sihanouk rightward. In December 1968, he ordered his army to tighten its control over the Vietnamese Communists operating in Cambodia, and in early 1969 he restored dialogue with Washington.[44] In April, the Nixon administration agreed to respect Cambodian "sovereignty and neutrality."[45] On June 11, diplomatic relations between the United States and Cambodia were reestablished. While Sihanouk was making diplomatic overtures to the United States, in a typical balancing act, he also elevated the NLF trade mission in Phnom Penh to the status of an embassy. Still wishing to steer his country away from the war, he declared in April 1969 that he would change his attitude toward Vietnam only when Communist pressure grew too strong for Cambodian forces to resist.[46]

Sihanouk's improved relations with the United States disturbed the Chinese leaders. Meeting with Dong in Beijing on April 20, 1969, Zhou gave a pessimistic assessment of the Cambodian situation. Noting the Nixon administration's recognition of Cambodia's borders, the Chinese premier said that Nixon's Cambodian policy "is more intelligent than" Johnson's. Showing distrust of Sihanouk, Zhou referred to the Cambodian leader's policy as "double dealing" and "tilting to the right."[47]

In late 1969, Pol Pot led a delegation to Hanoi for talks with Vietnamese leaders. Predicting that Lon Nol would seize power in Cambodia with American backing, the CPK leader contended that this would create favorable conditions for a Cambodian revolution because Sihanouk would then join with the Communists against the right and the United States. Not ready to concede that Sihanouk would be overthrown, the Vietnamese continued to subordinate the interests of the Cambodian revolution to those of the Vietnamese revolution. Le Duan asked the CPK delegation to avoid armed struggle and "wait until Vietnam wins victory. At that moment, we will strike one single blow and we will liberate Phnom Penh."[48]

Pol Pot's determination to press on with armed struggle in Cambodia demonstrated that he was no tool of either Hanoi or Beijing, and that local Khmer Rouge views and priorities ran counter to the regional perspectives and concerns of North Vietnam and China. The CPK's parochial outlook and localized interests made it better attuned to threats and opportunities in its immediate environment than were the Chinese and Vietnamese Communists, whose regional range of interests prevented them from giving full and protracted attention to specific local issues. To Pol Pot and his cohorts, local developments were an absolute, whereas to policymakers in Beijing and Hanoi, they constituted only one of many problems competing for attention and resources. The Khmer Rouge took advantage of the presence of the Vietnamese Communists in their country to advance their cause.

China's Reaction to the 1970 Coup

In early January 1970, Sihanouk traveled to Paris, ostensibly for his annual medical examination but actually planning to use his absence from Cambodia to outmaneuver his domestic opponent Sirik Matak and to employ his diplomatic skills in Moscow and Beijing, which he expected to visit on the way home, to ease Vietnamese pressure on his country. During his absence, Prime Minister Lon Nol stepped up anti-Vietnamese activities, including attacking North Vietnamese and NLF positions inside Cambodia. On March 11, massive protests occurred outside the DRV and NLF diplomatic missions in Phnom Penh. Demonstrators broke into the two installations, burning their contents and manhandling Vietnamese diplomats.[49]

The Chinese leaders watched extremely apprehensively the sharp turn to the right in Cambodia. On March 14, Zhou told the Cambodian ambassador to China, Nay Valentin, that "the Chinese government is disturbed by the recent events in Phnom Penh." After expressing regret over the sacking of the DRV and NLF diplomatic premises in Phnom Penh, the Chinese premier drew the ambassador's attention to the appearance of anti-Chinese slogans among the rioters and the rumors that similar actions would be taken against the Chinese Embassy. Zhou also voiced concern for Sihanouk's security: "It is reported that Prince Sihanouk plans to leave Moscow on the 16th and arrive in Beijing on the 17th. Therefore, it is all the more necessary for us to take measures to protect the prince's safety. We support the prince's policy of peace, neutrality, and independence."[50]

Anticipating possible anti-Chinese riots in Cambodia, on March 16 Zhou told the North Korean ambassador to China that, should the Chinese embassy in Cambodia be destroyed and telegraphic communications disrupted, Beijing hoped to maintain contacts with Cambodia through Pyongyang via the North Korean Embassy in Phnom Penh.[51]

Sihanouk prolonged his stay in the Soviet Union to hold further discussions with Russian leaders. In his memoirs, Sihanouk revealed that the Kremlin was prepared to provide military assistance to Cambodia.[52] On March 18, when the prince was still in Moscow, Lon Nol staged a coup, deposing him as head of state. The new regime demanded the withdrawal of all Vietnamese revolutionary forces from Cambodia.[53] En route to the Moscow airport, Soviet premier Alexei Kosygin informed Sihanouk that the National Assembly had voted him out of office, a move the prince termed unconstitutional and immoral, claiming that he would fight imperialism with all his strength.[54]

To sow discord between Sihanouk and China, Kosygin told the prince: "You can have absolute confidence in the Soviet Union's backing of your struggle. . . . You will see how it will be with the Chinese. They helped you while you were in power in Phnom Penh but now that you are no longer in power, you will see what they will do!" Still confident of China's endorsement, Sihanouk replied that "I will continue on to Peking and get the support of my old friend, Chou En Lai."[55] Moscow's readiness to offer military aid to Cambodia and Kosygin's attempt to drive a wedge between Sihanouk and Beijing indicated Soviet competition with the Chinese for influence over Cambodia.

After learning of Lon Nol's coup, Zhou immediately met with Mao to discuss China's response. Condemning the coup as an expansion of America's Indochina policy, Mao insisted that China would not recognize the Lon Nol regime and would still treat Sihanouk as the Cambodian chief of state when he arrived in Beijing. China would support the Cambodian people's struggle against the United States, Mao concluded. The next step was to see what position Sihanouk would adopt. To implement Mao's instructions, Zhou asked the Foreign Ministry to prepare to receive Sihanouk and to urge foreign ambassadors in Beijing to go to the airport to welcome him.[56]

On March 19, Zhou greeted the shaken Sihanouk at the Beijing airport. In a meeting shortly afterward, Zhou told the prince that China still recognized him as the Cambodian head of state. "After the occurrence of the incident," the Chinese premier continued, "you declared that you would return to Cambodia right away. Later you did not do that. We feel that it is better for you not to return." Sihanouk said that under present circumstances, he could not return, and that he therefore wished to stay in China for some time.[57]

After talking with Sihanouk, Zhou summoned the Politburo to discuss the Cambodian situation and the prince's requests to meet international reporters and distribute a written statement. The meeting decided to assist Sihanouk in his activities in Beijing, while preparing for the eventualities of the sacking of the Chinese Embassy in Phnom Penh and arrests of overseas Chinese in Cambodia. The next day, Zhou reported the meeting's conclusions to Mao, who approved them.[58] Meanwhile, Zhou signed a Foreign Ministry telegram to Wang Youping, the Chinese ambassador to the DRV, directing him to convey to Vietnamese leaders the results of his meeting with Sihanouk, to indicate China's support for the prince, and to solicit Hanoi's views on the Cambodian crisis.[59]

The coup in Cambodia clearly caught the Chinese leaders by surprise, and they believed that the U.S. Central Intelligence Agency had engineered it.[60] Although choosing to support Sihanouk, mainly to strengthen their position vis-à-vis the Soviets and the Vietnamese, they were unsure of the erratic and mercurial prince's long-term plans. Despite their statements of nonrecognition of the Lon Nol regime, they had not totally abandoned hope in the Cambodian general, who had visited Beijing the previous year to attend the October 1 celebration commemorating the twentieth anniversary of the PRC. This ambivalent attitude was clearly demonstrated when Zhou spoke with Dong in Beijing on March 21. After noting French interest in the continuation of Cambodia's neutral policy and the Lon Nol regime's cautious behavior toward Moscow and Beijing in the previous two days, including the implementation of security measures to protect the Chinese and Soviet embassies in Phnom Penh, Zhou told Dong:

> We should support Sihanouk for the time being and see how he will act. We should support him because he supports the anti-American struggle in Vietnam. . . . We will also see whether he really wants to establish a united front to oppose the U.S. before we support him. But because of the circumstances he may change his position. However, the more we can win his sympathy, the better.

The Chinese premier asked his DRV counterpart for his views on negotiations with the Lon Nol–Sirik Matak regime. Dong replied that before his trip to Beijing, the Hanoi leadership had already discussed the issue and concluded that "negotiations would not bring about any results, because they would eventually fight us."[61] Clearly, the North Vietnamese had no illusions about Lon Nol and Sirik Matak. The Zhou-Dong dialogue revealed how much the two parties differed over the treatment of the Lon Nol regime.

According to Nay Valentin, Dong assured Princess Monique, Sihanouk's wife, that North Vietnam's forces could help Sihanouk regain power within twenty-four hours.[62] Sihanouk himself later recalled that Dong asked to see him in Beijing. Sihanouk claimed that, during their meeting on the morning of March 22, he defined the conditions for cooperation, including Chinese assistance to the Khmer resistance, a summit conference of Indochinese peoples, and military training in Vietnam for his followers.[63] Clearly, the prince did not wish to depend solely on Hanoi's aid.

In the afternoon, Zhou met with Dong, undoubtedly to receive the latter's report on his negotiation with Sihanouk.[64] That evening, Zhou talked with Sihanouk, reaffirming China's support for his struggle. Commenting on the broadcast statement that the prince was to deliver the next day, the Chinese premier remarked that it would greatly inspire the Cambodian people.[65]

Realizing that Sihanouk lacked the military forces to oppose the United States, Chinese officials made every endeavor to persuade the Khmer Rouge to cooperate with him. At the time of Sihanouk's ouster, Pol Pot was making a secret visit to China. The Chinese leaders met with him several times, urging him to set aside his hatred against Sihanouk and form a united front with him to oppose the common enemy, the United States, to which Pol Pot agreed.[66]

On March 23, Sihanouk issued his first "Message to the Nation," urging Cambodians to take up arms against the Lon Nol regime and defy orders issued from Phnom Penh. He proposed a National Union Government, a National Liberation Army, and a National United Front of Kampuchea (NUFK), which would govern Cambodia on principles of "social justice, equality and fraternity."[67] Sihanouk's decision sealed his alliance with the Khmer Rouge, who would exploit his appeal and popularity among the Cambodian peasants for propaganda purpose, laying the groundwork for the eventual Khmer Rouge victory.[68]

The contrast between the reactions of Hanoi and Beijing to the Cambodian situation immediately after Sihanouk's overthrow was revealing. Between March 25 and 27, Hanoi released a formal statement in support of Sihanouk and withdrew its diplomats from Phnom Penh. The Chinese media and officials in Beijing refrained from commenting on Cambodian affairs, merely publicizing Sihanouk's statements. The Chinese ambassador, Kang Maozhao, remained in Phnom Penh after DRV and NLF representatives had left. Beijing lagged behind the DRV and Pathet Lao in accusing Washington of plotting Sihanouk's overthrow.[69] Not until April 5 did Zhou openly allege that the United States had engineered Sihanouk's ouster.[70]

Beijing's effort to restore the status quo in Phnom Penh, whether under Sihanouk or some other leader, ended in failure. During April, Ambassador Kang Maozhao informed Lon Nol that if he permitted the transportation of weapons through Cambodia, maintained sanctuaries for the Vietnamese Communist forces, and facilitated war propaganda, China would recognize his government, a request Lon Nol rejected. On May 5, the Chinese government finally broke relations with the Lon Nol regime and withdrew its diplomats from Phnom Penh.[71]

The Chinese leaders undoubtedly perceived events in Cambodia as linked to the recent escalation of fighting in Laos. On February 12, 1970, the combined forces of the People's Army of Vietnam and the Pathet Lao had launched an offensive to drive the government forces out of the Plain of Jars, deploying an additional 13,000 North Vietnamese soldiers to reinforce the 50,000 troops already there, who were now in a position to threaten Vang Pao's headquarters at Long Cheng. At Souvanna Phouma's request, U.S. B-52 bombers attacked northern Laos for the first time, halting the Communist advance.[72] Although the Chinese media denounced the American action,[73] North Vietnam's new initiative in Laos must have disturbed leaders in Beijing, because it threatened not only to expand the war but also, given the DRV's dependence on Soviet weapons, to extend Moscow's influence in tandem with that of Hanoi.[74] Though embracing the prospects of U.S. disengagement from Vietnam, Chinese policymakers were now concerned over the potential postwar domination of Indochina by Hanoi in alliance with the Soviet Union.

Primarily trying to compete with the Moscow and Hanoi for influence in Phnom Penh, Beijing, in the weeks immediately after the coup, adopted a two-track approach: to support Sihanouk and to explore the possibility of cooperation with the Lon Nol regime. It sought to keep its options open and to drive a wedge between Sihanouk and Moscow. When Sihanouk, during his March 28 talk with Zhou, expressed concern that the Soviet Union had behaved extremely cautiously toward him and that other socialist countries in Europe were following the Soviet example, the Chinese premier missed no opportunity to discredit the Kremlin. The Russians, Zhou asserted, had always acted thus; they "have not only treated Cambodia in this manner, but have also treated the DRV likewise." When the three Indochinese states eventually spoke out on the subject, Zhou continued, the Soviet Union "will be embarrassed."[75]

Driven by its rivalry with Beijing, Moscow had been unwilling to break diplomatic relations with the Lon Nol regime. To extend its influence in Cambodia, on April 17 the Soviet Union suggested calling another Geneva conference. The Summit Meeting of the Indochinese Peoples sponsored by China in late April, however, preempted the Soviet move. Beijing denounced the Soviet proposal on the day the summit opened.[76]

The Summit Meeting was held at the Conghua hot spring resort near Guangzhou on April 24 and 25, attended by Sihanouk; Souphanouvong of Laos; Pham Van Dong of the DRV; and Nguyen Huu Tho of the Provisional Revolutionary Government (PRG) of the Republic of South Vietnam, established by Hanoi in June 1969 as a diplomatic cover for the NLF and to serve as a formal alternative to the Nguyen Van Thieu regime.[77] Disputes broke out between the delegates to the meeting, and on the evening of April

24, Zhou flew to Guangzhou to help advance the conference, holding talks with Dong and Sihanouk to resolve their differences and work out the details of a joint declaration.[78]

On April 25, the summit concluded with the announcement of a joint statement, calling on the Indochinese people to join the common struggle against the United States and its lackeys. China, for its part, pledged to provide a "rear area" and "powerful backing" for the struggle against U.S. aggression.[79] Sihanouk also issued a proclamation condemning Washington and granting Hanoi and the NLF formal permission to use Cambodian territory.[80]

Zhou hosted a banquet in honor of the four Indochinese delegations. Congratulating them on a fruitful meeting, the Chinese premier announced the successful launching of China's first satellite the previous day.[81] Clearly, Zhou wanted to impress his listeners with China's latest achievement. By sheltering Sihanouk and sponsoring the summit, Beijing had stolen a diplomatic march on Moscow, at least temporarily reasserting China's influence in Indochina.

Nixon's decision to invade Cambodia in early May prompted a strong reaction from China. On May 11, Mao met with Le Duan in Beijing. According to Lu Huixiang, who took notes on the Mao-Duan conversation, the CCP chairman said that the main tendency in the world was revolution and that small countries should not fear U.S. imperialism.[82] On May 18, the Chinese government announced the cancellation of the forthcoming Warsaw talks with American diplomats scheduled to open two days later. At a mass rally in Tiananmen Square on May 20, Mao issued a statement expressing support for Sihanouk and denouncing U.S. aggression.[83] Significantly Mao's declaration, while rhetorically shrill, lacked substance and made no concrete commitments to the struggle in Indochina.[84] The address was primarily a propaganda gesture designed to serve three purposes: (1) to remind countries in the developing world that China remained their friend; (2) to embarrass the Russians by highlighting how, even though twenty countries had done so, the Soviet Union had not recognized the Royal Government of National Union of Kampuchea (RGNUK) led by Sihanouk; (3) to send a message to Nixon that any China-U.S. rapprochement would require reduced American involvement in Indochina.

When Mao delivered his speech, Chai Chengwen, the deputy head of the Chinese delegation to the Sino-Soviet negotiations, and Vasilu V. Kuznetsov, the head of the Soviet delegation to the negotiations, were also on the reviewing stand. Referring to the previous Soviet request for joint action in support of North Vietnam, Chai quipped to the Soviet diplomat: "You are always talking about 'united action.' Don't you think that the Soviet Union is lagging too far behind" in supporting Sihanouk?[85] Chai clearly felt that on Cambodia China had scored diplomatically over the Soviet Union.

The Cambodian crisis presented Beijing with both hazards and opportunities. On the one hand, to Chinese leaders, the American invasion of Cambodia—the first time during the Vietnam conflict Washington had employed ground combat forces outside Vietnam—seemed to suggest a reversal of the Nixon doctrine. Hesitant moves toward Sino-American accommodation ended abruptly after the invasion. On the other hand, by hosting the Summit Meeting of the Indochinese Peoples and facilitating the formation of the RGNUK, Beijing increased its influence in Indochina.

Because the Chinese leaders viewed Sihanouk as the major instrument for establishing China's influence in Cambodia, they did their utmost to accommodate his stay in China and facilitate his travels abroad, seeking to preserve and enhance his position as the legitimate leader of Cambodia. After the Cambodian coup, the Chinese Foreign Ministry established the Cambodian Office to coordinate Sihanouk's activities in China. After his return to Beijing in May 1970, Kang Maozhao became director of this office, which had a staff of about twelve people.[86] The Chinese government gave Sihanouk the former French embassy as his residence and constructed a heated swimming pool for him. His table was one of the fanciest in town, often laden with gifts of gooseberries and guinea fowl from Kim Il Sung of North Korea.[87]

Between May and July, 1970, Sihanouk visited North Vietnam and North Korea. On both occasions, Zhou went to the Beijing airport and railway station to see him off and welcome him back.[88] Seeking to underscore regional solidarity behind Sihanouk and enhance his international prestige, on July 5, Zhou hosted a state banquet in the Great Hall of the People—attended by representatives of the DRV, NLF, Pathet Lao, and North Korea—to celebrate the success of Sihanouk's trips.[89] In addition to his overseas journeys, the Chinese government also arranged frequent tours on which Sihanouk visited various parts of China, using extensive media coverage of these trips to project the image that Sihanouk was always treated warmly as the head of state.[90]

During their meetings with Sihanouk, the Chinese leaders attempted to influence his thinking in accordance with their own view of international affairs. In conversation with the prince on October 7, 1970, Zhou explained

Mao's theory of the two intermediate zones. According to Mao, two intermediate zones existed between the two superpowers. The first zone included developing countries in Asia, Africa, and Latin America and the second zone consisted of developed states in Europe, Canada, and Japan. Mao believed that countries in these two zones had conflicts with the United States and the Soviet Union and that peoples elsewhere who opposed superpower hegemony should join with these countries to form an international united front.[91] Although it remains unclear whether Sihanouk found Mao's theory persuasive, the change in China's policy toward the United States in 1971 and 1972 undoubtedly left him puzzled and unhappy.

In July 1971, U.S. national security adviser Henry A. Kissinger made a secret trip to Beijing to arrange for President Nixon's visit to China, holding lengthy talks with Zhou on a broad range of international issues. The Chinese premier blamed America for expanding the Vietnam War to Cambodia and Laos. Kissinger assured Zhou that the United States "did not produce, cause, or encourage" the coup against Sihanouk. At the time of Sihanouk's overthrow, Kissinger explained, the United States was negotiating with North Vietnam, and the coup "ruined negotiations that we were conducting and that we wanted to succeed." When Zhou asked whether the French were behind the coup, Kissinger replied: "That is conceivable, but it certainly was not done by us."[92]

During his historic meetings with Nixon in Beijing in February 1972, Zhou praised Sihanouk highly, telling the American president that although the Cambodian prince was a Buddhist, not a communist, China respected him. Asserting that he was different from Lon Nol, Sirik Matak, and Son Ngoc Thanh, Zhou informed Nixon that China supported him because he was a patriot, and the Chinese government had therefore allowed Sihanouk to publish messages to his people in the *People's Daily*.[93]

Sihanouk, however, could not understand why Beijing decided to invite President Nixon to visit China when American troops were still stationed on Taiwan. Unwilling to stay in the same city with Nixon, Sihanouk left Beijing for Hanoi before the American president's arrival on February 21, 1972, and only returned to China after Nixon's departure.[94]

The Emergence of Chinese–Khmer Rouge Solidarity

Beijing-Hanoi competition in Cambodia unfolded chiefly within the resistance movement. Geographical separation handicapped China's ability to maneuver within the NUFK, leading Beijing to concentrate its efforts on Sihanouk and the RGNUK. Through cooperation with Sihanouk, China hoped to maintain some leverage over Hanoi on the Cambodian issue. Beijing did not establish contacts with the resistance on the ground in Cambodia until Ieng Sary came to the Chinese capital as a special liaison in late 1971. The DRV relied on its military presence in Cambodia to maintain closer ties with the NUFK, hoping that Hanoi-trained Khmer returnees would establish domination over the resistance movement. Between 1970 and 1972, Hanoi's forces bore the main brunt of fighting Lon Nol's troops.[95]

China's concern over Hanoi's ability to influence events in Cambodia was clearly apparent in its reaction to the 1973 Paris Peace Agreement. During the American–North Vietnamese negotiations in Paris, both sides agreed that any settlement should include corresponding cease-fire arrangements in Cambodia and Laos. Confident of Hanoi's sway over the Pathet Lao, Le Duc Tho, the North Vietnamese negotiator, promised to implement a cease-fire in Laos within thirty days of the Vietnam cease-fire. On Cambodia, the Hanoi diplomat was less certain, claiming that North Vietnam possessed less influence over the Khmer Rouge.[96]

On January 27, 1973, the United States and North Vietnam signed the Paris Peace Agreement. Beijing had reservations about the agreement, especially its treatment of Cambodia and Laos. Chinese leaders had insisted that the Paris Agreement should cover only Vietnam and not extend to Cambodia and Laos, but, much to their disappointment, the final accord still brought up the situation in Cambodia and Laos. In a March 1973 internal speech, Zhou complained that the reference to the conflict in Cambodia and Laos in the Paris Agreement "was not good because we cannot impose the Vietnam settlement on these two countries."[97] Clearly Chinese leaders did not want to see Hanoi dictate peace terms for Cambodia and Laos.

Hanoi's influence over the Pathet Lao meant it quickly delivered the promised cease-fire in Laos. A Laotian armistice agreement was concluded within thirty days of the Paris Agreement on February 21, 1973. The Khmer Rouge, however, rejected cease-fire proposals. The Cambodian situation remained in flux. Anxiously and apprehensively, Chinese leaders watched developments in Cambodia, with their greatest fear being that the Soviet Union might exploit the uncertain Cambodian situation to enhance its presence there. They continued to oppose Lon Nol and support the Sihanouk–Khmer Rouge coalition and to rely on Sihanouk as the main instrument for maintaining China's influence in Cambodia, even though they also doubted his long-term reliability.

The Chinese leaders' uncertainty and apprehension over Cambodia were clearly apparent in meetings between Zhou and Kissinger held in Beijing from February 16 to 18, 1973. In these talks, Zhou conveyed China's fear of Soviet expansion in Indochina, its distrust of Lon Nol, and its uncertainty about Sihanouk's future orientation. He opened the February 16 meeting by noting that the Soviet ambassador had returned to Phnom Penh, and asking Kissinger why the United States refused to negotiate with Sihanouk. Kissinger replied that the United States could not engage in direct talks with Sihanouk while recognizing the Lon Nol government. He told Zhou that Lon Nol was "actually very anxious still to establish relations with you." The Chinese premier answered that "we wouldn't do that with such a person. You should also not deal with such a man who carries on subversive activities against the King." Realizing that Lon Nol was unacceptable to Beijing and Sihanouk, Kissinger then proposed the alternative of establishing an interim government in Cambodia, which would include elements from both the Sihanouk and Lon Nol groups. The United States was prepared to accept a government without Lon Nol, Kissinger continued, but that government should include the forces that he represented. Zhou contended that neither Sihanouk nor the Khmer Rouge would accept such a solution.[98]

During their February 17 talks, Kissinger assured Zhou that, once the Chinese had consulted Sihanouk, the United States was prepared to discuss with China "who might be acceptable negotiators on both sides and acceptable principles in an interim government." The point was to reach a settlement that was "consistent with the dignity of all sides," both the Lon Nol group and its opponents.[99] Kissinger later wrote in his memoirs that Zhou offered to convey his proposition of an interim government to the Cambodians.[100]

During their February 18 meeting, Zhou returned to the issue of Soviet policy toward Southeast Asia, drawing Moscow's intentions in Cambodia to Kissinger's attention: "The Soviet Union is . . . attempting to fabricate their own Red Khmer but they can't find many people. But it might in the future appear. So, in the future, if there is some information you would like to give us in this respect, we can also give you some too." Expressing China's support for Cambodia's ultimate goal of peace, independence, unity, sovereignty, and territorial integrity, Zhou stated that "it is impossible for Cambodia to become completely red now. If that were attempted, it would result in even greater problems." China wanted an independent Southeast Asia free from Soviet domination, Zhou went on, and "if we wish to see Southeast Asia develop along the lines of peace and neutrality and not enter a Soviet Asian security system, then Cambodia would be an exemplar country."[101] Clearly Zhou feared that, should Cambodia become communist at this time, Hanoi's influence would prevail there and, given Hanoi's close ties to Moscow, this would lead in turn to Soviet domination of Cambodia. Kissinger shared Zhou's concern over Soviet ambitions in Cambodia, telling the Chinese premier that the United States was prepared to exchange information regarding Soviet moves in the region.[102]

After this exchange of views on the prevention of Soviet interference in Cambodia, the conversation turned to assessing Sihanouk. Zhou said that although the prince had written an excellent poem terming China his second motherland, "we must be prepared for the day when he says it doesn't count! Anyway it was all written by him; it has nothing to do with us. Of course he is now saying I am one of his best friends. . . . It doesn't matter. That is only personal relations. He is still the Head of State of the Buddhist State of Cambodia." Although China endorsed Cambodia's goals of peace, unity, and independence, Zhou concluded, "we will still have to wait and see in which way these objectives can be realized." Kissinger replied that the United States was "in complete agreement with" the objective of an independent Cambodia and that "we have the same difficulty determining in exactly which direction to put our influence."[103] Kissinger clearly shared Zhou's frustration over the unpredictability of Cambodian politics, and both men regretted the limits upon their countries' power to determine events in Cambodia.

The Zhou-Kissinger talks were highly significant, revealing both convergences and divergences in Chinese and American policy toward Cambodia. The geopolitical calculations of Beijing and Washington with regard to Phnom Penh clearly converged. Both sides registered concern over Moscow's growing role in Southeast Asia, and both were willing to cooperate to block the Russians. A Sino-U.S. common front against the Soviet Union in Indochina was in the making. This cooperation would reach its high point during the 1979 Sino-Vietnamese War, when U.S. officials met the Chinese ambassador in Washington almost every day throughout the military conflict to turn over American intelligence on Soviet deployments.[104]

Although Beijing and Washington shared the goal of excluding the Soviets from Cambodia, they disagreed on future political arrangements in that country, looking to different Cambodian groups to advance their own interests there. Beijing viewed Sihanouk as the best guarantee of Cambodian independence, while Washington viewed the Lon Nol group as the best ally to protect American interests. Neither side was able to persuade the other to accept its choice in Cambodia.

Zhou must have gained increased confidence from his conversations with Kissinger, who had told him that the United States was determined to resist Soviet expansion in Southeast Asia and that American officials also distrusted Lon Nol. At the March 1973 party meeting, he expressed his sense of relief: "The current situation in Cambodia is . . . good. The Lon Nol regime now controls only a small piece of land, and moreover, it seems that the Americans do not respect this president very much. Lately the attitude of Prince Sihanouk has been tough and resolute."[105]

To enhance Sihanouk's image in a way that also reflected well on the Khmer Rouge, in February 1973, China, together with North Vietnam, arranged a visit by him to the Communist-controlled area of Cambodia. Sihanouk had for some time been demanding such a trip, a request Khmer Rouge leaders had repeatedly rejected with the excuse that the American bombing of the Ho Chi Minh Trail made it unsafe for him to do so. After the signing of the Paris Agreement, Sihanouk again raised the subject with Khieu Samphan, the deputy prime minister of the RGNUK, threatening to withdraw from the NUFK should the Khmer Rouge once again reject his proposal. This time Zhou Enlai intervened on Sihanouk's behalf, expounding to Ieng Sary the political advantages of allowing Sihanouk to visit Cambodia, and the Khmer Rouge eventually acceded to Chinese pressure. In late February, accompanied by Princess Monique and Ieng Sary, Sihanouk traveled in Soviet jeeps via the Ho Chi Minh Trail to Cambodia, where he met with Pol Pot and other Khmer Rouge leaders, watched a theatrical performance, and inspected Angkor Wat and other temples. On April 12, Zhou hosted a banquet to celebrate Sihanouk's return to Beijing, an occasion on which Zhou reaffirmed China's support for Sihanouk and condemned the United States for its continued bombing of Cambodia and support for the Lon Nol regime.[106]

Between late 1973 and early 1974, however, China's treatment of Sihanouk and the Khmer Rouge shifted substantially. Until the end of 1973, China had relied primarily on cooperation with Sihanouk to limit Soviet and Vietnamese influence in Cambodia and had been wary when dealing with the Khmer Rouge, because the latter were receiving aid from Hanoi to conduct their struggle. In 1974, however, China became more enthusiastic in supporting the Khmer Rouge. In April, Khieu Samphan visited Beijing and met with Mao Zedong, the first Khmer Communist to be granted this honor.[107] China signed an agreement to provide the RGNUK with military equipment and supplies. Beijing's decision to offer material aid to the Khmer Rouge may have been triggered by evidence that, despite Pol Pot's

efforts to eliminate pro-Vietnamese members from his party, Hanoi was trying to strengthen its position in Cambodia.[108] Beijing's warm reception of
Khieu Samphan marked a clear policy shift away from a political settlement, the formation of a neutral government led by Sihanouk, toward a military solution to the Cambodian problem.[109]

According to newly released documents from U.S. archives, the Gerald
Ford administration tried to enlist China's help in its efforts to preserve the
Lon Nol regime against the Khmer Rouge. In November 1974, Kissinger,
now the secretary of state, visited Beijing. In his conversations with Deng,
Zhou's chief aide, who had taken over many of his duties since Zhou was
seriously ill, Kissinger proposed Sihanouk's restoration to power in Cambodia as the head of an enlarged coalition that would include some of Lon
Nol's supporters. But Deng rejected this proposal. After stating China's support for Sihanouk and the Khmer Rouge, Deng told Kissinger that "we think
if the United States is to place its hopes on Lon Nol or on any force you
think would replace Lon Nol, that is not reliable."[110]

Why did Beijing become more eager to support the Khmer Rouge's
armed struggle in 1974? The primary reason was the Chinese leaders'
changing perceptions during this period of the ties between the Khmer
Rouge and North Vietnam. By 1974, Pol Pot had become increasingly independent of Hanoi, and major skirmishes had occurred between his forces
and North Vietnamese troops. Chinese policymakers were clearly no longer
apprehensive over the prospect that a Cambodia controlled by the Khmer
Rouge would align itself with Vietnam. Recognizing Khmer Rouge determination and strength, they apparently decided that, if they wished to outmaneuver the Vietnamese and the Russians in Cambodia, they must back
Pol Pot.

China played a significant role in helping the Khmer Rouge complete the
final phase of its struggle for power in Cambodia. Beijing assisted the early
1975 Khmer Rouge assault on Phnom Penh by helping to mine the Mekong
River, the Cambodian capital's key supply line.[111] On April 17, the Khmer
Rouge seized Phnom Penh.

In June 1975, shortly after seizing power in Cambodia, Pol Pot visited
Beijing and received a hero's welcome from his ideological mentor, Mao.
In conversations marked on both sides by false modesty and flattery, Mao
told Pol Pot: "You have achieved in one stroke what we failed with all our
masses." After praising the Khmer Rouge leader for having adopted a correct policy, Mao stated that many of the revolutionary efforts of the Cambodian party had far surpassed those of the CCP.[112] The victory of the

Khmer Rouge clearly excited the aging Mao, who, just as Stalin had felt reinvigorated in 1949 by the success of the young Chinese Communists, now saw in Pol Pot's triumph a return to his own revolutionary youth.[113] Mao told Pol Pot that the successful realization of communism was a tortuous process. Although Khrushchev and Leonid Brezhnev had deviated from Leninism, Mao continued, the Soviet Union would eventually return to Lenin's principles. The same was true for China; although it might turn to revisionism in the future, it would eventually return to the path of Marx and Lenin.[114]

Returning these compliments, Pol Pot said that as a youth he had begun to read Mao's writings, particularly those on people's war, and he had used Mao's ideas to guide his party. He told Mao that he would continue studying Chinese practices by paying close attention to class struggle. Mao concluded the conversation by asking Pol Pot not to copy the Chinese model in every respect and by presenting him with thirty books written by Marx, Engels, Lenin, and Stalin.[115] Eager to encourage Pol Pot's policy of seeking independence from Vietnam, Mao viewed Cambodia as a counterbalance to Vietnamese ambitions in Indochina. During Pol Pot's visit, China promised Cambodia more than $1 billion in economic and military assistance.[116]

Because the Khmer Rouge leadership was hostile to Sihanouk, they opposed his return to Cambodia. And Sihanouk demonstrated his displeasure by refusing to attend the mass celebration of the liberation of Phnom Penh that the Chinese government organized on April 19, 1975, asking Penn Nouth, the prime minister of the RGNUK, to speak on his behalf at this rally. In another angry gesture, in May Sihanouk left Beijing to live in Pyongyang.[117] Believing that the continuation of the united front with Sihanouk would help the Khmer Rouge to consolidate its domestic position, the Chinese leadership did not, however, endorse Pol Pot's treatment of Sihanouk. During talks with Pol Pot in Beijing in June 1975, Deng urged the Khmer Rouge to continue its policy of unity with Sihanouk to stabilize the Cambodian political situation, and he asked Pol Pot to permit Sihanouk to return to Phnom Penh.[118] Zhou, the prince's longtime patron, also pressured the Khmer Rouge to treat Sihanouk properly and to allow him back, personally meeting to discuss the prince's future on August 16 with Khieu Samphan and Ieng Sary in the Beijing hospital where he was receiving medical treatment.[119]

Under Chinese pressure, the Khmer Rouge finally relented. Pol Pot dispatched Khieu Samphan to North Korea to invite Sihanouk to return to Cambodia.[120] In August 1975, Sihanouk traveled back to Beijing. Before departing for Cambodia, on August 26 he and Penn Nouth had a hospital meeting with Zhou, who congratulated the Cambodians on their victory over the Americans, declaring that their triumph had validated Mao's theory that "small countries can defeat big countries and weak states can vanquish strong states." Zhou urged his Cambodian interlocutors to consolidate their victory and build their country independently.[121] Accompanied by Khieu Samphan, the following day Sihanouk also bid farewell to Mao, who expressed satisfaction with Cambodia's liberation, stating that he had not expected victory to be attained so quickly. Turning to Khieu Samphan, Mao prodded the Khmer Rouge to place unity over bickering when dealing with Sihanouk. He concluded by telling Sihanouk, half jocularly, that should the Khmer Rouge again mistreat him, he could count on "a warm welcome" in China.[122] After returning, Sihanouk remained the figurehead chief of state until he resigned in April 1976. He spent the following thirty-three months under house arrest in the Royal Palace in Phnom Penh. Zhou's death in January 1976 clearly removed a major force for restraint in the Khmer Rouge's treatment of Sihanouk.[123]

Conclusion

China's handling of the Cambodian conflict from 1970 to 1975 was conditioned primarily by its competition with the Soviet Union and North Vietnam in Indochina. After the Soviet invasion of Czechoslovakia in 1968 and the Sino-Soviet border clashes of 1969, Chinese leaders began to view the Soviet Union as the most dangerous threat to China—as demonstrated by chapters 1 and 9 in this volume by, respectively, Yang Kuisong and Niu Jun. Hanoi's increasing cooperation with Moscow in its war against the United States intensified their fears of Soviet encirclement of China. In 1970, they offered Sihanouk shelter and assistance to maintain their influence in Cambodia. Although Chinese officials were instrumental in the formation of the united front between Sihanouk and the Khmer Rouge, they remained uncertain as to the relationship between the Khmer Rouge and North Vietnam, and they initially backed Sihanouk. Once Pol Pot's break with Hanoi became clear in early 1974, they began to feel more enthusiasm for the Cambodian communists.

China and the United States had a common strategic interest in limiting Soviet influence in Indochina. In early 1973, Zhou and Kissinger reached an intelligence-sharing agreement, whereby they would keep each other informed of Soviet activities in Cambodia. Though in accordance on the general objective of minimizing the Soviet presence in Cambodia, the Chinese and the Americans diverged over which Cambodian group to support to realize that objective. The Chinese relied first on Sihanouk and subsequently on the Khmer Rouge. The Americans first supported Lon Nol while rejecting Sihanouk and the Khmer Rouge; later, they modified their position by agreeing to restore Sihanouk to an enlarged coalition government, which would also incorporate Lon Nol's supporters.

In early 1973 and again in the summer of 1975, China twice exerted pressure on the Khmer Rouge to treat Sihanouk with respect. In the first episode, Beijing insisted that the Khmer Rouge allow the prince to tour the liberated area of Cambodia, seeking to enhance Sihanouk's position because at that time Chinese leaders viewed him as the major instrument for maintaining China's influence in Cambodia. On the second such occasion, Beijing officials urged the Khmer Rouge government to permit Sihanouk to return to Cambodia on the grounds that he could fulfill useful united front functions.

Both times, the Khmer Rouge acceded to China's demands, demonstrating Beijing's influence in shaping developments in Cambodia and the Khmer Rouge's need for China's political and material support—first against the Americans and Lon Nol, later to withstand the Vietnamese. Once the Khmer Rouge had convincingly demonstrated that their movement looked to neither North Vietnam nor the Soviet Union for leadership, China's commitment to Sihanouk dwindled and faded. Beijing's assistance helped the Khmer Rouge seize power in Cambodia in 1975 and resist Vietnamese pressure until 1978. Throughout China's dealings with Cambodia, however, the pursuit of Chinese geopolitical and strategic interests in Indochina, especially its desire to minimize the influence of both Moscow and Hanoi, trumped considerations of ideological solidarity with a fraternal communist movement.

Notes

1. Pei Jianzhang, chief ed., *Zhonghua renmin gongheguo waijiaoshi, 1949–1956* [Diplomatic history of the People's Republic of China, 1949–1956] (Beijing: World Knowledge Press, 1994), 148; Roger M. Smith, *Cambodia's Foreign Policy* (Ithaca, N.Y.: Cornell University Press, 1965), 80; Michael Leifer, *Cambodia: The Search for Security* (New York: Praeger, 1967), 63; David P. Chandler, *The Tragedy of Cambodian History: Politics, War, and Revolution since 1945* (New Haven, Conn.: Yale University Press, 1991), 80; Milton Osborne, *Sihanouk: Prince of Light, Prince of Darkness* (Honolulu: University of Hawaii Press, 1994), 96.

2. Pei, *Zhonghua renmin gongheguo waijiaoshi,* 147–52; Xue Mouhong and Pei Jianzhang, chief eds., *Dangdai Zhongguo waijiao* [Contemporary Chinese diplomacy] (Beijing: Chinese Academy of Social Sciences Press, 1990), 169–70; Donald Kirk, *Wider War: The Struggle for Cambodia, Thailand, and Laos* (New York: Praeger, 1971), 48. For summaries of China's policy toward Cambodia, consult Melvin Gurtov, *China and Southeast Asia: The Politics of Survival* (Baltimore: Johns Hopkins University Press, 1971), chap. 3; and J. D. Armstrong, *Revolutionary Diplomacy: Chinese Foreign Policy and the United Front Doctrine* (Berkeley: University of California Press, 1977), chap. 6.

3. Pei, *Zhonghua renmin gongheguo waijiaoshi,* 149–52.

4. William J. Duiker, *China and Vietnam: The Roots of Conflict* (Berkeley: Institute of East Asian Studies, University of California, 1986), 51–52. Cambodia was the only professedly neutral country in the world where the United States maintained a Military Assistance Advisory Group.

5. Chae-Jin Lee, *Communist China's Policy toward Laos: A Case Study, 1954–67* (Lawrence: Center for East Asian Studies, University of Kansas, 1970), 31. On the shift in about 1953 in China's policy toward independent governments in the developing world, particularly in Asia and the Middle East, see Harry Harding, "China and the Third World: From Revolution to Containment," in *The China Factor: Sino-American Relations and the Global Scene,* ed. Richard H. Solomon (Englewood Cliffs, N.J.: Prentice-Hall, 1981), 260–61; Steven I. Levine, "China in Asia: The PRC as a Regional Power," in *China's Foreign Relations in the 1980s,* ed. Harry Harding (New Haven, Conn.: Yale University Press, 1984), 116.

6. Wang Taiping, chief ed., *Zhonghua renmin gongheguo waijiaoshi, 1957–1969* [Diplomatic history of the People's Republic of China, 1957–1969] (Beijing: World Knowledge Press, 1998), 50.

7. Mona K. Bitar, "Bombs, Plots and Allies: Cambodia and the Western Powers, 1958–59," *Intelligence and National Security* 14, no. 4 (Winter 1999): 149–80.

8. Zhou's talk with Sihanouk, August 17, 1958, in *Zhou Enlai nianpu, 1949–1976* [A chronology of Zhou Enlai's life, 1949–1976] (hereafter *Zhou Enlai nianpu*), 3 vols., ed. CCP Central Documentary Research Department (Beijing: Central Press of Historical Documents, 1997], vol. 2, 161–62; Diplomatic History Research Office of the PRC Foreign Ministry, ed., *Zhou Enlai waijiao huodong dashiji, 1949–1975* [A chronicle of Zhou Enlai's diplomatic activities, 1949–1975] (Beijing: World Knowledge Press, 1993), 240–41.

9. Memorandum, Eric Kocher (director of the Office of Southeast Asian Affairs) to Walter S. Robertson (assistant secretary of state for far eastern affairs), September 3, 1958, *Foreign Relations of the United States* (hereafter *FRUS*), *1958–1960, vol. 16: East Asia–Pacific Region; Cambodia; Laos* (Washington, D.C.: U.S. Government Printing Office, 1992), 248–49. According to this source, while visiting China, Sihanouk accepted offered additional economic aid equivalent to $5.6 million, which, added to existing economic assistance of $22.4 million, raised total Chinese aid to Cambodia to $28 million.

10. Bitar, "Bombs, Plots and Allies," 157–58.

11. Armstrong, *Revolutionary Diplomacy,* 191–92.

12. Wang, *Zhonghua renmin gongheguo waijiaoshi,* 50–51.

13. Wang, *Zhonghua renmin gongheguo waijiaoshi,* 51; See also Michael Leifer, "Cambodia and China: Neutralism, 'Neutrality,' and National Security," in *Policies to-*

ward China: Views from Six Continent , ed. A. M. Halpern (New York: McGraw-Hill, 1965), 345.

14. Zhou's talks with Penn Nouth, June 4, 1962, in *Zhou Enlai nianpu,* vol. 2, 481.

15. Wang, *Zhonghua renmin gongheguo waijiaoshi,* 51; Jin Chongji, chief ed., *Liu Shaoqi zhuan* [A biography of Liu Shaoqi], 2 vols. (Beijing: Central Press of Historical Documents, 1998), vol. 2, 938–40.

16. Elizabeth Becker, *When the War Was Over: Cambodia and the Khmer Rouge Revolution* (New York: PublicAffairs, 1998), 99–100.

17. Archives of the Chinese Foreign Ministry, ed., *Weiren de zuji: Deng Xiaoping waijiao huodong dashiji* [The footprints of a great man: A chronicle of Deng Xiaoping's diplomatic activities] (Beijing: World Knowledge Press, 1998), 48.

18. *Zhou Enlai nianpu,* vol. 2, 576, 582. J. D. Armstrong speculates that Sihanouk's adoption of China's position on the nuclear test ban treaty may have been intended as an indication of gratitude to Beijing for its help in pushing Hanoi to renounce in May 1963 its claim to the island of Phu Quoc, which Cambodia had for some time been disputing with Saigon. See Armstrong, *Revolutionary Diplomacy,* 195. No Chinese evidence, however, has surfaced to indicate that Beijing pressured Hanoi over Phu Quoc.

19. Qiang Zhai, "Opposing Negotiations: China and the Vietnam Peace Talks, 1965–1968," *Pacific Historical Review* 68, no. 1 (February 1999): 21–49.

20. *Zhou Enlai nianpu,* vol. 2, 731. On the circumstances leading to Sihanouk's decision to cut diplomatic ties with Washington, see, Kenton J. Clymer, "The Perils of Neutrality: The Break in U.S.–Cambodian Relations, 1965," *Diplomatic History* 23, no. 4 (Fall 1999): 609–31.

21. Wang, *Zhonghua renmin gongheguo waijiaoshi,* 52.

22. According to the French scholar Marie Alexanderine Martin, on November 25, 1965, General Lon Nol, chief of staff of the royal Khmer armed forces, visited Beijing on Sihanouk's orders and concluded with Luo Ruiqing, chief of staff of the People's Liberation Army, a military treaty, which stipulated: "(1) Cambodia would permit the passage and the refuge of Vietnamese combatants in the border regions, granting them protection if necessary and permitting them to establish command posts; (2) Cambodia would permit the passage of material coming from China and intended for Vietnam." See Marie Alexanderine Martin, *Cambodia: A Shattered Society* (Berkeley: University of California Press, 1994), 92–93. For a Chinese account of Beijing's use of Sihanoukville to send military supplies to the NLF between 1966 and 1967, see Kang Daisha, "Zai Jianpuzhai de rizi" [My days in Cambodia], in *Nu waijiaoguan* [Women diplomats], ed. Cheng Xiangjun (Beijing: People's Culture Press, 1995), 482–83. Kang Daisha is the wife of Chen Shuliang, who was China's ambassador to Cambodia between 1962 and 1967.

23. Anne Gilks and Gerald Segal, *China and the Arms Trade* (New York: St. Martin's Press, 1985), 50.

24. Sihanouk worked out an arrangement with Beijing and Hanoi in 1964 to retain 10 percent of the Chinese weapons delivered to the Vietnamese through Sihanoukville. Additional fees were charged for transporting food and other goods to the Vietnamese border in Cambodian army trucks and private vehicles contracted for that purpose. Many officers who had profited by trading with the Vietnamese Communists later supported General Lon Nol's coup against Sihanouk in 1970. Nayan Chanda, *Brother Enemy: The War after the War* (New York: Collier Books, 1986), 420; David P. Chandler, *The*

Tragedy of Cambodian History: Politics, War, and Revolution since 1945 (New Haven, Conn.: Yale University Press, 1991), 140.

25. Armstrong, *Revolutionary Diplomacy,* 204; Chandler, *Tragedy of Cambodian History,* 169, 347 n. 33.

26. Peter Edwards, *A Nation at War: Australian Politics, Society and Diplomacy during the Vietnam War, 1965–1975* (St. Leonards: Allen & Unwin, 1997), 144–45.

27. *Zhou Enlai nianpu,* vol. 3, 180; Diplomatic History Research Office of the PRC Foreign Ministry, *Zhou Enlai waijiao huodong dashiji,* 515. These two sources mention Zhou's meetings with Phurissara but do not describe the content of their conversations.

28. Zhou's quote in Chandler, *Tragedy of Cambodian History,* 169; see also Armstrong, *Revolutionary Diplomacy,* 204.

29. *Zhou Enlai nianpu,* vol. 3, 181–83.

30. Zhou's talks with the Cambodian ambassador, September 14, October 26, 1967, in *Zhou Enlai nianpu,* vol. 3, 185, 196.

31. *Black Paper: Facts and Evidences of the Acts of Aggression and Annexation of Vietnam against Kampuchea* (hereafter cited as *Black Paper*) (Phnom Penh: Department of Press and Information of the Ministry of Foreign Affairs of Democratic Kampuchea, 1978), 25–26. It should be noted that this pamphlet, believed to have been authored primarily by Pol Pot, was issued after the break of relations between the Khmer Rouge and Vietnam. It is thus a highly emotional and bitterly worded tract with a strong anti-Vietnamese bias, but it does reveal some specific factual information on Vietnamese–Khmer Rouge interactions.

32. Stephen Heder, "Kampuchea's Armed Struggle: The Origins of an Independent Revolution," *Bulletin of Concerned Asian Scholars* 11 (1979): 6–7; Ben Kiernan, *How Pol Pot Came to Power: A History of Communism in Kampuchea, 1930–1975* (London: Verso, 1985), 219–24.

33. David P. Chandler, *Brother Number One: A Political Biography of Pol Pot,* rev. ed. (Boulder, Colo.: Westview Press, 1999), 66, 71–73.

34. In reality, the Samlaut rebellion was primarily a localized occurrence. David Chandler writes that the revolt "sprang from local grievances against injustice and social change, corruption, and ham-fisted government behavior" and that the participants "did not respond to orders from the CPK central committee." Chandler, *Tragedy of Cambodian History,* 166. According to Milton Osborne, the rebellion "was more an outbreak of largely spontaneous resistance to government actions than the first orchestrated challenge from the radicals." Osborne, *Sihanouk,* 191. "Cambodia" and "Kampuchea" represent, respectively, English and Khmer pronunciations of the same word. The fullest account of the Samlaut rebellion is contained in Ben Kiernan, "The Samlaut Rebellion, 1967–68," in *Peasants and Politics in Kampuchea, 1942–1981,* ed. Ben Kiernan and Chanthou Boua (London: Zed Press, 1982), 166–205.

35. Odd Arne Westad, Chen Jian, Stein Tønnesson, Nguyen Vu Tung, and James G. Hershberg, eds., *77 Conversations between Chinese and Foreign Leaders on the Wars in Indochina, 1964–1977,* Cold War International History Project Working Paper 22 (Washington, D.C.: Woodrow Wilson International Center for Scholars, 1998), 101–4.

36. Westad et al., *77 Conversations,* 107–14; Diplomatic History Research Office of the PRC Foreign Ministry, *Zhou Enlai waijiao huodong dashiji* (pp. 510–11) records Zhou's conversations with Pham Van Dong on April 10 and 11, 1967, but it only includes their talks on the war in South Vietnam, ignoring the subject of Cambodia.

37. Gareth Porter, "Vietnamese Communist Policy toward Kampuchea, 1930–1970,"

in *Revolution and Its Aftermath in Kampuchea: Eight Essays,* Monograph Series 5, ed. David P. Chandler and Ben Kiernan (New Haven, Conn.: Yale University Southeast Asia Studies, 1983), 78–79.

38. Anne Gilks, *The Breakdown of the Sino-Vietnamese Alliance, 1970–1979* (Berkeley: Institute of East Asian Studies, University of California, 1992), 52.

39. Chandler, *Tragedy of Cambodian History,* 171. On the first two years of Pol Pot's revolutionary warfare, see Kiernan, *How Pol Pot Came to Power,* 268–88; Heder, "Kampuchea's Armed Struggle," 13–14; and Craig Etcheson, *The Rise and Demise of Democratic Kampuchea* (Boulder, Colo.: Westview Press, 1984), 82–84.

40. Chandler, *Tragedy of Cambodian History,* 171–74; Heder, "Kampuchea's Armed Struggle," 14.

41. Westad et al., *77 Conversations,* 135–37. Cambodian hostility increased when additional North Vietnamese regular units moved into Cambodia in mid-1968 following the Tet Offensive. These troops were more recognizably foreign than the previous NLF units on Cambodian soil, and they often treated the local population more abrasively. See Chandler, *Tragedy of Cambodian History,* 160.

42. Westad et al., *77 Conversations,* 135–37.

43. According to William Duiker, in 1968, Pol Pot, after a visit to China, launched an armed rebellion against Sihanouk. See Duiker, *China and Vietnam: The Roots of Conflict,* Indochina Research Monograph (Berkeley: University of California Institute of East Asian Studies, 1986), 53. Duiker drew upon his December 18, 1985, interview with Kong Korn, deputy foreign minister of the People's Republic of Kampuchea, on December 18, 1985, who claimed that Beijing instigated the insurrection.

44. Armstrong, *Revolutionary Diplomacy,* 209.

45. Etcheson, *Rise and Demise of Democratic Kampuchea,* 234.

46. Chandler, *Tragedy of Cambodian History,* 184.

47. Westad et al., *77 Conversations,* 158–59.

48. *Black Paper,* 32–34; Porter, "Vietnamese Communist Policy toward Kampuchea," 82–84.

49. Chandler, *Tragedy of Cambodian History,* 191–94. According to Marie Alexandrine Martin, while in France, "Sihanouk asked his prime minister to organize popular anti-Vietnamese demonstrations in support of his initiatives with the two Communist giants." Martin, *Cambodia,* 122–23.

50. Zhou's talk with Nay Valentin, March 14, 1970, in *Zhou Enlai waijiao huodong dashiji,* ed. Diplomatic History Research Office of the PRC Foreign Ministry, 548. See also *Zhou Enlai nianpu,* vol. 3, 354.

51. Zhou's talk with the North Korean ambassador, March 16, 1970, in *Zhou Enlai waijiao huodong dashiji,* ed. Diplomatic History Research Office of the PRC Foreign Ministry, 548–49.

52. Norodom Sihanouk, as related to Wilfred Burchett, *My War with the CIA: Cambodia's Fight for Survival* (London: Penguin Books, 1973), 24–25. Written after Sihanouk's deposition, this book has a strong anti-American tone.

53. Daniel S. Papp, *Vietnam: The View from Moscow, Peking, Washington* (Jefferson, N.C.: McFarland, 1981), 160; Duiker, *China and Vietnam,* 53.

54. Sihanouk, *My War with the CIA,* 26–27; Chandler, *Tragedy of Cambodian History,* 197.

55. Sihanouk, *My War with the CIA,* 27.

56. Zhang Qing, "Qingshen yizhong ershi zai: Zhou Enlai yu Xihanuke jiaowang

shilu" [Twenty years of deep friendship: A record of Zhou Enlai's contacts with Si-hanouk] in *Lao waijiaoguan huiyi Zhou Enlai* [Veteran diplomats remember Zhou Enlai], eds. Tian Zengpei and Wang Taiping (Beijing: World Knowledge Press, 1998), 151. Zhang Qing was an official in the Asian Department of the Chinese Foreign Ministry at the time.

57. Zhou's talk with Sihanouk, March 19, 1970, in *Zhou Enlai nianpu*, vol. 3, 356. See also Diplomatic History Research Office of the PRC Foreign Ministry, *Zhou Enlai waijiao huodong dashiji*, 549.

58. *Zhou Enlai nianpu*, vol. 3, 356.

59. *Zhou Enlai nianpu*, vol. 3, 356.

60. Kang Maozhao, "Zai peiban Xihanuke qingwang de rizili" [In the days of accompanying Prince Sihanouk], *Bainianchao* [Hundred-year tide], no. 2 (1999): 31–38. Kang Maozhao was China's ambassador to Cambodia at the time.

61. Westad et al., *77 Conversations*, 160–62.

62. Quoted in Chandler, *Tragedy of Cambodian History*, 200.

63. Quoted in Chandler, *Tragedy of Cambodian History*, 200.

64. Diplomatic History Research Office of the PRC Foreign Ministry, *Zhou Enlai waijiao huodong dashiji* (p. 549) mentions the Zhou-Dong meeting on March 22, but does not include its contents.

65. Zhou's talk with Sihanouk, March 22, 1970, in *Zhou Enlai nianpu*, vol. 3, 356. See also Diplomatic History Research Office of the PRC Foreign Ministry, *Zhou Enlai waijiao huodong dashiji*, 549.

66. Wang Taiping, chief ed., *Zhonghua renmin gongheguo waijiaoshi, 1970–1978* [Diplomatic history of the People's Republic of China] (Beijing: World Knowledge Press, 1999), 73–74. This source does not mention which Chinese leader negotiated with Pol Pot. The Khmer Rouge leader himself later claimed that he participated in the Zhou Enlai–Pham Van Dong discussions in Beijing and had been in Hanoi beforehand. See Chandler, *Tragedy of Cambodian History*, 200.

67. Chandler, *Tragedy of Cambodian History*, 200–1; Martin, *Cambodia*, 135–36.

68. Martin, *Cambodia*, 136.

69. Jay Taylor, *China and Southeast Asia: Peking's Relations with Revolutionary Movements*, expanded and updated ed. (New York: Praeger, 1976), 151–52; Eugene K. Lawson, *The Sino-Vietnamese Conflict* (New York: Praeger, 1984), 196; R. B. Smith, "The International Setting of the Cambodia Crisis, 1969–1970," *International History Review* 18, no. 2 (May 1996): 330.

70. Zhou made his remarks in Pyongyang at the welcome banquet hosted by Kim Il Sung. Xie Yixian, ed. *Zhongguo waijiao shi: Zhonghua renmin gongheguo shiqi, 1949–1979* [A Diplomatic History of China: The period of the People's Republic of China, 1949–1979] (Zhengzhou: Henan People's Press, 1988), 354.

71. Taylor, *China and Southeast Asia*, 152–53; Lawson, *Sino-Vietnamese Conflict*, 196; Armstrong, *Revolutionary Diplomacy*, 210; Gilks, *Breakdown of the Sino-Vietnamese Alliance*, 54. Kang Maozhao, in his recollection, said nothing about his negotiations with Lon Nol before his return to China. Kang Maozhao, "Zai peiban Xihanuke qingwang de rizili," 31–38.

72. Henry Kissinger, *White House Years* (Boston: Little, Brown, 1979), 448–57; Gilks, *Breakdown of the Sino-Vietnamese Alliance*, 54; Smith, "International Setting of the Cambodia Crisis," 319; Donald Kirk, *Wider War: The Struggle for Cambodia, Thailand, and Laos* (New York: Praeger, 1971), 46–47.

73. *Beijing Review,* March 13, 1970, 13.

74. Gilks, *Breakdown of the Sino-Vietnamese Alliance,* 54.

75. Zhou's talk with Sihanouk, March 28, 1970, in *Zhou Enlai waijiao huodong dashiji,* ed. Diplomatic History Research Office of the PRC Foreign Ministry, 550.

76. Gilks, *Breakdown of the Sino-Vietnamese Alliance,* 56.

77. Before the summit opened, Chinese vice foreign minister Han Nianlong led a team of officials to Guangzhou to make arrangements. See Zhang, "Qingshen yizhong ershi zai," 155. Zhang went with Han Nianlong to Guangzhou.

78. Zhang, "Qingshen yizhong ershi zai," 155. The author did not explain the nature of the differences between Pham Van Dong and Sihanouk. The actual proceedings of the summit remain murky and controversial. According to Western accounts, China and Sihanouk sought to establish a permanent organization to coordinate Cambodian resistance activities, a proposal Hanoi opposed because this organization would presumably be located in China. The North Vietnamese intended that the conference should serve only propaganda purposes and not become involved in planning operations. Taylor, *China and Southeast Asia,* 156; Lawson, *Sino-Vietnamese Conflict,* 198. Anne Gilks, conversely, implies that, although the conference failed to implement this, Hanoi initiated the call for "a joint military command, which would have considerably strengthened Vietnam's influence over the NUFK." Gilks, *Breakdown of the Sino-Vietnamese Alliance,* 57.

79. Xie, *Zhongguo waijiao shi,* 356–57; Papp, *Vietnam,* 161.

80. Truong Nhu Tang, *Journal of a Vietcong* (London: Jonathan Cape, 1985), 147.

81. Diplomatic History Research Office of the PRC Foreign Ministry, *Zhou Enlai waijiao huodong dashiji,* 552; Xie, *Zhongguo waijiao shi,* 357.

82. Editorial Group of the "Record of Mao Zedong's International Contacts," ed., *Mao Zedong guoji jiaowang lu* [The record of Mao Zedong's international contacts] (Beijing: CCP Central Party Material and History Press, 1995), 66–68.

83. Xue Mouhong and Pei Jianzhang, *Dangdai Zhongguo waijiao,* 219; Gong Li, *Kuayue honggou: 1969–1979 nian Zhong Mei guanxi de yanbian* [Crossing the chasm: The evolution of Sino-American relations, 1969–1979] (Zhengzhou: Henan People's Press, 1992), 56–57. See also William G. Hyland, *Mortal Rivals: Superpower Relations from Nixon to Reagan* (New York: Random House, 1987), 28.

84. As Kissinger pointed out to Nixon at the time, Mao's speech "makes no threats, offers no commitments, is not personally abusive toward you, and avoids positions on contentious bilateral issues." Absent from Mao's address was the standard phraseology that China was a "rear area" for the Indochinese struggle. Kissinger, *White House Years,* 695.

85. Chai Chengwen, Huang Zhengji, and Zhang Changjin, *Sanda Tupo: XinZhongguo zouxiang shijie de baogao* [Three breakthroughs: A report on New China's road to the world) (Beijing: PLA Press, 1994), 243.

86. Kang, "Zai peiban Xihanuke qingwang de rizili," 31–38.

87. William Shawcross, *Sideshow: Kissinger, Nixon and the Destruction of Cambodia* (New York: Simon & Schuster, 1979), 255.

88. Diplomatic History Research Office of the PRC Foreign Ministry, *Zhou Enlai waijiao huodong dashiji,* 555–58.

89. Before the evening started, Zhou Enlai asked Sihanouk not to salute Mao's portrait during the banquet Otherwise, Zhou continued, "we will feel embarrassed." See *Zhou Enlai nianpu,* vol. 3, 377.

90. Kang, "Zai peiban Xihanuke qingwang de rizili," 32–35.

91. *Zhou Enlai nianpu,* vol. 3, 399. Mao first developed the concept of the two intermediate zones during the period 1963–64. See Qiang Zhai, *China and the Vietnam Wars, 1950–1975* (Chapel Hill: University of North Carolina Press, 2000), 146.

92. Memorandum of conversation between Kissinger and Zhou Enlai, July 9, 1971, Kissinger Office Files, box 90, "China Visit: Record of Previous Meetings" File, Nixon Presidential Materials Project (NPMP), National Archives, Washington.

93. Nixon-Zhou talks, February 22, 24, 1972, President's Office Files, Memoranda for the President, box 87, "Beginning February 20, 1972" File, NPMP..

94. Kang, "Zai peiban Xihanuke qingwang de rizili," 35–36.

95. Gilks, *Breakdown of the Sino-Vietnamese Alliance,* 58–62; Chandler, *Tragedy of Cambodian History,* 205–10; Taylor, *China and Southeast Asia,* 156; Martin, *Cambodia,* 142.

96. Kissinger, *White House Years,* 1383; Gilks, *Breakdown of the Sino-Vietnamese Alliance,* 91.

97. For the complete text of Zhou's speech, see "Zhou Enlai's Internal Report to the Party on the Problems of the Current International Situation, March 1973," in *Chinese Foreign Policy during the Cultural Revolution,* ed. Barbara Barnouin and Yu Changgen (London: Kegan Paul International, 1998), appendix II, document 8b.

98. Memorandum of conversation between Kissinger and Zhou Enlai, February 16, 1973, in *The Kissinger Transcripts: The Top Secret Talks with Beijing and Moscow,* ed. William Burr (New York: New Press, 1998), 103–9.

99. *Kissinger Transcripts,* 109.

100. Kissinger, *Years of Upheaval* (Boston: Little, Brown, 1982), 343.

101. Memorandum of conversation between Kissinger and Zhou Enlai, February 18, 1973, in *Kissinger Transcripts,* ed. Burr, 109–11.

102. *Kissinger Transcripts,* ed. Burr, 109–11.

103. *Kissinger Transcripts,* ed. Burr, 109–11.

104. On Chinese-U.S. intelligence cooperation during the 1979 Sino-Vietnamese War, see James Mann, *About Face: A History of America's Curious Relationship with China, from Nixon to Clinton* (New York: Alfred A. Knopf, 1999), 100.

105. "Zhou Enlai's Internal Report to the Party," in *Chinese Foreign Policy,* ed. Barnouin and Yu.

106. Zhang, "Qingshen yizhong ershi zai," 168–70; *Zhou Enlai nianpu,* vol. 3, 586. See also Chandler, *Tragedy of Cambodian History,* 227–28; Wilfred P. Deac, *Road to the Killing Fields: The Cambodian War of 1970–1975* (College Station: Texas A&M University Press, 1997), 167.

107. Diplomatic History Research Office of the PRC Foreign Ministry, *Zhou Enlai waijiao huodong dashiji,* 699–700; *Zhou Enlai nianpu,* vol. 3, 660. During his meeting with Zhou Enlai, Khieu Samphan gave the Chinese premier a grenade launcher as a gift. Shawcross, *Sideshow,* 336.

108. Gilks, *Breakdown of the Sino-Vietnamese Alliance,* 125–26; Duiker, *China and Vietnam,* 60.

109. Etienne Manac'h, the French ambassador to China, also detected the shift in Beijing's policy in the spring of 1974. See Shawcross, *Sideshow,* 336.

110. Memorandum of conversation between Kissinger and Deng Xiaoping, November 26, 1974, in *Kissinger Transcripts,* ed. Burr, 289–93 (Deng's quotation is on 293).

111. The Khmer Rouge used rubber to pay for Chinese weapons. Kiernan, *How Pol Pot Came to Power,* 412; Deac, *Road to the Killing Fields,* 203.

112. Dan Tong, "Xihanuke, Boerbute yu Zhongguo" (Sihanouk, Pol Pot and China) in *Dangshi wenhui* (Collection of Party History Studies), no. 1 (2000): 35–38; Nayan Chanda, *Brother Enemy: The War after the War* (New York: Collier Books, 1986), 16–17.

113. On Stalin's euphoria over the victory of the Chinese Communist Party, see John Lewis Gaddis, *We Now Know: Rethinking Cold War History* (Oxford: Clarendon Press, 1997), 66–68.

114. Westad et al., *77 Conversations,* 194; Cheng Zhongyuan, "Mao Zedong de sanxiang zhishi he Deng Xiaoping zhuchi de 1975 nian zhengdun" [Mao Zedong's Three Instructions and the 1975 rectification directed by Deng Xiaoping] in *Dangdai Zhongguoshi yanjiu* [Studies on contemporary Chinese history], no. 1 (1997): 63–78.

115. Dan Tong, "Xihanuke, Boerbute yu Zhongguo," 38.

116. Neither Pol Pot's visit nor Chinese aid was publicized at the time. From China, Pol Pot journeyed to North Korea, where he obtained pledges of military aid. Returning to Beijing, he underwent medical treatment. David P. Chandler, *Brother Number One,* 105–6.

117. Zhang, "Qingshen yizhong ershi zai," 170.

118. Zhang, "Qingshen yizhong ershi zai," 170–71.

119. Diplomatic History Research Office of the PRC Foreign Ministry, *Zhou Enlai waijiao huodong dashiji,* 712; *Zhou Enlai nianpu,* vol. 3, 717. These two sources mention Zhou's meeting with Khieu Samphan and Ieng Sary but do not provide the content of their discussions.

120. Zhang, "Qingshen yizhong ershi zai," 171.

121. Diplomatic History Research Office of the PRC Foreign Ministry, *Zhou Enlai waijiao huodong dashiji,* 712; *Zhou Enlai nianpu,* vol. 3, 718.

122. Zhang, "Qingshen yizhong ershi zai," 171.

123. Chandler, *Brother Number One,* 106–10.

12

The Soviet-Chinese-Vietnamese Triangle in the 1970s: The View from Moscow

Stephen J. Morris

In November 1978, the Soviet Union and the Socialist Republic of Vietnam (SRV) signed a Treaty of Friendship and Cooperation. The treaty, following upon a series of events highlighted by Vietnam's admission into the Council for Mutual Economic Assistance (COMECON) the previous June, was the culmination of Vietnam's gradual integration into the Soviet bloc, which had begun in 1969.

The Hanoi government's alignment within the communist world had fluctuated over the years since the Soviet Union and the People's Republic of China (PRC) had abandoned their international solidarity against "imperialism." In early 1963, shortly after the open split between Moscow and Beijing, the North Vietnamese Communists gravitated to the Chinese side on a number of important issues under contention between the two communist powers. Then, following Nikita Khrushchev's ouster in October 1964, the Vietnamese tilt toward China quietly ended. The Vietnamese embraced a position of neutrality in the Sino-Soviet conflict throughout the years 1965–68. After 1968, the Vietnamese shifted to a pro-Soviet position, even though until 1978 the Soviet-Vietnamese relationship was extremely nuanced.

This chapter does not attempt any comprehensive causal analysis of the evolution in the relationship among the Soviet Union, China, and Vietnam. Instead, it seeks new insights into the triangular relationship by providing, through an examination of secret reports by Soviet officials stationed in North Vietnam, some of the behind-the-scenes texture of relations during the early to middle 1970s.[1]

The secret Soviet documents reveal, beneath the public posture of Soviet-Vietnamese friendship and solidarity that both sides' propaganda presented to the rest of the world, real tensions between patron and client, and is particularly interesting because during the period under analysis the Vietnamese leaders had shifted away from China and toward the Soviet "general line" on international affairs. The documents also reveal two contrasting aspects of Vietnamese-Chinese relations. First, Chinese anger with the Vietnamese tilt toward the Kremlin that exploded in a private meeting in 1975. Second, the Vietnamese leaders held a subtle and evolving set of attitudes toward China, attitudes far more complicated than those allowed by the broad explanatory concept of "Vietnamese nationalism" subscribed to by most Western academic and journalistic analysts and commentators.

Part of the complexity seems to have derived from factional splits within the Vietnamese leadership over the Communist Party's relationships with both the Soviets and the Chinese. Western analysts have long debated whether factional differences existed within the Vietnamese Communist Party (until 1976 the Vietnamese Workers' Party, VWP, or Lao Dong) and how important they were. The archives for the first time give us strong evidence of factional differences in Hanoi based at least in part upon attitudes toward China and the Soviet Union, as well as evidence of important policy splits that were not tied to this issue.

The source material for this chapter does not include all relevant documents available in the USSR, even for the time period examined, for several reasons. First and most important, there is the problem of inaccessibility to certain key archives, especially the Presidential Archive, where documentation of Soviet policy and strategy debates is to be found.[2] Second, because of time constraints on the author and the premature closure of the international affairs files of the Communist Party of the Soviet Union's (CPSU's) Central Committee archives (TSKhSD), the documents seen do not reflect an exhaustive examination of all relevant documents once made available in the TsKhSD files to the author but rather a concentration upon certain documents and certain years in the 1970s relevant to two other re-search projects the author was undertaking. Third, even within the frame-work of the TsKhSD files, only a small part of the archive's total collection was opened to researchers. For example, those files dealing with policy rec-ommendations by the Central Committee departments and most of the im-portant decisions of the Secretariat were not released. Finally, several re-quested files were denied to the author, allegedly on security grounds.

Thus, the material examined constitutes a skewed selection of the mate-rials in Russian archives on the Soviet-Chinese-Vietnamese triangle. It con-sists mostly of the reports from the Soviet Embassy in Hanoi, supplemented by a smaller number of Komitet Gosudarstvennoi Bezopasnosti (KGB) and the Soviet Armed Forces General Staff's Glavnoe Razvedivatel'noe Up-ravlenie (GRU) documents (only a fraction of those located in the KGB's and GRU's own archives) on Vietnam's foreign policy and internal condi-tions. The documents selected reflect the prejudices and political purposes of the Soviet observers. But they nevertheless constitute an invaluable his-torical source, for two reasons. First, they open a window into the secret in-teractions of the communist powers not previously visible to Western schol-ars. Second, the perspective is from the Soviet home, and thus gives us a very substantial part of Moscow's view of the relationships.

Background: Vietnam's Tilt toward the Soviet Union, 1968–1975

To evaluate the revelations from the archives one must examine the politi-cal context. In the late 1960s, North Vietnam tilted from a position of neu-trality in the Sino-Soviet dispute towads partial alignment with the Soviet Union. However, before 1978, no Western academic writer had perceived any Vietnamese Communist alignment with the Soviet Union.[3] Even seri-ous scholarly analyses produced after the Soviet-Vietnamese alliance had been publicly formalized in 1978 failed to discern that North Vietnam had already shifted before 1975.[4]

The failure of Western experts to detect a shift in North Vietnam's posi-tion, and their reiteration of a view of Hanoi's foreign policy as equidistant between Moscow and Beijing, stemmed, I argue, from a failure to examine and interpret correctly all the relevant evidence, namely, the Vietnamese Communists' positions on the issues dividing the Soviet Union and China. During the years 1968–75, Hanoi took a stand on several issues under contention between the USSR and the PRC that affected neither the national security nor economic well-being of the Vietnamese Communist state: (1) the Soviet invasion of Czechoslovakia in 1968;[5] (2) Soviet–West German détente in 1970;[6] (3) the attempted coup d'état of 1971 in Sudan;[7] (4) the 1974–75 military coup and political revolution in Portugal;[8] and (5) the civil war in Angola in 1975.[9]

A communist party's stand on any single issue alone does not provide evidence of alignment in the Sino-Soviet dispute. Only a *sequence* of stands indicates either alignment or independence. On all these issues, the Vietnamese had the opportunity to avoid taking any public stance by (1) mere factual reporting of events, (2) reporting both sides equally, or (3) reporting nothing at all. Yet in all these cases the Vietnamese chose a public stand in support of the Soviet line.

That the timing of the Vietnamese Communist tilt to the Soviet Union is roughly as I have suggested is corroborated by the published memoir of the former justice minister of the Provisional Revolutionary Government of South Vietnam, Truong Nhu Tang.

> I knew that the Vietnamese Communist Party had already decided to ally itself with the Soviets. Movement in that direction had begun as far back as 1969, and Ho Chi Minh's death had opened the way to formalizing the decision. Though nothing like an open declaration could be expected while there was still a need for Chinese aid, in fact, by 1974 the bitter infighting had resulted in a clear victory for the pro-Soviet faction led by Secretary General Le Duan and the Paris negotiator Le Duc Tho.[10]

Given the Vietnamese leaders' decision to tilt toward the Soviet Union, what is interesting is that the Soviets nevertheless found the alliance relationship difficult for the first few years. The archives provide fascinating new information on this subject.

Soviet Attitudes toward Vietnamese Foreign Policy, 1970–1975

One important source of Soviet thinking about Vietnam was the evaluations provided by Moscow's Embassy in Hanoi. It should be cautioned that the views of the Soviet Foreign Ministry did not determine the views of the CPSU Politburo. However, we should note that the CPSU Central Committee's Department for Relations with Communist and Workers' Parties in Socialist Countries was one source of information and analysis for the Politburo's deliberations. A large proportion of all the information provided to that Central Committee department came from the Foreign Ministry, especially the embassy reports. Moreover, the ambassador and other key figures in the Hanoi Embassy were always party functionaries. Thus the Foreign Ministry's embassy reports would have been one factor influencing Politburo deliberations. And they certainly illuminate diplomatic relations at the higher levels.

At the end of 1970, the Soviet Embassy in Hanoi showed little acknowledgment of Hanoi's foreign policy tilt toward the Soviet Union. The exception was their reference to a change in Vietnamese communist strategic thinking in 1968. In that year, the Vietnamese began to speak of three types of combat—military, political, and diplomatic—which the Soviets interpreted as a departure from China's position, which emphasized the military and "an acceptance of our views."[11] However, the embassy still perceived Hanoi as following a policy of balancing between Moscow and Beijing.[12]

Nevertheless, the bulk of the Soviet embassy's evaluation of Vietnamese foreign policy was highly critical. In the first place, the Soviet Union was eager to coordinate the two nations' foreign policies. By contrast, the Vietnamese were not only resistant to such an idea but also indicated explicitly that they would not inform the Soviets in advance on tactical aspects of specific foreign policy moves that they were undertaking, and that they would not consult on specific issues. This upset the Soviets, who had been providing the Vietnamese with information and advice on internal and foreign policy matters. But the lack of reciprocity by the Vietnamese had to be accepted, the Soviets felt, because the Chinese were also providing the Vietnamese with information and advice.[13] Yet some bitterness apparently remained:

> On account of the DRV's narrow national interests, which continue to exist among the Vietnamese leadership in relations with the Soviet Union and socialist countries of Eastern Europe, they are to this day not sufficiently sincere and trustworthy; they are not truly brotherly. Our friends were not adequately sincere with these countries concerning their plans for solving the Indochina problem. They have evaded agreeing and coordinating their actions with them.[14]

Soviet embassy analysts were also upset that the Vietnamese approached the Soviet and Eastern European allies separately, secretly making similar requests for assistance to more than one of these countries with a view to generating what the Soviets called "an unhealthy competition of a sort between socialist countries." The Soviets also felt that the DRV maintained closer relations with East Germany, Bulgaria, and Hungary, and also with North Korea and Cuba, than it did with the USSR.[15]

Despite substantial Soviet military aid—which was reequipping and providing training, repair, and maintenance support for the Vietnam People's Army—the 250 to 300 Soviet military specialists in the DRV faced difficulties. The Soviet embassy complained that the Vietnamese army command tried in every possible way to limit the Soviet specialists' activity to technical assistance only. Decisions on the combat use of military equipment and combat action tactics were reputedly jealously guarded from the influence of the Soviet specialists.[16]

However, particular distress was expressed over the working conditions of Soviet diplomats, who were allegedly subjected to a system of assorted bans and restrictions. Even though the Soviet Union was undertaking great efforts in support of the DRV, and hundreds of Soviet specialists were working for "the Vietnamese people," nevertheless "the Soviet embassy has been placed under unjust and severe conditions; it is under surveillance and suspicion."[17]

By the middle of 1971, the Soviet embassy had come to recognize a significant shift in Hanoi's foreign policy favorable to Moscow. In a political letter to Moscow in May, Ambassador I. Shcherbakov analyzed the shift as possessing two indices. First was the decision of the Vietnamese in 1968 to broaden their strategic approach to the war to incorporate military, political, and diplomatic forms of struggle (apparently connected to their decision to enter into negotiations with the United States in Paris). Second was the fact that the VWP "understands and apprehends more the policy of the CPSU."[18] Later in his report, the Soviet ambassador noted that "by leaning toward the Soviet Union, the VWP has endured the crude pressure of the Chinese leaders."[19]

The ambassador's main grievance was Hanoi's failure to exchange opinions and information on a future settlement for Indochina, and its refusal to arrange with the Soviet bloc socialist countries "a fully valuable coordination of actions, especially in the foreign policy sphere." The Hanoi leadership was accused of "trying to preserve for itself the exclusive right to a solution of the Vietnamese and Indochinese problems" and of "trying to impede, at least at the present stage, the broad involvement of the socialist countries on the matter."[20]

The embassy noted that in 1971 Chinese policy toward Indochina had begun to "acquire the appearance of moderation and some flexibility," which was reflected in Beijing's granting of supplementary aid that year, in China's public recognition of the program of the Provisional Revolutionary Government of the Republic of South Vietnam as a just basis for a Vietnam settlement, in China's indirect "rehabilitation" of the Paris peace negotiations, and also in Zhou Enlai's visit to Hanoi. These moves by Beijing were said to have brought some warming in Sino-Vietnamese relations. However, China's moves toward rapprochement with the United States—highlighted by the surprise July 1971 announcement that U.S. president Richard Nixon would visit Beijing—were said to have shaken the Vietnamese leaders, who feared new friction with the PRC and possibly renewed Chinese pressure. The Vietnamese tactical response was characterized as an attempt to compromise with the Chinese on minor matters of difference while avoiding concessions on the matters most important to them, especially on a settlement of the conflicts in Vietnam and Indochina generally.[21]

The Vietnamese Communists were said to have understood the connection between their primary task—finding a solution to the problem of Vietnam in Indochina—and receiving moral and material support from the Soviet Union and other socialist countries, including China.[22] Finally, the ambassador's report ended with two policy suggestions: (1) to inform the Vietnamese about Soviet-Chinese relations, and (2) to request the Vietnamese to mediate between the Soviet Union and China.[23]

By 1972, the Soviet embassy was reporting extensively on the tensions that had arisen between the Soviet Union and the DRV due to Nixon's May 1972 visit to Moscow, despite the American bombing of North Vietnam and the mining of North Vietnamese ports, and the efforts the Soviet side had made to diminish those tensions.

Although the Vietnamese Communist leaders had publicly supported Soviet détente with West Germany in 1970, in 1972 and 1973 they expressed a very different view on détente between the United States and the major communist powers:

> Nixon's policy of détente is aimed at achieving the objective of dividing the socialist camp in an attempt to weaken the revolution. In implementing a policy of "détente" with the big countries, the U.S. imperialists are scheming to "control" the socialist countries in their movement to develop the revolutionary offensive, while the United States is continuing its limited counteroffensives against the revolutionary movement in various areas and small countries.[24]

According to the Soviet Embassy in Hanoi, the Vietnamese leaders were most upset by Nixon's visit to Moscow in May 1972. They had been informed of the visit as early as October 1971, during a trip to Hanoi by a Soviet delegation headed by Nikolai Podgorny. According to the embassy, at that time the Vietnamese made no protest against the Nixon visit taking place. But as the time for the visit drew closer, the Vietnamese public stance changed.[25]

The Soviet embassy explained the anxiety of the Vietnamese over Nixon's visit to Moscow as a response to the unfavorable consequences of his visit to China for the Vietnamese Communists. That is, after Nixon visited Beijing in February 1972, the United States broke off negotiations in Paris, mined the sea approaches to North Vietnamese ports, and increased military pressure on Vietnam.[26] In reality, these American actions were a response to the North Vietnamese Easter Offensive, not the Nixon visit to China. But nevertheless, the Soviet Union experienced a negative reaction from the DRV. Hanoi feared that friendlier relations between its patrons and its main enemy would rebound on itself. This reaction, although restrained, demanded a response.

In 1972 several high-level Soviet and North Vietnamese delegations visited each other's capitals in an effort to smooth out the differences dividing the two countries. The most difficult period in their relationship was said to have been between April and September, the precise period of North Vietnam's Easter Offensive. But during the autumn of 1972, Vietnamese attitudes toward the Soviet Union improved.[27] Ultimately, it was the United States–China rapprochement, not United States–Soviet détente, that the Vietnamese would perceive as treacherous.

The Soviets also voiced dissatisfaction with the VWP's alleged policy of equally friendly relations with the USSR and PRC. The Soviets mentioned how the publication of news of polemics between Moscow and Beijing was prohibited in the DRV, while news of each country was presented evenly, policies that had inhibited the deepening of Soviet-Vietnamese relations. Interestingly, the embassy also remarked that "objectively one should recognize that the VWP for the present cannot foresee a single alternative to this policy." Soviet tolerance for Hanoi's situation was justified so far, the report noted. Yet the Maoists were said to be abusing this policy by trying to drive a wedge between the VWP and the CPSU. "One must hope that the VWP is aware of this."[28]

As in previous years, the embassy was most dismayed by what it termed Vietnamese Communist leaders' distrustful and deceitful behavior toward the Soviet Union. It was noted that unofficial contacts by Vietnamese with foreigners, even Soviets, were not permitted. But even in their official contacts, Vietnamese officials were said to be "insufficiently frank, they conceal a lot, they dissemble, etc." Even though the Soviet Union's leaders kept the Vietnamese leaders informed on many political issues, the Vietnamese were accused of withholding information on their foreign and internal policies. For example, the Vietnamese were said to inform the Soviets more candidly of developments at the Paris peace negotiations only when they needed Soviet assistance and support. Information provided on party building, on the country's economic situation, on losses due to American bombing, and on DRV ties with other countries was said to be of poor quality and acquired by the Soviets only with great difficulty.[29]

But the most telling example was provided by the experience of a Soviet delegation headed by Marshall P. F. Batitski, commander in chief of the Soviet Air Defense Forces, that visited North Vietnam in March 1972. According to the Soviet embassy, when the Vietnamese leaders requested Batitski to provide new arms, they omitted to mention that they were planning to launch the war's biggest military offensive immediately after his delegation departed.[30] This incident, if true—and it is hard to imagine why it would not be true—is a stunning reflection of Hanoi's distrust of its main patron at that time. Referring to these events, the Soviet embassy report concluded its evaluation of Soviet-Vietnamese relations for the year 1972:

> These and similar negative moments are gradually being overcome, but they are leaving certain impressions in our relations. However, on the whole we repeat that the leadership of the DRV continued on the course of strengthening ties with the Soviet Union, seeing in that the main buttress of its struggle and of peaceful construction.[31]

A year later, the Soviet embassy's view of the relationship was more upbeat. The embassy's annual report for 1973 spoke of the aspiration of "the Vietnamese comrades" to rely upon the Soviet Union in deciding the most important questions of domestic and foreign policy, during what was termed the transformative period from war to peace after the signing of the Paris Peace Agreement in January 1973.[32] The report claimed that the visit of a high-level Vietnamese Communist Party and government delegation to the USSR in 1973 helped to weaken Chinese influence in the DRV, in particular undermining its anti-Soviet propaganda.[33] The report explained only indirectly what might have been the decisive factor in this matter, when it specified the details of the August 14, 1973, agreement on new Soviet aid. The most significant feature of this agreement was the section in which the Soviet Union forgave the DRV a debt of $1.08 billion from earlier credit deliveries.[34] Trade relations involved the USSR providing goods worth 132.7 million rubles, of which 108 million rubles worth were on credit and 7.2 million rubles were an outright gift. Besides this, social organizations in the USSR sent free aid worth 10 million rubles.[35]

The embassy saw 1973 as the year in which Vietnamese leaders "began to take a significantly critical approach to several steps of the Maoists," thereby breaking from the previous VWP party line of standing aside from the "hostile, anti-Soviet line of Peking" and promoting "externally identical friendly relations with the Soviet Union and the DRV."[36] As noted above, the Vietnamese leaders actually began to take these steps much earlier, at some point between 1968 and 1970, even while they simultaneously continued to support "externally identical friendly relations with the Soviet Union and the PRC." The Soviet embassy had been less acutely cognizant of this trend than it should have been, and the Kremlin's desire for the unconditional loyalty of other communist states may have blinded it to more subtle tendencies, such as Hanoi's tilt. But in the aftermath of the tensions of 1972, it was now finally recognizing some change in Vietnamese foreign policy.

By the beginning of 1975, the Soviet embassy could speak of "the further closeness of the positions of both of our parties and countries on a whole series of important international problems." However, the embassy noted the continuing existence of "specific negative phenomena" in Vietnamese policy, among them the aspiration of the VWP leadership to remain "aloof from the struggle of the CPSU and other fraternal parties against Maoism." Moreover, although they had told USSR representatives that they were studying the question of their participation in this organization, the Vietnamese were uninterested in establishing broad ties with COMECON.[37]

The report recognized that the China factor was exercising a restraining influence on DRV cooperation with socialist countries. But so, too, was "the narrowly nationalistic path of the Vietnamese comrades," which caused them to formulate their attitude on the most important international problems "through the prism of the solution of the Vietnamese question." This was why Vietnamese leaders remained skeptical toward any Soviet-American dialogue. Yet, the report noted, their reaction to the 1974 Brezhnev-Nixon summit was calmer than before, because the Vietnamese leaders "are certain of the Soviet Union's position in relation to the Vietnamese people's struggle" and so regarded the meetings as "an internal [Soviet] affair."[38]

Political Factionalism within the Vietnamese Leadership

The issue of factionalism within the leadership of the Vietnamese Communist Party has long been a source of speculation among Western observers. Particular attention has often focused on the possibility of a split along pro-Chinese and pro-Soviet lines. As early as 1962, the British analyst P. J. Honey asserted that such a factional split existed, identifying the leaders of the pro-Soviet faction as Vo Nguyen Giap and Le Duan and the leaders of the pro-Chinese faction as Truong Chinh and Nguyen Duy Trinh.[39] Honey speculated that personal patronage and rivalries would place other Politburo members in one of the respective camps, and he specified that Le Duc Tho's rivalry with Duan was likely to make Tho pro-Chinese. Subsequently, the American analyst and former official W. R. Smyser criticized this view, asserting that there was "no definitive public evidence of such factions."[40] More recently, the expatriate Vietnamese analyst Thai Quang Trung revived Honey's interpretation, while using the advantage of hindsight to place Duan rather than Giap at the head of the pro-Soviet faction.[41]

Soviet Communist Party archives corroborate the view that the Vietnamese party was divided into factions, and that these included pro-Chinese and pro-Soviet groups. The archival evidence also indicates, however, that membership in either a pro-Chinese or pro-Soviet faction did not determine each party leader's stand on all important issues, because other factional divisions cut across the pro-Soviet / pro-Chinese divide.[42]

The most direct and credible evidence of pro-Chinese and pro-Soviet factions comes from party secretary Hoang Anh during his report to a 1971 VWP Central Committee plenum.[43] At several points during his report, Anh mentioned a small group of "opportunists" within the party who, he said, opposed the party leadership's line on a several issues, including agrarian policy, military policy, and foreign policy. He implied, though did not explicitly state, that on all these separate issues the opposition elements were comprised by the same group of people.[44] Evidence suggests that an obvious connection existed between the opposition faction's views on military and foreign policy.

On military policy, Anh stated that the "opportunists" sought to escalate the war and achieve a decisive military victory. To this end, the opposition faction wanted the Vietnamese government to invite the Chinese government to send troops to fight alongside the North Vietnamese forces in Laos and South Vietnam. On diplomatic policy, the so-called opportunists allegedly accused the party leadership of pursuing a concessionary line toward the Americans by pursuing negotiations with them in Paris. They also regarded the Soviet leadership as "revisionist" and supported China's Great Proletarian Cultural Revolution.[45] Anh's rebuttal of this line emphasized the importance of the patient and careful strategy of "people's war," which also incorporated political and diplomatic elements into military strategy.

One could be forgiven for a little confusion on this division of strategies into pro-Chinese and pro-Soviet, because the concept of "people's war" was originally a Maoist invention. It makes some sense, however, when one bears two points in mind. First, the Vietnamese themselves had co-opted the Maoist strategy and modified it to suit their own strategic and political situation. Second, in the wake of the Cultural Revolution, at that time China was still under the influence of a radical and optimistic phase of Maoism, emphasizing the primacy of violence over political and diplomatic approaches to conflict. Hence, being pro-Chinese and therefore Maoist in 1970 meant taking a more radical approach than the Maoist Chinese position of earlier periods.

Anh did not outline exactly how pervasive this "opportunist" faction was, but asserted that it included some of the higher military leaders and that its main party members included sixteen VWP Central Committee members. Six were identified by name: Le Liem, Nguyen Quang Toan, Ha Huy Giap, Bui Cong Trinh, Nguyen Van Vinh, and Song Khao, not all of whom were full members of the Central Committee. However, of these six the last was a lieutenant general and head of the DRV Defense Ministry's Main Political Administration, a most senior military position.[46] No Politburo member was identified as a member of this faction, although this does not preclude the possibility that one or more in fact were. It is worth remembering that one Politburo member of the period under review, Hoang Van Hoan, established that he was pro-Chinese when he defected to China in 1979.

Secondary evidence of a split within the Vietnamese leadership into pro-Chinese and pro-Soviet factions comes from a report of the Soviet military intelligence directorate, endorsed by the signature of Soviet chief of staff General Nikolai Ogarkov.[47] The GRU report, dated November 1972, does not refer to a pro-Soviet faction but instead to a "moderate group," which was said to have been in conflict with the "pro-Chinese group." These two groups were said to have been "finally formed" only in 1970–71, a somewhat surprising date given the long-standing historical factors that would have given rise to them, and that, as some Western analysts have previously speculated, should have promoted their emergence long before then.

But the most interesting feature of the GRU report is its specification of which Vietnamese leaders were members of which faction. The "moderate group" was said to have been headed by the first secretary of the Central Committee of the VWP, Le Duan, and Prime Minister and Politburo member Pham Van Dong. Politburo members said to have supported them included Defense Minister Vo Nguyen Giap, chairman of the VWP bureau for South Vietnam Pham Hung, Deputy Prime Minister Le Thanh Nghi, and unspecified others.[48] The "moderate group" was said to enjoy the support of "an overwhelming number of workers of the central apparatus and the intelligentsia."[49]

The head of the "pro-Chinese group" was said to be Politburo member Truong Chinh, ostensibly the party's leading theorist, and secretary general of the party until 1956. Those Politburo members alleged to have supported him were Foreign Minister Nguyen Duy Trinh, Hoan, and Tho, special adviser to the DRV delegation at the Paris negotiations. This group was said to include about twenty senior party, state, and military figures, and to have the support of party and administrative workers in agricultural regions, and pro-Chinese oriented elements in the central party and state organs. This group was claimed to favor resolving the Vietnam problem primarily by military means, closer intimacy with China, and a weakening of ties with the Soviet Union.[50] It is worth noting that the GRU analysis of membership of the two factions correlates closely with the factional membership analysis Honey published ten years earlier.

The GRU analysis considered these factional disagreements to be one of the main causes of what the GRU regarded as inconsistencies in North Vietnamese leaders' approach to solving important questions, "especially the Indochina problem." At the same time, the analysis asserted that the Politburo was "of one mind" in approving the plans for the spring 1972 military offensive. The subsequent failure of that military action led to a new split within the Politburo, which was especially pronounced from July 1972 on, over how to pursue the struggle—a split that brought a realignment of Politburo members into factions which in the West would be labeled "hawks" and "doves." These two new factions differed from and cut across the previous "moderate" and "pro-Chinese" split, with Le Duan and Chinh then joining in arguing for a primarily military solution to the conflict, and Pham Van Dong leading the faction, which included Tho, arguing for a political settlement.

A discrepancy exists between certain pieces of evidence considered here. On the one hand, some Western analysts and the 1972 GRU report place Tho in the pro-Chinese faction. On the other hand, Truong Nhu Tang identified Tho with a pro-Soviet orientation. How should one explain this discrepancy?

It may be that Tho was originally a member of the pro-Chinese faction but switched to the pro-Soviet faction in the early to mid-1970s. It may also be that Tang, who was a senior member of the southern revolutionary political front but not a Communist Party member, and thus acquired his information second-hand from friends within the party, erred on Tho's orientation. But if we accept that latter possibility, and that Tho was in fact pro-Chinese, then we have to explain how Tho retained and even enhanced his power after the Vietnamese party's shift to the side of the Soviet Union.

There is an easy explanation for this latter possibility. Most top party members of the Vietnamese Communist Party identified with the purported pro-Chinese faction submitted to the majority line. The major exception was Hoan, who after being dropped from the Politburo in December 1976, defected to China in 1979. In particular the alleged leader of the pro-Chinese faction, Chinh, retained his Politburo position until the 1986 Party Congress, which saw the nominal retirement of all the old guard leaders regardless of their purported factional membership. This evidence is consistent with the competing possibilities of Tho being pro-Chinese and then becoming pro-Soviet; or being pro-Chinese but, like Chinh, submitting to the Politburo majority.

The case of Chinh highlights the more important fact that these factional differences, even if they were significant political realities, were less important politically than the individual party member's commitment to the majority's "general line." The GRU document itself supports this view when it describes the purported leadership split in 1972 over the relative role of military versus political and diplomatic approaches to the struggle for South Vietnam. It thereby suggests that, because of the cross-cutting nature of party elite factional membership, factional identifications would not be decisive in any individual's decision on whether or not to adhere to the majority viewpoint. The existence of these factional splits within the Vietnamese party leadership suggests the lack of any one commanding figure within the Vietnamese Communist Party leadership, at least after Ho Chi Minh died in 1969.

China's Displeasure with Vietnam's Tilt toward the Soviet Union

Even before the North Vietnamese victory over South Vietnam, during private bilateral meetings, the Chinese had subtly indicated their grave displeasure with Hanoi's leaders.[51] The most serious private manifestation of tension between Vietnam and China, however, came in a secret meeting between the leaders of the two parties in September 1975, five months after the war ended; details of this meeting and a subsequent report by Le Duan to the Vietnamese Politburo were never published, but an account of both was conveyed to the Soviets in October 1975.[52]

From September 22 to 28, 1975, a Vietnamese Communist Party–government delegation, headed by Le Duan, visited China. The Vietnamese, in communications with the Soviets, indicated that this visit's goal was to improve Vietnamese-Chinese relations. In particular, they wanted to assure the Chinese that Vietnamese relations with the Soviet Union and China would remain as before.[53] This assurance apparently provided little comfort to Beijing. According to Hanoi, the Chinese leaders "openly and officially" showed their dissatisfaction with the conduct of Vietnamese foreign policy, especially over Vietnamese relations with the Soviet Union. Insofar as Vietnam continued this political line, they warned, it would not find support from China. Duan claimed that the visit enabled the Vietnamese leadership to show the Chinese, "officially and openly," that the VWP stood steadfastly by its political platform, regardless of the Chinese reaction. If relations between the two parties should deteriorate, Duan told the Soviets, the fault would lie entirely with the Chinese.[54]

At the same time, Duan noted, even if relations between the VWP and the Chinese Communist Party (CCP) deteriorated in the future, the VWP would act to support the principles of solidarity, mutual support, and unity of the world communist and workers' movement, and the "unity of all socialist countries." It would not insult China over its activities.

Yet Duan's overall evaluation of the results of the visit was grim. In his own words, a difficult period in relations between the Vietnamese and Chinese parties had set in. VWP-CCP relations were in an "alarming, critical condition." Therefore, the VWP must be careful, vigilant, and patient, and it must do all it could to avert a split between the two parties and countries.[55] Duan noted that no serious discussion of important political questions of mutual interest took place. The Chinese indicated that they did not want to discuss such questions and the Vietnamese did not insist on this. Thus there was no published document or communiqué confirming the results of the visit. However, Duan reminded the VWP Politburo, Vietnamese-Chinese discussions on the territorial water border in the Tonkin Gulf and the littoral continental shelf were due to commence at the beginning of October. The Vietnamese side intended to continue fishing on the shelf without waiting for the outcome of the negotiations. But Duan felt that the negotiations would be an important indicator of the future intentions of Chinese leaders on how they would develop relations with the Vietnamese. Duan's report demonstrated alarm over the decline of relations between the two parties and countries. Despite this concern, the Vietnamese leader opposed making any concession on the subject of most concern to China: Vietnam's relations with the Soviet Union.

China began to demonstrate its displeasure in tangible material ways. During the second half of 1975, Chinese assistance to North Vietnam declined rapidly. Several DRV departments reported to the Soviet embassy that the amount of freight unloaded off Chinese vessels in the port of Haiphong during those six months was half that unloaded during the comparable period of the previous year. Furthermore, the Vietnamese claimed, at the beginning of 1976 China recalled several groups of its specialists from Vietnam and delayed work on a number of projects being built with Chinese aid.[56]

By early 1976, the Vietnamese leaders were telling the Soviets that they were very anxious over their relations with China. They specifically cited the lack of any agreement for long-term economic aid from China, and the Chinese failure to settle outstanding territorial disputes, particularly over the Tonkin Gulf and the Paracel and Spratly Islands. Furthermore, Hanoi leaders were especially alarmed by the activities of Beijing, conducted through its contacts within the Chinese colony in South Vietnam, which was said to be "in conflict with the line of the revolutionary authorities." The Hanoi leaders claimed that they detected a connection between what they described as "the subversive appearances of the Maoists in Indochina" (a cryptic reference, possibly to the ideological orientation of the Cambodian communist leaders).[57] These anxieties led to repeated discussions of Vietnamese-Chinese relations at the highest level in the Central Committee of the VWP. Yet, despite their concern, Hanoi's leaders expressed to the Soviets their determination "not to withdraw from a principled political position," while at the same time attempting to "normalize relations with the PRC, in the first instance on a state-to-state basis."[58]

How then would the VWP repair relations with the Chinese and avoid a total split? Subsequent events suggested that the Hanoi leaders did not understand how to pursue that goal realistically.

The Fourth Vietnamese Party Congress and Hanoi's China Policy

The Vietnamese Communists held their Fourth Party Congress—their first after sixteen years of war—in December 1976. As with all party congresses, the meeting served to ratify political decisions already reached by the higher echelons of the party leadership. The CCP did not break its custom of not sending delegations to foreign party congresses, even though a Chinese delegation had attended the VWP's Third Congress in 1960, and even though on this occasion the Soviet Union sent a high-level delegation led by Politburo member and chief Soviet ideologist Mikhail Suslov.[59]

The Chinese informed the SRV Embassy in Beijing in advance of their decision not to send a delegation. However, Duan, in his conversation with Soviet ambassador B. Chaplin during November 1976, claimed that there were people in China who "are now expressing opinions against the orientation of the [Chinese ambassadorial] delegation in Hanoi." He noted, as if to support this point, that the Chinese had sent the VWP Central Committee a "long congratulatory telegram, in which was contained wishes for successes in the work of the Congress."[60]

It seems that Duan thought that Vietnam's problems with China were heavily rooted in the political outlook of the Chinese Embassy in Hanoi. Vietnamese leaders were acutely aware of the factional struggles in Beijing and deeply interested in their outcome. But insofar as they believed that their problems with China could be solved by the ascendancy of one Chinese political faction over another, the Vietnamese were greatly misinformed.

During the Fourth Party Congress, the Hanoi leaders removed the most pro-Chinese elements from the leadership. This included most notably the dropping from the Politburo and Central Committee of Hoang Van Hoan, the former Vietnamese ambassador to China (1950–57) and a founding member of the Indochinese Communist Party, who defected to China in 1979. Those dropped from the Central Committee also included Ngo Minh

Loan, Ngo Thuyen, Nguyen Trong Vinh, and Le Ban, all of whom had served in China, three as DRV ambassador.[61] Beijing could only have interpreted the downfall of these figures as a further and now overt repudiation of Chinese influence. Notwithstanding the demotion from alternate membership of the Central Committee of one former ambassador to the Soviet Union, the sacking of these prominent former ambassadors to China would have been interpreted as a further affirmation of Hanoi's desire to deepen its already close relations with Moscow. Finally, given its earlier explicit expressions of concern about the pro-Soviet drift of Vietnamese foreign policy, Beijing may well have considered these new Vietnamese party actions as a deliberate insult to China by the Vietnamese leadership. Thus, in February 1977, Beijing notified Hanoi that it was unable to provide any new economic aid.[62]

Hanoi's View of the Chinese
Political Succession Struggle

The Vietnamese leaders were not only aware of but also followed closely the factional political conflict in China. Their interest was linked to their belief that one faction rather than another would be more favorable toward Vietnam in foreign policy.

During a conversation with the Soviet ambassador in Hanoi in April 1976, Vietnamese foreign minister and Politburo member Nguyen Duy Trinh spoke of the factional struggle within China as one between "moderates"—including Deng Xiaoping—and "young activists." Trinh was impressed with the apparent strength of the "moderates" because they dared to criticize Jiang Qing, Mao's wife. He believed that their popularity derived from the fact that they had worked with Zhou Enlai.[63]

Later that year, in early November, SRV prime minister Pham Van Dong spoke favorably of the fall of the Shanghai group from power. Though he considered it still too early to draw conclusions as to the current situation in the PRC, he felt that so far "little had changed" in Chinese foreign policy. The only signs of possible improvement in Sino-Vietnamese relations were said to be the friendlier attitudes of the Chinese at meetings with Vietnamese representatives.[64]

The following year, the Vietnamese leadership was still uncertain and concerned by the evolution of the political situation in China. In October

1977, Duan told the Soviet ambassador in Hanoi that part of the Chinese leadership, especially Hua Guofeng, but also Li Xiannian, "do not understand us," whereas Deng "treats Vietnam with great understanding." Duan predicted that if Deng won the power struggle, then changes in Chinese policy could be expected because Deng did not follow in the footsteps of Mao and even expressed opposition to several of his ideas. Although, Duan noted, Deng's attitude toward the Soviet Union is "well known," nevertheless "his words in connection with the USSR show that . . . he is convinced that the Soviet Union is a socialist country." This, together with the restoration to key posts of purged former activists like Luo Ruiqing, the former army chief of staff who had previously expressed himself as favoring rapprochement with the USSR, seemed optimistic signs to Duan.[65]

Duan's interest in whether or not Chinese leaders favored a foreign policy of rapprochement with the USSR was not merely in response to Soviet inquiries. It had been a long-standing position of the Vietnamese Communists that international solidarity among all the "socialist countries"—particularly the USSR, PRC, and SRV—represented an important foreign policy goal, an objective that the top Vietnamese party leaders reiterated in their private meetings with the Chinese in November 1977.[66]

But by the end of 1978, with Sino-Vietnamese relations deteriorating rapidly, the Vietnamese attitude toward the Chinese leadership struggle had changed. Duan told the Soviet ambassador in September 1978 that while the Chinese leaders had serious disagreements on domestic policy, in foreign policy they shared a common viewpoint.[67]

Significantly, this information reveals that the Vietnamese Communist leaders were not imbued with an undiscriminating distrust of all Chinese Communist leaders, as Western analysts assumed. Initially, the Vietnamese leaders considered their political problems with China to be tied to the activities of the Maoist faction, which later came to be known as the Gang of Four. As a corollary, they were initially favorably disposed toward Deng. Zhou was a Chinese leader toward whom the Vietnamese were always favorably disposed. The Vietnamese evaluated each Chinese leader according to what they imagined to be his political line vis-à-vis Vietnam and the USSR. That the Vietnamese leaders changed their minds on Deng's views, and became more indiscriminately hostile toward the entire Chinese leadership, is in any case explained by the conflict that evolved over the different Chinese and Vietnamese foreign *policies,* especially toward the Soviet Union and Cambodia.

Aftermath

By the mid-1970s, Chinese-Vietnamese relations were exacerbated by the intensifying conflict between the Communist leaders of Vietnam and Cambodia, which erupted into major military battles between the armies of Vietnam and Cambodia in 1977, and the breaking of diplomatic relations between the two nations by the Khmer Rouge on December 31, 1977.

During 1978, Vietnamese-Chinese relations deteriorated even further, ostensibly due to Hanoi's policy of discrimination against and persecution of Vietnam's ethnic Chinese minority, though the struggle for Cambodia influenced both sides' view of the ethnic Chinese problem. In May 1978, China cut back aid and in June, after Vietnam joined COMECON, China cut off all its remaining economic assistance to Vietnam.[68]

In November 1978, Vietnam and the Soviet Union signed a Treaty of Friendship and Cooperation. Then, in December 1978, Vietnam launched a full-scale invasion of Cambodia, occupying Phnom Penh on January 9, 1979.

China, infuriated by Vietnam's invasion of Cambodia, decided to "teach Vietnam a lesson" by launching a cross-border invasion in February 1979. Though the Chinese army performed poorly in military terms during the three-week war, and Vietnam was not pressured to withdraw its army from Cambodia as China demanded, the episode had some impact on Vietnamese policy. The Chinese attack conveyed to the Vietnamese leaders the full significance of having China as an enemy, and by obliging Hanoi to keep troops in the north to repel a possible future Chinese attack, prevented Vietnam from applying its full military resources to winning the war in Cambodia.

Each of these different bilateral conflicts had its own origin. But Hanoi's decision to move toward a closer relationship with Moscow at the end of the 1960s, however fitfully and strangely applied in practice during the first half of the next decade, had a profound impact on all the other conflicts in the region.

Conclusions

The Vietnamese tilt toward the Soviet Union in the early 1970s marked a subtle policy shift with great ramifications. Though it did not satisfy Soviet expectations, it nevertheless managed to profoundly antagonize China.

Soviet archival evidence suggests that the North Vietnamese leaders proved extremely difficult clients to their major communist patrons.

The record of Soviet-Vietnamese relations in the first half of the 1970s was one of public amity coexisting with private enmity. In contrast to the public posture of deep friendship, the Soviet archives reveal a relationship marked by paranoid suspicion from one side and resentment from the other. The Soviets expected that in return for their considerable aid to North Vietnam, they would exert powerful influence over Vietnamese foreign policy and the form of a political settlement in Indochina. For many years, they were to be greatly disappointed. The Vietnamese did not treat the Soviet Union as a trustworthy ally, let alone a powerful sponsor, even though the Soviet Union was in fact a patron on which the VWP depended to achieve its political and military objectives in Indochina.

Part of the problem may have been political cleavages within the Vietnamese Communist Party's elite, who were, according to Soviet analysts, divided into "moderate" and "pro-Chinese" factions. But part of the problem was the paranoid political culture of the Vietnamese Communist Party leadership.

It is hard to imagine the United States tolerating from its clients the kind of treatment that the Hanoi leaders inflicted upon the Soviet representatives in North Vietnam. Of course, as the memoirs of U.S. and South Vietnamese policymakers show, tensions frequently hampered relations between Washington and Saigon.[69] But nothing in that difficult alliance compares with the recurrent duplicity and draconian security measures Hanoi imposed upon its Soviet ally. The Soviet Union's tolerance of its treatment, albeit reluctant and resentful, can be attributed to two factors. First, it needed to maintain a functioning relationship with the North Vietnamese to advance its strategic position against its two main adversaries, China and the United States. Second, though they may have personally resented their treatment, the Soviet representatives could hardly raise moral objections. After all, their own political system was hardly the embodiment of interpersonal trust and respect, and the Soviet Union's political leadership of the 1970s was itself a product of the same Stalinist moral and political upbringing as the North Vietnamese leadership. But an outsider may conclude that the Soviet-Vietnamese relationship in the early 1970s was a strange manifestation of international solidarity.

Still, the Soviet resentments toward the Vietnamese communists were minor compared with the anger of the Chinese. By 1975, the Vietnamese shift toward closer ties with the USSR had brought Chinese–Vietnamese relations close to breaking point. The Vietnamese privately expressed a desire to maintain a working relationship with China, if for no other reason than to ensure the flow of economic aid. But Hanoi soon antagonized Beijing even further by dropping some of the more pro-Chinese figures from the Vietnamese party leadership.

Yet the Hanoi officials seemed blithely unaware that their policies on several international issues were central to their future relations with China. They sought to maintain at least reasonable relations with China. But they took little account of their need to make hard choices, and for many years did not recognize that they could not achieve all their foreign policy goals while maintaining reasonable relations with China. Hanoi's decisionmakers mistakenly looked to the outcome of the factional power struggle within the Chinese leadership, not to their own policies, as a guide to prospects for their future relations with Beijing.

Notes

1. The only other studies of Soviet-Vietnamese relations using Soviet party archives are those of the Russian historian Ilya V. Gaiduk, *The Soviet Union and the Vietnam War* (Chicago: Ivan R. Dee. 1996), and *Confronting Vietnam: Soviet Policy toward the Indochina Conflict, 1954–1963* (Washington, D.C. and Stanford, Calif.: Woodrow Wilson Center Press and Stanford University Press, 2003). However, Gaiduk's ostensible topic is Soviet-Vietnamese relations spanning the years between 1954 and 1972—a period that overlaps with but is not identical with the period examined here. Moreover, he makes different references to Vietnamese-Chinese relations than are contained in my own research. In fact, Gaiduk's primary focus is on what may loosely be termed the American-Soviet-Vietnamese triangle.

2. This study is based upon documents from the former Communist Party of the Soviet Union's Central Committee (CPSU CC), found in the *Tsentr khraneniya sovremennoi dokumentatsii* (TsKhSD) [Center for the Storage of Contemporary Documentation], located within the former CPSU CC headquarters complex in Moscow. The main files within this archive relevant to the topic considered here are those of the *Otdel TsK KPSS po svyazyam s kommunisticheskimi i rabochimi partiyami sotsialisticheskikh stran* [Department of the CPSU CC for Ties with Communist And Workers' Parties of Socialist Countries]. The bulk of those seen were made available to researchers by TsKhSD in the winter of 1992–93, and subsequently closed to all researchers by the archives administration in the spring of 1993. On the circumstances surrounding this closure, see Mark Kramer, *Cold War International History Project Bulletin,* no. 3 (Fall 1993): 1. A few other files were among those that have been officially and permanently declassified by the Russian state archives since 1992.

Most of these documents are copies of reports originating in the embassies of the USSR, especially the Soviet Embassy in the Democratic Republic of Vietnam (DRV)—

renamed the SRV after the reunification of North and South Vietnam in 1976. The Soviet embassies in Beijing and Paris were also important sources of information on the political and military situation in Vietnam for the Foreign Ministry (MID) and hence the Central Committee, though obviously less important than the Hanoi embassy. Fortunately, some of the TsKhSD documents are copies of intelligence reports from the civilian and military intelligence agencies—the Komitet gosudarstvennoi bezopasnosti (KGB) and the Soviet Armed Forces General Staff's Glavnoe razvedivatel'noe upravlenie (GRU)— which has been forwarded to the Central Committee. They often provided both a supplement and a balance to the information available to the CPSU CC from the Foreign Ministry through its embassies.

Other Soviet Communist Party archives also contain important details of the shifting triangular relationship. The most important information is undoubtedly in the Presidential Archive, the Russian repository of documents dealing with policy decisions at the highest level. There were many important meetings between the top Soviet and Vietnamese leaders over the years, in both Moscow and Hanoi. The limited accounts of or references to these meetings contained in reports in TsKhSD suggest the vital importance of materials in the Presidential Archives—access to which is still tightly restricted—for a more comprehensive account of Soviet-Vietnamese (and Soviet-Chinese-Vietnamese) relations.

The separate archives of the KGB and GRU also contain documents of very great significance. The GRU materials are probably more important than those of the KGB, especially from 1969 onwards, because of the significant role of Soviet military advisers and specialists in assisting the Vietnamese armed forces after that time. The advisory function gave military officers more access to Vietnamese counterparts than would have been available to a KGB officer working under diplomatic cover, because of the restrictions discussed below the Vietnamese authorities placed upon movement by diplomats, even of allied nations.

Finally, the Ministry of Foreign Affairs (Ministerstvo Inostrannikh Del, MID) archive contains an enormous amount of material relevant to a study of the Soviet-Chinese-Vietnamese triangle. This judgment is based upon seeing copies of MID documents that have been lodged at the Central Committee archive. However, although the MID supposedly operates on a thirty-year secrecy rule, even the more important MID documents that are more than thirty years old still have not been made available to researchers through the MID's own archive. This is particularly unfortunate when one considers important historical events such as the Geneva Conferences of 1954 and 1962, and the planning for them, in which the ministry was an important participant, even if not a formulator of policy.

Unfortunately, the important Presidential, KGB, and GRU archives are not open to independent researchers, even under the constraints of a thirty-year rule. But the significance of these archives may be judged on the basis of the quality of the documents that were selectively provided to the Central Committee by these agencies.

　　3. E.g., Robert F. Turner, who has written a sober and empirically sound history of Vietnamese communism, stated in that book in 1974: "By 1973 North Vietnam was in a position approximately midway between China and the Soviet Union in the Sino-Soviet dispute, experiencing cooler relations with both than had been common during the previous decade." Robert F. Turner *Vietnamese Communism: Its Origins and Development* (Stanford, Calif.: Hoover Institution Press, 1975), 304. Ellen J. Hammer, author of a reputable history of French Indochina covering the period 1940 to 1955, wrote

STEPHEN J. MORRIS

in early 1976: "In early 1975, Ho Chi Minh's dictum that Vietnam should steer a middle course between the Soviet Union and China, accepting aid from both and alienating neither, was still the basis of Hanoi's foreign policy." Ellen J. Hammer, "Indochina: Communist But Nonaligned," *Problems of Communism* 25, no. 3 (May–June 1976): 7. Two years later, only months before the Vietnamese and Chinese conflicts became highly visible, the academic Carlyle Thayer wrote: "As a member of the socialist bloc Viet Nam has avoided taking sides in the Sino-Soviet dispute. Indeed the imperatives of Vietnamese nationalism dictate balancing Soviet and Chinese power." Carlyle Thayer, "Vietnam's External Relations," *Pacific Community* 9, no. 2 (January 1978): 230.

4. In the most careful of these, Robert Ross wrote that after Saigon's fall to the North Vietnamese, Soviet leaders tried "to move Hanoi away from its relatively centrist position in the Sino-Soviet conflict." Ross noted a shift by Vietnam toward the Soviet Union as taking place after August 1975. Robert Ross, *The Indochina Tangle: China's Vietnam Policy, 1975–1979* (New York: Columbia University Press, 1988), 30, 61. In a later work, Steven Hood noted Vietnam's move toward the Soviet Union as occurring in mid-1975. Steven J. Hood, *Dragons Entangled: Indochina and the China–Vietnam War* (Armonk, N.Y.: M. E. Sharpe, 1992), 30.

5. Hanoi Radio Domestic Service, August 21, 1968, in U.S. Foreign Broadcast Information Service Reports (hereafter identified with an "FBIS" number, as follows), *FBIS-APA-68-164,* August 21, 1968, p. K5.; Moscow TASS International Service, August 26, 1968, in *FBIS-APA-68-171,* August 30, 1968, p. K8.

6. Hanoi Radio VNA International Service in English, August 14, 1970, *FBIS-APA-70-159,* p. K1.

7. Hanoi Radio VNA International Service in English, July 29, 1971, *FBIS-APA-71-146,* July 29, 1971, p. K9. "We Vehemently Protest the Brutal Terrorist Acts of the Sudanese Authorities," Hanoi Radio domestic service, 30 July 1971, *FBIS-APA-71-152,* August 6, 1971, p. K22. Hanoi Radio VNA International Service in English, July 30, 1971, *FBIS-APA-71-152,* August 6, 1971, pp. K21-22.

8. Hanoi Radio VNA in English, June 13, 1975, *FBIS-APA-75-100,* June 17, 1975, pp. K3-K4; Hanoi Radio VNA, December 3, 1975, *FBIS-APA-75-233,* December 3, 1975, p. K3; Hanoi Radio VNA, January 28, 1976, *FBIS-APA-76-20,* January 29, 1976, p. K2.

9. Hanoi Radio VNA, October 30, 1975, *FBIS-APA-75-212,* November 3, 1975, p. K17; Hanoi Radio VNA, November 9, 1975, *FBIS-APA-75-218,* November 11, 1975, p. K9; Hanoi Radio VNA, November 12, 1975, *FBIS-APA-75-220,* November 13, 1975, p. K2; *Quan Doi Nhan Dan,* November 21, 1975, Hanoi in Vietnamese to Vietnam, November 21, 1975, *FBIS-APA-75-229,* November 26, 1975, p. K5; *Quan Doi Nhan Dan,* December 24, commentary: "The Angolan Revolution Is Steadily Advancing," *FBIS-APA-75-250,* December 29, 1975, p. K6.

10. Truong Nhu Tang, with David Chanoff and Doan Van Toai, *A Viet Cong Memoir* (New York: Harcourt Brace Jovanovich, 1985), 248.

11. "Politicheskii otchet posol'stvo SSSR v demokraticheskoi respublike v'etnam za 1970 god" ["Political report of the embassy of the USSR in the Democratic Republic of Vietnam for 1970"], TsKhSD, fond (f.) 5, opis' (op.). 62, delo (d.) 495, list (l., i.e., page) 100.

12. "Politicheskii otchet posol'stvo SSSR," l. 125.

13. "Politicheskii otchet posol'stvo SSSR," ll. 102–3.

14. "Politicheskii otchet posol'stvo SSSR," l. 164.

15. "Politicheskii otchet posol'stvo SSSR," l. 164.

16. "Politicheskii otchet posol'stvo SSSR," l. 109.

17. "Politicheskii otchet posol'stvo SSSR," ll. 190–91.

18. Posol'stvo SSSR v DRV, "O politike partii trudyashchikhsya v'etnama v reshenii problem indokitaya i nashikh zadachakh, vitekayushchikh iz reshenii XXIV s'ezda kpss" (Politicheskoye pis'mo) [Embassy of the USSR in the DRV, "About the Policy of the Vietnam Workers' Party Towards a Solution of the Problem of Indochina and Our Tasks, Flowing From the Decisions of the 24th Congress of the CPSU" (Political Letter)], 25 May 1971, p. 2. Located in TsKhSD, f. 89, op. 54, d. 10, l. 24.

19. Posol'stvo SSSR v DRV, "O politike partii trudyashchikhsya v'etnama," l. 13 (TsKhSD, f. 89, op. 54, d. 10, l. 24).

20. Posol'stvo SSSR v DRV, "O politike partii trudyashchikhsya v'etnama," l. 8 (TsKhSD, f. 89, op. 54, d. 10, l. 30).

21. Posol'stvo SSSR v DRV, "O politike partii trudyashchikhsya v'etnama," l. 7 (TsKhSD, f. 89, op. 54, d. 10, l. 29).

22. Posol'stvo SSSR v DRV, "O politike partii trudyashchikhsya v'etnama," l. 8 (TSKhSD, f. 89, op. 54, d. 10, l. 30).

23. I. Shcherbakov, in Posol'stvo SSSR v DRV, "O politike partii trudyashchikhsya v'etnama," l. 19 (TsKhSD, f. 89, op. 54, d. 10, l. 41).

24. *Quan Doi Nhan Dan* (Hanoi), November 24, 1973, p. 1. *FBIS-APA-73-234,* December 5, 1973, p. K2.

25. "Politicheskii otchet posol'stva SSSR v demokraticheskoi respublike v'etnam za 1972 god" ["Political report of the Embassy of the USSR in the Democratic Republic of Vietnam for 1972"], TsKhSD, f. 5, op. 64, d. 472, l. 17.

26. "Politicheskii otchet posol'stva SSSR v demokraticheskoi respublike v'etnam za 1972 god," l. 17.

27. "Politicheskii otchet posol'stva SSSR v demokraticheskoi respublike v'etnam za 1972 god," l. 17.

28. "Politicheskii otchet posol'stva SSSR v demokraticheskoi respublike v'etnam za 1972 god," l. 22.

29. "Politicheskii otchet posol'stva SSSR v demokraticheskoi respublike v'etnam za 1972 god," l. 22.

30. "Politicheskii otchet posol'stva SSSR v demokraticheskoi respublike v'etnam za 1972 god," l. 22.

31. "Politicheskii otchet posol'stva SSSR v demokraticheskoi respublike v'etnam za 1972 god," ll. 22–23.

32. "Politicheskii otchet posol'stva SSSR v demokraticheskoi respublike v'etnam za 1973 god" ["Political report of the Embassy of the USSR in the Democratic Republic of Vietnam for 1973"], TsKhSD, f. 5, op. 66, d. 781, l. 6.

33. "Politicheskii otchet posol'stva SSSR v demokraticheskoi respublike v'etnam za 1973 god," l. 9.

34. "Politicheskii otchet posol'stva SSSR v demokraticheskoi respublike v'etnam za 1973 god," l. 12.

35. "Politicheskii otchet posol'stva SSSR v demokraticheskoi respublike v'etnam za 1973 god," ll. 14–15.

36. "Politicheskii otchet posol'stva SSSR v demokraticheskoi respublike v'etnam za 1973 god," l. 10.

37. "Politicheskii otchet posol'stva SSSR v demokraticheskoi respublike v'etnam

za 1974 god" ["Political report of the Embassy of the USSR in the Democratic Republic of Vietnam for 1974"], TsKhSD, f. 5, op. 67, d. 655, l. 35.

38. "Politicheskii otchet posol'stva SSSR v demokraticheskoi respublike v'etnam
za 1974 god," ll. 35–36.

39. P. J. Honey, "The Position of the DRV Leadership and the Succession to Ho Chi
Minh," in *North Vietnam Today: Profile of a Communist Satellite,* ed. P. J. Honey (New
York: Frederick A. Praeger, 1962), 50, 58.

40. W. R. Smyser, *The Independent Vietnamese: Vietnamese Communism between
Russia and China, 1956–1969,* Papers in International Studies 55, Southeast Asia
(Athens: Center For International Studies, Ohio University, 1980), 122.

41. Thai Quang Trung, *Collective Leadership and Factionalism: An Essay on Ho
Chi Minh's Legacy* (Singapore: Institute of Southeast Asian Studies, 1985).

42. This matter is extremely complicated and will be the subject of another study by
the author.

43. Main Intelligence Directorate, General Staff of the Armed Forces of the USSR,
"Report of the VWP CC Secretary Hoang Anh to the 20th Plenum of the VWP CC, held
at the end of December 1970—beginning of January 1971," TsKhSD, f. 89, op. 54,
d. 8. Hereafter referred to as "Hoang Anh Report."
I am well aware that the numbering of the plenum at which this report was presented
as the 20th does not coincide with the public record, according to which this should have
been the 19th plenum. For reasons that I will explain in another article, it is, however,
my view that the public record is probably incorrect.

44. "Hoang Anh Report," l. 25 (TsKhSD, l. 209).

45. "Hoang Anh Report," ll. 10–11, 23, 26 (TsKhSD, ll. 194–95, 207, 210).

46. "Hoang Anh Report," l. 30 (TsKhSD, l. 214).

47. TsKhSD, f. 5, op. 64, d. 478.

48. TsKhSD, f. 5, op. 64, l. 168.

49. TsKhSD, f. 5, op. 64, l. 169.

50. TsKhSD, f. 5, op. 64, l. 169.

51. Truong, Chanoff, and Doan, *Vietcong Memoir,* 248–49.

52. The contents of the Vietnamese report to the Soviets on the details of this meeting are contained in "Results of the Visit of the Vietnamese Party-Government Delegation to China (1975)," TsKhSD, f. 5, op. 73, d. 1933.

53. "Results of the Visit of the Vietnamese Party-Government Delegation," l. 31.

54. "Results of the Visit of the Vietnamese Party-Government Delegation," ll.
31–32.

55. "Results of the Visit of the Vietnamese Party-Government Delegation," ll.
31–32.

56. V. Sviridov (second secretary, Embassy of the USSR in the SRV), "O nekotorikh
aspektakh v'etnamo–kitaiskikh otnoshenii" ["On several aspects of Vietnamese–
Chinese relations"], April 1976, TsKhSD, f. 5, op. 69, d. 2313, l.18.

57. Sviridov, "O nekotorikh aspektakh," ll. 18–19.

58. Sviridov, "O nekotorikh aspektakh," l.19.

59. For the best informed and detailed analysis of the Congress, see P. J. Honey, "The
Fourth Congress of the Lao Dong Party," *China News Analysis* 1072 (March 11, 1977).
See also William S. Turley, "Vietnam since Reunification," *Problems of Communism* 26,
no. 2 (March–April 1977): 36–54.

60. B. Chaplin, "Record of Conversation with the First Secretary of the CC of the VWP Le Duan," November 16, 1976, TsKhSD, f. 5, op. 69, d. 2314, ll. 112–13.

61. Honey, "Fourth Congress of the Lao Dong Party," 4.

62. *Beijing Review,* March 30, 1979, 22; cited in Pao-min Chang, *Beijing, Hanoi and the Overseas Chinese* (Berkeley: Institute of East Asian Studies, University of California, 1982), 21.

63. "Zapis' besedi s chlenom politburo TsK PTV, zam. prem'er-ministrom, ministrom inostrannikh del DRV Nguen Zui Chinem" [Report of a conversation with a member of the Politburo of the VWP CC, deputy Prime Minister, Minister of Foreign Affairs of the DRV, Nguyen Duy Trinh], April 6, 1976, TsKhSD, f. 5, op. 69, d. 2314, ll. 46–47.

64. "Zapis' besedi s chlenom politburo TsK PTV, Prem'er-ministrom SRV Pham Van Dongom" ["Report of a conversation with a member of the Politburo of the VWP CC, Prime Minister Pham Van Dong"], November 6, 1976, TsKhSD, f. 5, op. 69, d. 2314, l. 100.

65. "Zapis' besedi s generalnim sekretarom TsK VKP Le Zuanom" ["Report of a conversation with the General Secretary of the VCP CC Le Duan"], October 6, 1977, TsKhSD, f. 5, op. 73, d. 1409, ll. 122-3.

66. "Zapis' besedi s sekretarim TsK KPV, nachalnik otdela inostrannikh otnoshenakh Tsk KPV, Zuan Tuinom" ["Report of a conversation with secretary of the CPV CC, director of the Department of Foreign Relations of the CPV, CC Xuan Thuy"], TsKhSD, f. 5, op. 73, d. 1409, l. 133.

67. "Zapis' besedi s generalnim sekretarom TsK Kpv Le Zuanom" [Report of a conversation with general secretary of the CPV CC Le Duan], September 5, 1978, TsKhSD, f. 5, op. 75, d. 1061, l. 102.

68. The issues summarized in this and the previous paragraph are discussed and analyzed in great detail in my book, *Why Vietnam Invaded Cambodia* (Stanford, Calif.: Stanford University Press, 1999), esp. chaps. 4 and 7.

69. See, e.g., Henry A. Kissinger, *White House Years* (Boston: Little, Brown, 1979), esp. chaps. 33–34; and Nguyen Tien Hung and Jerrold L. Schecter, *The Palace File* (New York: Harper & Row, 1986).

13

Commentary: A Vietnamese Scholar's Perspective on the Communist Big Powers and Vietnam

Luu Doan Huynh

When writing on the two wars in Vietnam (1945–75), Vietnamese authors invariably make a point of expressing gratitude to the Soviet Union and China for their generous assistance to the cause of Vietnam's freedom. This is no mere lip service, but comes from the heart, because without this help victory would have been very difficult, if not impossible, to achieve.

But history also teaches us that such assistance invariably involved two components—namely, internationalist sentiment and the donor country's national interests—and that in the policymaking of these two great countries, the latter inevitably carried the greater weight. Therefore, even while Vietnam was striving to win the friendship and support of both the Soviet Union and China, Vietnam had to maintain its independence by all means possible—in spirit, in policy, in strategy, and in action—as a sine qua non of victory. In 1954, this was precisely what was lacking in the Democratic Republic of Vietnam (DRV).

These comments represent only the author's personal views.

433

The 1954 Conference on Indochina

On November 26, 1953, in a response to the Swedish newspaper *Expressen,* North Vietnam's preeminent leader, Ho Chi Minh, stated that "if the French Government have drawn a lesson from the war they have been waging these last few years and want to negotiate an armistice in Vietnam and solve the Vietnam problem by peaceful means, the people and Government of the Democratic Republic of Vietnam are ready to meet this desire." He also emphasized that "the negotiations for an armistice essentially concern the Government of the Democratic Republic of Vietnam and the French government." Yet a few months later, an ill-prepared Vietnam was dragged into an international conference that was manipulated by the big powers, and that resulted in the division of Vietnam against its will, with disastrous consequences for both that country and for peace.

The Year 1953: The Missing Link in Current
Research on Declassified Documents

Here, let me begin with some preliminary comments on sources, archives, and methodology. I entirely share the eagerness of the Cold War International History Project to use newly declassified documents and oral histories to research past events, and I greatly appreciate the hard work fellow researchers have already devoted to such efforts. One must, however, remember that it is important to use declassified documents from any individual country in combination with previous revelations and with declassified materials from other countries involved, and also to utilize relevant official statements and documents and contemporary press reports. Only by so doing can we obtain a comprehensive and accurate picture and avoid potential errors.

Except for a brief reference to a note sent by the Soviet Union to Western countries on September 28, 1953, calling for the convening of a conference on the Far East, and a statement by Chinese premier Zhou Enlai on October 8, 1953, supporting this move, when discussing the Geneva Conference, the Soviet scholar Ilya Gaiduk and Chinese researchers alike have focused on events from the early 1954 Berlin conference to July 1954, leaving untouched the entire period from the death of Joseph Stalin in March 1953 until the end of that year. Fragmentary reports seem to indicate that during this period the Sino-Soviet alliance solidified further, into something resembling a joint cochairmanship of the international socialist camp, united on a coordinated strategy based on peaceful coexistence and designed to reach a new modus vivendi with the West. Gaiduk, for example, describes how on September 28, 1953, the Soviet Union sent the Western powers a note stating that a "number of important questions concerning the situation of the countries of Southeast Asia and the Pacific" might be suitable topics for discussion at a forthcoming international conference. Yet, as early as July 28, 1953, *Renmin Ribao* had already carried an important editorial on the subject. The Chinese press reported much earlier than did equivalent Soviet media outlets that in June 1953 China suggested to a French economic delegation led by Bernard de Plas the advisability of a peaceful solution in Indochina, saying that the successful conclusion of the Korean armistice demonstrated that persevering in the spirit of consultation would eventually bring a compromise acceptable to all, and that other international disputes could likewise be resolved by these means.[1] Western reports, moreover, stated that as early as August 4, 1953, only one week after the Korean armistice agreement was finally signed, the Soviet Union had already launched its diplomatic demarche with the Western powers over Indochina.

All these developments are hints that preparatory Sino-Soviet exchanges of opinion on the subject may well have begun much earlier, perhaps some time after Georgi Malenkov's March 15, 1953, statement on peaceful coexistence. The works of François Joyaux, James Cable, and other scholars, and contemporary press reports all make it quite apparent that the United Kingdom and, even more, France deliberately sought to manipulate the conflicts among the national interests of China, the Soviet Union, and Vietnam—a strategy that would not have been possible if fertile ground for it had not existed within the socialist camp.[2] According to Gaiduk, on March 6, 1954, the French press reported that the Chinese ambassador in Moscow had requested Soviet foreign minister Vyacheslav Molotov to invite Ho Chi Minh to Moscow for discussions. Molotov told French foreign minister Georges Bidault that without Chinese participation it would prove impossible to resolve the Indochinese problem. Such reports seem to hint that China was the leading player, but it would be unfair and less than objective to reach so sweeping a conclusion on the basis of such fragmentary evidence. Gaiduk also wrote that, although in discussions with his Soviet counterpart the Vietnamese ambassador in Beijing did not advocate partition, the Soviet Union "seems to have been more sensitive to the needs of its Chinese ally" than to the interests of Vietnam.

Such reports give rise to several questions that it is necessary to elucidate to reach any accurate understanding of the 1954 Geneva Conference
and the resulting accords. Did this strong urge to reach a new agreement
with the West make it necessary for China and the Soviet Union to sacrifice
the interests of nationalist movements in Vietnam, Laos, and Cambodia?
Which of the two big powers took the initiative in proposing to the other
the idea of convening a conference to resolve the Indochina conflict on the
basis of a partition of Vietnam? Which power was primarily responsible for
the conference's blueprints? Which power was the most eager to reach an
agreement? Which power perceived the solution of partitioning Vietnam as
the core of its strategy, and to which did this simply represent a policy of
convenience? In the interests of fair play and objectivity and to accurately
explain Soviet and Chinese thinking on policy toward Vietnam and the
Geneva Conference, we need comprehensive analyses of the declassified
documentation of these two great powers in 1953, something Gaiduk and
Chinese scholars have not yet provided.

The Main Objectives of the Soviet Union
and China at the Geneva Conference

I find little to quarrel with in either the Soviet objectives of promoting détente with the West and countering the European Defence Community, or
the overarching Chinese intention of breaking the U.S. policy of isolation
and embargo toward China and reducing world tensions. I do, however, find
it difficult to accept or justify an additional Chinese objective: of trying to
reach agreements, even if these were only temporary ones, to avoid holding a fruitless conference, an idea set forth in a Chinese governmental "preliminary paper on the estimation of and preparations for the Geneva Conference" cited by former Chinese deputy foreign minister Han Nianlong
in his work *Contemporary Chinese Diplomacy*.[3] Shi Zhe, a member of the
Chinese delegation, recalled that at the preparatory meeting in Moscow preceding the Geneva Conference, Molotov cautioned Chinese premier Zhou
Enlai that, because the imperialist countries had "unshakable interests," he
should not entertain "unrealistic illusions" at Geneva.[4] This statement is
confirmed by Qu Xing's finding: "At the 1954 Geneva Conference, China
. . . insisted on pursuing all possible means to prevent the Geneva Conference from ending without any meaningful resolutions of its problems."[5]
Gaiduk likewise quoted the Chinese ambassador as informing Molotov that,

"if no great success should be achieved at the conference, any success would be important." Gaiduk added: "Zhou Enlai demonstrated that China was interested in reaching a peaceful resolution of the conflict . . . and excluded any possibility that might undermine the process of negotiations."[6]

The question arises: Did this overeagerness to reach a settlement reflect China's desire to promote its own far-reaching geopolitical and strategic objectives, or was fear of a major military confrontation with the United States the essential reason for these large and even unnecessary concessions? Of these two possible motives, which was the genuine and predominant one? If the fear of a military confrontation was genuine and China's first priority, why then did China raise no objection to Vietnamese efforts to destroy entirely the fortress of Dien Bien Phu and its garrison, at a time when the U.S. government publicly threatened to bomb Dien Bien Phu, and perhaps even to use atomic bombs, to save the beleaguered French troops? As it transpired, Vietnamese troops completely subjugated Dien Bien Phu, without provoking any military response from the United States.

Why did China and the Soviet Union fail to draw realistic conclusions from these events? American political scientists and historians have enumerated the various reasons why in 1954 the United States was neither willing nor able to move politically and militarily to launch any large-scale unilateral military intervention in Indochina. I find it particularly striking that, even though American writers have many disagreements over the Vietnam War, they are all virtually unanimous on this point. I therefore find it difficult to agree with those of my Chinese and Russian colleagues who repeatedly stress the danger of U.S. military intervention as a valid premise for the making of Soviet and Chinese policy at Geneva.[7] It is time to recognize that this policy premise was mistaken. Vietnamese leaders must also share the blame, because at that time they believed what their Chinese and Soviet allies told them on this point, even while disagreeing with them on other matters.

In this context, should one now take a different view of the events of June 15 and 16, 1954? As the conference reached stalemate on June 15, Western delegates ended the Korean negotiations and pressured the socialist countries to make concessions at the succeeding talks on Indochina, making statements threatening to terminate the conference entirely, and checking out of their hotels. On that same day, the Soviet and Chinese delegates impressed on their Vietnamese counterparts the need to make significant concessions, which Zhou announced on June 16, 1954. No detailed recitation of these concessions, whose terms have long been known, is necessary.

The main point is that the pressure from Western countries represented mere bluff, employing the empty threat of U.S. intervention to squeeze concessions from their opponents, which the socialist great powers immediately granted. Did the latter yield due to genuine fear of U.S. intervention, or just because that threat offered them a good opportunity to make these concessions and so move the conference forward following the fall of the French Joseph Laniel government on June 12 and the appointment on June 18 of Pierre Mendès-France as the new prime minister, a development that was full of promise for the Geneva Conference? I am therefore inclined to believe that the main driving force behind China's zeal to achieve an agreement at Geneva was its overeagerness to do so, in order to break the U.S. containment policy against China and join the world community as a big power. This accounted for the persistent Chinese attempts to induce the Vietnamese, in Yang Kuisong's words, and, as Tao Wenzhao put it, to "lower their asking price," and "to simplify matters, to avoid making issues complicated," so as to avoid, as Yang Kuisong stated, "losing the opportunity for a truce."[8]

Should Vietnam Have Been Partitioned at the Thirteenth or Seventeenth Parallel?

As mentioned by Gaiduk, at the April 1954 preparatory discussions in Moscow, the Soviet Union and China brought pressure to bear on Vietnamese leaders to accept the partition of Vietnam, a solution that, much though they disliked it, the latter were forced to accept. From June 1954 onward, secret military talks on this issue took place at Geneva. The French insisted that the demarcation line should be drawn at the 18th parallel of latitude, while DRV leaders held out for the 13th parallel, simultaneously demanding that Communist Pathet Lao forces should be allowed to control the eastern part of Laos, and the Khmer Issarak some territory in Cambodia.

Did Vietnam set the price too high by demanding that the 13th parallel serve as the temporary demarcation line? Did the 17th parallel correctly embody prevailing military realities? According to the French scholars Phillippe Devillers and Jean Lacouture, one high French Foreign Ministry official stated:

The July 20 agreement represents a way of adapting on the map the military situation existing on that date. This transposition was favorable to us on more than one account. On 20 July the existing military situation was most precarious. We were unable to hold Hanoi. The High Command notified us that even the dispatch of two more divisions of conscripts would not allow us to hold the capital of Tonkin. The City could be cut off from Haiphong in one day. The retreat of the garrison under artillery fire, we were told, would be very costly. Haiphong, the base to which we would have retreated, was undermined by the existence of a fifth column, which was further increased by a large number of refugees. The reality of the situation was that if the regroupment of forces was carried out within the limits of the Delta, which would be further reduced by our withdrawals from the Southern provinces (Nam Dinh, Phat Diem, Bui Chu), this would cause the Vietminh to withdraw from the regions we pretended to control an equivalent of two regular divisions. *Further, since all of our forces were concentrated in the North, in the South we were at the mercy of any incident* [emphasis added]. In view of these verified indications, one might well think that the line of demarcation at the Thirteenth Parallel would have reflected reality more closely than the Seventeenth, which we obtained.[9]

Well-informed French observers therefore concurred after the event with the Vietnamese view that in 1954 the 13th parallel would have accurately reflected the existing military situation in the country, suggesting that Chinese scholars' criticisms that the DRV held out for too high a price are unjustified.[10]

From June 1954 onward, the situation in the southern part of Central Vietnam, especially in the High Plateaux, the area near the 13th parallel, deteriorated dramatically for France. On June 1, Vietnamese forces attacked and destroyed one battalion and three companies of French forces in a cluster of strongholds lying between Phu Yen and Darlac provinces. On June 21, Vietnamese forces eliminated almost an entire enemy battalion in the town of Tuy Hoa, severely mauled three additional battalions, and destroyed more than 200 cars and other vehicles. Particularly noteworthy was an episode on June 25, when the 100th French mobile brigade, a battalion of artillery, and a battalion of auxiliary troops, withdrawing from An Khe to Pleiku, all fell victim to a major ambush on Highway Nineteen, in which 700 French troops were killed and wounded and almost 1,200 captured, together with massive amounts of weapons and ammunition. On June 25, another ambush cost French troops withdrawing from Pleiku to Chu Dreck about 500 casualties and 62 trucks. On July 19, a further major skirmish in Quang Nam province wiped out 700 French soldiers.[11] Many Vietnamese still remember how, when he learned of the conclusion of the Geneva Accords, General Nguyen Chanh, regional commander of the southern area of Central Vietnam, wept bitterly because he had been deprived of the opportunity to win a decisive victory.

In the Mekong Delta, in May and June 1954, DRV troops killed or captured more than 400 French soldiers in Go Cong in My Tho Province and destroyed several companies under French command in Chau Thanh and Ben Cat. In July 1954, Vietnamese troops under French officers deserted in large numbers, abandoning their outposts. According to Devillers and Lacouture, on July 13, 1954, secret reports that reached Paris from Saigon characterized the situation in South Vietnam as "disturbing," with "generalized guerrilla fighting" in progress.[12] On July 4, 1954, while attending a meeting with Chinese officials in Liuzhou, in Guangxi Province, southern China, Ho Chi Minh received secret reports that the military situation in North Vietnam had changed for the better. Under DRV pressure, the enemy had been forced to withdraw from substantial urban and rural areas south of the Red River Delta, with a population totaling between 2.5 and 3 million, while DRV troops were threatening the remaining areas of the Delta. James Cable, who served on the British delegation to the Geneva Conference, later wrote:

On July 1, the evacuation of French and Vietnamese troops—i.e., puppet troops—together with many thousands of civilians, from much of the Delta was begun. By 5 July, when the *Times* reported the news as being a shock to delegates in Geneva, the withdrawal had been successfully concluded and French Union forces now held only a salient based on the sea and embracing the cities of Hanoi and Haiphong. [Noncommunist South Vietnamese leader] Ngo Dinh Diem . . . was indignant but the desertion rate in the French-commanded Vietnamese army scarcely allowed him to put forward any alternative.[13]

The DRV High Command sought to exploit this situation by sending one or two divisions to South Vietnam, but in the end it could only dispatch one division, the 325th. When one of its constituent regiments reached Voeun Sai and Strungtreng in Cambodia, it found French-commanded Cambodian troops were fleeing and surrendering, but by then the Geneva Accords had been signed, and the division was forced to return, missing a major opportunity to fulfill the fears of French officials and alter the situation in the South.

In discussions with Chinese officials in Liuzhou from July 3 to 5, 1954, Ho Chi Minh and his top military commander, General Vo Nguyen Giap, stressed that they sought to gain the 13th parallel, but finally accepted the 16th parallel as the bottom line and dropped their ideas of regroupment according to the "leopard's spot" formula. They were also forced to acquiesce in the Chinese view that the Pathet Lao should only hold two provinces, while the Khmer Issarak of Cambodia were to be demobilized on the spot. Before concluding these discussions, Zhou said that he would try to obtain a demarcation line along the 16th parallel, but in case this proved impossible they would have to settle for the 17th parallel, with the partition running along the Ben Hai River.

Both Ho and Giap were astonished that while they, who were Vietnamese, had no idea of the precise location and course of the Ben Hai River, the Chinese Zhou should possess such an intimate knowledge of Vietnamese maps and geography. At the time they suspected that, without Vietnamese knowledge, China had already taken part in very detailed discussions with the French delegation at Geneva, some of whose members were extremely knowledgeable regarding Vietnam. At Geneva Vietnam's foreign minister, Pham Van Dong, was equally surprised when the Indian foreign minister V. K. Krishna Menon likewise suggested to him that the Ben Hai River, running roughly along the 17th parallel, represented an ideal course for a demarcation line.

Such secret understandings may well have been the reason why, in Franco-Vietnamese military discussions at Geneva, the French firmly insisted on a demarcation line following the 18th parallel, while the Vietnamese side were gradually forced to retreat, moving back from the 13th parallel on June 25, to somewhere between the 13th and 14th parallels by June 28, and so to the 14th parallel on July 9. After holding a long meeting with Dong during the night of July 12, the following day Zhou met with Mendès-France, informing the latter that, should France yield on a small concession, the DRV would make larger ones. When the French prime minister and Dong met later the same day, the latter agreed to shift the proposed demarcation line to the 16th parallel.

Even so, France still remained unsatisfied. On July 15, 1954, Jacques Guillermaz of the French delegation explained to Wang Bingnan of the Chinese delegation why France objected to setting the proposed demarcation line at the 16th parallel. On July 19, Wang informed Guillermaz that China and the DRV would accept a demarcation line running 10 kilometers north of the Quang Tri Road, a proposal Guillermaz rejected, on the grounds that this would entail complicated negotiations over boundary markers. Guiller-maz requested instead a line along the Ben Hai River, several kilometers north of the 17th parallel, and 20 kilometers north of the line set out in the seven-point message U.S. secretary of state John Foster Dulles had sent France in late June describing what he hoped would be the outcome of the Geneva Conference.[14]

Finally, on July 20, when British foreign minister Anthony Eden, Mendès-France, Molotov, Zhou, and Dong met at the offices of the French delegation, the Soviet cochairman of the conference proposed that they ac-cept the Ben Hai River as the demarcation line, and Dong was finally forced to agree. Thus, although, as Gaiduk has demonstrated, the Soviet Union and China originally proposed the 16th parallel as the line of partition, because the maximum demand of the Western powers was the 18th parallel and their bottom line the Ben Hai River, the two communist big powers had to settle for the latter.

At the Geneva Conference, the Western powers thus succeeded in win-ning what they had been unable to attain on the battlefield. The American historian Robert F. Randle quotes Walter Bedell Smith, head of the U.S. del-egation at Geneva, as describing the cease-fire agreements as "the best which we could have possibly gained under the circumstances. It is well to remember that diplomacy has rarely been able to gain at the conference table what cannot be gained or held on the battlefield." Randle added that Bedell Smith was only repeating Eden's words after the closing session of the Geneva Conference.[15]

The Chinese scholar Yang Kuisong wrote: "Zhou Enlai also believed that, given the Vietnamese Communist Party's reputation among the Viet-namese people, it was entirely possible that general elections would bring peace and reunification."[16] The argument that compromises on the line of demarcation were acceptable to obtain countrywide elections was probably employed at the time by Vietnam's Soviet and Chinese allies. Indeed, Ca-ble stated that, in exchange for making concessions on the line of partition, the DRV was promised that elections would take place within a two-year period.[17] In reality, however, it became clear that this was merely an argu-ment designed to induce the DRV to acquiesce in this line, because the United States and the Southern government based in Saigon would adamantly refuse to authorize any such elections, leaving the DRV to protest alone, denied forceful support from any other great power.

Because he had no real alternative, circumstances forced Ho to issue a statement welcoming the Geneva Accords, but at heart he felt very differently on the subject. At the end of the conference, Dong told the Western journalist Wilfred Burchett: "I don't know how we are going to explain all that has been decided here to our compatriots in the South."[18] When bidding farewell to those who were leaving for North Vietnam to regroup, the South Vietnamese population smiled at them and raised two fingers, meaning two years. The DRV official Le Duan, who witnessed this scene and was conscious that harsh enemy repression lay ahead, had tears in his eyes, stating: "It would be ten times longer than that."

Who Suffered? Who Gained? Who Paved the Way for a New and Greater War?

Vietnam paid a high price for accepting the line of peaceful struggle for national reunification in keeping with the Geneva Accords, as part of the broader strategy of peaceful coexistence. According to official Vietnamese statistics, as a result of savage repression by the Southern regime, between July 1954 and the end of 1958, in all Vietnam's southern provinces the Communist Party organization lost nine-tenths of its members. In South Vietnam (former Cochin China) alone, 70,000 party members were killed and 900,000 jailed, of whom 200,000 were left permanently injured by torture.[19]

In reality, the concessions made at Geneva in 1954 brought no genuine peace but only paved the way for a larger and more ferocious war. Having taken over responsibility for South Vietnam from the French, the United States made an open-ended commitment to defend the Saigon regime. As the situation there deteriorated, American officials felt that any concessions or failure there would have highly negative implications for its global strategy and credibility. This meant that large-scale U.S. intervention, which would have been extremely problematic in 1954, became almost inevitable in the 1960s.

Ultimately, Vietnam was only reunified after a devastating war, which lasted from 1959 to 1975, during which time North Vietnam suffered severe casualties: 1.1 million troops and 2 million civilians killed, 600,000 troops wounded and 300,000 missing, and 2 million civilians affected by poisonous chemicals.[20] To these figures must be added the casualties of the Saigon armed forces: almost 224,000 killed and 571,000 wounded.[21]

For all these losses, the 1954 Geneva Accords were to blame. In 1954, the Vietnamese leaders and people were thinking in terms of revolution and fraternal socialist ties, but the great socialist powers focused on their worldwide strategies and on such matters as creating and safeguarding buffer zones and zones of security and influence. Chen Jian came close to the truth when he wrote: "The creation of a communist-ruled North Vietnam would serve as a buffer zone between Communist China and the capitalist world in South-East Asia. In this respect, the difference between the Sixteenth and the Seventeenth parallels did not matter to China."[22] Eventually, the DRV probably received half of Vietnam and the Pathet Lao two provinces primarily because these areas fell within the Chinese buffer zone, or zone of security and influence, while the Khmer Liberation Front had to surrender their territory because it lay outside that zone. According to Chen, "The real winner at the Conference was China."[23]

It is difficult, therefore, to agree with Qu Xing, who argued that the disparities between the DRV and Chinese positions were only tactical differences. Yang Kuisong more frankly compared the 1954 Geneva accords with Soviet leader Stalin's attempts to compel the Chinese Communist Party to negotiate with Nationalist leader Jiang Jieshi (Chiang Kai-shek) in September 1945; he might also have mentioned Stalin's 1949 advice to the Chinese Communists, that they should not cross the Yangxi River. Yang added that on June 4, 1963, Mao Zedong told Le Duan that it had been wrong to conclude the Geneva Accords.[24] Qiang Zhai likewise quoted Zhou as making similar comments to the American journalists James Reston and Harrison Salisbury.[25] The Soviet Union also made gains at Geneva, strengthening the Sino-Soviet alliance, promoting détente, and gaining some influence over the future course of events in Southeast Asia. The European Defence Community scheme also eventually failed to materialize, though the reasons for this bore little relation to Soviet participation at Geneva.

France and the United Kingdom were, of course, the countries primarily responsible for the partitioning of Vietnam, an idea the United States initially rejected. Gaiduk nonetheless cites the view of the American historian Lloyd W. Gardner, that in May 1954, on the eve of the Geneva Conference, Washington indicated that partition might represent a middle course between what was unattainable and what was unacceptable.[26] Devillers and Lacouture also quoted Bedell Smith as stating, a few days into the conference, that partition was more or less inevitable.[27] Soon afterward, at the Anglo-American summit meeting in Washington from June 24 to 29, 1954, Dulles issued seven-point guidelines for the British and French delegations at Geneva, which stated that they must, among other things, ensure that the line of division fell below Dong Hoi town, that is, north of the 17th parallel. The United States emerged from Geneva with significant gains, leading Dulles to state that "Dien Bien Phu was a blessing in disguise." The 1954

Geneva Conference therefore represented a superpower diktat as to the fate of a smaller country, Vietnam.

The Anti-American War of Resistance
for National Reunification

By the 1960s, the situation in Vietnam had changed. The United States had to face the age-old nationalism of an entire people, while the decay and utter incompetence of the Saigon regime made it impossible for Washington to implement its strategy successfully in Vietnam. Moreover, America could not focus all its resources exclusively on the war in Vietnam for too protracted a period without increasingly negative consequences upon its global strategic posture, its economy, and its internal domestic politics, while the Vietnamese were determined to devote all their resources to the war for as long as possible, an aim in whose pursuit they developed appropriate strategies and tactics. The Sino-Soviet rift grew ever more acute, until it became irreconcilable, enabling the Vietnamese to implement a line toward both communist big powers that combined friendship and independence, and to bring their own strength and other advantages into full play, while the United States gradually found itself at an impasse, which climaxed in the sixty-day crisis following the 1968 Tet Offensive.

Rather than comment on these factors and developments, all of which are already well known to historians, I turn to the splits among Vietnam and its allies on the subject of peace negotiations. From February 1965 onward, on numerous occasions, the Soviet Union sought to convince North Vietnam to open peace talks with the United States as soon as possible, and to accept conditions considerably less favorable than those Vietnam demanded. In response, Vietnamese officials patiently explained their own stance and tactics, and the Soviet Union refrained from exerting undue pressure on them, and from 1968 onward contributed to the eventual success of the Paris peace talks, insofar as Vietnamese leaders found Soviet suggestions acceptable.

Apart from providing material aid, the Chinese government openly stationed troops in the northern portion of the DRV, hoping that these would act as a deterrent to any potential U.S. land invasion of North Vietnam, because this might have endangered Chinese security. Vietnam welcomed the Chinese forces as a valuable deterrent, and also made every effort to circumscribe the land war within South Vietnam. The precautions that Vietnam, the Soviet Union, and China took to avoid undue escalation of the conflict meant that both big communist powers could provide Vietnam with massive aid to counter U.S. aggression, without running the risk of provoking a major great-power confrontation. Coincidentally, these tactics effectively gave the lie to fears that, had hostilities continued in 1954, they might have led to such a confrontation at that time.

China sought to persuade Vietnam that it should not accept too much Soviet aid, be overly reliant on such assistance, or be too credulous of Soviet goodwill, repeatedly advising the DRV to fight both U.S. imperialism and Soviet revisionism. Despite its gratitude to China, there were many reasons why Vietnam could not accept such advice, including the crucial importance to the DRV of Soviet support and of the heavy, sophisticated weaponry the Soviet Union provided.

From 1965 onward, China also firmly opposed all attempts to open peace negotiations launched by the United States or its allies, together with the mediating efforts by the Soviet Union and other countries. Instead, China frequently endeavored to persuade the Vietnamese leadership to conduct a protracted small-scale guerrilla war in South Vietnam, rather than to open negotiations when, from the Chinese perspective, the situation was not yet ripe for these. The Vietnamese leaders recognized that China essentially sought to oppose all negotiations until China itself was ready to normalize relations with the United States and open talks with the latter on various problems, including the settlement of the Vietnam War, as it had done at Geneva in 1954. From the Vietnamese perspective, therefore, refusing to permit either the Soviet Union or China to interfere substantially in any peace negotiations, particularly if they tried to do so within the framework of big-power détente and through a large international conference, was a sine qua non of Vietnam's eventual victory.

On April 8, 1965, Vietnam announced a four-point plan designed to serve as a basis for subsequent talks with the United States at an appropriate time. From then until the end of 1966, Vietnam received numerous intermediaries and messages from the United States, enabling DRV officials to familiarize themselves with American negotiating positions and to discover how they could encourage the United States to open bilateral talks at a suitable moment in the war. By the end of 1966, they could discern serious signs that the United States was flagging and growing tired of the war. The DRV was willing to open talks if and when the United States unconditionally ceased all bombing and warlike acts against the DRV. If the United States responded to this offer, preparations for the early 1968 Tet Offensive would still continue, but the offensive itself could be postponed until a later date, if and when this became necessary in the future.

Because U.S. president Lyndon B. Johnson rejected this offer, clinging instead to his own earlier scheme of the conditional cessation of bombing and unconditional talks, no peace negotiations were possible in 1967. The DRV therefore launched the Tet Offensive, with the objective of bringing the United States to the table for bilateral peace negotiations. It is worth noting that China objected to the DRV foreign minister's January 1967 statement that North Vietnam would welcome peace talks, and that DRV officials concealed their plans to launch the Tet Offensive from both China and the Soviet Union. In 1967, the United States therefore believed that Vietnam did not want to open peace talks, while China believed that Vietnam was too eager to begin negotiations, and the DRV foreign minister's offer was premature.

In reality, Vietnam genuinely sought the beginning of peace talks, believing that the situation was already mature and the existing opportunity should not be missed. Once Johnson had made his March 31, 1968, offer to open peace negotiations, DRV leaders subsequently responded rapidly to this, primarily because the offer clearly involved an irreversible American trend toward the de-escalation of the war and a peaceful settlement, and also because they were eager to institutionalize bilateral Vietnamese-American talks and thereby preempt détente among the big powers and limit the harm this might do to Vietnam's own cause.

Vietnamese leaders took these measures despite Chinese opposition, not because they did not respect their great neighbor but because the supreme interests of the Vietnamese nation would not permit them to make any concessions on these matters. The issues at stake greatly surpassed simple tactical differences. On November 17, 1968, a high-level delegation including Dong and Nguyen Van Linh visited China to reassure Mao that their country was simply fighting while talking, a strategy also practiced by the American side. Mao did not share the critical attitude other Chinese leaders adopted toward this strategy, but in a statement made behind closed doors to the Vietnamese delegation on November 17, 1968, he told them that he approved of it. Mao's position was not simply the product of his thinking on bilateral Sino-Vietnamese dealings, but it was almost certainly formulated in a context carrying broader implications for Sino-American relations.

Nine days later, on November 26, 1968, an official Chinese spokesperson stated that his country wished to hold ambassadorial talks with the incoming administration of President Richard M. Nixon. Soon afterward, in

April 1969, the Chinese Communist Party held its Tenth Congress, which began the process of normalizing relations with the United States. Under the influence of the Tet Offensive and the subsequent Paris peace talks, the Chinese leadership was forced to readjust its strategy and begin the process of normalizing Sino-American relations sooner than had originally been planned.

It is well known that, due to many factors, from the early 1960s onward, there existed in Vietnam a situation in which the "tail wagged the dog," meaning that the United States and other big powers could not do just as they pleased and could not impose their own views on the smaller DRV as they had done in 1954. Eventually, the United States and the other great powers were forced to respect North Vietnam's legitimate demands: the four-point position, the unconditional cessation of bombing, and the unconditional withdrawal of American troops from Vietnam. With the signing of the Paris Peace Agreement in early 1973, the war in Vietnam once more became essentially a national struggle and a civil war, though some potential danger still existed of residual or new collusion and interference on the part of the bigger powers.

This trend, whereby the "tail wagged the dog," which prevailed for some years, until 1975, also generated considerable bitterness among the big powers. In the United States, it provoked a sense of humiliation and the mentality of a bad loser, and China felt fierce indignation over the "insolence" of this contemporary version of a tributary state, which had been expected to toe the line laid down by its suzerain. How Vietnam chose to deal with these problems and live with these legacies falls outside the framework of this commentary.

Notes

1. Editorial published in *Renmin Ribao* [People's Daily], June 28, 1953.
2. François Joyaux, *La Chine et le reglement du premier conflict d'Indochine, Génève, 1954* [China and the settlement of the first Indochina War, Geneva, 1954] (Paris: Publications de la Sorbonne, 1979); James Cable, *The Geneva Conference of 1954 on Indochina* (London: Macmillan, 1986).
3. Cited in Qiang Zhai, "China and the Geneva Conference of 1954," *China Quarterly,* no. 129 (March 1992): 107–8. In this article, Zhai utilized documentary sources, some of which were apparently still unavailable to other Chinese scholars in 2000.
4. Zhai, "China and the Geneva Conference," 114–15.
5. Qu Xing and Wan Tailei, "China and the Two Indochina Wars," paper delivered at International Workshop on "New Evidence on China, Vietnam, and the Wars in Indochina," University of Hong Kong, Hong Kong, January 2000.

6. Ilya Gaiduk, "From Berlin to Geneva: Soviet Views on the Settlement of the Indochina Conflict, January–April 1954," paper delivered at International Workshop on "New Evidence on China, Vietnam, and the Wars in Indochina," University of Hong Kong, Hong Kong, January 2000; also Ilya V. Gaiduk, *Confronting Vietnam: Soviet Policy toward the Indochina Conflict, 1954–1963* (Washington, D.C., and Stanford, Calif.: Woodrow Wilson Center Press and Stanford University Press, 2003), chaps. 1–3.

7. See Qu and Wan, "China and the Two Indochina Wars"; and Gaiduk, "From Berlin to Geneva." Also see Tao Wenzhao, "Containment and Counter-Containment: A Review of the Peaceful Resolution of the Indochina Wars at the Geneva Conference," paper delivered at International Workshop on "New Evidence on China, Vietnam, and the Wars in Indochina," University of Hong Kong, Hong Kong, January 2000; and chapter 1 of the present volume by Yang Kuisong, "Mao Zedong and the Indochina Wars."

8. See chapter 1 of the present volume; Tao, "Containment and Counter-Containment"; and Qu and Wan, "China and the Two Indochina Wars."

9. Philippe Devillers and Jean Lacouture, *Vietnam: De la guerre française à la guerre americaine* [Vietnam: From the French war to the American war] (Paris: Éditions de la Seuil, 1969), 329; particular attention should also be paid to the two maps on 322–23.

10. See esp. Qu and Wan, "China and the Two Indochina Wars"; and chapter 1 of the present volume.

11. Military History Institute of Vietnam, *The War of Resistance against the French Colonialists, 1945–1954* (Hanoi: Military History Institute of Vietnam, 1994), 291.

12. Devillers and Lacouture, *Vietnam,* 308.

13. Cable, *Geneva Conference,* 107–8.

14. Devillers and Lacouture, *Vietnam,* 311–12.

15. Robert F. Randle, *Geneva 1954: The Settlement of the Indochinese War* (Princeton, N.J.: Princeton University Press, 1969), 352.

16. See chapter 1 of the present volume.

17. Cable, *Geneva Conference,* 120.

18. Wilfred Burchett, *The China-Cambodia-Vietnam Triangle* (London: Zed Press, 1981), 40.

19. *Review of the Anti-United States War for National Salvation* (Hanoi, 1996), 192.

20. *Nhan Dan Daily,* September 22, 1995.

21. James Olson, ed., *Dictionary of the Vietnam War* (Westport, Conn.: Greenwood Press, 1987), 67.

22. Chen Jian, "China and the First Indochina War, 1950–54," *China Quarterly,* no. 133 (March 1993): 85.

23. Chen, "China and the First Indochina War," 110.

24. See Qu and Wan, "China and the Two Indochina Wars," and chapter 1 of the present volume.

25. Qiang, "China and the Geneva Conference of 1954," 113.

26. See Gaiduk, "From Berlin to Geneva."

27. Devillers and Lacouture, *Vietnam,* 181.

Part III

Documents

14

Le Duan and the Break with China

Introduced by Stein Tønnesson
Translated by Christopher E. Goscha

The decision to publish Christopher E. Goscha's translation of Secretary General Le Duan's lengthy 1979 statement about Sino-Vietnamese relations is a significant event. Until now, few Vietnamese documents of this kind have been made available to scholars. The latter have therefore tended to analyze the two Indochina wars and their role in the Cold War as a power game between Western powers, the Soviet Union, and China, and to overlook Vietnamese perspectives. Goscha's translation brings one such perspective into the scholarly debate.

Goscha, then a researcher with the Groupe d'Études sur le Vietnam Contemporain (Sciences Politique, Paris), consulted the document in the People's Army Library in Hanoi, copied it by hand, and translated it into English. He did so with full authorization. The text is undated, and the author's name is just given as "Comrade B." The content implies, however, that it was written in 1979, most probably between the Chinese invasion of northern Vietnam in February 1979 and the publication of the Vietnamese *White Paper* on Sino-Vietnamese relations on October 4 of the same year.[1]

It seems likely that the text was composed shortly after Deng Xiaoping's March 15, 1979, decision to withdraw the Chinese troops from their punitive expedition into northern Vietnam, but before the defection to China of the veteran Vietnamese communist leader Hoang Van Hoan in July 1979.

How can we know that the man behind the text is Le Duan? In it, Comrade B reveals that during a Politburo meeting in the Vietnamese Workers' Party (VWP, the name of the Vietnamese Communist Party from 1951 to 1976) he was referred to as Anh Ba (Brother Number Three), an alias we know was used by Duan. The document also refers frequently to high-level meetings between Chinese and Vietnamese leaders where the author (referred to in the text as "I," in Vietnamese *tôi*) represented the Vietnamese side in an authoritative way that few others than could have done. We know Duan did not write much himself, and the document has an oral style (a fact that has made its translation extremely difficult). It thus seems likely that the text is either a manuscript dictated by Duan to a secretary, or detailed minutes written by someone attending a high-level meeting where Duan made the statement.

The document can be used by the historian to analyze Duan's ideas and attitudes, the situation within the socialist camp in 1979, and the record of Le Duan's relations with China in the period 1952–79.

From a scholarly point of view, it is safest to use the text for the first and second purposes, because the document can then be exploited as an artifact, a textual residue from the past that the historian seeks to reconstruct. As such, it illuminates the views and attitudes of Vietnam's top leader in the crisis year 1979, and also some aspects of the situation within the socialist camp at that particular juncture. To use the text as a source on the earlier history of Duan's relations with China (the topic addressed in the text) is more problematic, because what Duan had to say in 1979 was deeply colored by rage. Thus he is likely to have distorted facts, perhaps even made up stories. As a source for events in the period 1952–79, the document must therefore be treated with tremendous caution, and compared with other available sources. Two similar sources, resulting from the same kind of outrage, are the official *White Paper*s published by Vietnam and China toward the end of 1979.[2] A third source, with a series of documents from the years 1964–77, is Working Paper 22, published by the Cold War International History Project in 1998, titled *77 Conversations between Chinese and Foreign Leaders on the Wars in Indochina, 1964–1977,* and edited by an international group of historians: Odd Arne Westad, Chen Jian, Stein Tønnesson, Nguyen Vu Tung, and James G. Hershberg. This collection contains 77 minutes of conversations or excerpts of such minutes between Chinese, Vietnamese, and other leaders in the period 1964–77 (presumably taken down during or shortly after each conversation, but compiled, excerpted, and possibly edited at later stages). The collection includes several conversations in which Duan took part. The editors of the *77 Conversations* write that the minutes have been compiled from "archival documents, internal Communist party documentation, and open and restricted publications from China *and other countries*" (emphasis added).[3] The editors do not tell which of the minutes were written, excerpted, and compiled in China and which in "other countries." It would seem possible that some of these minutes were used as background material for the preparation of the *White Paper*s in 1979, at least on the Chinese side. This would mean that the sources just mentioned are not altogether independent of each other. This fact and the obscure origin of the seventy-seven minutes means that they too must be treated with caution. Their main function may be to offer clues as to what the historian should look for when given access to the archives of the Chinese and Vietnamese Communist Parties.

Le Duan's Attitude

What does the text reveal about its originator, Le Duan? A striking feature of the text is its directness and the way in which the author comes across as an individual. This is not the normal kind of party document, where individual attitudes and emotions are shrouded in institutionalized rhetoric.[4] Duan seems to have addressed himself to a small group of party leaders, with the purpose of justifying his own actions vis-à-vis China and ensuring support for maintaining a hard line against Chinese pressures, possibly fighting another great war. Duan speaks of himself as "I," identifies each of his interlocutors on the Chinese side by name, and expresses his emotions toward Mao Zedong, Zhou Enlai, Deng, and other Chinese leaders. The author really likes the word "I," and he uses it even when referring to his talks with Ho Chi Minh. This is surprising because using *tôi* in relation to conversations with the uncle (*bác*) would probably be considered arrogant, even for people who worked closely with him. The proper term in that connection would perhaps be "*cháu*."[5] Throughout the document, it is Duan who does everything. The style is oral. It seems possible that the person who wrote down the text later deposited the document in the Army Library.[6]

Despite the refreshing directness of the text, one thing the author virtually never does is speak openly about internal disagreements among the Vietnamese leaders. The only other leaders mentioned by name are Ho and Nguyen Chi Thanh, who had both passed away long before 1979. There is not a word about Vo Nguyen Giap, Pham Van Dong, Nguyen Duy Trinh, Xuan Thuy, Hoang Van Hoan, or any of the others who had played prominent roles in Hanoi's tortuous relations with Beijing. Internal disagreements on the Vietnamese side are only mentioned on one occasion. Duan claims that everyone in the Politburo was always of the same mind, but that there had been one person who rose to question the Politburo, asking why Duan had talked about the need to not be afraid of the Chinese. On that occasion, says Duan, the one who stood up to support Anh Ba, was Nguyen Chi Thanh, the army commander in southern Vietnam, who had often been considered a supporter of Chinese viewpoints before his untimely death in 1967. The "comrade" asking the impertinent question was no doubt Hoan, and the fact that he is not mentioned by name may indicate that Duan's statement was made before this party veteran defected to China in July 1979.

As background to the analysis of the text, we should first establish what is generally known about Duan's life (1907–86) and career. He came from Quang Tre in Central Vietnam, and he based his party career on political work in the southern half of Vietnam. In the 1920s, he became a railway worker, joined the Indochinese Communist Party (ICP) at its foundation in 1930, and he spent the years 1931–36 in a French prison. During the Popular Front period in France, he was free again to work politically, and in March 1938 he became a member of the ICP Central Committee.[7] In 1940, he was arrested once more, and he belonged, with Pham Hung and Nguyen Duy Trinh, to the group of party leaders who spent the war years 1941–45 on the French prison island Poulo Condore.[8] He was released in 1945, and during the First Indochina War he served as secretary of the Nam Ba (southern region) Party Committee (from 1951, this was known as the Central Office for South Vietnam), with Le Duc Tho as his closest collaborator.

After the Geneva Accords of 1954, which established the division of Vietnam along the 17th parallel, Duan is known to have sent a letter to the party leaders, objecting to the concessions made. In 1957, after Truong Chinh had stepped down as secretary general of the VWP and President Ho himself had taken over the party leadership, Duan was called to Hanoi, where he became acting secretary general. He was the prime mover, in the years 1957–59, for resuming armed struggle in South Vietnam, and gaining Soviet and Chinese support for that policy. The decision of the Fifteenth Central Committee Plenum in January 1959 to move to active struggle in the South was a clear victory for Duan, and at the VWP's Third Congress in 1960 he was elected secretary general. It was more than fifteen years before the next, Fourth, Party Congress was held in 1976, and Duan died in office, half a year before the Sixth Congress in 1986.[9]

Le Duan was clearly the second most powerful Vietnamese communist leader of the twentieth century, after Ho, the founder of the Indochinese Communist Party in 1930 and president of the Democratic Republic of Vietnam from its foundation in 1945 to his death in 1969.

Duan must be characterized as an indigenous communist leader. He had not, like Ho, traveled around the world during his youth. He had not, like Dong, Giap, and Hoan, worked closely with Ho in building the Viet Minh front and the National Liberation Army in the area bordering China during World War II. Nor did he belonged to the group around Truong Chinh, who constituted the ICP's northern secretariat during the years from 1940 to the August Revolution of 1945. Ho's decision to leave the party leadership to Duan in the years 1957 to 1960, and to endorse his formal election in 1960, must be interpreted as a way to ensure national unity. At a time when Vietnam was divided in two, and many Southern cadres had been regrouped to the North, the safest way to ensure that the VWP would remain a party for all Vietnam was probably to make the leader of the Southern branch the leader of the whole party. Presumably this was the motive behind Ho's choice. The relationship between Ho and Duan was never characterized by the same kind of warmth as that between Uncle Ho and others among his party nephews.[10]

Duan's 1979 text shows that he combined an extremely strong national pride with an idea that the Vietnamese, as a particularly struggle-prone people, were playing a vanguard role in the world revolutionary struggle. The text does not reveal much admiration or respect for nations other than the Vietnamese, but it is deeply committed to the idea of national independence struggles, for all peoples, both small and great. His pride comes out even in the first paragraph, where he says that after "we" had defeated the Americans, there was no imperialist power that would dare to fight "us" again. Only some Chinese reactionary figures "thought they could." The terms "we" and "us" here denote the big national "we."

Duan's pride was of a moral nature, and the basic dichotomy in his moral universe was that between fear and courage. He seems to have despised those who did not "dare" to fight. If it had not been for the Vietnamese, he claimed, there would have been no one to fight the Americans, because at the time the Vietnamese were fighting the United States, the rest of the world was "afraid" of the Americans. The same kind of moral pride comes out in Duan's account of a meeting he had with Zhou in Hanoi, just after the latter had received Henry Kissinger in Beijing. Duan says he told Zhou that with the new Sino-American understanding, Richard Nixon would attack "me" even harder, but "I am not at all afraid." Later in the text, he comes back to the claim: "It was only Vietnam that was not afraid of the U.S." He also identifies the fearful. The first person to fear the Americans was Mao, he claims. The famous statement about the "paper tiger" is not present in this text. Mao is the one who always feared the Americans, discouraged the Vietnamese from fighting, and refused to offer support if this might entail a risk of U.S. retaliation against China. When China did intervene in Korea, this was not a sign of courage but simply something China had to do to defend its power interests.

Duan's admiration for courage reaches its crescendo in the following statement: "We are not afraid of anyone. We are not afraid because we are in the right. We don't even fear our elder brother. We also do not fear our friends. Even our enemies we do not fear. We have fought them already. We are human beings. We are not afraid of anyone. We are independent. All the world knows we are independent."

On the basis of his moral distinction between courage and fear, Duan claims that there was also a basic difference between Mao's military strategy and the strategy followed by the Vietnamese. The former was defensive, the latter offensive. The Vietnamese had not learned anything from the Chinese in military strategy. The Chinese had always been very weak. They did little to fight the Japanese. After Duan's first visit to China, which he claims occurred in 1952, Ho asked him what he had seen. Two things, he replied: "Vietnam is very brave, and they are not brave at all." From that day on, Duan had sensed the basic difference between the Chinese and the Vietnamese: "We were entirely different from them. Within the Vietnamese person there is a very courageous spirit, and thus we have never had defensive tactics. Every person fights."

There is little in the text to indicate that Duan felt more respect or sympathy for the Soviet Union than for China, although the Russians caused less worry. He complained about the Sino-Soviet split, but his reason for doing so was that it strengthened the United States' leverage in Vietnam. He complained that he had to explain so many things in China, going there "twice a year." Then he added that he had no such problem with the Soviets, because he just refrained from keeping them informed: "As for the Soviets, I did not say anything at all . . . I only spoke in general terms."[11]

Another important aspect of Duan's thinking is his ideologically motivated distinction between, on the one side, "the Chinese people," and on the other, reactionary Chinese figures. As has been seen, he had little admiration for the Chinese in general, but he did not want to blame the whole Chinese people for their leaders' aggressive policies: "We refer to them as a clique only. We do not refer to their nation. We did not say the Chinese people are bad towards us. We say that it is the reactionary Beijing clique."

Duan also distinguishes between individuals on the Chinese side, and here the criterion for judging people is their degree of understanding of Vietnam. The one who understood the least was Chairman Mao, whom Duan seems to have thoroughly disliked: "The most uncompromising person, the one with the Greater Han heart and the one who wanted to take Southeast Asia, was mainly Mao." He felt more sympathy both for Zhou and Deng. Duan claims that Zhou agreed, in the 1960s, on the need for a united front of socialist countries to back the struggle in Vietnam, but that Mao said this was not possible. Zhou helped Duan to understand what was going on in China, and he arranged for much assistance to be given to Vietnam: "I am indebted to him." Hua Guofeng did not understand Vietnam, but then again Deng had shown more understanding. This is somewhat surprising, because we know from *77 Conversations* that Deng was the one who most bluntly addressed the problems in the Sino-Vietnamese relationship in party-to-party conversations. Duan probably preferred Deng's straight, hard talk to Hua's evasiveness and Mao's eccentric allegories. Another source confirms Duan's admiration for Deng. In October 1977, he told the Soviet ambassador in Hanoi that Hua was one of those Chinese leaders who "does not understand us," but that Deng "treats Vietnam with great understanding." At that time Le Duan predicted that Deng Xiaoping would win the Chinese power struggle and that this would cause Sino-Vietnamese relations to improve.[12]

That Duan retained some of his positive attitude to Deng in 1979 is surprising, given that it was Deng who ordered the invasion of northern Vietnam. Duan claims that Deng sincerely congratulated the Vietnamese in 1975, when Vietnam won its struggle for national unification, whereas some other Chinese leaders were only grudging. And in 1977, Deng agreed with Duan on the need to start negotiations concerning border issues. Duan thought Deng was under pressure from other, less understanding Chinese leaders, and that he had to show resolution toward Vietnam to avoid accusations of revisionism: "Now he is rash and foolish. Because he wants to show that he is not a revisionist, he has struck Vietnam even harder. He went ahead and let *them* attack Vietnam" (italics added).[13]

The final aspect of Duan's attitude to be addressed here is his staunch internationalism. This may seem strange, given his almost parochially nationalist attitude, but he perceived Vietnam as the vanguard in a worldwide struggle for national liberation. This is not like the olden days, he says, when Vietnam stood alone against China. Now the whole world is closely knit together: "This is a time where everyone wants independence and freedom. [Even] on small islands, people want independence and freedom. All of humankind is presently like this. . . . To harm Vietnam was [is] to harm humanity, an injury to independence and freedom. . . . Vietnam is a nation that symbolizes independence and freedom."

The Year 1979

The next use that can be made of the document is to illuminate the situation in the year when it was written. The year 1979 marked the main turning point in the history of the international communist movement. By 1977–78, it was at the apex of its power, with some thirty Marxist governments worldwide. In 1979–80, international socialism entered a period of crisis that in a matter of twelve years would reduce the number of Marxist governments to only five: China, North Korea, Laos, Vietnam, and Cuba. The "disastrous" events of 1978–80 included not only the Vietnamese invasion of Cambodia, the Chinese punitive expedition into Vietnam, and the commitment of the Soviet Navy to the South China Sea, but also the election of the cardinal-archbishop of Krakow to the papacy and the founding of the Solidarity movement in Poland, the dismantling of collectivist agriculture and introduction of market forces in China, the creation of a de facto U.S.-Chinese alliance in East Asia, the establishment of an anticommunist Islamist regime in Iran, the crisis in Afghanistan leading to the Soviet invasion of December 1979, and the destabilization of several newly established Marxist regimes in Africa through anticommunist insurgencies. Most notably, this meant that the guerrilla weapon was turned around to become "low-intensity warfare" directed against socialist regimes. "Inverse Vietnams" were created in Cambodia, Afghanistan, Angola, Ethiopia, and elsewhere; and Leonid Brezhnev's Soviet regime took on so many international commitments that it entered a period of classic economic and imperial overstretch.

As of 1979, of course, neither Duan nor any other communist leader could foretell the approaching disaster. They were accustomed to success and were still deeply imbued with the fundamental Marxist belief that socialism represented a more advanced stage in human development than capitalism. The *White Paper* published by the Vietnamese Foreign Ministry in October 1979 claimed that "today the revolutionary forces have grown, and are in a most favorable position."[14] The victory of the Vietnamese Revolution was still fresh in their minds, and had been followed by the establishment of socialist regimes in the former Portuguese colonies in Africa and, most recently, in Central America. U.S. imperialism, claimed the *White Paper,* was sinking ever deeper into an irremediable general crisis, and could not even maintain its position in its apparently secure strongholds in Asia, Africa, and Latin America.[15] The Soviet and Vietnamese communist leaders no doubt interpreted the trouble in Cambodia and Afghanistan, the introduction of market forces in China, and China's alignment with the United States as temporary setbacks from the general course of global evolution, which would inevitably further strengthen socialist forces. Not until the mid-1980s did socialist leaders begin to realize that the trend had turned against socialism.

What does Duan's text reveal about the Vietnamese leadership's assessment of the general situation in 1979, and its expectations for the future? It shows that the Hanoi leaders were preparing for a larger war with China, and that Duan felt confident that Vietnam could survive such a war because the greater part of the Chinese army would be compelled to remain in place along the Soviet border. Duan prepared his comrades for a new protracted national resistance struggle, and he saw Vietnam as playing a crucial role in defending all Southeast Asia against Chinese expansionism. He intended to utilize the traditional strongholds of the Indochinese Communist Party in the north central provinces of Nghe An, Ha Tinh, and Thanh Hoa—where a disproportionate number of Vietnamese communist leaders had come from—as rearguard bases for the struggle against the northern enemy. "In the near future we will fight China. We are determined to win," Duan exclaimed, most probably after the end of the Chinese punitive expedition. To bolster his own and his comrades' determination, he resorted to his pride in his struggle-prone nation:

> The truth is that if a different country were to fight them, it is not clear that they would win like this. . . . We have never shirked from our historical responsibilities. . . . By guarding its own independence, Vietnam is also guarding the independence of Southeast Asian nations. Vietnam is resolved not to allow the Chinese to become an expansionist nation.

The recent battle was one round only. . . . If they bring one or two million troops in to fight us, we will not be afraid of anything. We have just engaged 600,000 troops, and, if, in the near future, we have to fight two million, it will not be a problem at all. We are not afraid. We will make each district a fortress, every province a battlefield. We have enough people. We can fight them in many ways. We are capable of taking two to three army corps to fight them fiercely in order to surprise them; thereby making them waver, while we still defend our land. If this is so desired, then every soldier must [give rise to or produce a] soldier and every squad a squad.

It seems that Deng calculated cleverly in March 1979, when he decided to withdraw Chinese troops, leaving the fight against Vietnam to the Khmer Rouge, while China concentrated on economic achievements.

The Record of Le Duan's Relations with China

The third, more difficult, use we can make of Duan's document is as a source on the author's relations with China and the Chinese leaders in the entire period from 1952 to 1979. In the absence of more reliable archival sources, it is tempting to make an attempt, but one should cherish no illusions as to the accuracy of what Duan has to say.

Duan tells that he first visited China to gain better health in 1952. In his account, he was struck by the fact that despite its huge population, the region he visited—which would probably have been Guangxi or Guangdong—had not waged any guerrilla struggle against Japan during the Japanese occupation. This fact is used in the text to draw the basic distinction between Vietnamese courage and Chinese pusillanimity. Duan claims that Ho confirmed his view. This story probably reveals more about Duan's attitude as of 1979 than about his real impressions at the time. We do not even know from other sources whether he went to China at all in 1952.

What he tells of his reaction to the Geneva Accords in 1954 is more reliable. At that time, he led the Central Office of South Vietnam in southern Vietnam, and there is little reason to doubt his disappointment at having to ask his comrades to refrain from any further fighting and resort only to political struggle or regroup north of the 17th parallel. In his 1979 text, he claims to have made an emotional outburst before Zhou, probably on July 13, 1971, when Zhou came to Hanoi to explain the Sino-American honeymoon. Duan had then spoken about his feelings in 1954, when he had been in Hau Nghia, northwest of Saigon, where the famous Cu Chi tunnel system would later be dug out. And, he says Zhou apologized, admitting his mistake.[16]

What is less certain, however, is if Duan already blamed China in 1954. At that time, China, the Soviet Union, and the North Vietnamese leadership stood firmly behind the agreement, and Duan may well have blamed his own national leaders more than Beijing and Moscow. It probably took some time before he discovered the crucial role played by Zhou in persuading the Democratic Republic of Vietnam leaders to accept the 17th parallel as the dividing line between North and South Vietnam. The individual most likely to have told him would be Pham Van Dong, who led the Vietnamese delegation in Geneva.[17]

The formative period for Duan's negative attitude toward China may well have been the late 1950s, when he led the effort to gain Soviet and Chinese support for a renewed armed struggle in South Vietnam. At that time, Mao was launching his Great Leap Forward, which plunged his country into a crisis that was not conducive to fulfilling international obligations, something Duan no doubt observed. In his 1979 text, he returns several times to how Zhou and Mao tried to prevent the Vietnamese from resuming an armed struggle in South Vietnam. Duan does not, however, mention the fact that the Soviet Union also believed in the Geneva Accords and discouraged the Vietnamese from taking any action that might make it easier for France and the South Vietnamese regime to disregard their obligations.[18]

Duan's text is not devoid of contradictions. First, he quotes Zhou as having said that whether or not the Vietnamese continued to fight was at their own discretion. Then he accuses him of having "pressured us to stop fighting." The first claim accords well with Chen Jian's conclusion about China's policy: "The Beijing leadership neither hindered nor encouraged Hanoi's efforts to 'liberate' the South by military means until 1962."[19] The second assertion seems more dubious. Duan also claims that he defied Chinese advice and went ahead with building armed forces in South Vietnam: "We were not of the same mind. We went ahead and clandestinely developed our forces." It was only when "we had already begun fighting that they then allowed us to fight." Duan conveniently refrains from mentioning differences between the views of the South-based cadres and some North Vietnamese leaders.

When coming to 1963–64, Duan turns the tables. The Chinese are no longer accused of trying to moderate the Vietnamese urge to fight, but instead of imposing themselves, building roads to facilitate the expansion of Chinese power into Southeast Asia, and sending troops to pave the way for controlling Vietnam. The main culprit is Mao.

We know of three occasions when Duan met Mao. The first was in 1963 in Wuhan, where Mao, according to the Vietnamese *White Paper,* received a delegation from the VWP. During that meeting, Duan claims to have recognized Mao's real intentions and to have warned him that Vietnam could well beat Chinese forces. Mao allegedly asked him: "Comrade, isn't it true that your people have fought and defeated the Yuan army?" Duan said: "Correct." "Isn't it also true, comrade, that you defeated the Qing army?" Duan replied: "Correct." Mao said: "And the Ming army as well?" It is then that Duan claims to have added boldly: "Yes, and you too. I have beaten you as well [or "and I'll beat yours as well"]. Did you know that? . . . I spoke with Mao Zedong in that way," Duan asserts, and Mao just said: "Yes, yes!"

This is a tricky conversation to interpret. On the one hand, it seems plausible that Mao, who liked to tease people in this manner, asked these questions. It seems highly unlikely, however, that Duan would have challenged Mao so openly. From the *77 Conversations,* it appears that Duan behaved rather like an obsequious servant before his master during his next two meetings with Mao, on August 13, 1964, and May 11, 1970.[20] In 1964, he said that "support from China is indispensable," and that "the Soviet revisionists want to make us a bargaining chip." In 1970, he requested Mao's instructions, and he ascribed Vietnam's successes to the fact that "we have followed the three instructions Chairman Mao gave us in the past," the first of which was "no fear, we should not fear the enemy."[21] The Duan who appears in some of the *77 Conversations* seems quite another person than the one portrayed in the 1979 account—but then the memory of one's own actions normally differs from others' perceptions at the time.

There is a major discrepancy between what Duan and the Vietnamese *White Paper* tell of Sino-Vietnamese relations in 1963–65, and what we know from Chinese sources. According to Duan's account, it was Mao who wanted to build roads into Vietnam, and to send troops there, while he himself wished only for material assistance. In all accounts based on Chinese sources, the request for roads and volunteer troops came from the Vietnamese side, and was expressed by Duan and Ho.[22] This is also confirmed by some of the *77 Conversations.* Duan's claim, that "I only asked that they send personnel, but they brought guns and ammunition," does not seem to conform to the evidence. After Chinese engineer troops and antiaircraft artillery units arrived, however, tensions soon emerged between the two sides, and once Premier Alexei Kosygin committed the Soviet Union to aid Vietnam substantially during a visit to Hanoi in February 1965, Vietnam assumed a more independent posture.

The tone in the *77 Conversations* turns sourer from that time onward. Duan's account of the late 1960s and the 1970s is more in line with what Chinese sources tell. By 1969, Duan claims to have summoned Vietnamese military cadres to warn them that China had joined hands with the U.S. imperialists, and that they must study this problem, that is, prepare themselves for future conflicts with China. Concerning Beijing's new line toward Washington, Duan makes the same accusation as the Vietnamese *White Paper:* "During that time, China made the announcement [to the United States]: 'If you don't attack me, I won't attack you.' Thus they left the United States with greater leverage in Vietnam." This undoubtedly makes sense, because China genuinely emphasized its own great-power interests to the detriment of North Vietnam.

The rhetorical highlight of Duan's text is the conversation he claims to have had with Zhou in Hanoi (probably in November 1971). Before Nixon went to China, says Duan, his goal was to disentangle the United States from Vietnam with the help of China, while enticing China over to the U.S. side in world affairs. Zhou allegedly told Duan: "At this time, Nixon is coming to visit me principally to discuss the Vietnamese problem, thus I must come to meet you, comrade, in order to exchange views."

Duan then claims to have answered: "Comrade, you can say whatever you like, but I still don't follow. Comrade, you are Chinese; I am a Vietnamese. Vietnam is mine; not yours at all." Duan again claims to have spoken harshly to his Chinese interlocutor, a claim that seems more reliable on this occasion, because it was far easier to speak harshly to Zhou in Hanoi in 1971 than to Mao in Wuhan in 1963. It would be interesting to see if Chinese reports of Zhou's November 1971 meetings in Hanoi reveal traces of Duan's nationalist credo.

A Remark on the Need for Archival Research

During the 1990s, the Sino-Vietnamese relationship improved tremendously. The year 1979 was the worst year, but China and Vietnam remained hostile throughout the 1980s, with troops massed on both sides of the border, no rails on the railways, and no open roads. Relations gradually improved from the mid-1980s, and the Vietnamese withdrawal from Cambodia in

1989 marked a huge step forward, paving the way for the normalization of diplomatic relations in 1991. On New Year's Eve 1999 (Western calendar), the two foreign ministers were able to sign a border treaty in Hanoi, and they renewed earlier promises to reach agreement on the delineation of maritime zones in the Gulf of Tonkin before the end of 2000. This fulfilled the tasks that Le Duan and Deng Xiaoping set for themselves in 1977, at that time without much hope of success. The railways are now open again, and border trade flourishes. Dealings between the two countries, the two parties, and the two armies have become more and more frequent, and the border provinces are playing a leading role in improving commercial and cultural ties. The Chinese and Vietnamese research communities also now communicate, as demonstrated at the huge Vietnam Studies Conference in Hanoi 1998, where Chinese and Vietnamese social scientists discussed highly tendentious issues, such as ethnicity in the border region between the two countries, in the presence of researchers from other countries.

What will this mean for the study of the history of contemporary Sino-Vietnamese relations? When two countries improve their relationship, this normally entails studies of their past difficulties. How will Vietnamese and Chinese historians set about studying their problematic historical relationship? One possibility is that each nation will generate its own separate historical studies—that Chinese historians working in Chinese archives will write books in Chinese about China's Vietnam policy, while Vietnamese researchers with access to Vietnamese archives will write Vietnamese books about Vietnam's difficulties with its northern neighbor. A second possibility is a bilateral process, with groups of Chinese and Vietnamese historians working together to explore the history of their relationship, and issuing common publications, preferably in both languages. This could be done in a highly formalized, closed manner, with trusted party historians on both sides forming a joint committee and gaining privileged access to sources screened by the two party leaderships; or it could be done more openly.[23] The third possibility is an open intellectual process, where all interested scholars gain access to Chinese and Vietnamese source material, and various competing books and articles are published in Chinese, Vietnamese, English, and other languages.

All three possibilities are premised on the assumption that the Chinese and Vietnamese authorities will become more self-assured than in the past, show more courage in jettisoning their fear of independent research, and allow access to key historical sources. Although both countries are—albeit slowly and gradually—making selected archival materials more readily accessible, each government has in recent years on occasion imposed severe penalties on scholars whose studies and writings it has considered unacceptable. This may prolong the current paradoxical situation, where scholars based outside China and Vietnam can have access to better sources than their colleagues on the inside and are freer to publish accounts arousing general interest. The only way to ensure that scholars based in China and Vietnam can play a significant role in researching the history of their mutual relations, in an international context, is to allow a new, more open intellectual climate, with declassification of documents, joint conferences, and the encouragement of independent scholarship.

* * * *

Document: Comrade B on the Plot of the Reactionary Chinese Clique against Vietnam

(*Source:* Army Library, Hanoi. Document obtained and translated by Christopher E. Goscha, Groupe d'Études sur le Vietnam Contemporain, Sciences Politique, Paris.)

Generally speaking, after we had defeated the Americans, there was no imperialist that would dare to fight us again.[24] The only persons who thought they could still fight us and dared to fight us were Chinese reactionaries. But the Chinese people did not want it like that at all. I do not know how much longer some of these Chinese reactionaries will continue to exist. However, as long as they do, then they will strike us as they have just recently done [meaning in early 1979]. If war comes from the north, then the [northern central] provinces of Nghe An, Ha Tinh, and Thanh Hoa will become the bases for the entire country. They are unparalleled as the most efficient, the best and the strongest bases. For if the Deltas [in the north] continued as an uninterrupted stretch, then the situation would be very complicated. Not at all a simple matter. If it had not been for the Vietnamese, there would not have been anyone to fight the USA, because at the time the Vietnamese were fighting the USA, the rest of the world was afraid of the USA. . . .[25] Although the Chinese helped [North] Korea, it was only with the aim of protecting their own northern flank. After the fighting had finished [in Korea] and when the pressure was on Vietnam, he [this appears to be a reference to Zhou Enlai as the text soon seems to suggest] said that if the Vietnamese continued to fight they would have to fend for themselves. He would not help any longer and pressured us to stop fighting.

When we had signed the Geneva Accords, it was precisely Zhou Enlai who divided our country into two [parts]. After our country had been divided into northern and southern zones in this way, he once again pressured us into not doing anything in regard to southern Vietnam. They forbade us from rising up [against the U.S.-backed Republic of Vietnam]. [But] they [the Chinese] could do nothing to deter us.

When we were in the south and had made preparations to wage guerrilla warfare immediately after the signing of the Geneva Accords, Mao Zedong told our Party Congress that we had to force the Lao to transfer immediately their two liberated provinces to [the] Vientiane government.[26] Otherwise the Americans would destroy them, a very dangerous situation [in the Chinese view]! Vietnam had to work at once with the Americans [concerning this matter]. Mao forced us in this way and we had to do it.[27]

Then, after these two [Lao] provinces had been turned over to Vientiane, the [Lao] reactionaries immediately arrested Souphanouvong. The Lao had two battalions which were surrounded at the time. Moreover, they were not yet combat ready. Later, one battalion was able to escape [encirclement]. At that time, I gave it as my opinion that the Lao must be permitted to wage guerrilla warfare. I invited the Chinese to come and discuss this matter with us. I told them, "Comrades, if you go ahead pressuring the Lao in this way, then their forces will completely disintegrate. They must now be permitted to conduct guerrilla warfare."

Zhang Wentian,[28] who was previously the Secretary General [of the Chinese Communist Party] and used the pen name Lac Phu, answered me: "Yes, comrades, what you say is right. Let us allow that Lao battalion to take up guerrilla war."

I immediately asked Zhang Wentian: "Comrades, if you allow the Lao to take up guerrilla war, then there is nothing to fear about launching guerrilla war in south Vietnam. What is it that frightens you so much so that you still block such action?"

He [Zhang Wentian] said: "There is nothing to be afraid of!"

That was what Zhang Wentian said. However, Ho Wei, the Chinese ambassador to Vietnam at that time, [and] who was seated there, was listening to what was being said. He immediately cabled back to China [reporting what had been said between Le Duan and Zhang Wentian]. Mao replied at once: "Vietnam cannot do that [taking up guerrilla war in the south]. Vietnam must lie in wait for a protracted period of time!" We were so poor. How could we fight the Americans if we did not have China as a rearguard base? [Thus], we had to listen to them, correct?[29]

However, we did not agree. We secretly went ahead in developing our forces. When [Ngo Dinh] Diem dragged his guillotine machine throughout much of southern Vietnam, we issued the order to form mass forces to oppose the established order and to take power [from the Diem government]. We did not care [about the Chinese]. When the uprising to seize power had begun, we went to China to meet with both Zhou Enlai and Deng Xiaoping. Deng Xiaoping told me: "Comrade, now that your mistake has become an accomplished fact, you should only fight at the level of one platoon downward." That was the kind of pressure they exerted on us.

I said [to the Chinese]: "Yes, yes! I will do that. I will only fight at the level of one platoon downward." After we had fought and China realized that we could fight efficiently, Mao suddenly had a new line of thinking. He said that as the Americans were fighting us, he would bring in [Chinese] troops to help us build roads. His essential aim was to find out about the situation in our country so that later he could strike us, and thereby expand into Southeast Asia. There was no other reason. We were aware of this matter, but had to allow it [the entry of Chinese troops]. But that was OK. They decided to send in their soldiers. I only asked that they send personnel, but these troops came with guns and ammunition. I also had to countenance this.

Later, he [Mao Zedong] forced us to permit 20,000 of his troops to come and build a road from Nghe Tinh into Nam Ba [the Vietnamese term for southern Vietnam]. I refused. They kept proposing, but I would not budge. They pressured me into permitting them to come, but I did not accept it. They kept on pressuring, but I did not agree. I provide you with these examples, comrades, so that you can see their long-standing plot to steal our country, and how wicked their plot is.

—After the Americans had introduced several hundred thousand troops into southern Vietnam, we launched a general offensive in 1968 to force them to de-escalate. In order to defeat the United States, one had to know how to bring them to de-escalate gradually. That was our strategy. We were fighting a big enemy, one with a population of 200 million people and who dominated the world. If we could not bring them to de-escalate step-by-step, then we would have floundered and would have been unable to destroy the enemy. We had to fight to sap their will in order to force them to come to the negotiating table with us, yet without allowing them to introduce more troops.

When it came to the time when they wanted to negotiate with us, Ho Wei wrote a letter to us saying: "You cannot sit down to negotiate with the

United States. You must bring United States troops into northern Vietnam to fight them." He pressured us in this way, making us extremely puzzled. This was not at all a simple matter. It was very tiresome every time these situations arose [with the Chinese].

We decided that it could not be done that way [referring to Ho Wei's advice not to negotiate with the United States]. We had to sit down back in Paris. We had to bring them [the United States] to de-escalate in order to defeat them. During that time, China made the announcement [to the United States]: "If you don't attack me, I won't attack you. However many troops you want to bring into Vietnam, it's up to you." China, of its own accord, did this and pressured us in this way.

They [the Chinese] vigorously traded with the Americans and compelled us to serve as a bargaining chip in this way. When the Americans realized that they had lost, they immediately used China [to facilitate] their withdrawal [from southern Vietnam]. Nixon and Kissinger went to China in order to discuss this matter.

—Before Nixon went to China, [the goal of his trip being] to solve the Vietnamese problem in such a way as to serve United States interests and to minimize the United States defeat, as well as to simultaneously allow him to entice China over to the United States [side] even more, Zhou Enlai came to visit me. Zhou told me: "At this time, Nixon is coming to visit me principally to discuss the Vietnamese problem, thus I must come to meet you, comrade, in order to discuss [it with you]."

I answered: "Comrade, you can say whatever you like, but I still don't follow. Comrade, you are Chinese; I am a Vietnamese. Vietnam is mine [my nation]; not yours at all. You have no right to speak [about Vietnam's affairs], and you have no right to discuss [them with the Americans].[30] Today, comrades, I will personally tell you something which I have not even told our Politburo, for, comrade, you have brought up a serious matter, and hence I must speak:

—In 1954, when we won victory at Dien Bien Phu, I was in Hau Nghia [province]. Bac [Uncle] Ho cabled to tell me that I had to go to southern Vietnam to regroup [the forces there] and to speak to the southern Vietnamese compatriots [about this matter].[31] I traveled by wagon to the south. Along the way, compatriots came out to greet me, for they thought we had won victory. It was so painful! Looking at my southern compatriots, I cried. Because after this [later], the United States would come and massacre [the population] in a terrible way.

Upon reaching the south, I immediately cabled Bac Ho to ask to remain [in the south] and not to return to the north, so that I could fight for another ten years or more. [To Zhou Enlai]: "Comrade, you caused me hardship such as this [meaning Zhou's role in the division of Vietnam at Geneva in 1954]. Did you know that, comrade?"

Zhou Enlai said: "I apologize before you, comrade. I was wrong. I was wrong about that [meaning the division of Vietnam at Geneva]."[32] After Nixon had already gone to China, he [Zhou] once again came to Vietnam in order to ask me about a number of problems concerning the fighting in southern Vietnam.

However, I immediately told Zhou Enlai: "Nixon has met with you already, comrade. Soon they [the United States] will attack me even harder." I am not at all afraid. Both sides [the United States and China] had negotiated with each other in order to fight me harder. He [Zhou] did not as yet reject this [view] as unfounded, and only said that "I will send additional guns and ammunition to you comrades."

Then he [Zhou] said [concerning fears of a secret U.S.-Chinese plot]: "There was no such thing." However, the two had discussed how to hit us harder, including B-52 bombing raids and the blocking of Haiphong [Harbor]. This was clearly the case.

—If the Soviet Union and China had not been at odds with each other, then the United States could not have struck us as fiercely as they did. As the two [powers of China and the Soviet Union] were in conflict, the Americans were unhampered [by united socialist bloc opposition]. Although Vietnam was able to have unity and solidarity both with China and the USSR, to achieve this was very complicated, for at that time we had to rely on China for many things. At that time, China annually provided assistance of 500,000 tons of foodstuffs, as well as guns, ammunition, money, not to mention dollar aid. The Soviet Union also helped in this way. If we could not do that [preserve unity and solidarity with China and the USSR], things would have been very dangerous. Every year I had to go to China twice to talk with them [the Chinese leadership] about [the course of events] in southern Vietnam. As for the Soviets, I did not say anything at all [about the situation in southern Vietnam]. I only spoke in general terms. When dealing with the Chinese, I had to say that both were fighting the United States. Alone I went. I had to attend to this matter. I had to go there and talk with them many times in this way, with the main intention to build closer relations between the two sides [meaning Chinese and Vietnamese]. It was precisely at this time that China pressured us to move away from the USSR, forbidding us from going with the USSR's [side] any longer.[33]

They made it very tense. Deng Xiaoping, together with Kang Sheng,[34] came and told me: "Comrade, I will assist you with several billion [presumably yuan] every year. You cannot accept anything from the Soviet Union."

I could not allow this. I said: "No, we must have solidarity and unity with the whole [socialist] camp."[35]

In 1963, when Nikita Khrushchev erred, [the Chinese] immediately issued a 25-point declaration and invited our Party to come and give our opinion.[36] Brother Truong Chinh and I went together with a number of other brothers. In discussions, they [the Chinese] listened to us for ten or so points, but when it came to the point of "there is no abandonment of the socialist camp,"[37] they did not listen . . . Deng Xiaoping said, "I am in charge of my own document. I seek your opinion but I do not accept this point of yours."

Before we were to leave, Mao met with Brother Truong Chinh and myself. Mao sat down to chat with us, and in the end he announced: "Comrades, I would like you to know this. I will be president of 500 million land-hungry peasants, and I will bring an army to strike downwards into Southeast Asia."[38] Also seated there, Deng Xiaoping added: "It is mainly because the poor peasants are in such dire straits!"

Once we were outside, I told Brother Truong Chinh: "There you have it, the plot to take our country and Southeast Asia. It is clear now." They dared to announce it in such a way. They thought we would not understand. It is true that not a minute goes by that they do not think of fighting Vietnam!

I will say more to you comrades so that you may see more of the military importance of this matter. Mao asked me:

—In Laos, how many square kilometers [of land] are there?
I answered:

—About 200,000 [square kilometers].

—What is its population? [Mao asked]:

—[I answered]: Around 3 million!

—[Mao responded:] That's not very much! I'll bring my people there, indeed!

—[Mao asked:] How many square kilometers [of land] are there in Thailand?.

—[I responded]: About 500,000 [square kilometers].

—And how many people? [Mao asked].

—About 40 million! [I answered].

—My God! [Mao said], Sichuan province of China has 500,000 square kilometers, but has 90 million people. I'll take some more of my people there, too [to Thailand]!

As for Vietnam, they did not dare to speak about moving in people this way. However, he [Mao] told me: "Comrade, isn't it true that your people have fought and defeated the Yuan army?" I said: "Correct." "Isn't it also true, comrade, that you defeated the Qing army?" I said: "Correct." He said: "And the Ming army as well?" I said: "Yes, and you too. I have beaten you as well.[39] Did you know that?" I spoke with Mao Zedong in that way. He said: "Yes, yes!" He wanted to take Laos, all of Thailand . . . as well as wanting to take all of Southeast Asia. Bringing people to live there. It was complicated [to that point].

—In the past [referring to possible problems stemming from the Chinese threat during these times], we had made intense preparations; it is not that we were unprepared. If we had not made preparations, the recent situation would have been very dangerous just recently. It was not a simple matter. Ten years ago, I summoned together our brothers in the military to meet with me. I told them that the Soviet Union and the United States were at odds with each other. As for China, they had joined hands with the United States imperialists. In this tense situation, you must study this problem immediately. I was afraid that the military did not understand me, so I told them that there was no other way to understand the matter. But they found it very difficult to understand. It was not easy at all. But I could not speak in any other way. And I did not allow others to grab me.[40]

—When I went to the Soviet Union, the Soviets were also tough with me about China. The Soviet Union had convened a conference of eighty [communist] Parties in support of Vietnam, but Vietnam did not attend this conference, for [this gathering] was not simply aimed at helping Vietnam, but it was also designed to condemn China. Thus Vietnam did not go. The Soviets said: "Have you now abandoned internationalism [or] what? Why have you done this?" I said: "I have not abandoned internationalism at all. I have never done this. However, to be internationalist, the Americans must be defeated first. And if one wants to defeat the Americans, then there must be unity and solidarity with China. If I had gone to this conference, then the Chinese would have created very severe difficulties for us. Comrades, please understand me."

—In China there were also many different and contending opinions. Zhou Enlai agreed on forming a front with the Soviet Union in order to oppose the Americans. Once, when I went to the USSR to participate in a national day celebration, I was able to read a Chinese cable sent to the Soviet

Union saying that "whenever someone attacks the USSR, then the Chinese will stand by your side."[41] [This was] because there was a treaty of friendship between the USSR and China dating from earlier times [February 1950]. Sitting next to Zhou Enlai, I asked him: "In this cable recently sent to the USSR, you have agreed, comrade, to establish a front with the Soviet Union, but why won't you form a front to oppose the United States?" Zhou Enlai said: "We can. I share that view. Comrades, I will form a front with you [on Vietnam]." Peng Zhen,[42] who was also seated there, added: "This opinion is extremely correct!" But when the matter was discussed in Shanghai, Mao said it was not possible, cancel it. You see how complicated it was.

—Although Zhou Enlai held a number of those opinions, he nonetheless agreed on building a front and [he] helped Vietnam a lot. It was thanks to him that I could understand [much of what was going on in China]. Otherwise it would have been very dangerous. He once told me: "I am doing my best to survive here, to use Li Chiang[43] to accumulate and provide assistance for you, comrades." And that there was [meaning that Zhou was able to use Li Chiang in order to help the Vietnamese]. My understanding is that without Zhou Enlai this would not have been possible at all. I am indebted to him.

However, it is not correct to say that other Chinese leaders shared Zhou Enlai's view at all. They differed in many ways. It must be said that the most uncompromising person, the one with the Greater Han mentality, and the one who wanted to take Southeast Asia, was mainly Mao. All of [China's] policies were in his hands.

The same applies to the current leaders of China. We do not know how things will turn out in the future, however, [the fact of the matter is that] they have already attacked us. In the past, Deng Xiaoping did two things which have now been reversed. That is, when we won in southern Vietnam, there were many [leaders] in China who were unhappy. However, Deng Xiaoping nonetheless congratulated us. As a result of this, he was immediately considered a revisionist by the others.

When I went to China for the last time,[44] I was the leader of the delegation, and I met with the Chinese delegation led by Deng Xiaoping. In speaking of territorial problems, including discussion of several islands, I said: "Our two nations are near each other. There are several areas of our territory which have not been clearly defined. Both sides should establish bodies to consider the matter. Comrades, please agree with me [on this]. He [Deng] agreed, but after doing so he was immediately considered a revisionist by the other group of leaders.

But now he [Deng] is crazy. Because he wants to show that he is not a revisionist, therefore he has struck Vietnam even harder. He let them go ahead in attacking Vietnam.

—After defeating the Americans we kept in place over one million troops, leading Soviet comrades to ask us: "Comrades, whom do you intend to fight that you keep such a large [standing] army?" I said: "Later, comrades, you will understand." The only reason we had kept such a standing army was because of China['s threat to Vietnam]. If there had not been [such a threat], then this [large standing army] would have been unnecessary. Having been attacked recently on two fronts, [we can see that] it would have been very dangerous if we had not maintained a large army.

(B) [The meaning of this "B" in the original text is unclear] —In the wake of World War II, everyone held the international gendarme to be American imperialism. They could take over and bully all of the world. Everyone, including the big powers, were afraid of the United States. It was only Vietnam that was not afraid of the United States.

I understand this matter for my line of work has taught me it. The first person to fear [the Americans] was Mao Zedong. He told me, that is, the Vietnamese and Lao, that: "You must immediately turn over the two liberated provinces of Laos to the [Vientiane] [government]. If you do not do so, then the United States will use it as a pretext to launch an attack. That is a great danger." As for Vietnam, we said: "We have to fight the Americans in order to liberate southern Vietnam." He [Mao] said: "You cannot do that. Southern Vietnam must lie in wait for a long period, for one lifetime, five-to-ten or even twenty lifetimes from now. You cannot fight the Americans. Fighting the United States is dangerous." Mao Zedong was scared of the United States to that extent. . . .

But Vietnam was not scared. Vietnam went ahead and fought. If Vietnam had not fought the United States, then southern Vietnam would not have been liberated. A country which is not yet liberated will remain a dependent one. No one is independent if only one-half of the country is free. It was not until 1975 that our country finally achieved its full independence. With independence would come freedom. Freedom should be freedom for the whole of the Vietnamese nation. . . .

—Engels had already spoken on people's war. Later the Soviet Union, China, and ourselves also spoke [on this matter]. However, these three countries differ a lot on the content [of people's war]. It is not true that just because you have millions of people you can do whatever you like. China also spoke on people's war, however, [they held that] "when the enemy advances, we must retreat." In other words, defense is the main feature, and war is divided into three stages with the countryside used to surround the cities, while [the main forces] remain in the forests and mountains only. . . . The Chinese were on the defensive and very weak [during World War II]. Even with 400 million people pitted against a Japanese army of 300,000 to 400,000 troops, the Chinese still could not defeat them.[45]

I have to repeat it like that, for before China had sent advisers to us [some of our Vietnamese] brothers did not understand. They thought the [Chinese] were very capable. But they are not so skilled, and thus we did not follow [the Chinese advice].[46]

In 1952, I left northern Vietnam for China, because I was sick and needed treatment. This was my first time abroad.[47] I put questions to them [the Chinese] and saw many very strange things. There were areas [which had been] occupied by Japanese troops, each with a population of fifty million people, but which had not [had] a single guerrilla fighter . . .

When I returned from China, I met Uncle [Ho]. He asked me:

—This was your first time to go abroad, isn't that right?

—Yes, I went abroad for the first time.

—What did you see?

—I saw two things: Vietnam is very brave and they [the Chinese] are not brave at all.

I understood this from that day on. We [the Vietnamese] were entirely different from them. Courage is inherent in the Vietnamese person, and thus we have never had a defensive strategy. Every inhabitant fights.

Recently, they [the Chinese] have brought several hundred thousand troops in to invade our country. For the most part, we have used our militia and regional troops to attack them. We were not on the defensive, and thus they suffered a setback. They were not able to wipe out a single Vietnamese platoon, while we wiped out several of their regiments and several dozen of their battalions. That is so because of our offensive strategy.

The American imperialists fought us in a protracted war. They were so powerful, yet they lost. But there was a special element, that is the acute contradictions between the Chinese and the Soviets. [Because of this,] they have attacked us hard like this.

—Vietnam fought the Americans, and fought them very fiercely, but we know that the United States was an extremely large country, more than capable of amassing 10 million troops and bringing all of its considerably powerful weapons in to fight us. Therefore we had to fight over a long period of time in order to bring them to de-escalation. We were the ones who could do this; the Chinese could not. When the American army attacked Quong Tre, the Politburo ordered troops to be brought in to fight at once. We were not afraid. After that I went to China to meet Zhou Enlai. He told me: "It [the attack in Quong Tre] is probably unparalleled, unique. In life there is only one [chance,] not two. No one has ever dared to do what you, comrades, have done."

. . . Zhou Enlai was the Chief of the General Staff. He dared to speak, he was more frank. He told me: "If I had known before the ways which you comrades employ, we would not have needed the Long March." What was the Long March for? At the beginning of the march there were 300,000 troops; and at the end of the Long March there were only 30,000 remaining. 270,000 people were lost. It was truly idiotic to have done it in this way. . . . [I] speak as such so that you, comrades, know how much we are ahead of them. In the near future, if we are to fight against China, we will certainly win. . . . However, the truth is that if a different country [other than Vietnam] were to fight against China, it is not clear that they would win like this [like Vietnam].

. . . If China and the USSR had been united with each other, then it is not certain that the United States would have dared to fight us. If the two had been united and joined together to help us, it is not certain that the United States would have dared to have fought us in the way in which they did. They would have balked from the very beginning. They would have balked in the same way during the Kennedy period. Vietnam, China, and the USSR all helped Laos and the United States immediately signed a treaty with Laos. They did not dare to send American troops to Laos, they let the Lao [People's Revolutionary] Party participate in the government right away. They did not dare to attack Laos any more.

Later, as the two countries [the USSR and China] were at odds with each other, the Americans were informed [by the Chinese] that they could go ahead and attack Vietnam without any fear. Don't be afraid [of Chinese retaliation]. Zhou Enlai and Mao Zedong told the Americans: "If you don't attack me, then I won't attack you. You can bring in as many troops into southern Vietnam as you like. It's up to you."[48]

. . . We are [presently] bordering on a very strong nation, one with expansionist intentions which, if they are to be implemented, must start with an invasion of Vietnam. Thus, we have to shoulder yet another, different historical role. However, we have never shirked from our historical tasks. Previously, Vietnam did carry out its tasks, and this time Vietnam is determined not to allow them to expand. Vietnam preserves its own independence, and by doing so is also safeguarding the independence of Southeast Asian nations. Vietnam is resolved not to allow the Chinese to carry out their expansionist scheme. The recent battle [with China] was one round only. Presently, they are still making preparations in many fields. However, whatever the level of their preparations, Vietnam will still win. . . .

Waging war is no leisurely walk in the woods. Sending one million troops to wage war against a foreign country involves countless difficulties. Just recently they brought in 500,000 to 600,000 troops to fight us, yet they had no adequate transport equipment to supply food to their troops. China is presently preparing 3.5 million troops, but they have to leave half of them on the [Sino-Soviet] border to deter the Soviets. For that reason, if they bring one or two million troops in to fight us, we will not be afraid of anything. We have just engaged 600,000 troops, and if in the near future we have to fight two million, it will not be a problem at all. We are not afraid.

We are not afraid because we already know the way to fight. If they bring in 1 million troops, they will only gain a foothold in the north. Descending into the midlands, the deltas, and into Hanoi and even further downwards would be difficult. Comrades, as you know, Hitler's clique struck fiercely in this way, yet when they [the German Nazis] arrived in Leningrad they could not enter. With the cities, the people, and defense works, it is impossible to carry out effective attacks against each and every inhabitant. Even fighting for two, three, or four years they will still not be able to enter. Every village there [in the north] is like this. Our guidelines are: Each district is a fortress, each province a battlefield. We will fight and they will not be able to enter at all.

However, it is never enough just to fight an enemy at the frontline. One must have a strong direct rearguard. After the recent fighting ended, we assessed that, in the near future, we must add several million more people to the northern front. But as the enemy comes from the north, the direct rear for the whole country must be Thanh Hoa, Nghe An, Ha Tinh . . . The direct rear to protect the capital must be Thanh Hoa and Nghe Tinh. We have enough people. We can fight them in many ways. . . . We can use two to three army corps to inflict a strong blow on them that will make them stagger, while we continue to hold our land. To this end, each soldier must be a real soldier and each squad a real squad.

—Having now fought one battle already, we should not be subjective. Subjectivism and underestimation of the enemy are incorrect, but a lack of self-confidence is also wrong. We are not subjective, we do not underestimate the enemy. But we are also confident and firmly believe in our victory. We should have both these things.

—The Chinese now have a plot to attack [us] in order to expand southward. But in the present era nothing can be done and then wrapped up tidily. China has just fought Vietnam for a few days, yet the whole world has shouted: ["]Leave Vietnam alone!["] The present era is not like the olden times. In those days, it was only us and them [meaning the Chinese]. Now the whole world is fastened closely together. The human species has not yet entered the socialist phase at all; instead this is a time where everyone wants independence and freedom. [Even] on small islands, people want independence and freedom. All of humankind is presently like this. That is very different than it was in olden times. In those days, people were not yet very aware of these things. Thus the sentence of Uncle Ho: "There is nothing more precious than independence and freedom" is an idea of the present era. To lay hands on Vietnam is to lay hands on humanity and infringe on independence and freedom. . . . Vietnam is a nation that symbolizes independence and freedom.

—When it came to fighting the United States, our brothers in the Politburo had to discuss together this matter to consider whether we dared to fight the United States or not. All were agreed to fight. The Politburo expressed its resolve: In order to fight the Americans, we must not fear the United States of America. All were of the same mind. As all agreed to fight the United States, to have no fear of the United States of America, we must also not fear the USSR. All agreed. We must also not fear China. All agreed. If we don't fear these three things, we can fight the United States. This was how we did things in our Politburo at that time.

Although the Politburo met and held discussions like this and everyone was of the same mind, there was later one person who told a comrade what I said. That comrade rose to question the Politburo, asking for what reason does Anh Ba[49] once again say that if we want to fight the Americans then we should not fear the Chinese? Why does he have to put it this way again?[50]

At that time, Brother Nguyen Chi Thanh, who thus far was suspected of being sympathetic to the Chinese, stood up and said: "Respected Politburo and respected Uncle Hò, the statement of Anh Ba was correct. It must be said that way [referring to the need not to fear the Chinese], for they [the Chinese] give us trouble on many matters. They blocked us here, then forced our hands there. They do not let us fight. . . ."[51]

While we were fighting in southern Vietnam, Deng Xiaoping stipulated that I [tôi] could only fight at the level of one platoon downward, and must not fight at a higher level. He [Deng] said: "In the south, since you have made the mistake of starting the fighting already, you should only fight at the level of one platoon downward, not at a higher level." That is how they brought pressure to bear on us.

—We are not afraid of anyone. We are not afraid because we are in the right. We do not fear even our elder brother. We also do not fear our friends.[52] Of course, we do not fear our enemies. We have fought them already. We are human beings; we are not afraid of anyone. We are independent. All the world knows we are independent.

We must have a strong army, because our nation is under threat and being bullied. . . . It cannot be otherwise. If not, then it will be extremely dangerous, but our country is poor.

—We have a strong army, but that does not in any way weaken us. The Chinese have several policies toward us: To invade and to occupy our country; to seek to weaken us economically and to make our living conditions difficult. For these reasons, in opposing China we must, first of all, not only fight, but also make ourselves stronger. To this end, in my view, our army should not be a force that wastes the resources of the state, but should also be a strong productive force. When the enemies come, they [the soldiers] grab their guns at once. When no enemy is coming, then they will produce grandly. They will be the best and highest symbol in production, producing more than anyone else. Of course, that is not a new story. . . .[53]

—At present, our army shoulders an historical task: to defend our independence and freedom, while simultaneously protecting the peace and independence of the whole world. If the expansionist policy of the reactionary Chinese clique cannot be implemented any longer, that would be in the interest of the whole world. Vietnam can do this. Vietnam has fifty million people already. Vietnam has Lao and Cambodian friends and has secure terrain. Vietnam has our camp and all of mankind on its side. It is clear that we can do this.

. . . Do our comrades know of anyone in our Party, among our people, who suspects that we will lose to China? No one, of course. But we must maintain our friendly relations. We do not want national hatred. I repeat: I say this because I have never felt hatred for China. I do not feel this way. It is they who fight us. Today I also want you comrades to know that in this world, the one who has defended China is myself! That is true. Why so? Because during the June 1960 conference in Bucharest, sixty Parties rose to oppose China, but it was only I who defended China.[54] Our Vietnamese people is like that. I will go ahead and repeat this: However badly they behave, we know that their people are our friends. As for our side, we have no evil feelings towards China. Yet the plot of several [Chinese] leaders is a different matter. We refer to them as a clique only. We do not refer to their nation. We did not say the Chinese people are bad towards us. We say that it is the reactionary Beijing clique. I again say it strictly like this.

Thus, let us keep the situation under firm control, remain ready for combat, and never relax in our vigilance. It is the same with respect to China. I am confident that in fifty years, or even in one hundred years, socialism may succeed; and then we will not have this problem any longer. But it will take such a [long] time. Therefore, we must prepare and stand ready in all respects.

At present, no one certainly has doubts any more. But five years ago I was sure there [were no] comrades who doubted] that China could strike us. But there were. That was the case because [these] comrades had no knowledge about this matter.[55] But that was not the case with us [Le Duan and the leadership].[56] We knew that China had been attacking us for some ten years or more. Therefore we were not surprised [by the January 1979 Chinese attack].

Notes

1. Ministry of Foreign Affairs, *The Truth Concerning Vietnamese-Chinese Relations over the Past 30 Years* (Hanoi: Ministry of Foreign Affairs, 1979). The *White Paper* was also published in foreign languages, and in this chapter we refer to the French version: Ministère des Affaires Etrangères, *La vérité sur les relations vietnamo-chinoises durant les trente dernières années* (Hanoi: Ministère des Affaires Etrangères, 1979).

2. The Vietnamese *White Paper* was countered by a similar Chinese publication: *On the Vietnamese Foreign Ministry's White Paper Concerning Viet Nam–China Relations* (Beijing: Foreign Languages Press, 1979.) According to the Chinese reply, the Vietnamese *White Paper* was an attempt to "distort, tamper with and fabricate history in an effort to convert the history between the two countries in the 30 years which was interwoven mainly with friendship and co-operation into one in which China tried to take control of Viet Nam" (pp. 2–3). Unfortunately, the Chinese found that the Vietnamese "lies" were "not worth refuting one by one." Thus the Chinese *White Paper* is less detailed and less interesting for the historian than the Vietnamese one.

3. Odd Arne Westad, Chen Jian, Stein Tønnesson, Nguyen Vu Tung, and James G. Hershberg, eds., *77 Conversations between Chinese and Foreign Leaders on the Wars in Indochina, 1964–1977,* Cold War International History Project Working Paper 22 (Washington, D.C.: Woodrow Wilson International Center for Scholars, 1998), 6.

4. A useful, meticulous study of Vietnamese official rhetoric, including Le Duan's official publications, is found in Eero Palmujoki, "Revolutionary Pragmatism and Formal Marxism-Leninism: An Analysis of Vietnam's Foreign-Policy Argumentation from

the Fall of Saigon to the Collapse of the Socialist World System," Ph.D. dissertation, Tampere University, Finland, 1995. The study also includes a number of documents from before 1975.

5. This is based on Christopher Goscha's observation to the author that it would be surprising if Le Duan actually used the word "*tôi*" when speaking to Ho Chi Minh. Goscha points to the fact that Ho had long established a revolutionary and hierarchical family in which each member had (or did not have) his place (*anh hai, ba,* etc.) as part of a special cast.

6. The arrogance Le Duan displayed seems to confirm some of Bui Tin's allegations in his *Following Ho Chi Minh: Memoirs of a North Vietnamese Colonel* (London: Hurst, 1995), 66. Bui Tin also says: "Le Duan scarcely ever seemed to write anything down. He just said what he thought on the spur of the moment. He also stammered a lot and was difficult to listen to. That was what everybody felt. They all became weary trying to understand what he was saying because he also spoke ungrammatically" (p. 105).

7. William J. Duiker, *The Communist Road to Power in Vietnam,* 2nd ed. (Boulder, Colo.: Westview Press, 1996), 385 n. 4.

8. Ralph B. Smith, "Appendix: The Vietnam Workers' Party and Its Leaders, in *An International History of the Vietnam War, Volume 1: Revolution versus Containment, 1955–61* (London: Macmillan, 1983), 263–71.

9. On Ho Chi Minh, see William F. Duiker, *Hò Chi Minh* (New York: Hyperion, 2000).

10. Ralph B. Smith goes so far as to claim that Ho Chi Minh and Le Duan were rivals. Smith, *International History of the Vietnam War,* 129. Pierre Asselin makes the same claim, asserting that by 1965, Ho Chi Minh had, due also to his rapidly deteriorating health, "for all intents and purposes been sidelined." Pierre Asselin, "Le Duan and the Creation of an Independent Vietnamese State," paper presented at International Conference on Vietnamese Studies, Hanoi, July 1998, 2. Bui Tin, whose hero is General Giap, claims that Le Duc Tho, Le Duan, and Pham Hung "progressively tried to neutralise Ho Chi Minh" as well as Pham Van Dong in their struggle to downgrade Giap's role and reputation. Bui Tin, *Following Ho Chi Minh,* 32.

11. Pierre Asselin claims that Le Duan "epitomized Vietnamese disrespect for the overlordship of both those countries," the Soviet Union and China, and that his death in 1986 opened the door to improve Vietnam's relationship not only with China but also with the Soviet Union. Pierre Asselin, "Le Duan and the Creation," 8. In view of Vietnam's heavy dependence on the USSR between 1978 and 1986, this seems exaggerated, but there may be a grain of truth in it. Soviet archives will eventually reveal the truth.

12. Stephen J. Morris, *Why Vietnam Invaded Cambodia: Political Culture and the Causes of War* (Stanford, Calif.: Stanford University Press, 1999), 181. Morris bases this information on Soviet archival sources.

13. There may be some truth in Le Duan's impression. Although Deng Xiaoping personally ordered the Chinese "self-defensive counterattack" against Vietnam, it was also he who called off the operation in March, after the Chinese had suffered more than 30,000 casualties. Deng was criticized afterward for not having broken the fingers of the Vietnamese but merely hurt them. See Richard Baum, *Burying Mao: Chinese Politics in the Age of Deng Xiaoping* (Princeton, N.J.: Princeton University Press, 1994), 80.

14. "Aujourd'hui, les forces révolutionnaires ont grandi et occupent une position des plus favorables"; *Vérité sur les relations vietnamo-chinoises,* 58.

15. *Vérité sur les relations vietnamo-chinoises,* 58.

16. Westad et al., *77 Conversations,* contains short excerpts of minutes from three meetings between Zhou Enlai and Le Duan in 1971 (March 7 in Hanoi, July 13 in Hanoi, and November in Beijing). None of the excerpts include references to Geneva, but both Mao and Zhou had allegedly admitted earlier, when talking with Ho Chi Minh and Pham Van Dong, that a mistake had been made in Geneva. See the September 7, 1971 conversation: *77 Conversations,* ed. Westad et al., 180.

17. See François Joyaux, *La Chine et le règlement du premier conflit d'Indochine, Genève 1954* (Paris: Publications de la Sorbonne, 1979).

18. See Mari Olsen, *Solidarity and National Revolution: The Soviet Union and the Vietnamese Communists, 1954–1960* (Oslo: Institutt for Forsvarsstudier, 1997); and Ilya V. Gaiduk, *The Soviet Union and the Vietnam War* (Chicago: Ivan R. Dee, 1996).

19. Chen Jian, "China's Involvement in the Vietnam War, 1964–69," *China Quarterly* 142 (June 1995): 356–87, esp. 357.

20. However, according to Bui Tin, Le Duan told his official biographers in an interview in 1983 that he had been better than Uncle Ho. Ho always said "Yes" to what Stalin and Mao told him. "As for me, I dared to argue with Khrushchev and Mao." Bui Tin, *Following Ho Chi Minh,* 43.

21. Westad et al., *77 Conversations,* 74 n. 117, 163–64.

22. Chen, "China's Involvement in the Vietnam War," 368–69. See also Westad et al., *77 Conversations,* 85, where Le Duan tells Liu Shaoqi on April 8, 1965: "We want some volunteer pilots, volunteer soldiers . . . and other volunteers, including road and bridge engineering units."

23. The comparison may perhaps be farfetched, but an open kind of cooperation between Norwegian and Swedish historians has been initiated to prepare for the 2005 centenary of the breakup of the Swedish-Norwegian Union.

24. This document is a translation of a copy of extracts from the original. It was copied by hand in the Library of the People's Army, Hanoi. The translator of this document, Christopher E. Goscha, had *full authorization* to do so. The text is attributed to "Comrade B." It may have been written by Comrade B himself, but is much more likely to be the typed notes of someone who listened to an oral presentation by Comrade B. In the text, Comrade B reveals that during a Politburo meeting, he was referred to as Anh Ba (Brother Number Three), the alias we know Secretary General Le Duan used within the Vietnam Workers' Party (from 1976 "Vietnamese Communist Party"). Although the document is undated, it is clear from the text that it was written some time in 1979, in the wake of the Chinese invasion of Vietnam. This is supported by another highly charged document, published in 1979 at the behest of the Vietnamese Communist Party, which chronicles Chinese perfidy and, not entirely surprisingly, mentions many of the same incidents Le Duan describes in this document. See Ministry of Foreign Affairs, *Truth Concerning Vietnamese-Chinese Relations over the Past 30 Years.* The endnotes include references to the page numbers of the French version of the same document: Ministère des Affaires Etrangères, *Vérité sur les relations vietnamo-chinoises durant les trente dernières années.* The translator would like to thank Thomas Engelbert, Stein Tønnesson, Nguyen Hong Thoch, and above all an anonymous Vietnamese reader for their invaluable suggestions and corrections. The translator is responsible for all errors.

25. All ellipses indicated as such are in the original; translator's ellipses and comments are in brackets: [. . .].

26. The Geneva Accords of 1954 allowed the Pathet Lao, closely allied with the Democratic Republic of Vietnam, to maintain a provisional presence in the two Lao

provinces of Phongsaly and Sam Neua. No similar concession was made to Khmers allied with the Vietnamese during the resistance against the French.

27. Ministry of Foreign Affairs, *Truth Concerning Vietnamese-Chinese,* puts these high-level discussions on Laos in August 1961. (*Vérité sur les relations vietnamo-chinoises,* 34.)

28. Zhang Wentian was one of the members of the Chinese delegation who was present when Comrade B made this remark. He was also then deputy foreign minister, as well as a longtime member of the Politburo of the Chinese Communist Party. During the 1950s, he had been an alternate member of the Politburo in charge of relations with socialist countries.

29. Ministry of Foreign Affairs, *Truth Concerning Vietnamese-Chinese,* described the meeting, thus: "In an exchange of opinions with the Vietnamese leadership, the Deputy Chinese Foreign Minister, Zhang Wentian, expressed his view that one could carry on with guerrilla warfare in southern Vietnam. But afterwards, in accordance with a directive from Beijing, the Chinese Ambassador to Hanoi informed the Vietnamese side that this had not been the official opinion of the Central Committee of the Chinese Communist Party, but rather a personal view." Ministry of Foreign Affairs, *Truth Concerning Vietnamese-Chinese,* 40 (*Vérité sur les relations vietnamo-chinoises,* 31).

30. See Ministry of Foreign Affairs, *Truth Concerning Vietnamese-Chinese,* 60 (*Vérité sur les relations vietnamo-chinoises,* 47).

31. Le Duan is referring to the task of explaining the repatriation of southern cadres to the north. Le Duan conveniently forgets to mention that the Chinese helped the Vietnamese to win at Dien Bien Phu in 1954.

32. See Ministry of Foreign Affairs, *Truth Concerning Vietnamese-Chinese,* 60, where the Vietnamese reportedly told the Chinese in November 1972: "Vietnam is our country, you comrades, are not to negotiate with the United States about Vietnam. You have already admitted your mistake of 1954, now you should not commit the same mistake again." (*Vérité sur les relations vietnamo-chinoises,* 47.)

33. One of Le Duan's close advisers, Tran Quyen, has recently circulated his memoirs in Vietnam, providing interesting details on Le Duan's policy toward the Sino-Soviet split and the divisions within the Vietnamese Worker's Party on this issue in the 1960s. Tran Quyen, *Souvenirs of Le Duan (Excerpts),* undated, privately published, copy in the translator's possession.

34. Kang Sheng (1903–75), one of the People's Republic of China's top national security experts. He had been trained by the Soviet NKVD in the 1930s, and had become Mao's closest adviser on the problem of interpreting Soviet policies. Kang Sheng was Secretary of the Central Committee of the Chinese Communist Party (CCP) in 1962, and a member of the CCP Politburo from 1969; between 1973 and 1975 he was a member of the Standing Committee of the Politburo.

35. See Ministry of Foreign Affairs, *Truth Concerning Vietnamese-Chinese,* 43, in which the Vietnamese claimed that in exchange for renouncing all aid from the Soviet Union, Deng Xiaoping promised to make Vietnam China's number one priority in foreign aid. (*La vérité sur les relations vietnamo-chinoises,* 33.)

36. See Ministry of Foreign Affairs, *Truth Concerning Vietnamese-Chinese,* 43 (*Vérité sur les relations vietnamo-chinoises,* 33); also Tran, *Souvenirs of Le Duan.*

37. In November 1966, the Soviets charged the Chinese with having abandoned the world communist line adopted at the 1957 and 1960 Moscow Conferences. See also Tran, *Souvenirs of Le Duan.*

38. Ministry of Foreign Affairs, *Truth Concerning Vietnamese–Chinese,* has Mao making this statement to a delegation of the Vietnamese Workers Party in Wuhan in 1963. Mao is quoted by the Vietnamese as saying: "I will be the Chairman of 500 million poor peasants and I will send troops down into Southeast Asia." (*Vérité sur les relations vietnamo-chinoises,* 9.)

39. This could also translate as "and I'll beat yours as well" or "I could beat yours as well."

40. It is not exactly clear to the translator to whom Le Duan is referring as the "military."

41. This appears to be a reference to the words relayed to the Soviets by the Chinese ambassador to Moscow, on February 14, 1965, on the occasion of the fifteenth anniversary of the Sino-Soviet Treaty of Friendship, Alliance, and Mutual Assistance. As Ambassador Pan Tzu-li told the Soviets: "If the imperialists dare to attack the Soviet Union, the Chinese people, without the least hesitation, will fulfill their treaty obligations and together with the great Soviet people . . . will fight shoulder to shoulder until the final victory." Quoted by Donald S. Zagoria, *Moscow, Peking, Hanoi* (New York: Pegasus, 1967), 139–40.

42. Peng Zhen was a member of the Politburo of the Central Committee of the CCP from 1951 to 1969.

43. Li Chiang was vice chairman of the Committee for Economic Relations with Foreign Countries within the Chinese State Council from 1965 to 1967. Between 1968 and 1973, he was vice minister of foreign trade, and from 1973 served as minister of foreign trade.

44. This is a reference to Le Duan's trip in November 1977.

45. Le Duan forgets that until March 1945 even fewer French had been able to rule Vietnam without too much trouble.

46. On Chinese advisers, see Qiang Zhai, *China & the Vietnam Wars, 1950–1975* (Chapel Hill: University of North Carolina Press, 2000); and Christopher E. Goscha, "Le contexte asiatique de la guerre franco-vietnamienne: Réseaux, relations et économie," thesis, Ecole Pratique des Hautes Etudes, La Sorbonne, Paris, 2000, section chinoise.

47. While Le Duan often traveled to northern Vietnam during the war against the French, he is normally assumed to have remained in southern Vietnam at this time, as the head of the southern branch of the party, which became COSVN in the early 1950s. The present translator doubts that Le Duan traveled to China in 1952. Ho Chi Minh did, but not Le Duan.

48. For details, see chapter 6 of this volume.

49. This confirms that Comrade B is the same person as "Anh Ba." With the knowledge that Anh Ba is another name for Le Duan, Comrade B, by extension, is Le Duan. From events described in the text, this is certain, and Tran, *Souvenirs of Le Duan,* confirms it.

50. This may be a reference to Hoang Van Hoan. For a contending view, one must consult *A Drop in the Ocean (Memoirs of Revolution)* (Beijing: NXB Tin Viet Nam, 1986).

51. See also Tran, *Souvenirs of Le Duan.*

52. This is perhaps an allusion to the Soviet Union.

53. This type of warfare had existed in China as well, and elsewhere in the world of guerrilla warfare.

54. This took place in June 1960. For more on Le Duan's position on this matter, see Tran, *Souvenirs of Le Duan.* After the Party Congress of the Romanian Communist Party in June 1960, the Soviets organized an on-the-spot meeting with the leaders of the foreign delegations present, during which Khrushchev severely criticized the Chinese, especially Mao, whom he denounced as a "dogmatist" for his views on the question of peaceful coexistence. See Adam B. Ulam, *The Communists: The Story of Power and Lost Illusions, 1948–1991* (New York: Macmillan, 1992), 211.

55. This seems to be a stab at Hoang Van Hoan and no doubt others.

56. This is probably a reference to the group of leaders listening to Le Duan's talk, and it can be taken as an indication that the pro-Chinese comrades referred to above were not part of the group listening. See also Tran, *Souvenirs of Le Duan.*

15

Selected Conversations of Asian Communist Leaders on Indochina

The following documents are transcripts or excerpts of official conversations from assorted archives and other sources in China and, in a few cases, Vietnam, whose precise provenance for the most part cannot yet be publicly identified. They have been selected from a larger collection of such materials translated and published by the Cold War International History Project, the compilation *77 Conversations between Chinese and Foreign Leaders on the Wars in Indochina, 1964–1977.*

Mao Zedong, Pham Van Dong,[1] and Hoang Van Hoan,[2] Beijing, October 5, 1964, 7–7:50 (P.M.?)

Mao Zedong: According to Comrade Le Duan,[3] you had the plan to dispatch a division [to the South]. Probably you have not dispatched that division yet.[4] When should you dispatch it, the timing is important. Whether or not the United States will attack the North, it has not yet made the decision.

Now, it [the U.S.] is not even in a position to resolve the problem in South Vietnam. If it attacks the North, [it may need to] fight for one hundred years, and its legs will be trapped there. Therefore, it needs to consider carefully. The Americans have made all kinds of scary statements. They claim that they will run after [you], and will chase into your country, and that they will attack our air force. In my opinion, the meaning of these words is that they do not want us to fight a big war, and that [they do not want] our air force to attack their warships. If [we] do not attack their warships, they will not run after you. Isn't this what they mean? The Americans have something to hide.

Pham Van Dong: This is also our thinking. The United States is facing many difficulties, and it is not easy for it to expand the war. Therefore, our consideration is that we should try to restrict the war in South Vietnam to the sphere of special war, and should try to defeat the enemy within the sphere of special war. We should try our best not to let the U.S. imperialists turn the war in South Vietnam into a limited war, and try our best not to let the war be expanded to North Vietnam. We must adopt a very skillful strategy, and should not provoke it [the U.S.]. Our Politburo has made a decision on this matter, and today I am reporting it to Chairman Mao. We believe that this is workable.

Mao Zedong: Yes.

Pham Van Dong: If the United States dares to start a limited war, we will fight it, and will win it.

Mao Zedong: Yes, you can win it.[5] The South Vietnamese [puppet regime] has several hundred thousand troops. You can fight against them, you can eliminate half of them, and you can eliminate all of them. To fulfill these tasks is more than possible. It is impossible for the United States to send many troops to South Vietnam. The Americans altogether have 18 army divisions. They have to keep half of these divisions, i.e., nine of them, at home, and can send abroad the other nine divisions. Among these divisions, half are in Europe, and half are in the Asian-Pacific region. And they have stationed more divisions in Asia [than elsewhere in the region], namely, three divisions. One [is] in South Korea, one in Hawaii, and the third one in [original not clear]. They also placed fewer than one division of marine corps in Okinawa in Japan. Now all American troops in South Vietnam belong to the navy, and they are units under the navy system. As far as the American navy is concerned, they have put more ships in the Western Pacific than in Europe. In the Mediterranean, there is the Sixth Fleet;

here [in the Pacific] is the Seventh Fleet. They have deployed four aircraft carriers near you, but they have been scared away by you.

. . . .

Mao Zedong: If the Americans dare to take the risk to bring the war to the North, how should the invasion be dealt with? I have discussed this issue with Comrade Le Duan. [First], of course, it is necessary to construct defensive works along the coast. The best way is to construct defensive works like the ones [we had constructed] during the Korean War, so that you may prevent the enemy from entering the inner land. Second, however, if the Americans are determined to invade the inner land, you may allow them to do so. You should pay attention to your strategy. You must not engage your main force in a head-to-head confrontation with them, and must well maintain your main force. My opinion is that so long as the green mountain is there, how can you ever lack firewood?

Pham Van Dong: Comrade Le Duan has reported Chairman Mao's opinions to our Central Committee. We have conducted an overall review of the situations in the South and the North, and our opinion is the same as that of Chairman Mao. In South Vietnam, we should actively fight [the enemy]; and in North Vietnam, we should be prepared [for the enemy to escalate the war]. But we should also be cautious.

Mao Zedong: Our opinions are identical. Some other people say that we are belligerent. As a matter of fact, we are cautious. But it is not totally groundless to say [that we are belligerent].

. . . .

Mao Zedong: The more thoroughly you defeat them, the more comfortable they feel. For example, you beat the French, and they became willing to negotiate with you. The Algerians defeated the French badly, and France became willing to come to peace with Algeria. It has been proven that the more badly you beat them, the more comfortable they feel.

. . . .

Mao Zedong: Is it true that you are invited to attend the [UN] Security Council meetings?

Zhou Enlai: This is still a secret. The invitation was made through U Thant.[6]

Mao Zedong: And U Thant made it through whom?

Zhou Enlai: The Soviets.

Mao Zedong: So the Soviet Union is the middleman.

Pham Van Dong: According to the Soviet ambassador to Vietnam, they met with U Thant on the one hand, and with [U.S. secretary of state Dean] Rusk on the other.

Mao Zedong: It is not completely a bad thing to negotiate. You have already earned the qualification to negotiate. It is another matter whether or not the negotiation will succeed. We have also earned our qualification to negotiate [with the Americans]. We are now negotiating with the Americans on the Taiwan issue, and the Sino-American ambassadorial talks are now under way in Warsaw. The talks have lasted for more than nine years.

Zhou Enlai: More than 120 meetings have been held.

Mao Zedong: The talks will continue. One time, during a meeting at Geneva, they did not want to continue the talks. They withdrew their representatives, leaving there only one person in charge of communication and liaison matters. We gave them a blow by sending them a letter, setting up a deadline for them to send back their representative. They did return to the talks later, but they did not meet the deadline we set for them: they were a few days late. They said that it was an ultimatum by us. At that time, some among ourselves believed that we should not set the deadline for them, nor should we make the harsh statement, and that by doing so it became an ultimatum. But we did, and the Americans did [return to the talks].

Source: Odd Arne Westad, Chen Jian, Stein Tønnesson, Nguyen Vu Tung, and James G. Hershberg, eds., 77 Conversations between Chinese and Foreign Leaders on the Wars in Indochina, 1964–1977, Cold War International History Project Working Paper 22 (Washington, D.C.: Woodrow Wilson International Center for Scholars, 1998), 74–77. Also available on Cold War International History Project Web site Virtual Archive: Collection New Evidence on the Vietnam/Indochina Wars (http://wwics.si.edu/index .cfm?topic_id=1409&fuseaction=library.document&id=83).

Zhou Enlai and Ho Chi Minh,[7] Hanoi, March 1, 1965

Zhou Enlai: When [Nikita] Khrushchev stepped down and the new leadership of the Soviet Party took power [in mid-October 1964], we thought that their policy would change somewhat in any case. This was why we proposed that we all should go to Moscow to celebrate, while at the same time observing the situation there. But the result made us greatly disappointed. As far as the new Soviet leadership is concerned, we believed that it was not sufficient to observe it just once, and we should observe for some more time. Now it is clear. The new Soviet Party leadership is carrying out nothing but Khrushchevism. It is absolutely impossible for them to change.

. . . .

Kosygin suggested that the socialist countries should have a joint statement in support of Vietnam.[8] I told him that each country had its own position and judgment, so it would also be good if each country had its own statement. However, during their visit to Vietnam they [the Soviets] could have a joint statement [with Vietnam].

. . . .

So in our course of revolution, and in our struggle against the U.S., the matters of top secrecy should not be disclosed to them. Of course, we can mention the principles which we also want to publicize. We oppose [the Soviet] military activities that include the sending of missile battalions and 2 MiG-21 aircraft as well as the proposal to establish an airlift using 45 planes for weapon transportation. We also have to be wary of the military instructors. Soviet experts have withdrawn, so what are their purposes [when they] wish to come back? We have had experience in the past when there were subversive activities in China, Korea, and Cuba. We, therefore, should keep an eye on their activities, namely their transportation of weapons and military training. Otherwise, the relations between our two countries may turn from good to bad, thus affecting cooperation between our two countries.

Source: Odd Arne Westad, Chen Jian, Stein Tønnesson, Nguyen Vu Tung, and James G. Hershberg, eds., *77 Conversations between Chinese and Foreign Leaders on the Wars in Indochina, 1964–1977,* Cold War International History Project Working Paper 22 (Washington, D.C.: Woodrow Wilson International Center for Scholars, 1998), 77–78. Also available on Cold War International History Project Web site Virtual Archive: Collection New Evidence on the Vietnam/Indochina Wars (http://wwics.si.edu/index.cfm?topic_id=1409&fuseaction=library.document&id=378).

Zhou Enlai and Pakistani President Ayub Khan,[9] Karachi, April 2, 1965

Zhou Enlai: I have recently visited two countries in Africa, they were both very much concerned about the development of the situation in Southeast Asia. I know that during [PRC Foreign Minister] Marshal Chen Yi's visit to Pakistan, he also had some discussion with Your Excellency.

Ayub Khan: We are very much worried. We don't know when the large-scale bombing will end.

Zhou Enlai: The Americans think that by expanding their aggression in

South Vietnam and escalating their bombing in North Vietnam, they can bring Vietnam to its knees. This kind of thinking will fail completely.

During my recent visit, the African and European friends were all concerned about this issue. In sum, there are three questions. (1) Under the circumstance that the United States is expanding its aggression and strengthening pressure, even if the people of Vietnam and Indo-China are able to resist America's aggression, they will suffer heavy losses; if they are unable to resist, they may compromise in the face of the tremendous threat. They (the friends in Africa and Europe) worry that if Vietnam is to yield to America's pressure, [the people] in other parts of the world will also suffer from heavy losses. (2) The worry that the war may expand, gradually developing into a world war. (3) Between compromise and world war, does there exist the possibility of [solving the issue through] negotiations?

I have analyzed and answered these questions.

(1) There exists no possibility that Vietnam will yield [to American pressure]. On March 22, the NLF [National Liberation Front] of South Vietnam issued an extremely strong statement. They firmly believe that they can defeat the puppet troops, and that the puppet troops in South Vietnam will collapse gradually. The troops the United States is able to send can only occupy a small portion of cities and sea ports. According to America's planning, they can only dispatch, at the most, three divisions to South Vietnam: one is an infantry division from America, one is a marine division from Okinawa, and the last one is put together by units from the Philippines, South Korea, and Thailand. These troops can only be used to defend sea ports, cities, and military bases in South Vietnam. The Americans hope to use these troops to replace the formal units of the puppet troops in South Vietnam, using the latter to deal with the people in South Vietnam. The NLF in South Vietnam is confident that the puppet troops will be eliminated. The American authorities worry what their troops should do if the puppet troops are eliminated. If they are far away from their strongholds, they will face the same fate of being defeated. Now their air and land forces are being eliminated continuously. The puppet regime in South Vietnam has changed about a dozen times, and the Americans can trust virtually none of them. The Ngo Dinh Diem brothers were assassinated by the Americans. The Americans are considering signing an agreement with the puppet regime, making it clear that America sends troops to Vietnam in accordance with the request of the puppet regime. But if the puppet regime in Saigon no longer exists, will the agreement still be effective? This indeed will become something unheard of. The United States signed many treaties with Jiang

Jieshi. But after the People's Liberation Army occupied Nanjing, these treaties could no longer be maintained—only Taiwan is an exception. Now the Americans again try to use agreements to serve their purpose in South Vietnam. In actuality, the United States has long realized that it will certainly be defeated in South Vietnam, but it is unwilling to withdraw, and it tries to use this tactic to put up a last ditch struggle.

On the other hand, the United States tries to use the bombardment of North Vietnam to force the North to surrender. In August and September last year, the United States bombed North Vietnam once or twice a week. From late March this year to now, there is bombing almost every day. In the face of this, the NLF in South Vietnam stated that no matter how long the bombing lasts, it will continue the fighting, until winning victory. The government of the Democratic Republic of Vietnam supports the NLF's statement, and is preparing to provide it with all kinds of assistance. The government of [North] Korea has also issued a statement to echo [that of the DRV]. China published an editorial on March 25 in *Renmin Ribao* [People's Daily], expressing determination to support the people in South Vietnam to win victory, preparing to offer all kinds of support, including weapons, to the people in South Vietnam. When the people in South Vietnam are in need, China will send its personnel to fight together with the people in South Vietnam. Although this is only an editorial, it has caused strong reaction in foreign opinions, especially in the United States. Foreign Minister Chen Yi, in his response to the foreign minister of the DRV, has also confirmed this stand. The public opinion in the world has condemned the United States. In the face of American bombardment, the DRV has started evacuating the population and is determined to support the brothers in South Vietnam to carry the resistance to the end.

Under these circumstances, what is America's policy? The propaganda in the United States has reflected the contradictions it is facing. On the one hand, American propaganda claims that if Vietnam does not stop its "aggression," the United States will expand the war of aggression. This is the most ridiculous bandit-style logic of imperialism. According to this logic, South Vietnam's resistance to American aggression is "aggression," and North Vietnam's support to South Vietnam is "aggression" against one's own compatriots. If so, the resistance by the NLF in Algeria to the French colonists becomes Algeria's "aggression" against Algeria, and Egypt's taking back the Suez Canal becomes the Egyptians' "aggression" against the Egyptians. This question became crystal clear as soon as I discussed it with the Algerians and Egyptians. This is nothing but America's bandit-style logic.

On the other hand, the United States is propagandizing that the expansion of the war will be limited to South Vietnam, and that it only wants North Vietnam to stop its support to South Vietnam. The United States is hoping to separate South Vietnam from North Vietnam, thus isolating the South.

When the United States escalates the bombardment of North Vietnam, it again claims that the expansion of the bombing will be limited to North Vietnam, and that it has no intention to fight a war with China. It has not only propagandized this way, it has also made statements along this line in the Sino-American ambassadorial talks in Warsaw. After meetings in Washington, the British foreign minister said that the United States had confirmed to Britain that it will not expand the war to China. The British prime minister thus said that he had no worries at all. This means that the United States now aims at separating China from Vietnam, making Vietnam isolated.

The policy of the United States is a wavering one. First, it asks the Vietnamese to stop "aggression" against the Vietnamese, this is groundless. Second, it has been wavering on expanding the war. Whenever it takes a step, it will look around for taking the next step. It does not have a fixed policy. [U.S. ambassador to South Vietnam Maxwell] Taylor[10] returned to Washington to discuss this issue, that is, whether it is beneficial for the United States to send troops to South Vietnam, and to what extent should the bombing be expanded.

After the publication of the *Renmin Ribao* editorial and response from Foreign Minster Chen Yi to the foreign minister of the DRV, the United States said that the Chinese were only paying lip service, which would play no role in the resistance by the people in South Vietnam. Sometimes the United States has said that it was uncertain if China would really enter the war. This means that America's policy is not established on a clearly defined foundation. It has conducted aggression, realizing however that reason is not on its side and that its position is not sound, yet it is unwilling to accept defeat and to withdraw. Because reason is not on its side, its policy is wavering. To withdraw is the best way for it to save face, but to continue to act recklessly will cause it to lose more face.

Ayub Khan: If the United States continues to put pressure on North and South Vietnam, China will have to send its troops. It seems that the United States has no doubt about this. What it doubts is whether or not the Soviet Union will provide support.

Zhou Enlai: What you have said has some basis. I will discuss it later when I discuss whether the war will develop into a world war. Now, let me first discuss the first question, namely, the question concerning American pressure. Vietnam will not surrender under pressure. America has devoted a large portion of its strength to Vietnam and the whole of Indo-China, the result can only be [America] being defeated and losing face.

When Your Excellency visits the United States, if the Americans ask what China will do, Your Excellency may convey the following three points to the United States:

First, China will not take the initiative to provoke a war against the United States. Taiwan is a case in point. We have every right to recover Taiwan, but we have never used armed force. Although the Seventh Fleet of the United States is stationed in the Taiwan Strait, still we have been conducting talks with the United States in Warsaw.

Second, China means what it says, and China will honor whatever international obligations it has undertaken.

Ayub Khan: We know this.

Zhou: There is proof for the second point. Less than one year after China's liberation [in October 1949], the United States initiated a war of aggression in Korea, while at the same time dispatching the Seventh Fleet into the Taiwan Strait, attempting to prevent China from recovering Taiwan. China, via India's then ambassador to China, told the United States: If the United States crossed the 38th parallel and approached the Yalu River, it is certain that China will not stand by without making a response. The Indian government indeed informed the U.S. government at that time. But the United States would not listen, not believing that China would support Korea. When Your Excellency visits the United States, please convey these points to them. Maybe they will again not believe us. Maybe, as Your Excellency has predicted, they will believe us. Both possibilities exist. However, our friend has changed this time, it is not India but Pakistan.

Ayub Khan: The United States should understand that if it puts too much pressure, China will provide support. Everyone with a mind should understand this. The United States says that it will not expand the war to China. It means to see to what extent the Soviets will be involved. The United States believes that probably the Soviet Union will not be involved, and whether or not it will expand the war will depend on to what extent the Soviet Union will provide support.

Zhou Enlai: (2) Will the war be expanded into a world war? Your Excellency is a marshal. You know that the rules of war are not based on human will. The United States believes that if it does not expand the war in Vietnam to China, China will not support Vietnam. Our position is that even if the war is not expanded to China, still China will support Vietnam, so long as the DRV requests it, so long as the NLF in South Vietnam requests it. When the war expands, it is impossible to draw a line. This is like the spread of a fire. The United States wants to play with fire and to take the risk. China hopes to extinguish the fire. The United States is not willing to do so, and is putting gas to the fire. As a result, the fire will be larger and larger. The expansion of the war is caused by the United States, not initiated by us. Although China has adopted an attitude of restraint, if the United States expands the war on this battlefield, the war flame will spread. The United States says that this is a regional war, and that it is doing limited bombing and limited expansion. But, even though it may want to limit the expansion of the war, in reality it cannot limit the war's expansion. Although the United States threatens that if the war in Indochina develops into a Korean-type war, it will not, as it did during the Korean War, limit itself to a regional war, but will expand the war to China, so that China will no longer be the shelter. We know this. China is prepared.

We are prepared. This is the third point Your Excellency may want to convey to the United States. The United States says that China has not made war preparations, using this to deceive its people. China does not want to fight a war with the United States. In the broadcast speech Your Excellency made yesterday, you said that China is a peace-loving country. When Your Excellency was visiting Beijing and Shanghai, you saw no signs of war preparations among the people there. But, in a military sense, we cannot but make due preparations. If the United States brings the war flame to our side, we have to extinguish it. The United States tries to scare China by saying that a Korean-type war will not be limited to the DRV and Indo-China, this is completely useless.

If the United States expands the war, the war will gradually be expanded to China. We are prepared both materially and spiritually. We hope that when our friends in Asia have the opportunity to talk to American people, they should tell them that they should see the danger involved in the American government's playing with fire. The possibility of an expanding war exists, and the American people will be brought into a great war.

The question is: After the expansion of the war, will it continue to expand? Your Excellency asked a moment ago if the war expands to China will the Soviet Union intervene. We are not going to answer this question, because you will be visiting the Soviet Union tomorrow. You can ask the Soviet friends, and let them answer it. As far as we are concerned, we are not considering this issue, and not expecting support from the Soviet Union.

If the United States expands the war to China, it will really suffer. Two marshals in the world have said this, you are the third marshal. Britain's Marshal [Bernard Law] Montgomery twice visited China. He advised his American friends that if America is to attack China, it may enter China, but will not get out. A new front is created on the front-line, but the rear will be in confusion. Before his death, [U.S. general Douglas] MacArthur also told this to Eisenhower and Kennedy. Johnson may remember this. If the United States imposes war on the Chinese people, the Chinese people will resist to the end, and there exists no other outcome. Under this circumstance, a faction in the United States says that the United States may only conduct bombing and will not use land forces. Your Excellency is a marshal, you know that a war fought in such a way will not solve the problem. If the United States conducts bombing from the air, we may carry out activities, using other strategy, everywhere on the ground. If the United States is to carry out extensive bombing in China, that is war, and a war has no boundaries. Every person in the military knows this. China will be [strong] enough to make the United States suffer, how can it expand the war to other parts of the world? Therefore, it is unnecessary to answer whether or not the Soviet Union will be involved, and we do not need to expect Soviet support. If the United States bases its policy on the premise that China and the Soviet Union will not cooperate to resist aggression and thus expand the war, it will cause an even earlier defeat. The Chinese people will bear more sacrifice for the interests of the people in the world, that is worth it.

To summarize, the three points are: (1) China will not provoke a war against the United States. (2) We Chinese mean what we say. (3) China is prepared.

We are intimate friends, and this is why I tell you the truth. Especially since you are going to visit the Soviet Union and the United States, it is even more necessary to tell you the truth in clear language.[11]

It is impossible for the United States to pass China's test. [If the war is to] expand into a world war, the United States will be defeated even more badly.

(3) Is it possible the problem will be solved through negotiations? China does not fundamentally oppose holding negotiations. Any question, in the final analysis, has to be solved through negotiation. However, the conditions and timing for holding negotiations on the South Vietnam question are not mature. The United States has introduced conditions to begin negotiations, that is, Vietnam should stop "aggression," the NLF in South Vietnam should stop resistance, so that the puppet regime will be given some breath-

ing space, and the United States will continue to oppress South Vietnam. The United States claims that any action on the part of the South Vietnamese people has been directed by North Vietnam. It is impossible to conduct negotiations under these conditions. Such negotiations will not solve the question even if they are to last for ten years.

The Chinese-American negotiations have lasted for ten years, and have resulted in nothing. We are patient. Taiwan is that much land, and will not grow any larger. Jiang Jieshi is getting older and older, and he will die sooner or later. China is becoming stronger day by day. Some day the question will be solved through negotiations. This is what is workable on the Taiwan question. But the same is not workable on the South Vietnam question. If the resistance is stopped, even if the negotiations will last for only one year, more people will die during this period than during war time. The NLF in South Vietnam points out that this is not the time for negotiations. This stand is correct.

Source: Odd Arne Westad, Chen Jian, Stein Tønnesson, Nguyen Vu Tung, and James G. Hershberg, eds., *77 Conversations between Chinese and Foreign Leaders on the Wars in Indochina, 1964–1977,* Cold War International History Project Working Paper 22 (Washington, D.C.: Woodrow Wilson International Center for Scholars, 1998), 79–85. Also available on Cold War International History Project Web site Virtual Archive: Collection New Evidence on the Vietnam/Indochina Wars (http://wwics.si.edu/index.cfm?topic_id=1409&fuseaction=library.document&id=38).

Zhou Enlai and Pham Van Dong, Beijing, October 9, 1965, 4 p.m.[12]

Zhou Enlai: . . . During the time Khrushchev was in power, the Soviets could not divide us because Khrushchev did not help you much. The Soviets are now assisting you. But their help is not sincere. The U.S. likes this very much. I want to tell you my opinion. It will be better without the Soviet aid. This may be an ultra leftist opinion. Yet, it is mine, not the CCP [Chinese Communist Party] Central Committee's.

. . . Now, the problem of international volunteers going to Vietnam is very complicated. But as you have mentioned this problem we will discuss it and then you can make your decision.

As you have asked for my opinion, I would like to tell you the following: I do not support the idea of Soviet volunteers going to Vietnam, nor [do I support] Soviet aid to Vietnam. I think it will be better without it. It is my own opinion, not the opinion of the Party Central Committee. Comrades Peng Zhen and Luo Ruiqing[13] who are present here today also agree with me.

[As to] Vietnam, we always want to help. In our mind, our thoughts, we never think of selling out Vietnam. But we are always afraid of the revisionists standing between us.[14]

Zhou Enlai: . . . The war has been expanded to North Vietnam. It is, therefore, impossible for Laos and Cambodia not to get involved. Sihanouk understands it. When we were on a sightseeing tour on the Yangtze, I asked him how he would deal with the situation and whether he needed weapons. At present, China has provided Cambodia with 28,000 pieces of weapons. Sihanouk told me that this amount was enough to equip Cambodian regular and provincial forces and that all U.S. weapons have been replaced.

I also asked him whether he needed more weapons. Sihanouk replied that because he could not afford to increase the number of troops, the weapons were enough. He only asked for anti-aircraft artillery and anti-tank weapons.

This is what he replied to my questions about weapons. He also added that if war broke out, he would leave Phnom Penh for the countryside where he had already built up bases. Last year, President Liu [Shaoqi] told Sihanouk: "Large-scale fighting in your country is not equal to the [fighting] at our border." If the U.S. launches attacks along the Chinese border, China will draw its forces there, thus reducing the burden for Cambodia. Sihanouk now understands and prepares to leave for the countryside and to regain the urban areas whenever good conditions prevail. That is what he thinks. Yet, whether his cadres can carry out this policy is a different thing.

These changes in the situation show that Sihanouk has been prepared to act in case of an invasion by the U.S. At present, Sihanouk strongly supports the NLF because he knows that the more you fight the U.S. the fewer difficulties there will be for the Cambodians. In addition, Sihanouk understands that he needs China. But at the same time, Sihanouk does not want to take sides because he is afraid of losing the support of France, losing his neutral position. At least, what he says shows that he seems to think of and understand the logic of the war: if the U.S. expands the war to North Vietnam, it will spread all over Indochina.[15]

Source: Odd Arne Westad, Chen Jian, Stein Tønnesson, Nguyen Vu Tung, and James G. Hershberg, eds., *77 Conversations between Chinese and Foreign Leaders on the Wars in Indochina, 1964–1977,* Cold War International History Project Working Paper 22

(Washington, D.C.: Woodrow Wilson International Center for Scholars, 1998), 89–91. Also available on Cold War International History Project Web site Virtual Archive: Collection New Evidence on the Vietnam/Indochina Wars (http://wwics.si.edu/index.cfm? topic_id=1409&fuseaction=library.document&id=283).

Zhou Enlai, Chen Yi, and Xuan Thuy,[16] Beijing, Great Hall of the People, May 7, 1968, 9:45 P.M.

Zhou Enlai: The situation of the negotiation on the Korean issue was different from your situation. At that time, [the Korean issue] concerned half of Korea, but the situation you are facing now concerns the unification of Vietnam. Half of Vietnam was the problem [we were facing] fourteen years ago. When Comrade Mao Zedong met President Ho Chi Minh the last time,[17] he said that it was possible that our signing the [1954] Geneva agreement was a mistake. After we signed the agreement, many soldiers of South Vietnam retreated to the North. The United States refused to sign the agreement. If we also refused to sign the agreement, there were reasons for us to do so. But President Ho said that there were benefits involved in [signing the agreement]. By doing so, after a period of difficulty, during which Ngo Dinh Diem made arrests, detentions, and suppression, causing the deaths of over 200,000, the people of South Vietnam, with this painful experience, had been awakened to make revolution, which led to today's situation. Therefore, the situation of the Korean negotiations was quite similar to the situation around the Geneva Conference of 1954. The Korean negotiations were conducted on the battlefield. The war lasted for almost three years, and the negotiations lasted for two years. But when the Korean issue was discussed at the Geneva Conference in 1954, the war had already stopped, and it was then difficult to solve the problem through negotiation. Whatever we said they would not agree. Therefore, the Korean negotiations resulted in only an armistice, and no other political agreement had been reached. On the issue of withdrawing [foreign] troops from Korea, they refused to discuss. We withdrew our troops [from Korea] in 1958, but they refused to withdraw their troops. The situation you are facing this time is different. You are negotiating with the Americans step by step. This might be fine. Take one step and you may watch for the next step. But the fundamental question is that what you cannot get on the battlefield, no matter how you try, you will not get at the negotiating table. Dien Bien Phu set up the 17th parallel, therefore the Geneva Conference could reach an agreement. Probably Comrade Pham Van Dong had conveyed our attitude after returning to Vietnam. It is our opinion that you have agreed to [negotiate] too fast and too hurriedly, which might have left the Americans with an impression that you are eager to negotiate. Comrade Mao Zedong told Comrade Pham Van Dong that negotiation is acceptable, but [first] you must maintain a lofty stance. Secondly, the Americans, the subordinate countries, and the puppets have a military force of over 1,000,000, and, before their backbone has been broken, or before five or six of their fingers have been broken, they will not accept the defeat, and they will not leave.

. . . .

Chen Yi: You should not inform the Soviets about developments in the negotiations with the U.S. because they can inform the U.S.

Zhou Enlai: You should not inform them what you plan to do as there have been cases of disclosure of military and diplomatic secrets by the revisionists. You should be highly vigilant.

Source: Odd Arne Westad, Chen Jian, Stein Tønnesson, Nguyen Vu Tung, and James G. Hershberg, eds., *77 Conversations between Chinese and Foreign Leaders on the Wars in Indochina, 1964–1977,* Cold War International History Project Working Paper 22 (Washington, D.C.: Woodrow Wilson International Center for Scholars, 1998), 134–35. Also available on Cold War International History Project Web site Virtual Archive: Collection New Evidence on the Vietnam/Indochina Wars (http://wwics.si.edu/index .cfm?topic_id=1409&fuseaction=library.document&id=312).

Chen Yi and Le Duc Tho,[18] Beijing, October 17, 1968[19]

Chen Yi: (1) Since last April when you accepted the U.S. partial cessation of bombing and held peace talks with them, you have lost the initiative in the negotiations to them. Now, you accept quadripartite negotiations. You lost to them once more. Therefore, this will cause more losses for the Vietnamese people, especially the people in the South.

(2) At present, Washington and Saigon are publicizing the negotiations, showing the fact that you have accepted the conditions put forward by the U.S. Your returning home for party instruction all the more proves it to the world's people. With your acceptance of the quadripartite negotiations, you handed the puppet government legal recognition, thus eliminating the National Liberation Front's status as the unique legal representative of the

people in the South. So, the Americans have helped their puppet regime to gain legal status while you have made the Front lose its own prestige. This makes us wonder whether you have strengthened the enemy's position while weakening ours. You are acting in contradiction to the teachings of President Ho, the great leader of the Vietnamese people, thus destroying President Ho's prestige among the Vietnamese people.

(3) This time, your acceptance of quadripartite negotiations will help Johnson and [U.S. vice president and Democratic Party presidential candidate Hubert H.] Humphrey win their elections, thus letting the people in the South remain under the rule of the U.S. imperialists and their puppets. You do not liberate the people in the South but cause them more losses. We do not want you to make another mistake. We believe that the people in the South of Vietnam do not want to surrender and they will win the war. But now the cause is more difficult and the price [for victory] more expensive.

(4) In our opinion, in a very short time, you have accepted the compromising and capitulationist proposals put forward by the Soviet revisionists. So, between our two parties and the two governments of Vietnam and China, there is nothing more to talk about. Nevertheless, as President Ho has said, our relationship is one of both comrades and brothers; we will therefore consider the changes of the situation in November and will have more comments.

Le Duc Tho: On this matter, we will wait and see. And the reality will give us the answer. We have gained experience over the past 15 years. Let reality justify.

Chen Yi: We signed the Geneva accords in 1954 when the U.S. did not agree to do so. We withdrew our armed forces from the South to the North, thus letting the people in the South be killed. We at that time made a mistake in which we [Chinese] shared a part.

Le Duc Tho: Because we listened to your advice.[20]

Chen Yi: You just mentioned that in the Geneva Conference, you made a mistake because you followed our advice. But this time, you will make another mistake if you do not take our words into account.

Source: Odd Arne Westad, Chen Jian, Stein Tønnesson, Nguyen Vu Tung, and James G. Hershberg, eds., *77 Conversations between Chinese and Foreign Leaders on the Wars in Indochina, 1964–1977,* Cold War International History Project Working Paper 22 (Washington, D.C.: Woodrow Wilson International Center for Scholars, 1998), 138–40. Also available on Cold War International History Project Web site Virtual Archive: Collection New Evidence on the Vietnam/Indochina Wars (http://wwics.si.edu/index.cfm? topic_id=1409&fuseaction=library.document&id=359).

Mao Zedong and Pham Van Dong,[21]
Beijing, November 17, 1968

Mao Zedong: You have been here some days, haven't you? I am a bit bureaucratic.

Pham Van Dong: How are you, Chairman Mao?

Mao Zedong: Not very well. I have had a cough for some days. It is time to go to Heaven. It seems that I am summoned to meet the Good God. How is President Ho?

Pham Van Dong: [He is] well. He is better than [when] he was in Beijing. The main reason is that he received good medical treatment in Beijing, and since he came back, he is doing well.

Mao Zedong: The weather in Beijing may not be suitable for President Ho.

Pham Van Dong: Very suitable.

Mao Zedong: In my opinion, maybe Guangzhou is better.

Pham Van Dong: On behalf of our President Ho, our Politburo, I would like to convey to you, Chairman Mao, Vice Chairman Lin and other comrades our honorable greetings.

Mao Zedong: Thank you.

Pham Van Dong: Today, in our delegation there are two comrades from the South (pointing to Comrade Muoi Cuc, and Comrade Le Duc Anh).[22]

Mao Zedong: Is it the first time Comrade Le Duc Anh came to China? (Shaking Muoi Cuc's hands, Chairman Mao said that they had met each other in 1966.)

Le Duc Anh: I came to China once, in 1962, but it is the first time I meet Chairman Mao.

Mao Zedong: I am bureaucratic. You came here, but I haven't met you. You may dismiss me from my post because of my being bureaucratic. We are going to convene a Party congress, and the congress may dismiss me. It may be good, too. Maybe now I should relax, only do small things such as sweeping my house. Recently, I haven't engaged in any battle.

You want to have talks with the U.S., and so do they with you. The U.S. has great difficulties in their undertaking. They have three problems to be dealt with, namely, the issues in America, mainly in the U.S., in Europe, and in Asia. They already have been involved in Asia for 4 or five years now. It is not even-handed. The U.S. capitalists who invested in Europe should be displeased and disagree. And in U.S. history, the Americans always let others engage in wars first and only get involved when the wars are half way over. But after the Second World War, they started fighting in Korea and then in Vietnam. They mainly fought these wars themselves, with little involvement of other countries. You call it a special war, a limited war, but for the U.S., they concentrate all their forces on it. At present their allies in Europe are complaining a lot, saying that [the United States] reduces the number of its troops [in Europe] and withdraws its experienced troops and good equipment [from Europe], not to mention the troops withdrawn from South Korea and Hawaii. The U.S. has a population of 200 million people, but it cannot stand wars. If they want to mobilize some tens of thousand of troops, they must spend a lot of time and money.

. . . .

Mao Zedong: After some years of struggling against them, you should consider not only your difficulties but also your enemy's. You have been fighting for more than a dozen of years. Twenty-three years have passed since the Japanese surrender in 1945 but your country is still existing. You have fought the Japanese, French, and now you are fighting the Americans. But Vietnam still exists like other countries, and more than that, it has developed to a greater extent.

Pham Van Dong: That is true.

Mao Zedong: Why was the Geneva Conference convened? ([he] asks Comrade Zhou Enlai).

In the past, I did say that we had made a mistake when we went to the Geneva conference in 1954. At that time, President Ho Chi Minh wasn't totally satisfied. It was difficult for President Ho to give up the South, and now, when I think twice, I see that he was right. The mood of the people in the South at that time was rising high. Why did we have the Geneva conference? Perhaps, France wanted it.

Zhou Enlai: It was proposed by the Soviet Union. Khrushchev at that time was in power. And in January 1954, the Soviets wanted to solve the problem.

Mao Zedong: Now, I cannot remember the whole story. But I see that it would be better if the conference could have been delayed for one year, so the troops from the North could come down [to the South] and defeat [the enemy].

Pham Van Dong: At that time, we were fighting in the whole country, having no division between the North and the South.

Mao Zedong: We had to fight in a sweeping manner. The world public opinion at that time also wanted to have this conference. In my opinion, at that time the French wanted to withdraw, the U.S. was not yet [ready] to come, and Diem was facing many difficulties.[23] I think that to withdraw our forces [to the North] meant that we lent them a helping hand. I once talked about it with President Ho, and today I talk about it again with you. Maybe my opinion is incorrect. But I think that we lost an opportunity, as in the treaty, there is a provision on the withdrawal of troops.

Zhou Enlai: To withdraw the armed forces.

Mao Zedong: But it is not a very serious problem. It is the simple question of killing. And killing led to war. When the war broke out, the Americans came, at first as advisers, and then as combat troops. But now, they again say that the Americans in Vietnam are advisers.

Pham Van Dong: It is impossible for them to be advisers.

Mao Zedong: I, however, think that they will be advisers.

Pham Van Dong: Let Comrade Muoi speak on that.

Muoi Cuc: Dear Uncle Mao! Our President Ho, Political Bureau and Party Central Committee give us the order to fight until there is no American left in our country, even as advisers. Our blood has been shed for several years now. Why do we have to accept them to stay as advisers?

Mao Zedong: So, it will take some time if you do not accept them as advisers.

Muoi Cuc: It is correct, Uncle Mao. We are persistently fighting until the South becomes entirely independent and free, until national unification is attained. By so doing, we adhere to the order by our President Ho as well as your [orders]. This is what our Party Central Committee thinks and also what the entire Vietnamese people desire.

Mao Zedong: It is good to think that way. It is imperative to fight and to talk at the same time. It will be difficult if you rely only on negotiations to request their departure.

Pham Van Dong: They will not go anywhere and just stay.

Mao Zedong: As far as fighting is concerned, the U.S. relies on its air force. There are about 9 or 10 U.S. divisions. The number of American troops fighting in the Korean War was bigger. It is said that they have 5 divisions—approximately 200 thousand troops—deployed in Europe. But this number is overstated. The number of airplanes has been reduced. Some troops have been sent to reinforce the Seventh Fleet. I do not know how many divisions are deployed in the U.S.

Wang Xinting: Nine divisions. [Ye Jianying corrected: 6 divisions and 4 regiments.]

Pham Van Dong: The best American divisions are deployed in South Vietnam.

Mao Zedong: [The United States faces three problems:] First the lack of troops; second the lack of equipment and last the lack of experienced people.

Zhou Enlai: They have 6 divisions and 6 regiments deployed in the U.S.

Mao Zedong: But the battlefield in Vietnam is of first priority. There, they have 9 divisions and 4 regiments. But as far as I remember, they had 7 divisions there.

Zhou Enlai: Later, they were reinforced.

Mao Zedong: I still have not understood why the U.S. imperialists went to Southeast Asia and what interests the American capitalists found there. Exploitation of natural resources? Of course, the region is rich in natural resources. Oil, rubber in Indonesia. Rubber in Malaysia. Is there rubber in your country?

Pham Van Dong: Plenty.

Mao Zedong: Rubber and tea. But I do not think that the U.S. needs food or plants.

Pham Van Dong: The U.S. is looking further than that when fighting in Vietnam.

Mao Zedong: They fight in the South, but target the North and further, China. They are not strong enough to target other areas.

Pham Van Dong: But they are imperialists.

Mao Zedong: Of course, imperialists must have colonies. They want countries like ours to become their colonies. Before, China used to be a semi-colony of imperialists for over 100 years. What did they rob us of? China's technology and agriculture did not develop.

Zhou Enlai: They robbed materials.

Mao Zedong: What materials?

Zhou Enlai: Soybean.

Mao Zedong: Britain exploited Chinese coal. The U.S. does not need Chinese coal. They say that China does not have oil. Basically, they do not involve themselves in steel production and engineering. They do some textile production, but Japan and Britain do the most. I, therefore, see that their target is to put out the fire, because fire has burst out in your country. Because the capitalists want to put out fire, they must design machinery to do so, thus making money. How much money do they spend in Vietnam every year?

Pham Van Dong: More than 30 billion [dollars].

Mao Zedong: The U.S. cannot prolong the war. Approximately 4 years at best. At present, the fire is not put out, but to the contrary, [it has] become fiercer. Some capitalist groups gain more benefits, but others do not. Since benefits have not been divided equally, they are at odds with each other. This contradiction can be exploited.

Additionally, the capitalists who enjoy fewer benefits now become less committed. I have seen this in different speeches during the election campaign. Recently, there was an article by an American reporter warning of another trap. The reporter's name is [Walter] Lippmann. [He wrote that] the U.S. is now trapped in Vietnam and trying to get of out the quagmire. Yet, it is afraid of getting into another quagmire. That is why your cause is hopeful. In 1964, in a 5-hour conversation with President Ho, I said that that year might be decisive because it was an election year in the U.S. Every presidential candidate has to face this problem. Will the U.S. continue to fight or get out of the quagmire? I think that it will be more difficult for them to continue to fight. But Europe has not participated, which is different from the Korean War.

Pham Van Dong: That's correct.

Mao Zedong: During the Korean War, Britain and Turkey participated.

Pham Van Dong: So did France.

Mao Zedong: Only nominally and really not much.

Pham Van Dong: There was a regiment from France.

Mao Zedong: We were not impressed by the French participation.

Zhou Enlai: There were a total of sixteen countries participating in the war, including South Korea.

Mao Zedong: Japan and Taiwan do not participate in the Vietnam war.

Pham Van Dong: They are wise. At times, we were very much afraid that Japan would.

Mao Zedong: Japan will not, generally. It may involve itself financially. At least, Japan benefits in terms of weapons.

The U.S. overestimated their forces. They again committed the same old mistake: scattering their forces. It is not my opinion but [U.S. president-elect Richard M.] Nixon's. He said that American forces were too scattered. Their forces are now scattered in America, Europe and Asia. Even in Asia, American forces do not concentrate. There are 70,000 American troops, including 2 divisions of marines, in South Korea. There is a division in Hawaii. Other naval and air bases need more reserve troops. You, therefore, can understand how the American ruling circles think. If you were American presidents, what would you think? I never thought that they would attack North Vietnam. But my prediction was wrong when they bombed the North. But now, when they stop, my prediction is proven right. If, in the future, they resume bombing, I will be wrong again. Anyway, I will be right one day.

It is good, nevertheless, that you have prepared for several alternatives. For all the years of fighting, the U.S. armies have not attacked the North, Haiphong port has not been blockaded, and the streets of Hanoi have not been bombed. It shows that the U.S. is keeping a card in reserve. At one time, they warned [that they would] pursue your planes to your air bases. But in fact, they did not. This shows that their warnings are empty.

Pham Van Dong: We have noticed this.

Mao Zedong: Later, they did not reiterate this warning. They did not mention the movement of your planes. They also know how many Chinese people are working in Vietnam, but do not mention this, just ignoring it. Maybe we should withdraw the [Chinese] troops which are not needed. Have you discussed that matter?

Zhou Enlai: We shall discuss this with Comrade Ly Ban, with our Ambassador and military experts.

Mao Zedong: In case they come, we will be back. There will be no big deal.

Pham Van Dong: Let us think again.

Mao Zedong: You do think again. Keep what you still need and we withdraw what you no longer need or do not yet need. In the future, when you need [assistance], we shall be back. The same will be with your air force: if you need China's air bases, you just use them; if you do not need them, you do not use them.

We agree with your slogan of fighting while negotiating. Some comrades worry that the U.S. will deceive you. But I tell them not to [worry]. Negotiations are just like fighting. You have drawn on experience, understood the rules. But sometimes they can deceive you. As you said, the U.S. did not keep their word.

Pham Van Dong: They are very wicked.

Mao Zedong: They in many cases even said that the signed treaties were worthless. But things have their rules. The Americans cannot do this all the time. Will you negotiate with them for 100 years? Our Comrade Prime Minister said: If Nixon cannot solve the problem in two years' time, he will be in trouble. Are you the chief representative in negotiations? (Asking Le Thanh Nghi)[24]

Zhou Enlai: Comrade Le Duc Tho is. This is Comrade Le Thanh Nghi.

Mao Zedong: Both have the family name of Le!

Pham Van Dong: As Chairman Mao said, we conduct fighting while negotiating. But fighting should be conducted to a certain extent before negotiations can start. Sitting at the negotiating table does not mean [we] stop fighting. On the contrary, fighting must be fiercer. In that way, we can attain a higher position, adopt the voice of the victorious and strong, who knows how to fight to the end and knows that the enemy will fail eventually. This is our attitude. If we think otherwise, we will not win. In this connection, the South must fight fiercely, at the same time carry out the political struggle. At present, conditions in the South are very good. The convening of talks in Paris represents a new source of encouragement for our people in the South. They say that if the U.S. fails in the North, they will definitely fail in the South.

Mao Zedong: Is it true that the American troops were happy when talks were announced?

Muoi Cuc:[25] I would like to tell you, Chairman Mao, that the Americans celebrate the news. Thousands of them gather to listen to radio coverage of the talks. When ordered to fight, some wrote on their hats: "I am soon going back home, please do not kill me." Saigon troops are very discouraged. Many of them openly oppose Thieu,[26] saying: "If Mr. Thieu wants to fight, just let him go to Khe Sanh and do it." The morale of the Saigon troops and government officials is very low. Our people, cadres, and troops in the South are encouraged and determined to fight harder. We see that because we are strong, we can force the U.S. to stop bombing the North. Therefore, [this] is the time we should fight more, thus defeating them. This is the common aspiration and spirit of our people, cadres, and troops in the South, Uncle Mao.

Mao Zedong: Is the number of American troops welcoming talks [and] wishing to go home big or small?

Muoi Cuc: Big. We will fight more, and at the same time, push the task of mobilizing the people and demoralizing the enemy.

Mao Zedong: That is good. I was told that the American troops have to stay in underground shelters. You also have to do so. How is it in the rainy season?

Muoi Cuc: We have to use water-proof cloth to cover [the soldiers].

Mao Zedong: How long is the rainy season?

Muoi Cuc: Six months each season, dry and rainy ones.

Mao Zedong: That long?

Muoi Cuc: But it rains most during three months.

Mao Zedong: Which months?

Muoi Cuc: May, June, and July.

Mao Zedong: Is it now the dry season?

Muoi Cuc: The end of rainy season and beginning of the dry one.

Pham Van Dong: Seasons are different in our country.

Mao Zedong: Seasons in the North are different from those in the South, aren't they?

Muoi Cuc: Uncle Mao, this time, like before, we are summoned to the North to report the situation in the South and receive new directives from President Ho and the Political Bureau. Then, President Ho and our Central Committee asked Comrade Le Duc Anh and me to accompany Comrades Pham Van Dong and Le Thanh Nghi to China to report to Chairman Mao, Vice-Chairman Lin Biao, and other Chinese leaders about the situation in the South. The day before yesterday, through Prime Minister Zhou Enlai, we know that Chairman Mao praised us. We felt very encouraged.

Mao Zedong: We mentioned it here, in this room.

Muoi Cuc: We know that every time when a victory is gained, Chairman Mao sends us a letter of praise. This is really a great encouragement for our people, cadres, and troops in the South. Our victories gained in the South are due, to a great extent, to the assistance, as well as the encouragement, of the Chinese people and your [encouragement], Chairman Mao.

Mao Zedong: My part is very small.

Muoi Cuc: Very big, very important.

Mao Zedong: Mainly because of your efforts. Your country is unified, your Party is unified, your armed forces are unified, your people, regardless in the South or North, are unified, which is very good.

Muoi Cuc: We hold that the spiritual support offered by China is most important. Even in the most difficult situations, we have the great rear area of China supporting us, which allows us to fight for as long as it takes. Material assistance is also very important. That we force the American troops into underground shelters [is] also because of pieces of artillery that China gave us.

Pham Van Dong: That is true.

Muoi Cuc: We even used Chinese weapons to attack Saigon. The enemy is frightened.

Mao Zedong: You seem to be receptive to the logic of weapons.

Pham Van Dong: It is true that we rely on Chinese weapons.

Muoi Cuc: We rely on the strength of our people, but without Chinese weapons, it will be more difficult.

Mao Zedong: Bare hands cannot do. There must be good weapons in [those] hands.

Muoi Cuc: As Uncle Mao said, we have to fight the enemy with guns and bags of rice.

Mao Zedong: Maybe I am receptive to the logic of weapons, too.

Pham Van Dong: China has provided us large amounts of weaponry and rice.

Muoi Cuc: Our troops are very moved when they know that Chairman Mao pays attention even to their health. In addition to weapons, we receive from China rice [and] food so that our troops can be better fed, thus being stronger.

Mao Zedong: Have the supplies arrived?

Muoi Cuc: Some have. For example, egg powder, soybean, seasoning.

Pham Van Dong: Very good.

Mao Zedong: More supplies may be available. We have to thank Sihanouk too.

Pham Van Dong: We have considered his role.

Mao Zedong: Some road-fees are needed. It is worth spending for this.

Pham Van Dong: We estimate that this amount is even bigger than that of American aid.

Muoi Cuc: Before, the U.S. gave Cambodia $20 million a year. Now, the amount China pays Sihanouk for rice and road-fees exceeds $20 million. In helping us, Sihanouk gains both good reputation and benefits.

Pham Van Dong: He also benefits from our defense of Cambodia's eastern border with the South of Vietnam.

Muoi Cuc: Plus Chinese sympathy.

Mao Zedong: As far as politics is concerned, he still sometimes surprises us. Recently, he may have felt abandoned by the U.S., so he has twice stated that the U.S. should withdraw some of its troops, but not all. Recently, he has stated on Paris Radio that the U.S. should withdraw its troops but not bring them to the U.S., and that the U.S. should not deploy its troops [in] Cambodia but in Thailand or in the Philippines, so that China will not invade his country. He often talks in an anti-Communist tone. According to what he said, there is evidence of the U.S. wanting to withdraw its troops. If they do withdraw, Sihanouk will be worried, and so will Thailand and the Philippines. In the South [of Vietnam], the first person to be worried is Thieu. Every one of them really wants U.S. troops to stay.

So, the world now is in great chaos. Those countries that lack their own strength need the help of superpowers, as in the case of Sihanouk. Even Japanese capitalists still need U.S. support. The Japanese seem to welcome negotiations. However, in fact, they do not, because as capitalists they get a lot of profit from the war. Many U.S. weapons are made in Japan.

Pham Van Dong: We have been attentive to this point. We are very surprised that Japan seemingly wants to make a contribution to solving the war. But we have to consider their real attitudes.

Mao Zedong: Some people talk one way and think another way. When the Korean war ended, many Japanese industries went bankrupt. When the U.S. starts to fight, Japan starts to benefit.

Pham Van Dong: It's the best policy of Japan.

Mao Zedong: The Filipino capitalists do the same. They do not contribute many troops to U.S. war efforts in South Vietnam. But since the U.S. troops are based in the Philippines, the Filipino capitalists gain a lot from that. So do the Thai capitalists.

Pham Van Dong: It's very clear in the case of Thailand. But it is not they who make decisions. It is the Vietnamese who decide whether the U.S. will stay or go. We, all the Vietnamese people, are determined to fight and to drive them away. We are preparing to concentrate our forces and fight the U.S. in the South. Probably, we will engage in large-scale battles in the coming period. Certainly, the war will be fiercer.

Mao Zedong: Early this spring you fought quite well. We have suggested that you fight large-scale battles like the one in Dien Bien Phu. At that time we didn't know that your liberated zones were terribly divided. Is this [still] the situation in every province?

Pham Van Dong: Yes, but this situation doesn't affect our efforts to encircle Saigon and other bases or blockade important points in their communication and transportation network. We have also thought of large-scale battles like Dien Bien Phu, but we must calculate carefully and thoroughly before we do so.

Mao Zedong: You should have your bases geographically interrelated with each other. Without this condition, it's difficult for you to concentrate your forces for large-scale battle. And there is another matter: Thieu's regime is afraid of the NLF. This fact proves that the NLF enjoys influence among the people in the South, not Thieu. Their mass media have talked about it, not in an official way, but based on official sources.

Which government has real prestige in South Vietnam? Nguyen Huu Tho's[27] or Nguyen Van Thieu's? Both of them have the family name of Nguyen. Recently, Thieu has tried to play hard, pretending that he didn't want to attend the Paris conference. But in fact, the U.S. has very clearly seen that the Vietnam problem cannot be solved without the participation of the NLF. You have read all these [facts], haven't you?

Muoi Cuc: They are perplexing.

Mao Zedong: The U.S. now respects the Party and Government in Vietnam led by President Ho, respects the NLF led by President Nguyen Huu Tho. The U.S. also does not think highly of the Thieu clique, considering them ineffective.

Pham Van Dong: That is correct.

Mao Zedong: The U.S. gives Saigon a lot of money, but much has been embezzled.

Pham Van Dong: In Paris, Thieu's representatives verbally opposed the U.S. We then asked the American representatives why the U.S. allowed Saigon to do so. [American negotiator W. Averell] Harriman replied that Saigon by so doing tried to show that they are not puppets.

Mao Zedong: They have been ordered to show opposition to the U.S., that's why. Maybe the Harriman team will be replaced. Nixon probably will assign new negotiators.

Pham Van Dong: Of course.

Le Duc Anh: Chairman Mao, our armies in the South are undergoing political education and military training. We are prepared to receive weapons provided for by Chairman Mao, [and] the Chinese Communist Party, and to set up battlefields for coming fierce campaigns. We are also prepared to inflict severe damage on several elite contingents of American troops in the South. Following the directives by President Ho, drawing on our most recent experience, we believe that we are going to achieve great victories.

Chairman Mao, since the beginning of this year, we have inflicted heavy casualties on some American elite contingents, such as the 25th Division, the 1st Division, and their armored vehicle units. In a battle in August in Tay Ninh alone, we killed and wounded 12,000 troops, the majority of which were Americans, destroyed 1,100 tanks, armored vehicles, more than 100 pieces of artillery. When our infantry troops were advancing, American tanks and armor retreated—they were very afraid of our troops equipped with weapons provided by Chairman Mao. Such weapons included [the] B-40, for example.

Mao Zedong: Is that weapon powerful?

Le Duc Anh: Very effective for fighting tanks.

Mao Zedong: Did we have this weapon before? (Asking Wang Xinting)

Wang Xinting: No, we did not.

Ye Jianying: We used the B-90 during the Korean War.

Pham Van Dong: Tanks will melt when they are hit by this weapon.

Le Duc Anh: And the drivers will be burnt to death.

Mao Zedong: Good. Can we produce more of this?

Wang Xinting: Yes, but to produce ammunition for this weapon is more difficult than to produce the weapon.

Le Duc Anh: The enemy has internal contradictions. Saigon troops criticize Americans for being cowards [and] do not believe in them any more.

Mao Zedong: Saigon troops criticize Americans?

Le Duc Anh: American and Saigon troops do not believe in each other. They are both afraid of the Liberation Armies.

Mao Zedong: It may well be so.

Le Duc Anh: In the recent incident occurring from October 25 to November 7, a unit of the American First Infantry Division refused to fight. During the August campaign, we killed a division commander. Troops in that division celebrated his death.

Muoi Cuc: This General was brutal.

Mao Zedong: Not civilized.

Le Duc Anh: In Tay Ninh, we eliminated fourteen companies of the 25th Division. The U.S. has acknowledged that.

Mao Zedong: Where is Tay Ninh?

Le Duc Anh: 60 kilometers northwest of Saigon and close to the border with Cambodia.

Mao Zedong: We know the 25th Division fairly well. We fought against it in Korea. At that time, due to the mistakes of Peng Dehuai, it was not totally crushed. Our 40th Army under the command of Ye Jianying first fought it. We do not know much about the First Division.

Ye Jianying: We terminated a regiment. At that time, the First Division had not been in Korea.

Mao Zedong: Do American cavalry units fight well? In fact they are infantry units, aren't they?

Le Duc Anh: They are cowardly infantry units.

Mao Zedong: In Korea, they were arrogant. But now, since being beaten by you, they also became cowards. Were they deployed in Western Korea? (Asking Ye Jianying)

Ye Jianying: In Eastern Korea.

Mao Zedong: The mistake we committed in Korea was that we wanted to swallow one or two divisions in a single battle. But we could not. The battles showed that we could only swallow a regiment. If we used all of our forces in order to terminate the 25th Division, it would take several weeks.

Hoang Van Thai:[28] At that time, there was not the B-40.

Mao Zedong: At that time, there were 800 pieces of artillery for each enemy division. On our side, there were 800 pieces of artillery for three armies. 9 Chinese divisions put together were not equal to one American division.

Pham Van Dong: At present, they are very well equipped.

Mao Zedong: Certainly, as 18 years have passed since 1950.

Le Duc Anh: Chairman Mao, we are now able to penetrate and fight anywhere. We can even penetrate the most heavily guarded bases.

Mao Zedong: That is why they curse you for fighting indiscriminately. They want to imply that they are the only ones that are discriminate.

Muoi Cuc: The more they are defeated, the more they curse us.

Le Duc Anh: Now, the American troops in Saigon and other cities cannot relax. They have to stay in underground shelters. They know that we are fighting them with Chinese weapons. So we are fighting more, focusing our forces on fighting them in the countryside as well as on their big bases. We are going to fight more fiercely.

Mao Zedong: It is necessary to have political education for your troops. You should take advantage of the negotiations for political education. Before every big battle, it is always an imperative to spend time on political education. There should be only two or three, or four at most, big campaigns every year. The regular troops should spend the remaining time on political education.

Pham Van Dong: That is what we do.

Mao Zedong: When we were fighting the Japanese in the war of liberation, every year, we only fought a couple of campaigns. However, we found that we still lacked time for political education. It is impossible to fight every month. We need time for military training, recruiting, and getting more supplies of weaponry and ammunition as well as consolidating the rear. There are a lot of things to do in-between battles.

Muoi Cuc: We are trying to be ready in every aspect. That is why we see the imperative of politically educating our troops.

Mao Zedong: It is necessary. There should be at least one big period of political education conducted. It may take two or three months, or several weeks. The interval between battles is the right time for that.

Muoi Cuc: It is what we are doing now. We are drawing experience, getting more prepared both materially and psychologically for the coming big battles and big victories. While negotiations are going on, we continue to fight as we see that it is the battlefield that decides the final outcome. During the period of political education, we have to prevent the thought of expecting too much to develop from negotiations.

Mao Zedong: This kind of thought can emerge. There always is a trend of thinking at any given time. But every trend is short-lived and temporary.

Muoi Cuc: This time, when we were summoned to the North, President Ho and the Poitburo told us that the enemy was suffering big defeats, so they had to accept negotiations even though they were still persistent. In this connection, we have to maintain the thought in favor of patience, of total revolution and of big battles. And we are strictly following this guidance.

Mao Zedong: Good.

Pham Van Dong: Comrades Muoi Cuc, Le Duc Anh, other comrades and I are grateful for the fact that you, Chairman Mao, have taken time to receive and talk with us. What the Chairman told us today and what Comrade Prime Minister Zhou Enlai and Comrade Kang Sheng told us the other day have made us all the more encouraged. We think that what Chairman Mao has said is very correct, very suitable for the situation in our struggle against the U.S. for national salvation.

Mao Zedong: Some [of my thinking] is not necessarily correct. We have to refer to the actual developments.

Pham Van Dong: Ultimately, it is we who make the decisions based on the actual situation in Vietnam and on how we understand the rules of the war. This is also what Chairman Mao has told President Ho and other Vietnamese comrades. Once again, we would like to reiterate before Chairman Mao and other leaders of the CCP that we are determined to fight until the final and total victory is gained. It is the best way to express our gratitude for the support and aid provided to us by Chairman Mao and the CCP as well as the fraternal Chinese people. We wish you, Chairman Mao, good health.

Mao Zedong: I wish President Ho good health, longevity. I also wish other comrades in your Politburo good health.

Pham Van Dong: Thank you, Chairman Mao.

Source: Odd Arne Westad, Chen Jian, Stein Tønnesson, Nguyen Vu Tung, and James G. Hershberg, eds., *77 Conversations between Chinese and Foreign Leaders on the Wars in Indochina, 1964–1977,* Cold War International History Project Working Paper 22 (Washington, D.C.: Woodrow Wilson International Center for Scholars, 1998), 140–54. Also available on Cold War International History Project Web site Virtual Archive: Collection New Evidence on the Vietnam/Indochina Wars (http://wwics.si.edu/index.cfm?topic_id=1409&fuseaction=library.document&id=444).

Mao Zedong and Le Duan,[29] Beijing,
Great Hall of the People, May 11, 1970, 6:45–8:15 P.M.

Mao Zedong: When did I meet you the last time?

Le Duan: In 1964. We see that Chairman Mao is in good health, and we all feel excited. This time Chairman Mao finds the time to meet us, we are very happy. At present, the situation in Vietnam and in Indo-China is complicated, and there exist some difficulties.

Mao Zedong: Every country is facing some difficulty. The Soviet Union has its [difficulty], and the United States has its [difficulty].

Le Duan: We are very much in need of getting Chairman Mao's instructions. If our Central Committee and Politburo learn that Chairman Mao has given instructions about how we should do our job, they will certainly be very happy.

Mao Zedong: You have done a very good job, and you are doing better and better.

Le Duan: We have tried our best to do our job. We have been able to do a good job because we have followed the three instructions Chairman Mao gave us in the past: first, no fear, we should not fear the enemy; second, we should break up the enemy one piece after another; third, we should fight a prolonged war.

Mao Zedong: Yes, a prolonged war. You should prepare to fight a prolonged war, but isn't it better if the war is shortened?

Who fears whom? Is it you, the Vietnamese, Cambodians, and the people in Southeast Asia, who fear the U.S. imperialists? Or is it the U.S. imperialists who fear you? This is a question which deserves consideration and study. It is a great power which fears a small country—when the grass bends as the wind blows, the great power will be in panic. It is true that during the Gulf of Tonkin Incident in 1964 you hit the U.S. imperialists, but it was not your intention to fight a war with the U.S. Navy. In actuality, you did not really hit it [the U.S. naval ship], but they themselves became nervous, saying that Vietnam's torpedo boats were coming and began opening fire. At the end, even the Americans themselves did not know if there had been a genuine [Vietnamese torpedo attack] or not. The journalists in various places of the United States believed that there had never been [such an attack], and that it was a false alarm. Since the war had already begun, there was no other choice but to fight it. The arms manufacturers and dealers are benefiting from it. American presidents have had much less sleep every night [since then]. Nixon says that he uses his main energy to deal with Vietnam.

Now there is another person, Prince Sihanouk. He is not an easy person to deal with either. When you offend him, he will come out to scold you.[30]

Some of our embassies, in my opinion, need to be rectified. Great-power chauvinism exists in some of the Chinese embassies. They only see the shortcomings of the others, paying no attention to the interests of the whole. Who was the last [Chinese] ambassador to Vietnam?

Zhou Enlai: Zhu Qiwen.[31]

Mao Zedong: Zhu Qiwen had very bad relations with you. As a matter of fact, Zhu Qiwen was a member of the Guomindang, and he planned to escape abroad. We did not know that he was a Guomindang member. Since you were coping with the Guomindang, how could he fail to make trouble for you? We did not know at that time, but we were not happy when we saw those telegrams [he sent back].

Le Duan: We Vietnamese people keep Chairman Mao's great goodness always in our mind. During the nine years of the war of resistance against the French, if there had not been the support from the Chinese Communist Party and Chairman Mao, it would have been impossible for us to win the victory. Why are we in a position to persist in fighting a prolonged war, especially in fighting a prolonged war in the South? Why dare we fight a prolonged war? This is mainly because we have been dependent upon Chairman Mao's works.

Mao Zedong: This is not necessarily true.

Le Duan: Of course this is true. We also need to apply [Chairman Mao's teachings] to Vietnam's practical situation.

Mao Zedong: You have had your own creations. How can one say that you do not have your own creation and experience? Ngo Dinh Diem murdered 160,000 [of your people]. This was reported to me, and I did not know if it was accurate, but I know that over 100,000 people had been killed.

Le Duan: Yes, 160,000 had been killed, and many others had been put into prison.

Mao Zedong: I think this is good. You can kill our people, why can't we kill your people?

Le Duan: Exactly. In 1969 alone we have killed and wounded 610,000 enemies, among whom 230,000 were Americans.

Mao Zedong: The Americans do not have enough manpower to spread around the world, since already they have been overextended. Therefore, when their people were killed their hearts were broken. The death of several dozens of thousands is a huge matter for them. You Vietnamese, both in the North and the South, in my opinion, it is inevitable for some of you also to be killed.

Le Duan: Our current ways of fighting cause low casualties. Otherwise, it is impossible for us to persist for a long time.

Mao Zedong: That is true. Maybe the situation in Laos is more difficult. . . . Southeast Asia is a hornets' nest. The people in Southeast Asia are awakening day by day. Some pacifists think that cocks like fighting. How can there be so many cocks? Now even hens like fighting.

Le Duan: There is no way out if one does not fight.

Mao Zedong: Yes, there is no way out if one does not fight. You [Mao speaks rhetorically to the Americans] compel the others [to fight] and leave them no other way to go. You are bullying them.

Le Duan: The people in Cambodia and Laos are believers in Buddhism who do not like fighting. Now they have also become fond of fighting.

Mao Zedong: This is true. You cannot say that they are not fond of fighting because they believe in Buddhism. The Chinese are also believers in Buddhism, but the 1911 Revolution was followed by seventeen years of fighting. Later it became the fighting between two factions [among the revolutionaries], and thus the people had been educated. Then the Northern Expedition War began, and then the Red Army emerged. Then the Japanese invaded China. After the surrender of the Japanese, Jiang Jieshi fought a war against us. The war lasted for less than four years, he could not continue and fled to Taiwan. He now claims at the United Nations that he represents all China. [Mao then reminisced about the Communists' close relationships with Jiang and the Guomindang during the 1920s and 1930s.]

. . . .

Le Duan: Recently Nixon claimed that the United States had never been defeated in the past 190 years. He meant that this time it would not be willing to be defeated by Vietnam.

Mao Zedong: Never defeated?

Le Duan: In actuality it has been defeated several times. In China, in Korea, and during the anti-French war in Indochina. The Americans covered 80 percent of France's military expenditures. Still it was defeated.

Mao Zedong: That is true. You mentioned a moment ago that first of all one should not fear the imperialists. After all, who really fears whom? Small countries. There exists such a problem on the part of small nations. It will gradually try. After trying for a few years, it will understand.

[. . . Mao recalled and discussed the Cultural Revolution].

Mao Zedong: . . . At that time, I also told you that if the Americans did not come to China's borders, and if you did not invite us, we would not dispatch our troops [to enter the war].

Le Duan: This was also what we thought. When we are still able to continue the fighting, we hope to make our "great rear" more stable. When we Vietnamese are fighting the Americans, China is our "great rear." Therefore, we once issued instructions that even though our planes had been attacked they should not land at the airports in China.

Mao Zedong: You can [land at our airports]. We do not fear. If the American air force come to attack the "shelters" of Vietnamese air force, let them come.

Le Duan: Although we issued such instructions, still we needed to rely on your support. At that time, you dispatched several divisions to Vietnam, also engaged in fighting American planes.

Mao Zedong: That is true. The Americans are afraid of being beaten, and they have no guts. You may negotiate [with the Americans]. I am not saying that you cannot negotiate, but your main energy should be put on fighting. Who sabotaged the two Geneva conferences? Both you and us truthfully abided by [the resolutions of the conferences]. But they did not. It is better that they did not.

Therefore, even Premier Kosygin of the Soviet Union, when making a public speech, had to say that as long as convening an international conference was concerned, Vietnam, Laos and Cambodia must be consulted. Many of their current leaders I am not familiar with, I do not know them. I know Kosygin and have talked with him. The newspapers in the West frequently make rumors about them, saying how divided is their leadership. I am not clear about this either. It is said that the common people are more interested in Kosygin as a leader.

Le Duan: We have also heard it.

Mao Zedong: You have also heard it? In my opinion, Stalin is alive again. The main tendency in the world today is revolution, including the whole world. There exists the possibility that the big powers may start a world war. But, because of a few atomic bombs, no one dares to start the war. This mainly concerns the two superpowers. At present many say that there are three big powers. China should not be included. China's study of making nuclear weapons is a recent experience.[32] We are at the stage of research. Why should someone fear us? China is populous and therefore they fear China. But we also have our own fear, we need to feed and to provide clothing for such a large population. Therefore we have now begun the study of birth control so that the large population will be reduced a little bit.

. . . .

Le Duan: We have been able to continue our fighting, this is because the Chairman has said that the 700,000,000 Chinese people are firmly backing the Vietnamese people. The United States is scared. This is very important.[33]

Mao Zedong: Why should it be scared? You invade another country, why is it wrong for us to back that country? You dispatch hundreds of thousands of naval, air and land forces to bully the Vietnamese people, who forbids China to become the rear [of the Vietnamese people]? Which law has set up this?

Le Duan: The Americans say that they can mobilize 12 million troops, but they can only dispatch half a million troops to Vietnam. They are scared to cross this limit.

Zhou Enlai: China has a large population, which makes them fear.

Mao Zedong: Because we have a large population sometimes we do not need to fear. In the final analysis, we do not have relations with you. You have occupied our Taiwan Island, but I have never occupied your Long Island.

Source: Odd Arne Westad, Chen Jian, Stein Tønnesson, Nguyen Vu Tung, and James G. Hershberg, eds., *77 Conversations between Chinese and Foreign Leaders on the Wars in Indochina, 1964–1977,* Cold War International History Project Working Paper 22 (Washington, D.C.: Woodrow Wilson International Center for Scholars, 1998), 164–69. Also available on Cold War International History Project Web site Virtual Archive: Collection New Evidence on the Vietnam/Indochina Wars (http://wwics.si.edu/index.cfm? topic_id=1409&fuseaction=library.document&id=8).

Mao Zedong and Pham Van Dong,[34]
Beijing, September 23, 1970

Mao Zedong: It seems to me that it is unlikely that a world war will erupt. The big powers do not want to fight such a war, they are afraid of each other. In the meantime, many countries in Europe, such as Britain, France, Italy, and West Germany, do not want to fight such a war.

. . . .

Mao Zedong: Why have the Americans not made a fuss about the fact that more than 100,000 Chinese troops help you building railways, roads and airports although they knew about it?

Pham Van Dong: Of course, they are afraid.

Mao Zedong: They should have made a fuss about it. Also, their estimate of the number of Chinese troops in Vietnam is less than their real number.

Pham Van Dong: We think that they find it difficult to deal with China.

Mao Zedong: If they did this, what would they do later? The Americans still want to go to Beijing for talks. It is what they propose. They said that Warsaw was not suitable and we replied that if they wanted to go to Beijing, [they should] just go. Later, they did not dare to go. Kissinger is a stinking scholar. I have read the report about the meeting between comrade Xuan Thuy and Kissinger.[35] The last part of it is very funny. Kissinger is a university professor who does not know anything about diplomacy. I think that he is not someone who can compete with Xuan Thuy, even though I have not met Xuan Thuy.

Pham Van Dong: We have two comrades who are good at diplomatic struggle. They are Xuan Thuy and Nguyen Thi Binh.

Mao Zedong: I see that you can conduct the diplomatic struggle and you do it well. Negotiations have been going on for two years. At first we were a little worried that you were trapped. We are no longer worried.

. . . .

Mao Zedong: Every Chinese province is now a fortress, ready in case of an American attack. But even in such a case, we still continue to help you because you are also in difficulties. Any one who says that we do not help you because we are also in difficulties is a reactionary. We have held the provinces of Guangdong, Guangxi, Yunnan, [and] Guangzhou responsible for helping you as well as the rest of the Southeast Asian region. The entire production by these provinces is for you. Cadres from these provinces will visit Vietnam to prepare for an American attack on China. Because you pin them down, they have not attacked China yet. In short, what I want to say is: You are fighting very well on the battlefield. Your policy for the diplomatic struggle is correct. We must give you what you want. I have no further comments.

Source: Odd Arne Westad, Chen Jian, Stein Tønnesson, Nguyen Vu Tung, and James G. Hershberg, eds., *77 Conversations between Chinese and Foreign Leaders on the Wars in Indochina, 1964–1977,* Cold War International History Project Working Paper 22 (Washington, D.C.: Woodrow Wilson International Center for Scholars, 1998), 177–78. Also available on Cold War International History Project Web site Virtual Archive: Collection New Evidence on the Vietnam/Indochina Wars (http://wwics.si.edu/index.cfm?topic_id=1409&fuseaction=library.document&id=178).

Le Duc Tho and Ieng Sary,[36] September 7, 1971, Place Not Provided

Le Duc Tho: We will always remember the experience in 1954. Comrade Zhou Enlai admitted his mistakes in the Geneva Conference of 1954. Two or three years ago, comrade Mao also did so. In 1954, because both the Soviet Union and China exerted pressure, the outcome became what it became. We have proposed that the Chinese comrades admit their mistakes and now I am telling you, the Cambodian comrades, about this problem of history.

We should be independent in thoughts, promote international solidarity and solidarity with the Soviet Union and with China. We have to fight a big imperialist country. If we take sides in the Sino-Soviet dispute, the situation will become more complicated. At present, China considers that it has two enemies, namely the Soviet Union and the U.S. It therefore will not be beneficial if we take sides.

Source: Odd Arne Westad, Chen Jian, Stein Tønnesson, Nguyen Vu Tung, and James G. Hershberg, eds., *77 Conversations between Chinese and Foreign Leaders on the Wars in Indochina, 1964–1977,* Cold War International History Project Working Paper 22 (Washington, D.C.: Woodrow Wilson International Center for Scholars, 1998), 180–81. Also available on Cold War International History Project Web site Virtual Archive: Collection New Evidence on the Vietnam/Indochina Wars (http://wwics.si.edu/index.cfm? topic_id=1409&fuseaction=library.document&id=113).

Zhou Enlai and Le Duc Tho, Beijing, July 12, 1972

Zhou Enlai: On the one hand, it is necessary to prepare for fighting. On the other hand, you have to negotiate. China has some experience with that. We also conducted fighting and negotiating with Jiang Jieshi. During the Korean War, we fought one year and negotiated two years. Therefore, your tactic of fighting and negotiating, that you have been conducting since 1968, is correct.

At first, when you initiated negotiations, some of our comrades thought that you had chosen the wrong moment. I even said to comrades Le Duan and Pham Van Dong that you had to choose the moment to start negotiations when you were in an advantageous position. Yet, comrade Mao said that it was correct to have negotiations at that time and that you were also

prepared to fight. Only you would know when the right moment for negotiations was. And your decision was correct, thus showing that comrade
Mao was more farsighted than we were.

We do not recognize Nguyen Van Thieu as he is a puppet of the U.S. Yet
we can recognize him as a representative of one of the three forces in the
coalition government. The coalition government will negotiate the basic
principles for it to observe and control the situation after the U.S. withdrawal of troops. The U.S. will see that Thieu is sharing power in that government, and therefore, find it easier to accept a political solution. In case
negotiations among the three forces fail, we will fight again. Similar situations can be found in Kashmir and the Middle East.

Le Duc Tho: But we still think of a government without Thieu.

Zhou Enlai: We are asking the U.S. to remove Thieu. However, if we hint
that Thieu can be accepted, the U.S. will be surprised because they do not
expect that. Of course, Thieu cannot be a representative of a government.
But in negotiations, surprise is necessary.

In the pro-American force, Thieu is a chieftain. He is the one that sells
out his country. Yet, he plays a decisive role in his party. We, therefore, cannot solve anything if we only talk with other figures in his party rather than
him. Of course how to solve this problem is your job. However, as comrades, we would like to refer to our experience: In the civil war, no result
would be gained if we insisted on talking with Jiang's ministers but not with
Jiang himself. In the Korean War, we talked with Eisenhower. At the
Geneva Conference, because [French Prime Minister Georges] Bidault was
stubborn, siding with the U.S., talks did not continue. When [Bidault's successor as Prime Minister in 1954, Pierre] Mendès-France came to power
and was interested in negotiations, the problem was solved. That means we
have to talk with the chieftains. Again, our talks with the U.S. did not proceed until the visit by Nixon to China. [North Korean Prime Minister] Comrade Kim Il Sung is also trying to talk directly with [South Korean Presi-
dent] Park Chung Hee. We do the same in our relations with Japan. These
are historical facts. The CCP Politburo has discussed this matter, but it is up
to you to decide.

May I put it another way: you can talk directly with Thieu and his deputy,
thus showing that you are generous to him when he is disgraced. Since
Thieu is still the representative of the Right faction, and there is not yet any-
one to replace him, the U.S. can be assured that their people are in power.
The NLF should also name its representative, who may be Mr. Nguyen Huu
Tho or Mr. Huynh Tan Phat,[37] and the neutralist faction should also do the

same. However, the real struggle will be between the NLF and the Right faction.

Le Duc Tho: We are asking Thieu to resign. If he does not, we will not talk with the Saigon government.

Zhou Enlai: If he does, who will replace him?

Le Duc Tho: We are ready to talk with anyone.

Zhou Enlai: That also means Thieu's policy without him.

Le Duc Tho: But they have to compromise.

Zhou Enlai: On general elections?

Le Duc Tho: We have not mentioned general elections. If they agree on a tripartite government and recognize the power of this government, then we agree to hold general elections.

Zhou Enlai: General elections will be very dangerous, maybe more dangerous than Thieu being the representative of the Right faction, not to mention international supervision and control of the elections.

Le Duc Tho: We hold that a tripartite government must be established. One of the duties of this government is to hold elections. And free elections require realization of democratic rights.

. . . .

Le Duc Tho: Another complicated question relates to the neutralist faction's participation in the coalition government. We have to discuss and define the term neutrality.

Zhou Enlai: Is Duong Van Minh[38] acceptable?

Le Duc Tho: This is a complicated problem. Duong Van Minh is not totally pro-American. Yet, the tripartite government is very provisional.

Zhou Enlai: Eventually, we have to fight again since the tripartite government is provisional.

Le Duc Tho: It also is difficult for France to become involved because of the U.S. influence.

Zhou Enlai: So the neutral position is both pro-French and pro-American.

Le Duc Tho: Duong Van Minh is exactly like this. But the important thing is how to make the U.S. accept the principle of the establishment of a tripartite government. And further discussion on dividing positions and power should take place after this.

Zhou Enlai: Chairman Mao has also spent much time talking with me on the question of a tripartite government. He told me to talk with you on this issue. We also have experience on this issue. A coalition government could be established, but we later had to resume fighting. The question is to play for time with a view to letting North Vietnam recover, thus getting stronger while the enemy is getting weaker.[39]

Source: Odd Arne Westad, Chen Jian, Stein Tønnesson, Nguyen Vu Tung, and James G. Hershberg, eds., *77 Conversations between Chinese and Foreign Leaders on the Wars in Indochina, 1964–1977,* Cold War International History Project Working Paper 22 (Washington, D.C.: Woodrow Wilson International Center for Scholars, 1998), 182–85. Also available on Cold War International History Project Web site Virtual Archive: Collection New Evidence on the Vietnam/Indochina Wars (http://wwics.si.edu/index.cfm?topic_id=1409&fuseaction=library.document&id=324).

Zhou Enlai and Le Duan, Pham Van Dong, and Le Thanh Nghi,[40] Beijing, June 5, 1973

Zhou Enlai: The world is now in a state of chaos. In the period after the Paris Agreements, the Indochinese countries should take time to relax and build their forces. During the next 5 to 10 years, South Vietnam, Laos, and Cambodia should build peace, independence, and neutrality. In short, we have to play for time and prepare for a protracted struggle. Each country has enemies of its own. So each has to prepare, both by increasing production and training armed forces. If we are not vigilant, the enemy will exploit our weakness. If we are well-prepared, then we will be ready for any move by the enemy.

At present, the cease-fire is well observed. The Cambodian problem is not solved. Yet, the people, after 20 years of fighting, wish to relax. So it is necessary that you restore production and effectively use the labor forces. These are big things to do. We agree with you that we have to restore production and train armed forces at the same time.

Le Duan: The U.S. was aiming at political objectives when fighting in Vietnam. Strategically speaking, they did not use a consistent strategy. Instead, in this neocolonial war, they changed several strategies, from one of special war to limited war and "Vietnamization." Their objective was not only to turn South Vietnam into their colony, but also to realize their global strategy in Vietnam. That means, they wished to control the South, then attack the North of Vietnam, thus damaging the defense system of socialism in Southeast Asia and threatening the national independence movement in the world.

Zhou Enlai: So you fought, and were not patient as Lin Biao advised. Patience is the maxim of Lin Biao's strategy. He knew of nothing else.

I would like to share with you some intelligence information that we have just received. The U.S. wants Saigon to decrease fighting. [U.S. envoy William] Sullivan[41] has to fly to Saigon to tell the same thing that he told Tran Van Huong[42]—Saigon's ambassador to Washington: Nixon is in trouble and Saigon should not make the situation more complicated. This is true, because it explains why Kissinger wants to have a joint declaration with you.

I also would like to stress that the U.S. should definitely drop Lon Nol to let the Cambodian people solve the problems themselves. This is a Cambodian civil war so the U.S. should leave Cambodia. As for FUNK, this war is to punish Lon Nol. So we have to consult with Prince Sihanouk whether to negotiate. We at the same time are not representing GRUNK.[43]

Le Duan: Cambodian comrades are making much progress. They are doing very well.

Zhou Enlai: There is still uncertainty in the situation. I recall that last year, Lon Nol went to China for the 20th anniversary celebration of the Chinese National Day and met with comrade Pham Van Dong. He was so confident. At that time, he still controlled all the transportation of materiel for South Vietnam.

Pham Van Dong: We did not anticipate that things would change in a very short time afterward. But he deserved it.

Zhou Enlai: Things always happen beyond our wishes. At that time, you had military and medical bases in Cambodia and we did not know about this. But Lon Nol did. And when Lon Nol asked for road fees for transportation of materiel via Cambodia, we had to pay.

Le Duan: We would like to talk about our policy in the South. The situation will be clear in three or four years' time. At any rate, the government there eventually must be a democratic and nationalist one. This government can exist for ten or 15 years. And then the name can be changed. So we are not in a hurry to turn South Vietnam into a socialist entity.

Pham Van Dong: In this struggle, our objective is independence and democracy. We are not in a hurry with the goal of national unification. One thing we should do is to highlight the NLF role and the Provisional Revolutionary Government with a neutral foreign policy.

Zhou Enlai: And the main problem is the leadership of the Party.

Pham Van Dong: That is correct. Lenin also discussed this problem in his book entitled "The Two Strategies." The whole problem is the leadership. We will highlight the NLF role both in internal and external policies.

Le Duan: In carrying out "Vietnamization," the enemies are clearly expanding the war. We hold that the U.S. has great strength and it can accept defeat to a certain extent. It is difficult to defeat the U.S. because it is a strong country. You have advised us to solve the problem of U.S. withdrawal first and solve the Saigon problem later. We think this is correct.

Source: Odd Arne Westad, Chen Jian, Stein Tønnesson, Nguyen Vu Tung, and James G. Hershberg, eds., *77 Conversations between Chinese and Foreign Leaders on the Wars in Indochina, 1964–1977,* Cold War International History Project Working Paper 22 (Washington, D.C.: Woodrow Wilson International Center for Scholars, 1998), 187–88. Also available on Cold War International History Project Web site Virtual Archive: Collection New Evidence on the Vietnam/Indochina Wars (http://wwics.si.edu/index.cfm? topic_id=1409&fuseaction=library.document&id=61).

Mao Zedong and Pol Pot, Beijing, June 21, 1975

[Mao Zedong:] During the transition from the democratic revolution to adopting a socialist path, there exist two possibilities: one is socialism, the other is capitalism. Our situation now is like this. Fifty years from now, or one hundred years from now, the struggle between two lines will exist. Even ten thousand years from now, the struggle between two lines will still exist. When Communism is realized, the struggle between two lines will still be there. Otherwise, you are not a Marxist. This is unity existing among opposites. If one only mentions one side of the two, that is metaphysics. I believe in what Marx and Lenin have said, that the path [of advance] would be tortuous. From the era of Lenin to the era of Khrushchev and Brezhnev, the Soviet Union has changed. But in the future it is certain that it will return to Lenin's path. China is also like this. It may turn to revisionism in the future, but it will eventually return to the path of Marx and Lenin. Our state now is, as Lenin said, a capitalist state without capitalists. This state protects capitalist rights, and the wages are not equal. Under the slogan of equality, a system of inequality has been introduced. There will exist a struggle between two lines, the struggle between the advanced and the backward, even when Communism is realized. Today we cannot explain it completely.

. . . .

You should not completely copy China's experience, and should think for yourself. According to Marx, his theory is a guideline for action, but not a doctrine.

Source: Odd Arne Westad, Chen Jian, Stein Tønnesson, Nguyen Vu Tung, and James G. Hershberg, eds., *77 Conversations between Chinese and Foreign Leaders on the Wars in Indochina, 1964–1977,* Cold War International History Project Working Paper 22 (Washington, D.C.: Woodrow Wilson International Center for Scholars, 1998), 194. Also available on Cold War International History Project Web site Virtual Archive: Collection New Evidence on the Vietnam/Indochina Wars (http://wwics.si.edu/index.cfm?topic_id=1409&fuseaction=library.document&id=537).

Deng Xiaoping and Le Duan, Beijing, September 29, 1975

Deng Xiaoping: There have been some problems in the relations between our countries. Some of them emerged when President Ho was still alive. We have to say that we are not at ease when we get to read Vietnamese newspapers and know [Vietnamese] public opinion. In fact, you stress the threat from the North. The threat from the North for us is the existence of Soviet troops at our northern borders, but for you, it means China.

Le Duan: We did not say that.

Deng Xiaoping: I still recall a meeting between President Ho and Premier Zhou and myself in which President Ho mentioned this problem. At that time, we had several hundred thousand troops stationed in Guangdong and Guangxi. Vietnamese people and cadres used history in order to imply the present, mentioning the threat from the North. The Soviet question was also mentioned. Premier Zhou then told President Ho straight: "You are threatening us." For my part I asked President Ho whether you were concerned that we were intimidating you. If you did think so, we would withdraw our troops from Guangdong and Guangxi and place them in the North. The reason we had to have them there was to prepare for a scenario like the Korean War. We had to consider the possibility of an American attack. Did President Ho tell you about that meeting?

Le Duan: To tell you the truth, we heard nothing about it from President Ho. Yet, I was told about that theater play.

Deng Xiaoping: There were at that time some articles and public discussions that hurt our bilateral relations. We told President Ho about that for the sake of relations between us. President Ho immediately replied: "I disagree with you that we are threatening you." He also did not agree with the withdrawal of our troops from these two provinces. Later, as the situation changed, we withdrew [them] and placed them elsewhere.

For the last few years, such things have still occurred and they seem to be more frequent than before. The threat from the North is the main theme, even in your textbooks. We are not at ease with this. Our relations are very profound. We have not annexed a centimeter of your territory.

Source: Odd Arne Westad, Chen Jian, Stein Tønnesson, Nguyen Vu Tung, and James G. Hershberg, eds., *77 Conversations between Chinese and Foreign Leaders on the Wars in Indochina, 1964–1977,* Cold War International History Project Working Paper 22 (Washington, D.C.: Woodrow Wilson International Center for Scholars, 1998), 194–95. Also available on Cold War International History Project Web site Virtual Archive: Collection New Evidence on the Vietnam/Indochina Wars (http://wwics.si.edu/index.cfm? topic_id=1409&fuseaction=library.document&id=51).

Notes

1. Pham Van Dong (1906–2000) was a long-standing member of the Indochinese Communist Party (ICP) who worked closely with Ho Chi Minh and was prime minister of the Democratic Republic of Vietnam (DRV) until 1980 (from 1976 the Socialist Republic of Vietnam, SRV).

2. Hoang Van Hoan (1905–94?) was a long-standing member of the ICP and a Politburo member of the Lao Dong (Vietnamese Workers' Party, VWP) from 1960 to 1976. Hoan was a crucial link between the DRV and China; ambassador to Beijing 1950–57; and led many delegations to China as vice chairman of the DRV National Assembly Standing Committee in the 1960s. He lost much of his influence after Ho Chi Minh's death in September 1969. In 1973, Hoan again went to China to arrange for a visit by Le Duan and Pham Van Dong. He defected to China in July 1979. In 1986, he published his memoirs (*A Drop in the Ocean*), which gave a rare glimpse into the inner life of the ICP/VWP.

3. Le Duan (1908–86) had been secretary of the Nam Bo (Southern Region) Party Committee, later the Central Office for South Vietnam (COSVN), during the first Indochina War. He sent a letter to party leaders objecting to the 1954 Geneva agreement. From 1956, he was acting general secretary of the Lao Dong (Ho Chi Minh was officially general secretary). He was the prime mover, in 1957–59, for a resumption of armed struggle in the South. From 1960 until his death in 1986, Le Duan served as general secretary of the VWP (in 1976 renamed the Vietnamese Communist Party, VCP).

4. Right after the Gulf of Tonkin Incident, Le Duan visited Beijing and met Mao on August 13, 1964. The two leaders exchanged intelligence reports on the two incidents. Le Duan confirmed to Mao that the first incident (that of August 2) was the result of the decisions made by the Vietnamese commander on the site, and Mao told Le Duan that according to the intelligence information Beijing had received, the second incident of August 4 was "not an intentional attack by the Americans" but caused by "the Americans' mistaken judgment, based on wrong information." Touching upon the prospect for the war to be expanded into North Vietnam, Mao thought that "it seems that the Americans do not want to fight a war, you do not want to fight a war, and we do not necessarily want to fight a war," and that "because no one wants to fight a war, there will be no war." Le Duan told Mao that "the support from China is indispensable, it is indeed related to the fate of our motherland. . . . The Soviet revisionists want to make us a bargaining chip; this has been very clear." (*Note:* In some of these notes, we have added additional information from the same sources as the documents themselves. The notes have also been slightly edited for bibliographic style.)

5. On January 22, 1965, Zhou Enlai told a Vietnamese military delegation: "As far

as the war in Vietnam is concerned, we should continuously eliminate the main forces of the enemy when they come out to conduct mopping-up operations, so that the combat capacity of the enemy forces will be weakened while that of our troops will be strengthened. We should strive to destroy most of the enemy's strategic hamlets by the end of this year. If this is to be realized in addition to the enemy's political bankruptcy, it is possible that victory would come even sooner than our original expectation."

6. U Thant (1909–74), secretary general of the United Nations, 1962–71.

7. Attending on the Chinese side were Zhou Enlai, Peng Zhen (member of the CCP Politburo and Mayor of Beijing), Yang Chengwu (deputy chief of staff of the People's Liberation Army (PLA), acting chief of staff until purged in March 1968); Wu Lengxi (director of the Xinhua News Agency and editor-in-chief of *Renmin Ribao* [People's Daily]); on the Vietnamese side: Ho Chi Minh, Le Duan, Pham Van Dong, Vo Nguyen Giap, and Pham Hung.

Vo Nguyen Giap (1912–) had set up the first unit of the People's Army of Vietnam (PAVN) in 1944 and had been commander-in-chief during the first Indochina War. Through the 1960s and most of the 1970s he was deputy premier, minister of defense, and commander-in-chief of the PAVN. He is generally thought to have been replaced by Van Tien Dung as minister of defense and commander-in-chief in 1980, but a military dictionary published in Hanoi in 1966 says that he was replaced by Dung already in early 1978. If this is correct, then Giap was not responsible for the decision to invade Cambodia, or for defending Vietnam against the Chinese attack in 1979. Giap remained on the VWP Politburo until 1982 and the Central Committee until 1991.

Pham Hung (1912–88), a member of the VWP Politburo from 1957, from 1967 directed the war in the South as secretary of the COSVN and as political commissar of the People's Liberation Armed Forces (PLAF). He was deputy premier from 1976 and prime minister of the SRV from June 1987 until his death in 1988.

8. On February 4–11, 1965, Soviet prime minister Aleksei Kosygin visited Beijing and Hanoi and held a series of talks with Chinese and Vietnamese leaders, including five meetings with Zhou Enlai and one meeting with Mao Zedong.

9. Muhammad Ayub Khan (1907–74), was the military leader and president (1958–69) of Pakistan.

10. Maxwell Taylor was the U.S. ambassador to South Vietnam from August 1964 to August 1965.

11. Khan's trip to the United States was subsequently postponed.

12. Pham Van Dong talked with Zhou Enlai in Beijing before he went on to visit Moscow. This was the third meeting of the Vietnamese delegation in Beijing.

13. Luo Ruiqing was a member of the CCP Central Secretariat and chief of staff of the PLA until he was purged in December 1965.

14. In talks held in Guangdong Province, November 8, 1965, Zhou told Ho Chi Minh that "the purposes of Soviet aid to Vietnam [are]: (1) to isolate China; (2) to improve Soviet-U.S. relations; and (3) to conduct subversive activities as well as acts of sabotage, make problems in China, and maybe also in Vietnam."

15. This conversation should be viewed in the light of the triangular relationship between the Chinese, Vietnamese, and Cambodian communist parties. Pol Pot (1923–98), who had become secretary general of the Workers Party of Kampuchea in 1963 (the party later changed its name to the Communist Party of Kampuchea, and was generally known as Khmer Rouge), had arrived in Hanoi in June 1965 and went on to Beijing in late 1965. In both countries, he met prominent party leaders. Serious disagreements de-

veloped between him and Le Duan in Hanoi: see Thomas Engelbert and Christopher E. Goscha, *Falling Out of Touch: A Study on Vietnamese Communist Policy towards an Emerging Cambodian Communist Movement, 1930–1975* (Clayton, Australia: Monash University, 1995); and also David Chandler, *Brother Number One: A Political Biography of Pol Pot* (Boulder, Colo.: Westview Press, 1992), 73–77. Pol Pot wanted already at this stage to take up armed fighting in Cambodia, but at this juncture both the Vietnamese and Chinese were keen to avoid any struggle against Sihanouk. They preferred to see Sihanouk continue his neutralist policy, and if the United States were to intervene in Cambodia, it hoped that Sihanouk and the Cambodian communists would join forces.

16. Xuan Thuy (1912–85), first worked as a journalist and senior official in communist front organizations during the First Indochina War. He was minister of foreign affairs in 1962–65, cabinet minister and head of the DRV delegation to the quadripartite negotiations in Paris in 1968–73.

17. Not specified, but possibly in the winter–spring of 1968, when Ho is reported to have been in Beijing for medical treatment. Thanks are due to William Duiker for clarification on this point.

18. Le Duc Tho (1910–90), was a senior member of the ICP who was deputy secretary of COSVN (under Le Duan) during the years 1949–54. He was a member of the Lao Dong Politburo from 1954. From 1963, he was the head of the committee for supervision of the South, held secret talks with Henry Kissinger in Paris from February 1970, and served as the DRV's chief negotiator during the peace talks in Paris. With Kissinger, in 1973 he was awarded the Nobel Peace Prize, which he declined.

19. On the way back from the Paris talks, Le Duc Tho stopped in Beijing. He met with and reported to Chinese foreign minister Chen Yi. He then asked the latter to inform Mao Zedong and Zhou Enlai, as well as the CCP Central Committee (CC) and the Leadership Group of the Cultural Revolution about the contents of the conversation. On October 17, Chen Yi met Le Duc Tho again to convey Zhou Enlai's personal comments based on general directives of Chairman Mao and the CCP CC.

20. See the introductory essay by Stein Tønnesson in *77 Conversations between Chinese and Foreign Leaders on the Wars in Indochina, 1964–1977,* Cold War International History Project Working Paper 22, ed. Odd Arne Westad, Chen Jian, Stein Tønnesson, Nguyen Vu Tung, and James G. Hershberg (Washington, D.C.: Woodrow Wilson International Center for Scholars, 1998), for a comment on the pronouns used in this exchange: "A conversation between Chinese Foreign Minister Chen Yi and North Vietnamese negotiator Le Duc Tho on 17 October 1968 reveals the limits to the kind of 'we' feeling that can exist between an elder and a younger brother. The word 'we,' as we know, can be used inclusively (we together) and exclusively (we as opposed to you). In this conversation, Chen Yi at first used the inclusive 'we' when describing what had been done in Vietnam: 'We withdrew our armed forces from the South to the North [after the Geneva agreement]. We at that time made a mistake in which [. . . and now he turned to the exclusive 'we':] we [Chinese] shared a part.' When Le Duc Tho answered, he used only the exclusive 'we': 'Because we [Vietnamese] listened to your [Chinese] advice' [the mistake was made in Geneva]. The elder thus went much further in his 'we' feeling than the younger."

21. In November 1968, a DRV delegation headed by Pham Van Dong (on his way back from Moscow) and a COSVN delegation headed by Muoi Cuc (Nguyen Van Linh) visited China. They had three meetings with Zhou Enlai, on November 13, 15, and 17, during which Pham Van Dong informed the Chinese about his talks with the Soviets and

the negotiations in Paris. After seeing Zhou Enlai, the delegations asked for a meeting with Chairman Mao Zedong. On the evening of November 17, Mao received the delegation at his home in Zhongnanhai. Present were Lin Biao, Zhou Enlai, Chen Boda, Kang Sheng, Wang Xinting (deputy chief of staff of the PLA), Ye Jianying, and others on the Chinese side, and Pham Van Dong, Le Thanh Nghi, Nguyen Van Linh, Le Duc Anh, and others on the Vietnamese side.

22. Le Duc Anh (1920–), an army officer, was PAVN deputy chief of the General Staff in 1963–64, chief of staff and subsequently PLAF deputy commander in 1964–68 (a function he still held when he visited China together with Nguyen Van Linh in 1968), and commander of Military Zone 9 (the Mekong Delta) in 1969–74. He was one of the deputy commanders of the Ho Chi Minh offensive in April 1975, and was overall commander of the forces invading Cambodia in 1978. He was a member of the VCP Politburo in 1982–97, and president of the Socialist Republic of Vietnam in 1992–97.

23. In fact, Ngo Dinh Diem first became prime minister on June 16, 1954, during the Geneva Conference.

24. Le Thanh Nghi (1911–89) was a long-standing member of the ICP who had been on the CC already during the First Indochina War. From the 1960s until the 1980s, he was a Politburo member and a deputy premier in charge of economic affairs, including economic assistance from foreign countries.

25. Nguyen Van Linh (Nguyen Van Cuc or Muoi Cuc) (1913–98) was a long-standing member of the ICP who originally came from northern Vietnam but spent most of his life in the south. He became the main party leader in the south when Le Duan went to Hanoi in 1957, and he later served as the principal deputy to Nguyen Chi Thanh and his successor Pham Hung in the COSVN leadership. After 1975, he became responsible for administering South Vietnam, and served as VCP general secretary during the reform period of 1986–91.

26. Nguyen Van Thieu (1924–2001), army general, was president of the Republic of Vietnam (South Vietnam) during the period 1967–75.

27. Nguyen Huu Tho (1910–95?), a lawyer and secret member of the ICP, was vice chairman of the Saigon Peace Committee following the 1954 Geneva agreements, and was detained by the Diem government for several years, then liberated by NLF forces. He was NLF chairman from its founding in 1960, and from 1969 was chairman of the advisory committee of the Provisional Revolutionary Government (PRG). He was SRV vice president in 1976–80.

28. Hoang Van Thai, alias Hoang Van Xiem (1906–86), was an army officer who directed a military-political school at the Viet Minh's HQ in Tan Trao before the August 1945 Revolution. He served as the first chief of the PAVN General Staff in 1945–53, commanded several of the main campaigns during the First Indochina War, became a member of the VWP CC in 1961, and a member of the National Defense Council in 1964. He was commander of Interzone 5 (south central Vietnam) in 1966–67. He was commander of the PLAF in 1967–73, deputy chief of the PAVN General Staff and deputy minister of defense in 1974–81. He was a member of the VWP/VCP CC in 1960–76, and again in 1982–86.

29. The participants on the Vietnamese side included Ly Ban (DRV vice minister of foreign trade) and Ngo Thuyen; on the Chinese side Lin Biao, Zhou Enlai, Kang Sheng, and Huang Yongsheng (CCP Politburo member and PLA chief of staff).

30. On May 5, Sihanouk had formed a Cambodian government in exile, based in Beijing.

31. Zhu Qiwen was Chinese ambassador to Vietnam from August 1962 to 1968, when he was purged and labeled a "Guomindang agent."

32. China exploded its first fission bomb in 1964 and its first thermonuclear weapon in 1967.

33. A week earlier, four American students, demonstrating against the war, had been shot to death by National Guard troops at Kent State University in Ohio.

34. On the Chinese side, Lin Biao, Zhou Enlai, Kang Sheng, Huang Yongsheng, and Li Xiannian were present.

35. Secret talks between Xuan Thuy and Kissinger had been going on alongside the official negotiations in Paris since August 4, 1969.

36. Ieng Sary (1930–) was Pol Pot's closest collaborator in the Cambodian Communist Party Politburo. He moved to Beijing in 1971, where he established the authority of the Khmer Rouge over Sihanouk's government in exile. He was responsible for foreign affairs in the government of Democratic Kampuchea after 1975. He defected to the Hun Sen–Ranaridh government in 1996.

37. Huynh Tan Phat (1913–89) was an architect who was twice arrested by the Diem government after 1954, NLF general secretary in 1964–66, and PRG president from its foundation in 1969 to 1976, when he became SRV deputy premier.

38. General Duong Van Minh (1916–2001) (also known as "Big" Minh) was one of the main figures in the coup against Ngo Dinh Diem 1963, and head of state in 1962–64, when he was deposed. In 1975 he became the last president of South Vietnam before the fall of Saigon.

39. In his peace plan of October 1972, Le Duc Tho actually dropped the demand for the resignation of President Thieu and the immediate formation of a coalition government.

40. Later that same day, Le Duan met with Mao Zedong (Zhou Enlai and Ye Jianying were also present). Records show the following exchange took place: "Le Duan: The chairman's correct judgment is for us a tremendous encouragement. Mao Zedong: Our Foreign Ministry has issued a circular, in which it says that the strategic emphasis of the United States lies in Asia and the Pacific. I say that this is not true. The United States has many problems in Europe, the Middle East, and America itself. Sooner or later it needs to withdraw some of its troops, and it will not stay in Asia and the Pacific forever. Therefore, Comrade Le Duc Tho's negotiation in Paris would result in something. Mao Zedong: Lin Biao knew only guerrilla warfare with a view to keeping the U.S. bogged down in Vietnam. I, however, wish to see you fighting mobile warfare and destroy their forces. Zhou Enlai: We mean their regular forces."

41. William Healy Sullivan (1922–) was deputy assistant secretary of state from the end of his term as U.S. ambassador to Laos in 1969 until he became ambassador to the Philippines in 1973; he later served as envoy to Iran until the Iranian Revolution in 1978–79.

42. Tran Van Huong (1903–82) was a former mayor of Saigon who twice served as prime minister in the Republic of Vietnam November 1964–January 1965, and May–August 1969. He later became vice president to Nguyen Van Thieu and served as president for seven days in April 1975.

43. The Beijing-based Royal Government of National Union of Kampuchea (Cambodia) was formed by Sihanouk and the Khmer Rouge in 1970.

About the Contributors

Chen Jian is Michael J. Zak Professor of China and Asia-Pacific Studies and History at Cornell University. He received his M.A. in history from Fudan University and East China Normal University (1982) and his Ph.D. from Southern Illinois University (1990). He has also taught at East China Normal University, Tibetan Nationality College, the State University of New York at Geneseo, and Southern Illinois University, and the University of Virginia. He was a Norwegian Nobel Institute Fellow and a U.S. Institute of Peace Senior Fellow. Among his many publications are *China's Road to the Korean War* (1994) and *Mao's China and the Cold War* (2001). He is now working on a short biography of Zhou Enlai, a history of Chinese-American diplomatic negotiations during the Cold War, and a comprehensive history of the external relations of Mao Zedong's China.

Christopher E. Goscha was educated at Georgetown University and La Sorbonne, and he is currently professor of international relations at the University of Quebec at Montreal. His major interests are in Indochinese history and Asian International Relations. His major publications include *Falling Out of Touch: A Study on Vietnamese Communist Policy towards an Emerging Cambodian Communist Movement, 1930–1975* (with Thomas Engelbert; 1995); *Vietnam or Indochina?: Contesting Concepts of Space in Vietnamese Nationalism, 1887–1954* (1995); and *Thailand and the Southeast Asian Networks of the Vietnamese Revolution, 1885–1954* (1999).

James G. Hershberg is associate professor of history and international affairs at George Washington University and director emeritus of the Cold War International History Project of the Woodrow Wilson International Center for Scholars. He is the author of *James B. Conant: Harvard to Hiroshima and the Making of the Nuclear Age* (1993, 1995) and of journal articles on various aspects of Cold War history. He is currently working on books dealing with the international history of the Cuban missile crisis and with secret communist peace initiatives during the Vietnam War.

Noam Kochavi is a lecturer at the International Relations Department, Hebrew University of Jerusalem. His doctoral dissertation from the History Department of the University of Toronto, where he studied with Ronald W. Pruessen, was published as *A Conflict Perpetuated: China Policy during the Kennedy Years* (2002). He has also published articles in the *Journal of American–East Asian Relations, Intelligence and International Security,* and *Diplomatic History.* His fields of interest include the history and historiography of U.S. foreign policy, U.S.-China relations, conflict resolution, and the international politics of human rights. His current research project examines various aspects of the American-Israeli dynamics with respect to Soviet Jewish emigration during the 1970s.

Li Danhui is a senior research fellow of the Contemporary China Institute, Chinese Academy of Social Sciences, and the editor-in-chief of the journal *Cold War International History Studies.* Her research interests include Sino-Soviet relations and China's foreign relations. Her major publications include the edited compilations *Beijing Yu Mo Si Ke: Cong Lianmeng Dao Duikang* [Beijing-Moscow: From Alliance to Confrontation] (2002) and *Zhongguo Yu Yidu Zhina Zhanzheng* [China and the Indochina Wars] (2000), as well as the articles "China-U.S. Détente and China's Aid to Vietnam to Resist U.S. Intervention" (in *Dang De Wenxian,* 2002), "The Sino-Soviet Clashes and Conflicts over the 'Aid Vietnam Resist America' Issue" (in *Dangdai Zhongguo Shi Yanjiu,* 2000), "A Historical Examination of the Origin of the 1962 I-Ta Incident Supported by Materials from Archives in Xinjiang" (in *Dangshi Yanjiu Ziliao,* 1999), and "Sino-Soviet Border Clash in 1969, the Origins and Results" (*Dangdai Zhongguo Shi Yanjiu,* 1996).

Li Xiangqian is the director of the Center for Political Party Research of the Party History Research Institute of the Chinese Communist Party Central Committee in Beijing. He is the author of *Mao's Exploration of the Chinese Socialist Road* (2003). He has written extensively on Chinese politics and foreign relations, and on leading Chinese Communist Party political figures. He is currently engaged in research on issues related to the Soviet Union and Eastern European countries during the communist era. He earned his undergraduate degree from the History Department of Renmin University, Beijing, and a master's degree from the Graduate School of the Chinese Academy of Social Sciences, Beijing.

Fredrik Logevall is professor of history at Cornell University. A native of Sweden, he received his Ph.D. in History from Yale University. Before coming to Cornell, he spent eleven years at the University of California, Santa Barbara, where he cofounded the Center for Cold War Studies. He has published numerous books and articles on U.S. foreign policy in the Cold War era, and he is currently working on a study of the French Indochina War of 1945–54 and its aftermath. He is also coauthor of *A People and A Nation: A History of the United States* (with Beth Bailey, David M. Katzman, David W. Blight, Howard P. Chudacoff, Mary Beth Norton, Thomas G. Paterson, and William M. Tuttle; 7th edition, 2004).

Luu Doan Huynh served in the Vietnamese anti-French resistance movement (1945–54) as a soldier and government official. From 1984, he was counselor of the Vietnamese Embassy in Canberra. He is currently a senior research fellow at the Institute of International Relations in Hanoi. He is coauthor of *President Ho Chi Minh and Vietnam's Diplomacy* (with other members of the Institute of International Relations, Vietnam Ministry of Foreign Relations; 1990) and coeditor of *The Vietnam War: Vietnamese and American Perspectives* (with Jayne S. Werner; 1993).

Stephen J. Morris is a fellow at the Foreign Policy Institute of Johns Hopkins University's Paul H. Nitze School of Advanced International Studies. He received his doctorate in political science from Columbia University, and he was awarded research grants by the Institute of East Asian Studies of the University of California at Berkeley. He has also held postdoctoral research appointments at Harvard University. He is the author of *Why Vietnam Invaded Cambodia: Political Culture and the Causes of War* (1999) and is currently writing a book on the Vietnam War during the Nixon years.

Niu Jun, a professor in the Institute of International Studies, Peking University, received his Ph.D. from the People's University of China in 1988. He teaches modern Chinese foreign policy and its making. His current research is focused on a project on the Cold War and the origin of New China's foreign policy, 1948–55. His major publications include *Cong yanan zouxiang shijie: Zhongguo gongchandang duiwai zhengce de qiyuan* [From Yan'an to the world: The origin and development of Chinese Communist foreign policy] (coedited with Zhang Baijia; 1992, 2005); *Towards a History of Chinese Communist Foreign Relations, 1920s–1960s* (coedited with Michael Hunt; 1995); and *Lengzhhan yu zhongguo* [The Cold War and China] (2002).

Mari Olsen studied at the University of Oslo and received her doctoral degree from the International Peace Research Institute, Oslo. She has also taught at the Norwegian Military Academy and has been affiliated with the Norwegian Institute for Defense Studies. She is currently a senior adviser in the Policy Planning Section, Security Policy Department, Norwegian Ministry of Defense. Her major publications include "The USSR and Vietnam, 1954–60" in *Viêt Nam: Sources et Approches* [Vietnam: Sources and approaches] (edited by Philippe Le Failler and Jean Marie Mancini; 1996); "Solidarity and National Revolution: The Soviet Union and the Vietnamese Communists, 1954–60" (published in *Defence Studies*); and *Soviet-Vietnam Relations and the Role of China, 1949–64: Changing Alliances* (2006).

Priscilla Roberts received her undergraduate and doctoral degrees from King's College, University of Cambridge. Since 1984, she has been a lecturer in history at the University of Hong Kong, where she is also honorary director of the Centre of American Studies. She has published numerous articles on twentieth-century diplomatic and international history, with a special interest in Anglo-American relations, in the *Business History Review, Journal of American Studies, Journal of American-East Asian Relations,* and other periodicals. She is the author of *The Cold War* (2000), and the editor of *Sino-American Relations since 1900* (1991) and *Window on the Forbidden City: The Beijing Diaries of David Bruce, 1973–1974* (2001).

She is associate editor of the *Encyclopedia of the Korean War* (2000), *Encyclopedia of World War II* (2004), *World War II: A Student Encyclopedia* (2005), *Encyclopedia of World War I* (2005), and *World War I: A Student Encyclopedia* (2005).

Shen Zhihua is a professor in the History Department of East China Normal University, Shanghai, and a visiting professor at Beijing University. His major publications include *Mao Zedong, Si Da Lin Yu Chaoxian Zhanzheng* [Mao Zedong, Stalin, and the Korean War] (2003); *Sulian Zhuanjia Zai Zhongguo* [Soviet experts in China, 1948–1960] (2003); *Chaoxian Zhanzheng: E'guo Dang'an Guan De Jiemi Wenjian* [The Korean War: Declassified Documents in Russian Archives] (editor; 2003); *Sulian Lishi Dang'an Xuanbian* [A Collection of Historical Documents of the Soviet Union] (editor; 2001–3); and *Zhongsu Tongmeng Yu Chaoxian Zhanzheng Yanjiu* [The Sino-Soviet Alliance and the Korean War] (1999).

Stein Tønnesson was educated as a historian at the University of Oslo. Since 2001, he has been director of the International Peace Research Institute, Oslo. His publications include *1946: Le déclenchement de la guerre d'Indochine* [The eruption of the Indochina war] (1987); *The Vietnamese Revolution of 1945* (1991); and *Asian Forms of the Nation* (editor; 1996). His research interests include revolution, war, and peace in Vietnam; the dispute in the South China Sea; and the geopolitics of energy security.

Yang Kuisong is a professor of history at Shanghai International Studies University. He was previously a professor of history at Beijing University. He has published widely on Chinese foreign policy and Cold War history, including "The Soviet Factor and the CCP's Policy toward the United States in the 1940s" (with Chen Jian, in *Chinese Historians;* 1992); "Chinese Politics and the Collapse of the Sino-Soviet Alliance," in *Brothers in Arms, The Rise and Fall of the Sino-Soviet Alliance, 1945–1963* (edited by Odd Arne Westad; 1998); *Mao zedong yu mosike de enen yuanyuan* [Cooperation and clash between Mao Zedong and Moscow] (1999); and "The Sino-Soviet Border Clash of 1969: From Zhenbao Island to Sino-American Rapprochement" (in *Cold War History,* 2000).

Zhai Qiang is professor of history at Auburn University, Montgomery, Alabama, where from 1997 to 2000 he was named Distinguished Research Professor. After obtaining bachelor's and master's degrees in China, he earned his doctorate from the University of Ohio in 1991, studying with John Lewis Gaddis. He is the author of *The Dragon, the Lion, and the Eagle: Chinese-British-American Relations, 1949–1958* (1994) and *China and the Vietnam Wars, 1950–1975* (2000). He has also published articles in the *International Journal of Historical Studies, China Quarterly, Journal of American–East Asian Relations, Journal of Military History, Pacific Historical Review,* and *Revue Historique des Armées.*

Shu Guang Zhang has been a professor of U.S. diplomatic and international history at the University of Maryland since 1993. He is the author of *Deterrence and Strategic Culture: Chinese-American Confrontations, 1949– 1958* (1992); *Mao's Military Romanticism: China and the Korean War, 1950–1953* (1994); and *Economic Cold War: America's Embargo against China and the Sino-Soviet Alliance, 1949–1963* (2001). He coedited *Chinese Communist Foreign Policy and the Cold War in Asia, 1944–1950: Documentary Evidence* (with Jian Chen; 1996). In 1990–91, he was an Olin Foundation postdoctoral fellow in international security at Yale University. He received a Norwegian Nobel Institute fellowship in international studies for the spring of 1995. He was also awarded a Distinguished Visiting Professorship at Shanghai International Studies University in 2000.

Index